Ethical Obligations and Decision Making in Accounting

Text and Cases

Sixth Edition

Steven M. Mintz, DBA, CPA
Professor Emeritus of Accounting
California Polytechnic State University,
San Luis Obispo

William F. Miller, Ed.D, CPA
Professor of Accounting
University of Wisconsin, Eau Claire

Mc
Graw
Hill
Education

ETHICAL OBLIGATIONS AND DECISION MAKING IN ACCOUNTING
Published by McGraw Hill LLC, 1325 Avenue of the Americas, New York, NY 10019. Copyright ©2023 by McGraw Hill LLC. All rights reserved. Printed in the United States of America. No part of this publication may be reproduced or distributed in any form or by any means, or stored in a database or retrieval system, without the prior written consent of McGraw Hill LLC, including, but not limited to, in any network or other electronic storage or transmission, or broadcast for distance learning.

Some ancillaries, including electronic and print components, may not be available to customers outside the United States.

This book is printed on acid-free paper.

1 2 3 4 5 6 7 8 9 LWI 27 26 25 24 23 22

ISBN 978-1-265-05961-3
MHID 1-265-05961-6

Cover Image: *Creativa Images/Shutterstock*

All credits appearing on page or at the end of the book are considered to be an extension of the copyright page.

The Internet addresses listed in the text were accurate at the time of publication. The inclusion of a website does not indicate an endorsement by the authors or McGraw Hill LLC, and McGraw Hill LLC does not guarantee the accuracy of the information presented at these sites.

mheducation.com/highered

Praise for Ethical Obligations and Decision Making in Accounting

As an accounting faculty member teaching ethics for the third time, I have to say that my first time using Professor Mintz's ethics textbook has been nothing short of an exhilarating experience. The textbook, in my mind, follows the Goldilocks' Rule—it is "just right" in terms of breadth and depth, striking a nice balance between accounting and business ethics. Given my preference for covering the increasingly important topic of whistleblowing, I was delighted to see real world examples such as Cynthia Cooper at WorldCom and Anthony Menendez at Halliburton, as well as numerous other real-world cases where whistleblowers were involved. The textbook also lends itself to being adapted flexibly depending upon course length and duration (for instance, I taught a one-half semester course). Eureka! I believe I have found the "ideal" textbook for my graduate course, and plan to use it going forward. Thanks to professor Mintz for doing an exceptional job of assembling such a fine textbook on a challenging, complex topic. I look forward to seeing the sixth edition co-authored with Bill Miller.

—Sri Ramamoorti, University of Dayton

There are not a lot of accounting ethics textbooks around that are designed to teach accounting students about ethics that incorporate contemporary accounting practice-related issues; this textbook does a masterful job integrating real-life ethical scenarios into cases that students can relate to and build an ethical foundation as they enter the accounting profession.

—Kevin Jones, University of California Santa Cruz

I have taught courses in Ethics in Accounting for over five years, and for the last several years I have used only the Mintz textbook. It combines ethics theories and case studies, and provides various types of assignment options, such as discussions, case studies, and multiple-choice questions. The textbook is thorough, concise, up-to-date, highly readable, and a superb platform on which to structure a syllabus for ethics in accounting. In particular, the case studies accompanying the lessons allow my students to take the subject matter in any direction—or to whatever depth—they wish.

—Ana Sturgess, Foothill College

To ensure students gain a thorough understanding of each chapter's content, I utilize the McGraw-Hill Connect software included with the Ethical Obligations and Decision Making in Accounting sixth edition. Prior to class, the students utilize the interactive SmartBook within the McGraw-Hill Connect software to read the material and answer questions to progress through the reading. The result is better prepared students; thus, allowing for more robust case study discussions in the classroom.

—Stacy L. Conrad, University of Texas at San Antonio

Dedication

We dedicate this book to all the students we have taught over the years, without whom our burning desire to teach ethics would lay dormant. In this book, we strive to stimulate a student's growth as a human being, awaken students' interest in ethics, and enhance their appreciation for the importance of ethical behavior. Our goals are to educate accounting students to be future leaders in the accounting profession and guide them along the path of ethical decision-making. We seek to have students gain the ability to not only know what the right thing to do is but have the courage to do it. Above all else, we seek to instill in students the desire to serve the public interest and meet their ethical obligations to society.

> "Educating the mind without educating the heart is no education at all."
>
> *Aristotle*

About the Authors

Courtesy of Steven Mintz

Steven M. Mintz, DBA, CPA, is a Professor Emeritus of Accounting from the Orfalea College of Business at the California Polytechnic State University–San Luis Obispo. Dr. Mintz received his DBA from George Washington University. His first book, titled *Cases in Accounting Ethics and Professionalism,* was also published by McGraw-Hill. Dr. Mintz has been acknowledged by accounting researchers as one of the top publishers of research papers on accounting ethics and accounting education. He was selected for the 2014 Max Block Distinguished Article Award in the "Technical Analysis" category by The CPA Journal and then again in 2018. Dr. Mintz received the 2015 Accounting Exemplar Award of the Public Interest Section of the American Accounting Association. He also has received the Faculty Excellence Award of the California Society of CPAs. Dr. Mintz writes three award-winning blogs under the names "ethics sage," "workplaceethicsadvice," and "higheredethicswatch."

Courtesy of William F. Miller

William F. Miller, EdD, CPA, CGMA, is a professor of accounting of the Accounting & Finance Department from the College of Business, University of Wisconsin, Eau Claire. Dr. Miller received his EdD from the University of Saint Thomas, Saint Paul, Minnesota. He also has over 23 years of professional accounting experience and maintains an active consulting practice. He has authored or co-authored over 20 publications, including a book on Giving Voice to Values in Accounting, and has won the Institute of Management Accountants Carl Menconi Ethics Case writing competition three times (2011, 2012, and 2015), and won the American Accounting Association's Public Interest Section best contribution to teaching award in 2015.

Both Professors Mintz and Miller have developed accounting ethics courses at their respective universities.

Foreword

By Mary C. Gentile, PhD

Creator/Director, Giving Voice To Values

University of Virginia Darden School of Business

Steven M. Mintz and William F. Miller's latest edition (and 6th) of *Ethical Obligations and Decision Making in Accounting: Text and Cases* is a comprehensive, readable, practical, fresh, and even inspiring text for students of accounting.

The authors cover all the relevant and even required bases for accounting ethics education—an accessible and clear introduction to ethical reasoning; the inclusion of recent and important insights from psychology and behavioral ethics; an impressive set of actual case studies—both short scenarios focused primarily on ethical challenges and longer cases that more clearly integrate values conflicts with financial analysis; discussions of ethical issues at both the organizational as well as the individual levels; examples of classic auditing ethics issues as well as reflection on the most current topics including the influence of social media, equity, diversity and inclusion, and so on—as well as review questions, assessments and all the other ancillary materials that any faculty member could desire.

However, one of the most compelling aspects of this impressive text is the fact that it goes well beyond simply raising awareness of all the ethical risks and choice points an accounting professional may face and providing analytical tools and lenses to aid in rigorously and consistently thinking through them. These are, of course, critical and required objectives for any accounting ethics educational experience. However, necessary as they are, they are not sufficient. Truly preparing future accountants for responsible and ethical practice also requires attention to questions of action: that is, developing the skills, competencies, literal scripts, confidence, and the habit of acting effectively on values-based positions. For this reason, I am pleased and proud to see that Mintz and Miller have thoroughly integrated the "Giving Voice to Values"[1] (GVV) pedagogy into their text.

"Giving Voice to Values" is an innovative approach to values-driven leadership development in business education and the workplace. Drawing on actual experience and scholarship, GVV fills a long-standing critical gap in the development of values-centered leaders. GVV is not about persuading people to be more ethical. Rather GVV starts from the premise that most of us already want to act on our values, but that we also want to feel that we have a reasonable chance of doing so effectively and successfully. This pedagogy and curriculum are about raising those odds. Rather than a focus on ethical *analysis*, the Giving Voice to Values (GVV) curriculum focuses on ethical *implementation* and asks the question: "What if I were going to act on my values? What would I say and do? How could I be most effective?"

GVV was developed for use in graduate business education and the goal was always to create a pedagogy and curriculum that would not be restricted to general ethics courses, but rather that lent itself to all the core functions of business and could easily and effectively be integrated into an accounting or a finance or a marketing or an operations course. The field of Accounting has been one of the most receptive to this approach and the authors of this text have played a major part in that integration. They have piloted the use of GVV in accounting teaching; researched and published on its impact; and built it into past texts. This latest edition is the most expansive and complete manifestation of that integration to date.

The goal here is for accounting students to not only understand the importance of ethical responsibility in their profession but to feel empowered and skillful enough to act on that insight. Through pre-scripting, rehearsal, and peer coaching, students normalize the voicing and enacting of values-based positions in their accounting careers but also learn how to frame their commitments in ways that are more likely to influence their intended audiences whether that may be a manager, a colleague, or a client. They anticipate the sorts of objections or "Reasons & Rationalizations" they are likely to encounter and pre-script effective ways to respond and neutralize them. And by having these conversations with their peers, they develop a comfort and confidence with this sort of discussion. Rather than merely a set of "thou shalt not's," ethical accounting becomes a process of innovation and of efficacy. They develop a "habit" of enacting their values, a "moral muscle memory."

Mintz and Miller have taken the core GVV concepts and put the accounting "meat on the bones." They have gone beyond ethical exhortations to the use of accounting vocabulary and frameworks and analytics to build persuasive action plans for values-driven practice. And rather than simply preaching to students and then pretending they can or will act ethically, these authors appeal to the professional aspirations their students already possess and provide them with the guidance and the practice to act on those aspirations successfully. This approach cannot *make* a future accountant act ethically but it goes a long way toward enabling them to know they truly have a choice and toward building their habit of making the ethical one.

Preface

Ethical Obligations and Decision Making in Accounting was written to guide students through the minefields of ethical conflict in meeting their responsibilities under the accounting professions' codes of conduct and ethical reasoning standards of conduct that have stood the test over time. Our book is devoted to helping students cultivate the ethical commitment needed to ensure that their work meets the highest standards of integrity, independence, objectivity, and professional skepticism. We hope that this book and classroom instruction will work together to provide the tools to inspire students to act in accordance with the rules and professional standards of behavior in everything they do. Here is a brief overview of enhancements to the sixth edition. Additional details follow.

Ethics Education

Most states require a CPA applicant to complete a professional ethics exam before licensure. The exam is often administered online at home and a passing score is considered a 90 percent or better. This exam generally must be completed within two years of passing the CPA Exam. Check your State Board for details.

Virtually, all states require continuing education in ethics after licensure. Generally, four hours are required every two years to include a course on state regulatory requirements. Some states allow a course on ethical reasoning.

Increasingly, more states are requiring a specific number of units in ethics education at the university level as a condition of licensing. For example, the Texas State Board of Accountancy says about course content that it must include: a framework of ethical reasoning, professional values, and attitudes for exercising professional skepticism and other behavior that is in the best interest of the public and profession. The course should provide a foundation for ethical reasoning and include the core values of integrity, objectivity, and independence. The California Board of Accountancy requires 10-semester hours of ethics study, three of which must be in a standalone Accounting Ethics course that addresses accounting ethics or accountants' professional responsibilities.

Overview of Sixth Edition

The sixth edition continues the trend of addressing societal ethics and civility in light of recent developments in the areas of equity, diversity, and inclusion. Students need to know about societal ethics issues along with those in business and accounting. One goal of our book is to develop the whole person and enhance their ethical decision-making skills in all aspects of their life—personal and professional. The "Giving Voice to Values" technique has a prominent role in the sixth edition to guide students on what they can do to counteract the pressures of top management to deviate from ethical and philosophical norms of behavior. GVV cases are clearly marked so instructors can easily determine whether to assign them in a given chapter.

The culture of an organization provides the foundation for ethical decisions in accounting. Accountants and auditors do not work in a vacuum. Instead, they are part of a larger organization within which ethical decisions are made. The sixth edition digs deeper into organizational ethics issues including corporate governance and discusses the link between internal controls over financial reporting and the role and responsibilities of accounting professionals. Ethical leadership concerns are addressed as well.

Ethics in the accounting profession is evolving. Independence issues are at the forefront of the discussions because of concerns that auditors are not paying enough attention to the importance of having an independent audit. The sixth edition addresses dozens of situations where auditor independence was questioned by the SEC in its regulatory actions. The Public Company Accounting Oversight Board has been concerned that independence impairments, along with integrity and a lack of professional skepticism, have led to high rates of audit deficiencies identified in PCAOB inspections of the Big Four.

The sixth edition has expanded coverage of accounting fraud and earnings management. Pressure to meet financial analysts' earnings projections and internal estimates of earnings and earnings per share create challenges for accounting professionals who must retain their integrity and professional skepticism as required by the AICPA Code of Professional Conduct.

There are many new cases in the book to diversify coverage and expand on what it takes to make ethical decisions and how to voice one's values when conflicts exist between what the organization wants to report and what the organization should report by following prescribed ethical standards. The reality is that the SEC and other regulatory bodies may investigate when material misstatements in the financial statements go undetected or organizations engage in earnings management through fraudulent accounting and financial reporting.

The book has been designed to meet the standards for ethical behavior by accounting professionals embodied in the AICPA Code and state board of accountancy regulations including:

- Encouraging students to make decisions in accordance with prescribed values, attitudes, and behaviors;
- Providing a framework for ethical reasoning, knowledge of professional values, and ethical decision making;
- Prescribing attributes for exercising professional skepticism and behavior that is in the best interest of the investing and consuming public and the profession;
- Putting the interests of the public ahead of those of an organization and self-interest; and
- Instilling the desire to do the right thing and adhere to the standards set forth in the AICPA Code.

Accounting students should strive to be the best accounting professionals possible. To that end, we seek to instill a sense of ethics and professionalism in everything they do.

What's New in the Sixth Edition?

In response to feedback and guidance from numerous accounting ethics faculty, the authors have made many important changes to the sixth edition of *Ethical Obligations and Decision Making in Accounting: Text and Cases,* including the following:

Connect

- **Connect is available** with assignable cases, test bank assessment material, and SmartBook. **SmartBook** is an excellent way to ensure that students are reading and understanding the basic concepts in the book and it prepares them to learn from classroom discussions. Several of the **Chapter Cases** are available in an auto-graded format to facilitate grading by instructors. The purpose of using the digital format is to better prepare students ahead of class to free up instructors to discuss a broader range of topics in their lectures and in the give-and-take between teacher and student. **Connect Insight Reports** will also give the instructor a better view into the overall class's understanding of core topics prior to class to appropriately focus lectures and discussion. The **Connect Library** also offers materials to support the efforts of first-time and seasoned instructors of accounting ethics, including a comprehensive Instructor's Manual, Test Bank, Additional Cases, and PowerPoint presentations.
- **Learning Objectives** have been added and linked to specific content material in each chapter.

End-of-Chapter Assignments

New to the sixth edition is the inclusion of five comprehensive discussion questions in addition to the 20 end-of-chapter discussion questions. The comprehensive questions were designed with three objectives in mind: (1) covering more than one topic in a discussion question; (2) adding to the discussion of chapter material by linking back to a topic covered in a previous chapter; and (3) requiring students to incorporate philosophical reasoning in answering a discussion question.

Ten cases cover a variety of topics deemed most important in each chapter. We have purposefully kept most of these cases short to provide ample time for discussion in class about the ethical issues and to not get too bogged down with financial analysis. However, we do provide many SEC cases that focus on the numbers and are more comprehensive. We hope the mixture will serve the interests of all instructors.

The major cases have been restructured in the sixth edition to provide a selection of short and long cases, all of which have one thing in common: through the questions at the end of each case students are given the opportunity to tie together important topics discussed in the text and apply their knowledge of ethical reasoning to more complex situations. We have included on the web some of the discussion questions, end-of-chapter cases, and major cases from the fourth and fifth editions not carried over to the sixth edition to make way for new cases and keep the book fresh and up to date. Instructors may find this material useful for assignment purposes. We have also revised and enhanced additional Instructor's Resource Materials and supplements.

Suggestions for Classroom Discussion

In addition to the customary pedagogical techniques of straight lecturing and class discussions, the authors have used the following techniques:

- Dividing students into groups to resolve ethical dilemmas posed by the facts of a case and discussing the resolution in class.
- Having students create their own case study and make a video to explain how to resolve the ethical dilemma.
- Requiring a role-playing exercise to practice responding to ethical dilemmas posed in case studies. This is particularly useful in Giving Voice to Values cases.
- Have students write a blog on an ethical issue and submit it for grading purposes. In the past, Professor Mintz has worked with instructors to review the blogs and decide whether it is appropriate for posting on his *Ethics Sage* blog site.
- Assign end-of-course projects where students work independently to write up the answers to cases and submit them for grading. The major cases have been used for this purpose.

Ethics IQ Test

An ethics IQ test appears at the end of Chapter 1. This was in the "Ethics Reflection" in the fifth edition. We felt having a different ethics reflection in the sixth edition would allow us to provide students with a better introduction to chapter one material. The IQ questions are designed to engage students in topics they care about such as sexual harassment, the use of marijuana, and dangers of posting material on social media. Instructors can use this test in the first few classes to get a sense of where students stand in their ability to identify and resolve ethical dilemmas. There is a scoring system to aid in this process.

Chapter-by-Chapter Enhancements

Chapter 1 Ethical Reasoning: Implications for Accounting

- Enhanced discussion of the difference between morals, ethics, and values.
- Expanded coverage of moral courage including a hazing incident at Louisiana State University.
- **New** case on "Operation Varsity Blues" where wealthy and well-connected parents made payments to a middleman to facilitate admission of their kids to prestigious colleges and universities.
- **New** case on "Getting Called Out on Social Media" that addresses the realities of the cancel culture.

Chapter 2 Cognitive Processes and Ethical Decision Making in Accounting

- Reorganization of the chapter to provide a roadmap to making ethical decisions in accounting.
- **New** section on What Makes for an Ethical Organization that addresses issues related to ethical culture and equity, diversity, and inclusion.
- Enhanced discussion of behavioral ethics and additional focus on the role of cognitive biases play in ethical decision making.
- Enhanced discussion of the GVV technique. Chapter 2 discusses the foundation of the approach including examples on applying the methodology. There are 18 GVV cases in the book.
- **New** case on equity, diversity, and inclusion surrounding automated screening of new hire candidates.
- Major update to case on the role of incrementalism in ethical decision making in accounting.

Chapter 3 Organizational Ethics and Corporate Governance

- Updated results from the Association of Certified Fraud Examiners 2020 Global Survey of Fraud.
- **New** discussion of conscious capitalism.
- **New** case on the fraud at Theranos that developed a blood testing system to facilitate obtaining the results at a cheaper cost only to find out the system did not work as intended.
- **New** case on the toxic sales culture at Wells Fargo that led to a massive fraud.
- Expanded coverage of corporate social responsibility including *sexual harassment.*
- **New** case about the cheating scandal at KPMG where partners cheated on an internal training exam to get credit for a continuing education course.

Chapter 4 AICPA Code of Professional Conduct

- Expanded coverage of independence including a new requirement in the United Kingdom to have accounting firms split off their consultancy services and auditing services into separate operating entities and implications for the SEC.
- **New** discussion of the loosening of independence rules by the SEC to focus more attention on objectivity and impartiality and less on strict independence.
- Expanded coverage of ethics in tax practice.
- **New** discussion of the expanded quality control requirements implemented by the Public Company Accounting Oversight Committee (PCAOB).
- **New** case on sexual harassment charges at Ernst & Young.
- **New** case where PricewaterhouseCoopers mischaracterized its nonaudit services to skirt the requirement not to perform certain nonaudit services for audit clients.

Chapter 5 Fraud in the Financial Statements and Auditor Responsibilities

- Expanded coverage of PCAOB's requirement for auditors to communicate in the audit report critical audit matters (CAMs) or state that none were determined to exist.
- **New** section on the use of automation, analytics, and artificial intelligence in the audit function.
- Expanded discussion of PCAOB audit inspection process and high rate of deficiencies of audit firms.
- **New** case on the allegations raised that Ernst & Young failed to detect fraudulent bank confirmations in its audit of Wirecard.
- **New** case on the risks surrounding the integration of audit analytic techniques into audit procedures.
- Major update to cases surrounding the uncovering of related party transactions and other fraudulent activities by an external auditor.

Chapter 6 Motivation for Fraudulent Financial Reporting

- The material in Chapter 7 of the fifth edition has been divided into two chapters. Chapter 6 discusses the motivation for fraudulent financial reporting, while Chapter 7 addresses the consequences of earnings management.
- **New** section on red flags and detecting fraudulent financial reporting.
- **New** section on using financial statement analysis to detect fraud.
- **New** case on fraud at BMW NA due to inaccurate disclosures of its retail vehicle sales volume in the United States.

Chapter 7 Consequences of Earnings Management: The Need for Ethical Leadership in Accounting

- Expanded discussion of restatements of financial statements and differences between a revising financial statements and reissuing them.
- **New** discussion of financial statement restatements including material misstatements at Kraft Heinz triggered by operational issues.
- **New** section on SEC clawbacks of executive compensation that are triggered by financial statement restatements.
- **New** section on the implications of financial statement restatements for corporate governance.
- **New** section on ethical leadership that has been condensed from the material in Chapter 8 of the fifth edition.
- **New** case that addresses issues related to the coronavirus pandemic including "PPP Loans: Free Money at a Cost."
- **New** case on professional skepticism and managing consensus earnings projections.
- **New** case about the fraud at Theranos that expands on the case in Chapter 3 by addressing failures in corporate governance and a lack of ethical leadership, all of which was triggered by a toxic corporate culture.

Chapter 8 Auditors' Legal Liabilities and Defenses

- The contents in this chapter in the sixth edition come from Chapter 7 of the fifth edition.
- Added exhibits to simplify learning of legal concepts.
- **New** section on income tax fraud versus tax negligence.
- **New** case that explores the legal liabilities of Alexion company because of improper payments made by its Turkish subsidiary to foreign government officials to gain new business and related failure of the internal controls.
- **New** case that addresses revenue recognition fraud caused by the structure of agreements with distributors of vaccines used to treat infectious diseases.

Acknowledgments

The authors want to express their sincere gratitude to these reviewers for their comments and guidance. Their insights were invaluable in developing this edition of the book.

- Stacy Conrad, *University of Texas at San Antonio*
- Carmela Gordon, *Trident Technical College*
- Kevin K. Jones, *University of California, Santa Cruz*
- Dr. Cedric Knott, *Wayne State University*
- William B. Mesa, *Metropolitan State University of Denver*
- Lewis Shaw, *Suffolk University*
- Dr. Anan Sturgess, *Foothill College*
- Kun Yu, *University of Massachusetts Boston*

We also appreciate the assistance and guidance given us on this project by the staff of McGraw-Hill Education, including Tim Vertovec, managing director; Rebecca Olson, portfolio manager; Lauren Schur, marketing manager; Elizabeth Pappas, product developer; Jolynn Kilburg, program manager; Lisa Bruflodt, content project manager; Shawntel Schmitt, content licensing specialist; and Sandy Ludovissy, buyer. We greatly appreciate the efforts of the copyeditor and proofreader of the book.

We wish to thank Tara Shawver, King's College, for her work in developing digital materials to accompany the book.

Finally, we would like to acknowledge the contributions of our students, who have provided invaluable comments and suggestions on the content and use of these cases.

If you have any questions, comments, or suggestions concerning *Ethical Obligations and Decision Making in Accounting,* please send them to Steve Mintz at smintz@calpoly.edu and/or Bill Miller at millerwf@uwec.edu.

Instructors: Student Success Starts with You

Tools to enhance your unique voice

Want to build your own course? No problem. Prefer to use an OLC-aligned, prebuilt course? Easy. Want to make changes throughout the semester? Sure. And you'll save time with Connect's auto-grading too.

65%
Less Time Grading

Laptop: McGraw Hill; Woman/dog: George Doyle/Getty Images

Study made personal

Incorporate adaptive study resources like SmartBook® 2.0 into your course and help your students be better prepared in less time. Learn more about the powerful personalized learning experience available in SmartBook 2.0 at **www.mheducation.com/highered/connect/smartbook**

Affordable solutions, added value

Make technology work for you with LMS integration for single sign-on access, mobile access to the digital textbook, and reports to quickly show you how each of your students is doing. And with our Inclusive Access program you can provide all these tools at a discount to your students. Ask your McGraw Hill representative for more information.

Padlock: Jobalou/Getty Images

Solutions for your challenges

A product isn't a solution. Real solutions are affordable, reliable, and come with training and ongoing support when you need it and how you want it. Visit **www.supportateverystep.com** for videos and resources both you and your students can use throughout the semester.

Checkmark: Jobalou/Getty Images

SUPPORT AT every step

Students: Get Learning that Fits You

Effective tools for efficient studying

Connect is designed to help you be more productive with simple, flexible, intuitive tools that maximize your study time and meet your individual learning needs. Get learning that works for you with Connect.

Study anytime, anywhere

Download the free ReadAnywhere app and access your online eBook, SmartBook 2.0, or Adaptive Learning Assignments when it's convenient, even if you're offline. And since the app automatically syncs with your Connect account, all of your work is available every time you open it. Find out more at **www.mheducation.com/readanywhere**

> *"I really liked this app—it made it easy to study when you don't have your text-book in front of you."*
>
> - Jordan Cunningham, Eastern Washington University

Everything you need in one place

Your Connect course has everything you need—whether reading on your digital eBook or completing assignments for class, Connect makes it easy to get your work done.

Calendar: owattaphotos/Getty Images

Learning for everyone

McGraw Hill works directly with Accessibility Services Departments and faculty to meet the learning needs of all students. Please contact your Accessibility Services Office and ask them to email accessibility@mheducation.com, or visit **www.mheducation.com/about/accessibility** for more information.

Top: Jenner Images/Getty Images, Left: Hero Images/Getty Images, Right: Hero Images/Getty Images

Case Descriptions

Chapter 1 Ethical Reasoning: Implications for Accounting

Case # Case Name/Description

1-1 Operation Varsity Blues
Rich and well-connected parents make improper payments to a middleman to gain admission to choice colleges for their kids.

1-2 Giles and Regas
Dating relationship between employees of a CPA firm jeopardizes completion of the audit.

1-3 Unintended Consequences
Ethical dilemma of a student who accepts an offer of employment from a firm but, subsequently, receives additional, attractive offers from other firms.

1-4 Lone Star School District
Failure to produce documents to support travel expenditures raises questions about the justifiability of reimbursement claims.

1-5 Lottery Bonanza
Two friends agree to share lottery winnings 50:50 no matter who wins but after winning, one friend considers backing out of the agreement.

1-6 Capitalization versus Expensing
Ethical obligations of a controller when pressured by the CFO to capitalize costs that should be expensed.

1-7 Eating Time
Ethical considerations of a new auditor who is asked to cut down on the amount of time that he takes to complete audit work.

1-8 Section 179 Deduction for Equipment Purchases
Ethical dilemma for audit firm after its tax client insists on improper depreciation deductions or else lose its audit and lucrative consulting services.

1-9 Cleveland Custom Cabinets
Ethical and professional responsibilities of an accountant who is asked to "tweak" overhead to improve reported earnings.

1-10 Getting Called-Out on Social Media
Calling out a classmate after a disagreement on social justice issues.

Chapter 2 Cognitive Processes and Ethical Decision Making in Accounting

Case # Case Name/Description

2-1 A Team Player? (a GVV case)
Ethical dilemma for audit staff member who discovers a deficiency in inventory procedures but is unable to convince the group to report it.

2-2 Liability Concerns (a GVV case)
Conflict between a chef and CFO over reporting bacteria found in food and FDA inspection results.

2-3 Taxes and the Cannabis Business (a GVV case)
Declaring the appropriate amount of sales revenue from cash transactions in the cannabis business and the impact on taxable income.

2-4 A Faulty Budget (a GVV case)
Ethical and professional responsibilities of an accountant after discovering an error in his sales budget.

2-5 Not so Diverse, Equitable or Inclusive (a GVV case)
Disproportionally high turnover rates for persons of color and women and the implications for diversity and inclusion.

2-6 **The Normalization of Unethical Behavior: The Harvey Weinstein Case**

Sexual harassment in the movie industry and the media and biases that influence whether such instances are reported.

2-7 **Milton Manufacturing Company**

Dilemma for top management on how best to deal with a plant manager who violated company policy but at the same time saved it $1.5 million.

2-8 **Chef's Delight: That Slope Looks Slippery (a GVV case)**

Pressure imposed by a CEO on external accountants to change financial statement classification of investments in securities to defer reporting a market loss in earnings.

2-9 **Racially Charged Language Inhibits Inclusive Cultures**

Equity, diversity, and inclusion policies (EDI) on college campuses and biases and stereotypes. Page xiii

2-10 **WorldCom**

Persistence of internal auditor Cynthia Cooper to correct accounting fraud and implications for Betty Vinson, a midlevel accountant, who went along with the fraud.

Chapter 3 Organizational Ethics and Corporate Governance

Case # Case Name/Description

3-1 **The Parable of the Sadhu**

Classic Harvard case about ethical dissonance and the disconnect between individual and group ethics.

3-2 **Rite Aid Inventory Surplus Fraud**

Dilemma of director of internal auditing whether to blow the whistle under Dodd-Frank on Rite Aid's inventory surplus sales/kickback scheme.

3-3 **United Thermostatic Controls (a GVV case)**

Acceptability of accelerating the recording of revenue to meet financial analysts' earnings estimates and increase bonus payments.

3-4 **Franklin Industries' Whistleblowing (a GVV case)**

Considerations of internal accountant how best to voice her values to convince others to act on questionable payments to a related-party entity.

3-5 **Theranos: A Cautionary Tale for Silicon Valley**

Falsification of the accuracy of blood-testing equipment to gain partners to promote the testing systems.

3-6 **Blow the Whistle or Don't Blow the Whistle**

Ethical dilemma for controller after discovering an embezzlement by the accounts payable clerk.

3-7 **Wells Fargo – A Toxic Sales Culture**

Setting up unauthorized accounts and making improper charges to bank customers to meet aggressive sales goals.

3-8 **Accountant takes on Halliburton and Wins!**

Violation of confidentiality in a whistleblowing case under SOX after Tony Menendez reported accounting improprieties to the SEC and was retaliated against by Halliburton.

3-9 **Expense or Capitalize Research and Development Costs (a GVV case)**

Improper capitalization of research and development costs and implications for meeting projected earnings per share.

3-10 **Cheating on Internal Training Exams at KPMG**

Coverup by lead engagement partner after providing questions and answers to an internal training exam to another engagement partner.

Chapter 4 AICPA Code of Professional Conduct

Case # Case Name/Description

4-1 **KBC Solutions**

Concerns about professional judgments made by audit senior after the review of workpaper files.

4-2   Beauda Medical Center
Confidentiality obligation of an auditor to a client after discovering a defect in a product that may be purchased by a second client.

4-3   Family Games, Inc. (a GVV case)
Ethical dilemma for a controller being asked to backdate a revenue transaction to increase performance bonuses in order to cover the CEO's personal losses.

4-4   Threats to Audit Independence
Threats to professional judgment because of biased feelings toward client and potential influence on integrity and objectivity, professional skepticism, and independence.

4-5   Han, Kang & Lee, LLC (a GVV case)
Pressure between audit partner who wants the client to write down inventory and other partners that want to keep the client happy.

4-6   Tax Shelters
Ethical dilemma of tax accountant in deciding whether to participate in tax shelter transactions targeted to top management of a client entity in light of cultural influences within the firm.

4-7   Sexual Harassment at EY
Sexual harassment claim by a staff member at EY charging her supervisor with making inappropriate comments and questions about firm culture.

4-8   Marcum LLP
Independence violations by a firm that promotes the interests of clients by setting up a conference to drum up new business for those clients.

4-9   PwC Mischaracterizes Nonaudit Services
PwC mischaracterized nonaudit services to avoid violating conflict of interest rules when providing prohibited nonaudit services to audit clients.

4-10   Johnson Pharmaceuticals (a GVV case)
Declining level of sales and earnings prompts former controller to sell stock in a company to avoid taking losses and profit from exercising stock options.

Chapter 5 Fraud in the Financial Statements and Auditor Responsibilities

Case # Case Name/Description

5-1   Loyalty and Fraud Reporting (a GVV case)
Employee who embezzles $50,000 seeks out the help of a friend to cover it up. Application of the fraud triangle and GVV.

5-2   ZZZZ Best
Fraudster Barry Minkow uses fictitious revenue transactions from nonexistent business to falsify financial statements.

5-3   Reauditing Financial Statements
Request to reaudit work of previous auditors.

5-4   GE Multibillion Insurance Charge
Threats to viability of insurance business after taking charges to earnings due to underestimating risk.

5-5   Audit Planning Gone Awry
Audit firm's use of artificial intelligence to improve audit quality and the inherent risks of doing so.

5-6   EY Target of German Regulators Over Suspected Audit Deficiencies at Wirecard
Collapse at Wirecard and questions about EY's audit after it was discovered that $2.1 billion was missing from the client's balance sheet amid the fabrication of false information including bank confirmations.

5-7   Diamond Foods: Accounting for Nuts
Application of the fraud triangle to assess corporate culture and analysis of fraud detection procedures.

5-8   Critical Audit Matters or Potentially Damaging Disclosure
Determination whether to communicate critical audit matters to the audit committee.

5-9   **Weatherford International** *Auditors' failure to detect deceptive income tax accounting, even though client was included in a high-risk category, and restatement of financial statements.*

5-10   **Potential Fraud at EP Sports**
Questions about related-party transactions and possible fraudulent behavior by the CEO.

Chapter 6 Motivation for Fraudulent Financial Reporting

Case # Case Name/Description

6-1   **Winners & Losers Inc.**
Managing earnings to meet or beat consensus estimates for EPS and showing earnings growth and related questions about whether forward-looking statements and earnings releases should be audited.

6-2   **Solutions Network, Inc. (a GVV case)**
Ethical challenges of a controller in voicing values when the company uses round-trip transactions to meet earnings targets.

6-3   **Allergan: Mind the GAAP**
Disagreements with the SEC about presentation of non-GAAP metrics in financial reports and press releases.

6-4   **The Potential Darkside of Using Non-GAAP Metrics (a GVV case)**
Acceptability of presenting multiple non-GAAP measures to "better" explain financial results and provide useful information to users of financial reports.

6-5   **Harrison Industries**
Concerns of a staff accountant asked to record accrued expenses without proper documentation and pressures applied by the supervisor to go along.

6-6   **Tier One Bank**
Failure of KPMG to exercise due care and proper professional judgment in gathering supporting evidence for loan loss estimates.

6-7   **Non-GAAP Metric Disclosure by General Electric: Value Added, Red Herring, or Red flag?**
Confusing disclosures of non-GAAP metrics by GE and SEC comment letter about inconsistencies with GAAP and potentially misleading information.

6-8   **BMW's Sales Reporting Practices**
Using excess reserves to manipulate the number of publicly reported vehicle sales.

6-9   **The North Face, Inc.**
Questions about revenue recognition on barter transactions and the role of Deloitte & Touche in its audit of the client.

6-10   **Beazer Homes**
Use of cookie jar reserves to manage earnings and meet EBIT targets.

Chapter 7 Consequences of Earnings Management: The Need for Ethical Leadership in Accounting

Case # Case Name/Description

7-1   **Should the Financial Statements be Reissued or Revised?**
Determining when to revise or reissue financial statements for errors in previously issued statements.

7-2   **PPP Loans: Free Money at a Cost (a GVV case)**
Questions about whether a company qualifies for PPT loan forgiveness during COVID-19 and ways for a new staff accountant to voice values and positively influence the decision.

7-3   **Managing Earnings and Putting Ethical Leadership to the Test**
Managing earnings to meet consensus EPS estimates and implications for ethical leadership.

7-4   **Monsanto Company Roundup**
Improper accounting for rebates offered to product distributors and retailers; auditing of restated financial statements.

7-5   Kraft Heinz

Appropriateness of restating financial statements to correct for misstatements in previously issued statements.

7-6   New Leadership at General Electric

Discussions about corporate culture, leadership style, and disappointing results in conference calls with financial analysts and investors.

7-7   Krispy Kreme Doughnuts Inc.

Using round-trip transactions to misrepresent earnings to meet earnings guidance and EPS estimates and related leadership failures.

7-8   Sunbeam Corporation

Use of cookie-jar reserves and channel stuffing by a turnaround artist to manage earnings.

7-9   KPMG Tax Shelter Scandal

Ethics of developing tax shelters for clients and a culture within KPMG that promoted making sales at all costs.

7-10   Theranos: Accounting for Bad Blood

Lack of ethical leadership and toxic corporate culture at Theranos trigger failures in corporate governance.

Chapter 8 Auditors' Legal Liabilities and Defenses

Case # Case Name/Description

8-1   Your Tax Client

Distinguishing between the legal standards of negligence, recklessness, and gross negligence.

8-2   Joker & Wild LLC

Auditor acceptance of management misrepresentations and alleged malpractice.

8-3   QSGI Inc.

Circumvention of internal controls by client management and false statement to auditors about operating effectiveness.

8-4   Anjoorian et al.: Third-Party Liability

Application of the foreseeability test, near-privity, and the restatement approach in deciding negligence claims against the auditor.

8-5   Vertical Pharmaceuticals Inc. et al. v. Deloitte & Touche LLP

Fiduciary duties and audit withdrawal considerations when suspecting fraud at a client.

8-6   Kay & Lee, LLP

Auditor legal liability when foreseen third party relies on financial statement.

8-7   Alexion

Improper payments to Turkish officials and violations of SEC rules. Determining whether there have been violations of the Foreign Corrupt Practices Act.

8-8   Disclosing Material Weakness in ICFR or Protecting the Firm from Litigation? (a GVV case)

Identified material weaknesses in internal controls and disclosure in the audit report.

8-9   Miller Energy Resources, Inc.

PCAOB investigation of KPMG and an audit partner for conducting a materially deficient audit and related legal liability.

8-10   Biotechnologies

Improper recognition of revenue on product shipment to accelerate revenue into the current period with the guarantee of the right to return in a subsequent period.

Major Cases: See this section at the back of the book for details.

Brief Contents

1 Ethical Reasoning: Implications for Accounting 1

2 Cognitive Processes and Ethical Decision Making in Accounting 46

3 Organizational Ethics and Corporate Governance 102

4 AICPA Code of Professional Conduct 174

5 Fraud in Financial Statements and Auditor Responsibilities 228

6 Motivation for Fraudulent Financial Reporting 282

7 Consequences of Earnings Management: The Need for Ethical Leadership in Accounting 345

8 Auditors' Legal Liabilities and Defenses 399

MAJOR CASES 449

NAME INDEX 472

SUBJECT INDEX 476

Table of Contents

Chapter 1

Ethical Reasoning: Implications for Accounting 1

Integrity: The Basis of Accounting 2

Religious and Philosophical Foundations of Ethics 4

    Greek Ethics 4

The Language of Ethics 5

    Difference between Morals and Ethics 5

    Difference between Values and Morals 6

    Ethics and Laws 7

    Laws and Ethical Obligations 7

    The Moral Point of View 8

    Student Cheating 8

    Social Networking 10

The Six Pillars of Character 11

    Virtues or Character Traits 11

    Trustworthiness 11

    Respect 13

    Responsibility 13

    Fairness 13

    Caring 13

    Citizenship 13

    Reputation 14

    Moral Courage 14

Modern Moral Philosophies 15

    Teleology 16

    Deontology 19

    Justice 20

    Virtue Ethics 21

Moral Relativism 23

The Public Interest in Accounting 24

    Regulation of the Accounting Profession 24

    The Public Interest in Accounting 24

    Ethics and Professionalism 25

AICPA Code of Conduct 26

Application of Ethical Reasoning in Accounting 27

    3D Printing Case Study 28

Scope and Organization of the Text 29

Chapter 1 Cases 37

    Case 1-1 Operation Varsity Blues 37

    Case 1-2 Giles and Regas 38

    Case 1-3 Unintended Consequences 39

    Case 1-4 Lone Star School District 40

    Case 1-5 Lottery Bonanza 41

    Case 1-6 Capitalization versus Expensing 41

    Case 1-7 Eating Time 42

    Case 1-8 Section 179 Deduction for Equipment Purchases 42

    Case 1-9 Cleveland Custom Cabinets 43

    Case 1-10 Getting Called-Out on Social Media 44

Chapter 2

Cognitive Processes and Ethical Decision Making in Accounting 46

Behavioral Ethics 48

    System 1 versus System 2 Thinking 49

    Cognitive Biases 49

    Additional Factors Impacting Our Decisions 53

Kohlberg and the Cognitive Development Approach 55

    Heinz and the Drug 56

Rest's Four-Component Model of Ethical Decision Making 59

    Moral Reasoning and Moral Behavior 59

    Moral Sensitivity 60

    Moral Judgment 60

    Moral Focus 61

    Moral Character 61

    Aligning Ethical Behavior and Ethical Intent 61

What Makes for an Ethical Organization? 63

    Organizational Influences on Ethical Decision Making 63

    Ethical Culture 63

    Ethical Climate 64

    Equity, Diversity, and Inclusion 64

    Diversity versus Inclusion 64

    Equality versus Equity 65

    Components of EDI Initiatives 65

    Sexual Harassment 66

    Uber Sexual Harassment Case 66

    Factors That Influence Ethical Decision Making 68

    Opportunity 70

Business Ethics Intentions, Behavior, and Evaluations 70

Ethical Decision-Making Models 70

Ethical Decision Making in Accounting and Auditing 71

Components of the Model 72

Integrated Ethical Decision-Making Process 73

Application of the Integrated Ethical Decision-Making Model: Ace Manufacturing 73

Giving Voice to Values 76

Reasons and Rationalizations 76

Levers 77

Application of GVV Methodology: Ace Manufacturing 77

Chapter 2 Cases 89

Case 2-1 A Team Player? (a GVV case) 89

Case 2-2 FDA Liability Concerns (a GVV case) 89

Case 2-3 Taxes and the Cannabis Business (a GVV case) 91

Case 2-4 A Faulty Budget (a GVV case) 92

Case 2-5 Not so Diverse, Equitable or Inclusive (a GVV case) 93

Case 2-6 The Normalization of Unethical Behavior: The Harvey Weinstein Case 94

Case 2-7 Milton Manufacturing Company 95

Case 2-8 Chefs Delight: That Slope Looks Slippery (a GVV case) 97

Case 2-9 Racially Charged Language Inhibits Inclusive Cultures 98

Case 2-10 WorldCom 100

Chapter 3

Organizational Ethics and Corporate Governance 102

Fraud in Organizations 103

Occupational Fraud 104

Financial Statement Fraud 107

Seven Signs of Ethical Collapse 109

Pressure to Maintain the Numbers 110

Fear of Reprisals 110

Loyalty to the Boss 110

Conflicts of Interest and the Board of Directors 111

Innovations 112

Goodness in Some Areas Atones for Evil in Others 112

Ethics in the Workplace 112

Compliance Function 113

Integrity: The Basis for Trust in the Workplace 113

Employees Perceptions of Ethics in the Workplace 114

Using Social Media to Criticize the Employer 114

Foundation of Corporate Governance Systems 115

Ethical and Legal Responsibilities of Officers and Directors 116

Components of Corporate Governance Systems 117

Executive Compensation 118

Corporate Governance Oversight and Regulation 120

Corporate Governance Responsibilities 123

Corporate Social Responsibilities 123

Sustainability 123

Triple Bottom Line (TBL) 123

Views of Millennials 123

Conscious Capitalism 124

Models of CSR 125

Examples of CSR 126

Impact of Governmental Regulations 127

Corporate Governance Structures and Relationships 128

Relationships between Audit Committee, Internal Auditors, and External Auditors 130

Internal Controls as a Monitoring Device 132

Equifax Data Breach 134

Whistleblowing 135

Morality of Whistleblowing 135

Rights and Duties 136

Anthony Menendez v. Halliburton, Inc. 137

Dodd-Frank Provisions 139

Whistleblowing Payouts 141

Implications of Supreme Court Decision in Digital Realty Trust, Inc. v. Somers 143

Whistleblowers Can Use Confidential Company Documents to Expose Fraud 144

Chapter 3 Cases 152

Case 3-1 The Parable of the Sadhu 152

Case 3-2 Rite Aid Inventory Surplus Fraud 156

Case 3-3 United Thermostatic Controls (a GVV case) 157

Case 3-4 Franklin Industries' Whistleblowing (a GVV case) 161

Case 3-5 Theranos: A Cautionary Tale for Silicon Valley 162

Case 3-6 Blow the Whistle or Don't Blow the Whistle 165

Case 3-7 Wells Fargo—A Toxic Sales Culture 165

Case 3-8 Accountant Takes on Halliburton and Wins! 167

Case 3-9 Expense or Capitalize Research and Development Costs (a GVV case) 171

Case 3-10 Cheating on Internal Training Exams at KPMG 172

Chapter 4

AICPA Code of Professional Conduct 174

What is Professional Judgment in Accounting? 176

KPMG Professional Judgment Framework 176

Link between Professional Judgment and Cognitive Processes 177

Link between Professional Judgment and AICPA Code of Professional Conduct 178

AICPA Code: Independence Considerations for Members in Public Practice 178

Introduction to Revised Code 179

Conceptual Framework for AICPA Independence Standards 179

Safeguards to Counteract Threats 181

Sarbanes-Oxely Act(SOX): Nonaudit Services 182

Relationships That May Impair Independence 183

SEC Actions on Auditor Independence 186

SEC Actions Against Big Four Audit Firms 186

Emerging Issues 188

AICPA Code: Ethical Conflicts 189

AICPA Code: Conceptual Framework for Members in Business 191

Threats and Safeguards 192

Link between Conceptual Framework and Giving Voice to Values 193

Rules for the Performance of Professional Services 194

General Standards Rule 194

Acts Discreditable 195

Contingent Fees 197

Commissions and Referral Fees 198

Advertising and Other Forms of Solicitation 198

Confidential Information 198

Form of Organization and Name 199

The Spirit of the Rules 200

Ethics and Tax Services 200

Statements on Standards for Tax Services (SSTS) 201

Treasury Circular 230 203

Tax Shelters 204

PCAOB Rules 207

Rule 3520—Auditor Independence 207

Rule 3521—Contingent Fees 207

Rule 3522—Tax Transactions 207

Rule 3523—Tax Services for Persons in Financial Reporting Oversight Roles 208

Rule 3524—Audit Committee Preapproval of Certain Tax Services 208

Rule 3525—Audit Committee Preapproval of Nonauditing Services Related to Internal Control over Financial Reporting 208

Rule 3526—Communication with Audit Committees Concerning Independence 209

PCAOB Inspections 210

Chapter 4 Cases 215

Case 4-1 KBC Solutions 215

Case 4-2 Beauda Medical Center 216

Case 4-3 Family Games, Inc. (a GVV case) 216

Case 4-4 Threats to Audit Independence 217

Case 4-5 Han, Kang & Lee, LLC (a GVV case) 218

Case 4-6 Tax Shelters 219

Case 4-7 Sexual Harassment at EY 220

Case 4-8 Marcum LLP 223

Case 4-9 PwC Mischaracterizes Nonaudit Services 225

Case 4-10 Johnson Pharmaceuticals (a GVV case) 227

Chapter 5

Fraud in Financial Statements and Auditor Responsibilities 228

Fraud in Financial Statements 231

Introduction 231

Nature and Causes of Misstatements 232

Errors, Fraud, and Illegal Acts 232

The Fraud Triangle and AU-C 240: Consideration of Fraud in a Financial Statement Audit 235

Incentives/Pressures to Commit Fraud 236

Opportunity to Commit Fraud 237

Rationalization for the Fraud 237

Frisch's Restaurant: Trust but Verify 238

Fraud Considerations and Risk Assessment 239

Fraud Risk Assessment 239

Assessing Management: Red Flags 240

Is There a Dark Triad Personality Risk? 240

Tyco Fraud 241

Internal Controls Over Financial Reporting 241

Audit Committee Responsibilities for Fraud Risk Assessment 243

Auditor's Communication with Those Charged with Governance 244

Management Representations and Financial Statement Certifications 245

Qwest Communications International Inc. 245

Audit Report and Auditing Standards 246

Background 246

Audit Report 247

PCAOB AS 1301: Communications with Audit Committees 250

PCAOB AS 3101: The Auditor's Report on an Audit of Financial Statements When the Auditor Expresses an Unqualified Opinion 251

Audit Opinions 252

Limitations of the Audit Report and the Future of the Audit Profession 255

Limitations of the Audit Report 255

Generally Accepted Auditing Standards (GAAS) 257

The Future of the Auditing Profession 259

Chapter 5 Cases 265

Case 5-1 Loyalty and Fraud Reporting (a GVV case) 265

Case 5-2 ZZZZ Best 266

Case 5-3 Reauditing Financial Statements 268

Case 5-4 GE Multibillion Insurance Charge 269

Case 5-5 Audit Planning Gone Awry 271

Case 5-6 EY Target of German Regulators Over Suspected Audit Deficiencies at Wirecard 271

Case 5-7 Diamond Foods: Accounting for Nuts 272

Case 5-8 Critical Audit Matters or Potentially Damaging Disclosure? 274

Case 5-9 Weatherford International 275

Case 5-10 Potential Fraud at EP Sports 280

Chapter 6

Motivation for Fraudulent Financial Reporting 282

Characteristics of Earnings Management 284

Motivation for Earnings Management 284

Income Smoothing 285

Ethical Choices 286

Acceptability of Earnings Management 287

How Managers and Accountants Perceive Earnings Management 287

Ethics of Earnings Management 288

Earnings Guidance 289

Audit Committee Responsibilities 290

Pull-In Sales 290

Using Social Media to Report Earnings Guidance and Financial Results 291

Red Flags 291

Earnings Quality 292

Financial Statement Analysis 293

Green Mountain Coffee Roasters 294

Revenue Recognition 295

Financial Shenanigans 298

Financial Statement Effects 298

Examples of Shenanigans 301

Non-GAAP Financial Metrics 305

Non-GAAP Financial Metrics 305

Revisiting Financial Shenanigans 310

Chapter 6 Cases 318

Case 6-1 Winners & Losers, Inc. 318

Case 6-2 Solutions Network, Inc. (a GVV case) 320

Case 6-3 Allergan: Mind the GAAP 322

Case 6-4 The Potential Darkside of Using Non-GAAP Metrics (a GVV case) 326

Case 6-5 Harrison Industries 328

Case 6-6 TierOne Bank 329

Case 6-7 Non-GAAP Metric Disclosure by General Electric: Value Added, Red Herring, or Red Flag? 331

Case 6-8 BMW's Sales Reporting Practices 333

Case 6-9 The North Face, Inc. 335

Case 6-10 Beazer Homes 339

Chapter 7

Consequences of Earnings Management: The Need for Ethical Leadership in Accounting 345

Characteristics of Financial Statement Restatements 347

Summary Reporting of Accounting Restatements 348

Restatements Due to Errors in Accounting and Reporting 350

Restatements Due to Operational Issues 352

MagnaChip Semiconductor, Ltd 353

SEC Clawback for Accounting Violations 355

Corporate Governance and Earnings Management 356

What Is Ethical Leadership? 357

Types of Leaders 361

Social Learning Theory 363

Ethical Skills of Leaders in Accounting Firms 364

Leadership Failures in the Accounting Profession 364

Ethical Leadership in the Accounting Profession 365

Chapter 7 Cases 374

Case 7-1 Should the Financial Statements be Reissued or Revised? 374

Case 7-2 PPP Loans: Free Money at a Cost (a GVV case) 374

Case 7-3 Managing Earnings and Putting Ethical Leadership to the Test 376

Case 7-4 Monsanto Company Roundup 377

Case 7-5 Kraft Heinz 380

Case 7-6 New Leadership at General Electric 383

Case 7-7 Krispy Kreme Doughnuts Inc. 385

Case 7-8 Sunbeam Corporation 387

Case 7-9 KPMG Tax Shelter Scandal 391

Case 7-10 Theranos: Accounting for Bad Blood 393

Chapter 8

Auditors' Legal Liabilities and Defenses 399

Legal Liabilities of Accountants: An Overview 401

Common-Law Liability 402

Liability to Clients—Privity Relationship 402

Professional Negligence 403

Defending Audit-Malpractice Cases 403

Recklessness 404

Negligent Misrepresentation 404

Liability to Third Parties 405

Actually Foreseen Third Parties 405

Reasonably Foreseeable Third Parties 406

Common-Law Liability For Fraud 407

Statutory Law Liability for Fraud 409

Liability for Fraudulent Misrepresentation 410

Income Tax Fraud versus Tax Negligence 411

Auditor Defenses to Negligence and Fraud 412

Auditor Defenses to Negligence 412

Auditor Defenses to Negligent Misrepresentation 413

Auditor Defenses to Fraud 414

Consideration of Fraud in a Financial Statement Audit 414

Statutory Liability 416

Securities Act of 1933 416

Section 11 Liability Under Securities Act of 1933 417

Section 11 Liability Standard for Auditors 418

Section 11 Auditors' "Opinion" Statements 418

Securities Exchange Act of 1934 419

Private Securities Litigation Reform Act (PSLRA) 422

Proportionate Liability 422

Establishing Scienter 423

SOX and Auditor Legal Liabilities 424

Section 404. Internal Control over Financial Reporting 425

Section 302. Corporate Responsibility for Financial Reports 426

Foreign Corrupt Practices Act (FCPA) 427

Chapter 8 Cases 436

Case 8-1 Your Tax Client 436

Case 8-2 Joker & Wild LLC 436

Case 8-3 QSGI, Inc. 437

Case 8-4 Anjoorian et al.: Third-Party Liability 439

Case 8-5 Vertical Pharmaceuticals Inc. et al. v. Deloitte & Touche LLP 441

Case 8-6 Kay & Lee, LLP 442

Case 8-7 Alexion 443

Case 8-8 Disclosing Material Weaknesses in ICFR or Protecting the Firm from Litigation? (A GVV case) 444

Case 8-9 Miller Energy Resources, Inc. 445

Case 8-10 Biotechnologies 446

Major Cases 449

Major Case 1: Colonial Bank 450

Major Case 2: Logitech International 452

Major Case 3: Kiley Nolan's Ethical Dilemma (a GVV case) 456

Major Case 4: Cendant Corporation 458

Major Case 5: Vivendi Universal 465

Major Case 6: Luckin Coffee 468

Name Index 472

Subject Index 476

CHAPTER 1
Ethical Reasoning: Implications for Accounting

LEARNING OBJECTIVES

After studying **Chapter 1**, you should be able to:

LO 1-1 Discuss the relationship between ethics, values, and ethical decision making.
LO 1-2 Explain how characteristic traits of behavior influence ethical decision making.
LO 1-3 Differentiate between moral philosophies and their effect on ethical reasoning in accounting.
LO 1-4 Describe how professional accountants serve the public interest and their obligations under the AICPA Code.
LO 1-5 Apply the AICPA Code and ethical reasoning methods to a case study.

Ethics Reflection

Solving Ethical Dilemmas in Accounting

Solving ethical dilemmas in accounting entails defining the relevant moral values that should guide ethical actions, identifying those who are or may be affected by the actions taken, analyzing each possible action using moral reasoning, and coming to a decision.

We might ask which professions rate high in moral values? The annual Gallup Poll on honesty and ethics in the professions rates nurses as #1, with a total score of 85 percent very high and high. This is an interesting result, given our recent battle with the coronavirus and all that nurses had to do. Notably, the 85 percent rating was before the pandemic. Following nurses are engineers (66%), and then medical doctors (65%) and pharmacists (64%), the latter two and nurses are in the helping professions.[1]

Accountants rate relatively high with a total score of 42 percent very high and high. This may seem low but it is not compared to other business professions. Indeed, accounting is rated #1 in that regard, dwarfing bankers with 28 percent and 21 percent for business executives. When we include the 48 percent rating of accountants in ethics and honesty, we might conclude that the total of 90 percent shows the public is satisfied with accountants' commitment to do the right thing.

What makes the accounting profession rated relatively high in the minds of many of the public? Most likely, it is a commitment to moral values in the performance of professional services including:

- Accountability
- Confidentiality
- Due care and competence
- Integrity
- Loyalty
- Reliability
- Trustworthiness

(continued)

continued   Ethics Reflection

Integrity is thought to be the whole of ethical behavior. According to Mintz, "Integrity is a fundamental trait of character that enables a CPA to withstand client and competitive pressures that might otherwise lead to the subordination of judgment."[2]

A person of integrity will act out of moral principle and not expediency. That person will do what is right, even if it means a loss of a job or client. In accounting, the public interest (i.e., investors and creditors) always must be placed ahead of one's own self-interest or the interests of others, including a supervisor or client.

Think about the following as you read the chapter: (1) How do we distinguish right from wrong? (2) What are the characteristic traits of behavior of an ethical person? (3) How do we reason through ethical dilemmas and distinguish between right versus wrong? (4) How can integrity reinforce the ethical reasoning?

> We look for three things when we hire people. We look for intelligence, we look for initiative or energy, and we look for integrity. And if they don't have the latter, the first two will kill you, because if you're going to get someone without integrity, you want them lazy and dumb."[3]
>
> _Source: Warren Buffet_

This quote by Warren Buffet emphasizes the importance of integrity, or principled behavior in those being recruited by his firm. That is because one has to act with integrity when making professional decisions otherwise pressure imposed on a new employee might steer them in the wrong direction.

Some people distinguish between the importance of ethics in their personal lives and professional lives, judging the latter as less important. However, ethics is not a spigot that can be turned on or off depending on one's whims or whether the matter at hand is personal or professional. As the ancient Greeks knew, we learn how to be ethical by practicing and exercising those virtues that enable us to lead a life of excellence. More will be said about this later.

In accounting, internal accountants and auditors may be pressured by superiors to manipulate financial results. The external auditors may have to deal with pressures imposed on them by clients to put the best face on the financial statements regardless of whether they conform to generally accepted accounting principles (GAAP). It is the ethical value of integrity that provides the moral courage to resist the temptation to stand by silently while a company misstates its financial statement amounts.

Integrity: The Basis of Accounting

According to Mintz (1995), "Integrity is a fundamental trait of character that enables a CPA to withstand client and competitive pressures that might otherwise lead to the subordination of judgment."[4] A person of integrity will act out of moral principle and not expediency. That person will do what is right, even if it means the loss of a job or client. In accounting, the public interest (i.e., investors and creditors) always must be placed ahead of one's own self-interest or the interests of others, including a supervisor or client.

Integrity means that a person acts on principle—a conviction that there is a right way to act when faced with an ethical dilemma. For example, assume that your tax client fails to inform you about an amount of earned income for the year, and you confront the client on this issue. The client tells you not to record it and reminds you that there is no W-2 or 1099 form to document the earnings. The client adds that you will not get to audit the company's financial statements anymore if you do not adhere to the client's wishes. Would you decide to "go along to get along"? If you are a person of integrity, you should not allow the client to dictate how the tax rules will be applied in the client's situation. You are the professional and know the tax regulations best, and you have an ethical obligation to report taxes in accordance with the law. If you go along with the client and the Internal Revenue Service (IRS) investigates and sanctions you for failing to follow the IRS Tax Code, then you may suffer irreparable harm to your reputation. An important point is that a professional must never let loyalty to a client cloud good judgment and ethical decision making.

WorldCom: Cynthia Cooper: Hero and Role Model

Cynthia Cooper's experience at WorldCom illustrates how the internal audit function should work and how a person of integrity can put a stop to financial fraud. It all unraveled in April and May 2002 when Gene Morse, an auditor at WorldCom, couldn't find any documentation to support a claim of $500 million in computer expenses. Morse approached Cooper, the company's director of internal auditing and Morse's boss, who instructed Morse to "keep going." A series of obscure tips led Morse and Cooper to suspect that WorldCom was cooking the books. Cooper formed an investigation team to determine whether their hunch was right.

In its initial investigation, the team discovered $3.8 billion of misallocated expenses and phony accounting entries.[5] Cooper approached the chief financial officer (CFO) Scott Sullivan, but was dissatisfied with his explanations. The chief executive officer (CEO) of the company, Bernie Ebbers, had already resigned under pressure from World-Com's board of directors, so Cooper went to the audit committee. The committee interviewed Sullivan about the accounting issues and did not get a satisfactory answer. Still, the committee was reluctant to take any action. Cooper persisted anyway. Eventually, one member of the audit committee told her to approach the outside auditors to get their take on the matter. Cooper gathered additional evidence of fraud, and ultimately KPMG, the firm that had replaced Arthur Andersen—the auditors during the fraud—supported Cooper. Sullivan was asked to resign, refused to do so, and was fired.[6]

One tragic result of the fraud and cover-up at WorldCom is the case of Betty Vinson. It is not unusual for someone who is genuinely a good person to get caught up in fraud. Indeed, we might ask: Why do good people sometimes do bad things? Vinson, a former WorldCom mid-level accounting manager, went along with the fraud because her superiors told her to do so. She was convinced that it would be a one-time action. It rarely works that way, however, because once a company starts to engage in accounting fraud, it feels compelled to continue the charade into the future to keep up the appearance that each period's results are as good as or better than prior periods. The key to maintaining one's integrity and ethical perspective is not to take the first step down the proverbial *ethical slippery slope.*

Vinson pleaded guilty in October 2002 to participating in the financial fraud at the company. She was sentenced to five months in prison and five months of house arrest. Vinson represents the typical "pawn" in a financial fraud: an accountant who had no interest or desire to commit fraud but got caught up in it when Sullivan, her boss, instructed her to make improper accounting entries. The rationalization by Sullivan that the company had to "make the numbers appear better than they really were" did nothing to ease her guilty conscience. Judge Barbara Jones, who sentenced Vinson, commented that "Ms. Vinson was among the least culpable members of the conspiracy at WorldCom. . . . Still, had Vinson refused to do what she was asked, it's possible this conspiracy might have been nipped in the bud."[7]

Accounting students should reflect on what they would do if they faced a situation similar to the one that led Vinson to do something that was out of character. Once she agreed to go along with making improper entries, it was difficult to turn back. The company could have threatened to disclose her role in the original fraud and cover-up if Vinson then acted on her beliefs. From an ethical (and practical) perspective it is much better to just do the right thing from the very beginning, so that you can't be blackmailed or intimidated later.

Vinson became involved in the fraud because she had feared losing her job, her benefits, and the means to provide for her family. She must live with the consequences of her actions for the rest of her life. On the other hand, Cynthia Cooper, on her own initiative, ordered the internal investigation that led to the discovery of the $11 billion fraud at WorldCom. Cooper did all the right things to bring the fraud out in the open. Cooper received the Accounting Exemplar Award in 2004 given by the Public Interest Section of the American Accounting Association and was inducted into the American Institute of Certified Public Accountants (AICPA) Hall of Fame in 2005. Therefore, we can say that doing the right thing can have positive consequences for the decision maker.

Cooper truly is a positive role model. She discusses the foundation of her ethics that she developed as a youngster because of her mother's influence in her book *Extraordinary Circumstances: The Journey of a Corporate Whistle-blower.* Cooper says: "Fight the good fight. Don't ever allow yourself to be intimidated. . . . Think about the consequences of your actions. I've seen too many people ruin their lives."[8]

Religious and Philosophical Foundations of Ethics

Virtually all the world's major religions contain in their religious texts some version of the Golden Rule: "Do unto others as you would wish them to do unto you." In other words, we should treat others the way we would want to be treated. This is the basic ethic that guides all religions. If we believe honesty is important, then we should be honest with others and expect the same in return. One result of this ethic is the concept that every person shares certain inherent human rights, which will be discussed later in this chapter.

We can think of the Golden Rule as a formal principle that serves as the general basis for other principles (duties) we have in an ethical system. **Exhibit 1.1** provides some examples of the universality of the Golden Rule in world religions provided by the character education organization Teaching Values.[9]

EXHIBIT 1.1   The Universality of the Golden Rule in the World Religions

Religion	Expression of the Golden Rule	Citation
Christianity	All things whatsoever ye would that men should do to you, Do ye so to them; for this is the law and the prophets	Matthew 7:12
Confucianism	Do not do to others what you would not like yourself. Then there will be no resentment against you, either in the family or in the state	Analects 12:2
Buddhism	Hurt not others in ways that you yourself would find hurtful	Uda–navarga 5,1
Hinduism	This is the sum of duty, do naught onto others what you would not have them do unto you	Mahabharata 5, 1517
Islam	No one of you is a believer until he desires for his brother that which he desires for himself	Sunnah
Judaism	What is hateful to you, do not do to your fellow man. This is the entire Law; all the rest is commentary	Talmud, Shabbat 3id
Taoism	Regard your neighbor's gain as your gain, and your neighbor's loss as your own loss	Tai Shang Kan Yin P'ien
Zoroastrianism	That nature alone is good which refrains from doing to another whatsoever is not good for itself	Dadisten-I-dinik, 94, 5

Greek Ethics

The origins of Western philosophy trace back to the ancient Greeks, including Socrates, Plato, and Aristotle. The ancient Greek philosophy of virtue deals with questions such as: What is the best sort of life for human beings to live? Greek thinkers saw the attainment of a good life as the *telos,* the end or goal of human existence. For most Greek philosophers, the end is *eudaimonia,* which is usually translated as "happiness." However, the Greeks thought that the end goal of happiness meant much more than just experiencing pleasure or satisfaction. The ultimate goal of happiness was to attain some objectively good status, the life of excellence. The Greek word for excellence is *arete,* the customary translation of which is "virtue." Thus for the Greeks, "excellences" or "virtues" were the qualities that made a life admirable or excellent. They did not restrict their thinking to characteristics we regard as moral virtues, such as courage, justice, and temperance that are learned primarily through habit and practice, but included others we think of as intellectual virtues, such as wisdom, which governs ethical behavior and understanding. The combination of these virtues are necessary to achieve moral excellence.[10]

The Language of Ethics

LO 1-1

Discuss the relationship between ethics, values, and ethical decision making.

The term *ethics* is derived from the Greek word *ethikos,* which itself is derived from the Greek word *ethos,* meaning "character." Morals is from the Latin word *moralis,* meaning "customs," with the Latin word *mores* being defined as "manners, morals, or ethics."

In philosophy, ethical behavior is that which is "good." The Western tradition of ethics is sometimes called "moral philosophy." The field of ethics or moral philosophy involves developing, defending, and recommending concepts of right and wrong behaviors. These concepts do not change as one's desires and motivations change. They are not relative to the situation. They are immutable.

In a general sense, ethics (or moral philosophy) addresses fundamental questions such as: How should I live my life? That question leads to others, such as: What sort of person should I strive to be? What values are important? What standards or principles should I live by?[11] There are various ways to define the concept of ethics. The simplest may be to say that ethics deals with "right" and "wrong." However, it is difficult to judge what may be right or wrong in a particular situation without some frame of reference.

Gaa and Thorne define ethics as "the field of inquiry that concerns the actions of people in situations where these actions have effects on the welfare of both oneself and others."[12] We adopt that definition and emphasize that it relies on ethical reasoning to evaluate the effects of actions on others—*the stakeholders.*

Ethics deals with well-based standards of how people ought to act, does not describe the way people actually act, and is prescriptive, not descriptive. Ethical people always strive to make the right decision in all circumstances. They may not always succeed, but their intentions are good ones. They do not rationalize their actions based on their own perceived self-interests and they take responsibility for those actions. The best way to understand ethics may be to differentiate it from other concepts.

Difference between Morals and Ethics

Ethics and morals relate to "right" and "wrong" conduct. While they are sometimes used interchangeably, there are differences. These differences may seem complicated at first but can be compared to each other to simplify ethical decision-making as shown in **Exhibit 1.2** below.

While morals are concerned with principles of right and wrong in general, ethics are related to right and wrong conduct of an individual in a particular situation. Whereas morals are customs established by a group of individuals, ethics defines the character of the individual. While morals represent what a person, group, or society believes people should do, ethics are guiding principles which help the individual or group decide what is good or bad. Morals are expressed in the form of general rules and statements. Ethics are abstract. They need context to decide what is right or wrong.

Moral principles include the following:

- Always tell the truth
- Do not cheat
- Treat others fairly
- Be kind to others

Ethical guiding principles, which will be discussed further in the next section, include the following:

- Truthfulness
- Honesty
- Integrity

- Fairness
- Respect
- Loyalty

One way of understanding the difference is to think of it this way. Ethics leans toward decisions based upon individual character and the more subjective understanding of right and wrong by individual, whereas morals emphasize the widely held communal or societal norms about right and wrong.[13]

EXHIBIT 1.2   Comparison of Morals and Ethics[14]

BASIS FOR COMPARISON	MORALS	ETHICS
Meaning	Morals are the beliefs of the individual or group as to what is right or wrong	Ethics are the guiding principles that help the individual or group to decide what is good or bad
Application	General principles set by group	Response to a specific situation
Governed By	Social and cultural norms	Individual or legal and professional norms
Deals with	Principles of right and wrong	Right and wrong conduct
Consistency	Morals may differ from society to society and culture to culture	Ethics are generally uniform
Expression	Morals are expressed in the form of general rules and statements	Ethics are abstract

Difference between Values and Morals

Values are basic and fundamental beliefs that govern our actions and represent the intention behind purposeful action. They are the foundation of the choices we make. We conceive of it as something that is important to an individual (personal values), a community (societal values), and to a profession (professional values). Values can be distinguished from morals as described in **Exhibit 1.3** below.

Values have intrinsic worth but are not necessarily universally accepted. For example, the right of free speech that is guaranteed by the U.S. Constitution is a community-wide norm that governs behavior in American society. In other countries, such as North Korea, citizens cannot practice free speech.

Moral values underlie what is considered right and wrong by an individual or community. It is the foundation of a person's ability to judge between right and wrong. In accounting, the values of the profession include independence, integrity, objectivity, professional skepticism, and due care. They define what it means to be a professional and provide a framework for the enforceable rules of professional conduct that are designed to serve the public interests above all else.

Moral values enable a person to make proper judgments in a specific situation. For example, cheating on a college exam is wrong while studying hard to ace the exam is right. Conversely, if someone values achievement and success over honesty, that person may opt to cheat on the exam in order to achieve the desired result. This relates to which value is "worth more" to the individual.

A person who values prestige, power, and wealth is likely to act out of self-interest, whereas a person who values honesty, integrity, and trust will strive to consider the interests of others in deciding what to do. It does not follow, however, that acting in the best interests of others always precludes acting in one's own self-interest. Indeed, the Golden Rule prescribes that we should treat others the way we want to be treated.

EXHIBIT 1.3   Comparison of Morals and Values

BASIS FOR COMPARISON	MORALS	VALUES
Meaning	Morals are the beliefs of the individual or group as to what is right or wrong	Values are fundamental beliefs that govern actions
Application	General principles set by group	Beliefs that reflect individual, community, and professional values
Governed By	Social and cultural norms	Individual and professional norms
Consistency	Morals may differ from society to society and culture to culture	Values are specific to an individual or group
Examples	Always tell the truth do not cheat, treat others fairly, be kind to others	Accounting Profession: independence, integrity, objectivity, professional skepticism, due care

Ethics and Laws

Laws are a collection of rules and regulations that come with penalties and punishments if not followed. Ethics, on the other hand, is a collection of societal or professional norms of behavior that are based on moral principles and values. Ethics is what should be done whereas laws deal with behavior that is compelled. Contrary to popular belief, we can and do legislate ethics. We have laws against stealing, kidnapping, etc., which are based on ethical standards. In accounting, we legislate ethics through a system of ethical duties established in state board of accountancy rules.

Being ethical is not the same as following the law. Although ethical people always try to be law-abiding, there may be instances where their sense of ethics tells them it is best not to follow the law. These situations are rare and should be based on sound ethical reasons.

> Assume that you are driving at a speed of 45 miles per hour (mph) on a two-lane divided roadway (double yellow line) going east. All of a sudden, you see a young boy jump into the road to retrieve a ball. The boy is close enough to your vehicle so that you know you cannot continue straight down the roadway and stop in time to avoid hitting him. You quickly look to your right and notice about 10 other children off the road. You cannot avoid hitting 1 or more of them if you swerve to the right to avoid hitting the boy in the middle of the road. You glance to the left on the opposite side of the road and notice no traffic going west or any children off the road. What should you do?
>
> **Ethical Perspective**
>
> If you cross the double yellow line that divides the roadway, you have violated the motor vehicle laws. We are told never to cross a double yellow line and travel into oncoming traffic. But the ethical action would be to do just that, given that you have determined it appears to be safe. It is better to risk getting a ticket than hit the boy in the middle of your side of the road or those children off to the side of the road.

There is a concept known as "ethical legalism," which holds that if an intended action is legal, it is, therefore ethical. However, there are situations where doing the right thing may not be the legal thing, and vice versa.

During the pre-Civil War years in the United States, the law did not prohibit slavery and slaves were considered personal property. Yet, few would say it was an ethical practice. Similarly, lying or betraying the confidence of a friend is not illegal, but most people would consider it unethical. The contrary is true as well. The law also prohibits acts that some groups would perceive as ethically neutral behavior—behavior that is ethically permissible but not itself ethical. For instance, speeding is illegal, but many people do not have an ethical conflict with exceeding the speed limit.

Laws and Ethical Obligations

Benjamin Disraeli (1804–1881), the noted English novelist, debater, and former prime minister, said, "When men are pure, laws are useless; when men are corrupt, laws are broken." A person of goodwill honors and respects the rules and laws and is willing to go beyond them when circumstances warrant. As indicated by the previous quote, such people do not need rules and laws to guide their actions. They always try to do the right thing. On the other hand, the existence of specific laws prohibiting certain behaviors will not stop a person who is unethical (e.g., does not care about others) from violating those laws. Just think about a Ponzi scheme, such as the $65 billion one engaged in by Bernie Madoff, whereby he duped others to invest with him by promising huge returns that, unbeknownst to each individual investor, would come from additional investments of scammed investors and not true returns.

Laws create a minimum set of standards but cannot cover every situation a person might encounter. When the facts are unclear and the legal issues uncertain, an ethical person should decide what to do on the basis of well-established standards of ethical behavior. This is where moral philosophies come in and, for accountants and auditors, the ethical standards of the profession.

A useful perspective is to ask these questions:

- What does the law require of me?
- What do ethical standards of behavior demand of me?
- How should I act to conform to both?

The Moral Point of View

When the rules are unclear, an ethical person looks beyond his/her own self-interest and evaluates the interests of the stakeholders potentially affected by the action or decision. Ethical decision making requires that a decision maker be willing, at least sometimes, to take an action that may not be in his/her best interest. This is known as the "moral point of view."

Sometimes people believe that the ends justify the means. In ethics it all depends on one's motives for acting. If one's goals are good and noble, and the means we use to achieve them are also good and noble, then the ends do justify the means. However, if one views the concept as an excuse to achieve one's goals through any means necessary, no matter how immoral, illegal, or offensive to others the means may be, then that person is attempting to justify the wrongdoing by pointing to a good outcome regardless of ethical considerations such as how one's actions affect others. The process you follow to decide on a course of action is just as important, if not more important, than achieving the end goal. If this were not true from a moral point of view, then we could rationalize all kinds of actions in the name of achieving a desired goal, even if that goal does harm to others while satisfying our personal needs and desires.

Imagine that you work for a CPA firm and are asked to evaluate three software packages for a client. Your boss tells you that the managing partners are pushing for one of these packages, which just happens to be the firm's internal software. Your initial numerical analysis of the packages based on functionality, availability of upgrades, and customer service indicates that a competitor's package is better than the firm's software. Your boss tells you, in no uncertain terms, to redo the analysis. You know what your boss wants, even though you feel uncomfortable with the situation, you decide to "tweak" the numbers to show a preference for the firm's package. The end result desired in this case is to choose the firm's package. The means to that end was to alter the analysis, an unethical act because it is dishonest and unfair to the other competitors (not to mention the client) to change the objectively determined results. In this instance, ethical decision making requires that we place the client's interests (to get the best software package for their needs) above those of the firm (to get the new business and not upset the boss).

Sometimes a moral point of view, such as cheating is bad, gets obscured by rationalizations by the decision-maker. Two examples are student cheating and social media activities.

Student Cheating

Kessler International surveyed students about cheating that shows students are cheating frequently using a variety of methods, many of which are chosen because of the advent of online schools and mobile devices. In total, Kessler surveyed 300 students from both public and private colleges and universities, including online universities.

The survey found:[15]

- 86 percent of the students surveyed claimed they cheated in some way in school.
- 54 percent of the students surveyed indicated that cheating was OK. Some went so far as to say it is necessary to stay competitive.

- 97 percent of the admitted cheaters say that they have never been identified as cheating.
- 76 percent copied word for word someone else's assignments.
- 79 percent of the students surveyed admitted to plagiarizing their assignments from the Internet or citing sources when appropriate.
- 42 percent indicated that they purchased custom term papers, essays, and thesis online.
- 28 percent indicated that they had a service take their online classes for them.
- 72 percent indicated that they had used their phone, tablet, or computer to cheat in class.
- Only 12 percent indicated that they would never cheat because of ethics.

It is disappointing to find out that only 12 percent used ethics to determine not to cheat. The rest seem oblivious to the fact that cheating is morally wrong. By cheating, students gain an unfair advantage over their honest classmates. Taken to its extreme, cheating your way through college may result in a higher grade point average but you learn less than one who acted morally. How will this help you to pass the certified professional accountant's exam (CPA)? Have you thought about interviewing for a job and starting by having a falsehood on your resume? How would you feel if your employer gives you an assignment, which should be easy for a student with a high GPA, but it is difficult for you because you never honestly studied and learned what the assignment is all about? These are questions that get to the core of ethics—making ethical judgments.

It is worth noting that at the time of this writing, Georgia Tech and Boston University were investigating whether students cheated during at-home online exams amid the COVID-19 pandemic. It appears that some students had others take exams for them and some shared answers to online exams. If students were caught cheating in this way it means they ignored the academic conduct code.

There are those occasions where faculty or the university promotes cheating even though they know it is wrong. A case in point is the so-called paper-class scandal in which 3,100 student-athletes at the University of North Carolina in Chapel Hill (UNC) were essentially allowed to take classes without attending classes and given grades good enough to keep them eligible to play men's football and basketball during a 20-year period.

University of North Carolina athletes weren't the only group benefiting from the 18-year, 3,100-student cheating scandal—fraternity members did, too. More than 700 fraternity brothers, and some sorority sisters, took the no-attendance, no-professor, one-assignment "paper classes" that earned them easy A's and B's. **Exhibit 1.4** provides additional information about the scandal.

EXHIBIT 1.4   Student Cheating Scandal at the University of North Carolina*

If you're a college sports fan, by now you have probably heard about the paper-class scandal that we call "Tar Heel Gate." For five years, UNC had insisted the paper classes were the doing of one rogue professor: the department chair of the African-American studies program, Julius Nyang'oro. However, an independent report found that five counselors actively used paper classes, calling them "GPA boosters," and that at least two counselors suggested to a professor the grade an athlete needed to receive to be able to continue to play.

Many of the academic-athletic staff who were named and implicated were also named by university learning specialist Mary Willingham. Willingham said that she had worked with dozens of athletes who came to UNC and were unable to read at an acceptable level, with some of them reading on par with elementary schoolchildren. She also said there were many members of the athletic staff who knew about the paper classes, and her revelations contradicted what UNC had claimed for years—that Nyang'oro acted alone in providing the paper classes.

Willingham went public with detailed allegations about paper classes and, after an assault on her credibility by the university, filed a whistleblower lawsuit. In March 2015, UNC announced it would pay Willingham $335,000 to settle her suit.

In an unusual twist to the story, the director of UNC's Parr Center for Ethics, Jeanette M. Boxill, was accused of steering athletes into fake classes to help them maintain their eligibility with the NCAA. Moreover, she covered up her actions after the fact. Boxill violated the most basic standards of academic integrity.

(continued)

The motivating factor at UNC was to keep student athletes eligible so that the sports programs would continue to excel and promote and publicize the school, not to mention earn millions of dollars in advertising. The investigation was completed in October 2017 and while the NCAA did not dispute that UNC was guilty of running one of the worst academic fraud schemes in college sports history, it did not impose any penalties because "no rules were broken." How could that be? Well, the panel that investigated the case determined that it could not punish the university or its athletic program because the paper classes were not available exclusively to athletes. Other students at UNC had access to the fraudulent classes, too.[16]

* Source: Marc Tracy, N.C.A.A.: North Carolina Will not Be Punished for Academic Scabdal, October 13, 2017, New York Times, Available at: https://www.nytimes.com/2017/10/13/sports/unc-north-carolina-ncaa.html

An ethical analysis of the scandal at UNC demonstrates ethical blindness. The athletic department and university failed to see the ethical violations of its actions in establishing a route for student-athletes to remain academically eligible. It acted in its own self-interest regardless of the impact of its behavior on affected parties including other students who did not benefit from the paper classes. The blind spots occurred because of a situational ethic whereby those who perpetrated the fraud and covered it up came to believe their actions were for the greater good of those involved in the athletic program and the UNC community. Honesty was ignored, integrity was not in the picture, and the athletes were not provided with the education they deserved.

The UNC situation illustrates an ends-justify-the-means approach to decision making in that some faculty rationalized cheating by saying it was necessary to maintain eligibility for student athletes.

Social Networking

The term "social network" is how we connect to other people using a platform that supports online communication, such as Facebook, Instagram, or Twitter. Video sharing services such as Snapchat and Tiktok are popular among millennials and the Generation Zers. The use of such social networking sites raises many questions that pertain to ethics.

It is not unusual to read critical, harsh, or hurtful comments on social networking sites. The harsh comments may be designed to embarrass someone or make them feel bad about themselves, making the recipient angry. They may want to lash out on social media in revenge. Before you know it the tone of the conversation goes from insulting to abusive.

Taken to an extreme, the harmful comments can lead to real danger including cyberbullying, especially when young adults are the target of the online abusers. Here, the words said take the form of aggressive behavior that is hostile to the recipient. Cyberbullying can lead to depression and even thoughts of suicide.

Today we see examples of calling-out someone on social media or cancelling them. Mintz points out that there is a difference between calling someone out and cancelling them. In the call-out culture a mistake, ill-advised statement, or other expression of one's views are taken to be a misstep—an error of judgment—that doesn't define that person. Oftentimes it occurred years ago. It might have been a questionable post on twitter. By calling-out the individual, we allow for the fact that they can learn and do better the next time.[17]

The motivation for cancelling someone is a lack of respect for something they said or did such as making offensive comments toward another. It is much more extreme than just calling them out. It has as its goal embarrassing them in their community. It's a form of social and cultural boycott driven by "groupthink" that manifests itself through intolerance of others with a point of view that diverges from group norms. Ironically, if a member of the cancelling group does not go along with the prevailing views of the group they may be canceled themselves.

The cancel culture can create an ethical slippery slope event. Where do we draw the line between a statement or action that should be canceled and one that should only be called-out or even ignored?

Cancelling someone promotes intolerance and stifles diversity of speech. It can promote shame and a feeling that one has committed an offense that likely would be universally condemned by offended parties and society in general.

Cancelling is the opposite of being understanding, kind, and compassionate. After all, we should be willing to forgive others if they admit their mistake, are remorseful, make amends, promise not to do again, and change their behavior accordingly.

Examples of the cancel culture range from those who seem to deserve to be expelled from the Hollywood community, such as Harvey Weinstein, to those who make comments offensive to some people or groups. Weinstein, who was accused by more than 40 women of sexual abuse and harassment, exacted sexual favors from actresses in return for stardom.

Many well-known people have been cancelled because of racist tweets including actor Kevin Hart and television star Rosanne Barr. While these abhorrent comments may justify cancelling the offender, a valid question is: How far should we go to cancel someone? After all, the right to free speech is guaranteed by the U.S. Constitution. However, this raises the ethical point that just because someone has a right to do or say something that doesn't mean it is the right thing to do.

The Six Pillars of Character

LO 1-2
Explain how characteristic traits of behavior influence ethical decision making.

It has been said that ethics is all about how we act when no one is looking. In other words, ethical people do not do the right thing because someone observing their actions might judge them otherwise, or because they may be punished as a result of their actions. Instead, ethical people act as they do because their "inner voice" or conscience tells them that it is the right thing to do.

Assume that you are leaving a shopping mall, get into your car to drive away, and hit a parked car in the lot on the way out. Let's also assume that no one saw you hit the car. What are your options? You could simply drive away and forget about it, or you can leave a note for the owner of the parked car with your contact information. What would you do and why? Would your action change if your son or daughter were in the car? Now just imagine your car was hit. Further, it's a brand new car. What would you want the motorist to do and why? The point is The Golden Rule asks us to think about ethics as if we are the recipient of possible unethical behavior.

Virtues or Character Traits

According to "virtue ethics," there are certain ideals, such as excellence or dedication to the common good, toward which we should strive and which allow the full development of our humanity. These ideals are discovered through thoughtful reflection on what we as human beings have the potential to become.

Virtues are attitudes, dispositions, or character traits that enable us to be and to act in ways that develop this potential. They enable us to pursue the ideals we have adopted. Honesty, courage, compassion, generosity, fidelity, integrity, fairness, self-control, and prudence are all examples of virtues in Aristotelian ethics. A quote attributed to Aristotle is, "We are what we repeatedly do. Therefore, excellence is not an act. It is a habit."[18]

The Josephson Institute of Ethics identifies Six Pillars of Character that provide a foundation to guide ethical decision making. These ethical values include trustworthiness, respect, responsibility, fairness, caring, and citizenship. Josephson believes that the Six Pillars act as a multilevel filter through which to process decisions. So, being trustworthy is not enough—we must also be caring. Adhering to the letter of the law is not enough; we must accept responsibility for our actions or inactions.[19]

Trustworthiness

The dimensions of trustworthiness include being honest, acting with integrity, being reliable, and exercising loyalty in dealing with others.

Honesty

Honesty is the most basic ethical value. It means that we should express the truth as we know it and without deception. There are two elements of honesty: (1) not making a statement that deceives others, or a lie of commission, and (2) failing to mention something that someone has a right to know or purposefully leaving it out, which is a lie by omission.

Some people believe "white lies" are acceptable behavior when it is a lie about a small or unimportant matter that someone tells to avoid hurting another person. For example, someone gives you a gift for your birthday you don't like. Do you say you don't like it or something such as "Thanks for the thoughtful gift?" Here, we could justify the latter because kindness and caring about the other person outweighs being truthful. So, two of these values may conflict and a decision made which is more important. The danger of telling a white lie is we may have to perpetuate the lie or continue to create more lies to cover our tracks.

Integrity

The integrity of a person is an essential element in trusting that person. A person of integrity takes time for self-reflection, so that the events, crises, and challenges of everyday living do not determine the course of that person's moral life. Such a person is trusted by others because that person is true to their word.

Ultimately, integrity means to act on principle rather than expediency. If my superior tells me to do something wrong, I will not do it because it violates the ethical value of honesty. If my superior pressures me to compromise my values just this one time, I will not agree because one time can lead to another and a slide down the proverbial *ethical slippery slope.*

Reliability

The promises that we make to others are relied on by them, and we have a moral duty to follow through with action. A reliable person can be counted on because they are dependable and always try to do the right thing. Our ethical obligation for promise keeping includes avoiding bad-faith excuses and unwise commitments. For example, you should not agree to go out on a date with someone and then back away because something better comes up.

Loyalty

Loyalty requires that friends not violate the confidence we place in them. In accounting, loyalty requires that we keep financial and other information confidential when it deals with our employer and client. For example, if you are the in-charge accountant on an audit of a client for your CPA firm-employer and you discover that the client is "cooking the books," you shouldn't telephone the local newspaper and tell the story to a reporter. Instead, you should go to your supervisor and discuss the matter and, if necessary, go all the way up to the partner in charge of the engagement and tell them. Your ethical obligation is to report what you have observed to your supervisor and let them take the appropriate action. However, the ethics of the accounting profession allow for instances whereby informing those above your supervisor is expected, an act of internal whistleblowing, and, in rare circumstances, going outside the organization to report the wrongdoing. Whistleblowing obligations will be discussed in **Chapter 3**.

There are limits to the confidentiality obligation. For example, let's assume that you are the accounting manager at a publicly owned company and your supervisor (the controller) pressures you to keep silent about the manipulation of financial information. You then go to the CFO, who tells you that both the CEO and board of directors support the controller. Out of a misplaced duty of loyalty in this situation, you might rationalize your silence as did Betty Vinson. Here ethical values conflict. Loyalty is the one value that should never take precedence over other values such as honesty and integrity. Otherwise, we can imagine all kinds of cover-ups of information in the interest of loyalty or friendship.

Respect

All people should be treated with dignity. We do not have an ethical duty to hold all people in high esteem, but we should treat everyone with respect, regardless of their circumstances in life. In today's slang, we might say that respect means giving a person "props." The Golden Rule encompasses respect for others through notions such as civility, courtesy, decency, dignity, autonomy, tolerance, and acceptance.[20]

Respect is an element of the cancel culture. When someone acts in an offensive way it could lead to the loss of respect and being cancelled. On the other hand, we should respect those who have earned our admiration by doing things that conform to the ethical values.

It seems more and more today that we are having trouble talking to each other in a civil manner. Arguments break out because of differences of opinion. Name calling is on the rise. We, must, as a society, learn how to disagree with each other without being disagreeable.

Responsibility

Josephson points out that our capacity to reason and our freedom to choose make us morally responsible for our actions and decisions. We are accountable for what we do and who we are.[21]

The judgments we make in life reflect whether we have acted responsibly. Eleanor Roosevelt, the former first lady, puts it well: "One's philosophy is not best expressed in words; it is expressed in the choices one makes . . . and the choices we make are ultimately our responsibility." We should never blame another person for our failings in life. We need to accept responsibility for our actions and be accountable for them.

Fairness

Fairness is a subjective concept but typically involves issues of equality, impartiality, and due process. As Josephson points out, "Fairness implies adherence to a balanced standard of justice without relevance to one's own feelings or inclinations."[22]

The problem sometimes is what seems fair to one person or group seems unfair to another. For example, if a department head has limited funds for bonuses and chooses one group of people over another, those passed over may think they have been unfairly treated while those receiving bonuses believe they deserved it.

Caring

The late Edmund L. Pincoffs, a philosopher who formerly taught at the University of Texas at Austin, believed that virtues such as caring, kindness, sensitivity, altruism, and benevolence enable a person who possesses these qualities to consider the interests of others.[23] Such people gain empathy for others. They are able to "walk a mile in someone else's shoes," meaning that before judging another person, you must first understand that person's experiences and thought processes. Josephson believes that caring is the "heart of ethics and ethical decision making."[24]

Kind people are willing to go out of their way to help others and they do not expect anything in return. The act itself is enough and can enhance their feeling of self-worth. One form of kindness is a random act of kindness that is unplanned; they are spontaneous. You may do them because of the way you feel at the moment. For example, you may offer to cover the shift of a coworker who just found out their child is sick and needs to be picked up at school.

Citizenship

Josephson points out that "citizenship includes civic virtues and duties that prescribe how we ought to behave as part of a community."[25] An important part of good citizenship is to obey the laws, be informed about the issues, volunteer in your community, and vote in elections.

Another important part of citizenship is to act in the common good. A good example is the call to action to wear a mask and practice social distancing during the recent COVID-19 pandemic. We were not only doing it for ourselves but for the health and welfare of others in our community.

Civility is an important part of being a good citizen. It is much more than acting politely and respectfully toward others. It means to avoid harmful actions toward others. Verbal or physical attacks on others, cyber bullying, rudeness, religious intolerance, discrimination, and vandalism are just some of the acts that are generally considered acts of incivility. By acting civilly toward other, we can foster civic discourse in society.

The 2019 annual poll on civility in society by Weber Shandwick continues to show that a vast majority of Americans—93 percent—identify incivility as a problem in society, with most classifying it as a "major" problem (68%). According to the poll, the consequences of incivility include: (1) cyberbullying (89%); (2) harassment (88%); (3) violent behavior (88%); (4) hate crimes (88%); (5) intimidation and threats (87%); (6) intolerance (87%); (7) people feeling less safe in public places (87%); (8) discrimination and unfair treatment of certain groups of people (84%); (9) less community engagement (79%); and (10) feelings of isolation and loneliness (78%).[26]

Virtues such as respect, kindness, caring, empathy, and responsibility are all elements of a civil society. Those who practice it would never engage in these acts and should speak out when others do as well.

Reputation

It might be said that judgments made about one's character contribute toward how another party views that person's reputation. In other words, what is the estimation in which a person is commonly held, whether favorable or not?

Often when we cover up information in the present, it becomes public knowledge later. The consequences at that time are more serious because trust has been destroyed. A good example is Lance Armstrong, who for years denied taking performance-enhancing drugs while winning seven Tour de France titles. In 2012, he finally admitted to doing just that, and as a result, all those titles were stripped away by the U.S. Anti-Doping Agency. Armstrong's reputation took a hit and the admiration many in the public had for him fell by the wayside.

There is a saying that it takes a long time to build a reputation for trust but not very long to lose it. Lance Armstrong is a case in point.

Moral Courage

Moral Courage means to act for moral reasons and stand up for what you believe regardless of any negative consequences for yourself, such as ridicule, punishment, loss of job, or social status.

A good example of when it would have been important to act with moral courage is the hazing incident that occurred at Louisiana State University in the 2018 fall semester. Members of Delta Kappa Epsilon forced pledges to lie in piles of broken glass, kicked them with steel-toed boots, urinated on them, and committed acts of abuse.

Imagine you are a fraternity brother witnessing these incidents. Recognizing the dangers to the pledges, you want to do something about it but are concerned about the reaction of your fraternity brothers. If you act at that moment, you may suffer abuse either verbal or physical. If you fail to act, then you have given in to fear of the consequences rather than doing the right thing. If you act with moral courage, you would do something about the situation while also minimizing the risk of harm to yourself.

So, what are your choices? Speaking to the brothers and discussing the dangers is a start. You could report it to the university administration if the brothers fail to act. Much like whistleblowing, the first attempt should be to take care of the matter internally among those involved. If that does not work, reporting the matter to the Interfraternity Council might be the next step even though it involves external whistleblowing where you could be labeled disloyal. But remember loyalty should never be used to mask higher ethical values such as caring and concern for others and one's responsibility to right a wrong.

Modern Moral Philosophies

LO 1-3

Differentiate between moral philosophies and their effect on ethical reasoning in accounting.

The ancient Greeks believed that reason and thought precede the choice of action and that we deliberate about things we can influence with our decisions. The ability to reason through ethical dilemmas and act on moral intent is a necessary but sometimes insufficient skill to make ethical decisions. This is because, while we believe that we should behave in accordance with certain moral principles, peer pressure, pressure from one's superior(s), and a culture that favors the client's interest above the public interest together create a barrier to acting in accordance with those principles. For example, accountants know inventory obsolescence should be recorded at year-end. But what if the client insists on holding off on the write-down due to concerns about a low level of earnings? Will we stand by our moral principles? Will we satisfy our obligation to honor the public trust? Or will we go along to get along and be a "team player"?

The noted philosopher James R. Rest points out that moral philosophies present guidelines for "determining how conflicts in human interests are to be settled for optimizing mutual benefit of people living together in groups." However, there is no single moral philosophy everyone accepts.[27]

Moral philosophies provide specific principles and rules that we can use to decide what is right or wrong in specific instances. There are many such philosophies and they are quite complex. We limit the discussion to what is necessary for students to learn in order to apply these methods to a variety of conflict situations that occur in accounting. Later in this chapter we will address the ethical standards embedded in the profession's ethics codes. It is the combination of the two that establish the ethical expectations of the public for the accounting profession. We do not favor any one of these philosophies because there is no one correct way to resolve ethical issues in accounting. **Exhibit 1.5** presents the underlying framework for ethical decision making for each of the moral philosophies. It describes how each method is used to make ethical judgments. Students should use this exhibit as a road map to ethical decision making as it simplifies the discussion in the text of complex philosophical issues.

EXHIBIT 1.5   Understanding Ethics as a Framework for Guiding Behavior

Philosophical Method	Proponents →	Basis for Moral Behavior →	Achieving Moral Excellence →	End Goal
Classic Greek Virtue Ethics	Aristotle, Plato, Socrates	**Virtues** Develop ethical character traits	Develop moral and intellectual virtues	Human excellence/a life of virtue
Modern Philosophies Deontology (Rights Theory)	Kant	**Moral Principle** Categorical Imperative/ Universality	Satisfying duties to oneself and others	Treat humanity as an end in itself not a means to an end
Teleology (Act Utilitarianism)	Bentham, Mill	**Moral Action** Greatest good for the greatest number	Make decisions that produce the best consequences for oneself and others	Maximize well-being for all concerned
(Rule Utilitarianism)		Actions that conform to general rules	Make decisions that produce the best consequences for oneself and others without violating certain rules	
Egoism (Rational Egoism)	Rand	**Moral Principle** The virtue of rationality	Make decisions that promote one's own interests in accordance with reason	Rational Selfishness

(continued)

Philosophical Method	Proponents → Basis for Moral Behavior → Achieving Moral Excellence → End Goal			
(Enlightened Egoism)	Alexis de Tocqueville	**Moral Concept** Self-interest rightly understood	Pursue self-interest to maximize general prosperity	Allow for the well-being of others in pursuing one's own interest
Justice	Rawls	**Moral Principles** Liberty Principle Difference Principle	Fair treatment: Treat equals, equally; unequals, unequally	Give each person what they deserve

Teleology

In *teleology,* an act is considered morally right or acceptable if it produces some desired result such as pleasure, the realization of self-interest, fame, utility, wealth, and so on. Teleologists assess the moral worth of behavior by looking at its consequences, and thus moral philosophers often refer to these theories as *consequentialism.* Consequentialism is a theory about outcomes, not motives or intentions. Two important teleological philosophies are egoism and utilitarianism.

Egoism

Egoism defines right or acceptable behavior in terms of its consequences for the individual. *Egoists* believe that they should make decisions that maximize their own self-interest, which is defined differently by each individual. In other words, the individual should "[do] the act that promotes the greatest good for oneself."[28] Many believe that egoistic people and companies are inherently unethical because they ignore the moral point of view: they are short-term-oriented and will take advantage of others to achieve their goals. We discuss three forms of egoism below: ethical egoism, enlightened egoism, and rational egoism.

ETHICAL EGOISM

As a brand of egoism, *ethical egoism* claims that the promotion of one's own good is in accordance with morality. It may or may not be moral to never promote it based on the version used. Thus, there are conditions in which the avoidance of personal interest may be a moral action.[29]

The ethical egoist ranks as most important duties that bring the highest payoff to oneself. Standard moral theories determine importance, at least in part, by considering the payoff to those helped. The conclusion is what brings the highest payoff to me will not, necessarily, bring the highest payoff to those helped.[30]

Ethical egoism as a moral theory creates conflicts of interest that are difficult to resolve. It is argued that pursuing my own interest can conflict with another's interest—my actions may bring about a cost to others. Specifically, a critic may contend that personal gain logically cannot be in one's best interest if it entails doing harm to another: doing harm to another would be to accept the principle that doing harm to another is ethical—that is, one would equate doing harm with one's own best interest. The ethical egoist could logically pursue their interests at the cost of others.[31]

Egoism/ethical egoism is not an acceptable standard for decision making in accounting. How could we justify ignoring the public interest because it is in our own best interest not to go against the client's wishes?

ENLIGHTENED EGOISM

Enlightened self-interest was discussed by Alexis de Tocqueville in his work *Democracy in America.* The notion he held was that Americans voluntarily join together in associations to further the interests of the group and, thereby, to serve their own interests.[32] This certainly accurately characterizes the role and purpose of the accounting profession.

Alexis de Tocqueville used "self-interest rightly understood" to describe this concept. He combined the right of association with the virtue to do what was right.

Enlightened self-interest poses the question of whether or not it is to the advantage of a person to work for the good of all.

Enlightened egoism is one form of egoism that emphasizes more of a direct action to bring about the best interests of society. Enlightened egoists take a long-range perspective and allow for the well-being of others because they help achieve some ultimate goal for the decision maker, although their own self-interest remains paramount. For example, enlightened egoists may abide by professional codes of ethics, avoid cheating on taxes, and create safe working conditions. They do so not because their actions benefit others, but because they help achieve some ultimate goal for the egoist, such as advancement within the firm.[33] In other words, enlightened egoism is advocated as a means rather than an end, based on the belief that for everyone to pursue their own interests will maximize general prosperity.

Let's examine the following example from the perspectives of egoism and enlightened egoism. The date is Friday, January 17, 2021, and the time is 5:00 p.m. It is the last day of fieldwork on an audit, and you are the staff auditor in charge of receivables. You are wrapping up the test of subsequent collections of accounts receivable to determine whether certain receivables that were outstanding on December 31, 2020, and that were not confirmed by the customer as being outstanding, have now been collected. If these receivables have been collected and in amounts equal to the year-end outstanding balances, then you will be confident that the December 31 balance is correct and this aspect of the receivables audit can be relied on.

However, one account receivable for $1 million has not been collected, even though it is 90 days past due. You go to your supervisor and discuss whether to establish an allowance for uncollectibles for part of or the entire amount. Your supervisor contacts the manager in charge of the audit who goes to the CFO to discuss the matter. The CFO says in no uncertain terms that you should not record an allowance of any amount. The CFO does not want to reduce earnings below the current level because that will cause the company to fail to meet financial analysts' estimates of earnings for the year. Your supervisor informs you that the firm will go along with the client on this matter, even though the $1 million amount is material. In fact, it is 10 percent of the overall accounts receivable balance on December 31, 2020.

The junior auditor faces a challenge to integrity in this instance. The client is attempting to circumvent GAAP. The ethical obligation of the staff auditor is not to subordinate judgment to others' judgment, including that of top management of the firm. Easier said than done, no doubt, but it is the standard of behavior in this situation.

If you are an egoist, you might conclude that it is in your best interests to go along with the firm's position, to support the client's presumed interests. After all, you do not want to lose your job. An enlightened egoist would consider the interests of others, including the investors and creditors, but still might reason that it is in their long-run interests to go along with the firm's position to support the client because they may not advance within the firm unless they are perceived to be a team player. Moreover, you don't want the firm to lose a client if it does not go along with the client's wishes. While the interests of others are seen as a means to an end—maximize one's own self-interests—enlightened egoism has value in accounting decision making because the public interest can (and should) be considered in evaluating the competing interests in the course of maximizing one's own interests.

RATIONAL EGOISM

Rational egoism is a particular brand of ethical egoism that claims the promotion of one's own interest is always in accordance with reason. Rational egoism, also called rational selfishness, is the principle that an action is rational if and only if it maximizes one's self-interest. One of the most well-known proponents of rational egoism is the contemporary philosopher Ayn Rand (1905–1982).

Rand's philosophy is an ethics of choice, guided by reason, with human survival as its goal. This is diametrically opposed to altruism. Altruism, according to Rand, is a morality of the past. It is irrational to expect people to be motivated to act in whole or in part for the sake of another's interest(s). According to Rand, humans must choose their own values, goals, and actions in order to maintain their lives. Without the ability to choose, there could be no morality because morality deals only with issues requiring a decision (i.e., the use of free will).

In Rand's *The Virtue of Selfishness: A New Concept of Egoism,* rationality is conceived of as man's basic virtue, the source of all other virtues. The virtue of rationality means the recognition and acceptance of reason as one's only source of knowledge, one's only judge of values, and one's only guide to action. It means a commitment to the reality of one's existence, that is, to the principles that all of one's goals, values, and actions take place in reality and, therefore, that one must never place any value or consideration whatsoever above one's "perception of reality."[34]

It is popular today to link Rand's philosophy with the basic tenets of capitalism. She describes the capitalist system as the essence of individualism with a laissez-faire attitude in which the function of government is solely to protect individual rights, including property rights. The idea is for the government to have a hands-off approach and let each individual act in their rational self-interest and somehow this will lead to the ultimate best interests of society. Thus, Rand had a vision of capitalism as a moral ideal. Of course, this is a controversial issue today as many critics talk about the evils of capitalism and the unequal distribution of resources and wealth born out of a pursuit of self-interest mentality of corporations and well-heeled individuals.

The problem we see with Rand in the accounting arena is it is a profession where one's individual values need to conform to the profession's ethical standards and, if they do not, the individual runs the risk of acting in their own best interests but not the public interest. Moreover, individuals may have a different perception of reality and those perceptions may change with each new situation. Actions become more relativistic and this makes it difficult to have a consistent set of ethical standards such as exists in the AICPA Code of Professional Conduct (AICPA Code). The reality for accounting students to consider in evaluating Rand's philosophy is the ethical standards of the accounting profession are not up for debate.

Utilitarianism

Like egoism, *Utilitarianism* is concerned with consequences, but unlike the egoist, the utilitarian seeks to make decisions that bring about the greatest good for the greatest number of people affected by a decision.[35]

Utilitarians follow a relatively straightforward method for deciding the morally correct course of action for any particular situation. First, they identify the various courses of action that they could perform. Second, they determine the utility of the consequences of all possible alternatives and then select the one that results in the greatest net benefit. In other words, they identify all the foreseeable benefits and harms (consequences) that could result from each course of action for those affected by the action, and then choose the course of action that provides the greatest benefits after the costs have been taken into account.[36] Given its emphasis on evaluating the benefits and harms of alternatives on stakeholders, utilitarianism requires that people look beyond self-interest to consider impartially the interest of all persons affected by their actions.

The utilitarian theory was first formulated in the eighteenth century by the English writer Jeremy Bentham (1748–1832) and later refined by John Stuart Mill (1806–1873). As their basis for moral behavior evolved over the years, Utilitarians differed in their views about the kind of question we ought to ask ourselves when making an ethical decision. Some believe the proper question is: What effect will my doing this action in this situation have on the general balance of good over evil? If lying would produce the best consequences in a particular situation, we ought to lie.[37] These *act-utilitarians* examine the specific action itself, rather than the general rules governing the action, to assess whether it will result in the greatest utility. For example, a rule in accounting such as "don't subordinate judgment to the client" would serve only as a general guide for an act-utilitarian. If the overall effect of giving in to the client's demands brings net utility to all the stakeholders, then the rule is set aside.

Rule-utilitarians, on the other hand, claim that we must choose the action that conforms to the general rule that would have the best consequences. In other words, we must ask ourselves: What effect would everyone's doing this kind of action (subordination of judgment) have on the general balance of good over evil? For the rule-utilitarian, actions are justified by appealing to rules such as "never compromise audit independence." According to the rule-utilitarian, an action is selected because it is required by the correct moral rules that everyone should follow. For example, a general rule such as "don't deceive" (an element of truthfulness) might be interpreted as requiring the full disclosure of the possibility that the client will not collect on a material, $1 million receivable. A rule-utilitarian might reason that the long-term effects of deceiving the users of financial statements are a breakdown of the trust that exists between the users and preparers and auditors of financial information. Notwithstanding differences between act- and rule-utilitarians, most hold to the general principle that morality must depend on balancing the beneficial and harmful consequences of conduct.[38]

While utilitarianism is a very popular ethical theory, there are some difficulties in relying on it as a sole method for moral decision making because the utilitarian calculation requires that we assign values to the benefits and harms resulting from our actions. But it is often difficult, if not impossible, to measure and compare the values of certain benefits and costs. Let's go back to our receivables example. It would be difficult to quantify the possible effects of going along with the client. How can a utilitarian measure the costs to the company of possibly having to write off a potential bad debt after the fact, including possible higher interest rates to borrow money in the future because of a decline in liquidity? What is the cost to one's reputation for failing to disclose an event at a point in time that might have affected the analysis of financial results? On the other hand, how can we measure the benefits to the company of *not* recording the allowance? Does it mean the stock price will rise and, if so, by how much?

Deontology

The term *deontology* is derived from the Greek word *deon,* meaning "duty." *Deontology* refers to moral philosophies that focus on the rights of individuals and on the intentions associated with a particular behavior, rather than on its consequences.

Deontologists believe that moral norms establish the basis for action. Deontology differs from rule-utilitarianism in that the moral norms (or rules) are based on reason, not outcomes. Fundamental to deontological theory is the idea that equal respect must be given to all persons.[39] In other words, individuals have certain inherent rights and I, as the decision maker, have a duty (obligation, commitment, or responsibility) to respect those rights. Philosophers claim that rights and duties are correlative. That is, my rights establish your duties and my duties correspond to the rights of others.[40]

As with utilitarians, deontologists may be divided into those who focus on moral rules and those who focus on the nature of the acts themselves. Unlike utilitarians, deontologists argue there are things we should not do, even to maximize utility. We should not deceive investors and creditors by going along with improper accounting even if it enables a client to gain needed financing, expand operations, add jobs to the payroll, and, ultimately, earn greater profit for the company. To do so would violate the rights of investors and creditors to full and fair financial information to assist in their decision-making needs (i.e., buy/sell stock, loan money/don't loan).

Rule deontologists believe that conformity to general moral principles based on logic determines ethicalness. Examples include Kant's categorical imperative, discussed next, and the Golden Rule.

Rights Principles

A *right* is a justified claim on others. For example, if I have a right to freedom, then I have a justified claim to be left alone by others. Turned around, I can say that others have a duty or responsibility to leave me alone.[41] In accounting, because investors and creditors have a right to accurate and complete financial information, I have the duty to ensure that the financial statements "present fairly" the financial position, results of operations, and changes in cash flows.

One of the most important and influential interpretations of moral rights is based on the work of Immanuel Kant (1724–1804), an eighteenth-century philosopher. Kant maintained that each of us has a worth or dignity that must be respected. This dignity makes it wrong for others to abuse us or to use us against our will. Kant expressed this idea as a moral principle: Humanity must always be treated as an end, not merely as a means. To treat a person as a mere means is to use them to advance one's own interest. But to treat a person as an end is to respect that person's dignity by allowing each the freedom to choose for themselves.[42]

An important contribution of Kantian philosophy is the so-called categorical imperative: "Act only according to that maxim by which you can at the same time will that it should become universal law."[43] The "maxim" of our acts can be thought of as the intention behind our acts. The maxim answers the question: What am I doing, and why? In other words, moral intention is a driver of ethical action. The categorical imperative is a useful perspective: How would I want others to decide the issue in similar situations for similar reasons? If I can confidently answer that question, then my decision would meet the universality standard.

Kant believed that truth telling could be made a universal law, but lying could not. If we all lied whenever it suited us, rational communication would be impossible. Thus, lying is unethical. Imagine if every company falsified its financial statements. It would be impossible to evaluate the financial results of one company accurately over time and in comparison to other companies. The financial markets might ultimately collapse because reported results were meaningless, or even misleading. This condition of universality, not unlike the Golden Rule, prohibits us from giving our own personal point of view special status over the point of view of others. It is a strong requirement of impartiality and equality for ethics.[44]

One problem with deontology is when the rights of two groups conflict. For example, it is still legal for a private golf club to permit one group to join, such as men, but deny the same right to others, namely women. A private membership club, as it is sometimes called, is one that is explicitly *not* open to the public. In these situations, either club's rights are violated or individual rights are violated by not being allowed to join. Here, social or personal costs must be identified and weighed; rights cannot be the only consideration when making ethical choices.

In accounting, we may have to differentiate between the rights of one party versus another and should rely on our duties/obligations to each under the Principles in the AICPA Code that are discussed later. But, never forget that the rights of investors and creditors must come first and not be masked by perceived obligations to ourselves and others.

Justice

Justice is usually associated with issues of rights, fairness, and equality. A just act respects your rights and treats you fairly. Justice means giving each person what they deserve. *Justice* and *fairness* are closely related terms that are often used interchangeably, although differences do exist. While *justice* usually has been used with reference to a standard of rightness, *fairness* often has been used with regard to an ability to judge without reference to one's feelings or interests.

Justice as Fairness

John Rawls (1921-2002) developed a conception of justice as fairness using elements of both Kantian and utilitarian philosophy. He described a method for the moral evaluation of social and political institutions based on Liberty and Difference principles.[45]

Rawls argues that the rational individual would only choose to establish a society that would at least conform to the following two rules:

1. *Each person is to have an equal right to the most extensive basic liberty compatible with similar liberty for others.*
2. *Social and economic inequalities are to be arranged so that they are both:*

    (a) reasonably expected to be to everyone's advantage and

    (b) attached to positions and offices open to all.

The first principle—often called the *Liberty Principle*—is very Kantian in that it provides for basic and universal respect for persons as a minimum standard for all just institutions. But while all persons may be morally equal, we also know that in the "real world" there are significant differences between individuals that under conditions of liberty will lead to social and economic inequalities.

The second principle—called the *Difference Principle*—permits such inequalities and even suggests that it will be to the advantage of all (similar to the utility principle), but only if they meet the two rules. Thus the principles are not strictly egalitarian, but they are not laissez-faire either. Rawls is locating his vision of justice in between these two extremes.

When people differ over what they believe should be given, or when decisions have to be made about how benefits and burdens should be distributed among a group of people, questions of justice or fairness inevitably arise. These are questions of *distributive justice.*[46]

The most fundamental principle of justice, defined by Aristotle more than 2,000 years ago, is that "equals should be treated equally and unequals unequally." In other words, individuals should be treated the same unless they differ in ways that are relevant to the situation in which they are involved. The problem with this interpretation is in determining which criteria are morally relevant to distinguish between those who are equal and those who are not. It can be a difficult theory to apply in business if, for example, a CEO of a company decides to allocate a larger share of the resources than is warranted (justified), based on the results of operations, to one product line over another to promote that operation because it is judged to have more long-term expansion and income potential. If I am the manager in charge of the operation getting fewer resources but producing equal or better results, then I may believe that my operation has been (I have been) treated unfairly. However, it could be said that the other manager deserves to receive a larger share of the resources because of the long-term potential of that other product line. That is, the product lines are not equal; the former deserves more resources because of its greater upside potential.

For purposes of future discussions about ethical decision making, we elaborate on the concept of *procedural justice.* Procedural justice is the idea that fairness in the processes should resolve disputes and allocate resources. When there is strong employee support for decisions, decision makers, organizations, and outcomes, procedural justice is less important to the individual. In contrast, when employees' support for decisions, decision makers, organizations, or outcomes is not very strong, then procedural justice becomes more important.[47] Consider, for example, a potential whistleblower who feels confident about bringing her concerns to top management because specific procedures are in place to support that person. Unlike the Betty Vinson situation at WorldCom, an environment built on procedural justice supports the whistleblower, who perceives the fairness of procedures used to make decisions.

Virtue Ethics

One of the differences between virtue theory and the other moral philosophies is that virtue theory focuses on both the person engaging in the act and the act itself, whereas the latter focuses only on the act. This philosophy is called *virtue ethics,* and it posits that what is moral in a given situation is not only what conventional morality or moral rules require but also what a well-intentioned person with a "good" moral character would deem appropriate.

Virtue theorists place less emphasis on learning rules and instead stress the importance of developing *good habits of character,* such as kindness. Plato emphasized four virtues in particular, which were later called *cardinal virtues:* wisdom, courage, temperance, and justice. Other important virtues are fortitude, generosity, self-respect, good temper, and sincerity. In addition to advocating good habits of character, virtue theorists hold that we should avoid acquiring bad character traits, or vices, such as cowardice, insensibility, injustice, and vanity. Virtue theory emphasizes moral education because virtuous character traits are developed in one's youth. Adults, therefore, are responsible for instilling virtues in the young.

The philosopher Alasdair MacIntyre states that the exercise of virtue requires "a capacity to judge and to do the right thing in the right place at the right time in the right way." Judgment is exercised not through a routinizable application of the rules, but as a function of possessing those dispositions/tendencies (i.e., virtues) that enable choices to be made about what is good for people and by holding in check desires for something other than what will help achieve this goal.[48]

At the heart of the virtue approach to ethics is the idea of "community" and all who practice in it. MacIntyre relates virtues to the rewards of a practice. He differentiates between the external rewards of a practice (such as money, fame, and power) and the internal rewards, which relate to the intrinsic value of a particular practice. MacIntyre points out that every practice requires a certain kind of relationship between those who participate in it. The virtues are the standards of excellence that characterize relationships within the practice. To enter into a practice is to accept the authority of those standards, obedience to the rules, and commitment to achieve the internal rewards.[49] The accounting profession is a community with standards of excellence embodied in state board rules of conduct and the AICPA Code.

We have emphasized moral intent as an essential ingredient of ethical behavior. Moral intent is necessary to deal with the many conflicts in accounting among the interests of employers, clients, and the public interest. We realize that for students, it may be difficult to internalize the concept that, when forced into a corner by one's supervisor to go along with financial wrongdoing, you should stand up for what you know to be right, even if it means losing your job. However, ask yourself the following questions: Do I even want to work for an organization that does not value my professional opinion? If I go along with it this time, might the same demand be made at a later date? Will I begin to slide down that ethical slippery slope where there is no turning back? How much is my reputation for honesty and integrity worth? Would I be proud if others found out what I did (or didn't do)? To quote the noted Swiss psychologist and psychiatrist, Carl Jung: "You are what you do, not what you say you'll do."

By way of summarizing the material in this section, we present an analysis of ethical reasoning methods that form the basis for ethical judgments and related implementation issues in **Exhibit 1.6**. We elaborate on these judgments throughout the book. Students should use this exhibit as a road map to how ethical decisions should be made as it simplifies the discussion in the text of complex ethical reasoning methods.

EXHIBIT 1.6   Ethical Reasoning Method Bases for Making Ethical Judgments

	Teleology			Deontology		Virtue Ethics
	Egoism	**Enlightened Egoism**	**Utilitarianism**	**Rights Theory**	**Justice**	
Ethical Judgments	Defines "right" behavior by consequences for the decision maker	Considers well-being of others within the scope of deciding on a course of action based on self-interest	Evaluates consequences of actions (harms and benefits) on stakeholders	Considers "rights" of stakeholders and related duties to them	Emphasizes rights, fairness, and equality	Only method where ethical reasoning methods—"virtues" (internal traits of character)—apply both to the *decision maker* and the *decision*
			Act Evaluate whether the intended *action* provides the greatest net benefits	*Rule* Select the action that conforms to the correct *moral rule* that produces the greatest net benefits	Treats people as an end and not merely as a means to an end	Those with equal claims to justice should be treated equally; those with unequal claims should be treated unequally	Judgments are made not by applying rules, but by possessing those traits that enable the decision maker to act for the good of others
					Universality Perspective: Would I want others to act in a similar manner for similar reasons in this situation?		Similar to Principles of AICPA Code and IMA standards
Problems with Implementation	Fails to consider interests of those affected by the decision	Interests of others are subservient to self-interest	Can be difficult to assign values to harms and benefits	Relies on moral absolutes—no exceptions; need to resolve conflicting rights	Can be difficult to determine the criteria to distinguish equal from unequal claims	Virtues may conflict, requiring choices to be made

Moral Relativism

Moral relativism is the view that moral or ethical statements, which vary from person to person, are all equally valid and no one's opinion of right and wrong is actually better than any others.[50] In moral relativism, there is no ultimate standard of good or evil, so every judgment about right and wrong is purely a product of a person's preferences and environment.

Moral relativism moves away from the notion there are fixed standards of behavior based on moral principles and toward a subjective approach to decision making. In this view, morals depend on one's culture, religion, place, and time in which they occur. Three examples are ethical relativism, cultural relativism, and situation ethics.

Ethical Relativism

Moral relativism and *ethical relativism* are often thought of as the same concept. *Ethical relativism* is the philosophical view that what is right or wrong and good or bad is not absolute but variable and relative, depending on the person, circumstances, or social situation. Slavery is a good example of ethical relativism, an immoral act that some might feel is ethically acceptable.

Relativists point to certain beliefs in making their case.[51]

- What's right for you may not be what's right for me.
- What's right for my culture won't necessarily be what's right for your culture.
- No moral principles are true for all people at all times and in all places.

Cultural Relativism

Cultural relativism holds that morality is relative to the norms of one's culture. That is, whether an action is right or wrong depends on the moral norms of the society in which it is practiced. The same action may be morally right in one society but be morally wrong in another. If cultural relativism is correct, then there can be no common framework for resolving moral disputes or for reaching agreement on ethical matters among members of different societies.

A basic tenet of cultural relativism is that one cannot fully understand certain actions or customs without also understanding the culture from which those actions are derived. A good example is bullfighting, a traditional spectacle of Spain, Portugal, and some Latin American countries. Proponents claim it is a cultural art form. The highly regarded American novelist, Ernest Hemingway, said about bullfighting that it is "a decadent art in every way. . .[and] if it were permanent it could be one of the major arts."[52] The opposite view shared by many cultures is bullfighting is an indecent form of torture. Is one view right and the other wrong? It depends on your perspective.

Most ethicists reject the theory of moral relativism. Some philosophers criticize it because if it is true then one must obey the norms of one's society and to diverge from them is to act immorally. This means if I am a member of a society that believes sexist practices are morally permissible, then I must accept those practices as morally right. Such a view promotes social conformity and leaves no room for moral reform or improvement in a society.[53]

Just imagine we are back in 1920 before the Congressional ratification of the 19th Amendment to the U.S. Constitution that gave women the right to vote. If I were a firm believer in women's suffrage then, under cultural relativism, I must accept the fact that before that time it was morally appropriate that women were denied the right to vote.

Situation Ethics

Situation ethics, a term first coined in 1966 by an Episcopalian priest, Joseph Fletcher, is a body of ethical thought that takes normative principles—like the virtues, natural law, and Kant's categorical imperative that relies on the universality of actions—and generalizes them so that an agent can "make sense" out of one's experience when confronting ethical dilemmas. Unlike ethical relativism that denies universal moral principles, claiming the moral codes are strictly subjective, situational ethicists recognize the existence of normative principles but question whether they should be applied as strict directives (i.e., imperatives) or, instead, as guidelines that agents should use when determining a course of ethical conduct. In other words, situationists ask: Should these norms, as generalizations about what is desired, be regarded as intrinsically valid and universally obliging of all human beings? For situationists, the circumstances surrounding an ethical dilemma can and should influence an agent's decision-making process and may alter an agent's decision when warranted. Thus, situation ethics holds that "what in some times and in some places is ethical can be in other times and in other places unethical."[54]

A classic case of situation ethics is that of Anne Frank and her Jewish family that was hiding in a sealed-off area in the home of a Christian family in Amsterdam to escape Nazi terror back in World War II. Imagine if you were the person hiding Anne Frank and her family. One day Nazi soldiers came banging on your door and demanded, "Do you know where the Frank's are? A strict application of rights theory requires that you tell the truth. However, isn't this situation one in which an exception to the rule should come into play for humanitarian reasons? In other words, situational ethics is looking past the standard of right and wrong and performing what the circumstances demand.

The Public Interest in Accounting

LO 1-4
Describe how professional accountants serve the public interest and their obligations under the AICPA Code.

Regulation of the Accounting Profession

Professions are defined by the knowledge, skills, attitudes, behaviors, and ethics of those in the (accounting) profession. Regulation of a profession is a specific response to the need for certain standards to be met by the members of the profession. The accounting profession provides an important public service through audits and other assurance services (together, attest services) and those who choose to join the community pledge to act in the public interest.

Regulations exist to address the knowledge imbalance between the client and the provider of services, who has professional expertise. Regulation also helps when there are significant benefits or costs from the provision of accountancy services that accrue to third parties, other than those acquiring and producing the services.

In the United States, the state boards of accountancy are charged with protecting the public interest in licensing candidates to become CPAs. The behavior of licensed CPAs and their ability to meet ethical and professional obligations is regulated by the state boards. Regulatory oversight is based on the statutorily defined scope of practice of public accountancy. There are 55 state boards (50 states, plus the District of Columbia, Guam, Commonwealth of Northern Mariana Islands, Puerto Rico, and the U.S. Virgin Islands). Since it is impracticable to review all 55 state board rules, and many of them are similar, we will refer to the ethics standards of the American Institute of Certified Professional Accountants (AICPA) in **Chapter 4** to illustrate those rules.

The Public Interest in Accounting

Following the disclosure of numerous accounting scandals in the early 2000s at companies such as Enron and WorldCom, the accounting profession, professional bodies, and regulatory agencies turned their attention to examining how to rebuild the public trust and confidence in financial reporting. Stuebs and Wilkinson point out that restoring the accounting profession's public interest focus is a crucial first step in recapturing the public trust and securing the profession's future.[55] Copeland believes that in order to regain the trust and respect the profession enjoyed prior to the scandals, the profession must rebuild its reputation on its historical foundation of ethics and integrity.[56]

The CPA license has "public" in its title to remind all that the primary obligation of CPAs is to the public interest. Keeping the public interest in mind helps a CPA determine dilemmas such as: who is the primary client—the public, company, management, or shareholders; to whom ethical loyalty is owed; when services and clients present conflicts of interests; and when confidentiality must be upheld. The Principles in the AICPA Code state that "members should accept the obligation to act in a way that will serve the public interest, honor the public trust, and demonstrate commitment to professionalism" (AICPA 0.300.030.01, 2014). The responsibility to the public overrides the responsibilities to the clients or those who hire and pay them. The public interest includes those who rely on financial statements for lending, investing, and pension decisions.[57]

Ethics and Professionalism

The accounting profession is a community with values and standards of behavior. These are embodied in the various codes of conduct in the professional bodies, including the AICPA. The AICPA is a voluntary association of CPAs with more than 431,000 members in 130 countries, including CPAs in business and industry, public accounting, government, education; student affiliates; and international associates. CPA state societies also exist in the United States. Even though regulation of the profession and licensing is through state boards and state board rules of conduct, the AICPA Code of Professional Conduct is typically recognized as having accepted standards of behavior.

The Institute of Management Accountants (IMA) has a global network of accountants and financial professionals with more than 125,000 members from organizations of all sizes and structure, including family-run businesses, private firms, not-for-profit organizations, government and academic institutions, small and large publicly traded companies, and multi-national corporations. The IMA represents itself as The Association of Accountants and Financial Professionals in Business. Its Statement of Ethical Professional Practice provides guidelines for ethical conduct and is unique in that it provides guidelines to resolve ethical conflicts. The IMA standards appear in **Exhibit 1.7**.

EXHIBIT 1.7   **Institute of Management Accountants Statement of Ethical Professional Practice**

Members of IMA shall behave ethically. A commitment to ethical professional practice includes overarching principles that express our values and standards that guide member conduct.

Principles

IMA's overarching ethical principles include: Honesty, Fairness, Objectivity, and Responsibility. Members shall act in accordance with these principles and shall encourage others within their organizations to adhere to them.

Standards

IMA members have a responsibility to comply with and uphold the standards of Competence, Confidentiality, Integrity, and Credibility. Failure to comply may result in disciplinary action.

I. Competence

1. Maintain an appropriate level of professional leadership and expertise by enhancing knowledge and skills.
2. Perform professional duties in accordance with relevant laws, regulations, and technical standards.
3. Provide decision support information and recommendations that are accurate, clear, concise, and timely. Recognize and help manage risk.

II. Confidentiality

1. Keep information confidential except when disclosure is authorized or legally required.
2. Inform all relevant parties regarding appropriate use of confidential information. Monitor to ensure compliance.
3. Refrain from using confidential information for unethical or illegal advantage.

III. Integrity

1. Mitigate actual conflicts of interest. Regularly communicate with business associates to avoid apparent conflicts of interest. Advise all parties of any potential conflicts of interest.
2. Refrain from engaging in any conduct that would prejudice carrying out duties ethically.
3. Abstain from engaging in or supporting any activity that might discredit the profession.
4. Contribute to a positive ethical culture and place integrity of the profession above personal interests.

(continued)

IV. Credibility

1. Communicate information fairly and objectively.

2. Provide all relevant information that could reasonably be expected to influence an intended user's understanding of the reports, analyses, or recommendations.

3. Report any delays or deficiencies in information, timeliness, processing, or internal controls in conformance with organization policy and/or applicable law.

4. Communicate professional limitations or other constraints that would preclude responsible judgment or successful performance of an activity.

Resolving Ethical Issues

In applying the Standards of Ethical Professional Practice, the member may encounter unethical issues or behavior. In these situations, the member should not ignore them, but rather should actively seek resolution of the issue. In determining which steps to follow, the member should consider all risks involved and whether protections exist against retaliation.

When faced with unethical issues, the member should follow the established policies of their organization, including use of an anonymous reporting system if available.

If the organization does not have established policies, the member should consider the following courses of action:

• The resolution process could include a discussion with the member's immediate supervisor. If the supervisor appears to be involved, the issue could be presented to the next level of management.

• IMA offers an anonymous helpline that the member may call to request how key elements of the *IMA Statement of Ethical Professional Practice* could be applied to the ethical issue.

• The member should consider consulting their own attorney to learn of any legal obligations, rights, and risks concerning the issue.

If resolution efforts are not successful, the member may wish to consider disassociating from the organization.

Other professional organizations include The Institute of Internal Auditors (IIA), Association of Certified Fraud Examiners (ACFE), and The International Federation of Accountants IFAC. Similar to the IMA code, internal auditors are held to standards that address their competence, integrity, and objectivity (credibility). Both codes contain a provision for confidentiality because internal accountants and auditors gain access to sensitive financial and operating information that should not be disclosed because it might negatively affect the company's financial and operating positions.

Regulation in the accounting profession is a necessary but insufficient condition to ensure ethical and professional behavior occurs; ethics education on an ongoing basis is an essential ingredient through ethics courses in college and in continuing professional education. The key is to develop an ethical culture to support ethical behavior by setting an ethical tone at the top. This will be further explored in **Chapters 2** and **3**.

AICPA Code of Conduct

Principles in the Code

The Principles of the AICPA Code are aspirational statements that form the foundation for the Code's enforceable rules. The Principles guide members in the performance of their professional responsibilities and call for an unyielding commitment to honor the public trust, even at the sacrifice of personal benefits. While CPAs cannot be legally held to the Principles, they do represent the expectations for CPAs on the part of the public in the performance of professional services. In this regard, the Principles are based on values of the profession and traits of character (virtues) that enable CPAs to meet their obligations to the public.

The Principles include (1) Responsibilities, (2) The Public Interest, (3) Integrity, (4) Objectivity and Independence, (5) Due Care, and (6) Scope and Nature of Services.[58]

The umbrella statement in the Code is that the overriding responsibility of CPAs is to exercise sensitive professional and moral judgments in all activities. By linking professional conduct to moral judgment, the AICPA Code recognizes the importance of moral reasoning in meeting professional obligations.

The second principle defines the public interest to include "clients, credit grantors, governments, employers, investors, the business and financial community, and others who rely on the objectivity and integrity of CPAs to maintain the orderly functioning of commerce."[57] This principle calls for resolving conflicts between these stakeholder groups by recognizing the primacy of a CPA's responsibility to the public as the way to best serve clients' and employers' interests. In discharging their professional responsibilities, CPAs may encounter conflicting pressures from each of these groups. According to the public interest principle, when conflicts arise, the actions taken to resolve them should be based on integrity, guided by the precept that when CPAs fulfill their responsibilities to the public, clients' and employers' interests are best served.

As a principle of CPA conduct, integrity recognizes that the public trust is served by (1) being honest and candid within the constraints of client confidentiality, (2) not subordinating the public trust to personal gain and advantage, (3) observing both the form and spirit of technical and ethical standards, and (4) observing the principles of objectivity and independence and of due care.

Objectivity requires that all CPAs maintain a mental attitude of impartiality and intellectual honesty and be free of conflicts of interest in meeting professional responsibilities. Objectivity pertains to all CPAs in their performance of all professional services. Independence applies only to CPAs who provide attestation services, not tax and advisory/consulting services. The audit opinion is relied on by external users–investors and creditors–thereby triggering the need to be independent of the client entity to enhance assurances. In tax and advisory engagements, the service is provided primarily for the client (internal user) so that the CPA might become involved in some relationships with the client that might otherwise impair audit independence but do not come into play when providing nonattest services; nonattest services do require objectivity in decision making and the exercise of due care.

The due care standard calls for continued improvement in the level of competency and quality of services by (1) performing professional services to the best of one's abilities, (2) carrying out professional responsibilities with concern for the best interests of those for whom the services are performed, (3) carrying out those responsibilities in accordance with the public interest, (4) following relevant technical and ethical standards, and (5) properly planning and supervising engagements. A key element of due care is professional skepticism, which means to have a questioning mind and critical assessment of audit evidence.

The importance of the due care standard is as follows. Imagine if a CPA were asked to perform an audit of a school district and the CPA never engaged in governmental auditing before and never completed a course of study in governmental auditing. While the CPA or CPA firm may still obtain the necessary skills to perform the audit–for example, by hiring someone with the required skills–the CPA/firm would have a hard time supervising such work without the proper background and knowledge.

Recall from the introduction that accountants are rated high in honesty and ethics. There is no doubt that part of the reason is a commitment to professionalism through the AICPA Code. Beyond that, regardless of the form of practice all accounting professionals should be able to apply moral reasoning to resolve ethical dilemmas that may exist between accountants and auditors, and top management and clients in order to act in the public interest.

Application of Ethical Reasoning in Accounting

LO 1-5
Apply the Principles of the AICPA Code of Conduct and ethical reasoning methods to a case study.

In this section, we discuss the application of ethical reasoning to a common dilemma faced by accountants. The case deals with the classic example of prematurely recording revenue to inflate earnings and make it look as though the company is doing better than it really is.

3D Printing Case Study

3D Printing, a privately held company, was formed in March 2020 after a successful Kickstarter funding campaign. The project to develop the first jet fusion printer brought in $1.1 million, 10 percent above its goal. The company has struggled through its first full year of operations and is now preparing its financial statements for fiscal year end September 30, 2021. Kyle Bloom is the chief executive officer (CEO) of the company. He reports to a 12-member board of directors. Madison Rose is the chief financial officer (CFO). She holds the CPA certificate.

Kyle is meeting with Madison on October 5, 2021, to review the financial statements. The key issue being discussed is recording revenue on a $200,000 order from A-1 Printers. It seems the product won't be shipped until October 15, 2021, yet Kyle wants Madison to include the $200,000 in the current year earnings since that amount was received on September 30, 2021.

The following is an overview of the October 5 meeting.

Kyle:	Madison, you have to include the $200,000 from A-1 Printers in revenue for this year
Madison:	I can't. Generally Accepted Accounting Principles (GAAP) require at least shipment of the product to A-1 as of September 30
Kyle:	You know we will ship the product in ten days. What's the big deal? You know our Kickstarter funds have run out so I'm in negotiations with our bank to borrow $10 million for continued expansion of our product line. Omitting the $200,000 means our net income will be $50,000, 80 percent below the target we announced. There's no way we'll get the loan. Production will be halted and layoffs will begin
Madison:	I understand and don't want to be held responsible for missing our targets. Still, it's better to take the hit to earnings now and record the revenue next year when it can put us over the top with respect to targeted earnings
Kyle:	I'll worry about next year, next year. If you prefer, we can adjust out the $200,000 in the first quarter of fiscal year 2022 as a prior period adjustment to retained earnings
Madison:	Has the board of directors approved it?
Kyle:	Don't worry about the board. I'll take care of them

At this point, the meeting broke up and Madison was told to make the adjustment and include the $200,000 revenue this year. The last thing Kyle said to Madison was that she is expected to be a team player.

What should Madison do?

Principles of the AICPA Code of Professional Conduct

Madison is an internal accountant so the independence standard doesn't apply.

Objectivity requires that Madison should make decisions impartially and based on professional standards, and not allow herself to be pressured by Kyle. She knows that recording premature revenue in the current fiscal year is wrong under GAAP.

Integrity requires that Madison should not subordinate her judgment to that of Kyle regardless of the personal and professional costs. If she gives in to Kyle now, then further down the line he may expect her to do the same. She may wind up sliding down the ethical slippery slope where there is no turning back.

Ethical Reasoning Methods

<u>Categorical Imperative:</u> (Rights Theory): Madison knows that Kyle's proposed revenue recognition is not a universally accepted method. It accelerates revenue into an earlier period than justified. She would not want (or expect) other accountants to record the revenue as proposed, so why should she? Kyle is promoting an "ends justify the means" approach to decision making (consequentialism) in that the revenue needs to be recorded in fiscal year ended 2021 to obtain the needed financing regardless of the method used to do it. The Public Interest is represented by current investors and creditors, and the bank financing the $10 million. They have an ethical right to receive accurate and reliable financial statements and Madison has an ethical duty to see to it that the financial statements do just that.

<u>Utilitarianism:</u> Act Utilitarianism could be used to justify recording the revenue in fiscal 2021 reasoning the benefits to be derived from getting the loan now (continued financing, no production stoppage, avoid layoffs) exceeds the potential costs if the bank finds out about the improper reporting. The costs might include lying to the bank about when the revenue should be recorded, which can have major implications in the financial community. Also, the company might be sanctioned for not adhering to ethical and professional standards. A Rule Utilitarian approach would come to a different conclusion because, much like Rights Theory, certain rules should never be violated regardless of utilitarian benefits. The relevant rule is never to falsify financial statement information.

The Act Utilitarianism approach can be used to rationalize otherwise unethical behavior. This is why the Rule Utilitarianism approach often is the best to use especially because the overriding rule in accounting is to protect the public interest.

Madison should also consider whether the board of directors have a right to know what is going on and if she has an ethical obligation to tell them. In all cases the board should know because it is ultimately responsible to ensure the financial statements are accurate and reliable.

Decision

Madison should do whatever it takes to delay the recording of revenue until fiscal year ended September 30, 2022. She needs to counteract Kyle's statement of being a team player by pointing out her ultimate loyalty is not to the team or the organization but to the public (investors, creditors,) that relies on accurate financial statements to make credit and investment decisions. She needs to take her concerns to the board and explain her position. If the board goes along with Kyle, then her only other option is to go outside the company (i.e., external auditors, regulatory agencies). Doing so entails whistleblowing, an action that could have severe consequences for Madison. More will be said about that in **Chapter 3**.

Scope and Organization of the Text

Ethical decision making in accounting is predicated on moral reasoning. In this chapter, we have attempted to introduce the complex moral reasoning methods that help to fulfill the ethical obligations of accounting professionals. In **Chapter 2**, we address behavioral ethics issues and lay the groundwork for discussions of professional judgment. We introduce a model that provides a framework for ethical decision making and can be used to help analyze cases presented at the end of each chapter. We also explain the "Giving Voice to Values" methodology that has become an integral part of ethical behavior since a decision maker who possesses the abilities to express personal and professional values in an effective manner may be able to positively influence superiors who advocate improper financial reporting. In **Chapter 3**, we transition to the culture of an organization and how processes and procedures can help to create and sustain an ethical organization environment, including effective corporate governance systems. We also address whistleblowing considerations for accounting professionals.

The remainder of this book focuses more directly on accounting ethics. **Chapter 4** addresses the AICPA Code and provisions that establish standards of ethical behavior for accounting professionals. In **Chapter 5**, we address fraud in financial statements, including the Fraud Triangle, and the obligations of auditors to assess the risk of material misstatements in the financial statements. The motivation for fraudulent financial reporting is discussed in **Chapter 6** in the context of using techniques to manipulate earnings. These "financial shenanigans" threaten the reliability of the financial reports and can lead to legal liabilities for accountants and auditors. Auditors can be the target of lawsuits because of business failures and deficient audit work. In **Chapter 7**, we look at the consequences of earnings management including financial statement restatements and implications for corporate governance. We also address the consequences for ethical leadership, the heart and soul of an ethical organization. Since auditors and audit firms can be sued by the SEC when their audits fail to meet regulatory standards, in **Chapter 8** we examine the various legal liability issues for auditors, SEC regulations, and examples of how legal liability standards are applied to actual cases.

Concluding Thoughts

We live in a world where being an ethical person has its challenges because some people put their own self-interest above doing the right thing and pressures exist to act contrary to ethical standards. Knowledge of what ethics is and what being ethical tries to accomplish can positively influence behavior. This is one of the goals of **Chapter 1**.

The accounting profession has, for the most part, been viewed as having strong ethical requirements built on a foundation of protecting the public interest. There aren't many professions that put the best interests of the public ahead of the obligation of confidentiality to the client. For example, lawyers put the best interest of the client ahead of disclosing improper/illegal behavior that can harm the public.

Financial scandals, unreported sexual harassment cases in Hollywood, the media and Congress, government misuse of funds, and other improprieties litter the stage of life these days with unabated examples of bad behavior. When was the last time you picked up a newspaper and read a story about someone doing the right thing because it was the right thing to do? It is rare these days. We seem to read and hear more about pursuing one's own selfish interests, even to the detriment of others. It might be called the "What's in it for me?" approach to life. Nothing could be more contrary to leading a life of virtue.

We want to conclude on a positive note. We need to praise good deeds and professional, ethical behavior more so the public will know. Heroes in accounting do exist: brave people who have spoken out about irregularities in their organizations, such as Cynthia Cooper from WorldCom, whom we have already discussed. Another such hero is David Walker, who served as comptroller general of the United States and head of the Government Accountability Office from 1998 to 2008. Walker appeared before an appropriations committee of the U.S. Senate in 2008 and spoke out about billions of dollars in waste spent by the U.S. government, including on the Iraqi war effort. Then there was auditor Joseph St. Denis, who spoke out about improper accounting practices at his former company, AIG, which received a $150 billion bailout from the U.S. government during the financial crisis of 2008.

A final note for students. Keep in mind that you may be in a position during your career where you feel pressured to remain silent about financial wrongdoing. You might rationalize that you didn't commit the unethical act, so your hands are clean. That's not good enough, though, as your ethical obligation to the public and the profession is to do whatever it takes to prevent a fraud from occurring and, if it does, take the necessary steps to correct and, if necessary, report the matter to higher-ups and government agencies.

We hope that you will internalize the ethical standards of the accounting profession and look at the bigger picture when pressured by a superior to do something that you know in your gut is wrong. Trust your common sense. Trust your conscience. Don't make a decision that might haunt you the rest of your life.

We leave you with this thought: The pattern of a person's judgments made spontaneously under pressure is the best sign of a person's moral compass.

Ethics IQ Test

What Is Your Ethics IQ?

The concept of an "Ethics IQ" has been discussed by Bruce Weinstein, The Ethics Guy. Your Ethics IQ measures your level of ethics intelligence. This is not an exact science but does provide insight into your ability to reason through ethical dilemmas and make the right choice. Answer these questions honestly. Otherwise, you will not know where you stand at the beginning of this course. Each question below has three possible answers. Each question is scored from 1 (least appropriate) to 3 (most appropriate). The scores are totaled and an Ethics IQ will be provided by your instructor.

Grab a pen and paper and let's get started!

Choose the "best" answer for each question.

Questions:

1. Employees often work in teams to create marketing campaigns, develop new products, or fine-tune services, yet rarely does everyone in the group contribute equally to the final product. If three members of a five-person team did all the work, should those three members demand to receive FULL credit?

A.) Yes, they should demand to receive full credit.

B.) No, each member should receive credit since it's a team effort.

C.) No, the three members must work with the other two on other projects and don't want to rock the boat.

2. You are a student in Government 101 and are scheduled to take an essay final at 2:00 p.m. While online, you notice a friend of yours in the 9:00 a.m. section shared an Instagram photo of the essay questions. You are spending the time between 10:00 a.m. and 2:00 p.m. in your study group. You need to ace this class to graduate with honors. What would you do?

A.) Use the posting to prepare for the exam but don't tell the group members about it.

B.) Inform the group members and use the posted information to prepare for the exam.

C.) Ignore the posting.

3. You have discovered through a reliable third party that your best friend is cheating on his wife. Your wife asks whether you know anything about it after seeing your friend with another woman at a restaurant. What would you do?

A.) Confide in her that the cheating is going on.

B.) Deny you know anything about it.

C.) Tell her your friend hasn't said anything to you about it.

4. Your boss comes on to you at work. He constantly asks about your dating life and if you're seeing anyone regularly. He regularly stares at you. His behavior makes you feel uncomfortable. But you are up for a promotion and he has the final say. What would you do?

A.) Ignore it, at least until you get the promotion.

B.) Tell him his behavior is unwanted and you feel uncomfortable.

C.) Inform the Human Resources Department.

5. Your best friend was diagnosed with cancer a year ago. You have seen him deteriorate and deal with excruciating pain since then. His doctor can't prescribe marijuana, which might alleviate the pain, because it is illegal to do so in your state. You are thinking about crossing state lines and buying marijuana in a state that has medical and recreational-use marijuana laws even though it is illegal to do so under the federal Controlled Substances Act. What would you do?

A.) Cross state lines where buying and using marijuana is permitted and give it to your friend.

B.) Don't cross state lines because it is illegal under the federal Controlled Substances Act.

C.) Tell your friend to move to a state that has medical marijuana laws.

6. You work for a small business and do a lot of travel and entertaining of potential clients. The company issues a credit card for all employees to simplify the accounting function. The card is to be used solely for business expenses. One day while on an out-of-town trip and after business hours, you use the business card to go to the spa to get a massage to alleviate painful arthritis, a problem you have been dealing with for years. What would you do when questioned about this charge by the Accounting Department?

A.) Explain that the out-of-town trip included a five-hour flight that created stress for your condition. The massage is a legitimate business expense and should be reimbursed.

B.) Explain to the responsible person in the Accounting Department that you know it is a personal expense but ask that it be reimbursed this one time since you have a cash flow problem.

C.) Offer to reimburse the company for the massage.

7. You have just been fired from your job. On the way out, you contemplate downloading some proprietary information about a new R&D project of your employer. You worked on the project so figure you had a right to do so. What would you do?

A.) Don't download the information.

B.) Download the information about the project.

C.) Ask your employer for permission to download the information.

8. You are one of five workers on a team that performs financial calculations for your company. In advance of a meeting between the team and your supervisor, you discover a member of the team, who is your boyfriend, made a mistake in a calculation. The mistake made it look like the company was making more money than it was. What would you do assuming you are convinced the mistake was an honest one?

A.) Ignore it: You don't want to get your friend in trouble.

B.) Speak to your friend: Give him the opportunity to correct the mistake.

C.) Inform the supervisor since it's your job to report what you have observed.

9. You manage a group of six employees. One day one of those employees calls in sick. Later that day you notice she posted photos at a restaurant to Instagram. What would you do?

A.) Speak to the employee the next day when she comes to work.

B.) Let it go and say nothing.

C.) Fire the employee.

10. You are a manager at a fast food restaurant and monitor your employee's social media posts on company equipment. You just read a Facebook post by an employee who commented that the working conditions were oppressive. Other employees commented; some agreeing and others disagreeing. Assuming you work in an "at will" employment state (either the employer or the employee may terminate employment at any time). What would you do?

A.) Fire the employee who posted the critical comments.

B.) Ignore the comments.

C.) Meet with the employee(s) to discuss the comments.

Discussion Questions

Instructions: Be sure to provide ethical reasoning in answering the following questions.

1. Is it ever appropriate to lie to someone? Explain why or why not using ethical reasoning. Give one example of when you believe lying might be justified.

2. Is there a difference between cheating on a math test, pocketing an extra $10 from the change given to you at a restaurant, and using someone else's ID to get a drink at a bar?

3. Sir Walter Scott (1771–1832), the Scottish novelist and poet, wrote: "Oh what a tangled web we weave, when first we practice to deceive." Comment on what you think Scott meant by this phrase.

4. One explanation about rights is that there is a difference between what we have the right to do and what the right thing to do is. Explain what you think is meant by this statement. Do you believe that if someone attacks your credibility on social media that gives you the right to attack them?

5. Do you think it is ethical for a prospective employer to investigate your social media footprint in making a hiring decision? What about monitoring social networking activities of employees while on the job?

6. According to the website *Indeed,* one question to ask the interviewer when you are interviewing for a job is: "What are the characteristics of someone who would succeed in this role?" Why might you ask such a question?

7. Some people believe that promise keeping is the essence of ethical behavior. Do you agree?

8. David Starr Jordan (1851–1931), an educator and writer, said, "Wisdom is knowing what to do next; virtue is doing it." Explain the meaning of this phrase as you see it.

9. Answer the following with regard to egoism. (a) Do you think it is the same to act in your own self-interest as it is to act in a selfish way? (b) Do you think "enlightened self-interest" is a contradiction in terms, or is it a valid basis for all actions?

10. What does the term "civility" mean to you? Do you think it is civil behavior to shout down a speaker with whom you do not agree? What about cancelling someone because you don't agree with their message?

11. Distinguish between ethics, morals, and values.

12. MacIntyre, in his account of Aristotelian virtue, states that integrity is the one trait of character that encompasses all the others. How does this relate to the Principles in the AICPA Code of Professional Conduct?

13. Distinguish between ethical rights and obligations from the perspective of accountants and auditors.

14. Do you think the "Resolution of Ethical Issues" section in The IMA Statement of Ethical Professional Practice is a helpful part of its ethical standards?

15. One morning a student telephones her professor that she won't be able to take a scheduled exam because her car broke down on the way home from an out-of-town trip. She asks to take it at another time. What would you do if you were the professor and why?

16. Assume that a CFO asks you, as the accountant for the company, to omit certain financial figures from the balance sheet that may paint the business in a bad light. Because the request does not involve a direct manipulation of numbers or records, would you agree to go along with the request? Would you ever consider blowing the whistle on the CFO? What ethical considerations exist for you in deciding on a course of action?

17. Do you think a CPA should be able to justify allowing the unethical behavior of a supervisor, by claiming "It's not my job to police the behavior of others?

18. Why do bad things sometimes happen to good people? Does this mean they are a bad person?

19. Consider the ethical principle of praising the good and ignoring the bad. Is this a good way to foster ethical behavior?

20. Mark Twain once said, "If you tell the truth, you don't have to remember anything." Explain what you think Twain meant by this statement and how it addresses one's character.

Comprehensive Questions

1. A common ethical dilemma used to distinguish between philosophical reasoning methods is the "Trolley Problem." Imagine that you are standing on a footbridge spanning some trolley tracks. You see that a runaway trolley is threatening to kill five people. Standing next to you, in between the oncoming trolley and the five people, is a railway worker wearing a large backpack. You quickly realize that the only way to save the people is to push the man off the bridge and onto the tracks below. The man will die, but the bulk of his body and the pack will stop the trolley from reaching the others. (You quickly understand that you can't jump yourself because you aren't large enough to stop the trolley, and there's no time to put on the man's backpack.) Legal concerns aside, would it be ethical for you to save the five people by pushing this stranger to his death? Use the deontological and teleological methods to reason out what you would do and why.

2. Another ethical dilemma deals with a runaway trolley heading for five railway workers who will be killed if it proceeds on its present course. The only way to save these people is to hit a switch that will turn the trolley onto a side track, where it will run over and kill one worker instead of five. Ignoring legal concerns, would it be ethically acceptable for you to turn the trolley by hitting the switch in order to save five people at the expense of one person? Use the deontological and teleological methods to reason out what you would do and why.

3. For years, the Baseball Hall of Fame has officially steered clear of the question as to how voters should handle the candidacies of players connected to performance-enhancing drugs. Initially, two of the game's best players—Roger Clemens and Barry Bonds—could only muster about one-half of the 75 percent approval needed to be voted in. In 2019, both players received more than 50 percent, a significant threshold that has historically indicated future

election, although their support only increased to 59.5 percent and 59.1 percent, respectively. However, their approval rating increased to over 60 percent in 2020: Clemens, 61.0 percent; Bonds, 60.7 percent. Do you believe Clemens and Bonds should be voted into the Hall of Fame? Use ethical reasoning to answer this question.

4. Your best friend is from another country. One day after a particularly stimulating lecture on the meaning of ethics by your instructor, you and your friend disagree about whether culture plays a role in ethical behavior. You state that good ethics are good ethics, and it doesn't matter where you live and work. Your friend tells you that in her country it is common to pay bribes to gain favor with important people. Comment on both positions from an ethical point of view. What do you believe and why?

5. Do you agree with our decision to omit Rand's Rational Egoism as a basis for making ethical judgments in accounting? Compare it to other ethical reasoning methods.

Endnotes

1. Gallup, *Honesty/Ethics in the Professions*, December 2–15, 2019, https://news.gallup.com/poll/1654/Honesty-Ethics-Professions.aspx?version=print.

2. Steven M. Mintz, "Virtue Ethics and Accounting Education," *Issues in Accounting Education* 10, no. 2 (Fall 1995), p. 257.

3. Marcel Schwantes, Warren Buffet Says Look for This 1 Trait if You Want to Hire the Best People, August 26, 2019. Available at: https://www.inc.com/marcel-schwantes/warren-buffett-says-look-for-this-1-trait-if-you-want-to-hire-best-people.html

4. Mintz, p.257.

5. Susan Pulliam and Deborah Solomon, "Ms. Cooper Says No to Her Boss," *The Wall Street Journal* (October 30, 2002), p. A1.

6. Lynne W. Jeter, *Disconnected: Deceit and Betrayal at WorldCom* (Hoboken, NJ: Wiley, 2003).

7. Jeff Clabaugh, Washington Business Journal, WorldCom's Betty Vinson gets 5 months prison, August 5, 2005, https://www.bizjournals.com/washington/stories/2005/08/01/daily51.html.

8. Cynthia Cooper, *Extraordinary Circumstances* (Hoboken, NJ: Wiley, 2008).

9. Teaching Values, *The Golden Rule in World Religions,* Available at: www.teachingvalues.com/goldenrule.html.

10. William J. Prior, *Virtue and Knowledge: An Introduction to Ancient Greek Ethics* (London: Routledge, 1991).

11. William H. Shaw and Vincent Barry, *Moral Issues in Business* (Belmont, CA: Wadsworth Cengage Learning, 2010).

12. James C. Gaa and Linda Thorne, "An Introduction to the Special Issue on Professionalism and Ethics in Accounting Education," *Issues in Accounting Education* 1, no. 1 (February 2004), p. 1.

13. Paul Walker and Terry Lovat, *You Say Morals, I Say Ethics—What's the Difference*, September 17, 2014, Available at: https://theconversation.com/you-say-morals-i-say-ethics-whats-the-difference-30913.

14. Source: Difference Between Morals and Ethics, https://keydifferences.com/difference-between-moral-and-ethics.html.

15. Andrew Simmons, *Why Students Cheat—and What to Do About It*, February 6, 2017, Cision PR Newswire, Available at: https://www.prnewswire.com/news-releases/survey-shows-cheating-and-academic-dishonesty-prevalent-in-colleges-and-universities-300402014.html.

16. Marc Tracy, *N.C.A.A.: North Carolina Will Not Be Punished for Academic Scandal*, October 13, 2017, New York Times, Available at: https://www.nytimes.com/2017/10/13/sports/unc-north-carolina-ncaa.html.

17. Steven Mintz, *Diversity of Thought Under Attack By the Cancel Culture*, https://www.ethicssage.com/2020/08/diversity-of-thought-under-attack-by-the-cancel-culture.html.

18. Aristotle, *Nicomachean Ethics,* trans. W. D. Ross (Oxford, UK: Oxford University Press, 1925).

19. Michael Josephson, *Making Ethical Decisions,* rev. ed. (Los Angeles: Josephson Institute of Ethics, 2002).

20. Josephson.

21. Josephson.

22. Josephson.

23. Edmund L. Pincoffs, *Quandaries and Virtues against Reductivism in Ethics* (Lawrence: University Press of Kansas, 1986).

24. Josephson.

25. Josephson.

26. Weber Shandwick, *Civility in America 2019: Solutions for Tomorrow,* https://www.webershandwick.com/wp-content/uploads/2019/06/CivilityInAmerica2019SolutionsforTomorrow.pdf.

27. James R. Rest, *Moral Development: Advances in Research and Theory* (New York: Praeger, 1986).

28. O.C. Ferrell, John Fraedrich, and Linda Ferrell, *Business Ethics: Ethical Decision Making and Cases,* 11th ed. (Mason, OH: South-Western, Cengage Learning, 2011), p. 159.

29. Internet Encyclopedia of Philosophy, *Egoism,* Available at: http://www.iep.utm.edu/egoism/.

30. Stanford Encyclopedia of Philosophy, *Egoism,* Available at: https://plato.stanford.edu/entries/egoism/.

31. Internet Encyclopedia of Philosophy.

32. Alexis de Tocqueville, *Democracy in America* (Originally published 1835) (Chicago, ILL: University of Chicago Press, 2000).

33. Ferrell et al., p. 159.

34. Ayn Rand, *The Virtue of Selfishness: A New Concept of Egoism (*New York, NY: New American Library, 1964).

35. Ferrell et al., p. 159.

36. Manuel Velasquez, Claire Andre, Thomas Shanks, and Michael J. Meyer, "Calculating Consequences: The Utilitarian Approach to Ethics," *Issues in Ethics* 2, no. 1 (Winter 1989), Available at: www.scu.edu/ethics.

37. Velasquez et al.

38. Velasquez et al.

39. Velasquez et al.

40. Velasquez et al.

41. Claire Andre and Manuel Velasquez, "Rights Stuff," Markkula Center for Applied Ethics," *Issues in Ethics* 3, no. 1 (Winter 1990), Available at: www.scu.edu/ethics/publications/iie/v3n1/.

42. Velasquez et al.

43. Immanuel Kant, *Foundations of Metaphysics of Morals,* trans. Lewis White Beck (New York: Liberal Arts Press, 1959), p. 39.

44. Velasquez, et al.

45. Spencer J. Maxcy, *Ethical School Leadership* (Plymouth, United Kingdom: Rowman & Littlefield Education, 2002).

46. Manuel Velasquez, Claire Andre, Thomas Shanks, and Michael J. Meyer, "Justice and Fairness," *Issues in Ethics* 3, no. 2 (Spring 1990).

47. Ferrell et al., p. 165.

48. MacIntyre, pp. 187–190.

49. MacIntyre, pp. 190–192.

50. Moral Relativism, Available at: https://www.allaboutphilosophy.org/moral-relativism.htm.

51. Ethical Relativism, Available at: https://www.allaboutphilosophy.org/ethical-relativism-faq.htm.

52. Ernest Hemingway, *Death in the Afternoon* (Scribner; Reprint edition, April 6, 1996: New York, N.Y.).

53. Manuel Velasquez, Claire Andre, Thomas Shanks, S.J., and Michael J. Meyer, *Ethical Relativism* (Markkula Center for Applied Ethics), Available at: https://www.scu.edu/ethics/ethics-resources/ethical-decision-making/ethical-relativism/.

54. Joseph Fletcher, *Situation Ethics: The New Morality* (Louisville: KY: Westminster John Knox Press, 1966).

55. Martin Stuebs and Brett Wilkinson, "Restoring the Profession's Public Interest Role," *The CPA Journal* 79, no. 11, (2009), pp. 62–66.

56. James E. Copeland, Jr., "Ethics as an Imperative," *Accounting Horizons* 19, no. 1 (2005), pp. 35–43.

57. American Institute of CPAs (AICPA), *AICPA Code of Professional Conduct, Effective,* December 15, 2014, Available at: https://www.aicpa.org/content/dam/aicpa/research/standards/codeofconduct/ downloadabledocuments/2014december15contentasof2016august31codeofconduct.pdf.

58. American Institute of Certified Public Accountants, *Code of Professional Conduct* at June 1, 2012 (New York: AICPA, 2012); Available at: www.aicpa.org/Research/Standards/CodeofConduct/Pages/default.aspx.

Chapter 1 Cases

Case 1-1 Operation Varsity Blues

What motivates a parent to bribe key people to get their kid admitted to a prestigious university? That is the ethical question of "Operation Varsity Blues."

In March 2019, the story broke of an alarming fraudulent scheme by parents to pay off middleman, William "Rick" Singer, and athletic coaches to give favored treatment to the children of rich and well-connected people.

Singer, CEO of a college admissions prep company, The Key, took in large amounts of money and laundered them as contributions to a foundation he controlled, Key Worldwide Foundation, which only pretended to help underprivileged students. Using Singer's connections, the parents bribed coaches and administrators at some of the most prestigious institutions in the United States.

Singer helped parents craft fake documentation to allow students to be admitted as recruited athletes even though they never participated in a sport, and he developed an elaborate system to help students cheat on their college entrance exams. He then paid coaches and administrators to look the other way.

Singer pled guilty to four felony counts, admitting he accepted some $25 million in bribes to rig the admissions process in what he described as a "side door" into college.

The Department of Justice charged 55 parents, coaches, and administrators with fraud that enabled children of wealthy parents to gain admission to colleges they were not qualified to attend. These included Georgetown, Stanford, UCLA, USC, and the University of Texas at Austin.

When the story first broke all attention was on two Hollywood actresses Lori Laughlin and Felicity Huffman. At her sentencing, Huffman was very contrite saying "I am in full acceptance of my guilt–deep regret and shame." She also said her daughter had no idea of the scheme. She was sentenced to two weeks in prison.

Laughlin was convicted of conspiracy to commit wire and mail fraud. She was sentenced to 2 months in prison, a $150,000 fine, 2 years of supervised released, and 100 hours of community service.

Laughlin's husband, Giannulli, was convicted of paying $500,000 in bribes to facilitate his children's acceptance to USC. He earlier had pleaded guilty to conspiracy to commit wire and mail fraud.

In another case, California investor Todd Blake and his wife, Diane, pled guilty admitting they paid $250,000 to get their daughter into the University of Southern California as a purported volleyball recruit even though she didn't play volleyball in any organized way.

At USC, athletic director Donna Heinel and men's and women's water polo coach Jovan Vavic were fired after allegedly receiving bribes totaling more than $1.3 million and $250,000, respectively, to help parents take advantage of relaxed admissions standards for athletes at USC even though their kids were not being recruited as athletes.

In one audacious scheme, Singer bribed test administrators in Houston and Los Angeles to allow Mark Riddell, a very bright individual, to secretly take the ACT and SAT tests in place of the children of the parents that Singer represented. He scored 35 out of 36 on the ACT, which put him in about the 99th percentile of ACT takers.

Some of the students were expelled. Others had their admissions revoked. Some of the coaches have been fired. They faced charges—athletic coaches who were involved in misrepresenting people as being recruits.

Of the 55 people charged only a handful are still fighting the charges. The first trial was scheduled to begin in October 2020 but has been delayed due to COVID-19. It was expected to begin in January 2021 at the earliest.

Questions

1. Examine the behavior of the parents from the perspective of moral relativism. Is it fair to say the parents believed the rules should not apply to them? Explain.

2. Evaluate the actions of the parents using teleology, deontology, and justice.

3. What is your takeaway from Operation Varsity Blues?

Case 1-2 Giles and Regas

Ed Giles and Susan Regas have never been happier than during the past four months since they have been seeing each other. Giles is a 35-year-old CPA and a partner in the medium-sized accounting firm of Saduga & Mihca. Regas is a 25-year-old senior accountant in the same firm. Although it is acceptable for peers to date, the firm does not permit two members of different ranks within the firm to do so. A partner should not date a senior in the firm any more than a senior should date a junior staff accountant. If such dating eventually leads to marriage, then one of the two must resign because of the conflicts of interest. Both Giles and Regas know the firm's policy on dating, and they have tried to be discreet about their relationship because they don't want to raise any suspicions.

While most of the staff seem to know about Giles and Regas, it is not common knowledge among the partners that the two of them are dating. Perhaps that is why Regas was assigned to work on the audit of CAA Industries for a second year, even though Giles is the supervising partner on the engagement.

As the audit progresses, it becomes clear to the junior staff members that Giles and Regas are spending personal time together during the workday. On one occasion, they were observed leaving for lunch together. Regas did not return to the client's office until three hours later. On another occasion, Regas seemed distracted from her work, and later that day, she received a dozen roses from Giles. A friend of Regas's who knew about the relationship, Ruth Revilo, became concerned when she happened to see the flowers and a card that accompanied them. The card was signed, "Love, Poochie." Regas had once told Revilo that it was the nickname that Regas gave to Giles.

Revilo pulls Regas aside at the end of the day and says, "We have to talk."

"What is it?" Regas asks.

"I know the flowers are from Giles," Revilo says. "Are you crazy?"

"It's none of your business," Regas responds.

Revilo goes on to explain that others on the audit engagement team are aware of the relationship between the two. Revilo cautions Regas about jeopardizing her future with the firm by getting involved in a serious dating relationship with someone of a higher rank. Regas does not respond to this comment. Instead, she admits to being distracted lately because of an argument that she had with Giles. It all started when Regas had suggested to Giles that it might be best if they did not go out during the workweek because she was having a hard time getting to work on time. Giles was upset at the suggestion and called her ungrateful. He said, "I've put everything on the line for you. There's no turning back for me." She points out to Revilo that the flowers are Giles's way of saying he is sorry for some of the comments he had made about her.

Regas promises to talk to Giles and thanks Revilo for her concern. That same day, Regas telephones Giles and tells him she wants to put aside her personal relationship with him until the CAA audit is complete in two weeks. She suggests that, at the end of the two-week period, they get together and thoroughly examine the possible implications of their continued relationship. Giles reluctantly agrees, but he conditions his acceptance on having a "farewell" dinner at their favorite restaurant. Regas agrees to the dinner.

Giles and Regas have dinner that Saturday night. As luck would have it, the controller of CAA Industries, Mark Sax, is at the restaurant with his wife. Sax is startled when he sees Giles and Regas together. He wonders about the possible seriousness of their relationship, while reflecting on the recent progress billings of the accounting firm. Sax believes that the number of hours billed is out of line with work of a similar nature and the fee estimate. He had planned to discuss the matter with Herb Morris, the managing partner of the firm. He decides to call Morris on Monday morning.

"Herb, you son of a gun, it's Mark Sax."

"Mark. How goes the audit?"

"That's why I'm calling," Sax responds. "Can we meet to discuss a few items?"

"Sure," Morris replies. "Just name the time and place."

"How about first thing tomorrow morning?" asks Sax.

"I'll be in your office at 8:00 a.m.," says Morris.

"Better make it at 7:00 a.m., Herb, before your auditors arrive."

Sax and Morris meet to discuss Sax's concerns about seeing Giles and Regas at the restaurant and the possibility that their relationship is negatively affecting audit efficiency. Morris asks whether any other incidents have occurred to make him suspicious about the billings. Sax says that he is only aware of this one instance, although he sensed some apprehension on the part of Regas last week when they discussed why it was taking so long to get the audit recommendations for adjusting entries. Morris listens attentively until Sax finishes and then asks him to be patient while he sets up a meeting to discuss the situation with Giles. Morris promises to get back to Sax by the end of the week.

Questions

1. Assess the personal responsibility of Ed Giles and Susan Regas for the relationship that developed between them. Who do you think is mostly to blame?

2. If Giles were a person of integrity but just happened to have a "weak moment" in starting a relationship with Regas, what do you think he will say when he meets with Herb Morris? Why?

3. Assume that Ed Giles is the biggest "rainmaker" in the firm. What would you do if you were in Herb Morris's position when you meet with Giles? In your response, consider how you would resolve the situation in regard to both the completion of the CAA Industries audit and the longer-term issue of the continued employment of Giles and Regas in the accounting firm.

Case 1-3 Unintended Consequences

Veronica Betterman, a fifth-year accounting major at Anywhere University, wakes up in a cold sweat. Like many accounting majors, Veronica did an internship in public accounting the previous spring resulting in a full-time job offer with Anywhere CPAs to start after she graduates this spring which she readily accepted.

Now in her fifth and final year, Veronica decided she wanted to see what other job opportunities might be out there. So, she went through her university's career fair just two weeks before and was invited to participate in six on-campus interviews. Five of those potential employers then invited her to their offices for another round of interviews. She received full-time job offers from four of the five and has yet to hear from the last. Her deadline for deciding on the first of those offers is two days away and she does not know what to do.

While everyone tells her that she should be excited, she is not. She is scared. Worried she may make the wrong decision, she seeks advice from her academic advisor. Her advisor listens to Veronica's dilemma and to Veronica's surprise the advisor tells her that she should never have gone through the career fair, done any of those recent interviews, or be contemplating anything other than starting at the firm she interned with.

The advisor stated that she has made a commitment with that company that she has to honor. To do otherwise would be a breach of ethics and is not only an indication of a lack of integrity on Veronica's part, but could cause irreparable harm to the university. He requests that Veronica meet with him again the next day after she prepares a list of all the potential consequences that could happen (to her, the internship program, the other employers, the university, other students) should she take a job with one of the other potential employers.

Veronica gets out of bed, opens up her laptop, and starts working on the list of consequences.

Questions

1. What potential consequences are there for Veronica, the internship program, the other employers, the university, and other students should Veronica not honor her commitment?

2. Analyze Veronica's actions using the Six Pillars of Character. What do Veronica's actions tell you about her character? Do you think her advisor handled the situation appropriately?

3. Assume Anywhere CPAs is in an "employment-at-will" state, which allow employers to fire an employee under most circumstances and this law is generally applied to employer rescinded job offers as well. Should that affect Veronica's decision to take a job with one of the other potential employers? Why or why not?

4. If Veronica decided to accept one of those other job offers, and that employer subsequently learned about her backing out of her previous commitment, how might they react?

Case 1-4 Lone Star School District

Jose and Emily work as auditors for the state of Texas. They have been assigned to the audit of the Lone Star School District. There have been some problems with audit documentation for the travel and entertainment reimbursement claims of the manager of the school district. The manager knows about the concerns of Jose and Emily, and he approaches them about the matter. The following conversation takes place:

Manager:	Listen, I've requested the documentation you asked for, but the hotel says it's no longer in its system
Jose:	Don't you have the credit card receipt or credit card statement?
Manager:	I paid cash
Jose:	What about a copy of the hotel bill?
Manager:	I threw it out
Emily:	That's a problem. We have to document all your travel and entertainment expenses for the city manager's office
Manager:	Well, I can't produce documents that the hotel can't find. What do you want me to do?

Jose and Emily have heard rumors about a sexual relationship between the manager and a subordinate. They are wondering whether it had anything to do with the payment of cash by the manager.

Questions

1. Assume that Jose and Emily are CPAs and members of the AICPA. What ethical standards in the Code of Professional Conduct should guide them in dealing with the manager's inability to support travel and entertainment expenses?

2. Evaluate the statements and behavior of the manager from an ethical perspective.

   a. Assume that Jose and Emily report to Sharon, the manager of the school district audit. Should they inform Sharon of their concerns? Why or why not?

   b. Assume that they don't inform Sharon, but she finds out from another source. What would you do if you were in Sharon's position?

Case 1-5 Lottery Bonanza

Sam and John have been friends for 20 years. They met in college and worked together for 10 of the 20 years. During that time, each made a promise that if they won a lottery they would share the winnings 50:50. Even though they drifted apart over the years, they had a bond of friendship that neither forgot.

One day Sam plays the Lotto and wins $2 million. He remembers the agreement with John. Sam tells his wife he will call John and give him the good news that he will get $1 million from their good fortune. His wife is astonished. She reminds Sam that they have thousands of dollars of unpaid bills and $2 million would more than cover them. She tells Sam to forget about contacting John, with whom they haven't spoke for three years, and keep all the winnings.

Sam is trying to decide what to do. He would like to share his good fortune with John but doesn't want to upset his wife. Paying off the bills will bring them peace of mind.

Questions

Drawing upon the concepts and ethical theories presented in the chapter respond to the following questions.

1. Assume you are in Sam's position. What would you do and why?
2. Would your decision change if any of the following situations existed? Each question is independent of the others.
   a. You have grown apart from John over the years and haven't spoken to him for two years.
   b. Your child has a medical condition that requires surgery and your insurance carrier has refused to cover the costs.
   c. You won $20 million in the lottery not $2 million.

Case 1-6 Capitalization versus Expensing

Gloria Hernandez is the controller of a public company. She just completed a meeting with her superior, John Harrison, who is the CFO of the company. Harrison tried to convince Hernandez to go along with his proposal to combine 12 expenditures for repair and maintenance of a plant asset into one amount ($1 million). Each of the expenditures is less than $100,000, the cutoff point for capitalizing expenditures as an asset and depreciating it over the useful life. Hernandez asked for time to think about the matter. As the controller and chief accounting officer of the company, Hernandez knows it's her responsibility to decide how to record the expenditures. She knows that the $1 million amount is material to earnings and the rules in accounting require expensing of each individual item, not capitalization. However, she is under a great deal of pressure to go along with capitalization to boost earnings and meet financial analysts' earnings expectations, and provide for a bonus to top management including herself. Her job may be at stake, and she doesn't want to disappoint her boss.

Questions

Assume both Hernandez and Harrison hold the CPA and CMA designations.

1. What are the loyalty obligations of both parties in this case?
2. Assume that you were in Gloria Hernandez's position. What would motivate you to speak up and act or to stay silent? Would it make a difference if Harrison promised this was a one-time request?
3. Assume that you were in Gloria Hernandez's position. What would you do and why?

Case 1-7 Eating Time

Kevin Lowe is depressed. He has been with the CPA firm Stooges LLP for only three months. Yet the partners in charge of the firm—Bo Chambers and his brother, Moe—have asked for a "sit-down." Here's how it goes:

> "Kevin, we asked to see you because your time reports indicate that it takes you 50% longer to complete audit work than your predecessor," Moe said.
>
> "Well, I am new and still learning on the job," replied Lowe.
>
> "That's true," Bo responded, "but you have to appreciate that we have fixed budgets for these audits. Every hour over the budgeted time costs us money. While we can handle it in the short run, we will have to bill the clients whose audit you work on a larger fee in the future. We don't want to lose clients as a result."
>
> "Are you asking me to cut down on the work I do?" Lowe asked.
>
> "We would never compromise the quality of our audit work," Moe said. "We're trying to figure out why it takes you so much longer than other staff members."
>
> At this point, Lowe started to perspire. He wiped his forehead, took a glass of water, and asked, "Would it be better if I took some of the work home at night and on weekends, completed it, but didn't charge the firm or the client for my time?"
>
> Bo and Moe were surprised by Kevin's openness. On one hand, they valued that trait in their employees. On the other hand, they couldn't answer with a yes. Moe looked at Bo, and then turned to Kevin and said, "It's up to you to decide how to increase your productivity on audits. As you know, this is an important element of performance evaluation."
>
> Kevin cringed. Was the handwriting on the wall in terms of his future with the firm?
>
> "I understand what you're saying," Kevin said. "I will do better in the future—I promise."
>
> "Good," responded Bo and Moe. "Let's meet 30 days from now and we'll discuss your progress on the matters we've discussed today and your future with the firm."

In an effort to deal with the problem, Kevin contacts Joyce, a friend and fellow employee, and asks if she has faced similar problems. Joyce answers "yes" and goes on to explain she handles it by "ghost-ticking." Kevin asks her to explain. "Ghost-ticking is when we document audit procedures that have not been completed." Kevin, dumbfounded, wonders, what kind of a firm am I working for?

Questions

1. Kevin is not a CPA yet. What are his ethical obligations in this case?
2. Given the facts in the case, evaluate using deontological and teleological reasoning whether Kevin should take work home and not charge it to the job. What about engaging in ghost-ticking?
3. What would you do if you were Kevin and why? How would you explain your position to Bo and Moe when you meet in 30 days?

Case 1-8 Section 179 Deduction for Equipment Purchases

Section 179 of the IRS tax code allows qualifying businesses to deduct the full cost of "eligible property" on their income taxes as an expense, rather than requiring the cost of the property to be capitalized and depreciated over its useful life. The provision was adopted into law to help businesses.

For 2020, the deduction limit was $1,040,000 and applies to new and used equipment, as well as off-the-shelf software. The rules state that the deduction can only be taken if the equipment was financed or purchased and put into service between January 1, 2020, and December 31, 2020. The code says a business has to be profitable to use the deduction, and it needs to elect it; it's not automatic. The business cannot deduct more than its business income for the year.

Madison just transferred into to the tax department of Cohn and Klein, CPAs. She wants to get off to a good start. Madison has just come across a situation where their client, So What Inc., deducted the full cost of three equipment purchases for its 2020 tax return. The amount in total is $560,000.

Madison traced the deduction back to the original invoices and found that the company met all of Section 179 rules except one that still had to be determined. That was whether the equipment was put into service between January 1 and December 31, 2020. She was able to find some documentation in the production department that said it was purchased on December 30, 2020 and put into service on January 4, 2021.

Madison knew this made the property ineligible for Section 179 treatment. She approached the production manager and confirmed the January 4 date. At this point, Madison decided to discuss the matter with David, the senior on the tax engagement. David agreed with Madison. They went to discuss the matter with the tax manager who explained to them that So What had been hemorrhaging cash. The deduction would enable it to save $118,000 ($560,000 × 21% tax rate). Given that its net income for the year was $120,000, the deduction would all but wipe out taxable income.

The tax manager, Mark, went to see the CFO of So What. The CFO in no uncertain terms told Mark to deduct the full $560,000 in 2020. The explanation was simple: The equipment was purchased in 2020 and even though it wasn't put into service until January 4, 2021, there was no way the IRS would know.

Cohn and Klein decided to go along with the client for fear of losing not only the tax engagement but audit work as well and lucrative consulting services.

Mark explained the matter to David who explained it to Madison. David advised Madison to go along and not take the matter further. However, Madison always considered herself to be an ethical person and knew what was being asked of her was wrong.

Assume you are in Madison's place. Answer the following questions.

Questions

1. What are Madison's ethical obligations under the AICPA Code of Professional Conduct assuming she is a CPA?
2. Drawing upon the concepts and ethical theories presented in the chapter answer the following question: What should Madison do next and why?

Case 1-9 Cleveland Custom Cabinets

Cleveland Custom Cabinets is a specialty cabinet manufacturer for high-end homes in the Cleveland Heights and Shaker Heights areas. The company manufactures cabinets built to the specifications of homeowners and employs 125 custom cabinetmakers and installers. There are 30 administrative and sales staff members working for the company.

James Leroy owns Cleveland Custom Cabinets. His accounting manager is Marcus Sims, who reports to the director of finance. Sims manages 15 accountants. The staff is responsible for keeping track of manufacturing costs by job and preparing internal and external financial reports. The internal reports are used by management for decision making. The external reports are used to support bank loan applications.

The company applies overhead to jobs based on direct labor hours. For 2022, it estimated total overhead to be $4.8 million and 80,000 direct labor hours. The cost of direct materials used during the first quarter of the year is $600,000, and direct labor cost is $400,000 (based on 20,000 hours worked). The company's accounting system is old and does not provide actual overhead information until about four weeks after the close of a quarter. As a result, the applied overhead amount is used for quarterly reports.

On April 10, 2022, Leroy came into Sims's office to pick up the quarterly report. He looked at it aghast. Leroy had planned to take the statements to the bank the next day and meet with the vice president to discuss a $1 million working capital loan. He knew the bank would be reluctant to grant the loan based on the income numbers in **Exhibit 1**. Without the money, Cleveland could have problems financing everyday operations.

EXHIBIT 1   **Cleveland Custom Cabinets**

Net Income for the Quarter Ended March 31, 2022	
Sales	$6,400,000
Cost of goods sold	4,800,000
Gross margin	$ 1,600,000
Selling and administrative expenses	1,568,000
Net income	$32,000

Leroy asked Sims to explain how net income could have gone from 14.2 percent of sales for the year ended December 31, 2021, to 5.0 percent for March 31, 2022. Sims pointed out that the estimated overhead cost had doubled for 2022 compared to the actual cost for 2021. He explained to Leroy that rent had doubled and the cost of utilities skyrocketed. In addition, the custom-making machinery was wearing out more rapidly, so the company's repair and maintenance costs also doubled from 2021.

Leroy wouldn't accept Sims's explanation. Instead, he told Sims that the quarterly income had to be at least the same percentage of sales as of December 31, 2021. Sims looked confused and reminded Leroy that the external auditors would wrap up their audit on April 30. Leroy told Sims not to worry about the auditors. He would take care of them. Furthermore, "as the sole owner of the company, there is no reason not to 'tweak' the numbers on a one-time basis. I own the board of directors, so no worries there." He went on to say, "Do it this one time and I won't ask you to do it again." He then reminded Sims of his obligation to remain loyal to the company and its interests. Sims started to soften and asked Leroy just how he expected the tweaking to happen. Leroy flinched, held up his hands, and said, "I'll leave the creative accounting to you."

Questions

1. Do you agree with Leroy's statement that it doesn't matter what the numbers look like because he is the sole owner? Even if it is true that Sims "owns" the board of directors, what should be their role in this matter? What about the external auditors? Should Sims simply accept Leroy's statement that he would handle them?

2. a. Assume that Sims is a CPA. Put yourself in Sims's position. What are your ethical considerations in deciding whether to tweak the numbers?

   b. Assume you do a utilitarian analysis to help decide what to do. Evaluate the harms and benefits of alternative courses of action. What would you do? Would your analysis change if you use a rights theory approach?

3. Think about how you would actually implement your chosen action. What barriers could you face? How would you overcome them? Is it worth jeopardizing your job in this case? Why or why not?

Case 1-10 Getting Called-Out on Social Media

Jenna was irritated after class today. A classmate, Ben, had argued about the need for social justice reform that included defunding the police. Jenna was offended by the comments in part because her father was a policeman. She spoke to others in her circle of friends who agreed. Jenna decided that someone had to react to Ben's statement that the money to fund the police would be better spent on youth initiatives and social services.

Jenna decided to call-out Ben by name so that it would be taken more seriously. She also wanted to show her commitment to her group's values and that she went along with their prevailing views. This was Jenna's way of fitting in.

One of the comments made by Jenna was to attack Ben as an extremist who was willing to go too far in reforming the social justice system. Defunding the police was akin to asking for trouble in our streets, Jenna commented. However, then it turned super critical and personal.

Jenna made up a story that Ben was a sexist and had made insensitive comments outside of class. None of this was true. She got hundreds of Likes of her comments on Facebook.

Later that day, Ben went online and attacked Jenna as a racist. Nothing could be further from the truth.

Jenna was furious and considered posting a doctored image of Ben portraying him in an unflattering way.

Questions

1. Discuss the ethical values that are illustrated by the case.
2. Assume Jenna asks for your advice. Use ethical reasoning to decide what you would say to her and why?

CHAPTER 2
Cognitive Processes and Ethical Decision Making in Accounting

LEARNING OBJECTIVES

After studying **Chapter 2**, you should be able to:

LO 2-1   Analyze the thought processes involved in, and the impact cognitive biases have on, making decisions and taking ethical action.

LO 2-2   Describe Kohlberg's stages of moral development.

LO 2-3   Explain Rest's Model and how its components influence ethical decision making.

LO 2-4   Describe the link between organizational culture, ethical climate, ethical leadership, and ethical decision making.

LO 2-5   Distinguish between Equity, Diversity, and Inclusion.

LO 2-6   Apply both the Integrated Ethical Decision-Making Model and the Giving Voices to Values Methodology to a case study.

Ethics Reflection

Enron's Fall From Grace

Enron was once celebrated as one of Americas best companies winning *Fortune* magazine's 'America's most innovative company' award six years in a row between 1996 and 2001.[1] According to Dobson, the three most senior Enron executives, Ken Lay (CEO & Chairman of the Board), Jeff Skilling (President and COO who eventually replaced Lay (2001) as CEO & Chairman of the Board) and Andy Fastow (CFO) were frequently lauded by the financial press as representing "everything good and right about corporate America" and for creating a corporate culture second to none.[2]

In a rather surprising twist of fate, these same executives will forever be remembered as having orchestrated one of the largest financial frauds in history and resulting in the demise of Arthur Andersen, one of the then five largest and well-respected public accounting firms in the world. Within 18 months of Enron's shares hitting a record high of $90 in August of 2000 (making it the seventh largest company in the world at the time), the company's shares plummeted to just $.20 per share on November 30, 2001, just a few days before declaring bankruptcy.[3]

Sherron Watkins, who is generally viewed as the whistleblower who eventually took action and helped bring the facts about Enron to light, stated she was aware of questionable accounting practices at Enron going as far back as 1996.[4] Watkins, who had been an Auditor for Arthur Andersen before taking a job at Enron's Finance Division in 1993, reported to Fastow. In a 2003 interview with Damian Wild of Accountancy Age,[5] she explained that after expressing concerns over certain accounting practices in 1996 to both Fastow and the auditors, she was reprimanded and told they were not her concern. She worked in the Finance department and was told not to stick her nose in the Accounting departments business.[6]

After being reprimanded by Fastow, she transferred to another division within Enron to get away from these questionable practices.[7] In June 2001, Watkins once again found herself working for Fastow in his Mergers and Acquisition group. Very shortly after joining this group, she discovered just how bad the situation had become, including the covering up of some $800 million in losses over a two-year period.[8]

According to Watkin's "What I stumbled across was hiding losses. It shocked me to my core."[9] That is when she decided she had to speak up and bring the matter to Ken Lay. She further states that she had been "incredibly naive, to the point of stupidity" about Lay's knowledge of what had been going on. She indicated that he tried to whitewash it away.[10]

Our focus in this chapter is not on the accounting practices used to commit this fraud, but rather the cognitive decision-making processes that possibly led to it, and the role that corporate culture may have played in these decisions as well. What led the senior executives at Enron to commit fraud? Why would partners and employees from one of the most highly reputable accounting firms in the world effectively agree to go along? Why didn't anyone at Enron speak up sooner?

We can look at decision making at Enron as being influenced by cognitive biases. A cognitive bias refers to a systematic pattern of deviation from norms or rationality in judgment that manifests itself as a mistake in reasoning, evaluating, reflecting, and other cognitive processes. Individuals create their own social reality from their perception of the input rather than an objective analysis of it.[11] Cognitive biases can fool an individual into thinking, depending on how an issue is framed, that one is not even facing a moral or ethical dilemma.[12] This often times results in an underestimation of risk.

While the senior executives, their legal counsel, their board, and their auditors have all been vilified for their role in enabling the fraud, Sherron Watkins has generally been viewed as the hero of this story. Watkins, however, regrets a number of things, including her decision not to pursue her concerns from 1996 further at the time. She has indicated she never thought about quitting back then, as she was fearful she would not be able to find a new job.[13] In fact, the reason she has given for eventually going to Lay in 2001 was that she was concerned that the accounting fraud would come to light and result in the company imploding and that her years at Enron would not be worth anything on her resume.

While Watkins is generally viewed positively for her actions, her motives appear to have been somewhat self-serving. She also regrets selling some $47,000 of company stock in 2001 after discovering the extent of the fraud. She believes that with so many truly bad characters in the Enron story, that she got made into the heroine of it, whether deserved or not.[14]

The goal of **Chapter 2** is to help prepare you for making ethical decisions in your future leadership roles in the accounting profession. To accomplish this goal, it is essential that you gain an understanding of: (1) How people think (Behavioral Ethics); (2) How people develop morally (Cognitive Development); (3) How people make ethical decisions (Ethical Decision Making); (4) How Organizations can Influence your Ethical Decisions (Ethical Organizations); and (5) How to make Ethical Decisions in Accounting (Ethical Decision-Making Models). This and each of the chapters following provide ample opportunity for you to practice and hone your ethical decision-making skills through end of chapter discussion questions and case studies.

The Road to Making Ethical Decisions in Accounting

Think about the following questions as you read the chapter: (1) How can cognitive processes and biases influence your decision making? (2) In terms of ethical decisions you have made in the past, where do you rank yourself and your peers in terms of moral development? (3) What you would do if your attitudes and beliefs about right and wrong were being tested by pressures within an organization? (4) What factors might increase the likelihood that you would speak up if you encountered an ethical dilemma?

> As we practice resolving dilemmas we find ethics to be less a goal than a pathway, less a destination than a trip, less an inoculation than a process.
>
> *Source: Ethicist Rushworth Kidder (1944–2012)*

Kidder believed that self-reflection was the key to resolving ethical dilemmas, and a conscious sense of vision and deep core of ethical values provide the courage to stand up to the tough choices. The pathway one takes can be influenced by biases we have about ourselves and others that need to be understood and acted upon to successfully continue the journey to ethical decision making.

Behavioral Ethics

LO 2-1

Analyze the thought processes involved in, and the impact cognitive biases have on, making decisions and taking ethical action.

The field of behavioral ethics emphasizes the need to consider how individuals actually make decisions, rather than how they would make decisions in an ideal world. Per Simon Longstaff of the Ethics Resource Center, "It is not that most people are inherently unethical. Instead, the problem is that many people are unconscious of the fact that nearly everything that they do has an ethical dimension."[15] Knowledge of behavioral ethics is important to understand the way individuals think and process information, and how they deal with biases that can influence ethical decision making.

System 1 Versus System 2 Thinking

Research in behavioral ethics reveals that our minds have two distinct modes of decision making— "System 1" and "System 2" thinking.[16] Daniel Kahneman, the Nobel Prize–winning behavioral economist, points out that System 1 thinking is our intuitive system of processing information: fast, automatic, effortless, and emotional decision processes; on the other hand, System 2 thinking is slower, conscious, effortful, explicit, and a more reasoned decision process. Walter points out that the dominant role of System 1 in ethical decision making is evidenced by the fact that children, even babies, have a basic moral sense that is ingrained into their brains before they are taught morality by their parents and society.[17] For example, infants at the earliest levels of moral development in Kohlberg's model, discussed later, are aware of the importance of rules and the need to yield to authority figures.

Kahneman's fundamental proposition is that we identify with System 2, "*the conscious, reasoning self that has beliefs, makes choices and decides what to think about and what to do.*" But the one that is really in charge is System 1 as it "*effortlessly originates impressions and feelings that are the main sources of the explicit beliefs and deliberate choices of System 2.*"[18]

What follows is an example of using System 1 thinking instead of the more deliberate approach of System 2, and drawing the wrong conclusion as a result. To illustrate, answer the following question: A baseball bat and ball together cost $110. If the bat costs $100 more than the ball, how much does the ball cost? Most people say $10. They decide quickly, without doing the math or thinking through the question. However, it is the wrong answer. The ball actually costs $5, and the bat costs $105.

The broader point of this exercise is to explain how System 1 thinking can lead to snap decisions that make it more difficult to resolve an ethical dilemma in a morally appropriate way. It may occur because you lack important information regarding a decision, fail to notice available information, or face time and cost constraints. You don't have the time or inclination and fail to see the dangers of deciding too quickly. However, both System 1 and System 2 thinking may be negatively impacted because cognitive biases can shape people's ethical decision making in ways they often do not understand or notice.

Cognitive Biases

Understanding the unconscious biases that people may have is an important first step to preventing unethical behavior. Unconscious or cognitive biases are biases that all humans have to some degree. Karen Wynn, Director of the Infant Cognition Center at Yale University has spent most of her career studying the cognition of infants. She along with her colleagues have demonstrated that infants not only have these types of biases,[19] but they are also ingrained with a basic sense of morality (the difference between right and wrong).[20] With a simple Google search, you will discover that Wynn's work has been highlighted on a number of television shows including Sixty Minutes, Anderson Cooper360, The Discovery Channel, and PBS's The Human Spark.[21]

Messick and Bazerman have categorized our biases suggesting that we have cognitive biases about the world, other people, and ourselves which can negatively influence our decision-making process. Understanding our own biases, and those of others, can help us avoid them and improve our ethical decision making.[22]

These biases are often compounded by the false belief that the world is more predictable/controllable than it is (Deterministic Bias). This illusion of control causes us to underestimate the risks involved with our decisions. Memories of past-experiences change to support this erroneous belief (Hindsight Bias). A hindsight bias might develop where people tend to believe that they expected a past outcome before it occurred (even when they did not).

Theories about the world also suggest that we tend to blame individuals for events, rather than their work environment, policies and procedures, or incentive programs (Attribution Bias). The attribution bias often leads to problems being framed inaccurately and can result in decisions which do not correct and may even exacerbate the problem (Framing Bias). People have a tendency to make different decisions based upon how an issue is framed so that other factors are framed as more important than ethical standards[23] (i.e., meet or beat financial statement earnings goals). Therefore, it is important to accurately frame the problem to maximize the probability of finding a solution for it.

Framing was an important factor in the Enron case. Top executives were fixated on share price, which caused them to focus on earnings projections. Knowing that missing earnings targets would lead to a steep reduction in share price, they engaged in accounting maneuvers to keep the stock price up. Ethical considerations were completely disregarded, despite Enron's code of ethics.

In a 2016 presentation to Certified Fraud Examiners, Fastow stated "At Enron, I found every loophole in the finance and accounting area. My title was chief financial officer, but I should have been called chief loophole officer. I undermined every principle possible."[24] He went on to say he never considered these decisions to involve ethics, simply one of following the rules, and described the rules as amoral. Had the company's officers managed to keep ethics in their decision analysis, they might have acted differently.[25]

Theories About the World

According to Messick and Bazerman, people have a tendency to simplify complex issues to make decision making easier. This oversimplification bias can lead to underestimating risk and making poor decisions by ignoring low-probability events; failing to identify all stakeholders impacted; ignoring the possibility the public will find out; not thinking about long-term consequences; and undervaluing the magnitude of the consequences in total.[26]

A good example of the damage underestimating risk can have is the "Dieselgate" scandal at Volkswagen (VW). The scandal broke in July 2015 when the California Air Resources Board (CARB) shared its findings about carbon dioxide emissions from diesel vehicles produced by VW. CARB and the Environmental Protection Agency (EPA) refused to certify VW's 2016 diesel vehicles. VW at first blamed software irregularities. An increasing number of negative reports about VW's diesel vehicles and VW's culpability led to the auto company's admission in September 2015 that the cars were "designed and manufactured with a defeat device to bypass, defeat, or render inoperative elements of the vehicles emission control system."[27] The system was set to report levels of emission that would pass lab tests, even though they emitted as much as 40 times the legal limit of pollutants on the road.[28]

Instead of stepping back and looking for other ways to increase their revenues and meet their goals, senior management focused solely on how to still enter the U.S. market with their not so clean diesel vehicles. They did not frame the problem as needing to find a way to capture more market share, but rather one of finding a way for their vehicles to pass the U.S. emissions test while still delivering the promised fuel efficiency. Senior management at VW then approved and ordered the installation of software in each of the vehicles which would make it appear to meet the U.S. emission standards.

In addition to not framing the problem correctly, VW's senior management significantly underestimated not only the risk of getting caught, but what it would cost them if they did. Falling victim to the deterministic bias previously discussed, VW executives incorrectly thought they could accurately predict the future. Reviewing previous cases of violations of environmental regulations by auto manufacturers in the United States, they predicted that the likely fines posed "only a moderate cost risk." They cited the highest fine, imposed against Hyundai/Kia as amounting to "barely $91 per vehicle" and added, "fines in this amount are not even remotely capable of influencing the share price of a globally operative company such as Volkswagen."[29]

In reality, the financial penalties of previous cases ranged from $98 to $292 per vehicle. These previous penalties were well below the maximum allowable penalty of $37,500 and the $29,000 per vehicle that VW actually was fined.[30] VW management's cognitive shortcomings also included miscalculating the risk of getting caught and the other consequences of reporting fraudulent emissions data. This is why cost–benefit analyses are risky.

It is also worth mentioning, when the issue was first brought into the public eye, Martin Winterkorn tried to blame the problem on a couple of "rogue" engineers. This is an example of Winterkorn trying to use people's own attribution biases to his advantage. As we have a tendency to blame people rather than systems for problems, his attempts to hide the facts surrounding the issue might seem reasonable. This act is also an example of Winterkorn being overconfident in his abilities to continue to keep all the facts from coming to light. Moreover, his blaming of others for the scandal, illustrates a self-serving bias as well.

One of the most common biases that people have is to defer to those in authority. This authoritative bias was at play at VW. In fact, it was raised during the trial of several of those indicted for their roles in this fraud. We might also consider this to be an example of bounded ethicality.[31] This is a concept that our ethics are bounded or limited by internal or external pressures, like authoritative figures or our loyalty to the success of the company. While most people know the difference between right and wrong and are generally ethical, the importance they place on being ethical may be less than the importance they place on other factors.

This scenario is similar to what we saw at Enron. A management team focused on a single goal which resulted in their being blind to the ethical aspects of the decisions they were making. At VW this resulted in billions in fines, lost reputation and revenues far into the future, and for many of its senior executives and managers, both fines and/or jail time. We might sum up this case by saying VW was guilty of having a blind spot where ethics was concerned. It used an ends justifies the means approach to ethical decision making but failed to incorporate the costs of their actions. They violated the trust of the driving public and the company paid dearly for its lapse in judgment.

Theories About Other People

Business today operates in a global environment rich in diversity with people who speak different languages, have different customs, mores, cultural beliefs, religious beliefs, laws, and accepted ways of behavior. Unfortunately, people have a tendency to think of themselves and the groups they belong to or share their beliefs with as better than those they don't belong to whether based on factors of race, religion, nationality, political affiliation, and so on.

This perception that "our way" is normal and preferred and that other ways are somehow inferior has been called ethnocentrism. In the ethnocentric view, the world revolves around our group, and our values and beliefs become the standard against which to judge the rest of the world.

Ethnocentrism is best described an "us versus them" mentality that is pervasive in most societies. Having national pride or being affiliated with a religious group is natural and there is nothing wrong with that. The problem lies in our tendency to inaccurately believe that our group is better than any other without taking the time to thoroughly analyze whether these beliefs are valid. People often exacerbate this tendency by making up derogatory stories or comments about those that are not part of "their" group. This is where stereotypes come from. Stereotypes are unconscious beliefs we have about certain people within certain groups. These beliefs or stereotypes can exaggerate the differences between groups and can unconsciously negatively influence the decisions we make.

In business, these unconscious beliefs can manifest themselves through discriminatory hiring and promotion practices and favoritism for white employees over employees of color and one gender over another. Understanding the role that stereotypes can play in our decision-making process is critical if we hope to avoid their negative manifestations. It is essential, in an increasingly diverse workforce, to mold individuals with these differences into a coherent whole. This is the essence of ethical leadership.

Theories About Ourselves

People have a tendency to overestimate their positive attributes and to underestimate their weaknesses (Superiority/ Overconfidence Bias). This bias can be caused or exacerbated by the hindsight bias discussed previously. This can result in executives being overconfident in their abilities to make decisions based on incomplete or inaccurate information. The best decisions surrounding complex matters are made through consultation and inclusion of other points of view.

People also have a tendency to believe that they are more ethical than they actually are, which can cause them to make decisions with serious ethical implications without proper reflection.[32] Overconfidence bias is important in accounting because auditors overconfident in their (conservative) risk assessments about certain areas of the audit (i.e., the risk of failure of internal controls) may fail to seek additional information to update their knowledge. One cost of overconfidence is a reluctance to learn more about how the internal controls work before determining whether they are working as intended.[33]

In addition, people have a tendency to detest losses (Loss Aversion Bias) even more than they enjoy gains. Research has shown that many people will make immoral decisions to avoid what they perceive to be a potential loss.[34]

Matousek identifies two of the most common social and organizational pressures that can cause well-intentioned people to make poor ethical choices: the tendencies to be overly obedient to authority and to conform excessively to the ethical judgments and actions of peers.

Stanley Milgram's classic 1963 study involving a person's willingness to administer increasingly more severe electrical shocks to others as punishment demonstrates our tendency to subjugate our will to authoritative figures. The experiment shows that people have a tendency to follow the instructions of those they perceive to be in authority, even when those instructions conflict with their own values.[35] This bias can result in a person unconsciously giving more weight to their loyalty to their employer than their own integrity when making a decision as to whether to go along with an unethical request made by that employer.

In accounting, it is important to follow superiors' instructions, especially if they are seen as being ethical.[36] However, the desire to please authority can bias one's outlook on a financial reporting issue, suspend one's own ethical judgment about right versus wrong, and bend to the wishes of a superior. Obedience to authority played a role in the Enron case. Andy Fastow, the Enron CFO, and David Duncan, the Andersen auditor who went along with Enron's improper accounting, explicitly raised the defense that they were just following orders. In fact, this was the rallying cry for many in the era of financial frauds at companies such as WorldCom (Betty Vinson) and other leading figures in the Enron-era scandals.[37] Despite sensing she was being asked to do something wrong by WorldCom's CFO, Scott Sullivan, Betty Vinson rationalized that since he was the CFO, Sullivan must know better than herself what was the proper accounting. The authoritative bias may also help explain why Sherron Watkins did not do more back in 1996 when she initially raised concerns over the accounting practices at Enron.

In regard to peers, Asch found that people have a tendency to yield to group pressure, even when they know the majority view is incorrect. The greater the number of people in the majority, the more likely those in the minority change their view to conform with the majority. "Group Think" speaks to an unconscious need for approval and avoidance of conflict within the groups we belong. This bias can result in individual group members not sharing concerns they may have about potential consequences a decision may have, leading to poor decisions being made.[38] **Table 2.1** provides a summary of the all the biases highlighted above.

Table 2.1	Cognitive Biases	
Bias by Category	**Description**	**Potential Issues**
Theories About the World		
Deterministic Bias	Belief that the world is more deterministic/predicable than it actually is	Underestimating risk
Hindsight Bias	Tendency to believe past outcomes were expected/known before they occurred	Underestimating risk, not gathering all the relevant facts
Framing Bias	Tendency to place blame on people rather than systems or processes	Treating people poorly, and never solving the underlying problem

Bias by Category	Description	Potential Issues
Attribution Bias	Tendency to define issues incorrectly, often cause by the attribution bias	Not solving the underlying problem
Oversimplification Bias	Tendency to simplify issues in order to make faster decisions	Increasing risk and making poor decisions
Theories About Other People		
Ethnocentrism	Tendency to believe ourselves, and the groups we belong, to be better than all others	Excluding valid data and perspectives in our decision-making process
Stereotypes	Stereotypes are derived from the stories we tell ourselves about others to inflate our own self or group worth caused from Ethnocentrism	Discrimination, poor corporate culture and discriminatory hiring practices
Theories About Ourselves		
Authoritative Bias	Tendency to subordinate one's own judgment to those perceived to be authoritative figures	People going along with unethical practices and incrementalism
Superiority/ Overconfidence Bias	Tendency to overestimate one's positive attributes and underestimate weaknesses	Underestimating risk, and making decisions with incomplete or inaccurate information
Loss Aversion Bias	Tendency to place more weight on items that eliminate losses than other factors	Ignoring better alternatives and making poor decisions
Group Think Bias	Tendency to go along with the majority and not speak up if in the minority	Not contributing to problem analysis/ discussion, and ignoring facts needed to make the best decision

Additional Factors Impacting Our Decisions

Whether the result of authoritative bias or that of succumbing to group pressure, small bad decisions can snowball into much larger ones. Kahneman and Tversky point out that incrementalism (the slippery slope) may influence the behavior of even well-intentioned people who find themselves in situations in which ethical corners are being cut. It can be difficult to notice gradual changes in one's environment so that cutting corners grow until violations of the law occur.[39]

Sherron Watkins decision to transfer out of the Finance Division of Enron in 1996 was driven by a fear of Incrementalism. She compared herself to a frog in boiling water indicating that she jumped out of the pot when the water got lukewarm.[40] While she is happy she did, she indicated some of her friends were not so lucky. She described their situation as walking along the shell of an egg, with each step looking very similar to the last. Never realizing the peril you are in.

A good example of incrementalism is the case of Aaron Beam, the first CFO at HealthSouth Corporation—a company that had a $2.7 million accounting fraud in the 1990s. One day in 1996 the time came when the company couldn't make its projected earnings and CEO Richard Scrushy refused to report a bad quarter. Instead, he instructed the chief accountant to scatter false assets and revenues throughout the company's 1,500 ledgers to hit their targets. Beam watched this go on for years. He watched as pressure was applied on CFOs to go along with the fraud.

Beam knew what he was about to do was wrong but went along perhaps because of the authoritative bias discussed earlier in this chapter. He also experienced fear and guilt and was concerned what Scrushy might do if he did not agree. Beam put his own reputation at risk when he agreed to falsely certify the financial statements to the SEC, even though he knew they were fraudulent. He did not consider how his silence would affect others but found out the hard way on March 26, 2003, when HealthSouth's shares lost 97 percent of their value as news of the accounting fraud surfaced.[41] Beam was sentenced to three months in prison after pleading guilty to going along with the fraud.

Beam never considered that Scrushy would continue to pressure him to manipulate the numbers. He suddenly realized he had begun the slide down the slippery slope of reporting false numbers and the need to cover them up, and there was no turning back.

Some people fall victim to self-serving biases in their decision making whereby they tend to gather, process, and even remember information in a way that advances their perceived self-interest and to support preexisting views. People can readily notice how the self-serving bias might affect others' decisions on ethical matters, but they are often nearly blind in perceiving how they themselves might be affected. This kind of ethical blindness occurs because we fail to perceive or think about how the ethical issues and contextual factors blinds us to right and wrong, such as occurred for Aaron Beam.

Situational Factors

Situational factors (the context of the situation), as discussed under **Situation Ethics** in **Chapter 1**, can also influence ethical decision making and the actor may not even be aware of the effect. Studies show that when people are under time pressure, they will often act less ethically than in situations when they are not. They will not realize the impact that time pressure has on their decision making and actions, but the impact is still there.[42] For example, a lead engagement auditor might be hustling to complete an audit on time and under budget and not realize certain steps in the audit process have not been properly completed.

Transparency is another important factor. Novelist C. S. Lewis famously said: "Integrity is doing the right thing, even when no one is watching." Research shows that if people feel that they are not being watched, they will tend to act less ethically.[43] A greater number of people will try to get away with wrongdoing if they feel they won't get caught. It's logical to conclude that the accounting frauds that took place in the late 1990s and early 2000s were masterminded by people who never thought they would be caught doing the deed. Bernie Madoff most likely would not have conned his investors out of $65 billion using a Ponzi scheme if he thought he was being watched by the authorities.

Cognitive Dissonance

How we think we should behave is often different from how we decide to behave. This creates a problem of *cognitive dissonance,* a term first coined by Leon Festinger in 1956. The inconsistency between our thoughts, beliefs, or attitudes and our behavior creates the need to resolve contradictory or conflicting beliefs, values, and perceptions.[44]

Cognitive dissonance suggests that we have an inner drive to hold all our attitudes and beliefs in harmony and avoid disharmony. When there is inconsistency between attitudes and behaviors (dissonance), something must change to eliminate the dissonance. Festinger posits that dissonance can be reduced in one of three ways: (1) change one or more of the attitudes, behavior, or beliefs so as to make the relationship between the two elements a consonant one; (2) acquire new information that outweighs the dissonant beliefs; or (3) reduce the importance of the cognitions (beliefs, attitudes).[45]

The Betty Vinson situation illustrates the dangers of reducing dissonance by changing one's attitudes and behaviors. It also illustrates how situational factors and social and organizational pressures can create biased behavior. Vinson knew it was wrong to "cook the books." She felt it in her inner being, but she did not act on those beliefs. Instead, she followed the orders from superiors and later justified her behavior by rationalizing it as a one-time act and demanded by people who knew accounting better than herself. In a sense, she reduced the importance of her own intuitions about the appropriateness of what she was asked to do.

Bystander Effect

People also have a tendency to not report incidents of wrong doing they may witness if they believe (or hope) others will report it. Each individual may think that others will come to the aid of the threatened person. This bias is known as the bystander effect. Studies have shown that the greater the number of people present, the fewer the incidents of assistance; we take our cues from the behavior of others, and that is, after all, less stress and hassle to ourselves to assume others will intervene.[46]

One example of the bystander effect at work is an incident that occurred on a subway platform in New York City on December 3, 2012. During a disagreement between two passengers waiting for the train, Ki-Suck Han was pushed off the platform by Naeem Davis. Han was killed by an oncoming train while observers did nothing to help him off the tracks. One such observer, R. Umar Abbasi, a freelance photographer, took pictures of the incident. When questioned, Abbasi said he was shocked that people nearer to Han didn't try to help in the 22 seconds before the train struck. He figured others were closer and could have grabbed him and pulled him to safety.

Another example of the bystander effect is the rash of sexual harassment charges during 2017, first against Hollywood moguls such as Harvey Weinstein, then media personalities like Matt Lauer, and finally, a large number of Congressmen, many of whom resigned, including Minnesota Senator Al Franken. In each of these cases, the women alleging sexual harassment did not come forward initially because they feared for their career. Moreover, consciously or unconsciously, they assumed others similarly affected would report the wrongdoing.

The bystander effect could manifest itself in accounting if a fraud occurs and those in the know don't report it believing others, such as higher-ups, would do so. Failing to report fraud violates the integrity principle in the AICPA Code. An accountant or auditor cannot turn a blind eye to wrongdoing that affects the accuracy and reliability of the financial statements. Perhaps, the bystander effect also helps to explain why Sherron Watkins did not do more when she first encountered the questionable accounting practices at Enron in 1996.

Bazerman and Gino ask: What makes even good people cross ethical boundaries?[47] Wittmer asks: Do individuals in organizations always act and behave consistently with what they know or believe to be the right thing to do?[48] The behavioral approach to ethics leads to understanding and explaining moral and immoral behavior in systematic ways. In reality, whether behaviors are viewed legally or ethically, we hold individuals accountable for their behaviors and choices, at least in part because they *should have* known better. Even if we agree on what someone should ethically do in a given situation, our judgment is often clouded by other factors that cause us to act against our intuition of what good sense dictates.

Why did CEO Richard Scrushy certify HealthSouth Corporation's financial statements when he knew or was reckless in not knowing they were materially false and misleading? What influenced him to behave unethically? Once we start asking these questions, we shift our attention from inquiring about what the right thing to do is, or what a good person should do. Rather, we are attempting to understand why such an individual acted the way he did, trying to identify the factors that influenced or caused the behaviors. We have moved from a prescriptive framework, such as with the philosophical reasoning methods, to a more descriptive mode of analysis. Such a perspective is important in leading organizations toward more ethical behavior.[49] It requires identifying levers at both the individual and the institutional level to change ethically questionable behaviors when individuals are acting in unethical ways that they would not endorse with greater reflection.[50]

Many decisions in business and accounting have ethical challenges. This is because of the impacts of those decisions and the fact that outcomes are likely to affect stakeholders in different ways and will express different ethical values. A decision-making model built on System 2 thinking can provide a more systematic analysis that enables comprehensible judgment, clearer reasons, and a more justifiable and defensible action than otherwise would have been the case.

Our awareness of situations that create bias is important in the audit function. Auditors need to understand how they might utilize their understanding of biases to improve their ethical decision making. We build on our discussion of biases from this chapter in **Chapter 4** where we discuss the link between KPMG's Professional Judgment Framework and our cognitive processes.

Kohlberg and the Cognitive Development Approach

LO 2-2

Describe Kohlberg's stages of moral development.

Cognitive development refers to the thought process followed in one's moral development. An individual's ability to make reasoned judgments about moral matters develops in stages. The psychologist Lawrence Kohlberg concluded, on the basis of 20 years of research, that people develop from childhood to adulthood through a sequential and hierarchical series of cognitive stages that characterize the way they think about ethical dilemmas. Moral reasoning processes become more complex and sophisticated with development. Higher stages rely upon cognitive operations that are not available to individuals at lower stages, and higher stages are thought to be "morally better" because they are consistent with philosophical theories of justice and rights.[51] Kohlberg's views on ethical development are helpful in understanding how individuals may internalize moral standards and, as they become more sophisticated in their use, apply them more critically to resolve ethical conflicts.

Kohlberg developed his theory by using data from studies on how decisions are made by individuals. The example of Heinz and the Drug, given here, illustrates a moral dilemma used by Kohlberg to develop his stage-sequence model.

Heinz and the Drug

In Europe, a woman was near death from a rare type of cancer. There was one drug that the doctors thought might save her. It was a form of radium that a druggist in the same town had recently discovered. The drug was expensive to make, but the druggist was charging 10 times what the drug cost him to make: It cost $200 for the radium, and he charged $2,000 for a small dose of the drug. The sick woman's husband, Heinz, went to everyone he knew to borrow the money, but he could get together only about $1,000—half the cost. He told the druggist that his wife was dying and asked him to sell it cheaper or let him pay later. But the druggist said, "No, I discovered the drug and I'm going to make money from it." Heinz got desperate and broke into the man's store to steal the drug for his wife.

Should the husband have done that? Was it right or wrong? Most people say that Heinz's theft was morally justified, but Kohlberg was less concerned about whether they approved or disapproved than with the reasons they gave for their answers. Kohlberg monitored the reasons for judgments given by a group of 75 boys ranging in age from 10 to 16 years and isolated the 6 stages of moral thought. The boys progressed in reasoning sequentially, with most never reaching the highest stages. He concluded that the universal principle of justice is the highest claim of morality.

The dilemma of Heinz illustrates the challenge of evaluating the ethics of a decision. **Table 2.2** displays three types of responses.[52]

Table 2.2	Three Sample Responses to the Heinz Dilemma
A:	It really depends on how much Heinz likes his wife and how much risk there is in taking the drug. If he can get the drug in no other way and if he really likes his wife, he'll have to steal it.
B:	I think that a husband would care so much for his wife that he couldn't just sit around and let her die. He wouldn't be stealing for his own profit; he'd be doing it to help someone he loves.
C:	Regardless of his personal feelings, Heinz has to realize that the druggist is protected by the law. Since no one is above the law, Heinz shouldn't steal it. If we allowed Heinz to steal, then all society would be in danger of anarchy.

Kohlberg considered how the responses were different and what problem-solving strategies underlie the three responses. Response A (Preconventional) presents a rather uncomplicated approach to moral problems. Choices are made based on the wants of the individual decision maker (egoism). Response B (Conventional) also considers the wife's needs. Here, Heinz is concerned that his actions should be motivated by good intentions (i.e., the ends justifies the means). In Response C (Postconventional), a society-wide perspective is used in decision making. Law is the key in making moral decisions[53] (e.g., rule utilitarianism; justice orientation).

The examples in **Table 2.3** demonstrate the application of Kohlberg's model of cognitive development to possible decision making in business.

Table 2.3	Kohlberg's Stages of Moral Development

Level 1—Preconventional
At the preconventional level, the individual is very self-centered. Rules are seen as something external imposed on the self.

Stage 1: Obedience to Rules; Avoidance of Punishment

At this stage, what is right is judged by one's obedience to rules and authority.

Example: A company forbids making payoffs to government or other officials to gain business. Susan, the company's contract negotiator, might justify refusing the request of a foreign government official to make a payment to gain a contract as being contrary to company rules, or Susan might make the payment if she believes there is little chance of being caught and punished.

Stage 2: Satisfying One's Own Needs

In Stage 2, rules and authority are important only if acting in accordance with them satisfies one's own needs (egoism).

Example: Here, Susan might make the payment even though it is against company rules if she perceives that such payments are a necessary part of doing business. She views the payment as essential to gain the contract. Susan may believe that competitors are willing to make payments, and that making such payments are part of the culture of the host country. She concludes that if she does not make the payment, it might jeopardize her ability to move up the ladder within the organization and possibly forgo personal rewards of salary increases, bonuses, or both. Because everything is *relative,* each person is free to pursue her individual interests.

Level 2—Conventional
At the conventional level, the individual becomes aware of the interests of others and one's duty to society. Personal responsibility becomes an important consideration in decision making.

Stage 3: Fairness to Others

In Stage 3, an individual is not only motivated by rules but seeks to do what is in the perceived best interests of others, especially those in a family, peer group, or work organization. There is a commitment to loyalty in the relationship.

Example: Susan wants to be liked by others. She might be reluctant to make the payment but agrees to do so, not because it benefits her interests, but in response to the pressure imposed by her supervisor, who claims that the company will lose a major contract and employees will be fired if she refuses to go along.

Stage 4: Law and Order

Stage 4 behavior emphasizes the morality of law and duty to the social order. One's duty to society, respect for authority, and maintaining the social order become the focus of decision making.

Example: Susan might refuse to make the illegal payment, even though it leads to a loss of jobs in her company (or maybe even the closing of the company itself), because she views it as her duty to do so in the best interests of society. She does not want to violate the law.

Level 3—Postconventional
Principled morality underlies decision making at this level. The individual recognizes that there must be a society-wide basis for cooperation. There is an orientation to principles that shape whatever laws and role systems a society may have.

(continued)

Table 2.3	Kohlberg's Stages of Moral Development

Stage 5: Social Contract

In Stage 5, an individual is motivated by upholding the basic rights, values, and legal contracts of society. That person recognizes in some cases that legal and moral points of view may conflict. To reduce such conflict, individuals at this stage base their decisions on a rational calculation of benefits and harms to society.

Example: Susan might weigh the alternative courses of action by evaluating how each of the groups is affected by her decision to make the payment. For instance, the company might benefit by gaining the contract. Susan might even be rewarded for her action. The employees are more secure in their jobs. The customer in the other country gets what it wants. On the other hand, the company will be in violation of the Foreign Corrupt Practices Act (FCPA), which prohibits (bribery) payments to foreign government officials. Susan then weighs the consequences of making an illegal payment, including any resulting penalties, against the ability to gain additional business. Susan might conclude that the harms of prosecution, fines, other sanctions, and the loss of one's reputational capital are greater than the benefits.

Stage 6: Universal Ethical Principles

Kohlberg was still working on Stage 6 at the time of his death in 1987. He believed that this stage rarely occurred. Still, a person at this stage believes that right and wrong are determined by universal ethical principles that everyone should follow. Stage 6 individuals believe that there are inalienable rights, which are universal in nature and consequence. These rights, laws, and social agreements are valid not because of a particular society's laws or customs, but because they rest on the premise of universality. Justice and equality are examples of principles that are deemed universal. If a law conflicts with an ethical principle, then an individual should act in accordance with the principle.

An example of such a principle is Immanuel Kant's categorical imperative, the first formulation of which can be stated as: "Act only according to that maxim [reason for acting] by which you can at the same time will that it would become a universal law."[54] Kant's categorical imperative creates an absolute, unconditional requirement that exerts its authority in all circumstances, and is both required and justified as an end in itself.

Example: Susan would go beyond the norms, laws, and authority of groups or individuals. She would disregard pressure from her supervisor or the perceived best interests of the company when deciding what to do. Her action would be guided only by universal ethical principles that would apply to others in a similar situation.

Relating Kohlberg's stages to cognitive biases, individual's reasoning at Stage 3 could be affected by "groupthink." Groupthink manifests itself in group decision making that discourages individuality and personal responsibility. In this stage, peer pressure influences decision making. A good example is the case of Cynthia Cooper at WorldCom. Cooper was pressured not only by the CFO, Scott Sullivan, but also the audit committee that initially backed away from any support for her position. Still, she persisted and eventually uncovered and reported the fraud at the company. Cooper's reasoning was at the postconventional level.

Let's return to the receivables example in **Chapter 1** that applies ethical reasoning to the methods discussed in **Exhibit 1.6** (Ethical Reasoning Method Bases for Making Ethical Judgments). In the receivables example, an auditor who reasons at Stage 3 might go along with the demands of a client out of loyalty or because they think the company will benefit by such inaction. At Stage 4, the auditor places the needs of society and abiding by the law (GAAP, in this instance) above all else, so the auditor will insist on recording an allowance for uncollectibles.

An auditor who reasons at Stage 5 would not want to violate the public interest principle embedded in the profession's ethical standards, which values the public trust above all else. Investors and creditors have a right to know about the uncertainty surrounding collectibility of the receivables. At Stage 6, the auditor would ask whether she would want other auditors to insist on providing an allowance for the uncollectibles if they were involved in a similar situation. This creates an objective standard for determining the right decision. The auditor reasons that the orderly functioning of markets and a level playing field require that financial information should be accurate and reliable, so another auditor should also decide that the allowance needs to be recorded. The application of the ethical principles of objectivity and integrity in the AICPA Code enables them to carry out the ethical action and act in a responsible manner.

Kohlberg's model suggests that people continue to change their decision priorities over time and with additional education and experience. They may experience a change in values and ethical behavior.[55] In the context of business, an individual's moral development can be influenced by corporate culture, especially ethics training.[56] Ethics training and education have been shown to improve managers' moral development. More will be said about corporate culture later in this chapter.

Kohlberg maintains that his stage sequence is universal; it is the same in all cultures. William Crain addresses whether different cultures socialize their children differently, thereby teaching them different moral beliefs.[57] He points out that Kohlberg's response has been that different cultures do teach different beliefs, but that his stages refer not to specific beliefs, but to underlying modes of reasoning. We might assume, then, in a collectivist society, which exists in many Asian cultures, blowing the whistle on a member of a work group would be considered improper because of the "family" orientation or team player mentality (Stage 3), while in a more individualistic one, such as exists in the United States, it is considered acceptable because it is in the best interests of society (Stage 4). Thus, individuals in different cultures at the same stage-sequence might hold different beliefs about the appropriateness of whistleblowing but still reason the same because, from a fairness perspective, it is the right way to behave.

Rest's Four-Component Model of Ethical Decision Making

LO 2-3
Explain Rest's model and how its components influence ethical decision making.

Moral Reasoning and Moral Behavior

Within the cognitive-developmental paradigm the most distinguishing characteristic of morality is the human capacity to reason. Moral judgment has long been regarded as the single most influential factor—and the only truly moral determinant—of a person's moral behavior.[58] By definition, morality requires that a person's actions be rational, motivated by purpose or intent, and carried out with autonomous free will. Kohlberg maintained that it is as a result of development in moral reasoning that one becomes truly a moral person in both mind and deed.[59]

Kohlberg's work is not without its critics. Some philosophers complain it draws too heavily from Rawls's Theory of Justice and makes deontological ethics superior to other ethical perspectives. They note that the theory applies more to societal issues than to individual ethical decisions. A number of psychologists have challenged the notion that people go through "rigid" stages of moral reasoning, arguing instead that they can engage in many ways of thinking about a problem, regardless of their age.[60]

Although he later admitted to having underestimated the complexity of the relation between moral stage and action and revised his thinking to include two intervening cognitive functions to explain it—a prescriptive judgment of the moral right and a personal judgment of responsibility to act accordingly—Kohlberg still contended that it is the logic of a person's reasoning that most strongly influences their moral behavior. Thus, reason constitutes the essential core and strength of character of a person's moral maturity in Kohlberg's theory.[61]

Kohlberg's commitment to reason has been challenged by some who claim he disregarded other factors also associated with moral functioning, such as emotion[62] and traits of character.[63] Others have criticized Kohlberg's emphasis on reason without considering its interaction with other components of morality, and its link to moral behavior in particular.[64] Still others claim the over-reliance on dilemmas, such as Heinz and the Drug, to evaluate moral reasoning shortchanges the role of virtue ethics and its focus on the character of individuals and their overall approach to life.[65]

Noted moral psychologist James Rest attempted to address some of the problems that are recognized in Kohlberg's work, and in doing so has moved from the six-stage model to one with three levels of understanding: personal interest, maintaining norms, and postconventional. Rest focuses on the maintaining norms (similar to the conventional level) and postconventional schemas. By maintaining norms, Rest means recognizing the need for society-wide norms; a duty orientation; the need for cooperation; uniform and categorical application of norms, laws, and rules; and that individuals will obey the norms and laws and expect others to do the same even though it may not benefit all affected parties equally.[66]

Rest's conception has particular appeal for accountants who, at this level of moral development, recognize the importance of various laws and standards, comply with them, understand that sometimes compliance would benefit them and sometimes not, but recognize that obeying these norms is important for society. Rest recognized that, while operating at this level would be ideal for an accountant, it does not ensure that the accountant can make good decisions when there are options and ambiguities within accounting and auditing standards, nor does it ensure that they will have the ability to make good decisions when business circumstances arise that are outside the current laws, norms, or standards.[67]

A higher level of understanding is needed to deal with these different perspectives. The postconventional schema integrates such issues by recognizing that accountants do not have to follow the norms but should seek the moral criteria behind the norms for guidance in action. In accounting, this means the fair presentation of financial information in a way that benefits society—that is, the public interest.

Cognitive-developmental researchers have attempted to understand the process of ethical decision making. In particular, Rest asserts that ethical actions are not the outcome of a single, unitary decision process, but result from a combination of various cognitive structures and psychological processes. Rest's model of ethical action is based on the presumption that an individual's behavior is related to their level of moral development. Rest built on Kohlberg's work by developing a four-component model of the ethical decision-making process. The four-component model describes the cognitive processes that individuals use in ethical decision making; that is, it depicts how an individual first identifies an ethical dilemma and then continues through to their moral motivation and finally finds courage to behave ethically. Each component of the model must be present before the moral action will be undertaken.[68]

Rest built his four-component model by working backward. He started with the end product—to take ethical action—and then determined the steps that produce such behavior. He concluded that ethical action is the result of four psychological processes: (1) moral sensitivity (recognition), (2) moral judgment (reasoning), (3) moral focus (motivation), and (4) moral character (action).

Moral Sensitivity

The first step in moral behavior requires that the individual interpret the situation as moral. Absent the ability to recognize that one's actions affect the welfare of others, it would be virtually impossible to make the most ethical decision when faced with a moral dilemma.

Aaron Beam was unable to spot the ethical issues. He felt uncomfortable with what Richard Scrushy had asked him to do and that it was wrong to manipulate the numbers, yet he went along anyway; perhaps because of the **authoritative bias** discussed earlier in this chapter. He also was thinking at **Stage 2** of Kohlberg's stages of cognitive development. He did not consider how his silence would affect others but found out the hard way on March 26, 2003, when HealthSouth's shares lost 97 percent of their value as news of the accounting fraud surfaced. His concerns appeared to be himself and what the impact of complying with or not complying with Scrushy's request would mean to him personally.

Moral Judgment

An individual's ethical cognition of what "ideally" ought to be done to resolve an ethical dilemma is called *prescriptive reasoning*.[69] The outcome of one's prescriptive reasoning is their ethical judgment of the ideal solution to an ethical dilemma. Generally, an individual's prescriptive reasoning reflects their cognitive understanding of an ethical situation as measured by their level of moral development.[70] Once a person is aware of possible lines of action and how people would be affected by the alternatives, a process aided by the philosophical reasoning methods, a judgment must be made about which course of action is more morally justifiable (which alternative is just or right).

Moral judgment relates to developing moral reasoning abilities over time. Kohlberg believed that people engage in more complex reasoning as they progress up the stages and become less self-centered and develop broader definitions of morality. Rest added that developing moral judgment is a social and cognitive construct that progressed from a self-focused view of moral issues through a group-based moral perspective to a reliance on postconventional moral principles and a primary factor in the understanding of moral actions and emotions.

Moral Focus

After concluding what course of action is best, decision makers must be focused on taking the moral action and follow through with ethical decision making. Moral values may conflict with other values. Moral motivation reflects an individual's willingness to place ethical values (e.g., honesty, integrity, trustworthiness, caring, and empathy) ahead of nonethical values (e.g., wealth, power, and fame) that relate to self-interest. An individual's ethical motivation influences their intention to comply or not comply with their ethical judgment in the resolution of an ethical dilemma.

Sometimes individuals want to do the right thing but are overwhelmed by countervailing pressures that may overpower their ethical intentions because of perceived personal costs. The loss of a job or a client can be motivating factors that compromise integrity and block ethical action. With Betty Vinson, fear for her job and ability to support her family tainted her motivation to do the right thing and refuse to record improper accounting.

Emotions also play a part in moral motivation. Organizations should create ethically rewarding environments to increase moral motivation. To reduce the costs of behaving morally, policies and procedures should be instituted that make it easier to report unethical behavior, prevent retaliation, and create an ethical culture in the organization. Leaders have to inspire employees and build confidence that their ethical intentions are supported by organizational systems.

Moral Character

As we learned in the discussion of cognitive dissonance, individuals do not always behave in accordance with their ethical intention. An individual's intention to act ethically and their ethical actions may not be aligned because of pressures or biases that influence decision making. Individuals with strong ethical character will be more likely to carry out their ethical intentions with ethical action than individuals with a weak ethical character because they are better able to withstand any pressures (i.e., have courage and maintain integrity to do otherwise).

Executing a plan of action takes character. Moral agents have to overcome indifference and opposition, resist distractions, cope with fatigue, and develop tactics and strategies for reaching their goals. Johnson points out that this helps to explain why there is only a moderate correlation between moral judgment and moral behavior. Many times deciding does not lead to doing.[71]

The four components of Rest's model are processes that must take place for moral behavior to occur. Rest does not offer the framework as a linear decision-making model, suggesting instead that the components interact through a complicated sequence of "feed-back" and "feed-forward" loops. An individual who demonstrates adequacy in one component may not necessarily be adequate in another, and moral failure can occur when there is a deficiency in any one component.[72] For example, an individual who has good moral reasoning capacity, a skill that can be developed (Component 2), may fail to perceive an ethical problem because they do not clearly understand how others might feel or react—a lack of empathy (Component 1).

Aligning Ethical Behavior and Ethical Intent

One question that arises from Rest's model is how to align ethical behavior with ethical intent. The answer is through the exercise of virtue, according to a study conducted by Libby and Thorne.[73] The authors point out that audit failures at companies such as Enron and WorldCom demonstrate that the rules in accounting cannot replace auditors' professional judgment. Transactions such as the special-purpose entities at Enron can be structured around rules, and rules cannot be made to fit every situation. The rules may be unclear or nonexistent, in which case professional judgment is necessary for decisions to be made in accordance with the values of the profession as embodied in its codes of conduct. Professional judgment requires not only technical competence but also depends on auditors' ethics and virtues that inform ethical decision making.

Libby and Thorne surveyed members of the Canadian accounting community with the help of the Canadian Institute of Chartered Accountants (CICA), the equivalent of the AICPA in the United States, to develop a set of virtues important in the practice of auditing.[74] The authors divided the virtues into two categories: intellectual virtues which indirectly influence an individual's intentions to exercise professional judgment and instrumental virtues which directly influence an individual's actions. The most important intellectual virtues were found to be integrity, truthfulness, independence, objectivity, dependability, being principled, and healthy skepticism. The most important instrumental virtues were diligence (i.e., due care) and being alert, careful, resourceful, consultative, persistent, and courageous. The authors concluded from their study that virtue plays an integral role in the intention to exercise professional judgment, the exercise of professional judgment, and the necessity of possessing both intellectual and instrumental virtues for auditors.

Intellectual virtues aim at cognitive goods through the pursuit of truth, knowledge, and understanding. They can be thought of as qualities of mind and character that enable an auditor to act with good purpose. Intellectual virtues are developed over time by gaining knowledge and skills through experiences that develop one's ability to reason through difficult situations, develop good judgment, and ultimately gain practical wisdom.

Returning now to Rest's model, Thorne contends that the model fails to provide a theoretical description of the role of personal characteristics, except for level of moral development, in auditors' ethical decision processes. Thorne develops a model of individuals' ethical decision processes that integrates Rest's components with virtue-based characteristics, which, taken together, tend to increase the decision maker's propensity to exercise sound ethical judgment. Thorne believes that virtue theory is similar to the approach advocated by the cognitive-developmental perspective in three ways. First, both perspectives suggest that ethical action is the result of a rational decision-making process. Second, both perspectives are concerned with an individual's ethical decision-making process. Third, both perspectives acknowledge the critical role of cognition in individuals' ethical decision making. **Exhibit 2.1** presents Thorne's integrated model of the ethical decision-making process.[75]

Exhibit 2.1 indicates that moral development and virtue are both required for ethical behavior. In her examination of the model, Armstrong suggests that moral development comprises sensitivity to the moral content of a situation or dilemma and prescriptive reasoning, or the ability to understand the issues, think them through, and arrive at an ethical judgment. Similarly, virtue comprises ethical motivation which describes an individual's willingness to place the interests of others ahead of their own interest and ethical character which leads to ethical behavior.[77]

EXHIBIT 2.1   Thorne's Integrated Model of Ethical Decision Making[76]

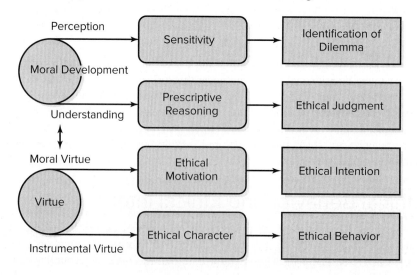

Even though virtue is a critical component of ethical behavior, other factors may get in the way of taking ethical action, including situational pressures, business norms, and the moral intensity of the issue itself that influences ethical decision making. Also, one's strength of character deepens with experience, and reflection on ethical dilemmas can bolster one's resolve.

What Makes for an Ethical Organization?

Organizational Influences on Ethical Decision Making

Organizational ethics can be thought of as the generally accepted principles and standards that guide behavior in business and other organizational contexts. High ethical standards require both organizations and individuals to conform to sound moral principles. In organizations, a critical component of creating an ethical organization environment is the culture that includes shared values, beliefs, goals, norms, and problem-solving mechanisms.

Ethical Culture

Corporate culture starts with an explicit statement of values, beliefs, and customs from top management. The statement provides the framework for top management on how to manage themselves and other employees, and how they should conduct their business(es). A code of ethics builds on those values and serves as a guide to support ethical decision making. It clarifies an organization's mission, values, and principles, linking them with standards of professional conduct. **Exhibit 2.2** highlights Microsoft's Standards of Business Conduct.

EXHIBIT 2.2   Microsoft's Standards of Business Conduct

Microsoft has been designated as one of the 132 companies in the 2020 list of the World's Most Ethical Companies by Ethisphere. *Ethisphere* is an organization that makes the designation based on an Ethics Quotient rating system that includes the following factors: Ethics and Compliance Program; Corporate Citizenship and Responsibility; Culture of Ethics; and Leadership, Innovation, and Reputation. Microsoft has been included in the list for the last nine years.[78]

Microsoft's Standards of Business Conduct define what it stands for: "We are more likely to make ethical choices when integrity, honesty, and compliance guide our decision making." It links building trust with applying the company's culture and values to build lasting relationships inside and outside the company: "Our values are the enduring principles that we use to do business with integrity and win trust every day. Our culture is our operating framework—who we are and how we behave."[79]

An important element of ethical culture is the tone at the top. Tone at the top refers to the ethical environment that is created in the workplace by the organization's leadership. An ethical tone creates the basis for standards of behavior that become part of the code of ethics. Microsoft has established a tone that reflects a commitment to ethical practices.

The tone set by managers influences how employees respond to ethical challenges and is enhanced by ethical leadership. When leaders are perceived as trustworthy, employee trust increases; leaders are seen as ethical and as honoring a higher level of duties. Employees identify with the organization's values and the likely outcome is high individual ethics, high organization ethics, and a lack of dissonance.[80]

If the tone set by management upholds ethics and integrity, employees will be more inclined to uphold those same values. However, if top management appears unconcerned about ethics and focuses solely on the bottom line, employees will be more prone to act unethically (i.e., Sexual Harassment at Uber) or commit fraud (i.e., in fraudulent financial reporting as occurred with Aaron Beam and Betty Vinson).

Ethical Climate

The ethical climate of an organization plays an important role in organizational culture. Whereas an organization's overall culture establishes ideals that guide a wide variety of member behaviors, the ethical climate focuses specifically on issues of right and wrong. We have seen how a toxic climate, such as the one at both Enron and Volkswagen, can corrupt virtually all the systems and negate checks and balances designed to ensure ethical standards are followed.

As discussed in the **Behavioral Ethics** section of the chapter, theories about the world suggest that top management tends to blame individuals for events, rather than their work climate, operational policies and procedures, or incentive programs. This often leads to problems being framed inaccurately and can result in unethical decisions.

Organizational ethical climate refers to the moral atmosphere of the work environment and the level of ethics practiced within a company. Leaders determine organizational climate, establish character, and define norms. Character plays an important role in leadership. Leaders of good character have integrity, courage, and compassion. They are careful and prudent. Their decisions and actions inspire employees to think and act in a way that enhances the well-being of the organization, its people, and society in general. Ralph Waldo Emerson, the American essayist, poet, and philosopher, said, "Our chief want is someone who will inspire us to be what we know we could be."

There is no one size fits all for ethical climates. Johnson believes that an organization must first identify principles and practices that characterize positive ethical climates and then adapt them to a particular organization setting. He identifies key markers of highly ethical organizations including humility, zero tolerance for individual and collective destructive behaviors, justice, integrity, trust, a focus on process, structural reinforcement, and social responsibility. An ethical climate is enhanced through a values-driven organization that encourages openness and transparency and provides a supportive environment to voice matters of concern without fear of retribution or retaliation.[81] An ethical climate should also support policies related to equity, diversity, and inclusion.

Equity, Diversity, and Inclusion

LO 2-5
Distinguish between equity, diversity, and inclusion.

We hear a lot about equity these days. It tends to be thought of as one of three key values necessary in the twenty-first century workplace. Equity, Diversity, and Inclusion (EDI) loosely means to give each person the same opportunity, accepting people from different races, genders, religions, and nationalities, and inviting those who have been historically locked out of society to come in. EDI policies can help promote ethical behavior and mitigate cognitive biases that might influence the fair treatment of all people.

Diversity Versus Inclusion

Diversity and inclusion are often viewed the same way. However, there are important differences. The U.S. government's Office of Personnel Management indicates that diversity is hiring and retaining employees that "reflect America's diversity," while inclusion is making them feel motivated, and a true part of the organization.[82]

The concept of diversity encompasses acceptance and respect. It means to treat each person as unique and to recognize our individual differences. It means understanding each other and moving beyond simple tolerance to embracing and to celebrating the rich dimensions of individuality. A diverse workforce is one where similarities and differences among employees in terms of different dimensions are molded together to produce the best outcome.

Inclusion has often been defined in the context of a society that leaves no one behind. It is one in which the cultural, economic, political, and social life of all individuals and groups can take part. The United Nations report, *Creating an Inclusive Society: Practical Strategies to Promote Social Integration,* points out: An inclusive society is one that overrides differences of race, gender, class, generation, and geography, and ensures inclusion and equality of opportunity, as well as capability of all members of the society to determine an agreed set of social institutions that govern social interaction.[83]

Equality Versus Equity

People tend to think about equality of opportunity and fairness in treatment as one and the same. It means having the same rights, social status, etc. Equality aims to ensure that everyone gets the same things in order to enjoy full, healthy lives. Like equity, equality aims to promote fairness and justice, but it can only work if everyone starts from the same place and needs the same things. But when we place it next to equity, that's when the lines get blurred. Equity can be thought of in terms of equal opportunity that fits a person's circumstances and abilities. It may mean giving a group of people different access to resources, as with disabled individuals who deserve special access for entry or different testing procedures in the classroom. In the workplace, it means to provide accommodations as needed.

A good analogy is to think of runners sprinting around an oval track during a competition. The concept of equality would mean treating runners the same way; having them start at the same place on the track. While this may seem fair at first, we quickly realize that those starting from an inside position have an advantage over runners in the outside lanes because the distance they have to travel is shorter. As a result, equality—starting at the same place—doesn't result in fairness. The concept of equity would mean the starting positions should be staggered so runners in the outer lanes have an equal chance to win the competition. In this case, different or tailored treatment leads to fairness and justice, not the same treatment.[84]

Components of EDI Initiatives

Our view is that creating a sense of belonging at work is the outcome of three mutually reinforcing attributes. Workers should feel *comfortable* at work, including being treated fairly and respected by their colleagues. They should feel *connected* to the people they work with and the teams they are part of. And they should feel that they *contribute* to meaningful work outcomes—understanding how their unique strengths are helping their teams and organizations achieve common goals.

Deloitte's 2020 Global Human Capital Trends survey results offer support for this view. Twenty-five percent of survey respondents identified fostering an environment where workers feel they are treated fairly and can bring their authentic selves to work (feeling comfortable) as the biggest driver of belonging. Thirty-one percent said that having a sense of community and identifying with a defined team (feeling connected) was the biggest driver. And 44 percent reported that feeling aligned to the organization's purpose, mission, and values and being valued for their individual contributions (feeling their contributions matter) was the biggest driver of belonging at work.

EDI policies are an integral part of ethics because the way we treat people with different demographic characteristics says a lot about the culture of an organization. The underlying principles of fairness and justice provide the foundation for EDI policies. The virtues of caring, kindness, and empathy should drive behavior in an ethical organization that wants to be known as a welcoming and supportive place to work.

According to the Deloitte survey, *Global Human Capital Trends,* employee belonging tops the list of the most important issues in 2020.[85] Seventy-two percent of respondents indicated that fostering a sense of belonging in the workplace was important to the success of their organization over the next 12 to 18 months. Why have diversity and inclusion efforts become so important? One answer is, in today's global business environment, it is common to have a diverse workforce that needs to be managed in ways that recognize equity and fairness in treatment. A diverse workforce poses challenges in the way people of different religions, genders, generations, and other types of diversity blend together to create an ethical corporate culture that values individuals from many walks of life.

The Deloitte survey indicates that 93 percent of respondents believe a sense of belonging drives organizational performance. This coincides with a 2019 survey by Better Up which found that workplace belonging can lead to a 56 percent increase in job performance, a 50 percent reduction in the risk of turnover, and a 75 percent decrease in the number of employees calling in sick.[86] They also found that one single incidence of a micro-exclusion can result in a 25 percent reduction in productivity. Yet, despite the importance of belonging, only 13 percent of respondents to the Deloitte 2020 Survey reported being ready to address this. Solving diversity challenges is very difficult. Also, trending upward is a focus on eliminating measurable bias from talent processes, including hiring, promotion, performance management, leadership development, succession, and compensation.

In an effort to minimize the impact of cognitive biases, many companies have moved to "Artificial Intelligence" systems for the initial screening of applicants in corporate onboarding. Artificial Intelligence is a fancy way of saying a computer program is used to screen big sets of data for particular attributes (it is the engine that drives Data Analytics). According to O'Neil,[87] 60 percent to 70 percent of perspective workers in the United States now use this type of screening. Unfortunately, the algorithms used to screen candidates very often are biased as well. Artificial Intelligence and Data Analytics in Accounting will be discussed in detail in **Chapter 5**.

In another survey by Deloitte—the 2017 *Inclusion Pulse Survey*—it was found that 72 percent of working Americans surveyed would or may consider leaving an organization for one they think is more inclusive. Thirty percent of millennials surveyed say they have already left a job for one with a more inclusive culture.[88]

The Deloitte Pulse survey gathered online responses during April 13–20, 2017, from more than 1,300 full-time employees from different sized companies across the United States. The survey reported that inclusivity was perceived differently by different groups, but when it comes to workplace culture, most respondents relate more to the way inclusion "feels" over how it may "look." Nearly half of all respondents (47%) chose "an environment that makes me feel comfortable being myself" as one of the top three attributes of an inclusive workplace.

EDI policies are significantly more important in the twenty-first century than ever before. One reason is young adults and millennials have grown up in a culture that talks about these issues even though they may be lacking in reality. Deloitte's 2020 *Global Human Capital Trends* survey reports that diversity and inclusion at the workplace are CEO-level issues, but they continue to be frustrating for many companies.

Effective EDI policies help to create an ethical culture by valuing the contribution of each individual and treating them as members of a community. The expectations are high for an inclusive environment and the failure to create one can have negative consequences as the survey results indicate. One example of EDI policies at work is sexual harassment. In the past few years, charges of sexual harassment have touched many companies including Uber discussed below.

Sexual Harassment

Issues of equality, equity, and fairness are front and center when men (or women) with power and influence use their positions to extract favors from subordinates of the same or other sex. The allegations of sexual harassment and its relation to the bystander effect illustrates an environment where treating women (or men) equally might be dependent on whether they are willing to accept sexual overtones and other forms of threatening behavior.

Sexual harassment oftentimes implies a "quid pro quo"—something for something. A harassed woman may come to believe that their boss could stifle their career advancement unless they tolerate such behavior . . . and maybe more.

Sexual harassment is unwelcome behavior of a sexual nature that is severe, pervasive, or persistent enough to create a hostile or intimidating work environment. It can include physical touching, verbal comments, non-verbal conduct such as leering or e-mails, or a combination of these things.

As far as biases go, harassing behavior can create the belief that the recipient will not be treated equally and have the same opportunities unless they give in to sexual advances.

Uber Sexual Harassment Case

Charges of sexual harassment lodged against Uber by Susan Fowler in 2017 led to an investigation of the company's practices and corporate culture. Fowler's blog post, "Reflecting on one very, very strange year at Uber," detailed allegations of harassment, discrimination, and retaliation during her employment at Uber, and the ineffectiveness of the then-existing policies and procedures. **Exhibit 2.3** provides details of Fowler's experiences and the role and responsibilities of the Covington law firm that investigated these practices and their recommendations in general.

EXHIBIT 2.3   Sexual Harassment Charges at Uber

Sexual harassment charges at Uber came to light on February 19, 2017, when former Uber engineer, Susan Fowler, published a blog post about behavior toward women at Uber.[89] Fowler detailed how, after joining Uber, she became part of a team. Her manager quickly sent her a string of messages about the open relationship he had with his girl-friend, and how he wasn't having as much luck as she was in finding sexual partners. Fowler took this as a blatant attempt by her superior to get her to sleep with him. She took a screenshot of his come-on and reported him. Human Resources told her even though this was harassment, nothing would be done. The manager was highly regarded and it was his first offense. Fowler was told her choice was to forget about it, be reassigned, or stay put even though the manager, who knew he had been reported, might give her a poor performance review.

Reassigned, Fowler wrote she later found out that the manager was openly propositioning female team members. She also discovered and wrote about a sexist corporate culture where women saw their performance evaluations retroactively downgraded when it suited male managers.

Ultimately, in response to Fowler's claim of sexual harassment and similar accusations, Uber fired 20 employees, including senior executives, and reprimanded 40 more employees. Uber commissioned an investigation of its work-place practices by Covington & Burling LLP ("Covington"), which was headed by Eric Holder, former Attorney General of the United States. Specifically, Covington was asked to conduct a thorough and objective review regarding "the specific issues relating to work place environment raised by Fowler, as well as diversity and inclusion at Uber more broadly."[90]

The sexual harassment case took a strange turn on November 30, 2017, when one of Uber's early investors and Hyperloop co-founder, Shervin Pishevar, was accused by at least five women of sexual harassment or assault. Pishevar allegedly made unwanted sexual advances or harassed them. The women accused Pishevar of exploiting a professional connection or offering the prospect of a job or investment to commit sexual assaults.[91]

The Covington report lays out a strong case for a company that lacked guidelines on issues of diversity and inclusion and an indifference to what was going on in the company. Holder suggested that Uber change its written cultural values to promote positive behavior, inclusion, and collaboration. That means doing away with values that justified poor behavior, such as "Let Builders Build," "Always Be Hustlin'," Meritocracy and Toe-Stepping" and "Principled Confrontation."

The recommendations in the report are designed to improve Uber's culture, promote fairness and accountability, and establish processes and systems to ensure the mistakes of the past would not repeated. The goal is to rebuild trust with Uber employees, riders, and drivers. Specifically, the new plan calls for Uber to forbid "any type of romantic or intimate relationship between individuals in a reporting relationship."[92]

The recommendations for Uber were numerous and covered areas such as changing senior leadership and board oversight to develop and oversee diversity and inclusion policies, strengthening internal controls, reformulating Uber's cultural values, mandatory training for managerial personnel and the human resources department, diversity and inclusion enhancements in recruiting women and other underrepresented minority groups, providing an effective compliance process, recognizing and supporting efforts of employees to improve the workplace environment, and eliminating bias and misuse of the performance evaluation system.

Ferrell et al. point out that people can act unethically by failing to identify the ethical dimensions of a situation. Ethical blindness results from individuals who fail to sense the nature and complexity of their decisions.[93] Decision making at Uber with respect to how female employees were treated illustrates what can happen when a company has a blind spot with respect to equity, diversity, and inclusion. The Covington report identifies the areas of risk for Uber and concludes that if the company commits to following their recommendations, Uber should be better positioned to create a corporate culture that values EDI and commits to incorporating it into their strategic policies.

Perhaps, the Covington report was correct. Uber settled the EEOC Sexual Harassment probe in December of 2019, and agreed to establish a $4.4 million fund to compensate female employees who are found to have suffered harassment or retaliation.[94] In addition, Uber agreed to track harassment claims by person accused to quickly identify repeat offenders, and to add specific questions to employee exit interviews surrounding sexual harassment and retaliation. The company agreed to conduct employee surveys on workplace conditions as well in hopes of identifying and resolving any issues of this nature quickly.

Is there a difference between ethical decision making in general, as we discussed previously, and ethical decision making in an organizational setting? We believe there are important differences that incorporate both individual and organizational factors into the process.

Factors That Influence Ethical Decision Making

Individual Factors

When people need to resolve issues in their daily lives, they often make their decisions based on their own values and principles of right or wrong. Values of individuals can be derived from moral philosophies, such as those discussed in **Chapter 1**. These provide principles or rules people use to decide what is right or wrong from a moral and personal perspective. Although an individual's intention to engage in ethical behavior relates to individual values, organizational and social forces also play an important role by shaping behavioral intentions and decision making.[95]

Values applied to business can also be used in negative rationalizations, such as "Everyone does it" or "We have to do what it takes to get the business."[96] We learned how Enron set unrealistic sales goals and pressured employees to go along by rationalizing their behavior as "I'm just following orders."

Organizational Factors

Research has established that in the workplace, the organization's values often have a greater influence on decisions than a person's own values. Ethical decisions in the workplace are made jointly in work groups or other organizational settings. The strength of personal values, the opportunities to behave unethically, and the exposure to others who behave ethically or unethically influence decision making. An alignment between an individual's own values and the values of the organization helps create positive work environments and organizational outcomes.[97]

An important component of organizational culture is the company's ethical culture. Ethical culture reflects the integrity of decisions made and results from corporate policies, top management's leadership on ethical issues, the influence of coworkers, and the opportunity for unethical behavior. Research indicates that ethical values integrated into the organization's culture are positively correlated to employees' commitment to the firm and their sense that they fit into the company.[98] The more employees perceive an organization's culture to be ethical, the less likely they are to make unethical decisions.

Ethical Dissonance Model

Jones and Hiltebeitel conducted a study of organizational influence on moral decisions and proposed a model that demonstrated organizational influence on the moral decision-making process.[99] They based their model on Rest's moral reasoning and Kohlberg's moral development theory.

The Jones-Hiltebeitel model looks at the role of one's personal code of conduct in ethical behavior within an organization. When an employee was called upon to perform routine tasks—those with no internal conflict or cognitive dissonance—the actions taken were almost automatic. However, when those tasks diverged from the routine, the employee would refer to their personal code of conduct for ethical cues. The implications for ethical behavior within the organization are significant because an unethical individual might act dishonestly in one case, while a virtuous person would act in a truthful, trustworthy manner.

According to the model, when one's personal code is insufficient to make the necessary moral decision, the individual will look at the factors that influenced the formation of the code, including professional and organizational influences to resolve the conflict. The influences that are strongest are the ones that determine the reformation of the individual's code of conduct. The implications for the culture of an organization are significant because an organization that values profits above all else might elicit one kind of response, such as to go along with improper accounting, while an organization that values integrity above all else might lead to questioning improper accounting and doing what one can to reverse false and misleading financial results.[100]

Burchard points out that the Jones-Hiltebeitel model and others like it pay too little attention to the examination of ethical person-organization fit upon the person-organization exchange, within each of the four potential fit options. Burchard presents what she calls the Ethical Dissonance Cycle Model to illustrate the interaction between the individual and the organization, based on the person-organization ethical fit at various stages of the contractual relationship in each potential ethical fit scenario.[101] The model is complex, so we restrict our coverage to the basics of the person-organization interchange and its implications for ethical behavior within organizations. This is an important consideration because the ethics of an individual influences the values that one brings to the workplace and decision making, while the ethics (through its culture) of an organization influences that behavior. To keep it simple, we adopt the idea that there can be a dissonance between what is considered ethical and what may actually be "best" for the subject inviting ethical consideration.

Of the four potential fit options, two possess high person-organization fit: (1) high organizational ethics, high individual ethics (High-High), and (2) low organizational ethics, low individual ethics (Low-Low); and two possess low person-organization fit: (1) high organizational ethics, low individual ethics (High-Low) and (2) low organizational ethics, high individual ethics (Low-High).[102]

Let's pause for a moment and consider the practical implications of this model. Imagine that you are interviewing for a position with a mid-sized company in your town. You can easily find out information about the company on the Internet to prepare for the interview, such as the scope of its operations, products and services, customer base, and geographical locations. However, it is less easy to find out about its reputation for ethics, although reports in the media about specific events might be of some use. Now, let's assume that you knew (and understood) what is meant by organizational fit and in this case the fit is Low-High. Would that affect whether you interview with the company? Might you ask questions to better understand why that fit exists? Would it affect your final decision whether to work for the company? The information you might gather during the process could be invaluable when you face ethical dilemmas in the workplace.

In two of the fit options (High-High and Low-Low), no ethical dissonance exists. Person-organization fit is optimal, and the organization is highly effective, either to constructive or destructive ends. The other two (High-Low and Low-High) demonstrate a lack of person-organization fit in the realm of ethics and values.[103]

High Organizational Ethics, High Individual Ethics (High-High)

Assume that you know your values and beliefs are an ethical match for the company you work for. You are likely to continue to stay employed in the organization. The issue for us is how you might assess organizational ethics. Koh and Boo identified three distinct measures of organizational ethics: support for ethical behavior from top management, the ethical climate of the organization, and the connection between career success and ethical behavior.[104] These three factors relate to the culture of the organization and may have implications for actions such as whistleblowing, as discussed later on. Koh and Boo found that positive ethical culture and climate produce favorable organizational outcomes by setting down the ethical philosophy and rules of conduct and practices (i.e., code of ethics).

Low Organizational Ethics, Low Individual Ethics (Low-Low)

When both the individual and organization possess low moral and ethical development, the fit is there, but it turns in a negative direction. A culture of corruption is difficult to change, and, for the employee, it takes more conscious effort to stop the corruption than to participate in it. You might say that the employee adopts the attitude of going along to get along. Padilla et al. contend that "dysfunctional leader behaviors and susceptible followers interacting in the context of a contributing environment produce negative organizational outcomes in which 'followers must consent to, or be unable to resist, a destructive leader.'"[105]

High Organizational Ethics, Low Individual Ethics (High-Low)

According to Hamilton and Kelman, if the individual possesses lower ethics than that which is held by the organization, the discovery of an individual's lack of person-organization fit is often pointed out by socialized members within the ethical organization.[106] Those assimilated members of the organization may attempt to socialize the individual to the ways of the organization to alleviate the ethical dissonance. Once this dissonance is discovered, the likelihood that the mismatched employee will leave the company rises. The more the individual's personal decisions are seen to be in conflict with the ethical decisions that are perceived to be encouraged by the organization, the greater the discomfort of the individual. Imagine, for example, a newly hired employee thought there was nothing wrong with accepting free gifts from contractors doing business with one's employer, but the employer has a code of ethics forbidding such practices. The culture of the organization conflicts with the individual's low ethical standards in this instance, and others in the organization that identify with organizational values may attempt to resolve the dissonance and alter the employee's behavior. If the employee's behavior does not change, the employee may be let go for cause or insubordination.

Low Organizational Ethics, High Individual Ethics (Low-High)

A reduction in job satisfaction is likely if an employee striving to be ethical perceives little top management support for ethical behavior, an unfavorable ethical climate in the organization, and/or little association between ethical behavior and job success.[107] Once this ethical dissonance is discovered, the likelihood of employee turnover rises. Sims and Keon found a significant relationship between the ethical rift between one's personal decisions and the perceived unwritten/informal policies of the organization, and the individual's level of comfort within the organization. The greater the difference between the decisions that the individual made and the decisions perceived as expected and reinforced by the organization, the greater levels of discomfort the individual would feel, and the more likely the individual would be to report these feelings of discomfort.[108] The case of Cynthia Cooper, discussed in **Chapter 1**, illustrates the low organizational, high individual ethics environment. Cooper reported her concerns to top management, and once she was convinced that nothing would be done to address the improper accounting for capitalized costs, she blew the whistle by going to the audit committee and external auditors.

Opportunity

Ferrell et al. point out that opportunity describes the conditions in an organization that limit or permit ethical or unethical behavior.[109] Opportunity results from conditions that either provide internal or external rewards or fail to erect barriers against unethical behavior. The opportunities that employees have for unethical behavior in an organization can be reduced or eliminated with aggressive enforcement of rules and codes of ethics.

Business Ethics Intentions, Behavior, and Evaluations

Ethical dilemmas involve problem-solving situations where the rules governing decisions are often vague or in conflict. The results of an ethical decision are often uncertain; it is not always immediately clear whether or not we made the right decision. Moreover, the decision we make may not always comport with the one we intended to make because of pressures within the organization.

One's intentions influence the final decision but our actions may not match our intentions because of pressures from our organizations. This is where learning how best to evaluate an ethical dilemma and how best to raise an issue when you encounter one comes in.

Ethical Decision-Making Models

LO 2-6
Apply both the Integrated Ethical Decision-Making Model and the Giving Voice to Values Methodology to a Case Study.

Ethical Decision Making in Accounting and Auditing

A commitment to serve the public interest is the bedrock of the accounting profession. Snoeyenbos, Almeder, and Humber have described this as a "social contract" in which the professional discharges their obligation by operating with high standards of expertise and integrity. When the profession does not maintain these standards, the social contract is broken, and society may decide to limit the role or the autonomy of the profession. This occurred in the aftermath of the accounting scandals when Congress passed the Sarbanes-Oxley Act (SOX) and established the Public Company Accounting Oversight Board (PCAOB) to oversee the auditing, ethics, and independence practices of CPA firms that audit companies with stock listed on the New York Stock Exchange (NYSE) and NASDAQ. For nonpublicly owned companies, the standards of the AICPA still apply.[110]

The ethical domain for accountants and auditors usually involves four key constituent groups, including (1) the client organization that hires and pays for accounting services; (2) the accounting firm that employs the practitioner, typically represented by the collective interests of the firm's management; (3) the accounting profession, including various regulatory bodies such as the Securities and Exchange Commission (SEC) and the PCAOB; and (4) the general public, who rely on the attestations and representations of the practitioner and the firm.[111] Responsibilities to each of these groups may conflict. For example, fees are paid by the client organization rather than by the general public, including investors and creditors who are the direct beneficiary of the independent auditing services, so the public interest may conflict with client interests. These conflicts might influence the cognitive development of auditors, thereby influencing their ethical reasoning.

The accounting profession's codes of conduct that were discussed in **Chapter 1** encourage the individual practitioner's ethical behavior in a way that is consistent with the stated rules and guidelines of the profession. These positive factors work in conjunction with an individual's attitudes and beliefs and ethical reasoning capacity to influence professional judgment and ethical decision making. Biases can creep into decision making, leading the auditor to be overconfident about their ability to properly assess risk on the audit.

One type of bias that fits into the discussion of moral development is conformity bias. In every aspect of their lives, people take cues from those around them about the proper way to act. By observing others in the workplace, new hires learn the culture of the organization and expected behavior. The conformity bias strongly pushes people to conform their judgments to those of their reference group. A good example is at Enron where freshly minted MBAs were acculturated into Enron's fast-and-loose corporate style without fully recognizing the ethical implications of company practices. At Enron, the "everybody else is doing it" explanation was used to justify the earnings manipulations.[112]

Kohlberg's theory of ethical development provides a framework that can be used to consider the effects of conflict areas on ethical reasoning in accounting. For example, if an individual accountant is influenced by the firm's desire to "make the client happy," then the result may be reasoning at Stage 3. The results of published studies during the 1990s by accounting researchers indicate that CPAs reason primarily at Stages 3 and 4. One possible implication of these results is that a larger percentage of CPAs may be overly influenced by their relationship with peers, superiors, and clients (Stage 3) or by rules (Stage 4). A CPA who is unable to apply the technical accounting standards and rules of conduct critically when these requirements are unclear is likely to be influenced by others in the decision-making process.[113] If an auditor reasons at the postconventional level, then that person may refuse to give in to the pressure applied by the supervisor to overlook the client's failure to follow GAAP. This is the ethical position to take, although it may go against the culture of the firm to "go along to get along."

Empirical studies have explored the underlying ethical reasoning processes of accountants and auditors in practice. Findings show that ethical reasoning may be an important determinant of professional judgment, such as the disclosure of sensitive information[114] and auditor independence.[115] Results also show that unethical and dysfunctional audit behavior, such as the underreporting of time on an audit budget, may be systematically related to the auditor's level of ethical reasoning.[116] In reviewing these and other works, Ponemon and Gabhart conclude that the results imply that ethical reasoning may be an important cognitive characteristic that affects individual judgment and behavior under a wide array of conditions and events in extant professional practice.[117]

The role of an accountant is to tell a story—to make an account—of a series of business activities. This story can be told from a variety of perspectives (i.e., employer or client) and can therefore result in many accounts. It is the role of the accountant to determine the perspective that will fairly present the information in accordance with laws and accounting standards, but they contain options and ambiguities. A higher level of understanding is required to deal with these different perspectives, the options and ambiguities that exist within the standards, and the uncertainties of business life. This higher level of understanding is encapsulated in the postconventional level of reasoning.[118]

Components of the Model

Dealing with moral issues can be perplexing. How, exactly, should we think through an ethical issue? What questions should we ask? What factors should we consider? The philosophical methods of moral reasoning suggest that once we have ascertained the facts, we should ask ourselves five questions when trying to resolve a moral issue:

- What benefits and what harms will each course of action produce, and which alternative will lead to the best overall consequences?
- What moral rights do the affected parties have, and which course of action best respects those rights?
- Which course of action treats everyone the same, except where there is a morally justifiable reason not to, and does not show favoritism, discrimination, or other biased behaviors?
- Which course of action advances the common good?
- Which course of action develops moral virtues?

In commenting on these questions, Velasquez points out that they do not provide an automatic solution to moral problems. They are not meant to. The reasoning is merely meant to help identify most of the important ethical considerations. In the end, we must deliberate on moral issues for ourselves, keeping a careful eye on both the facts and on the ethical considerations involved.[119]

Ethicist Rushworth Kidder suggests evaluating ethical decisions using various tests to assess right-versus-wrong issues. **Exhibit 2.4** displays Kidder's tests as well as one of our own.

EXHIBIT 2.4   Tests to Apply to Ethical Decisions

Smell Test. It relies on intuition. If you have an uneasy feeling about the decision or course of action, chances are it involves right-versus-wrong issues.

Front Page Test. Ask how you would feel if your decision made it to the front page of the local newspaper. If you feel uncomfortable about it, then you should consider choosing another alternative.

Mom Test. Ask how you would feel if your mother or some other important role model became aware of your choice. If you have a queasy feeling, then it is best to reconsider your choice.

Ours—*Social Media Test*. Ask how you would feel if others called you out for your decision by posting critical comments online. Are you prepared to deal with the reactions of others through trolling behavior?

Decision-making guidelines can help us make better ethical choices. Johnson points out that taking a systematic approach encourages teams and individuals to carefully define the problem, gather information, apply ethical standards and values, identify and evaluate alternative courses of action, and follow through on their choices. They are also better equipped to defend their decisions.

We believe that we need a decision-making process specific to accounting that helps to organize one's thoughts about the ethical issues that accounting professionals face and can serve as a basis for analysis in many of the cases in this book. The integrated model explained below draws on Rest's Model and Kidder's Tests to provide a basis for ethical decision making when accounting issues create ethical dilemmas. Consideration is given to moral intensity and how intellectual and instrumental virtues enable ethical action to occur.

The integrated model links to Rest's framework as follows:

Integrated Ethical Decision-Making Process

1. **Identify the ethical and professional issues (ethical sensitivity).**
   - *What are the ethical and professional issues in this case (i.e., GAAP and GAAS)?*
   - *Who are the stakeholders (i.e., investors, creditors, employees, management, the organization)?*
   - *Which ethical/professional standards apply (i.e., AICPA Code Principles, IMA Ethical Standards)?*

2. **Identify and evaluate alternative courses of action (ethical judgment).**
   - *What legal issues exist?*
   - *What can and cannot be done in resolving the conflict under professional standards?*
   - *Which ethical reasoning methods apply to help reason through alternatives (i.e., rights theory, utilitarianism, justice, and virtue)?*

3. **Use ethical reasoning to evaluate the alternative courses of action (ethical motivation).**
   - *Evaluate the magnitude of the consequences if specific actions are taken; likelihood of those consequences; ability to effect ethical responses by one's actions; consensus view within the profession about the appropriateness of the intended actions (Utilitarianism).*
   - *Consider whether anyone's rights are at stake and how they manifest in the decision-making process (Rights Theory).*
   - *Consider how virtue motivates ethical actions (Virtue Theory).*

4. **Take action (ethical behavior).**
   - *Evaluate social and organizational pressures and its effect on decision making.*
   - *Decide on a course of action consistent with one's professional obligations.*
   - *What steps can I take to strengthen my position and argument?*
   - *How can I counter reasons and rationalizations that mitigate against taking ethical action? Who can I go to for support?*

Reflection would follow after the decision has been made. What was the outcome? How should it affect my approach to ethical decision making? How can I do better in the future?

Application of the Integrated Ethical Decision-Making Model: Ace Manufacturing

In order to illustrate the use of the model, a short case appears in **Exhibit 2.5**. The facts of the case and ethical issues are analyzed below using the Integrated Model. It is not our intention to cover all points; instead, it is to illustrate the application of the model and consideration of Rest's framework, moral intensity, and the virtues previously discussed and identified in Thorne's study.

EXHIBIT 2.5   Ace Manufacturing

Ace Manufacturing is a privately held company in Anytown, USA. There are three stockholders of the company—Joe Smith, Sue Williams, and Jack Jones. Jones manages the business, including the responsibility for the financial statements. Smith and Williams are in charge of sales and marketing. Each owner has a one-third stake in the business.

Jones recently hired his son, Paul, to manage the office. Paul has limited managerial experience, but his father hopes Paul will take over in a few years when he retires, and this is a good opportunity for Paul to learn the business.

(continued)

Paul is given complete control over payroll, and he approves disbursements, signs checks, and reconciles the general ledger cash account to the bank statement balance. Previously, the bookkeeper was the only employee with such authority. However, the bookkeeper recently left the company and Jack Jones needed someone he could trust to be in charge of these sensitive operations. He did ask his son to hire someone as soon as possible to help with these and other accounting functions. Paul hired Larry Davis shortly thereafter based on a friend's recommendation. While Davis is relatively inexperienced, he did graduate with honors in Accounting from Anytown University and recently passed all parts of the CPA Exam.

On March 21, one year after hiring Davis, Paul discovered that he needed surgery. Even though the procedure was fairly common and the risks were minimal, Paul planned to take three weeks off after the surgery because of other medical conditions that might complicate the recovery. He told Davis to approve vouchers for payment and present them to his father during the three-week period for payment. Paul had previously discussed this plan with his father, and they both agreed that Davis was ready to assume the additional responsibilities. They did not, however, discuss the matter with either Smith or Williams.

The bank statement for March arrived on April 4. Paul did not tell Davis to reconcile the bank statement. In fact, he specifically told Davis to just put it aside until he returned. But Davis looked at the March statement while trying to trace a payment to a vendor who had billed the company for an invoice that Davis thought had already been paid, which was true. In the course of examining the bank statement, Davis noticed five separate payments to Paul, each for $2,000, during March. He became suspicious because Paul's salary was $3,950 per month. What's more, a check for that amount appeared on the statement.

Curiosity got the better of Davis and he decided to trace the checks paid to Paul to the cash disbursements journal. He looked for supporting documentation but couldn't find any. He noticed that the five checks were coded to different accounts including supplies, travel and entertainment, office expense, and two miscellaneous expenses. He then reviewed the banks statements for January and February and found five separate check payments each month to Paul each for $2,000.

Davis didn't know what to do at this point. He was quite certain there was no business justification for the $30,000 payments to Paul for the first three months of the year and he was concerned that if the same pattern continued unabated for the next three months, the total of $60,000 payments to Paul might threaten the ability of the company to secure a $100,000 loan for working capital.

What would you do if you were in the position of Larry Davis? Use the Integrated Ethical Decision-Making Model to craft your responses.

Ace Manufacturing: Integrated Ethical Decision-Making Process

1. **Identify the ethical and professional issues (ethical sensitivity).**

GAAP

- Appears there may be fraud in the financial statements. Expense accounts were charged for personal withdrawals.
- Financial statements do not fairly present financial position and results of operations due to improper expensing of personal expenditures.
- Taxable income may be similarly misstated.

STAKEHOLDERS/INTERESTS

- Owners including Jack Jones
- Paul Jones (son)
- Larry Davis (new accountant/CPA)
- IRS
- Banks that may be approached about the loan
- Smith and Williams were not informed of Davis's increased responsibilities during Paul's recovery.

ETHICAL/PROFESSIONAL STANDARDS

- Objectivity: Davis should not permit bias or influence, because of Paul's authority position, to interfere with making the right choice.
- Integrity: Don't subordinate judgment to Paul even though he is your boss.
- Due care: Professional skepticism has been exercised; carry through diligently and insist on supporting evidence for the recorded expenditures.

2. **Identify and evaluate alternative courses of action (ethical judgment).**

LEGAL ISSUES

- Lacking evidence to the contrary, GAAP appears to have been violated and the financial statements are fraudulent. Legal liabilities may exist.
- Tax payments will be understated assuming the improper accounting carries over to taxable income.
- Jack Jones (through his son's actions) may have some liability to the other owners.

ALTERNATIVES/ETHICAL ANALYSIS

- Do nothing: Davis knows about the highly questionable personal withdrawals by Paul. He can't stand idly by and do nothing. That would violate the integrity standard in the AICPA Code.
- Confront Paul and insist on an explanation: (a) allow him to repay the amount if he agrees to do so, (b) insist on adjusting entries, and/or (c) bring the matter to the attention of the owners and let them deal with it.
- Report the matter to Jack Jones—let Paul's dad deal with it: He may pay back the amounts for his son, which sweeps the ethical problem under the rug; he may read the riot act to his son.
- Report the matter to all of the owners without confronting Paul. Possible outcomes: (a) Jack Jones may insist Davis should be fired; (b) The other owners may insist Paul must be fired; (c) Paul's dad makes good on the amount owed to the company by his son's wrongdoing.

Prevailing ethical theories: Rule utilitarianism dictates that certain rules should never be violated (i.e., GAAP) regardless of any utilitarian benefits. Owners have a right to know about Paul's ethical lapse. Davis has an ethical obligation to the owners to make them aware of the situation. Davis has a professional, ethical obligation to avoid subordinating his judgment to Paul and/or his father. Justice requires Paul suffer the consequences of his action. If a different employee submitted improper expenses for reimbursement, that employee would (should be) reported to top management—the owners.

3. **Use ethical reasoning to evaluate the alternative courses of action. (Consider what would motivate me to act in this situation)**

- Do I want to be responsible for getting Paul in trouble with his dad, possibly fired? Paul may be prosecuted for his actions. The consequences for Ace are severe so I need to be sure of my decision.
- I want to do the right thing but will my actions do irreparable harm to others? What organizational pressures exist that may influence my decision?
- Can I ever trust Paul again? What he did is wrong and I shouldn't become a party to a cover-up. I need to avoid the slippery slope.
- I am accountable for my actions; I need to maintain my integrity.
- I need to avoid the effects of cognitive dissonance and not act in a manner that is inconsistent with the way I think I should act as an ethical person.
- What are my responsibilities given the company's pending bank loan?

4. **Take action (ethical behavior).**

- I should give Paul an opportunity to explain why he did what he did, out of fairness, but be prepared to approach the owners if his explanation and intended actions are not satisfactory.
- I should insist that steps be taken to correct the accounting and have the courage to stand up for my beliefs.

Giving Voice to Values

Once I decide what to do and why, I need to assess how best to express myself and be true to my values. Close to 60 percent of all workplace misconduct goes unreported.[120] Mary Gentile suggests that most people already know what the right thing to do is and want to take action, but either lack the confidence, or the knowledge on how best, to speak up.[121] This results in most unethical practices going unreported.

I should expect the person whose behavior I want to change to come up with reasons and rationalizations for what they did or are currently doing. I need to be prepared to counter them using sound judgment. This is where a "Giving Voice to Values" framework comes in handy.

"Giving Voice to Values" (GVV) is a behavioral ethics approach that builds on the traditional philosophical reasoning methods and emphasizes developing the capacity to effectively express one's values to ensure ethical action is taken. There is a need to develop an approach to express one's values in a way that positively influences others by finding the levers to effectively voice and enact one's values.[122] GVV asks the protagonist to think about the arguments others might make that create barriers to expressing one's values and how best to counteract these "reasons and rationalizations."[123]

GVV links to ethical intent and ethical action in Rest's Model. An ethical decision maker should start by committing to expressing their values. The intent is there, but it may fall short of the mark of taking ethical action unless a pathway can be found to effectively express what one believes is the proper course of action in workplace dilemma situations. It is the pathway to that action that GVV addresses.

GVV is used post–decision making; that is, you have already decided what to do and have chosen to voice your values. According to Mary Gentile who developed the GVV methodology, "It shifts the focus away from awareness and analysis to action by addressing a series of questions for protagonists after identifying the right thing to do,"[124] including: How can you get it done effectively and efficiently? What do you need to say, to whom, and in what sequence? What will the objections or pushback be and, then, what will you say next? What data and examples do you need to support your point of view?[125]

The underlying theme of GVV is that we can effectively voice values in the workplace if we have the proper tools to do so. GVV relies on developing arguments and action plans and rehearsing how to voice/enact not just any values, but moral values specifically. For our purposes, the six pillars of character strengthened by virtue-based decision making are our target behaviors.

Reasons and Rationalizations

An important part of the GVV methodology is to develop ways to confront barriers we may encounter when value conflicts exist in the workplace. These barriers often appear in the form of "reasons and rationalizations" that can confound our best attempts to fulfill our sense of organizational and personal purpose. These are the objections one might hear from colleagues when attempting to point out an ethical problem in the way things are being done, as Sherron Watkins experienced at Enron and Cynthia Cooper experienced in the WorldCom case. Or sometimes you do not hear them because they are the unspoken assumptions of the organization.[126]

GVV provides a framework to deal with the opposing points of view based on the following series of questions.[127]

- What are the main arguments you are trying to counter? That is, what are the *reasons and rationalizations* you need to address?
- What is at *stake* for the key parties, including those who disagree with you?
- What *levers* can you use to influence those who disagree with you?
- What is your most *powerful and persuasive response* to the reasons and rationalizations you need to address? To whom should the argument be made? When and in what context?

Gentile identifies the most frequent categories of argument or rationalization that we face when we speak out against unethical practice.

Expected or Standard Practice: "Everyone does this, so it's really standard practice. It's even expected. It is in the best interest of the company."

Materiality: "The impact of this action is not material. It doesn't really hurt anyone."

Locus of Responsibility: "This is not my responsibility; I'm just following orders here."

Locus of Loyalty: "I know this isn't quite fair to the customer, but I don't want to hurt my reports/team/boss/company."

An additional argument we include is:

Isolated Incident: "This is a one-time request; you won't be asked to do it again."

Think back to the Enron case and we see that management was driven by the goal of share price maximization and rationalized their actions as expected or standard practice. They viewed their actions as being in the best interest of the company.

The GVV process includes advance planning of the conversation or conversations you will have when you raise an issue. The idea being that the more prepared you are, the more comfortable and confident you will be addressing the issue. Gentile suggests using the responses you determine to the questions above to script out the possible things the person you raise the issue to will say, and what your responses to each of those points will be.

Levers

The final ingredient included in the GVV methodology are the tools necessary to speak up and voice your values in a way that is comfortable to you. Gentile calls these tools levers and according to Shawver and Miller some common ones include:[128]

- Asking for help—Seeking advice from friends, family, mentors, and professional organizations.
- Finding Allies—Identifying those in the organization who can provide support and probably will have similar concerns to yours.
- Identifying Risk—Consider both short- and long-term consequences of the issue.
- Researching the topic—Collecting support for your concern whether that be evidence of the issue, authoritative literature surrounding the proper treatment or policy and procedures manuals, etc.
- Providing solutions rather than complaints—Always better to provide a resolution to a problem than complain about the existence of one.
- Considering what is unique about you or the situation that you can use to your advantage like a new employee being able to raise a concern by starting with, "I need your help in understanding something. As a new employee, I probably am misunderstanding or misinterpreting this, but. . ."
- Identifying the impact stakeholders—both primary and secondary to the issue.
- Highlighting the benefits of the proposed solution.

While Cynthia Cooper successfully was able to voice her values at WorldCom, Sherron Watkins at Enron was not. As we saw, when Watkins first raised her concerns in 1996, she was told it was not her job (not her responsibility) and to effectively back off: which she did. Had she been trained in the use of GVV, perhaps things might have turned out quite differently for both Enron and Arthur Andersen.

Application of GVV Methodology: Ace Manufacturing

We assume that Davis has decided to give Paul a chance to explain why he is receiving $10,000 a month with coding the expenditures to different accounts and no further substantiation. Giving Paul the opportunity to explain enhances the GVV methodology because Davis needs to be prepared to counter the arguments provided by Paul.

Davis needs to find a way to communicate his values powerfully and persuasively in the face of strong countervailing organizational or individual norms, reasons, and rationalizations. In other words, how can Davis find a way to effectively articulate his point of view so that others can be convinced of its rightness? He may need to find a way not only to counteract Paul's position but that of his dad as well if he provides reasons to go along with what he and Paul decide is best in this situation.

Kohlberg argues that higher moral development requires role-taking ability. Role-taking ability involves understanding the cognitive and affective (i.e., relating to moods, emotions, and attitudes) aspects of another person's point of view. Davis needs to consider how Paul might react, what he might say, and how Davis might counter those statements when he meets with Paul.

We assume Paul and Davis will meet to discuss the matter. Using the GVV framework, what follows is a brief explanation of how such a meeting might go.

What are the main arguments you are trying to counter? That is, what are the reasons and rationalizations you need to address?

These could be addressed from the perspective of Paul trying to convince Davis to remain silent about the apparent misappropriation of company cash. Developing a script, such as the one below, can help Davis get to the next step, which is to understand the full scope of his dilemma, and then develop responses to Paul and other detractors with an opposing view (i.e., his dad) followed by involving other parties that can serve as enablers for his position.

- Davis was told to put bank statements aside and not to do reconciliations.
- The company is privately owned, no one gets hurt by what he did.
- The use of company cash for personal purposes is a common practice in the company because it's not publicly owned. (*Expected or Standard Practice*)
- He needed the money to pay for hospitalization costs.
- The amount of money involved is not significant. (*Materiality*)
- His monthly salary is low for someone in his position; he's not being compensated adequately.
- It was a one-time event and won't happen again. (*Isolated Incident*)
- His dad knows about it and has approved the withdrawals.
- He promises to pay the money back as soon as he gets out of the hospital (no harm, no foul).

What is at stake for the key parties, including those who disagree with you?

- Paul's reputation is on the line because he committed a fraud on the company.
- Jack Jones will feel embarrassed for himself and his son if Davis discloses what Paul has done to the other owners.
- The other owners have a right to know what has happened and may feel betrayed if no one discloses the problem.
- Davis may lose his job if he confronts Paul even if he drops the matter later on.
- The ability of the company to secure the $100,000 loan is at stake.
- Davis' reputation for integrity is at stake.

What levers can you use to influence those who disagree with you?

- Davis can ask Paul for supporting documentation to back up the coding of expenses to different accounts; he can share with Paul his analysis of the bank statements. When faced with the evidence, Paul may agree to repay the amount and not do it again.
- Davis can try to convince Paul that his actions are harmful to the company and potentially very embarrassing for his dad; he needs to come forward sooner rather than later and correct the "mistake."
- Davis can try to convince Paul that he needs to look at the long-term effects of taking money from the company that has not been properly authorized, rather than focus on short-term gain such as covering hospital bills. He certainly could have asked his dad to pay for these amounts.
- Davis should try and convince Paul of the dangers of producing financial statements with fraudulent expenses both in terms of the bank loan and taxes.

- Davis can use the leverage of threatening to go to all the owners if Paul doesn't admit the mistake and take corrective action; his loyalty obligation is to the three owners, not just Paul. They are the ones with the most at stake.

- Davis can enlist the help of Smith and Williams to serve as supporters to help counteract the reasons and rationalizations provided by Paul for his actions.

- Davis' reputation is at stake: he cannot violate the ethics of the profession; the accounting is wrong and needs to be corrected; he needs to explain about his ethical obligations as a CPA.

What is your most powerful and persuasive response to the reasons and rationalizations you need to address? To whom should the argument be made? When and in what context?

- Davis should explain to Paul that he was acting diligently when he looked at the bank statements because he didn't want to pay the same vendor twice and needed to see whether the first check had cleared the bank statement. In fact, Davis saved the company money by examining the bank statements and identifying the duplicate request for payment by a vendor.

- He should explain that using company cash for personal purposes is never acceptable unless Paul can demonstrate that the other owners knew about it and approved it.

- He should stress to Paul that taking company funds without offsetting business expenditures is a personal withdrawal, not an operating expense.

- Davis should challenge Paul's statement that his dad knows about it and approved it by suggesting they both go to Jack Jones and discuss the matter; he is calling Paul's bluff. Paul may back off at this point, which confirms the asset misappropriation.

- He should explain to Paul that it is not enough to simply pay the money back. Davis doesn't want to get caught up in a cover-up. He should ask himself: What if Paul persists in his actions even after repaying the $30,000? If he doesn't inform the owners now, Davis could be accused of being part of the problem and dismissed from his job. While this may seem remote at the time, Davis needs to ask himself: How would I feel if the state board of accountancy is contacted?

Role-playing Exercise

The script is developed and now it's time to turn it into a role-playing exercise where key participants can practice voicing their beliefs in a contentious situation.

Assume that Larry Davis calls Paul Jones and they set a 2:00 p.m. meeting on Friday at Paul's home where he is convalescing. The meeting goes like this:

"Paul, how are you feeling?"

"OK, Larry. What's happening at work?"

"That's why I wanted to see you."

"Yeah, why's that?"

"I noticed $10,000 payments to you each month for the first three months of the year. I can't find any supporting documentation for these amounts."

Paul immediately becomes indignant. "I told you not to look at the bank statements. You ignored my orders and disrespected my position. Your job is on the line here."

Davis is taken aback. He hesitates at first but explains about the vendor billing and tells Paul he saved the company $40,000 by detecting the duplicate billing. Paul abruptly says: "Don't you think I would have found this discrepancy?" Davis can tell Paul's anger is growing so he tries to defuse the situation.

"Paul, I may have overstepped my bounds here, and I apologize, but I believe, on balance, that I did the right thing."

Paul starts to get tired and Davis can tell he's stressed out so they agree to meet in Paul's office on Monday when he returns to work.

Paul's final comment is, "Tell no one about this meeting!" Davis returns to the office and starts to reflect on the meeting. He is not sure what to do at this point. He is thinking about his options, including not waiting for the meeting with Paul before acting.

What would you do if you were in Davis's position? You might seek out some advice at this point. Perhaps you have a trusted friend or adviser who can bring a fresh perspective to the situation? *The role-playing exercise might be extended for such a discussion.*

Cognitive issues play a role in what Davis decides to do. He needs to follow a Systems 2 approach, which he has already begun to do, by carefully evaluating the possible consequences of his actions for himself and others. He knows what the right thing to do is and must be certain his actions reflect his intentions and beliefs. To help insure this, he needs to consider how organizational influences, and the culture at Ace may be impacting his ultimate decision on how to proceed. As previously discussed, ethical decision making is complex and influenced by both individual and organizational factors. The GVV methodology helps maximize the probability of acting on one's beliefs.

Concluding Thoughts

Good intentions are a necessary but insufficient condition to ensure that ethical action occurs. You have learned in the first two chapters that an ethical person knows what the right thing to do is but can struggle doing it. Sometimes biases influence our actions and decisions. At other times, organizational pressures dissuade us from the rightful course. In the end, it is a matter of conforming our beliefs with our actions.

We have shown you how important working at an organization that has a strong ethical tone at the top and that shares your values is. The example set by organizational leadership is mirrored by the employees, thus creating the real ethical culture of the organization. When your individual values do not match those of the organization you work for, you run the risk of subordinating your values to those of the organization to avoid conflict, resulting in your decent down a rather slippery slope.

Ethical decisions are not made in a vacuum. Pressures exist in the real world of business and accounting; cultures may support or work against ethical behavior; and individuals react differently to the reasons and rationalizations given for not taking the ethical path. Therefore, it is important to understand how best to make your case when faced with an ethical dilemma. You need to learn how to overcome obstacles and effectively deal with those who would distract you from the goal of making the ethical choice and following through with ethical action. This is where the GVV framework is most valuable.

You will face dilemmas in the workplace; all of us do. You may make some mistakes, but in truth the only mistake is not trying to correct wrongdoing. In this chapter, we have tried to provide you with the tools to deal with ethical conflicts in the workplace. We've given you a pathway to serve as part of a process for making ethical decisions. We hope you will put these lessons to good use and avoid the lifetime of regrets that failing to do the right thing can lead to, like Aaron Beam and Health South Corporation and so many others have.

Perhaps the least likely person to choose for our final inspirational quote is Kristi Loucks, a sports writer, author, and freelance pastry chef who also covers the National Hockey League team Chicago Blackhawks. Loucks has said, "The road to success is littered with failures, but the lessons learned are crucial in plotting your course to success!"

Discussion Questions

1. Why do you think good people sometimes do bad things? Explain.
2. Do you believe all sexual relationships should be forbidden in the workplace? Use ethical reasoning to support your view.

3. Why are Equity, Diversity, and Inclusivity considered to be important for businesses today?

4. How do you assess at what stage of moral development in Kohlberg's model you reason at in making decisions? Do you believe your level of reasoning is consistent with what is expected of an accounting professional? How does the stage you indicate relate to the findings of research studies discussed in this chapter about moral reasoning in accounting?

5. In his research into the components of ethical decision making, Rest raised the following issue: Assuming someone possesses sound moral reasoning skills, "Why would they ever choose the moral alternative, especially if it involves sacrificing some personal value or suffering some hardship? What motivates the selection of moral values over other values?" How does Rest's model deal with such a question? How would you answer it from the point of view of an accounting professional?

6. In the text, we point out that Rest's model is not linear in nature. An individual who demonstrates adequacy in one component may not necessarily be adequate in another, and moral failure can occur when there is a deficiency in any one component. Give an example in accounting when ethical intent may not be sufficient to produce ethical behavior and explain why that is the case.

7. In teaching about moral development, instructors often point out the threefold nature of morality: It depends on emotional development (in the form of the ability to feel guilt or shame), social development (manifested by the recognition of the group and the importance of moral behavior for the group's existence), and cognitive development (especially the ability to adopt another's perspective). How does this perspective of morality relate to ethical reasoning by accountants and auditors?

8. Do you believe that our beliefs trigger our actions, or do we act and then justify our actions by changing our beliefs? Explain.

9. In this chapter, we discuss the study by Libby and Thorne of the association between auditors' virtue and professional judgment. The most important virtues identified were truthful, independent, objective, and having integrity. The authors note that the inclusion of these virtues in professional codes of conduct (such as the Principles of the AICPA Code) may account for their perceived importance. Explain how these virtues relate to an auditor's intention to make ethical decisions.

10. You are in charge of the checking account for a small business. One morning, your accounting supervisor enters your office and asks you for a check for $150 for expenses that he tells you he incurred entertaining a client last night. He submits receipts from a restaurant and lounge. Later, your supervisor's girlfriend stops by to pick him up for lunch, and you overhear her telling the receptionist what a great time she had at dinner and dancing with your supervisor the night before. What would you do and why?

11. Explain the components of Burchard's Ethical Dissonance Model and how it describes the ethical person-organization fit at various stages of the contractual relationship in each potential fit scenario. Assume a *Low Organizational Ethics, High Individual Ethics (Low-High)* fit. How might this relationship influence your motivation to blow the whistle on corporate wrongdoing?

12. Sharon is an intern with a local CPA firm. Prior to returning to school, her supervisor goes on sick leave and asks her to do some complicated reconciliation work for him. She is given what seems to her to be an unrealistic deadline. Sharon looks at the workpapers and supporting documentation and realizes she doesn't have the skills to complete the work without help. She contacts her supervisor who tells her to talk to Holly, a good friend of Sharon and former intern at the firm, for help. Holly returned to school one semester ago. What ethical considerations do you have in this matter? What would you do and why?

13. Identify the ethical issues in each of the following situations and what your ethical obligations are, assuming you are faced with the dilemma.

    a. A consultant for a CPA firm is ordered by her superior to downgrade the ratings of one company's software package being considered for a client and increase the ratings for another company, which is run by the superior's wife. What would you do and why?

    b. A tax accountant is told by his superior to take a position on a tax matter that is not supportable by the facts in order to make the client happy. This is a common practice in the firm and the likelihood of the IRS questioning it is remote. Would you go along with your supervisor?

    c. An auditor for a governmental agency concluded a contractor's accounting system was inadequate; her supervisor changed the opinion to adequate in order to minimize the audit hours on the job and make the process seem more efficient. Would you go above your supervisor in this matter and bring your concerns to high-ups in the agency?

14. One expression in particular seems to sum up why the accounting frauds at companies such as Enron, WorldCom, and HealthSouth were allowed to persist for so long: "If I Do It, I Must Do It Again." Explain what is meant by this statement in the context of ethical decision making.

15. Explain why the process of ethical decision making depends on a number of moral, social, psychological, and organizational factors.

16. Sherron Watkins regrets not taking more action back in 1996 when she first concluded that Enron's accounting might not be in accordance with GAAP. Explain how GVV training might have helped her bring the matter to a successful resolution at that time.

17. How do the reasons and rationalizations of GVV influence the culture of the organization?

18. Explain how an overconfidence bias might influence an auditor's judgment about the proper balance sheet value of inventory?

19. Explain what you think each of the following statements means in the context of moral development.

    a. How far are you willing to go to do the right thing?

    b. How much are you willing to give up to do what you believe is right?

    c. We may think we would blow the whistle on client wrongdoing but what should we do if firm management tells us to drop the matter?

20. A major theme of this chapter is that our cognitive processes influence ethical decision making. Use the theme to comment on the following statement, which various religions claim as their own and has been attributed to Lao Tzu and, some say, the Dalai Lama:

> "Watch your thoughts; they become your words.
> Watch your words; they become your actions.
> Watch your actions; they become your habits.
> Watch your habits; they become your character.
> Watch your character; it becomes your destiny."

Comprehensive Questions

1. How do theories about the world, other people, and ourselves influence ethical decision making?

2. On November 21, 2017, a story broke that *New Yorker* reporter Ronan Farrow had alleged that Harvey Weinstein used lengthy nondisclosure agreements attached to hefty monetary settlements to prevent accusers from coming forward with reports of his alleged sexual activities. Do you think it would be right or wrong for someone who alleges Weinstein sexually harassed them to violate the nondisclosure agreement in order to get their story out in the press and potentially help other victims? Explain using ethical reasoning.

3. Back in August 2017, a leaked memo by Google employee James Damore alleged that the company was discriminating in its hiring practices based on race or gender. He claimed that Google was "pressing individual managers to increase diversity" and is "using race or gender" to decide which workers are promoted and with which teams' job candidates are placed. Damore made controversial statements like: "Women, on average, have more openness directed toward their feelings and esthetics rather than ideas. Women generally also have a stronger interest in people rather than things, relative to men. . . These two differences in part explain why women relatively prefer jobs in social or artistic areas. More men like coding because it requires systemizing and even within software engineers, comparatively more women work on the front end, which deals with both people and esthetics."[129] Google's CEO, Sundar Pichai, criticized the memo that claimed women had biological issues that prevented them from being as successful as men in technology. He said Damore's statements had "crossed the line

by advancing harmful gender stereotypes in our workplace."[130] Damore was fired by Google after 3 1/2 years for writing the memo critical of the company's diversity efforts. Damore then filed a suit against Google and filed a claim with the National Labor Relations Board (NLRB) for discrimination against white men. Evaluate Damore's statements with respect to the discussion in this chapter of equity, diversity, and inclusion.

4. In 2016, an incident of price gouging raised issues similar to those in the Heinz and the Drug discussion in this chapter. Turing Pharmaceuticals purchased the right to the prescription drug Diaprim, a life-saving drug that treats toxoplasmosis, an infection that affects people with compromised immune systems, particularly those with HIV/AIDS and some forms of cancer. Lacking competition for their drug, Turing raised the price from $13.50 per tablet to $750 per tablet, or an increase of 5,000 percent. The reason given for the increase was to help the company fund its research work on toxoplasmosis, along with new education programs for the disease. Turing's CEO, Martin Shkreli, explained that it was a great business decision that benefited the company's stakeholders. From an ethical perspective, what's wrong with a pharmaceutical company charging whatever price the market will bear?

5. Michael just graduated with a degree in Accounting from State University. He worked hard in school but could only achieve a 2.95 GPA because he worked 40 hours a week to pay his own way through college. Unfortunately, Michael was unable to get a job because the recruiters all had a 3.0 GPA cut-off point. Michael stayed with his college job for another year but is anxious to start his public accounting career. One day he reads about a job opening with a local CPA firm. The entry-level position pays little but it's a way for Michael to get his foot in the door. However, he knows there will be candidates for the position with a higher GPA than his so he is thinking about using his overall GPA, which was 3.25 including two years of community college studies, rather than his major GPA and the GPA at State, even though the advertisement asks for these two GPAs. Michael asks for your opinion before sending in the résumé. Use Ethical Reasoning to determine what you would say to Michael and why?

Endnotes

1. J. Dobson, Enron: The Collapse of Corporate Culture. In *Enron and World Finance,* eds. P.H. Dembinski, C. Lager, A. Cornford, J.M. Bonvin. London: Palgrave Macmillan, 2006. https://doi.org/10.1057/9780230 518865_12.

2. J. Dobson.

3. J. Dobson.

4. Damian Wild, *Profile: Sherron Watkins, Enron whistleblower, Accountancy Age* (December 18, 2003).

5. Damian Wild.

6. Whistleblower Recalls Enron Crisis, *BBC News,* September 12, 2006, retrieved 9/5/2020 from: http://news.bbc.co.uk/2/hi/business/5335214.stm.

7. J. Dobson.

8. Whistleblower Recalls Enron Crisis, *BBC News,* September 12, 2006, retrieved 9/5/2020 from: http://news.bbc.co.uk/2/hi/business/5335214.stm.

9. Whistleblower Recalls Enron Crisis.

10. Whistleblower Recalls Enron Crisis.

11. Martie G. Haselton, Daniel Nettle, and Paul W. Andrews, The Evolution of Cognitive Bias. In *The Handbook of Evolutionary Psychology,* ed. D.M. Buss. Hoboken, NJ: John Wiley & Sons Inc., 2005, pp. 724–746.

12. The Psychology of Enron, https://peopletriggers.wordpress.com/2014/06/29/the-psychology-of-enron/.

13. Damian Wild.

14. Whistleblower Recalls Enron Crisis.

15. Longstaff, S. (1997) An Ethical Dilemma for Accountants. Ethics Resource Center. Retrieved September 8, 2020: https://ethics-dilemma-for-accountants/

16. Richard F. West and Keith Stanovich, "Individual Differences in Reasoning: Implications for the Rationality Debate," *Behavioral & Brain Sciences* 23 (2000), pp. 645–665.

17. Chip Walter, *Last Ape Standing* (NY: Bloomsbury, 2013).

18. Leon Festinger, A Theory of Cognitive Dissonance (Evanston, IL: Row & Peterson, 1957).

19. N. Mahajan and K. Wynn, The Origins of Us vs Them: Prelinguistic Infants Prefer Similar Others, *Cognition* 2, 124 (2012), pp. 227–233.

20. Kiley-Hamlin, J. and K. Wynn, Young infants prefer prosocial to antisocial others, *Cognitive Development* 26, no. 1 (2011), pp. 30–39.

21. See Karen Wynn's Bio with links to videos: https://psychology.yale.edu/people/karen-wynn.

22. David M. Messick and Max H. Bazerman, "Ethical Leadership in the Psychology of Decision Making," *Sloan Management Review,* 37 (1996), pp. 9–22.

23. Max H. Bazerman and Ann E. Trebunsel, *Blind Spots* (Princeton, NJ: Princeton University Press, 2011).

24. Coonan, Clifford (2016) Former Enron CFO Andrew Fastrow: "You can follow all the rules and still commit fraud' The Irish Times, January 6, 2016: Retrieved 9/5/2020 from: https://www.irishtimes.com/business/companies/former-enron-cfo-andrew-fastrow-you-can-follow-all-the-rules-and-still-commit-fraud-1.2485821

25. Robert A. Prentice, "Ethical Decision Making: More Needed Than Good Intentions," *Financial Analysts Journal* 63, no. 6, https://www.cfapubs.org/doi/pdf/10.2469/faj.v63.n6.4923.

26. Messick et al.

27. VW Notice of Violation, Clean Air Act. United States Environmental Protection Agency, Septe. 18, 2015.

28. Volkswagen Emissions Scandal – Timeline, December 15, 2015, https://www.theguardian.com/business/2015/dec/10/volkswagen-emissions-scandal-timeline-events.

29. Jack Ewing, Faster, Higher, Farther: The Volkswagen Scandal. (NY: W. W. Norton & Co., Inc., 2017).

30. Drew Kodjak, "Taking Stock of the VW Settlement Agreement," *The International Council on Clean Transportation* (July 15, 2016), https://www.theicct.org/blogs/staff/taking-stock-vw-settlement-agreement.

31. University of Texas, Volkswagen's Emissions Evasion Case Study, Ethics Unwrapped, Retrieved September 6, 2020, https://ethicsunwrapped.utexas.edu/video/volkswagens-emissions-evasion.

32. Cordelia Fine, *A Mind of Its Own* (NY: W.W. Norton & Co, 2006).

33. Messick and Bazerman.

34. Cass Sunstein, *Simpler: The Future of Government* (NY: Simon & Schuster, 2013).

35. Stanley Milgram, "Behavioral Study of Obedience," *Journal of Abnormal and Social Psychology* 67, no. 4 (1963), pp. 371–378.

36. Mark Matousek, *Ethical Wisdom* (NY: Anchor Books, 2011).

37. Robert A. Prentice.

38. Solomon Asch, Effects of Group Pressure Upon the Modification and Distortion of Judgement. Chapter 5 in Eleanor Maccoby, *Readings in Social Psychology* (NY: Holt, 1958). A summary and video of the experiment can be found here: http://www.psychologyconcepts.com/solomon-aschs-conformity-study/.

39. Daniel Kahneman and Amos Tversky, "Choices, Values and Frames," *American Psychologist* 39 (1984), pp. 341–350.

40. Damian Wild.

41. Amber Walkowiak, "The Wagon to Disaster: Aaron Beam on Fraud in HealthSouth and the Price He Paid," *McCombs TODAY* (April 21, 2010), http://www.today.mccombs.utexas.edu/2010/04/the-wagon-to-disaster-aaron-beam-on-fraud-in-healthsouth-and-the-price-he-paid.

42. John M. Darley and Daniel Bateson, "From Jerusalem to Jericho": A Study of Situational and Dispositional Variables in Helping Behavior," *Journal of Personality and Social Psychology* 27, no. 1, pp. 100–108.

43. Adam Alter, *Drunk Tank Pink* (NY: Oxford University Press, 2013).

44. Leon Festinger, *A Theory of Cognitive Dissonance* (Evanston, IL: Row & Peterson, 1957).

45. Leon Festinger.

46. Kristy Mathewson, "Whistleblowing and Bystander Apathy: Connecting Ethics with Social Responsibility," *The Corporate Social Responsibility Newswire*, Posted August 7, 2012, http://www.csrwire.com/blog/posts/494-whistleblowing-and-bystander-apathy-connecting-ethics-with-social-responsibility.

47. Max H. Bazerman and Francesca Gino, "Behavioral Ethics: Toward a Deeper Understanding of Moral Judgment and Dishonesty," *Annual Review of Law and Social Science* 8 (December 2012), pp. 85-104.

48. Dennis P. Wittmer, "Behavioral Ethics in Business Organizations: What the Research Teaches Us," in *Encyclopedia of Business Ethics and Society,* ed. Robert W. Kolb. NY: Sage Publications, 2008.

49. Dennis P. Wittmer.

50. Max H. Bazerman and Francesca Gino, "Behavioral Ethics: Toward a Deeper Understanding of Moral Judgment and Dishonesty," *Annual Review of Law and Social Science* 8 (December 2012), pp. 85-104.

51. Lawrence Kohlberg, "Stage and Sequence: The Cognitive Developmental Approach to Socialization," in *Handbook of Socialization Theory and Research,* ed. D. A. Goslin. Chicago: Rand McNally, 1969, pp. 347-480.

52. James R. Rest and Darcia Narvaez, editors, *Moral Development in the Professions: Psychology and Applied Ethics,* Lawrence Erlbaum Associates, Inc. Note 53 should say what Note 60 does. That's the first mention of this citation. Note 60 would then be" Rest et al.

53. James R. Rest, Darcia Narvaez, Muriel J. Bebeau, and Stephen J. Thoma, *Postconventional Moral Thinking: A Neo-Kohlbergian Approach* (Mahwah, NJ: Lawrence Erlbaum, 1999).

54. Muriel J. Bebeau and S.J. Thoma, "Intermediate Concepts and the Connection to Moral Education," *Educational Psychology Review* 11, no. 4 (1999), p. 345.

55. O.C. Ferrell, John Fraedrich, and Linda Ferrell, *Business Ethics: Ethical Decision Making and Cases* (Mason, OH: South-Western, Cengage Learning, 2009 Update), pp. 162-163.

56. Clare M. Pennino, "Is Decision Style Related to Moral Development Among Managers in the U.S.?" *Journal of Business Ethics* 41 (December 2002), pp. 337-347.

57. William Crain, *Theories of Development: Concepts and Applications,* 6th ed. (Upper Saddle River, NJ, 2010).

58. Lawrence Kohlberg, *Essays on Moral Development: Vol. II: The Psychology of Moral Development: The Nature and Validity of Moral Stages* (San Francisco: Harper & Row, 1984).

59. Mary Louise Arnold, "Stage, Sequence, and Sequels: Changing Conceptions of Morality, Post-Kohlberg," *Educational Psychology Review,* 12, no. 4 (2000), pp. 365-383.

60. Rest et al.

61. Mary Louise Arnold, pp. 367-368.

62. John C. Gibbs, "Toward an Integration of Kohlberg's and Hoffman's Moral Development Theories," *Human Development* 34 (1991), pp. 88-104.

63. Richard S. Peters, *Moral Development and Moral Education* (London: George Allen & Unwin, 1982).

64. Augusto Blasi, "Bridging Moral Cognition and Moral Action: A Critical Review of the Literature," *Psychological Bulletin* 88, no. 1 (1980), pp. 1-45.

65. William Damon and Anne Colby, "Education and Moral Commitment," *Journal of Moral Education* 25, no. 1 (1996), pp. 31-37.

66. Craig E. Johnson, *Organizational Ethics: A Practical Approach,* 3rd ed. (NY: Sage Publications, Inc., 2015).

67. Plummer, K. (2005). Improving ethical judgment through deep learning. In Campbell T. & Houghton K. (Eds.), *Ethics and Auditing* (pp. 242-244). ANU Press.

68. James R. Rest, "Morality," in *Handbook of Child Psychology: Cognitive Development,* Vol. 3, series ed. P.H. Mussen and vol. ed. J. Flavell. New York: Wiley, 1983, pp. 556-629.

69. Lawrence Kohlberg, *The Meaning and Measurement of Moral Development* (Worcester, MA: Clark University Press, 1979).

70. Rest and Narvaez, p. 24.

71. Craig E. Johnson, *Meeting the Ethical Challenges of Leadership* (New York: Sage Publications, 2011).

72. Steven Dellaportas, Beverly Jackling, Philomena Leung, and Barry J. Cooper, "Developing an Ethics Education Framework for Accounting," *Journal of Business Ethics Education* 8, no. 1 (2011), pp. 63-82.

73. Theresa Libby and Thorne Linda. "The Development of a Measure of Auditors' Virtue," *Journal of Business Ethics* (2007), pp. 89-99, doi:10.1007/s10551-006-9127-0.

74. Libby and Thorne.

75. Libby and Thorne.

76. Libby and Thorne.

77. Mary Beth Armstrong, J. Edward Ketz, and Dwight Owsen, "Ethics Education in Accounting: Moving Toward Ethical Motivation and Ethical Behavior," *Journal of Accounting Education* 21 (2003), pp. 1–16.

78. https://ethisphere.com/2020-wmec-application-process/.

79. Microsoft Standards of Business Conduct, https://www.microsoft.com/en-us/leagl/compliance/sbc/download.

80. Cam Caldwell, Linda A. Hayes, and Do Tien Long, "Leadership, Trustworthiness, and Ethical Stewardship," *Journal of Business Ethics* 96 (2010), pp. 497–512.

81. Johnson, pp. 321–323.

82. U.S. Government Office of Personnel Management, Diversity and Inclusion, https://www.opm.gov/policy-data-oversight/diversity-and-inclusion/.

83. United Nations Department of Economic and Social Affairs, *Creating an Inclusive Society: Practical Strategies to Promote Social Integration*, 2009, http://www.un.org/esa/socdev/egms/docs/2009/Ghana/inclusive-society.pdf.

84. SGBA e-Learning Resource: Rising to the Challenge, "Distinguish Between Equity and Equality," http://sgba-resource.ca/en/concepts/equity/distinguish-between-equity-and-equality/.

85. https://www2.deloitte.com/cn/en/pages/human-capital/articles/global-human-capital-trends-2020.html.

86. https://get.betterup.co/rs/600-WTC-654/images/BetterUp_BelongingReport_091019.pdf.

87. Cathy O'Neil, *"Weapons of Math Destruction: How Big Date Increases Inequality and Threatens Democracy"* (Broadway Books, 2017).

88. Deloitte, Seventy-Two Percent of Working Americans Surveyed Would or May Consider Leaving an Organization for One They Think is More Inclusive, Deloitte Poll Finds, https://www.prnewswire.com/news-releases/seventy-two-percent-of-working-americans-surveyed-would-or-may-consider-leaving-an-organization-for-one-they-think-is-more-inclusive-deloitte-poll-finds-300469961.html. The well-being pulse survey is available at: https://www2.deloitte.com/us/en/pages/about-deloitte/articles/well-being-survey.html.

89. Susan Fowler, "Reflecting on One Very, Very Strange Year at Uber," https://www.susanjfowler.com/blog/2017/2/19/reflecting-on-one-very-strange-year-at-uber.

90. "Uber CEO Travis Kalanick says the company has hired former Attorney General Eric Holder to probe allegations of sexism." Vox Media, Feb. 20, 2017

91. Seung Lee, Uber investor Shervin Pishevar accused of sexual misconduct, report says, *The Mercury News,* http://www.mercurynews.com/2017/11/30/uber-investor-shervin-pishevar-accused-of-sexual-misconduct-report-says/.

92. Tom Krisher and Barbara Ortutay, The Last Straw: Uber Loyalists Tested by String of Scandals," November 22, 2017, https://apnews.com/article/8a46cfd33602421a9d82281d05900d63.

93. O.C. Ferrell, John Fraedrich, and Linda Ferrell, *Business Ethics: Decision Making for Personal Integrity & Social Responsibility* (Boston, MS: Cengage Learning, 2018), p. 3.

94. https://www.eeoc.gov/newsroom/uber-pay-44-million-resolve-eeoc-sexual-harassment-and-retaliation-charge.

95. Ferrell et al., pp. 131–132.

96. Ferrell et al., p. 132.

97. Ferrell et al., pp. 133–134.

98. Sean Valentine, Lynn Godkin, and Margaret Lucero, "Ethical Context, Organizational Commitment, and Person-Organization Fit," *Journal of Business Ethics* 41, no. 4 (December 2002), pp. 349–360.

99. Scott K. Jones and Kenneth M. Hiltebeitel, "Organizational Influence in a Model of the Moral Decision Process of Accountants," *Journal of Business Ethics* 14, no. 6 (1995), pp. 417–431.

100. Jones and Hiltebeital.

101. MaryJo Burchard, "Ethical Dissonance and Response to Destructive Leadership: A Proposed Model," *Emerging Leadership Journeys*, no.1, pp. 154-176.

102. Burchard, pp. 158–159.

103. Lawrence A. Pervin, "Performance and Satisfaction as a Function of Individual-Environment Fit," *Psychological Bulletin* 69, no. 1 (January 1968), pp. 56–68.

104. Hian Chye Koh and El'fred H. Y. Boo, "Organizational Ethics and Job Satisfaction and Commitment," *Management Decision* 4, nos. 5 and 6 (2004), pp. 677–693.

105. Art Padilla, Robert Hogan, and Robert B. Kaiser, "The Toxic Triangle: Destructive Leaders, Susceptible Followers, and Conducive Environments," *Leadership Quarterly* 18, no. 3 (2007), pp. 176–194.

106. V. Lee Hamilton and Herbert Kelman, *Crimes of Obedience: Toward a Social Psychology of Authority and Responsibility* (New Haven, CT: Yale University Press, 1989).

107. Koh and Boo.

108. Randi L. Sims and Thomas L. Keon, "The Influence of Ethical Fit on Employee Satisfaction, Commitment, and Turnover," *Journal of Business Ethics* 13, no. 12 (1994), pp. 939–948.

109. Ferrell et al.

110. Milton Snoeyenbos, Robert F. Almeder, and James M. Humber, *Business Ethics, Corporate Values and Society* (Buffalo, NY: Prometheus Books, 1983). pp. 239–264.

111. Lawrence A. Ponemon and David R.L. Gabhart, "Ethical Reasoning Research in the Accounting and Auditing Professions," in *Moral Development in the Professions: Psychology and Applied Ethics,* eds. James R. Rest and Darcia Narvaez. New York: Psychology Press, 1994, pp. 101–120.

112. Robert A. Prentice.

113. See Michael K. Shaub, "An Analysis of the Association of Traditional Demographic Variables with the Moral Reasoning of Auditing Students and Auditors," *Journal of Accounting Education* (Winter 1994), pp. 1–26; and Lawrence A. Ponemon, "Ethical Reasoning and Selection Socialization in Accounting," *Accounting, Organizations, and Society* 17 (1992), pp. 239–258.

114. David Arnold and Larry Ponemon, "Internal Auditors' Perceptions of Whistle-blowing and the Influence of Moral Reasoning: An Experiment," *Auditing: A Journal of Practice and Theory* (Fall 1991), pp. 1–15.

115. Larry Ponemon and David Gabhart, "Auditor Independence Judgments: A Cognitive Developmental Model and Experimental Evidence," *Contemporary Accounting Research* (1990), pp. 227–251.

116. Larry Ponemon, "Auditor Underreporting of Time and Moral Reasoning: An Experimental-Lab Study," *Contemporary Accounting Research* (1993), pp. 1–29.

117. Ponemon and Gabhart, 1994, p. 108.

118. Plummer, p. 244.

119. Manuel Velasquez, Claire Andre, Thomas Shanks, and Michael J. Meyer, "Thinking Ethically: A Framework for Moral Decision Making," Available at: http://www.scu.edu/ethics/practicing/decision/thinking.html#sthash.zMGI3C7i.dpuf.

120. https://www.cfoinnovation.com/risk-management/major-risks-60-workplace-misconduct-being-unreported.

121. M.C. Gentile, *Giving Voice to Values: How to Speak Your Mind When You Know What's Right* (New Haven, CT: Yale University Press, 2010). Can renumber.

122. The University of Texas uses a program, "Ethics Unwrapped," to teach GVV to its students. Videos are available on the following Web site: http://ethicsunwrapped.utexas.edu/.

123. Materials to teach GVV and cases are available on the GVV Web site: http://www.babson.edu/Academics/teaching-research/gvv/Pages/curriculum.aspx.

124. M.C. Gentile.

125. M.C. Gentile.

126. M.C. Gentile et al.

127. M.C. Gentile et al.

128. T.J. Shawver, W.F. Miller, *Giving Voice to Values in Accounting* (London: Routledge, 2019), https://doi.org/10.4324/9781351107495.

129. "Column: What we can learn from a Google employee's epic failure to understand gender differences." NewsHour Productions LLC, August 9, 2017.

130. Swisher, K., Google has fired the employee who penned a controversial memo on women and tech, August 7, 2017, https://www.recode.net/2017/8/7/16110696/firing-google-ceo-employee-penned-controversial-memo-on-women-has-violated-its-code-of-conduct.

131. Jodi Kantor and Megan Twohey, Harvey Weinstein Paid Off Sexual Harassment Accusers for Decades. *New York Times* October 5, 2017: https://www.nytimes.com/2017/10/05/us/harvey-weinstein-harassment-allegations.html.

132. Ronan Farow, From Aggressive Overtures to Sexual Assault: Harvey Weinstein's Accusers Tell Their Stories. *The New Yorker,* October 10, 2017: https://www.newyorker.com/news/news-desk/from-aggressive-overtures-to-sexual-assault-harvey-weinsteins-accusers-tell-their-stories.

133. https://www.npr.org/2017/11/15/564310240/times-reporters-describe-how-a-paper-trail-helped-break-the-weinstein-story.

134. Ashley Lee, Seth MacFarlane Explains 2013 Oscars Jab at "Abhorrent, Indefensible" Harvey Weinstein, *The Hollywood Reporter,* October 11, 2017, https://www.hollywoodreporter.com/news/seth-macfarlane-explains-harvey-weinstein-at-2013-oscars-jab-1047829.

135. Cynthia Littleton, Ashley Judd Gives First TV Interview on Harvey Weinstein: 'I Had No Warning.', October 26, 2017, http://variety.com/2017/biz/news/ashley-judd-harvey-weinstein-good-morning-america-diane-sawyer-1202599726/.

136. Zaniewski, Ann. "Racist fliers found, removed at Eastern Michigan University." Detroit Free Press, Sept. 7, 2017. https://www.freep.com/story/news/2017/09/07/racist-fliers-found-removed-eastern-michigan-university/644473001/

137. Cabrini's Response to Hate Speech. Cabrini University, Sept. 18, 2017. http://www.phillytrib.com/news/racial-epithets-reported-at-cabrini-university/article-6e46de74-2f6c-5813-bae5-cfe0553955ad.html.

138. Racism Response: Timeline & Updates. Framingham State University. https://www.framingham.edu/the-fsu-difference/inclusive-excellence/bias-education-response-team/racism-response

139. http://www.statesman.com/news/local/updated-racist-flyers-found-say-around-blacks-never-relax/J0sDeYiBgauXj7oS3pWyUP/.

140. http://wtnh.com/2017/11/01/pd-university-of-hartford-student-arrested-for-bullying-roommate/

141. David K. Katz and Julia Homer, "WorldCom Whistle-blower Cynthia Cooper," CFO Magazine. February 1, 2008. Available at: www.cfo.com/article.cfm/10590507.

142. Susan Pulliam, "Ordered to Commit Fraud, a Staffer Balked, Then Caved: Accountant Betty Vinson Helped Cook the Books at WorldCom," *The Wall Street Journal,* June 23, 2003. Available at: www.people.tamu.edu/‾jstrawser/acct229h/Current%20 Readings/E.%20WSJ.com%20-%20A%20Staffer%20Ordered%20to%20Commit%20Fraud,%20Balked.pdf.

143. McClam, Erin. "Judge Sentences Two Former WorldCom Accounting Officials." The Washington Post, August 5, 2005.

144. U.S. Securities and Exchange Commission. Betty L. Vinson, CPA: Admin. Proc. Rel. No. 33.

Chapter 2 Cases

Case 2-1 A Team Player? (a GVV case)

Barbara is working on the audit of a client with a group of five other staff-level employees. After the inventory audit was completed, Diane, a member of the group, asks to meet with the other employees. She points out that she now realizes a deficiency exists in the client's inventory system whereby a small number of items were double counted. The amounts are relatively minor and the rest of the inventory observation went smoothly. Barbara suggests to Diane that they bring the matter to Jessica, the senior in charge of the engagement. Diane does not want to do it because she is the one responsible for the oversight. Three of the other four staff members agree with Diane. Haley is the only one, along with Barbara, who wants to inform Jessica.

After an extended discussion of the matter, the group votes and decides not to inform Jessica. Still, Barbara does not feel right about it. She wonders: What if Jessica finds out another way? What if the deficiency is more serious than Diane has said? What if it portends other problems with the client? She decides to raise all these issues but is rebuked by the others who remind her that the team is already behind on its work and any additional audit procedures would increase the time spent on the audit and make them all look incompetent. They remind Barbara that Jessica is a stickler for keeping to the budget and any overages cannot be billed to the client.

Questions

1. Explain how cognitive shortcomings play a role in Diane's position.
2. Explain what Barbara should do if she reasons at each of the six stages of Kohlberg's model.
3. Assume you are in Barbara's position. What would you do and why? Consider the following in answering the question:
   - How can you best express your point of view effectively?
   - What do you need to say, to whom, and in what sequence?
   - What do you expect the objections or pushback will be and, then, what would you say next?

Case 2-2 FDA Liability Concerns (a GVV case)

Gregory and Alex started a small business based on a secret-recipe salad dressing that got rave reviews. Gregory runs the business end and makes all final operational decisions. Alex runs the creative side of the business.

Alex's salad dressing was a jalapeno vinaigrette that went great with barbeque or burgers. He got many requests for the recipe and a local restaurant asked to use it as the house special, so Alex decided to bottle and market the dressing to the big box stores. Whole Foods and Trader Joe's carried the dressing; sales were increasing every month. As the business grew, Gregory and Alex hired Michael, a college friend and CPA, to be the CFO of the company.

Michael's first suggestion was to do a five-year strategic plan with expanding product lines and taking the company public or selling it within five to seven years. Gregory and Alex weren't sure about wanting to go public and losing control, but expanding the product lines was appealing. Michael also wanted to contain costs and increase profit margins.

At Alex's insistence, they called a meeting with Michael to discuss his plans.

> "Michael, we hired you to take care of the accounting and the financial details," Alex said. "We don't understand profit margins. On containing costs, the best ingredients must be used to ensure the quality of the dressing. We must meet all FDA requirements for food safety and containment of food borne bacteria, such as listeria or e. coli, as you develop cost systems."

> "Of course," Michael responded. "I will put processes in place to meet the FDA requirements."

At the next quarterly meeting of the officers, Alex wanted an update on the FDA processes and the latest inspection. He was concerned whether Michael understood the importance of full compliance.

"Michael," Alex said, "the FDA inspector and I had a discussion while he was here. He wanted to make sure I understood the processes and the liabilities of the company if foodborne bacteria are traced to our products. Are we doing everything by the book and reserving some liabilities for any future recalls?"

Michael assured Alex and Gregory that everything was being done by the book and the accounting was following standard practices. Over the next 18 months, the FDA inspectors came and Michael reported everything was fine.

After the next inspection, there was some listeria found in the product. The FDA insisted on a recall of batch 57839. Alex wanted to recall all the product to make sure that all batches were safe.

"A total recall is too expensive and would mean that the product could be off the shelves for three to four weeks. It would be hard to regain our shelf advantage and we would lose market share," Michael explained.

Alex seemed irritated and turned to Gregory for support, but he was silent. He then walked over to where Michael was sitting and said, "Michael, nothing is more important than our reputation. Our promise and mission is to provide great-tasting dressing made with the freshest, best, organic products. A total recall will show that we stand by our mission and promise. I know we would have some losses, but don't we have a liability reserve for recall, like a warranty reserve?"

"The reserve will not cover the entire expense of a recall," Michael said. "It will be too expensive to do a total recall and will cause a huge loss for the quarter. In the next six months, we will need to renew a bank loan; a loss will hurt our renewal loan rate and terms. You know I have been working to get the company primed to go public as well."

Alex offered that he didn't care about going public. He didn't start the business to be profitable. Gregory, on the other hand, indicated he thought going public was a great idea and would provide needed funds on a continuous basis.

Alex told Michael that he needed to see all the FDA inspection reports. He asked, "What is the FDA requiring to be done to address the issue of listeria?"

"I'm handling it, Alex," Michael said. "Don't worry about it. Just keep making new salad dressings so that we can stay competitive."

"Well, Michael, just answer what the FDA is asking for."

"Just to sterilize some of our equipment, but it shouldn't be too bad."

"Michael, it's more than that," Alex responded. "The FDA contacted me directly and asked me to meet with them in three days to discuss our plans to meet the FDA requirements and standards. We will be fined for not addressing issues found in prior inspections. I want to see the past inspection reports so I can better understand the scope of the problem."

"Listen, Alex," Michael said. "I just completed a cost–benefit analysis of fixing all the problems identified by the FDA and found the costs outweighed the benefits. We're better off paying whatever fines they impose and move on."

"Michael, I don't care about cost–benefit analysis. I care about my reputation and that of the company. Bring me all the inspection reports tomorrow."

The three of them met the following day. As Alex reviewed the past inspection reports, he realized that he had relied on Michael too much and his assurances that all was well with the FDA. In fact, the FDA had repeatedly noted that more sterilization of the equipment was needed and that storage of the products and ingredients needed additional care. Alex began to wonder whether Michael should stay on with the company. He also was concerned about the fact that Gregory had been largely silent during the discussions. He wondered whether Gregory was putting profits ahead of safety and the reputation of the company.

Questions

Alex knows what the right thing to do is. As Alex prepares for a meeting on the inspection reports the next day, he focuses on influencing the positions of Michael and Gregory, both of whom will be involved in the meeting. Put yourself in Alex's position and answer the following questions.

1. What are the main arguments you are trying to counter? That is, what are the reasons and rationalizations you need to address?

2. What is at stake for the key parties, including those who disagree with you?

3. What levers can you use to influence those who disagree with you?

4. What is your most powerful and persuasive response to the reasons and rationalizations you need to address? To whom should the argument be made? When and in what context?

Case 2-3 Taxes and the Cannabis Business (a GVV case)

Hailey Declaire, a CPA, just sent the tax return that she prepared for a client in the marijuana growing and distribution business, Weeds 'R' Us, to Harry Smokes the manager of the tax department. Harry had just fielded a phone call from the president of Weeds 'R' Us who gave him an ear full because Hailey insisted on reporting all of the cash sales from the marijuana business on the 2020 tax return. Hailey arrives at Harry's office and the following conversation ensues.

"Hailey, come in," Harry said.

"Thank you, Harry," Hailey responded.

"Do you know why I asked to see you?"

"I'm not sure. Does it have something to do with the tax return for Weeds 'R' Us?" asked Hailey.

"That's right," answered Harry.

"Is there a problem?" Hailey asked.

Harry answered: "I just spoke with the company's president. He said you insisted on reporting 100% of the cash sales from the marijuana business. He's upset. He wants to hold back 25% of that amount and figures no one will be the wiser because marijuana is a cash business. The company can't get a bank account in the state because, even though the cannabis business is legal in the state, it still is prohibited under federal law under the Controlled Substances Act."

"Why would we risk our reputation by going along with the client's position?" Hailey asked.

"It's not that simple," Harry responded. "The client needs an audit report under state regulations. We have been pushing hard to get that business. It's lucrative and may open the door to even more services including personal financial planning."

Harry knew he could simply change the tax return and submit it for the client. However, he wanted Hailey to get onboard because the firm intended to go after other clients in the marijuana business. So, Harry asked Hailey to meet with him and the partner in charge of the tax practice first thing on Monday morning. Hailey says she'll be there and returns to her office.

Questions

Assume you are in Hailey's position and answer the following questions.

1. Explain how social and organizational pressures might influence your position at Monday's meeting.

2. What role might cognitive dissonance play in developing your position?

3. Think of your response in the context of developing a script and consider the following:

   • What are the main arguments you are trying to counter? That is, what are the reasons and rationalizations you need to address?

   • What is at stake for the key parties?

   • What levers can you use to influence those who disagree with you?

   • What is your most powerful and persuasive response to the reasons and rationalizations you need to address? To whom should the argument be made? When and in what context?

Case 2-4 A Faulty Budget (a GVV Case)

Jackson Daniels graduated from Lynchberg State College two years ago. Since graduating from college, he has worked in the accounting department of Lynchberg Manufacturing. Lynchberg is publicly owned with an 11-member board of directors.

Daniels was recently asked to prepare a sales budget for the year 2021. He conducted a thorough analysis and came out with projected sales of 250,000 units of product. That represents a 25 percent increase over 2020.

Daniels went to lunch with his best friend, Jonathan Walker, to celebrate the completion of his first solo job. Walker noticed Daniels seemed very distant. He asked what the matter was. Daniels stroked his chin, ran his hand through his bushy, black hair, took another drink of scotch, and looked straight into the eyes of his friend of 20 years. "Jon, I think I made a mistake with the budget."

"What do you mean?" Walker answered.

"You know how we developed a new process to manufacture soaking tanks to keep the ingredients fresh?"

"Yes," Walker answered.

"Well, I projected twice the level of sales for that product than will likely occur."

"Are you sure?" Walker asked.

"I checked my numbers. I'm sure. It was just a mistake on my part."

Walker asked Daniels what he planned to do about it.

"I think I should report it to Pete. He's the one who acted on the numbers to hire additional workers to produce the soaking tanks," Daniels said.

"Wait a second, Jack. How do you know there won't be extra demand for the product? You and I both know demand is a tricky number to project, especially when a new product comes on the market. Why don't you sit back and wait to see what happens?"

"Jon, I owe it to Pete to be honest. He was responsible for my hire."

"You know Pete is always pressuring us to 'make the numbers.' Also, Pete has a zero tolerance for employees who make mistakes. That's why it's standard practice around here to sweep things under the rug. Besides, it's a one-time event—right?"

"But what happens if I'm right and the sales numbers were wrong? What happens if the demand does not increase beyond what I now know to be the correct projected level?"

"Well, you can tell Pete about it at that time. Why raise a red flag now when there may be no need?"

As the lunch comes to a conclusion, Walker pulls Daniels aside and says, "Jack, this could mean your job. If I were in your position, I'd protect my own interests first."

Jimmy (Pete) Beam is the vice president of production. Jackson Daniels had referred to him in his conversation with Jonathan Walker. After several days of reflection on his friend's comments, Daniels decided to approach Pete and tell him about the mistake. He knew there might be consequences, but his sense of right and wrong ruled the day. What transpired next surprised Daniels.

"Come in, Jack" Pete said.

"Thanks, Pete. I asked to see you on a sensitive matter."

"I'm listening."

"There is no easy way to say this so I'll just tell you the truth. I made a mistake in my sales budget. The projected increase of 25 percent was wrong. I checked my numbers and it should have been 12.5 percent. I'm deeply sorry, want to correct the error, and promise never to do it again."

Pete's face became beet red. He said, "Jack, you know I hired 20 new people based on your budget."

"Yes, I know."

"That means ten have to be laid off or fired. They won't be happy and once word filters through the company, other employees may wonder if they are next."

"I hadn't thought about it that way."

"Well, you should have." Here's what we are going to do . . . and this is between you and me. Don't tell anyone about this conversation."

"You mean not even tell my boss?"

"No," Pete said. "JB can't know about it because he's all about correcting errors and moving on. Look, Jack, it's my reputation at stake here as well."

Daniels hesitated but reluctantly agreed not to tell the controller, JB, his boss. The meeting ended with Daniels feeling sick to his stomach and guilty for not taking any action.

Questions

1. What are Daniels's options in this situation? Use ethical reasoning to identify the best alternative. What would you do if you were in Daniels's position?
   Assume that you have decided to take some action, based on the ethical analysis, even though you had agreed not to do so. Consider the following in deciding what your next step should be.
2. What is at stake for the key parties?
3. Based on your chosen action, develop a list of the main arguments you are likely to encounter in making the strongest case possible to the relevant stakeholders?
4. What is your most powerful and persuasive response to the reasons and rationalizations you may need to address? To whom should the argument be made? When and in what context?

Case 2-5 Not so Diverse, Equitable or Inclusive (a GVV Case)

You are the Controller for Mountain Manufacturing which produces specialized components used in the manufacturing of cell phones sold by Apple, Motorola, and Samsung. The company is located in Southglenn Colorado, a suburb of Denver. Demand for your products continues to grow year over year. However, due to a high level of employee turnover, it has become increasingly difficult to keep up with demand for your products. In addition, the costs involved in employee onboarding (the process of finding, screening and hiring employees) has skyrocketed in the last couple of years.

An analysis you performed shows overall turnover to be 25 percent annually, with turnover to be much higher (40%) for employees in their first year with the company. You are really concerned due to manufacturing delays caused by the personnel shortage that you might lose one of your three primary customers which would be catastrophic to the company and its investors. To see if you could learn anything else from the employment data, you did queries on employee age, gender, race, home zip code, and wage comparing those to the employee's number of months of employment.

Your analysis indicated that turnover of employees of color is five times that of the company's white employees. This finding is of great concern to you, as the company describes itself as having a high level of diversity among its staff and as being a very open and inclusive company. There also seemed to be a much higher level of turnover of employees who live in one particular zip code. You know that particular area is not considered to be a desirable place to live with a very low median income, low real estate values, a high level of crime and the worst schools in the area.

You share your findings during a meeting with the company's CEO and the Director of Human Resources. The Director of Human Resources said she was aware of the disproportionately high turnover for persons of color and women, but did not know what could be done to improve the situation. She shared that last year she and her staff had screened over 25,000 resumes, interviewed close to 3,000 candidates, and hired over 2,500 new employees. She stated the high amount of overall and new hire turnover results in a continuous recruitment effort with no time left to concentrate on improving the work environment for all the employees. She described it as somewhat of a vicious cycle that she did not think they could break.

At this point, the CEO cleared his throat and stated he knew exactly what to do. He said they had a similar situation at his last place of employment and they simply stopped hiring employees who lived in the areas with the highest turnover. He said it worked great. Retainage immediately improved as did their overall hiring costs. He also suggested using a third-party company to perform the initial screening of resumes for the HR department. He said they use computers to scan and read every resume and screen them for the specific qualifications and other parameters the employer would like them screened for. He said it is a great way to screen out those who you do not think will be a good fit to start with. Zip code of residence could be one of the attributes the computer uses to eliminate candidates from the pool.

The CEO concludes the meeting stating he was glad he could help solve that problem, and to let him know if you need help with anything else.

Questions

1. What biases if any did you identify as possibly being at play in the above scenario? Be sure to explain what the bias is and how it may be involved in this case.
2. Do you think implementing the CEO's proposed solution is a good idea? Why or why not.
3. Regardless of how you answered question number 2, what would you do if asked to implement this policy (refer to the GVV methodology in responding)?

Case 2-6 The Normalization of Unethical Behavior: The Harvey Weinstein Case

On October 5, 2017, New York Times investigative reporters Jodi Kantor and Megan Twohey broke the story "Harvey Weinstein Paid Off Sexual Harassment Accusers for Decades."[131] Harvey Weinstein was one of the most powerful and influential movie executives in Hollywood. Weinstein co-founded both the Weinstein Company and Miramax Films. His movies have garnered over 300 Oscar nominations. Ronan Farrow suggests in his article, "From Aggressive Overtures to Sexual Assault: Harvey Weintein's Accusers Tell Their Stories," that Weinstein has been publicly thanked at award ceremonies more than anyone else in movie history (with the exception of Steven Spielberg and God).[132] The allegations against Weinstein span three decades and range from sexual harassment to sexual assault and rape.

Kantor's and Twohey's report found at least eight women in which Weinstein entered into settlement agreements with to presumably keep from pursuing any further legal action against him. The release of this article resulted in a flood of women coming forward and telling their stories regarding similar encounters with Weinstein. It also led to the resignation of four of the Weinstein Companies Board members and the firing of Weinstein himself. NPR interviewed Kantor and Twohey about their investigation of Weinstein and is available via podcast.[133]

On October 10, 2017, The New Yorker published Farrow's article, which corroborates what is in the report of Kantor and Twohey with 3 of the 13 women he interviewed accusing Weinstein of rape. As with the Kantor and Twohey article, Farrow suggests that Weinstein's exploits were common knowledge throughout the entertainment industry. They point toward a systemic problem in the industry where people turned a blind eye to what was happening and even normalized this behavior in their responses to it. In fact, Seth MacFarlane while announcing the Best Supporting Actress Nomination's at the 2013 Oscars joked "Congratulations, you five ladies no longer have to pretend to be attracted to Harvey Weinstein."[134]

One of the first women to be interviewed was Ashley Judd. The actress was interviewed by ABC News' Diane Sawyer about her experiences. She expressed regret that she didn't come forward sooner about her allegations of sexual harassment in a hotel room years ago from Weinstein. In the segment that first aired on ABC's "Good Morning America," Judd said she wished she had a "magic wand" that would allow her to change the past, for her and others. "I wish I could prevent it for anyone, always." Judd did tell her parents and other people in Hollywood, including agents and actors, but didn't think she would be believed by going public. "Who was I to tell," she said. "I knew it was disgusting. Was I going to tell the concierge who sent me up to the room?"[135]

Emboldened by what had become a scandal of epic proportions in the entertainment industry, dozens of women started to speak out and tell their story. It motivated actress Alyssa Milano to tweet a call-out to victims "so we might give people a sense of the magnitude of the problem." The hashtag #MeToo caught fire and became the rallying cry for all women similarly abused.

The bravery exhibited by these women empowered other women throughout the entertainment industry, media, and politics to step forward and finally tell their stories about gender sexual harassment, bullying, and rape. Time magazine named these brave women the 2017 Person(s) of the Year "Silence Breakers—the voices that launched a movement." Over the rest of 2017, we witnessed an unprecedented number of men being accused of and fired or being forced to resign because of sexual harassment allegations. These include the firing of CBS Good Morning America's host Charlie Rose, NBC's News Anchor Matt Lauer, PBS's Tavis Smiley, and a host of other high-profile media figures. Congress had its own problems with the resignation of Rep. John Conyers Jr. (D-MI.) and Senator Al Franken (D-MN).

Questions

1. Why do you think this type of behavior was allowed to go on for nearly 30 years?
2. What biases do you think may have played a role in the decisions made by both victims and others who were aware of Weinstein's crimes but did nothing?
3. What responsibility did the Weinstein board of directors have to the victims? What about agents who continued to send their clients to meetings with him? What about the Screen Actors Guild-American Federation of Television and Radio Artists (SAG-AFTRA) that claims to have a zero-tolerance policy on sexual harassment?
4. Is it fair to judge a person on his/her worst act after a lifetime of seemingly doing good things?

Case 2-7 Milton Manufacturing Company

Milton Manufacturing Company produces a variety of textiles for distribution to wholesale manufacturers of clothing products. The company's primary operations are located in Long Island City, New York, with branch factories and warehouses in several surrounding cities. Milton Manufacturing is a closely held company, and Irv Milton is the president. He started the business in 2008, and it grew in revenue from $500,000 to $5 million in 12 years. However, the revenues declined to $4.5 million in 2020. Net cash flows from all activities also were declining. The company was concerned because it planned to borrow $20 million from the credit markets in the fourth quarter of 2021.

Irv Milton met with Ann Plotkin, the chief accounting officer (and also a CPA), on January 15, 2021, to discuss a proposal by Plotkin to control cash outflows. He was not overly concerned about the recent decline in net cash flows from operating activities because these amounts were expected to increase in 2021 as a result of projected higher levels of revenue and cash collections. However, that was not Plotkin's view.

Plotkin knew that if overall negative capital expenditures continued to increase at the rate of 40 percent per year, Milton Manufacturing probably would not be able to borrow the $20 million. Therefore, she suggested establishing a new policy to be instituted on a temporary basis. Each plant's capital expenditures for 2021 for investing activities would be limited to the level of those capital expenditures in 2018, the last year of an overall positive cash flow. Operating activity cash flows had no such restrictions. Irv Milton pointedly asked Plotkin about the possible negative effects of such a policy, but in the end, he was convinced that it was necessary to initiate the policy immediately to stem the tide of increases in capital expenditures. A summary of cash flows appears in **Exhibit 1**.

EXHIBIT 1   Milton Manufacturing Company

Summary of Cash Flows		
For the Years Ended December 31, 2020 and 2019 (000 omitted)		
	December 31, 2020	December 31, 2019
Cash Flows from Operating Activities		
Net income	$ 372	$ 542

(continued)

Summary of Cash Flows		
For the Years Ended December 31, 2020 and 2019 (000 omitted)		
Adjustments to reconcile net income to net cash provided by operating activities	(2,350)	(2,383)
Net cash provided by operating activities	$(1,978)	$(1,841)
Cash Flows from Investing Activities		
Capital expenditures	$(1,420)	$(1,918)
Other investing inflows (outflows)	176	84
Net cash used in investing activities	$(1,244)	$(1,834)
Cash Flows from Financing Activities		
Net cash provided (used in) financing activities	$ 168	$1,476
Increase (decrease) in cash and cash equivalents	$(3,054)	$(2,199)
Cash and cash equivalents—beginning of the year	$3,191	$5,390
Cash and cash equivalents—end of the year	$ 147	$3,191

Sammie Markowicz is the plant manager at the headquarters in Long Island City. He was informed of the new capital expenditure policy by Ira Sugofsky, the vice president for operations. Markowicz told Sugofsky that the new policy could negatively affect plant operations because certain machinery and equipment, essential to the production process, had been breaking down more frequently during the past two years. The problem was primarily with the motors. New and better models with more efficient motors had been developed by an overseas supplier. These were expected to be available by April 2021. Markowicz planned to order 1,000 of these new motors for the Long Island City operation, and he expected that other plant managers would do the same. Sugofsky told Markowicz to delay the acquisition of new motors for one year, after which time the restrictive capital expenditure policy would be lifted. Markowicz reluctantly agreed.

Milton Manufacturing operated profitably during the first six months of 2021. Net cash inflows from operating activities exceeded outflows by $1,250,000 during this time period. It was the first time in two years that there was a positive cash flow from operating activities. Production operations accelerated during the third quarter as a result of increased demand for Milton's textiles. An aggressive advertising campaign initiated in late 2020 seemed to bear fruit for the company. Unfortunately, the increased level of production put pressure on the machines, and the degree of breakdown was increasing. A big problem was that the motors wore out prematurely.

Markowicz was concerned about the machine breakdown and increasing delays in meeting customer demands for the shipment of the textile products. He met with the other branch plant managers, who complained bitterly to him about not being able to spend the money to acquire new motors. Markowicz was very sensitive to their needs. He informed them that the company's regular supplier had recently announced a 25 percent price increase for the motors. Other suppliers followed suit, and Markowicz saw no choice but to buy the motors from the overseas supplier. That supplier's price was lower, and the quality of the motors would significantly enhance the machines' operating efficiency. However, the company's restrictions on capital expenditures stood in the way of making the purchase.

Markowicz approached Sugofsky and told him about the machine breakdowns and the concerns of other plant managers. Sugofsky seemed indifferent but reminded Markowicz of the capital expenditure restrictions in place and that the Long Island City plant was committed to keeping expenditures at the same level as it had in 2018. Markowicz argued that he was faced with an unusual situation and he had to act now. Sugofsky hurriedly left, but not before he said to Markowicz, "You and I may not agree with it, but a policy is a policy."

Markowicz reflected on his obligations to Milton Manufacturing. He was conflicted because he viewed his primary responsibility and that of the other plant managers to ensure that the production process operated smoothly. The last thing the workers needed right now was a stoppage of production because of machine failure.

At this time, Markowicz learned of a 30-day promotional price offered by the overseas supplier to gain new customers by lowering the price for all motors by 25 percent. Coupled with the 25 percent increase in price by the company's supplier, Markowicz knew he could save the company $1,500, or 50 percent of cost, on each motor purchased from the overseas supplier.

After carefully considering the implications of his intended action, Markowicz contacted the other plant managers and informed them that, while they were not obligated to follow his lead because of the capital expenditure policy, he planned to purchase 1,000 motors from the overseas supplier for the headquarters plant in Long Island City.

Markowicz made the purchase at the beginning of the fourth quarter of 2021 without informing Sugofsky. He convinced the plant accountant to record the $1.5 million expenditure as an operating (not capital) expenditure because he knew that the higher level of operating cash inflows resulting from increased revenues would mask the effect of his expenditure. In fact, Markowicz was proud that he had "saved" the company $1.5 million, and he did what was necessary to ensure that the Long Island City plant continued to operate.

The acquisitions by Markowicz and the other plant managers enabled the company to keep up with the growing demand for textiles, and the company finished the year with record high levels of profit and net cash inflows from all activities. Markowicz was lauded by his team for his leadership. The company successfully executed a loan agreement with Second Bankers Hours & Trust Co. The $20 million borrowed was received on October 3, 2021.

During the course of an internal audit of the 2021 financial statements, Beverly Wald, the chief internal auditor (and also a CPA), discovered that there was an unusually high number of motors in inventory. A complete check of the inventory determined that $1 million worth of motors remained on hand.

Wald reported her findings to Ann Plotkin, and together they went to see Irv Milton. After being informed of the situation, Milton called in Sugofsky. When Wald told him about her findings, Sugofsky's face turned beet red. He told Wald that he had instructed Markowicz *not* to make the purchase. He also inquired about the accounting since Wald had said it was wrong.

Wald explained to Sugofsky that the $1 million should be accounted for as inventory, not as an operating cash outflow: "What we do in this case is transfer the motors out of inventory and into the machinery account once they are placed into operation because, according to the documentation, the motors added significant value to the asset."

Sugofsky had a perplexed look on his face. Finally, Irv Milton took control of the accounting lesson by asking, "What's the difference? Isn't the main issue that Markowicz did not follow company policy?" The three officers in the room nodded their heads simultaneously, perhaps in gratitude for being saved the additional lecturing. Milton then said he wanted Wald and Plotkin to discuss the alternatives on how best to deal with the Markowicz situation and present the choices to him in one week.

Questions

Use the Integrated Ethical Decision-Making Process to guide you in answering the following:

1. Identify the ethical and professional issues of concern to Beverly Wald and Ann Plotkin.
2. Identify and evaluate alternative courses of action using ethical reasoning.
3. Decide on a course of action to present to Milton. Why did you select that alternative?

Case 2-8 Chefs Delight: That Slope Looks Slippery (a GVV case)

"I'm sorry, Jen. That's the client's position," Travis said.

"I just don't know if I can go along with it, Travis," Jen replied.

"I know. I agree with you. But, Chefs Delight is our biggest client, Jen. They've warned us that they will put the engagement up for bid if we refuse to go along with the reclassification of marketable securities," Travis explained.

Jen asked, "Have you spoken to the engagement review partners about it?"

"They recommended giving in to the client on this matter," Travis responded.

"Listen, I understand the pressures of being the engagement partner and the need to keep the client happy, but this goes too far" Jen said.

The previous scene took place in the office of Trending Upwards, a large CPA firm in Beverly Hills, California. Jen is the Senior Manager on the engagement of Chefs Delight, a publicly owned global manufacturer of Chef's cookware. Travis is the Partner in charge of the engagement. The engagement review partners make final judgments on difficult accounting issues, especially when there is a difference of opinion with the client. All of these individuals are CPAs.

Travis is preparing for a meeting with Chef Norman, the CEO of Chefs Delight. Travis knows that the company expects to borrow $5 million next quarter and it wants to put the best possible face on its financial statements to impress the banks. That would explain why the company reclassified a $2 million market loss on a trading investment to the available-for-sale category so that the "loss" would now show up in stockholder's equity, not as a charge against current income. The result was to increase earnings in 2021 by 8 percent. Travis knows that without the change, the earnings would have declined by 2 percent and the company's stock price would have taken a hit.

In the meeting, Travis decides to overlook the recommendation by the engagement review partners. He felt Jen made valid points. Travis points out to Chef that the investment in question was marketable, and in the past, the company had sold similar investments in less than one year. Travis adds there is no justification under GAAP to change the classification from trading to available-for-sale.

What happened next shocked Travis back to reality. The conversation between Chef Norman and Travis went this way.

"I hate to bring it up, Travis, but do you recall what happened last year at about the same time?"

"What do you mean?" Travis replied.

Chef then stated "You agreed that we could record $1 million as revenue for 2020 based on a sale of our product that we held at an off-site distribution warehouse until the client asked for delivery, which occurred in 2021."

Travis remembered all too well. It almost cost the firm the Chefs Delight account. "Are you going to throw that in my face?" Travis said rather heatedly.

"No, Travis. Just a gentle reminder that you had agreed to go along with what we had asked at that time. We believe there is enough gray area to do the same here. Who knows, we may hold on to the investment for more than one year." Chef said calmingly.

The meeting broke up when Chef received a confidential phone call. They agreed to continue it first thing in the morning. Chef Norman's parting words were "we value loyalty in our accountants."

Questions

1. Explain how incrementalism might influence Travis's position with respect to the not so subtle statement by Chef Norman.
2. Assume you are in Travis's position and preparing for the meeting with Chef Norman in the morning. Consider the following in crafting a response to him.

- What are the main arguments you are trying to counter?
- What is at stake for the key parties?
- What levers can you use to influence Chef Norman?
- What is your most powerful response to the reasons and rationalizations you need to address? To whom should the argument be made? When and in what context?

Case 2-9 Racially Charged Language Inhibits Inclusive Cultures

Leaving home for the first time and going off to college is an exciting and stressful time for tens of thousands of students across the United States each year. Leaving the familiarity of family, friends, and community behind and entering an often much more diverse community filled with people with different social, political, religious, racial, national, and sexual orientation backgrounds can create challenges. Luckily, there is currently an effort across the

United States to reduce the impact of potential biases by educating people on and promoting the benefits of having diversity in communities, businesses, schools, and social groups people belong to. These efforts are more commonly known as Equity, Diversity, and Inclusion (EDI) Initiatives. One example of a college that seems to have it right with respect to EDI policies is the University of Wisconsin, Eau Claire. A brief review of those policies and programs appears in **Exhibit 1**.

EXHIBIT 1   Equity, Diversity, and Inclusion Policies and Programs at UWEC

Faculty and staff at the University of Wisconsin, Eau Claire (UWEC) have incorporated EDI initiatives into their core mission. The core mission is to create an inclusive community where all students thrive and find the programs and support needed to reach their full potential. Too often, members of underrepresented groups feel alienated and/or are unconsciously or consciously discriminated against resulting in them transferring schools or dropping out completely.

To operationalize this mission, the faculty, staff, and administration came together setting goals surrounding student enrollment and retainment specifically for underrepresented groups. The faculty have common language surrounding EDI within all course syllabi and encourage all their students to help make the classroom environment more welcoming and inclusive to all. They have all agreed to participate in EDI initiatives in some way and to have that participation be a part of their annual performance review. In 2017, they created the first office of EDI and hired an Assistant Chancellor of Equity, Diversity, and Inclusion to lead the effort.

UWEC has also developed a 12-week training program called Circles of Change to start an open in-person dialogue about race throughout the region the university is located within. Launched as a pilot in the Spring of 2017, the fall of 2017 had more than 120 people participating in Circles of Change action groups, gathering weekly to discuss race relations on campus and in the community. "The goal is to help make the Chippewa Valley a more welcoming place for everyone."

As discussed in **Chapter 2**, some people have unconscious biases and stereotypical beliefs that can lead to making poor decisions. This can be magnified by instances of bias on college campuses. Many colleges and universities across the country have implemented freshman orientation programs to help students transition into college life and to make them feel welcome.

There is a need for diversity and inclusivity training. During 2017, there were many reported instances of racial bias through the use of racial slurs on college and university campuses. Many were reported during the September to December 2017 period, magnifying the growing need for EDI programs on campus. The following examples were chosen not only to illustrate the hateful speech but to describe admirable responses by the universities affected.

1. At Eastern Michigan University, racial fliers promoting a white supremacist organization were found posted on several buildings. Officials removed them because they ran counter to the school's values. According to a spokesperson, "The fliers and the hateful, racist causes they promote run completely counter to Eastern's core values of diversity, inclusiveness and respect."[136]

2. At Cabrini University in Radnor, PA, a number of instances were reported of the words "N-word go away" written on the dormitory room door of a female black student and a second occurrence stating "go away too" just a few days later. The reaction of the university was: "As we ensure a thorough investigation into the incident, we want to remind everyone that hate has no home on our campus—hate speech of any kind goes against who we are as an institution and as a diverse community of learners."[137]

3. A few racial incidents occurred between October and December 2017 at Framingham State University in Framingham, MA. In one such incident, a flyer defaced with racially offensive writing was found under an African-American student's door. The President of the University responded: "Framingham State University draws strength from its diversity. We are an institution where individuals of differing cultures, perspectives, and experiences are welcomed, respected, valued, and supported. In response to recent events, we must not allow those with hate in their hearts to divide us. The best way to stand up to this type of vile behavior is by uniting as a community against it."[138]

4. Flyers containing a racist slogan and anti-African-American imagery were found at the University of Texas at Austin. The flyers depict a racist caricature of a Black man holding a knife and bear the words "Around blacks . . . never relax." The University was quick to condemn such hatred and pointed to their new Hate and Bias Policy that addresses such issues.[139]

A good illustration of a proactive response to incidents of hatred occurred at the University of Hartford in West Hartford, CT. In response to an incident of racial harassment and bullying, Gregory Woodward, president of the University, stated that "the harsh reality is that racism in America is part of our reality. It is here on our campus and on campuses across the country. We are a reflection of the society at large. It is disturbing and inexcusable, and needs our constant attention and vigilance. We must all speak up, speak out, and be relentless in our pursuit of a more inclusive environment for our students. Acts of racism, bias, or other abusive behaviors will not be tolerated in any way, shape, or form on this campus."[140]

Questions

1. Identify which biases and/or stereotypes might exacerbate the type of behavior described in this case.
2. What responsibility does a college or university have in ensuring all students feel safe and welcome at their institutions? Answer this question using Rights Theory and theories of Justice.
3. Why is it important for EDI policies to be implemented in the workplace? Refer to the Deloitte surveys in answering this question.

Case 2-10 WorldCom

The WorldCom fraud was the largest in U.S. history, surpassing even that of Enron. Beginning modestly during mid-year 1999 and continuing at an accelerated pace through May 2002, the company—under the direction of Bernie Ebbers, the CEO; Scott Sullivan, the CFO; David Myers, the controller; and Buford Yates, the director of accounting—"cooked the books" to the tune of about $11 billion of misstated earnings. Investors collectively lost $30 billion as a result of the fraud.

The fraud was accomplished primarily in two ways:

1. Booking "line costs" for interconnectivity with other telecommunications companies as capital expenditures rather than operating expenses.
2. Inflating revenues with bogus accounting entries from "corporate unallocated revenue accounts."

During 2002, Cynthia Cooper, the vice president of internal auditing, responded to a tip about improper accounting by having her team do an exhaustive hunt for the improperly recorded line costs that were also known as "prepaid capacity." That name was designed to mask the true nature of the costs and treat them as capitalizable costs rather than as operating expenses. The team worked tirelessly, often at night and secretly, to investigate and reveal $3.8 billion worth of fraud.

Soon thereafter, Cooper notified the company's audit committee and board of directors of the fraud. The initial response was not to take action, but to look for explanations from Sullivan. Over time, Cooper realized that she needed to be persistent and not give in to pressure that Sullivan was putting on her to back off. Cooper even approached KPMG, the auditors that had replaced Arthur Andersen, to support her in the matter. Ultimately, Sullivan was dismissed, Myers resigned, Andersen withdrew its audit opinion for 2001, and the Securities and Exchange Commission (SEC) began an investigation into the fraud on June 26, 2002.

In an interview with David Katz and Julia Homer for *CFO Magazine* on February 1, 2008, Cynthia Cooper was asked about her whistleblower role in the WorldCom fraud. When asked when she first suspected something was amiss, Cooper said: "It was a process. My feelings changed from curiosity to discomfort to suspicion based on some of the accounting entries my team and I had identified, and also on the odd reactions I was getting from some of the finance executives."[141]

Cooper did exactly what is expected of a good auditor. She approached the investigation of line-cost accounting with a healthy dose of skepticism and maintained her integrity throughout, even as Sullivan was trying to bully her into dropping the investigation.

When asked whether there was anything about the culture of WorldCom that contributed to the scandal, Cooper laid blame on Bernie Ebbers for his risk-taking approach that led to loading up the company with $40 billion in debt to fund one acquisition after another. He followed the same reckless strategy with his own investments, taking out loans and using his WorldCom stock as collateral. Cooper believed that Ebbers's personal decisions then affected his business decisions; he ultimately saw his net worth disappear, and he was left owing WorldCom some $400 million for loans approved by the board.

Betty Vinson, the company's former director of corporate reporting, was one of five former WorldCom executives who pleaded guilty to fraud. At the trial of Ebbers, Vinson said she was told to make improper accounting entries because Ebbers did not want to disappoint Wall Street. "I felt like if I didn't make the entries, I wouldn't be working there," Vinson testified. She said that she even drafted a resignation letter in 2000, but ultimately she stayed with the company. It was clear she felt uneasy with the accounting at WorldCom.

Vinson said that she took her concerns to Sullivan, who told her that Ebbers did not want to lower Wall Street expectations. Asked how she chose which accounts to alter, Vinson testified, "I just really pulled some out of the air. I used some spreadsheets."[142]

Her lawyer urged the judge to sentence Vinson to probation, citing the pressure placed on her by Ebbers and Sullivan. "She expressed her concern about what she was being directed to do to upper management, and to Sullivan and Ebbers, who assured her and lulled her into believing that all was well,"[143] he said.

On December 6, 2002, the SEC reached an agreement with Betty Vinson about her role in the WorldCom fraud and suspended her from appearing or practicing before the Commission as an accountant. In its Administrative Proceeding, the SEC alleged that: "At the direction of WorldCom senior management, Vinson and other WorldCom employees caused WorldCom to overstate materially its earnings in contravention of GAAP for at least seven successive fiscal quarters, from as early as October 2000 through April 2002." The overstatement included improperly capitalized line costs to overstate pre-tax earnings by approximately $3.8 billion. The agreement went on to say: "Vinson knew, or was reckless in not knowing, that these entries were made without supporting documentation, were not in conformity with GAAP, were not disclosed to the investing public, and were designed to allow WorldCom to appear to meet Wall Street analysts' quarterly earnings estimates."[144]

Questions

1. Explain the role of cognitive shortcomings in the WorldCom fraud and how social and organizational pressures influenced Betty Vinson's actions.

2. The SEC action against Vinson was deemed "appropriate and in the public interest." How was the public interest affected by what Vinson did and WorldCom's actions broadly?

3. In a presentation at James Madison University in November 2013, Cynthia Cooper said, "You don't have to be a bad person to make bad decisions." Discuss what you think Cooper meant and how it relates to our discussion of ethical and moral development in the chapter.

Organizational Ethics and Corporate Governance

Ethics Reflection

What is Fraud?

Fraud can be defined as a deliberate misrepresentation to gain an advantage over another party or have them do something they might not ordinarily do. For example, if you were to apply for a home mortgage loan and include a source of income as part of your earnings that doesn't exist, you have committed fraud. Your objective is to get the bank to qualify you for a loan that might not be accepted if the income had been reported honestly.

Fraud comes in many different forms including the misappropriation of assets (i.e., theft), fraud in financial statements, and disclosure fraud. In each case, a deceptive practice is used to mask the fraud and internal controls are either nonexistent or overridden by the perpetrator of the fraud.

The Association of Certified Fraud Examiners (ACFE) studies the costs and effects of occupational fraud (or workplace fraud) and issues an annual survey, *The 2020 Global Study of Occupational Fraud and Abuse*. The study looked at 2,504 cases from 125 countries and found total losses of more than $3.6 billion and an average loss per case of $1.5 million. The ACFE estimates that organizations lost five percent of revenue to fraud each year.[1]

Some organizations experience two or more kinds of occupational fraud. Asset misappropriation occurs in 86 percent of the cases and is implemented by billing fraud (20%), noncash fraud (18%), expense reimbursements (14%), and others. Corruption is one of the most significant frauds for many organizations (43%) causing a median loss of $100,000. This includes conflicts of interest, bribery, illegal gratuities, and economic extortion.

Financial statement fraud is the least common (10%) but most costly fraud ($954,000 median loss). These occur through the understatement of expenses and liabilities, overstatement of revenues, and improper asset valuation.

The most common way to detect fraud is by tip (43%). Organizations with hotlines detected fraud more often (49%) than those without a hotline (31%). The supervisor was the most common individual within the organization to receive an initial whistleblowing report (28%). Other findings of the study will be discussed later in the chapter.

In order to combat fraud, organizations need strong corporate governance mechanisms including an efficient system of internal controls to prevent and detect fraud, an active audit committee to work with the internal and external auditors to ensure appropriate standards are followed, and a whistleblowing process that takes allegations of fraud seriously. In essence, the organization must establish an ethical tone at the top and clear guidelines that misbehavior and improper financial reporting will not be tolerated.

From an ethical perspective, fraud occurs because of a loss of integrity. According to Mintz (1995), "Integrity is a fundamental trait of character that enables a CPA to withstand employer or client pressures that might lead to the subordination of judgment."[2]

Think about the following as you read the chapter: (1) How can an organization create an ethical culture? (2) What are the signs that occupational fraud might exist? (3) How can corporate governance systems prevent fraud from happening? (4) What are the options available to a whistleblower including external reporting considerations?

> The thing I have learned at IBM is that culture is everything. Underneath all the sophisticated processes, there is always the company's sense of values and identity.
>
> *Source: Louis V. Gerstner, Jr., former CEO, IBM*

This statement by former IBM chief executive officer (CEO) Louis Gerstner highlights one of the themes of this chapter: The culture of an organization establishes the boundaries within which ethical decisions must be made. As we learned from previous chapters, it is one thing to know that you should behave in a certain way, but it is quite another to do it (or even want to do it) given the pressures that may exist from within the organization.

Overview of Chapter

There are several moving parts to this chapter. In order to guide you through it, **Exhibit 3.1** depicts how the information flows and the systems involved.

Don't worry about following all the steps depicted in the chapter to get from basic corporate governance systems (i.e., how the organization is managed) to the issuance of financial statements and audit opinions, influenced by the AICPA Code of Professional Conduct. We will discuss them as we go. You can use this exhibit to refer back to as a roadmap through the chapter.

Fraud in Organizations

LO 3-1
Describe the causes of fraud, detection methods, and preventative controls.

Fraud can be defined as a deliberate misrepresentation to gain an advantage over another party. Fraud comes in many different forms, including fraud in financial statements, the misappropriation of assets (theft) and subsequent cover-up, and disclosure fraud. We introduce the concept of fraudulent financial statements in this chapter and discuss it more fully in **Chapter 5**. We begin by examining the results of the *2020 Global Study on Occupational Fraud and Abuse: Report to the Nations,* conducted by the Association of Certified Fraud Examiners (ACFE).

EXHIBIT 3.1   Integration of Corporate Governance Structures

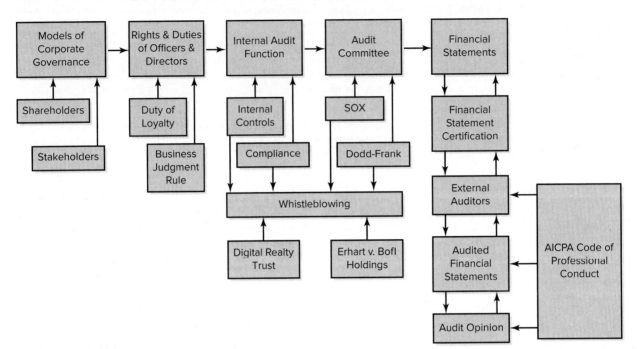

Occupational Fraud

The 2020 ACFE survey that was discussed in the Introduction provides interesting information about the initial detection of fraud, frequency of anti-fraud controls, behavioral red flags exhibited by perpetrators, and reporting by whistleblowers.[3]

How Occupational Fraud Is Committed and Detected

Asset misappropriation schemes include when an employee steals or misuses resources, such as charging personal expenses to the company while traveling on business trips. Corruption schemes include misusing one's position or influence in an organization for personal gain, something that Dennis Kozlowski was known for doing. Kozlowski and CFO Mark Swartz were convicted on June 21, 2005, of taking bonuses worth more than $120 million without the approval of Tyco's directors, abusing an employee loan program, and misrepresenting the company's financial condition to investors to boost the stock price while selling $575 million in stock.

The most common method of detection was a "tip," with 43 percent reporting. In organizations with hotlines, 49 percent come from a tip but declines to 31 percent in organizations with no hotline. Internal audit was next with 15 percent followed by management review with 12 percent. Taken together these results indicate the need for strong internal controls to help prevent and detect fraud. More effective internal audits serve to strengthen internal controls, a goal of Section 404 of SOX. **Exhibit 3.2** shows the frequency of detection methods as reported by survey respondents.

EXHIBIT 3.2   Initial Detection of Occupational Frauds from the *ACFE 2020 Global Study on Occupational Fraud and Abuse*

Detection Method	Percentage Reported	Median Loss
Tip	43%	$145,000
Internal Audit	15%	$100,000
Management Review	12%	$100,000
Other	6%	N/A
By Accident	5%	$200,000
Account Reconciliation	4%	$81,000
External Audit	4%	$150,000
Document Examination	3%	$101,000
Surveillance/Monitoring	3%	$44,000
Notified by Law Enforcement	2%	$900,000
IT Controls	2%	$80,000
Confession	1%	$225,000

An important point is that controls such as management reviews and internal audits account for a significant percentage of detection methods (27%), while the external audit accounts for only 4 percent. The point is that companies should not rely on the external audit to detect fraud but should put in place internal mechanisms to prevent and detect it.

The results indicate that tip, internal audit, and management review accounted for 70% of fraud detection. That's not bad but organizations should be able to do better by strengthening their audit committee and ensuring an independent board of directors.

Survey respondents provided information about how perpetrators were internally punished or dealt with. Not surprisingly, termination was the most common disciplinary action taken in occupational fraud cases (66%).

Frequency of Anti-Fraud Controls

The survey points out that while the presence of internal controls does not guarantee protection against fraud, it can help to both mitigate losses and deter some potential fraudsters by enhancing the perception of detection. Consequently, enacting internal controls specifically designed to prevent and detect fraud is a necessary part of a fraud risk management program.

With 43 percent of frauds being detected by tips, hotlines should play an essential role in organizations' anti-fraud programs. However, only 64 percent had a hotline mechanism in place and 13 percent provided rewards for whistleblowers.

It may seem counterintuitive that while the external audit only detects fraud four percent of the time, it is the most common anti-fraud control with 83 percent of respondents indicating its usage as such. We might conclude that the financial statement audit is conducted not so much to detect fraud, as previously discussed, but because the SEC requires public companies to have such an audit.

Exhibit 3.3 summarizes the frequency of anti-fraud controls.

EXHIBIT 3.3   Frequency of Anti-Fraud Controls: *2020 ACFE Global Fraud Survey*

Anti-Fraud Control	Percentage Reported
External Audit of Financial Statements	83%
Code of Conduct	81%
Internal Audit Department	79%
Management Certification of Financial Statements	73%
External Audit of Internal Controls over Financial Reporting	68%
Management Review	65%
Hotline	64%
Independent Audit Committee	62%
Anti-Fraud Policy Employee Support Programs	56%
Employee Support Programs	55%
Fraud Training for Employees	55%
Fraud Training for Managers/Executives	52%
Dedicated Fraud Department, Function, or Team	44%
Formal Fraud Risk Assessments	41%
Surprise Audits	38%
Proactive Data Monitoring/Analysis	38%
Job Rotation/Mandatory Vacations	23%
Rewards for Whistleblowers	13%

Red-Flag Warnings of Fraud

Individuals who are engaged in occupational fraud schemes often exhibit certain behavioral traits or warning signs associated with their illegal activities. These are presented in **Exhibit 3.4**. Of particular note is living beyond one's means (42%) and financial difficulties (26%). The question is how can the anti-fraud controls identify these behavioral indicators of fraud? These behavioral red flags might show up through personal and workplace relationships. There may be warnings signs such as internal and external relationships that create pressures to carry out one's obligations ethically.

EXHIBIT 3.4   Behavioral Red Flags Displayed by Perpetrators: *2020 ACFE Global Fraud Survey*

Behavioral Indicators of Fraud	Percentage Reported
Living Beyond Means	42%
Financial Difficulties	26%
Unusually Close Association with Vendor/Customer	19%
Control Issues, Unwillingness to Share Duties	15%
No Behavioral Red Flags	15%
"Wheeler-Dealer" Attitude	13%
Irritability, Suspiciousness, or Defensiveness	13%

Behavioral Indicators of Fraud	Percentage Reported
Divorce/Family Problems	12%
Addiction Problems	9%
Complained About Inadequate Pay	8%
Excessive Pressure from Within the Organization	7%
Refusal to Take Vacations	7%
Past Employment-Related Problems	6%
Social Isolation	6%
Past Legal Problems	5%
Complained about Lack of Authority	5%
Excessive Family/Peer Pressure for Success	4%
Other	4%
Instability in Life Circumstances	4%

The results of the survey clearly indicate that internal auditors should have their "eyes wide open" with respect to whether managers have personal and work pressures that create conflicts of interest, one of the signs of ethical collapse. Similarly, the internal auditors need to be aware of financial and/or personal problems of employees that might create pressures to misappropriate cash and/or create fictitious entries to cover up occupational fraud.

Example of Occupational Fraud

What follows is a description of a payroll fraud scheme. According to the ACFE study, payroll schemes accounted for 9.0 percent of the asset misappropriations, had a median cost of $62,000, and lasted a median of two years before being detected.

> The head of a department distributed paychecks to their employees on a weekly basis. Typically, the department head received the payroll checks each week from a payroll processing company and then distributed them to employees. One day another employee noticed the department head had locked their door after the checks were received and wondered about it. The employee became suspicious and reported it to their manager. A payroll audit discovered that several former employees were still receiving paychecks. It was discovered that the department head had the ability to access and edit electronic time keeping records for hourly employees and knew the passwords to the payroll system for their supervisors. They used this access to falsify hours, and thus paychecks, for previous employees. They then took the paychecks to check cashing companies to redeem them. The department head ultimately confessed to over 100 instances of payroll fraud over a 10-month period totaling almost $100,000.

In this case, a lack of proper internal controls contributed to the fraud. The company lacked a proper separation of duties, did not regularly monitor payroll records for "ghost employees," did not require that employees regularly change their passwords, and allowed the department head who distributed the checks to also accept them from the payroll service. Perhaps a fraud hotline for employees to report suspicious behavior would have led to earlier reporting of the fraud.

Financial Statement Fraud

A variety of factors discourage the reporting of fraud according to a report by the Anti-Fraud Collaboration including[4]:

- Poor tone at the top.
- Dominating and intimidating personalities.
- Mistrust.

- Excessive team loyalty.
- Management does not want to hear about problems.
- A lack of sound policies and procedures.
- Perception that wrongdoing will not be addressed if misconduct is reported.

Participants in the study identified the following factors that potentially discourage employees from coming forward and reporting fraud:

- Fear of the unknown.
- Fear that the report will not be handled anonymously or confidentially.
- Fear that the reporter's identity will be revealed to others in the organization.
- Concern that the person perpetrating the misconduct will not be held responsible.

The potential consequences to reporting suspected fraudulent financial reporting include:

- Retaliation by coworkers.
- Termination.
- Future reputation.
- Impact on others.
- Results of investigation determine that the misconduct is unsubstantiated.
- Emotional cost of whistleblowing.

Looking at the overall results of the study, it becomes clear why employees may be reluctant to report suspected fraudulent financial reporting. Concerns whether their reports will do any good and the potential consequences for them both professionally and personally discourage reporters from coming forward. A perceived lack of support makes it more difficult to want to do the right thing and report the fraud. It all comes down to the culture of the organization and whether top management genuinely encourages the reporting of financial statement fraud or just gives lip service to it.

Financial statement fraud is discussed in greater detail in **Chapter 5**. Here, we introduce the term and give examples of fraud techniques to provide context for the types of transactions that raise concerns for those in the corporate governance system.

Financial statement fraud schemes occur because an employee—typically a member of top management—causes a misstatement or omission of material information in the organization's financial reports. Examples include recording fictitious revenues, understating reported expenses, artificially inflating reported assets, failing to accrue expenses at the end of the year, and accelerating the recording of revenue into an earlier period as occurred in the 3D Printing case in **Chapter 1**.

A report by Ernst & Young, *Detecting Financial Statement Fraud: What Every Manager Needs to Know*,[5] provides examples of common methods to overstate revenue, understate expenses, and make improper asset valuations. Revenue overstatements include the following:

- Recording gross, rather than net, revenue.
- Recording revenues of other companies when acting as a "middleman."
- Recording sales that never took place.
- Recording future sales in the current period.
- Recording sales of products that are out on consignment.

Another would be recording revenue from increases in asset values that are not in accordance with GAAP, as Enron did by using mark-to-market accounting for a fixed asset—power plants.

Common methods of understating expenses include the following:

- Reporting cost of sales as a nonoperating expense so that it does not negatively affect gross margin.
- Capitalizing operating costs, recording them as assets on the balance sheet instead of as expenses on the income statement (i.e., WorldCom).
- Not recording some expenses at all, or not recording expenses in the proper period.

Examples of improper asset valuations include the following:

*   Manipulating reserves.
*   Changing the useful lives of assets.
*   Failing to take a write-down when needed.
*   Manipulating estimates of fair market value.

Why Does Financial Statement Fraud Occur?

Why does financial statement fraud occur? This question has been examined since the 1980s when well-publicized financial statement frauds occurred at companies including ZZZZ Best, Miniscribe, Phar-Mor, Cendant, and Waste Management. Theoretically, there are three factors that appear to be present in every case of financial statement fraud that are addressed in auditing standards.[6]

Situational pressure. Situational pressures may prompt an otherwise honest person to commit fraud. It typically occurs as a result of immediate pressure within either the internal or the external environment. For example, financial analysts project earnings and companies feel the pressure to meet or exceed these amounts. An accountant may come to believe they have no option other than to go along with the fraud. The Betty Vinson situation at WorldCom is a case in point. She did not know where to turn; she was unequipped to deal with the fraud.

Perceived opportunity. The opportunity to commit fraud and conceal it must exist. People do not normally commit fraud believing they will get caught. They do it because they believe they can get away with it (i.e., have access to the underlying financial information or override internal controls). The opportunity to commit fraud and conceal it often involves the absence of or improper oversight by the board of directors or audit committee, weak or nonexistent internal controls, unusual or complex transactions, accounting estimates that require sufficient subjective judgment by management, and ineffective internal audit staff.

Rationalization. People who commit financial statement fraud are able to rationalize the act. Being able to justify the act makes it possible. The individual must first convince themself that the behavior is temporary or is acceptable. They may believe it is in the best interest of the company to commit the fraud, perhaps because a needed loan will not be secured without financial statements to back it up. There is often the belief that everything will return to normal after the trigger event has passed.

Financial statement fraud does not occur in a vacuum. It is enabled by the absence of an ethical culture. Oftentimes, a culture is created and a tone at the top established that presents the image of a company willing to do whatever it takes to paint a rosy picture about financial results. Effective oversight and strong internal controls give way to greed, moral blindness, and inattentiveness to the important details that help to prevent and detect fraud. As with most situations in business, the desire to succeed crowds out ethical behavior. Those in the way are pressured to be team players; go along just this one time; and, in the end, compromise their values.

Seven Signs of Ethical Collapse

LO 3-2

Describe the signs that an organization has collapsed ethically.

We can think of the ethical culture of an organization as a piece of the overall organizational culture. So, if the organizational culture represents "how we do things around here," the ethical culture represents "how we do things around here in relation to ethics and ethical behavior in the organization." The ethical culture represents the organizations "ethics personality." A strong ethical culture is essential in creating an organization that supports people making good ethical decisions and behaving ethically at all times and in all decisions. When all relevant organizational systems are pushing people in the same ethical direction, ethical failure is much less likely.[7]

In her book *The Seven Signs of Ethical Collapse,* Marianne Jennings analyzes the indicators of possible ethical collapse in companies and provides advice on how to avoid impending disaster. She starts with a description of ethical collapse, saying that it "occurs when any organization has drifted from the basic principles of right and wrong," and she uses financial reporting standards and accounting rules as one area where this might occur. She points out that "not all companies that have drifted ethically have violated any laws."[8] Enron did not necessarily violate GAAP in treating the effects of *some* of its transactions with special-purpose entities off-balance-sheet. However, the company ignored conflicts of interest of Andy Fastow who managed some of the entities while wearing a second hat as CFO of Enron during the time the two entities had mutual dealings.

According to Jennings, "When an organization collapses ethically, it means that those in the organization have drifted into rationalizations and legalisms, and all for the purpose of getting the results they want and need at almost any cost."[9] A good example is Dennis Kozlowski at Tyco International who misappropriated company resources for personal purposes without the approval of the board of directors and rationalized that he was just doing what those before him had done. Thus, he invoked one of the reasons and rationalizations that we discussed in GVV—Expected or Standard Practice. Jennings links the rationalizations and legalisms to a culture that leads to behavior based on the notion "It's not a question of should we do it." It is a culture of "Can we do it legally?" This mentality occurs because of the combination of the seven factors working together to cloud judgment.[10]

Jennings identifies seven common ethical signs of moral meltdowns in companies that have experienced ethical collapse. The common threads she found that make good people at companies do really dumb things include (1) pressure to maintain numbers; (2) fear and silence; (3) young 'uns and a bigger-than-life CEO (i.e., loyalty to the boss); (4) weak board of directors; (5) conflicts of interest overlooked or unaddressed; (6) innovation like no other company; and (7) goodness in some areas atones for evil in others.[11] We briefly review them next.

Pressure to Maintain the Numbers

Jennings points out that the tension between ethics and the bottom line will always be present. The first sign of a culture at risk for ethical collapse occurs when there is not just a focus on numbers and results, but an unreasonable and unrealistic obsession with meeting quantitative goals. This "financial results at all costs" approach was a common ethical problem at both Enron and WorldCom. At WorldCom, the mantra was that financial results had to improve in every quarter, and the shifting of operating expenses to capitalized costs was used to accomplish the goal regardless of the propriety of the accounting treatment. It was an "end justifies means" culture that sanctioned wrongdoing in the name of earnings. Accountants like Betty Vinson got caught up in the culture and did not know how to extricate herself from the situation.

Fear of Reprisals

A culture of fear and silence can easily mask ethical problems. Employees may be reluctant to raise issues of ethical concern because they may be ignored, treated badly, transferred, or worse. Others might rationalize leaving it up to the next employee to report it, or the bystander effect. The whistleblowing process in many organizations does not work as intended because while ethical employees want to blow the whistle, they are reluctant to do so because they fear reprisals, so they stay silent. One aspect of such a culture is a "kill the messenger syndrome," whereby an employee brings bad news to higher-ups with the best intentions of having the organization correct the matter, but instead the messenger is treated as an outcast. The employee finds themselves in a situation where their ethics are high but the organization's is low.

Loyalty to the Boss

Dennis Kozlowski, the dominant, larger-than-life CEO of Tyco, had an appetite for a lavish style of living. He surrounded himself with young people who were taken by his stature and would not question his actions. Kozlowski, who once spent $6,000 on shower curtains for an apartment paid for by the company, made sure these "young'uns" received all the trappings of success so they would be reluctant to speak up when ethical and legal issues existed for fear of losing their expensive homes, boats, and cars and the prestige that comes along with financial success at a young age. Jennings quoted Kozlowski as saying, "I hire them just like me: smart, poor, and want to be rich." Kozlowski selected them for their positions based on their inexperience, possible conflicts of interest, and unlikelihood to question the boss's decisions. Of course, not all bigger-than-life CEOs are unethical (e.g., Warren Buffett).

Conflicts of Interest and the Board of Directors

A conflict of interest occurs when a person holds a position of trust that requires them to exercise judgment on behalf of others, but where their personal interests and/or obligations conflict with those of others. Andy Fastow was making a lot of money as the general partner of the off-balance-sheet entities that did many deals with Enron. Some at Enron felt the deals were not in its best interests. Still, Fastow was able to convince the Enron board that the entities couldn't exist without his working both sides of the table. Consequently, the board repeatedly gave Fastow a limited waiver of the company's conflict of interest rules in its code of ethics so he could run the off-balance-sheet entities and, simultaneously, serve as Enron's CFO.

A weak board of directors characterizes virtually all the companies with major accounting frauds in the early part of the 2000s. One example is HealthSouth. Richard Scrushy surrounded himself with a weak board so that when he made decisions as CEO that contributed to an accounting scandal where the company's earnings were falsely inflated by $1.4 billion, the board would go along, in part because of their interrelationships with Scrushy and HealthSouth that created conflicts of interest. Jennings identifies the following conflicts of interest that are described in **Exhibit 3.5**.[12]

EXHIBIT 3.5   Conflicts of Interest Between the CEO and Board of Directors

- One director earned $250,000 per year from a consulting contract with HealthSouth over a seven-year period.
- Another director had a joint investment venture with Scrushy on a $395,000 investment property.
- Another director's company was awarded a $5.6 million contract to install glass at a hospital being built by HealthSouth.
- MedCenter District, a hospital-supply company that was run online, did business with HealthSouth and was owned by Scrushy, six directors, and the wife of one of those directors.
- The same three directors had served on both the audit committee and the compensation committee for several years.
- Two of the directors had served on the board for 18 years.
- One director received a $425,000 donation to their favorite charity from HealthSouth just prior to them going on the board.

Conflicts of interest between directors and top management are indicators that fraud may be more likely to occur and the corporate governance system has holes in it. Weak boards can often indicate an organization's ethical collapse, simply because they lack the experience or cohesiveness to challenge an unethical CEO or senior management team.

Conflicts of interest were pronounced before the passage of the Sarbanes-Oxley Act (SOX) and revision of the New York Stock Exchange corporate governance rules that call for the splitting of the roles of CEO and chair of the board of directors. The problem with having a single person perform dual roles is the CEO is also setting the agenda for the board, thereby creating an inherent conflict because the board is supposed to supervise the CEO. Moreover, it is the board's responsibility to vote on executive compensation packages, so when the CEO is also the chair, they are voting on their own compensation package. Publicly held corporations in the U.S. are required to have a board of directors to oversee top management and ensure top management decisions reflect shareholder interest. In 2010, the SEC under the Dodd-Frank Financial Reform Act adopted rules that require companies to disclose in their proxy statements why the board chair and CEO positions are unified or separated.

Innovations

Too many companies that dissolve in fraud and other wrongdoings felt they were above the fray because they were so innovative. In entering a guilty plea to fraud, Sanjay Kumar, former CEO of Computer Associates, remarked: ". . . standard accounting rules [were] not the best way to measure [CA's] results because it had changed to a new business model offering its clients more flexibility."[13]

The innovators may come to believe they are immune from the business cycle and almost untouchable. In a sense, they become blind to the ethical issues that arise during and after the innovation process.

Goodness in Some Areas Atones for Evil in Others

Does it make sense that a company steeped in good works for a community and socially responsible behavior should be given a pass if it gets involved in wrongful acts? Many companies rely on their culture of diversity, safety, volunteerism, or environmentally conscious operations as evidence of their overall ethical goodness, despite improprieties elsewhere as if two "rights" undo a "wrong." Jennings quotes John Rigas, the founder of Adelphia Communications that had a multi-billion dollar fraud in 2002 that included $2.3 billion of co-borrowing between Adelphia subsidiaries and some Rigas family-owned entities: "It's more than money. You've got to give back to the community that supported you." Jennings points out that while he was CEO of Adelphia, John Rigas "gave back" it was to his daughter and others in business with him.[14]

Ethics in the Workplace

LO 3-3

Discuss compliance, integrity, and employee views about ethics in the workplace.

When we think about workplace ethics, the first thing that comes to mind is a code of conduct that influences the development of an ethical culture and provides direction to steer the ethical climate toward right behavior. A code goes beyond what is legal for an organization and provides normative guidelines for ethical conduct. Support for ethical behavior from top management is a critical component of fostering an ethical climate. Employees who sense that top managers act unethically quickly lose trust in those managers. The result can be to become disillusioned with the goals of the organization and question whether the corporate culture is one that is consistent with individual, personal values and beliefs.

Here is a list of measures that should be taken to establish an ethical culture:

1. Establish clear policies on ethical conduct including a code of ethics.
2. Develop an ethics training program that instills a commitment to act ethically and explains code provisions.
3. Assign a top-level officer, such as the Chief Ethics and Compliance Officer (CECO), to oversee compliance with ethics policies.
4. Use the internal auditors to investigate whether ethics policies have been followed in practice.
5. Establish strong internal controls to prevent and detect unethical behaviors, such as fraud.
6. Establish whistleblowing policies, including reporting outlets.
7. Establish an ethics hotline where employees can discuss questionable behavior on an anonymous basis.
8. Have employees sign a statement that they have complied with ethics policies.
9. Enforce ethics policies fairly and take immediate action against those who violate the policies.
10. Reward ethical behavior by including it in the performance evaluation system.

Compliance Function

On August 4, 2015, it was announced that the Ethics Resource Center (ERC), the oldest nonprofit advancing high ethical standards and practices in public and private institutions, and the Ethics Compliance and Officer Association (ECOA), a member-driven association for practitioners responsible for their organization's ethics and compliance programs, joined together to form a strategic alliance to become the go-to organization for ethics and compliance resources in the workplace. The resulting Ethics Compliance Initiative (ECI) provides leading ethics and compliance research and best practices, networking opportunities, and certification to its membership.

According to a Deloitte study, *Building world-class ethics and compliance programs,* there are five factors that separate the "good" from the "great" compliance programs including the following[15]:

- Tone at the top.
- Corporate culture.
- Risk assessments.
- The Chief Compliance Officer (CCO).
- Testing and monitoring.

With respect to the tone at the top, the board of directors and senior management should do more than pay "lip service" to ethics and compliance. They need to provide the necessary tools for individuals who have day-to-day responsibilities to mitigate risks and build organizational trust. Along these lines, a culture of integrity is critical to any effective ethics and compliance program.

Integrity: The Basis for Trust in the Workplace

Albert Camus, the French Nobel Prize winning author, journalist, and philosopher, said, "Integrity has no need of rules." People of integrity are self-driven to do the right thing. Leaders of integrity act on the knowledge that their actions are ethical and provide the basis for others in the workplace to follow their lead.

KPMG's *Integrity Survey 2013* provides an inside look at organizational misconduct based upon responses from more than 3,500 U.S. working adults. Key findings from the report include[16]:

- Nearly three out of four employees reported that they had observed misconduct within their organizations in the previous 12 months.
- More than half of employees reported that what they observed could potentially cause a significant loss of public trust if discovered.
- Some of the driving forces behind fraud and misconduct in the corporate environment include pressure to do "whatever it takes" to meet targets, not taking the code of conduct seriously, believing employees will be rewarded based upon results and not the means used to achieve them, and fear of losing one's job for not meeting performance targets.
- Nearly half of employees were uncertain that they would be protected from retaliation if they reported concerns to management. And more than half suggested a lack of confidence that they would be satisfied with the outcome.
- Ethics and compliance programs continue to have a favorable impact on employee perceptions and behaviors.

Employees were asked what they would do if they observed a violation of their organization's standards of conduct. The results were: 78 percent would notify their supervisor or another manager; 54 percent would try resolving the matter directly; 53 percent would call the ethics or compliance hotline; 26 percent would notify someone outside the organization; and 23 percent would look the other way or do nothing.

It's encouraging to learn that over three-fourths would inform their supervisor, in part because it is the generally recognized initial step in considering whether to blow the whistle. It is somewhat troubling that almost one-quarter of the workers would look the other way or do nothing. Perhaps they do not believe they would be taken seriously or a "kill the messenger" culture exists in the organization. There is also the possibility that dissonance exists if the individual has a high ethics orientation while the organization's is low.

The tone at the top set by top management is a determining factor in creating organizational commitment to high ethics and integrity. Employees were asked whether the chief executive officer and other senior executives exhibited characteristics attributable to personal integrity and ethical leadership. Approximately two-thirds of the employees agreed that their leaders set the right tone regarding the importance of ethics and integrity and served as positive role models for their organization, leaving one-third unsure or in disagreement.

Perhaps not surprisingly, a large percentage (64 percent) indicated that the root cause of misconduct was pressure to do "whatever it takes" to meet business objectives, while 59 percent said they believed they would be rewarded for results, not the means used to achieve them. In such instances, the corporate culture does not foster integrity or ethical behavior; instead, expedience and self-interest drive workplace behavior. Moreover, the findings seem to indicate a majority of respondents believe their organizations follow an end justifies the means approach to decision making: what is most important is results, not the way they were achieved.

Employees Perceptions of Ethics in the Workplace

A record number of U.S. workers say they feel pressure to cut ethical corners on the job, and a record number also say they have experienced retaliation after reporting corporate misconduct—and for both issues, those numbers have essentially doubled in just three years.

The *2021 Global Business Ethics Survey,* a sweeping survey of employee perceptions of ethics in the workplace released every few years by the ECI has several troubling findings for corporate ethics and compliance officers.[17]

The good news for the U.S. is that 21 percent of employees say they work in organizations with a strong ethical culture, the same number who said so in ECI's 2017 report. Even better, the number of employees who said they were likely to report misconduct they saw in the workplace rose from 69 percent in 2017 to 86 percent this year.

Now the bad news. Thirty percent of employees said they felt pressure to compromise ethical standards at work—up from 14 percent in 2017, and the highest number ever recorded for this question since ECI began conducting the survey more than 20 years ago.

Separately, 79 percent of U.S. employees who reported misconduct said they then suffered some form of retaliation. That's up from 44 percent in 2017 and 21 percent in 2011; and, again, is the highest number ECI has ever recorded for this question.

The results on the global mirror those in the U.S. although the global medians are lower in all cases. Here is a summary of the results.

2021 Global Business Ethics Survey

Survey Questions	Results	
	U.S.	Global Median
% of employees that work in a strong ethics culture	21%	N/A
% of employees who feel pressure to compromise ethical standards	30%	29%
% of employees who observed misconduct in the workplace	49%	33%
% of employees who were likely to report misconduct	86%	81%
% of employees who reported misconduct felt retaliation	79%	61%

Source: Credit: 2021 Global Business Ethics Survey.

Using Social Media to Criticize the Employer[18]

What can employees do if they observe misconduct and want to vent their action on social media? The National Labor Relations Act protects the rights of employees to act together in a concerted manner to address conditions at work, with or without a union. This protection extends to certain work-related conversations conducted on social media, such as Facebook and Twitter. Employees who act together on workplace issues—by, for example, meeting with a manager to lobby for better benefits or having a group discussion about the company's safety record—are protected from employer retaliation.

An activity is concerted only if it involves more than one employee's concerns. For example, employees discussing working conditions is protected. An employee who complains, after consulting with or on behalf of coworkers, that the company's performance evaluation system unfairly penalizes employees who speak up in safety meetings is engaged in concerted activity. However, an employee who complains about their own performance evaluation is not taking concerted action. As the National Labor Relations Board (NLRB) puts it, "personal gripes" are not protected. Even if employees are clearly acting in a concerted way, they won't be protected if they cross the line from constructive behavior to malicious or reckless actions.

As an example of what not to do: The former employee handbook of fast-food chain Wendy's included a rule requiring authorization before workers could make comments on social media about Wendy's business, policies, or employees especially if it negatively reflected on Wendy's. This direction was deemed too broad and the internal complaint mechanism chilled employee rights.

In 2010, the NLRB began receiving charges related to employer social media policies and to specific instances of discipline for Facebook postings. Following investigations, the agency found reasonable cause to believe that some policies and disciplinary actions violated federal labor law, and the NLRB Office of General Counsel issued complaints against employers alleging unlawful conduct. In other cases, investigations found that the communications were not protected and so disciplinary actions did not violate the Act.

On September 28, 2012, the NLRB found that the firing of a BMW salesman for photos and comments posted to his Facebook page did not violate federal labor law. The question came down to whether the salesman was fired exclusively for posting photos of an embarrassing accident at an adjacent Land Rover dealership, which did not involve fellow employees, or for posting mocking comments and photos with coworkers about serving hot dogs at a luxury BMW car event. Both sets of photos were posted to Facebook on the same day; a week later, the salesman was fired. The Board ruled that the salesman was fired solely for the photos he posted of a Land Rover incident, which was not concerted activity and so was not protected.

The best advice for any employee when it comes to what they post on social media is to take a step back and think about the ramifications. You might be engaging in protected speech, and you might not.

Oftentimes an employer will claim that an employee who was fired ostensibly for comments on social media was fired instead for legitimate performance reasons. In these cases, the employer must prove it would have fired them even if they had not engaged in protected concerted activity.

Human Resource managers can't infringe on employee rights or individual rights to freedom of speech, but they can help educate employees about how to properly conduct themselves in the workplace. In this digital age, employers must develop a social media policy so employees know just what is the expected standard of behavior.

Foundation of Corporate Governance Systems

LO 3-4

Describe the scope and role of corporate governance systems in the ethical decision-making process.

In his book *Corporate Governance and Ethics,* Zabihollah Rezaee points out that corporate governance is shaped by internal and external mechanisms, as well as policy interventions through regulations. Internal mechanisms help manage, direct, and monitor corporate governance activities to create sustainable stakeholder value. Examples include the board of directors, particularly independent directors; the audit committee; management; internal controls; and the internal audit function. External mechanisms are intended to monitor the company's activities, affairs, and performance to ensure that the interests of insiders (management, directors, and officers) are aligned with the interests of outsiders (shareholders and other stakeholders). Examples of external mechanisms include the financial markets, state and federal statutes, SEC regulations, court decisions, and shareholder proposals.[19] Three noteworthy points are: (1) independent directors enhance governance accountability; (2) separation of the duties of the CEO and board chair minimizes conflicts of interest; and (3) separate meetings between the audit committee and external auditors strengthen control mechanisms.

Ethical and Legal Responsibilities of Officers and Directors

Duty of Care—Managers and Directors

Directors and officers are deemed fiduciaries of the corporation because their relationship with the corporation and its shareholders is one of trust and confidence. As fiduciaries, directors and officers owe ethical—and legal—duties to the corporation and to the shareholders. These fiduciary duties include the duty of care and the duty of loyalty.

The standard of *due care* provides that a director or officer act in good faith, exercise the care that an ordinarily prudent person would exercise in similar circumstances, and act in the way that is considered to be in the best interests of the corporation. Directors and officers who have not exercised the required duty of care can be held liable for the harms suffered by the corporation as a result of their negligence. Notice how this standard ties into Kant's Categorical Imperative: Act only according to that maxim whereby you can, at the same time, will that it should become a *universal law.* The universal standard is one of due care.

The duty of care also involves the exercise of reasonable care by a board member to ensure that the corporate executives with whom they work carry out their management responsibilities and comply with the law in the best interests of the corporation.[20]

Duty of Loyalty

The *duty of loyalty* requires faithfulness; a director must place the interests of the corporation ahead of personal interests. For example, directors must not use corporate funds or confidential corporate information for personal advantage. A conflict occurs when a board member hears of a potential deal that might affect the selling price of company stock (up or down). The board member's attempt to profit from this knowledge is called insider trading; it's illegal as well as being a conflict of interest.[21] Another conflict would be if a board member is involved in a personal relationship with an employee of the company. The employee's position with the company might be affected by the relationship and allegations of sexual harassment could harm corporate interests.

Duty of Good Faith

The obligation of *good faith* requires an honesty of purpose that leads to caring for the well-being of the constituents of the fiduciary. Vice Chancellor Leo Strine of the Delaware Chancery Court linked good faith to fiduciary analysis in the Enron fraud by suggesting that the Enron case might influence courts to look more carefully at whether directors have made a good faith effort to accomplish their duties. He connected good faith with directors' "state of mind." Strine identified certain kinds of director conduct that may call good faith into question. These include "a failure to monitor if [the directors'] laxity in oversight was so persistent and substantial that it evidences bad faith." It can also arise in situations where "committee members knew that their inadequate knowledge disabled them from discharging their responsibilities with fidelity."[22]

Business Judgment Rule

A corporate director or officer may be able to avoid liability to the corporation or to its shareholders for poor business judgments under the *business judgment rule.* Directors and officers are expected to exercise due care and to use their best judgment in guiding corporate management, but they are not insurers of business success. Honest mistakes of judgment and poor business decisions on their part do not make them liable to the corporation for resulting damages.

To obtain the business judgment rule's protection, directors must be independent and disinterested as to the matter acted upon. Directors must act with due care and good faith. The due care inquiry is process-oriented, and due care is measured by a standard of gross negligence (i.e., reckless behavior), not simple negligence. The burden of proof is on the party challenging the board's decision, to establish facts rebutting the presumption in favor of upholding the decision. Unless a plaintiff succeeds in rebutting the rule, the court will not substitute its views for those of the board's if the latter's decision can be "attributed to any rational business purpose."

The business judgment rule generally immunizes directors and officers from liability for the consequences of a decision that is within managerial authority, as long as the decision complies with management's fiduciary duties and as long as acting on the decision is within the powers of the corporation. Therefore, if there is a reasonable basis for a business decision, it is unlikely that a court will interfere with that decision, even if the corporation suffers as a result.

The Chancery Court located in Delaware is the preeminent forum for the resolution of commercial business litigation matters including the duties of officers and directors. The Court's fundamental purpose is to be an equity court—to provide relief suited to the circumstances when no adequate remedy is available at law.

Components of Corporate Governance Systems

An essential part of creating an ethical organization environment is to put in place effective corporate governance systems that establish control mechanisms to ensure that organizational values guide decision making and that ethical standards are being followed. Corporate governance entails developing formal systems of accountability, oversight, and control. Strong corporate governance mechanisms lessen the opportunity for employees to make unethical decisions. Research has shown that corporate governance has a positive relationship with social responsibility. Moreover, firms with strong corporate governance mechanisms that call for the disclosure of social responsibility initiatives can establish legitimacy and trust among their stakeholders.[23]

There are many ways to look at what corporate governance should do. We like the characterization by Ferrell et al.[24] described below:

> Accountability refers to how closely workplace decisions align with a firm's strategic direction and its compliance with ethical and legal considerations. Oversight provides a system of checks and balances that limit employees' and managers' opportunities to deviate from policies and strategies aimed at preventing unethical and illegal activities. Control is the process of auditing and improving organizational decisions and actions.*

Models of Corporate Governance

Differences exist about the role of corporate governance in business. Some organizations take the view that as long as they are maximizing shareholder wealth and profitability, they are fulfilling their core responsibilities. Other firms take a broader view based on the stakeholder perspective.

The shareholder model of corporate governance is founded on classic economic precepts, including maximizing wealth for investors and creditors. In a public corporation, firm decisions should be oriented toward serving the best interests of investors. Underlying these decisions is a classic agency problem, in which ownership (investors) and control (managers) are separate. Managers act as the agents of the investors (principals), who expect those decisions to increase the value of the stock they own.[25] However, managers may have motivations beyond stockholder value such as increasing market share or more personal ones including maximizing executive compensation. In these instances, decisions may be based on an egoist approach to ethical decision making that ignores the interests of others. An enlightened egoist approach is more in keeping with capitalistic theory whereby other interests are considered by managers prior to deciding how best to serve their own interests. For example, it could be that managers believe an increase in the corporate dividend serves their interest because it may convince shareholders that managers are acting like responsible agents.

Albrecht et al. point out that the principal-agent relationship involves a transfer of trust and duty to the agent, while also assuming that the agent is opportunistic and will pursue interests that are in conflict with those of the principal, thereby creating an "agency problem."[26] Because of these potential differences, corporate governance mechanisms are needed to align investor and management interests. A fundamental challenge underlying all corporate governance affairs dates back to the days of Adam Smith. In *The Wealth of Nations,* Smith said that "the directors of companies, being managers of other people's money, cannot be expected to watch over it with the same vigilance with which they watch over their own."

One traditional approach is for shareholders to give the CEO shares or options of stock that vest over time, thus inducing long-term behavior and deterring short-term actions that can harm future company value. When the interests of top management are brought in line with interests of shareholders, agency theory argues that management will fulfill its duty to shareholders, not so much out of any sense of moral duty to shareholders, but because doing what shareholders have provided incentives for maximizes their own utility.[27]

Jensen and Meckling demonstrate how investors in publicly traded corporations incur (agency) costs in monitoring managerial performance. In general, agency costs arise whenever there is an "information asymmetry" between the corporation and outsiders because insiders (the corporation) know more about a company and its future prospects than do outsiders (investors).[28]

Agency costs can occur if the board of directors fails to exercise due care in its oversight role of management. Enron's board of directors did not monitor the company's incentive compensation plans properly, thereby allowing top executives to "hype" the company's stock so that employees would add it to their 401(k) retirement plans. While the hyping occurred, often through positive statements about the company made by CEO Ken Lay, Lay himself sold about 2.3 million shares for $123.4 million.

The agency problem can never be perfectly solved, and shareholders may experience a loss of wealth due to divergent behavior of managers. Investigations by the SEC and U.S. Department of Justice of 20 corporate frauds during the Enron-WorldCom era indicate that $236 billion in shareholder value was lost between the time the public first learned of the first fraud and September 3, 2002, the measurement date.

An alternative to agency theory is stewardship theory. In this theory, managers and directors are viewed as stewards of their companies and have a fiduciary duty to act in the best interests of the shareholders. The theory holds that as stewards, managers and directors will choose the interests of shareholders, perhaps psychologically identified as the best interests of "the company," over self-interests, regardless of personal motivations or incentives.[29] Contrary to agency theory, stewardship theory believes that directors do not inevitably act in a way that maximizes their own personal interests: They can and do act responsibly with independence and integrity. Even though some will fail, it does not invalidate the theory.[30]

Stewardship advocates recognize that directors need to consider a broader range of interests, including employees, customers, suppliers, and other legitimate stakeholders, but under the law their first responsibility is to the shareholders. They argue that conflicts of interest between stakeholder groups and the company should be met by competitive pressures in free markets, backed by legislation and legal controls to protect various stakeholder interests (i.e., environmental law, health and safety law, employment discrimination law).

Executive Compensation

One of the most common approaches to the agency problem is to link managerial compensation to the financial performance of the corporation in general and the performance of the company's shares. Typically, this occurs by creating long-term compensation packages and stock option plans that tie executive wealth to an increase in the corporation's stock price. These incentives aim to encourage managers to maximize the market value of shares. One of the biggest issues that corporate boards of directors face is executive compensation as is the case in the Tesla example discussed next. It has been found that most boards spend more time deciding how much to compensate top executives than they do ensuring the integrity of the company's financial reporting systems.[31]

Tesla's Lucrative Incentive-Based Compensation Package for Elon Musk

The Chancery Court ruled on November 5, 2019 that Tesla's board of directors must defend at a trial a compensation package for Elon Musk, its chair, CEO, and controlling shareholder. The Court held that the board's decision was subject to entire fairness review despite approval of the award by an independent board committee and ratification of 47 percent of the disinterested shareholders.[32]

The ruling follows a shareholder challenge to the lucrative equity grant to Musk, claiming that the director's decision to approve the pay package breached their fiduciary duties. The compensation consisted of stock options that only vested upon Tesla's achievement of market cap and operational milestones, with a value to Musk of up to $55.8 billion rising to a market value to as much as $650 billion over the next decade.

The Chancery Court acknowledged that although the ratifying shareholder vote would justify business judgment review in ordinary circumstances, it was insufficient in the case of compensation granted to a controlling shareholder where the shareholder vote is made on a fully informed basis. As a result, the Court denied the directors' motion to dismiss the lawsuit, holding that the exacting "entire fairness" standard of review was warranted in the circumstances, in part because fewer than a majority of the disinterested shareholders voted to ratify the award.

Executive Pay Packages

A problem arises when top management purposefully manipulates earnings amounts to drive up the price of stock so they can cash in more lucrative stock options. During the financial crisis of 2008–2009, Congress charged executives at some of the nation's largest companies with gaining pay packages in the millions while their companies suffered losses, and they may have even accepted funds from the government to keep them liquid.

The disparity between the pay of CEOs and average worker is stunning. In 2019, it was reported that CEOs saw their pay grow 1,000 percent in the last 40 years, now making 278 times the average worker. Is it any wonder that statistics such as these trigger clawback lawsuits by shareholders?

Clawbacks

The Dodd-Frank Wall Street Reform and Consumer Protection Act (H.R. 4173)[33] was signed into federal law by President Barack Obama on July 21, 2010. Passed as a response to the late-2000s recession, it brought the most significant changes to financial regulation in the U.S. since the regulatory reform that followed the Great Depression. Two areas where Dodd-Frank relates to corporate governance are in executive compensation and in whistleblowing procedures, which will be discussed later on.

Clawbacks have been on the regulatory radar screen in a big way since 2002, when SOX gave the SEC power to recover compensation and stock profits from CEOs and CFOs of public companies in the event of financial restatements caused by misconduct. Clawback policies among Fortune 100 companies were already on the rise before the financial crisis, jumping from 17.6 percent in 2006 to 42.1 percent in 2007. In 2010, the year Dodd-Frank was passed, 82.1 percent of the Fortune 100 had them. In 2012, 86.5 percent of the Fortune 100 firms had adopted publicly disclosed policies. Now, about 90 percent have such policies. The ethical justification for clawbacks is the breach of fiduciary duty owed by top management to shareholders and inequities when they benefit from their own wrongful acts.

On July 1, 2015, the SEC proposed rules directing U.S. stock exchanges to create listing standards requiring listed companies to implement policies to recover or "claw back" incentive-based compensation received by executive officers as a result of materially incorrect financial statements.

Clawback provisions are contract clauses designed to ensure that company executives don't manipulate financial information to hit certain earnings targets linked to their compensation payments. Essentially, a clawback requires executives to pay back bonuses they received if the incentive was based on a performance benchmark that later turned out to be an incorrect number. A good example of how it works is the case of Morris Maxwell, the CEO of publicly traded Carp Corp., who received a bonus due to higher-than-expected reported earnings in 2019.

The bonus to Maxwell consisted of a cash payment, a stock award, and options with a total value of $1 million. However, Maxwell or others at the company used several accounting tricks or manipulations to achieve this reported result. The auditors didn't discover this initially, but Carp Corp. had to restate its financial statements a year later. If the company had included a clawback provision in its executives' contracts, then Maxwell might have been required to repay all or some of the $1 million bonus payment.

Say on Pay

Dodd-Frank includes say-on-pay provisions (Section 951) that require SEC-registered issuers to provide shareholders at least once every three calendar years as a separate nonbinding say-on-pay vote regarding the compensation of the company named executive officers (i.e., CEO and CFO) and the company's three other most highly compensated officers. Although the vote on compensation is nonbinding, the company must include a statement in the "Compensation Discussion and Analysis" of the proxy statement whether its compensation policies and decisions have taken into account the results of the shareholder say-on-pay vote and, if so, how. The idea is for the vote of the shareholders to be taken seriously not only by the company, but also by other companies in the same marketplace.

A good example of how this works is Citigroup's shareholders that voted against CEO Vikram Pandit's $15 million compensation package for 2011, a year when the bank's stock tumbled. At the time of the vote, Pandit had received nearly $7 million in cash for 2011, with the remainder to be paid in restricted stock and cash over the next few years (and thus subject to possible restructuring by the board). Citigroup's shareholders expressed concerns that the compensation package lacked significant and important goals to provide incentives for improvement in the shareholder value of the institution.

There is little need for shareholder oversight of executive pay if directors do a good job providing oversight themselves or have strong incentives to do a good job. However, conflicts of interest, such as when the CEO and CFO also serve on the board of directors, creates an element of lack of accountability. Issues related to fairness and justice dictate that the oversight of executive compensation packages by shareholder groups is the right thing to do. The ethical question is: How can oversight be done in a way that protects shareholder and other stakeholder needs?

Corporate Governance Oversight and Regulation

Following the large number of frauds and business failures in the later 1990s and early 2000s, regulators turned to the systems in place to monitor corporate behavior. This led to developing policies and procedures to strengthen the oversight and regulation of corporate governance mechanisms, in particular the board of directors and audit committee. One control mechanism is appointing nonexecutive directors to the audit committee.

An outside or nonexecutive director is a member of a company's board of directors who is not part of the executive team. Nonexecutive directors, also known as external directors, independent directors, or outside directors, do not hold executive level or managerial positions. These directors are thought to hold the interests of the company in higher regard than executive directors, who may have an agency problem or conflict of interest between management and stockholders. A nonexecutive director typically does not engage in the day-to-day management of the organization, but is involved in policy making and planning exercises. In addition, nonexecutive directors' responsibilities include the monitoring of the executive directors and acting in the interest of the company stakeholders.

Requirements for Public Company Boards in the United States

Public companies in the United States that list their equity securities on the New York Stock Exchange (NYSE) or the Nasdaq Stock Market (Nasdaq) are required to have in place a board of directors with the following features[34]:

INDEPENDENT DIRECTORS

Independent directors must comprise a majority of the board. An "independent director" is one who has no material relationship with the company either directly or as a partner, shareholder, or officer of an organization that has a relationship with the company. The company must have a minimum three-member audit committee composed of entirely independent directors.

AUDIT COMMITTEE

In addition to the independence requirements above, the audit committee must meet the independence requirements enumerated in Section 301 of SOX and the Securities Exchange Act Rule 10A-3(b)(1). This prohibits a director from accepting any direct or indirect consulting, advisory, or other compensatory fee from the listed company other than compensation for director service and not being affiliated with the company or its subsidiaries.

Not addressed by the NYSE, SEC Regulation S-K requires disclosure in annual reports whether or not the audit committee includes at least one "financial expert." An audit committee financial expert has an understanding of the financial statements and GAAP; experience in preparing, auditing, analyzing, or evaluating financial statements of companies comparable to the company or experience in actively supervising one or more persons engaged in such activities; experience in applying GAAP to accounting for estimates, accruals, and reserves; and an understanding of internal accounting controls, procedures for financial reporting, and audit committee functions. **Exhibit 3.6** describes audit committee duties and responsibilities.

EXHIBIT 3.6   Audit Committee Duties and Responsibilities

Audit committee duties and responsibilities include, among others:

- Meet at least annually with the independent auditor and review the audit report describing independent auditor's internal quality control procedures.
- Discuss any material issues raised by the auditor's most recent internal quality control review or peer review of the firm, or by any inquiry or investigation by governmental or professional authorities within the preceding five years with regard to one or more independent audits carried out by the firm and steps taken to deal with any such issues.
- Discuss all relationships between the independent auditor and the company to enable assessment of the auditor's independence.
- Meet and discuss with the independent auditor and management the annual audited financial statements and quarterly financial statements, including review of Management's Discussion and Analysis of Financial Condition and Results of Operations.
- Discuss earnings press releases and financial information and earnings guidance given to analysts and rating agencies.
- Discuss policies with respect to risk assessment and risk management.
- Meet separately, from time to time, with management, with internal auditors, and with independent auditors.
- Review with the independent auditor any audit problems or difficulties and management's response to such issues.
- Set clear hiring policies for employees or former employees of the independent auditor.
- Report regularly to the board of directors.
- Evaluate work of the audit committee annually.

Public companies also should have a compensation committee composed only of independent directors. It's best not to have the same members serve on the audit and compensation committees to reduce the likelihood of any conflict of interest.

Corporate Governance Failures at Lehman Brothers

The Great Recession that officially lasted from December 2007 to June 2009, ushered in a period of bank failures and fraud that shook the economy of the U.S. Many people blamed excessive risk taking and failed corporate governance systems. Some point out that "moral hazard" was a major contributing factor. *Moral hazard* occurs where one party is responsible for the interests of another, but has an incentive to put its own interests first. The banks used collateral debt obligations (CDOs) to repackage individual mortgage loans into a product sold to investors on the secondary market. By so doing, Lehman transferred the risk of nonpayment on these financial instruments to other parties. Given the transfer of risk, Lehman initially issued loans to uncreditworthy borrowers, knowing the bank would not be responsible if the homeowners defaulted. Unfortunately, the extra liquidity created an asset bubble in housing, credit cards, and auto debt. Housing prices skyrocketed beyond their actual value. People bought homes so they could sell them. The easy availability of debt meant people used their credit cards too much. That drove credit card debt to almost $1 trillion in 2008.

For two and a half years, the U.S. Senate focused on the role of financial institutions in the financial crisis that started with the failure of Lehman Brothers. A bankruptcy examiner's report issued on April 12, 2011, shed light on the role of auditing firms in the financial meltdown. The report was written by Jenner & Block Chairman Anton Valukas.

At the Senate Banking Committee hearings on the Lehman failure and subsequent financial crisis, Valukas (U.S. Senate Committee on Banking, Housing, and Urban Affairs) spoke about the general principle that auditors play a critical role in the proper functioning of public companies and financial markets. He said:

> Boards of directors and audit committees are entitled to rely on external auditors to serve as watchdogs—to be important gatekeepers who provide an independent check on management. And the investing public is entitled to believe that a 'clean' report from an independent auditor stands for something. The public has every right to conclude that auditors who hold themselves out as independent will stand up to management and not succumb to pressure to avoid rocking the boat. I found that [valid] claims exist against Lehman's external auditor in connection with Lehman's issuance of materially misleading financial reports.*

The Lehman failure illustrates how things can go so wrong when sound corporate governance mechanisms are not in place or not working as intended. **Exhibit 3.7** briefly describes those failures, many of which were in the area of corporate risk management.

EXHIBIT 3.7   Corporate Governance Failures at Lehman

Lehman's corporate governance systems broke down as a result of the following:

- Failed risk management procedures brought on by excessive use of CDOs with exposure that far exceeded Lehman's understanding of the inherent risks.
- Ignoring warnings signs of liquidity risk.
- Failure to disclose material information on foreseeable risk factors.
- The Valukas report indicated that Lehman repeatedly exceeded its own internal risk limits and controls.
- Richard S. Fuld, Jr. served as chairperson and CEO.
- Makeup of the board was inadequate given the complex nature of Lehman's financial transactions: only two of ten members had direct experience in the financial services industry.
- Significant payments were made to members of the board, which did not result from remuneration granted to them. These were payments from investment activity of limited partnerships set up by the company and that directors could engage.
- Top executive managers at Lehman received about $1 billion from cash bonuses and equity sales between 2000 and 2008; chairperson Fuld received close to $500 million just four days before the collapse.
- The staff owned four percent of the bank in 1994 when it went public and about 30 percent by 2006, mostly due to stock and options, the equivalent of $11 billion on paper.
- Ernst & Young know of potential accounting irregularities and failed to raise the issue with Lehman's board.

The relationships and activities described above illustrate a breakdown in ethics and failure of the board to exercise objective independent judgment on bank affairs. The board did not effectively monitor activities and did not meet the corporate governance standard of accountability to shareholders. It failed to meet its fiduciary responsibilities and duty of care to the shareholders. During the court process the Lehman officers stated that "Ernst & Young did not approve the Accounting Policy," instead the firm "became comfortable with the Policy for purposes of auditing financial statements."

Corporate Governance Responsibilities

LO 3-5
Explain the models of corporate governance and ethical expectations of organizations.

Corporate Social Responsibilities

It's clear that business has a social responsibility to obey the law. Relationships with employees, customers, suppliers, creditors, etc. create contractual obligations. Legal obligations also exist to avoid negligence, fraud, and other liabilities under tort law. Economists point out that business has a social responsibility to produce the goods and services required for society to function. The philosopher and ethicist, Chris MacDonald, believes the primary question of corporate social responsibilities (CSR) is the extent to which business organizations and their managers have ethical responsibilities that go beyond producing needed goods and services within the law.[35]

For our purposes, when we address issues of CSR, we are referring to the ethical expectations that society has for business. Ethical responsibilities are those things that we ought to, or should do, even if we prefer not to.[36] A business may not want to develop the systems to remove toxic waste because of cost concerns, but it chooses to do so to garner goodwill through environmentally friendly policies and act in society's interests. We also address the more obligatory sense of ethical responsibility to prevent harm. A good example is developing (and enforcing) policies against sexual harassment in the workplace.

Sustainability

Concepts such as sustainability and the triple bottom line are the forerunners of conscious capitalism. Here is a brief review of what they mean.

Sustainability describes the ability to maintain various systems and processes—environmentally, socially, and economically—over time. Sustainability originated in natural resource economics but has since gained broader focus over time into sustainable development and social equality. Economic sustainability addresses the need for financial resources to maintain independent communities around the globe and provide economic activities available to everyone to secure sources of livelihood. It has been reported that 86 percent of the Standard & Poor's 500 Index companies published sustainability/responsibility reports in 2018.

Triple Bottom Line (TBL)

Three aspects of sustainability, often referred to as the three "P's"—people, planet, and profit—has received increased attention from non-governmental organizations, management, consultants, and investors seeking to invest in socially responsible companies. TBL describes the scope of reporting in three broad areas affecting society: economic including financial reporting, ecological including the environment, and social including social responsibility. Investors use them and their own measurements for valuing companies. Accountability for environmental, social, and economic impacts of a company is increasingly part of every manager's job. TBL is an important part of disclosure and enhances transparency of financial reporting. TBL is consistent with the broad stakeholder perspective of CSR that includes shareholders, creditors, employees, the community, the environment, government, and society in general. TBL's mission is to disseminate knowledge to engender and catalyze TBL practices.

Views of Millennials

Socially responsible workplace policies and socially responsible investments can help with millennial engagement. Millennials are passionate about social causes. According to a 2015 Cone Communications Millennial CSR Study, more than 9-in-10 millennials would switch brands to one associated with a cause, and millennials are "prepared to make personal sacrifices to make an impact on issues they care about, whether that's paying more for a product, sharing products rather than buying, or taking a pay cut to work for a responsible company."[37]

A 2016 study produced the following key findings[38]:

- 76% of Millennials consider a company's CSR commitments when deciding where to work.
- 64% won't take a job if a company doesn't have strong CSR values.
- 83% would be more loyal to a company that helps them contribute to social and environmental issues.
- 88% say their job is more fulfilling when they are provided opportunities to make a positive impact on social and environmental issues.

Socially responsible companies should leverage Millennials' commitment to engage in practices that, we might say, illustrate "Doing Good by Being Good."

Conscious Capitalism

Conscious capitalism is a relatively new concept but a natural part of the evolution of what it means to have CSR. Corporations need to embrace conscious capitalism if they want to be relevant as an engine for economic growth. The main difference between conscious capitalism and CSR is that the former is a more comprehensive and holistic approach to the relationship between business and society.

Conscious capitalism as a business philosophy comes from John Mackey, co-founder and CEO of Whole Foods Market, and professor Raj Sisodia, who together wrote a book on the concept and founded Conscious Capitalism, Inc. It goes beyond the bottom line and holds that money isn't the only goal for the company. It is about making ethical decisions that positively impacts the entire ecosystem surrounding the company. The ecosystem basically reflects the stakeholders of a company including investors, customers, employees, vendors, and the environment. Conscious capitalism is becoming committed to the TBL.[39]

The framework of conscious capitalism starts by clarifying a company's purpose and core values. Having clear values provides the pathway to satisfying stakeholder needs. Understanding that when consumers purchase a product or service it not only improves their lives, but those who work for the company and the environment builds a sense of community around the brand and strengthens close relationships with integrity.

While conscious capitalism still pursues a profit, it does so in light of stakeholder needs. Conscious capitalism goes beyond standalone programs and it promotes an ongoing, integrated approach to social responsibility, self-awareness, and purposeful decision making.

Northeastern University describes the framework of conscious capitalism using four guiding principles.[40]

1. *Higher purpose:* While profits are essential for a sustainable business, conscious capitalism focuses on purpose beyond profit.
2. *Stakeholder orientation:* Conscious companies operate with their entire business ecosystems in mind, meaning they concentrate on optimizing equal values for all of their stakeholders.
3. *Conscious leadership:* With a "we" rather than a "me" mentality, conscious leaders embrace the company's purpose, create value for all stakeholders, and inspire actions that contribute to a conscious culture.
4. *Conscious culture:* Conscious capitalism contributes to a culture of trust, care, and cooperation among the company's employees and all other stakeholders.

The logical question to ask is whether any companies are following the conscious capitalism framework. As would be expected, Whole Foods does. Their website is quite explicit on what it means:

> *Whole Foods Market's purpose is to nourish people and the planet. We realize that selling high quality food is not enough, that we also have a responsibility to the people, communities, and environment where we source and sell our products. We make our decisions based on this stakeholder model. Making sure we consider and balance the needs of all the stakeholders in our business.*

Models of CSR

Corporate Governance Models typically include those with a shareholder-orientation or those that emphasize the needs of stakeholders that can include shareholders, customers, employees, the community, and others who benefit from ethical corporate governance systems. These models link to the rights and duties of officers and directors that should reflect the type of model in effect. **Exhibit 1** that was presented in the Introduction depicts their role in decision making.

Economic Model

A business exists to serve the interests of society. This may mean to produce goods and services needed, create jobs, and providing wealth for investors. The economic model of CSR holds that businesses' sole social responsibility is to fulfill the economic functions they were designed to serve. As R. Edward Freemen points out, managers are employees, or agents, of those owners and must work to further the owners' interests. He identifies this perspective as the dominant model of CSR and refers to it as "managerial capitalism."[41]

The economic model of CSR places the shareholders at the center of the corporation and the ethical responsibility of management is to serve those shareholders. Specifically, managers have a primary responsibility to pursue profit within the law. Nobel Prize-winning economist Milton Friedman's classic 1970 *New York Times* article, "The Social Responsibility of Business is to Increase Profits," argues for the economic model.

Some critics contend that Friedman ignored the ethical dimension of business in his statement: "There is one and only one social responsibility of business—to use its resources and engage in activities to increase profits so long as it stays within the rules of the game, which is to say, engages in open and free competition without deception or fraud."[42] Friedman certainly recognized the importance of staying within the law. Beyond that, it may seem Friedman's statement implies that decisions that are not driven by fraud or deception are likely to be ethical decisions. Perhaps, but there's more to it than that interpretation. Specifically, we should question whether it's ethical to cut wages in order to maximize profits. There's no deception or fraud, but is it right to harm another to accomplish one's self-interest goals? Is this end justify the means approach ethical when employees work hard, haven't had a pay raise for five years, and must contend with rising consumer prices?

Did Friedman intend to recognize the moral responsibilities of business and somehow link them to profit-making activities? Hartmann et al. believe so. They state that contrary to popular belief, Friedman does not ignore ethical responsibilities in his analysis but suggested that managers fulfill their ethical responsibility by increasing shareholder wealth and pursuing profit.[43] In other words, so long as shareholder wealth and profitability increase or are benefited by managers' actions, the corporation has met its ethical responsibilities to society. But what happens when laws are passed that impose costs on business and do not increase profits, yet they have an ethical basis to them? Does that mean the company can't meet its ethical responsibilities to shareholders?

A good example is the Sarbanes-Oxley Act (SOX) that was enacted into law on July 30, 2002. Section 404 of the Law imposes significant costs on business to develop internal controls to help prevent and detect wrongful behavior, including fraud, and to minimize the risk that CEOs and CFOs will sign off on financial statements that contain material misstatements. A study by Charles River Associates in 2004 shows that on average, companies in the sample were estimated to have spent $7.8 million each to implement Section 404, including $1.9 million of audit and compliance fees. Some business leaders observed that the costs of compliance exceed the benefits in terms of improved internal control systems over financial reporting and they have urged regulators to modify the implementation rules to reduce the costs associated with Section 404.[44] Of course, determining the benefits is no easy task because how can we know the "savings" by having in place strong controls that cut down on instances of fraud? It is worth noting that compliance costs have been decreasing for many companies that have implemented COSO's *Internal Control - Integrated Framework*. More will be said about that later.

Stakeholder Model

A second perspective on CSR is known as the stakeholder model. The stakeholder model takes a broader view than the shareholder model and recognizes that business exists to create value for a range of parties, including employees, customers, suppliers, and communities as well as investors and stockholders. Business managers have responsibilities to all those who have a stake in the success or failure of the company, not only those who have invested financially.[45]

Freeman's version of stakeholder theory is widely recognized as the most influential. Stakeholder theory begins by recognizing that every business decision affects a wide variety of people, benefiting some and imposing costs on others. Think about the Volkswagen case discussed in **Chapter 2**. The decision makers probably thought the company would benefit by not having to redesign the diesel engines to meet pollution requirements. Most likely they thought profits would be higher as a result. Beyond that, the costs were more significant since customers were cheated, communities were harmed, and, ultimately, shareholder value was lost.[46]

Stakeholder theory recognizes that every business decision imposes costs on someone that must be recognized. A manager who seeks to maximize profits is imposing costs on employees, consumers, and suppliers because the maximization is, typically, driven by price increases or cost reductions. The dominant economic model argues that these costs are justified because management owes an ethical duty to shareholders. The stakeholder model acknowledges this but argues that other ethical duties have an equal claim on managerial decision making.[47]

Examples of CSR

The Case of the Ford Pinto

Even though it is now decades old, the case of the Ford Pinto illustrates a classic example of how a company can make a fatal mistake in its decision making by failing to consider the interests of the stakeholders adequately. The failure was due to total reliance on utilitarian thinking instead of the universality perspective of rights theory, to the detriment of the driving public and society in general. **Exhibit 3.8** provides background on the case.

EXHIBIT 3.8   Background on Ford Pinto Case

The Pinto was Ford Motor Company's first domestic North American subcompact automobile, marketed beginning on September 11, 1970. It competed with the AMC Gremlin and Chevrolet Vega, along with imports from makes such as Volkswagen, Datsun, and Toyota. The Pinto was popular in sales, with 100,000 units delivered by January 1971, and was also offered as a wagon and Runabout hatchback. Its reputation suffered over time, however, especially from a controversy surrounding the safety of its gas tank.

The public was shocked to find out that if the Pinto cars experienced an impact at speeds of only 30 miles per hour or less, they might become engulfed in flames, and passengers could be burned or even die. Ford faced an ethical dilemma: what to do about the apparently unsafe gas tanks that seemed to be the cause of these incidents. At the time, the gas tanks were routinely placed behind the license plate, so a rear-end collision was more likely to cause an explosion (whereas today's gas tanks are placed on the side of the vehicle). However, the federal safety standards at the time did not address this issue, so Ford was in compliance with the law. Ford's initial response was based on ethical legalism—the company complied with all the laws and safety problems, so it was under no obligation to take any action.

Eventually, Ford did use ethical analysis to develop a response. It used a risk–benefit analysis to aid decision making. This was done because the National Highway Traffic Safety Administration (NHTSA) excused a defendant from being penalized if the monetary costs of making a production change were greater than the "societal benefit" of that change. The analysis followed the same approach modeled after Judge Learned Hand's ruling in *United States v. Carroll Towing* in 1947 that boiled the theory of negligence down to the following: If the expected harm exceeded the cost to prevent it, the defendant was obligated to take the precaution, and if he (or it, in the case of a company) did not, liability would result. But if the cost was larger than the expected harm, the defendant was not expected to take the precaution. If there was an accident, the defendant would not be found guilty.[48] A summary of the Ford analysis follows.

FORD'S RISK–BENEFIT ANALYSIS[49]

Benefits of Fixing the Pintos

Savings: 180 burn deaths, 180 serious burn injuries, 2,100 burned vehicles

Unit cost: $200,000 per death (figure provided by the government); $67,000 per burn injury and $700 to repair a burned vehicle (company estimates)

Total benefits: 180 × ($200,000) + 180 × ($67,000) + 2,100 × ($700) = **$49.5 million**

Costs of Fixing the Pintos

Sales: 11 million cars, 1.5 million light trucks

Unit cost: $11 per car, $11 per light truck

Total cost: 11,000,000 × ($11) + 1,500,000 × ($11) = **$137 million**

Based on this analysis and other considerations, including not being required by law to change its product design, Ford decided not to change the placement of the fuel tank.

Ford's risk–benefit analysis relied only on act-utilitarian reasoning, an approach that ignores the rights of various stakeholders. A rule-utilitarian approach might have led Ford to follow the rule "Never sacrifice public safety." A rights theory approach would have led to the same conclusion, based on the reasoning that the driving public has an ethical right to expect that their cars will not blow up if there is a crash at low speeds.

In the aftermath of the scandal, it is interesting to consider whether any of the Ford executives who were involved in the decision-making process would have predicted in advance that they would have made such an unethical choice. Dennis Gioia, who was in charge of recalling defective automobiles at Ford, did not advocate ordering a recall. Gioia eventually came to view his decision not to recall the Pinto as a moral failure—what De Cremer and Tenbrunsel call a failure to think outside his prevailing background narrative or script at the point of decision. "My own schematized (scripted) knowledge influenced me to perceive recall issues in terms of the prevailing decision environment and to unconsciously overlook key features of the Pinto case . . . mainly because they did not fit an existing script." While personal morality was very important to Gioia, he admits that the framing narrative of his workplace "did not include ethical dimension."[50] The moral mistake was that there were other, better choices that he could have made—albeit ones outside the purview of Gioia's framing narrative.

LESSONS LEARNED?

Has the automobile industry learned a lesson from Ford's experience with the Pinto? The answer is an unequivocal no. We've learned about the VW defeat device case, and here is another example of moral blindness by a supplier of parts to an automobile company.

On September 1, 2017, Honda agreed to a $605 million so-called economic loss settlement covering up to 16.5 million U.S. vehicles with potentially faulty Takata air bag inflators. The settlement covers damages linked to inflators, including claims that vehicles were inaccurately represented to be safe, and that buyers had overpaid for cars with defective or substandard air bags. At least 18 deaths and 180 injuries worldwide have been tied to the defect that led to Takata filing for bankruptcy protection. At the time of this writing, 19 automakers had recalled more than 42 million vehicles in the largest auto safety callback in history. Takata expects 125 million vehicles worldwide will eventually be recalled due to its defect-prone inflators.[51] Various reports indicate that Honda and Takata knew about the faulty inflators since 2004 but failed to notify the National Highway Traffic Safety Administration in previous recalls (which began in 2008) that the affected airbags actually ruptured or were linked to injuries or deaths.

Impact of Governmental Regulations

LO 3-6

Explain how the provisions of the Sarbanes-Oxley Act relate to corporate governance, including relationships with key parties.

Corporate Governance Structures and Relationships

In response to accounting scandals at Enron and WorldCom that caused huge losses to shareholders and led to a crisis of confidence in the financial markets, the U.S. Congress adopted the SOX in 2002. **Exhibit 3.9** summarizes the key requirements under SOX.[52]

EXHIBIT 3.9   Summary of Key Requirements of SOX

Section 301

Section 301 requires publicly traded corporations to "establish procedures" for accepting employee complaints (both anonymously and nonanonymously) concerning "questionable accounting or auditing matters." Section 301 also requires independent audit committees to oversee the procedures for receiving and handling confidential whistle-blower reports including (1) the receipt, retention, and treatment of reports received by the issuer regarding accounting, internal accounting controls, or auditing matters and (2) the confidential, anonymous submission by employees of the issuer of concerns regarding questionable accounting or auditing matters.

Section 302

Section 302 requires that principal executive and financial officers certify that they have reviewed the findings of annual or quarterly reports, and find the statements within to be accurate and free of any material errors. Those officers, normally the CEO and CFO, must also certify that they understand their responsibility for creating and monitoring internal controls within their organization, and have evaluated the effectiveness of those controls within 90 days prior to the report being issued.

Section 404

Section 404 requires public companies to include in their annual reports a report of management on the company's internal control over financial reporting. The internal control report must include a statement of management's responsibility for establishing and maintaining adequate internal control over financial reporting for the company and management's assessment of the effectiveness of those controls. The external auditor must evaluate management's conclusions and issue its own report on the assessment of internal controls.

Section 406

Section 406 outlines code of ethics requirements for senior financial officers. A code for financial officers comprises the standards necessary to promote honest and ethical conduct; full, fair, accurate, timely, and understandable disclosure in periodic reports; and compliance with applicable governmental rules and regulations.

Section 806

Section 806 links to section 12 of the Securities Exchange Act of 1934 and prohibits "any officer, employee, contractor, subcontractor, or agent of such company" to "discharge, demote, suspend, threaten, harass, or in any other manner discriminate against an employee in the terms and conditions of employment because of any lawful act done by the employee. This includes providing information concerning any conduct which the employee reasonably believes constitutes a violation of any rule or regulation of the SEC, or any provision of federal law relating to fraud against shareholders, when the information or assistance is provided to or the investigation is conducted by federal officials, members of Congress, and "a person with supervisory authority over the employee (or such other person working for the employer who has the authority to investigate, discover, or terminate misconduct.)"

SOX also establishes the Public Company Accounting Oversight Board (PCAOB) to: (1) oversee the audit of public companies that are subject to the securities laws; (2) establish audit report standards and rules; and (3) inspect, investigate, and enforce compliance on the part of registered public accounting firms, their associated persons, and certified public accountants. PCAOB also establishes (or modifies) the auditing and related attestation standards, quality control, and the ethics standards used by registered public accounting firms to prepare and issue audit reports.

Section 906

Section 906 requires a "written statement by the CEO and CFO (or equivalent thereof) of the issuer that the periodic report containing the financial statements fully complies with the requirements of section 13(a) or 15(d) of the Securities Exchange Act of 1934, *and* that information contained in the periodic report fairly presents, in all material respects, the financial condition and results of operations of the issuer."

The section requires a certification that is broader than the typical outside auditor's report, which generally states that the company's financials are fairly presented in all material respects in accordance with GAAP. Any individual who "certifies any 906 statement *knowing* that the periodic report accompanying the statement does not comport with all the 906 requirements shall be fined not more than $1,000,000 or imprisoned not more than 10 years, or both." For any person who "*willfully* certifies" such a statement "knowing" that it does not comply, the penalties are much higher, up to $5 million and/or 20 years.

False Certifications of Financial Statements

There have been very few cases of false certifications of financial statements under section 302 and 906 of SOX that have led to sanctions by the SEC. In fact, perhaps the best-known case is one of failure to impose sanctions when sanctions were warranted. Richard Scrushy, the former HealthSouth Corporation CEO, falsely certified the financial statements of the company that had a $2.8 billion accounting fraud but was not sent to jail for that crime. On the other hand, HealthSouth CFO Weston L. Smith was sentenced in 2005 to 27 months in prison for his role in the fraud. Smith had pleaded guilty to one count each of conspiracy to commit wire and securities fraud, falsely certifying a financial report, and falsifying a report to the SEC.

The SEC's disclosure on July 30, 2014, of an enforcement action against two corporate executives of a small Florida-based computer equipment company exemplifies the type of emerging theory of fraud it is now pursuing. The commission went after both the CEO and CFO of Quality Services Group Inc. (QSGI) solely for alleged misrepresentations in public disclosures about the company's internal controls environment, which are required by SOX.

The SEC alleged that QSGI's CEO (Marc Sherman) and former CFO (Edward Cummings) knew of significant internal controls issues in the company's inventory practices that they failed to disclose to auditors and investors. Central to the SEC's theory of fraud is that Sherman and Cummings (1) signed Form 10-Ks (annual financial statements filed with the SEC) with management reports on internal controls that falsely omitted issues and (2) signed certifications in which they falsely represented that they had evaluated the management report on internal controls and disclosed all significant deficiencies to auditors.[53]

The SEC found that Sherman falsely certified in the certifications attached to the Forms 10-K and 10-K/A for the fiscal year December 31, 2008, and 10-Q (quarterly statements) forms for the quarter ended March 31, 2009, respectively, that he had: (1) evaluated QSGI's internal controls over financial reporting and (2) disclosed all significant deficiencies to the external auditors which were reasonably likely to adversely affect QSGI's ability to record, process, summarize, and report financial information. As a result, Sherman violated Securities Exchange Act Rule 13a-14 by signing false Section 302 certifications. Sherman was sanctioned by the SEC and prohibited from committing or causing any future violations of specified Securities Exchange Act rules, prohibited for five years from acting as an officer or director of any issuer that has a class of securities registered under the Exchange Act, and ordered to pay a civil monetary penalty in the amount of $7,500.[54]

So, the question in the end is, why have there not been more prosecutions under Sections 302 and 906? Allison Frankel believes that the answer may lie partly in how corporations have responded to SOX. Most major corporations have implemented internal compliance systems that make it very difficult to show that the CEO or CFO knowingly signed a false certification. When prosecutors have enough evidence to show that those internal systems failed and top executives knowingly engaged in wrongdoing, they often prefer, for strategic reasons, to charge crimes other than false certification.[55]

After SOX was passed, most large corporations put in place multiple layers of subcertification, requiring lower-level officials to attest to the accuracy of financial reports all the way up the chain of command to the CEO and CFO. The subcertifications forces corporations to be more vigilant about financial reporting at all levels but it also insulates CEOs and CFOs from false certification charges.

The SEC seems to be going after CFOs now because they typically mastermind financial frauds. Emboldened by legislative expansions of liability for financial executives under SOX and Dodd-Frank, the SEC increasingly is pursuing claims against CFOs that do not allege actual wrongdoing. It does so by alleging that the CFO's subordinates violated securities laws and that the CFO either certified the resulting reports or failed to implement adequate internal safeguards.

Relationships between Audit Committee, Internal Auditors, and External Auditors

The corporate governance systems previously discussed include the responsibilities of internal auditors, audit committees, and the external auditors all of which are charged with ensuring that the financial statements are free of material misstatements including fraud and present fairly the financial position, net income, and cash flows. Internal controls exist to support reliable financial statements that comply with the rules of the accounting profession including GAAP, generally accepted auditing standards, which is discussed in **Chapter 5**, and the ethical provisions in the AICPA Code of Professional Conduct that is discussed in **Chapter 4**. Refer back to **Exhibit 3.1** to see the flow of information through the corporate governance system.

Following the passage of SOX, the audit committee was seen as the one body that was (or at least should be) capable of preventing identified fraudulent financial reporting. The audit committee has an oversight responsibility for the financial statements. The internal auditors should have direct and unrestricted access to the audit committee so that they can take any matters of concern directly to that group without having to go through top management. The external auditors rely on the support and actions of the audit committee to resolve differences with management over proper financial reporting. The goal of such relationships should be to establish an ethical corporate culture that supports good corporate governance. **Exhibit 3.10** depicts the ideal relationship between the internal auditors and audit committee. The framework is identified in the Treadway Commission Report titled *Report of the National Commission on Fraudulent Financial Reporting.*[56]

EXHIBIT 3.10   Internal Control Environment—"Corporate Culture"

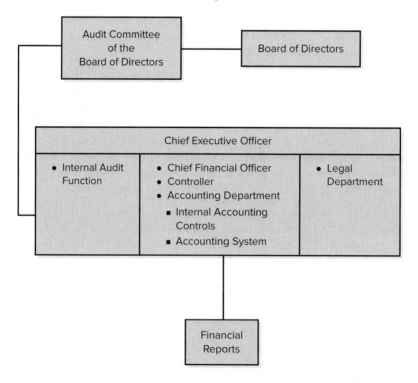

Audit Committee

In the accounting scandals of the early 2000s, the audit committee either didn't know about the fraud or chose to look the other way. A conscientious and diligent audit committee is an essential ingredient of an effective corporate governance system—one that takes its role in financial statement oversight to heart and follows basic principles of responsibility, accountability, and transparency.

An effective device to ensure audit committee independence is for the committee to meet separately with the senior executives, the internal auditors, and the external auditors. The perception of internal auditors as the "eyes and ears" of the audit committee suggests that the head of the internal audit department attend all audit committee meetings. Recall the role of Cynthia Cooper, the director of internal auditing at WorldCom. She informed the audit committee every step of the way as her department uncovered the fraud, and ultimately, she gained the support of the external auditors.

The audit committee's duties include: (1) monitor the integrity of the financial statements; (2) review any formal announcements relating to the company's financial performance; (3) review significant financial reporting judgments contained in the statements and performance statements; (4) review the company's internal financial controls and risk management procedures; (5) monitor the effectiveness of the company's internal audit function; (6) review the company's whistleblower processes and compliance program; and (7) review and monitor the external auditor's independence and objectivity and the effectiveness of the audit process.

The audit committee should also seek assurances from the CEO and CFO, as part of the CEO/CFO financial statement certification process under Sections 302 and 906 of SOX, that they have put in place effective disclosure controls and procedures to ensure that all reports have been prepared and filed properly with the appropriate authorities in accordance with applicable requirements.

SOX calls on audit committees to create formal procedures to collect, track, and process hotline claims received by the issuer company related to accounting, internal controls, or auditing matters. Additionally, SOX holds audit committees responsible for establishing a channel for employees to submit confidential, anonymous concerns regarding questionable accounting or auditing matters through the whistleblower hotline. However, the legislation did not provide prescriptive guidance for establishing effective whistleblower programs. Because the SEC has not mandated specific processes and procedures, the audit committee plays a critical role in determining the processes appropriate for its organization.

Internal Auditors

Internal auditors interact with top management and, as such, should assist them to fulfill their role in developing accurate and reliable financial statements, ensure the effectiveness of internal control systems, and monitor compliance with laws and regulations. Specific obligations include: (1) monitor corporate governance activities and compliance with organization policies; (2) review effectiveness of the organization's code of ethics and whistleblower provisions; (3) assess audit committee effectiveness and compliance with regulations; and (4) oversee internal controls and risk management processes. Internal auditors should provide objective assurance on how effectively the organization assesses and manages its risks. A growing area of importance is to provide assurance with data security and privacy controls as will be discussed below in the Equifax data breach.

External Auditors

External auditors have an obligation to the public interest that underlies their corporate governance responsibilities. One of the primary roles of external auditors in corporate governance is protecting the interests of shareholders. This is possible because external audits should be conducted independent of any influence of management or the board of directors of the company. External audits should be designed to introduce a measure of accountability into the financial reporting process.

The PCAOB has recognized the importance of two-way communication between audit committees and external auditors with the adoption of Auditing Standard No. 16, *Communications with Audit Committees* ("AS 16"). Required communications include:

- Matters relating to the company's accounting policies and practices, including why certain accounting policies and practices are considered critical.

- Estimates made by management and the process used to develop these estimates, including significant changes to the process used by management to develop estimates, reasons for the changes, and the effects on the financial statements.

- The auditor's judgment about the quality of the entity's financial reporting, including the auditor's evaluation of and conclusions about the qualitative aspects of the company's significant accounting policies and practices. Auditors should also discuss significant unusual transactions and their opinion on the business rationale thereof.

- Whether the audit committee is aware of matters relevant to the audit including, but not limited to, violations or potential violations of laws or regulations, including fraud risks.

A company's audit committee is the primary link between the board of directors, management, and the independent auditors. Improving communication among these parties will play a vital role in improving the overall value of the audit for all stakeholders.

Internal Controls as a Monitoring Device

The internal controls that are established by management should help prevent and detect fraud, including materially false and misleading financial reports, asset misappropriations, and inadequate disclosures in the financial statements. These controls are designed to ensure that management policies are followed, laws are strictly adhered to, and ethical systems are built into corporate governance.

The internal control report required by Section 404 of SOX must include a statement of management's responsibility for establishing and maintaining adequate internal control over financial reporting for the company, management's assessment of the effectiveness of the company's internal control over financial reporting as of the end of the company's most recent fiscal year, a statement identifying the framework used by management to evaluate the effectiveness of the company's internal control over financial reporting, and a statement that the registered public accounting firm that audited the company's financial statements included in the annual report has issued an attestation report on management's assessment of the company's internal control over financial reporting.

An internal control system, no matter how well conceived and operated, can provide only reasonable—not absolute—assurance to management and the board of directors regarding achievement of an entity's objectives. The likelihood of achievement is affected by a variety of factors including: judgments in decision making can be faulty; breakdowns can occur due to simple mistakes and errors in the application of controls; and controls can be circumvented by the collusion of two or more people. Management override of internal controls may be a problem as well, similar to what happened at Enron and WorldCom. Indeed, the ACFE Fraud Survey found that organizations that lacked internal controls were more susceptible to asset misappropriation schemes, while corruption schemes more often involved an override of existing controls. Further, a poor tone at the top was much more likely to contribute to a financial statement fraud scheme than either of the other two categories of occupational fraud.

COSO Framework

The system of internal controls and whether it operates as intended enables the auditor to either gain confidence about the internal processing of transactions or create doubt for the auditor that should be pursued. *Internal Control—Integrated Framework,* published by the Committee of Sponsoring Organizations (COSO) of the Treadway Commission in 1992, establishes a framework that defines internal control as a process, effected by an entity's board of directors, management, and other personnel, designed to provide reasonable assurance regarding the achievement of the following objectives: (1) effectiveness and efficiency of operations; (2) reliability of financial reporting; and (3) compliance with applicable laws and regulations.[57]

The COSO report states that management should enact five components related to these objectives as part of the framework: (1) the control environment; (2) risk assessment; (3) control activities; (4) monitoring; and (5) information and communication. Each component is described in **Exhibit 3.11**.

EXHIBIT 3.11   Components of the COSO Framework

1. The *control environment* sets the tone of an organization, influencing the control consciousness of its people. It is the foundation for all aspects of internal control, providing discipline and structure.
2. *Risk assessment* is the entity's identification and evaluation of how risk might affect the achievement of objectives.
3. *Control activities* are the strategic actions established by management to ensure that its directives are carried out.
4. *Monitoring* is a process that assesses the efficiency and effectiveness of internal controls over time.
5. *Information and communication* systems provide the information in a form and at a time that enables people to carry out their responsibilities.

COSO updated the framework in 2013 that acknowledges that there are limitations related to a system of internal control. For example, certain events or conditions are beyond an organization's control, and no system of internal control will always do what it was designed to do. Controls are performed by people and are subject to human error, uncertainties in judgment, management override, and their circumvention due to collusion. An effective system of internal control recognizes their inherent limitations and addresses ways to minimize these risks by the design, implementation, and conduct of the system of internal control. However, an effective system will not eliminate these risks. An effective system of internal control (and an effective system of internal control over financial reporting) provides reasonable assurance, not absolute assurance, that the entity will achieve its defined operating, reporting, and compliance objectives.[58]

Enterprise Risk Management

In 2001, COSO initiated a project, and engaged PwC, to develop a framework that would be readily usable by managements to evaluate and improve their organizations' enterprise risk management. The need was there following a large number of business scandals born out of a failure of internal controls, corporate governance systems, and risk management.

According to the report, enterprise risk management enables management to effectively deal with uncertainty and associated risk and opportunity, enhancing the capacity to build value. Value is maximized when management sets strategy and objectives to strike an optimal balance between growth and return goals and related risks and efficiently and effectively deploys resources in pursuit of the entity's objectives. Of particular importance, enterprise risk management encompasses[59]:

- Aligning risk appetite and strategy—Management considers the entity's risk appetite in evaluating strategic alternatives, setting related objectives, and developing mechanisms to manage related risks.
- Enhancing risk response decisions—Enterprise risk management provides the rigor to identify and select among alternative risk responses—risk avoidance, reduction, sharing, and acceptance.

Deloitte discusses the value of risk management by pointing out that management and the Board of Directors must know beforehand the firm's capacity for risk-taking, the previously specified amount of different risks they want the firm to take, and the current and targeted risk profile relative to the desired level and capacity–to be able to evaluate and take action. This is the essence of what a risk appetite framework can do for an organization. Information needs to flow up to the Board and be presented in a timely way that drives decision making.[60]

The capabilities inherent in enterprise risk management help management achieve the entity's performance and profitability targets and prevent loss of resources. Enterprise risk management helps ensure effective reporting and compliance with laws and regulations and helps avoid damage to the entity's reputation and associated consequences. In sum, enterprise risk management helps an entity get to where it wants to go and avoid pitfalls and surprises along the way.

COSO updated its enterprise risk management positions in *ERM Framework, Enterprise Risk Management–Integrating with Strategy and Performance.* The September 2017 revisions to the ERM framework highlight the importance of enterprise risk management in strategic planning. According to COSO's Chair, Robert B. Hirth Jr., COSO's "overall goal is to encourage a risk-conscious culture." PwC developed the framework and according to Miles Everson, PwC's Global Advisory Leader and Engagement Leader: "The Framework addresses the evolution of ERM, the benefits that can be achieved, and the need for organizations to improve their approach to managing risk."[61]

Drilling down on the Framework with respect to corporate culture, ERM suggests that each entity should link its culture—shared behaviors, emotions, and mindsets in the organization—to its strategy and risk appetite. The problem here is the ERM framework does not place sufficient emphasis on the ethical dimension of making strategic decisions opting, instead, for a focus on the entity's "hunger" for risk in terms of its strategic objectives. This tail-wagging-the-dog approach to developing an ethical culture allows management to create a culture in each situation after first determining its willingness to accept risk in developing strategic activities. Our concern is this approach sounds too much like ethical relativism because it allows each entity to define its own risk appetite rather than creating a standard built on ethical values.

Equifax Data Breach

In September 2017, Equifax disclosed that a flaw in a tool designed to build web applications created a security breach that had occurred two months prior and hackers gained access to its data. Some of the information hackers had access to included names, social security numbers, birth dates, addresses, and some driver's license numbers. The tool is called Apache Struts, and it's used by many large businesses and government organizations. A cybersecurity arm of the U.S. Department of Homeland Security "identified and disclosed" the flaw in March 2017, according to an Equifax statement. The company's security department "was aware of this vulnerability at that time, and took efforts to identify and to patch any vulnerable systems." Yet, the company admitted that hackers exploited the flaws months later. Equifax was widely criticized for waiting almost two months to alert its customers and shareholders about the hack.[62]

Congress conducted hearings to discover why the breach occurred and why it took so long for the company to inform the public about the hack of the personal information of 143 million consumers. Equifax responded by announcing that its chief information officer and chief security officer were "retiring," and that was followed by the chief executive and two other senior managers. An investigative journalist and accounting professor analyzed the Equifax data breach and gave her views about the event, which are summarized in **Exhibit 3.12**.

EXHIBIT 3.12   Views of Experts on the Equifax Data Breach

Francine McKenna, an investigative journalist who covers the accounting and auditing profession and writes a column called the *Dig* and is an Adjunct Professor at the American University, points out that a company's external auditor is supposed to be an objective independent watchdog, the first line of defense for shareholders and the public when company executives and the board fail to protect them. She explains that even before the external auditors, Ernst & Young (EY), audited the financial statements of Equifax, it should have made sure the company executives set the right "tone at the top" about controls, including of its information technology systems. This was necessary to ensure Equifax was protecting its biggest asset—the consumer information it sells to banks and other organizations, which generates most of its revenues.[63]

Was EY asleep at the wheel? It was aware that the SEC had scrutinized Equifax for inadequate disclosures of its cyber risk and poor overall disclosure controls. That was based on correspondence between the SEC and Equifax CEO and CFO dating from 2011 to 2014. In January 2014, the SEC asked Equifax's CEO about inadequate disclosures regarding a material weakness in internal controls over financial reporting in 2013. In its response, Equifax provided the SEC with a detailed timeline of its evaluation of the control weaknesses and concluded that its interim quarter disclosure controls were also ineffective. McKenna points out that EY's audit partner for Equifax was copied on the response to the SEC from the company's controller, along with the rest of the company's top executives. Therefore, it appears, EY knew about the data security problems but did nothing about it.

In yet another embarrassing event for Equifax management, the U.S. Department of Justice (DOJ) announced in September 2017 that it had opened a criminal investigation into Equifax officials' stock sales just before the public disclosure of the security breach. DOJ is considering whether officials dumped nearly $1.8 million in stock just after the company discovered the breach and one month before it was announced. The company maintains the officials didn't know about the breach when they sold the stock. The SEC also announced it is investigating the possibility of insider trading.

The Equifax scandal raises some important questions in light of our discussion about internal controls, risk assessment, and the role of the internal auditors and audit committee in the data breach fiasco. A few items to consider are:

- External auditors rely on the work of internal auditors. What steps did Equifax's internal auditors take to ensure the information technology systems were operating as intended? Did it communicate this matter with the audit committee? The external auditors?

- Did the EY auditors adequately consider whether problems with the information security systems also affected the internal control systems thereby raising doubts whether the financial statements did or did not contain any material misstatements? A problem in one area of the audit heightens the possibility of problems in other areas.

- Did the company (i.e., CEO and CFO) adequately consider the controls when they certified under Section 302 that the internal controls over financial reporting were operating as intended?

- Should the SEC go after top officials of Equifax to claw back some of its executive compensation during the period nothing was done about the data breach even though the company was well aware of it?

The Equifax case illustrates what can happen when management seeks to protect its own interests and that of the company without regard to its responsibilities to consumers and the public. The audit deficiencies seem to be a fallout of the fraud. One concern we have is whether the EY auditors made a good faith attempt to understand information technology controls and how they may have influenced the internal controls over financial reporting.

We also are concerned about the role that "risk tolerance" may have played in the company's evaluations. The ERM document says that each entity should link its culture to its strategy and risk appetite, focusing on its "hunger" for risk. Does this mean that Equifax might have, knowingly or unknowingly, decided the risk of a data breach was acceptable because its risk tolerance was very high?

Whistleblowing

LO 3-7

Discuss whistleblowing procedures under Dodd-Frank and concerns about the program.

There is a symbiotic relationship between whistleblowing and an organization's culture. Effective internal whistleblowing processes are an important part of a healthy corporate culture. Internal auditors have a critical role to play in monitoring whistleblowing procedures, given the nature of internal control. The audit committee should ensure that matters of concern are raised through appropriate channels and promptly dealt with. Whistleblowing should be part of the internal control environment and an effective corporate governance system.

There is no one set definition of whistleblowing, although most definitions characterize the practice as disclosing to others in an organization an action that violates organizational norms or the law. Near and Miceli take a broad view of whistleblowing as "the disclosure by organization members (former or current) of illegal, immoral, or illegitimate practices under the control of their employers, to persons or organizations that may be able to effect action."[64] This definition includes whistleblowers who use internal channels (e.g., a hotline or ombudsperson) or external channels (e.g., the external auditors or the SEC) to blow the whistle. They identify four elements of the whistleblowing process: the whistleblower, the whistleblowing act or complaint, the party to whom the complaint is made, and the organization against which the complaint is lodged. In discussing the act itself, they label it as an act of "dissidence" somewhat analogous to civil disobedience.[65]

Morality of Whistleblowing

Given that the act of whistleblowing is a personal choice, the key to whether an individual will blow the whistle on wrongdoing is whether the whistleblower perceives organizational policies are designed to encourage moral autonomy, individual responsibility, and organizational support for whistleblowers.

Whistleblowing always involves an actual or at least declared intention to prevent something bad that would otherwise occur. It always involves information that would not ordinarily be revealed. Most ethicists agree whistleblowing is an ethical action. According to the "standard theory" on whistleblowing of Michael Davis, whistleblowing is morally required when it is required at all; people have a moral obligation to prevent serious harm to others if they can do so with little costs to themselves.[66]

DeGeorge analyzes when whistleblowing is a moral act. His starting position is based on the universal ethical principle that "corporations have a moral obligation not to harm." DeGeorge identifies five criteria when whistleblowing is morally permitted: (1) the firm's actions will do serious and considerable harm to others; (2) the whistleblowing act is justifiable once the employee reports it to her immediate supervisor and makes her moral concerns known; (3) absent any action by the supervisor, the employee should take the matter all the way up to the board, if necessary; (4) documented evidence must exist that would convince a reasonable and impartial observer that one's views of the situation is correct and that serious harm may occur; and (5) the employee must reasonably believe that going public will create the necessary change to protect the public and is worth the risk to oneself.[67]

DeGeorge's criteria establish the foundation for moral behavior to occur when contemplating whistleblowing. He rejects the position that external whistleblowing is *always* morally justifiable, and also rejects the position that external whistleblowing is *never* morally justifiable. Basically, his position is that the whistleblower should have a moral motivation to engage in the act (i.e., to expose unnecessary harm and illegal or immoral actions).

Rights and Duties

Researchers have posed the question of whether workplace whistleblowing is a right, and thus allows for responsible behavior, or whether it is an imposed corporate duty, thus resulting in liability of workers. If an organization institutes an internal whistleblowing policy, it is because it perceives moral autonomy to be weak so that employees need direction when and how whistleblowing should occur. When businesses then implement the policy, it leads to the conclusion that moral autonomy is strong, and employees are expected to blow the whistle.[68] Therefore, if employees do not blow the whistle in accordance with corporate policy, they then become liable for not doing so, rendering the policy a tool that controls employee behavior. Responsibility for misdeeds then shifts from the organization to the individual, and employees are further stripped of the right to moral autonomy.[69]

Miceli and Near's research has shown that what whistleblowers hope and believe their speaking out will achieve is the correction of what they perceive as an organizational wrongdoing (e.g., fraudulent financial statements). This research also found that not everyone who perceives a wrongdoing acts upon that perception. In fact, only 42 percent stated they were ready to blow the whistle. Those who observe wrongdoing but would not do so identify a "retaliatory climate" in their organizations as the primary barrier to blowing the whistle on corporate wrongdoing, while those who say they would speak up about it were confident that they "would not experience managerial retaliation if they blew the whistle."[70]

Whistleblowing regulations attempt to protect individuals when they behave responsibly toward society in light of irresponsible behavior by their organizations. This certainly is the motivation for the anti-retaliation provisions of both SOX and Dodd-Frank. The acknowledgement of the need for such protection, however, implies that moral agency, autonomy, and responsibility are problematic in organizations, or at the very least, that they do not come naturally and are not welcomed when they arrive. When organizations establish an ethical culture and anonymous channels to report wrongdoing, they create an environment that supports whistleblowing and whistleblowers while controlling for possible retaliation.[71]

According to the 2020 ACFE study, a variety of mechanisms are used to report improprieties. An interesting result is that telephone hotlines declined by nine percent between 2018 and 2020 while web-based reporting using an online form increased nine percent. The shift may be due to the relative ease of using an online form and/or perceived lessened stigma of doing so. **Exhibit 3.13** provides a summary of the mechanisms for reporting and the percent used by whistleblowers.

EXHIBIT 3.13   Whistleblower Reporting Mechanisms[72]

Mechanism	Percentage Reported
Telephone Hotline	33%
E-Mail	33%
Web-Based/Online Form	32%
Mailed Letter/Form	12%
Other	9%
Fax	1%

Whistleblower reporting methods vary from the direct supervisor (28%) to the external audit (1%). **Exhibit 3.14** details those reporting mechanisms and the percentage reported.

EXHIBIT 3.14   To Whom Did Whistleblowers Initially Report?

Reporting Method	Percentage Reported
Direct Supervisor	28%
Other	15%
Fraud Investigation Team	14%
Internal Audit	12%
Executive	11%
Coworker	10%
Law Enforcement or Regulator	7%
Owner	7%
Board or Audit Committee	6%
Human Resources	6%
In-House Counsel	4%
External Audit	1%

Reporting to the direct supervisor is the right thing to do and the expected reporting outlet under AICPA rules as will be discussed later. However, there is a U.S. Supreme Court ruling that will be discussed later as well that whistleblowers are not protected from retaliation under Dodd-Frank unless they report the matter to the SEC, even if they use internal channels. The importance of this ruling cannot be overstated as it implies that a whistleblower will forfeit their right to compensation under Dodd-Frank unless first reporting to the SEC. The problem is the direct supervisor and board of directors are not likely to support this approach as it places external reporting above internal reporting.

Anthony Menendez v. Halliburton, Inc.[73]

Doing the right thing and blowing the whistle does not always pay off and can be an arduous task. A case in point is what happened to Anthony Menendez in his whistleblowing ordeal with Halliburton. One day in February 2006, he received an e-mail from Halliburton's chief accounting officer, Mark McCollum, that was addressed to much of the accounting department. It read, "The SEC has opened an inquiry into the allegations of Mr. Menendez." Everyone was told to retain their documents until further notice. Menendez had been outed. Thus, began a nine-year ordeal to clear his name.

The key accounting issue was how to recognize revenue when goods are held for the customer in the seller's warehouse and not shipped pending customer request. Halliburton was engaging in "bill-and-hold" transactions. To meet the GAAP requirements to recognize revenue on these transactions, the following four criteria must be met: (1) the risks of ownership must have passed to the buyer; (2) delivery must be for a fixed date; (3) the seller must not retain any significant performance obligations; and (4) the goods or equipment must be complete and ready for shipment. Menendez knew the first criteria couldn't be met and in most cases neither could the second. All efforts to convince the company it was prematurely recognizing revenue were met with resistance because the company was under pressure to meet financial analysts' earnings projections. The KPMG auditors went along despite Menendez's efforts to convince them of the GAAP violation. Once he had been retaliated against, Menendez decided to lodge a complaint with the SEC under SOX.

The facts of the case are summarized in **Exhibit 3.15**. (An expanded version of this case with multiple areas for discussion appears in Case 3-8).

EXHIBIT 3.15   Accountant Takes on Halliburton and Wins

Tony Menendez was the Director of Technical Accounting Research and Training at Halliburton. Halliburton contracts with energy companies like Royal Dutch Shell and BP to find and exploit huge oil and gas fields. It sells services of its geologists and engineers who work intricate machinery that Halliburton built and sold to its customers. The company's accountants had been allowing the company to count the full value of the equipment right away as revenue, sometimes even before it had assembled the equipment. But the customers could walk away in the middle of the contracts. Menendez knew that if the equipment were damaged, Halliburton, not the customer, absorbed the loss. Menendez recommended the company wait until the work was completed to record the equipment sales as revenue.

Even though top Halliburton accounting executives, including Halliburton's chief accounting officer, Mark McCollum, agreed with Menendez's analysis, they didn't act to correct the accounting because of concern about its impact in slowing revenue growth. McCollum tried to dissuade Menendez by reminding him of the need to be a team player and that his persistence was not well received by colleagues. He told Menendez that the Halliburton team, working with the external auditors from KPMG, had reached a different conclusion. He also offered that Menendez shouldn't put things in writing and had to be more "circumspect about the use of e-mail to communicate." He finished by telling Menendez that he wasn't asking him to compromise his ethics and compromise the position he felt so strongly about.

Menendez waited to see what would happen. Given that billions in equipment sales were involved, he knew this was no trivial matter. Finally, in the fall he realized nothing would happen. Menendez agonized and several days later filed a confidential complaint with the SEC in November 2005.

He spoke to the SEC about the matter and was told to go to the audit committee. Menendez assumed the SEC would take action, but nothing seemed to occur, until February 4, 2006, when he heard the SEC was poking around.

Unbeknownst to Menendez, his complaint went to the Halliburton legal department as well as the board committee, an apparent violation of company policy. The audit committee was supposed to keep such reports confidential. A few days later, the SEC notified the company that it had opened an investigation into the company's revenue recognition. Then, the e-mail from McCollum got distributed. Halliburton's general counsel said "the SEC is investigating Mr. Menendez's complaints" to the company's chief financial officer, KPMG, other top executives, and McCollum. McCollum had forwarded it to at least 15 of Menendez's colleagues in accounting. As far as Halliburton was concerned, they had a traitor in their ranks.

The ramifications were immediate. Menendez was stripped of his responsibilities and became a pariah at the firm. Halliburton contracted with an outside law firm to conduct an "investigation." Not surprisingly, it cleared the company. The SEC informed Halliburton it would not bring any enforcement action against it.

Menendez went back to the SEC to no avail. The commission wouldn't even accept the documents he had provided. Finally, he felt he had to leave Halliburton having been punished for blowing the whistle. He brought a claim under SOX in May 2006 based on retaliation, but the government would not take up his case. He brought separate lawsuits, but lost. He persisted even when others told him he had no chance of prevailing. No one would take his case. Finally, he decided to represent himself in the appeals process. It went on for more than five years. In September 2011, the administrative laws appeals panel had ruled. It overturned the original trial judge.

> Halliburton appealed the reversal. Another two years went by and in April 2013, the appeals panel ruled that he had been retaliated against for blowing the whistle, just as he had argued all along.
>
> Menendez acted on principle in his quest for the truth. He only wanted to be proven right so he had asked for a token sum. The panel, noting the importance of punishing retaliations against whistleblowers, awarded him $30,000.

Menendez's case was filed before Dodd-Frank became effective. It is interesting to contemplate what might have happened had he filed a whistleblower claim under the act. Would he have been rewarded for his efforts?

Dodd-Frank Provisions

From time to time, accountants and auditors are faced with situations that motivate them to blow the whistle on financial wrongdoing. The provisions included in SOX, that were discussed in the previous section, provide a roadmap to whistleblowing that is depicted in Exhibit 3.1. The Dodd-Frank Wall Street Reform and Consumer Protection Act was adopted by Congress on January 5, 2010, and became effective on August 12, 2011.[74] It changes the regulatory landscape for internal accountants and auditors, and external auditors and auditing firms, by protecting whistleblowers that "voluntarily" provide the SEC with "original information" about a violation of federal securities laws that leads to a successful enforcement proceeding. Under the United States Code, the enforcement action must result in monetary sanctions of more than $1 million.[75]

Dodd-Frank defines a whistleblower as any individual who provides information to the SEC relating to a violation of the securities laws that has occurred, is ongoing, or is about to occur. *Voluntarily* means the whistleblower has provided information prior to the government, a self-regulatory organization, or the PCAOB asking for it directly from the whistleblower. Original information must be based upon the whistleblower's independent knowledge or independent analysis, not already known to the SEC and not derived exclusively from an allegation made in a judicial or administrative hearing or a governmental report, hearing, audit, or investigation.[76]

In December 2020, the SEC announced a change in how it determines the eligibility of whistleblowers for an award under Dodd-Frank to clarify what it means by original information. The new interpretation is that a whistleblower's tip has to offer insight "beyond what would be reasonably apparent" to the agency from publicly available information. This could make it harder for tipsters from outside a company to be awarded for their disclosure.

It appears the motivation for the rule change is to cut down on the number of tips the SEC receives. Through December 2020, the Commission had received a total of 40,200 tips since its inception. There is no doubt the volume of the tips stretches an already lean SEC budget. Still, that's not the best reason to change the standards.

The motivation of the whistleblower program should be to increase the likelihood that bad actors are caught and punished for their crimes. The idea that the information has to go beyond what a reasonable person might infer builds in a standard that is, at best, difficult to apply as is the case in any reasonable basis criteria. It smacks of ethical relativism and not to interpret a rule in a way that is responsive to the need of the public given it has a right to know about fraudulent reporting.

Under Section 922 of the Dodd-Frank Act, the award for whistleblowers (who meet the criteria) is "not less than 10 percent and not more than 30 percent, in total, of what has been collected of the monetary sanctions imposed in the section."[77] Kastiel believes the award incentivizes whistleblowing and provides a bounty hunter's payment for disclosing the relevant information to the SEC.[78] This raises the question: Is it ethical to provide financial incentives to motivate employees to come forward and report financial wrongdoing? This is not an easy question to answer.

One major concern with Dodd-Frank is that it may cause would-be whistleblowers to go external with the information rather than internally using the organization's prescribed reporting mechanisms. The disclosure of confidential information about clients raises questions about a possible violation of Section 1.320.001 of the AICPA Code and of state privilege laws.[79] The external disclosure of confidential information can, under certain circumstances, be treated as an exception to the rule if disclosure is linked to compliance with applicable laws and government regulations, which include Dodd-Frank. The act defines the circumstances under which the disclosure of confidential information by external auditors will not violate confidentiality and entails a good faith effort to get the company or client to alter the accounting that triggers the concern.

We believe that once the internal reporting process has played out and nothing has been done to correct for the wrongdoing, from an ethical perspective, external whistleblowing is the proper course of action, especially if it is the *only* way for the public to know. An employee should not fall victim to the bystander effect and assume others will report it. Along with knowledge comes the responsibility to correct wrongdoings, which is in the best long-term interests of the organization.

Internal Accountants' Eligibility

Under Dodd-Frank, internal accountants are excluded from receiving whistleblower awards because of their pre-existing legal duty to report securities violations.[80] This includes individuals with internal compliance or audit responsibilities at an entity who receive information about potential violations since it is part of their job responsibilities to report suspicion of illegal acts and fraud to management.

Internal accountants are eligible to become Dodd-Frank whistleblowers in three situations: (1) disclosure to the SEC is needed to prevent "substantial injury" to the financial interest of an entity or its investors; (2) the whistleblower "reasonably believes" the entity is impeding investigation of the misconduct (e.g., destroying documents or improperly influencing witnesses); or (3) the whistleblower has first reported the violation internally and at least 120 days have passed with no action.

The substantial injury provision does not require the whistleblower to reasonably believe that the entity might commit a "material violation"; rather, the whistleblower will generally only need to demonstrate that responsible management or governance personnel at the entity were aware of an "imminent violation" and were not taking steps to prevent it. The 120-day "look-back" period begins after the internal accountant or auditor either provided information of a possible violation to the relevant entity's management (i.e., audit committee, chief legal officer, or chief ethics and compliance officer), or at least 120 days have elapsed since the whistleblower received the information, if the whistleblower received it under circumstances indicating that these people were already aware of the information. The internal accountant cannot become eligible for a whistleblower award by learning of possible misconduct, realizing that those responsible for the entity's compliance are not aware of the possible misconduct, failing to provide the information to them, waiting for the 120-day period to run, and then reporting the information to the SEC (SEC 2010).[81]

External Auditor Eligibility

External auditors are generally prohibited from blowing the whistle on their clients because the information gained during a mandated audit would not be considered to derive from an individual's independent knowledge or analysis. The Dodd-Frank Act prohibits an external auditor who is already obligated to report information to the SEC from personally profiting from reporting that same information as a whistleblower. However, for auditors and their firms, the whistleblower rules allow the auditor or an employee associated with the auditor to make a whistleblower submission alleging that the firm failed to assess, investigate, or report wrongdoing in accordance with Section 10A or that the firm failed to follow other professional standards.

Section 10A of the Securities Exchange Act sets out prescribed steps to take before deciding whether to inform the SEC of fraud.

1. Determine whether the violations have a material effect, quantitatively or qualitatively, on the financial statements.
2. If yes, has management, or the board of directors, caused management to take remedial action, including reporting externally if necessary?
3. If no, then the auditor must make a formal report of its conclusions and provide the report to the board. The board then has one business day to inform the SEC and provide a copy of the communication to the external auditor. If the auditing firm does not receive a copy within one business day, then it has two choices:

    a. Provide a copy of its own report to the SEC within one business day, or

    b. Resign from the engagement and provide a copy of the report to the SEC within one business day of resigning.

If the whistleblower makes such a submission to the SEC based on the firm's failure to follow Section 10A, the whistle-blower will be able to obtain an award not only from a successful enforcement action against the auditing firm, but also from any successful action against the firm's engagement client. In allowing such claims, the goal of the SEC is to "help insure that wrongdoing by the [accounting] firm (or its employees) is reported on a timely fashion." According to the SEC, this goal is paramount "because of the important gatekeeper role that auditors play in the securities markets."[82]

Rosenthal and Smith point out that several members of the public accounting profession, including KPMG, Ernst & Young, PricewaterhouseCoopers, and the Center for Audit Quality, believe that permitting CPAs to obtain monetary rewards for blowing the whistle on their own firms' performance of services for clients could create several significant problems including: (1) undermining the ethical obligations of CPAs not to divulge confidential client information by providing a financial reward for whistleblowing; (2) harming the quality of external audits because client management might restrict access to client information for fear the financial incentive for whistleblowing could lead to reporting client-specific information to the SEC; (3) overriding the firms' internal reporting mechanisms for audit-related dis-agreements; and (4) incentivizing an individual to bypass existing programs to report disagreements including hot-lines.[83]

Integrity Considerations

The Integrity and Objectivity rule in the AICPA Code requires that "In the performance of any professional service, a member shall maintain objectivity and integrity, shall be free of conflicts of interest, and shall not knowingly misrepresent facts or subordinate their judgment to others [1.100.001]."[84] This rule includes subordination of judgment issues when differences of opinion exist either between an internal accountant and their supervisor within the client entity as well as differences between an external auditor and the audit firm. The process to follow is depicted in **Exhibit 3.16**.

If the internal accountant concludes that safeguards cannot eliminate or reduce the threats to integrity and objectivity to an acceptable level or other appropriate action was not taken, then the accountant should consider whether the relationship with the organization should be terminated including possibly resigning one's position. These steps are necessary to prevent subordination of judgment.

The ethical standards in the AICPA Code, SOX provisions, and Dodd-Frank reporting requirements are all part of a healthy corporate governance system. The rules provide the foundation for professional obligations and when to report differences within the corporate governance system. SOX provides steps to ensure the underlying features of a strong corporate governance system exist and are operating as intended. Dodd-Frank addresses whistleblowing considerations when the corporate governance system has not worked as intended to rectify deficiencies in the financial statements. An ethical company is one that embraces these requirements and instills them in the corporate culture.

Whistleblowing Payouts

On June 4, 2020 the SEC announced a nearly $50 million whistleblower award to an individual who provided detailed, firsthand observations of misconduct by a company, which resulted in a successful enforcement action that returned a significant amount of money to harmed investors. This was the largest amount ever awarded to one individual under the SEC's whistleblower program since issuing its first award in 2012.[85] This brings the total awarded to whistleblowers by the SEC to nearly $600 million as of January 14, 2021.

While we believe the whistleblowing program is the right thing to do to protect the public interest, we are concerned about two things:

1. A self-interested and opportunistic person may be induced to reveal company information to the SEC after following the prescribed internal compliance process, that led to no action by the company, with inadequate safeguards as to the quality of the information provided, and

2. Permitting compliance officers to become whistleblowers merely because of the passage of time (i.e., 120 days), rather than on a case-specific consideration of whether the company adequately addressed the underlying compliance issues in good faith, can erode corporate culture and trust in compliance officials; the result may be to subvert the overarching objectives of preventing, detecting, and remediating corporate misconduct on an enterprise-wide basis.[86]

We agree with others who have pointed out that, by reporting through the internal compliance process, others in the organization become informed of the facts and become potential whistleblowers.[87] As a practical matter, there may be no way around widening the circle of those in the know, but organizations should, at a minimum, take steps to protect the identity of the whistleblower.

EXHIBIT 3.16   Ethical Responsibilities of CPAs to Avoid Subordination of Judgment*

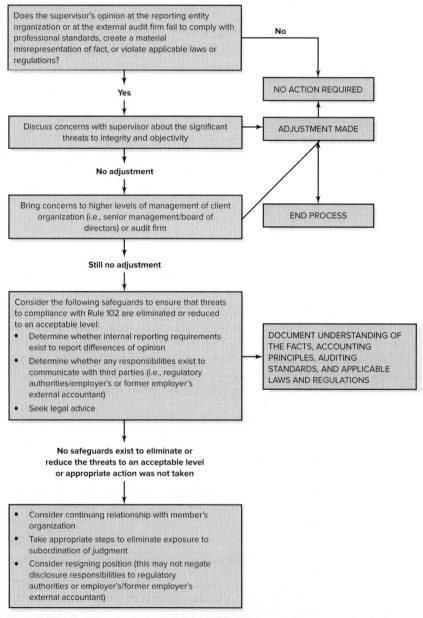

* Source: was developed by the author from AICPA Code Section 1.130.020

Implications of Supreme Court Decision in *Digital Realty Trust, Inc. v. Somers*

Two cases illustrate the challenges for accountants and auditors in deciding whether to blow the whistle on financial wrongdoing. The Digital Realty case emphasizes the need to report the matter to the SEC as a precondition to being able to benefit from the protections under Dodd-Frank. The *Erhart v. BofI Holdings* case provides protections for whistleblowers with respect to using company documents to blow the whistle and, at the same time, not violating their confidentiality requirement. These relationships were depicted back in Exhibit 3.1 and discussed below.

On February 21, 2018, the U.S. Supreme Court issued an opinion in *Digital Realty Trust, Inc. v. Somers*[88] that whistle-blowers are not protected against retaliation under Dodd-Frank unless they report the matter to the SEC, even if they report wrongdoing internally. The Court overruled a decision by the 9th Circuit Court of Appeals that sided with Paul Somers, formerly a vice-president of Realty Trust, who was terminated as a result of his reports to senior management regarding possible securities law violations. The lower Court ruled in his favor but the Supreme Court reversed the decision because Somers did not make any disclosure of the alleged misconduct to the SEC.

The controversial decision lessens protections for employees under Dodd-Frank who are retaliated against and may drive them to the SEC sooner rather than later. That may not be a good thing for employers who saw the *Digital Realty* decision as a win. It appears that employees can still qualify for the bounty hunter award under Dodd-Frank because they have to report the alleged wrongdoing to the SEC to enable it to institute legal action against the employer.

The key issue in the *Digital Realty* case was the interpretation of who is a whistleblower under Dodd-Frank and when does a would-be whistleblower qualify for protection against retaliation. The statute defines a whistleblower as a person who reports potential violations of the securities laws to the SEC. Under the anti-retaliation provisions, an employer is prohibited from discharging, harassing or otherwise discriminating against a whistleblower because of the whistle-blower's having made protected disclosures in any of three situations: (1) providing information to the SEC, (2) testifying or assisting in the SEC's investigation, and (3) "making disclosures that are required or protected under" SOX, the Securities Exchange Act, specified criminal anti-retaliation prohibitions or "any other law, rule, or regulation subject to the jurisdiction of the Commission."[89]

The SEC had been interpreting the Act with respect to the retaliation provision broadly thereby allowing the protections to apply to internal company reporting even if the individual did not report to the SEC. The Supreme Court disagreed with that interpretation. Writing for the Court in its 9-0 unanimous decision, Justice Ruth Bader Ginsburg put it this way: "A whistleblower is any person who provides . . . information relating to a violation of the securities laws *to the Commission*" [emphasis added]. "That definition," she added, "describes who is eligible for anti-retaliation protection if the individual engages in any of the protected conduct enumerated in the three clauses." Moreover, she observed, "this interpretation is consistent with the 'core objective' of Dodd-Frank's robust whistleblower program," . . . [which] is 'to motivate people who know of securities law violations to *tell the SEC.*'" That's why, for example, the program provides for substantial monetary rewards for SEC reporting. By comparison, SOX had a broader mission to "disturb the 'corporate code of silence' that 'discourage[d] employees from reporting fraudulent behavior not only to the proper authorities, such as the FBI and the SEC, but even internally.'"[90]

As for auditors, attorneys and other employees who are subject to internal-reporting requirements, they are protected under the provision as soon as they also report to the SEC. This has significant implications for accountants and auditors who are CPAs. Rule 1.130.020 of the AICPA Code, that is depicted in **Exhibit 3.15**, calls for accounting professionals to first meet their internal reporting obligations and then and only then to determine whether any responsibilities exist to communicate with third parties (i.e., the SEC). Consider what might happen if a controller uses the internal reporting mechanisms and, during the process, is fired by the company. It would seem to be too late at that point to inform the SEC and qualify for whistleblower protection. Filing under the Sarbanes-Oxley Act may be an option but there is only a 180-day window of opportunity after the date on which the employee became aware of the violation. Dodd-Frank actions have a shelf life of three years in most cases.

The bottom line on the Supreme Court decision, at least for most employees, is whether they go to the SEC immediately even before they report the matter internally to ensure they qualify for Dodd-Frank protections. Accounting professionals have a tougher decision since they are professionally and ethically obligated to use the internal chain of command first before reporting to the SEC. The Supreme Court may have turned Dodd-Frank, and whistleblowing in general, on its head. Only time will tell whether employees rush off to the SEC to seek protection rather than try and resolve differences internally first. For now, a cynic might say you should go to the SEC and report wrongdoing then risk being fired and then go back to the SEC and claim retaliation.

Whistleblowers Can Use Confidential Company Documents to Expose Fraud

On January 26, 2018, Charles Matthew Erhart struck a blow for all would-be whistleblowers when he achieved a significant win on a critical challenge that nearly all corporate whistleblowers often face—whether they can use confidential company documents to expose fraud and other illegality. District Court Judge Cynthia Bashant's decision in *Erhart v. BofI Holdings*[91] clarifies that employer confidentiality agreements do not supersede federal whistleblower rights and signals that retaliatory lawsuits against whistleblowers are unlikely to succeed. The decision also provides important guidance to corporate whistleblowers concerning precautions to take in using company documents to blow the whistle.

Erhart worked for BofI Federal Bank (BofI) as an internal auditor and sued BofI under the Sarbanes-Oxley Act and other whistleblower protection laws. Erhart alleged that BofI terminated his employment in retaliation for disclosing to the bank and federal regulators numerous violations of federal and state law. In particular, Erhart's whistleblower retaliation complaint alleged that he opposed the bank's decision to withhold information that was clearly responsive to an SEC subpoena and disclosed improprieties in the CEO's personal accounts and potential violations of bank rules.

Shortly after Erhart filed his retaliation claim, BofI further retaliated against him by suing him for alleged theft and dissemination of BofI's confidential information. In particular, BofI brought claims for (1) breach of contract; (2) conversion; (3) breach of the duty of loyalty; (4) negligence; (5) fraud; (6) violation of the Computer Fraud and Abuse Act; (8) unfair business practices; and (9) other violations of federal and state law.

The key aspects of the decision follow.

Confidentiality Agreements Do Not Trump Whistleblower Rights

The public policy protecting whistleblowers from retaliation, which is reflected in the Dodd-Frank Financial Reform Act and Sarbanes-Oxley, precludes companies from interfering with or preventing whistleblowing. In particular, an SEC rule implementing the Dodd-Frank whistleblower reward program bars companies from "enforcing, or threatening to enforce, a confidentiality agreement" to impede communicating with the SEC. Judge Bashant held that the "public policy in favor of whistleblower protection clearly outweighs the interest in the enforcement of [BofI's confidentiality] agreement, and the agreement is unenforceable."

Appropriating Company Documents is Protected Whistleblowing in Certain Circumstances

Judge Bashant held that whistleblowers are permitted to take company documents to disclose fraud to the government for two reasons. First, "whistleblowers often need documentary evidence to substantiate their allegations." Second, "[a]llowing a whistleblower to appropriate documents supporting believed wrongdoing also mitigates the possibility that evidence of the wrongdoing will be destroyed before an investigation can be conducted."

However, Judge Bashant also held that if a whistleblower engages in wholesale stripping of confidential documents or where the appropriation of confidential documents is "vast and indiscriminate," the public policy in favor of whistleblower might not immunize the whistleblower from potential liability. Here, Judge Bashant declined to reject Erhart's whistleblower defense to the appropriation claims because (1) Erhart testified in a declaration that he "was very careful in [selecting] the information [he] accessed and turned over; (2) Each document was specifically related to one of the allegations of wrongdoing [he] had discussed with [his supervisor] and then reported to federal law enforcement"; and (3) Erhart states that "every document" he used was one he "had properly accessed in the course of performing [his] work as an internal auditor."

Disclosure of Confidential Information in a Retaliation Complaint Should Be Limited to What is Reasonably Necessary to Pursue the Claim

Judge Bashant rejected BofI's position that its confidentiality agreement barred Erhart from using any confidential information to pursue his retaliation claims and also noted that Erhart should be permitted to disclose BofI's information in his complaint if doing so was "reasonably necessary" to pursue his retaliation claim.

Taken together with the *Digital Realty Trust, Inc. v. Somers* ruling, these two court decisions seek to protect whistleblowers at the cost of harming employer interests. It remains to be seen whether these rulings result in more whistleblower activity against employers and increased involvement of the SEC at an earlier stage to shut down financial wrongdoing sooner rather than later.

Concluding Thoughts

It is essential for all organizations to take reasonable steps to ensure that they develop an ethical culture, enhance ethical climate by clearly defining right behavior through a code of ethics and ethics policies, and set an ethical tone at the top that encourages responsible behavior. Corporate governance is a key element of an ethical environment. Strong internal controls, an independent audit committee, periodic meetings between independent directors and the external auditors, and a clearly defined whistleblowing policy all contribute to an effective corporate governance system. Research supports the proposition that "strong ethical cultures" diminish organizational misconduct and thereby the need for employees to blow the whistle internally or externally.[92]

Creating an ethical culture is a necessary but insufficient condition to ensure that ethical behavior occurs. Individuals within the organization may attempt to subvert the systems and pressure others to look the other way or go along with wrongdoing under the guise of being a team player or accepting a one-time fix to a perceived problem. In these situations, outlets should exist for employees to voice their values when they believe unethical or fraudulent behavior has occurred. Just imagine how Anthony Menendez's experiences would have changed had Halliburton created such a supportive environment.

Employees who have made a good faith effort to report material misstatements in the financial statements or violations of applicable laws and regulations to top management and the board of directors to no avail now have the option of informing the SEC under SOX and be protected against retaliation. Dodd-Frank provides a whistleblower award to incentivize internal accountants and external auditors to report fraud after following the prescribed procedures so that management has an opportunity to adjust the financial statements. These are important parts of a healthy corporate governance system but may not solve the underlying problem, which is a tone at the top that says: This is the way things are done around here. It takes a strong commitment to ethics of those in the organization to change the culture and align ethical action with ethical beliefs.

The end result of the corporate governance system is to provide audited financial statements that comply with the professions' ethical rules of conduct embodied in the AICPA Code as depicted in **Exhibit 3.1**. The public relies on ethical auditors to render an objective opinion on the company's financial statements. This builds trust and confidence in the company' financial reporting.

Discussion Questions

1. In her book *The Seven Signs of Ethical Collapse,* Jennings explains: "When an organization collapses ethically, it means that those in the organization have drifted into rationalizations and legalisms, and all for the purpose of getting the results they want and need at almost any cost." How does her statement relate to the discussions about ethical culture?

2. Explain the role of integrity in workplace ethics.

3. Organizational culture can influence moral behavior. Explain how this might work and lead to a defense of subordinates' behavior we might call "They made me do it."

4. What are the indicators that occupational fraud might exist? Explain.

5. According to the 2020 Global Study on Occupational Fraud and Abuse, a tip is the most common way to report fraud. What should be the ethical considerations for employees before deciding whether to blow the whistle on wrongdoing through a tip or organization hotline?

6. Do you believe that employees who observe more occupational fraud in their organizations are more likely to engage in occupational fraud themselves?

7. The following questions are about corporate governance and executive compensation: (a) How does agency theory address the issue of executive compensation? (b) How might stakeholder theory argue against the current model of executive compensation in the United States? (c) What is meant by the statement, "Compensation systems always become in part *end* and not simply *means*"?

8. Explain how internal auditors' sensitivity to ethical dilemmas might be influenced by corporate governance mechanisms.

9. What is the role of the board of directors in developing an ethical organization culture?

10. While on a lunch break following a dispute with a supervisor, an employee updated her Facebook status to an expletive and the name of the employer's company. Several coworkers "liked" her status. She later posted that the employer didn't appreciate its employees; no coworkers responded to this online. Do you believe the employee should be fired for her actions? Explain why or why not.

11. How does the Sarbanes-Oxley Act seek to create an ethical organization culture?

12. How do the concepts of cognitive dissonance and organizational/ethical dissonance that was discussed in Chapter 2 relate to whether an accountant might choose to blow the whistle on corporate wrongdoing?

13. Just because an accountant or auditor has a right to blow the whistle, does that mean they should blow the whistle? How might she make that determination?

14. An important factor in an individual's decision whether to become a whistleblower is their sense of duty and loyalty. Imagine a CPA discovers that their supervisor is committing fraud to make the company's financial statements appear better than they really are. How might duty and loyalty influence that decision?

15. Do you believe the U.S. Supreme Court decision in *Digital Realty Trust, Inc. v. Somers* was the "right" decision? Explain the basis for your answer from a whistleblower's perspective.

16. Should whistleblowers be allowed to use confidential company documents to expose fraud and other illegality? Use the ruling in *Erhart v. BofI Holdings* to guide the discussion.

17. Given the requirements of the Dodd-Frank Act to receive an award, what factors should a potential whistleblower consider before blowing the whistle to the SEC on financial wrongdoing from an ethical reasoning perspective?

18. Review the facts related to the reporting of financial statement fraud by Tony Menendez at Halliburton. In commenting on his actions, Menendez said one reason for bringing a claim under SOX was to be proven right about his views on the premature recognition of revenue on equipment. Is "proven right" a valid ethical reason to blow the whistle in this case? Explain.

19. It has been said that recent graduates from a business school majoring in accounting and just entering the profession are especially vulnerable to ethical missteps because they are often naive and may not see the ethical aspects of situations they confront. Explain the various dimensions of such alleged ethical challenges in the workplace?

20. Is business ethics an oxymoron? Why or why not?

Comprehensive Questions

1. Do you believe that the Dodd-Frank whistleblower program that incentivizes reporting fraud and other wrongdoings in return for a monetary reward is ethical? Use the ethical reasoning methods discussed in **Chapter 1** to answer the question.

2. The issue of the size of executive compensation packages is explored in the text. In 2019, Elon Musk at Tesla was the highest paid CEO with combined compensation from all sources (i.e., salary, bonuses, and stock options) of $595 million. The next highest was Tim Cook at Apple with $134 million. Do you believe these compensation packages are excessive? Answer with respect to the discussion in the chapter of the Foundation of Corporate Governance Systems.

3. A CEO and CFO of a public company filing a quarterly or annual report with the SEC must consider the requirements of Section 302 of the Sarbanes-Oxley Act. In addition, the Section 302 certification requirement also calls for the top officials to develop and implement internal disclosure controls and procedures designed to guarantee that its quarterly and annual reports are accurate and complete in preparation for having to disclose its CEO's and CFO's evaluation of such controls in its quarterly and annual reports. How do these requirements help to establish an effective system of corporate governance and an ethical organization culture?

4. "Conscious Capitalism" has become a buzz word for corporate governance in recent times. Explain the concept of conscious capitalism in the context of corporate social responsibilities.

5. During the past few years, surveys of millennials' opinions about work have taken front and center in the focus on CSR. In one survey, 86 percent of millennials (those between the ages of 22 and 37) would consider taking a pay cut to work at a company whose mission and values align with their own. Only 9 percent of baby boomers (those between the ages of 54 and 72) would. In another survey, only 31 percent of millennials say they would leave their current job if their employer were to ask them to do something they would find morally or ethically questionable compared to 51 percent of baby boomers. Based on these results, can we conclude that millennials are purpose-driven at work but relatively unethical, especially in comparison to baby boomers? Comment on these findings based on your own beliefs.[93]

Endnotes

1. Association of Certified Fraud Examiners, *2020 Global Study on Occupational Fraud and Abuse: Report to the Nations,* https://www.acfe.com/report-to-the-nations/2020.

2. Steven M. Mintz, "Virtue Ethics and Accounting Education," *Issues in Accounting Education* 10, no. 2 (Fall 1995), p. 257.

3. ACFE.

4. Encouraging the Reporting of Misconduct, http://www.antifraudcollaboration.org/wp-content/uploads/2017/11/AFC_report_encouraging_reporting_misconduct_2017-11.pdf.

5. Ernst & Young, *Detecting Financial Statement Fraud: What Every Manager Needs to Know* (Center for Audit Quality, October 2010).

6. AICPA Professional Standards, *Consideration of Fraud in a Financial Statement Audit* (AU-C Section 240) (NY: AICPA, 2014).

7. Corporate Culture, *Ethical Systems,* http://www.ethicalsystems.org/content/corporate-culture.

8. Marianne M. Jennings, *The Seven Signs of Ethical Collapse: How to Spot Moral Meltdowns in Companies Before It's Too Late* (New York: St. Martin's Press, 2006).

9. Marianne M. Jennings, *The Seven Signs of Ethical Collapse: How to Spot Moral Meltdowns in Companies Before It's Too Late* (New York: St. martin's Press, 2006).

10. Jennings et al.

11. Jennings et al.

12. Jennings et al., pp. 138–139.

13. Marianne M. Jennings, The Seven Signs of Ethical Collapse, Markkula Center for Applied Ethics, April 4, 2007, https://www.scu.edu/ethics/focus-areas/business-ethics/resources/seven-signs-of-ethical-collapse/.

14. Jennings, Markkula Center for Applied Ethics.

15. Deloitte, Building world-class ethics and compliance programs: Making a good program great, https://www2.deloitte.com/content/dam/Deloitte/us/Documents/risk/us-aers-g2g-compendium.pdf.

16. *KPMG Integrity Survey 2013,* https://assets.kpmg.com/content/dam/kpmg/pdf/2013/08/Integrity-Survey-2013-O-201307.pdf.

17. ECI, *The State of Ethics & Compliance in the Workplace*, March 2021, https://www.ethics.org/global-business-ethics-survey/.

18. This section is taken from a blog posted by Steven Mintz: "Beware of Posting Critical Comments About Your Employer on Facebook," March 1, 2017, http://www.ethicssage.com/2017/03/beware-of-posting-critical-comments-about-your-employer-on-facebook.html.

19. Zabihollah Rezaee, *Corporate Governance and Ethics* (New York: Wiley, 2009).

20. Hartman, pp. 508–509.

21. Jean Murray, *Why a Conflict of Interest Policy is Needed for Corporate Boards*, September 9, 2016, https://www.thebalance.com/conflict-of-interest-policy-for-your-corporate-board-397464.

22. Leo L. Strine, Jr., "Derivative Impact? Some Early Reflections on the Corporation Law Implications of the Enron Debacle," *57 Business Lawyer,* 1371, no. 1373 (2002).

23. O.C. Ferrell, John Fraedrich, and Linda Ferrell, *Business Ethics: Ethical Decision Making and Cases* (Stamford, CT: Cengage Learning, 2015), p. 44.

24. Ferrell et al., pp. 44.

25. Ferrell et al., pp. 44.

26. W. Steve Albrecht, Conan C. Albrecht, and Chad O. Albrecht, "Fraud and Corporate Executives: Agency, Stewardship, and Broken Trust," *Journal of Forensic Accounting* 5 (2004), pp. 109–130.

27. Lex Donaldson and James H. Davis, "Stewardship Theory," *Australian Journal of Management* 16, no. 1 (June 1991).

28. Michael Jensen and William H. Meckling, "Theory of the Firm: Managerial Behavior, Agency Costs, and Ownership Structure," *Journal of Financial Economics* (1976), pp. 305–360.

29. Chamu Sundaramurthy and Marianne Lewis, "Control and Collaboration: Paradoxes and Government," *Academy of Management Review* 28, no. 3 (July 2003), pp. 397–416.

30. Tricker, Bob. Corporate Governance: Principles, Policies, and Practices. 3rd ed., Oxford, 2015.

31. John A. Byrne with Louis Lavelle, Nanette Byrnes, Marcia Vickers, and Amy Borrus, "How to Fix Corporate Governance," *BusinessWeek* (May 6, 2002), pp. 69–78.

32. Chancery Court Requires Entire Fairness Review of Tesla CEO Compensation, https://www.lexology.com/library/detail.aspx?g=7d951872-d49c-42d1-9dcd-04318dbf0466.

33. Dodd-Frank Wall Street Reform and Consumer Protection Act (H.R. 4173), www.sec.gov/about/laws/wallstreet reform-cpa.pdf.

34. New York Stock Exchange, *NYSE Corporate Governance Guide*, 2014, https://www.nyse.com/publicdocs/nyse/listing/NYSE_Corporate_Governance_Guide.pdf.

35. Chris MacDonald, BP and Corporate Social Responsibility, *The Business Ethics Blog,* https://business ethicsblog.com/2010/09/01/bp-and-csr/.

36. Laura P. Hartman, Joseph DesJardins, and Chris MacDonald, *Business Ethics: Decision Making for Personal & Social Responsibility* (New York: McGraw Hill Education, 2018), pp. 177–180.

37. Kelsey Chong, Millenials and the Rising Demand for Corporate Social Responsibility, Berkely Haas, https://cmr.berkeley.edu/blog/2017/1/millennials-and-csr/.

38. 2016 Cone Communications Millennial Employee Engagement Study, https://www.conecomm.com/research-blog/2016-millennial-employee-engagement-study.

39. *Why Conscious Capitalism is The Future*, July 20, 2020, https://chipperfieldmedia.com/blogs/why-conscious-capitalism–is-the-future.

40. *What is Conscious Capitalism, and How Does it Differ from Corporate Social Responsibility?*, https://online business.northeaster.edu/what-is-conscious-capitalism-and-how-does-it-differ-from-corporate-social-responsibility/.

41. R. Edward Freeman, "Managing for Stakeholders," https://papers.ssrn.com/sol3/papers.cfm?abstract_id=1186402.

42. Milton Friedman, "The Social Responsibility of Business is to increase its Profits," *NY Times*, September 13, 1970, http://www.nytimes.com/1970/09/13/archives/article-15-no-title-html.

43. Hartman et al., pp. 180–182.

44. Charles River Associates, *Sarbanes-Oxley Section 404 Costs and Remediation of Deficiencies: Estimates from a Sample of Fortune 1000 Companies*, April 2005, https://www.sec.gov/spotlight/soxcomp/soxcomp-all-attach.pdf.

45. Hartman et al., pp. 185–187.

46. Freeman.

47. Hartman et al., pp. 183–187.

48. *United States v. Carroll Towing*, 159 F.2d 169 (2d Cir. 1947).

49. Douglas Birsch and John H. Fiedler, *The Ford Pinto Case: A Study in Applied Ethics, Business, and Technology* (Albany: State University of New York, 1994).

50. David De Cremer and Ann E. Tenbrunsel, *Behavioral Business Ethics: Shaping an Emerging Field* (New York: Routledge, 2012).

51. Honda Settles Takata Air Bag Claims for $605 Million, *Reuters*, September 1, 2017, http://fortune.com/2017/09/01/honda-takata-air-bag-lawsuit-settlement/.

52. House of Representatives Financial Services Committee, HR 3763-Sarbanes-Oxley Act of 2002, July 24, 2002, https://www.congress.gov/bill/107th-congress/house-bill/3763.

53. Securities and Exchange Commission, "SEC Charges Company CEO and Former CFO With Hiding Internal Controls Deficiencies and Violating Sarbanes-Oxley Requirements," July 30, 2014.

54. *In the Matter of Marc Sherman, Respondent,* Securities Exchange Act of 1934, Release No. 74765, April 20, 2015, https://www.sec.gov/litigation/admin/2015/34-74765.pdf.

55. Alison Frankel, "Sarbanes-Oxley's Lost Promise: Why CEOs Haven't been Prosecuted," *Reuters.com On the Case* blog, July 27, 2012, Available at: http://blogs.reuters.com/alison-frankel/2012/07/27/sarbanes-oxleys-lost-promise-why-ceos-havent-been-prosecuted/.

56. Report of the National Commission on Fraudulent Financial Reporting (Treadway Commission), October 1987, https://www.coso.org/Documents/NCFFR.pdf.

57. Committee of Sponsoring Organizations of the Treadway Commission (COSO), 2013 *Internal Control–Integrated Framework,* Report Available at: http://www.coso.org/documents/Internal%20Control-Integrated%20Framework.pdf.

58. Internal Control – Integrated Framework: Executive Summary, May 2013, https://www.coso.org/Documents/990025P-Executive-Summary-final-may20.pdf.

59. COSO, Enterprise Risk Management–Integrated Framework, September 2004, https://www.coso.org/Documents/COSO-ERM-Executive-Summary.pdf.

60. Deloitte, Risk Appetite Frameworks: How to Spot the Genuine Article, https://www2.deloitte.com/content/dam/Deloitte/au/Documents/risk/deloitte-au-risk-appetite-frameworks-financial-services-0614.pdf.

61. COSO, Enterprises Risk Management Framework: Integrating with Strategy and Performance, https://www.cosco.org/Documents/COSO-ERM-Presentation-September-2017.pdf.

62. Jackie Wattles and Selena Larson, How the Equifax data breach happened: What we know now, *CNNTech,* September 16, 2017, http://money.cnn.com/2017/09/16/technology/equifax-breach-security-hole/index.html.

63. Francine McKenna, Equifax auditors are on the hook for data security risk controls," *Market Watch,* October 3, 2017, http://money.cnn.com/2017/09/16/technology/equifax-breach-security-hole/index.html.

64. Janet P. Near and Marcia P. Miceli, "Organizational Dissidence: The Case of Whistle-blowing," *Journal of Business Ethics* 4 (1985), pp. 1–16.

65. Near and Miceli.

66. Michael Davis, "Some Paradoxes of Whistleblowing," *Business and Professional Ethics Journal* 15, no. 1 (1996), https://philosophia.uncg.edu/media/phi361-metivier/readings/Davis-Paradoxes%20of%20Whistle-Blowing.pdf.

67. Richard T. De George, *Business Ethics,* 7th ed. (NY: Prentice-Hall, 2010).

68. Marion Mogielnicki, "Hunting for 'Bounty' and Finding 'Moral Autonomy': The Dodd-Frank Act Expansion of Whistle Blower Protections," *Academy of Business Research* 2 (2011), pp. 74–84.

69. Eva Evdokia Tsahuridu, *Moral Autonomy in Organizational Decisions*, https://core.ac.uk/download/pdf/41536179.pdf.

70. Miceli and Near, pp. 698–699.

71. Tsahuridu et al.

72. Difference Between Morals and Ethics, https://keydifferences.com/difference-between-moral-and-ethics.html.

73. Jesse Eisinger, "The Whistleblower's Tale: How an Accountant took on Halliburton and Won," *Pro Publica* (April 21, 2015).

74. Dodd-Frank Wall Street Reform and Consumer Protection Act (H.R. 4173), www.sec.gov/about/laws/wallstreetreform-cpa.pdf.

75. SEC, "Implementation of the Whistleblower Provisions of Section 21F of the Securities Exchange Act of 1934," Available at: https://www.sec.gov/rules/final/2011/34-64545.pdf.

76. Dodd-Frank Wall Street Reform and Consumer Protection Act (H.R. 4173).

77. Kobi Kastiel, "Elements of an Effective Whistleblower Hotline," *Harvard Law School Forum on Corporate Governance and Financial Regulation*, October 25, 2014. Available at: http://corpgov.law.harvard.edu/2014/10/25/elements-of-an-effective-whistleblower-hotline/.

78. Kobi Kastiel.

79. AICPA, *Code of Professional Conduct,* December 15, 2014, Available at: https://www.aicpa.org/content/dam/aicpa/research/standards/codeofconduct/downloadabledocuments/2014december15contentasof2016august31codeofconduct.pdf.

80. SEC, "Implementation of the Whistleblower Provisions of Section 21F of the Securities Exchange Act of 1934," Available at: https://www.sec.gov/rules/final/2011/34-64545.pdf.

81. SEC.

82. SEC.

83. Jason Rosenthal, Esq. and Lesley Smith, Esq, "Should CPAs be Financially Rewarded As Whistleblowers?" *CPA Insider,* 2011, Available at: https://www.cpa2biz.com/Content/media/PRODUCER_CONTENT/Newsletters/Articles_2011/CPA/Jul/Whistleblowers.jsp

84. AICPA Code.

85. SEC Awards Record Payout of Nearly $50 Million to Whistleblower, June 4, 2020, https://www.sec.gov/news/press-release/2020-126.

86. Philip Stamatakos and Ted Chung, "Dodd-Frank's Whistleblower Provisions and the SEC's Rule: Compliance and Ethical Considerations," *Corporate Governance Advisor,* September/October 2011.

87. Daniel Hurson, "United States: Ten 'Rules' For Becoming A Successful SEC Whistleblower," September 11, 2013, Available at: http://www.mondaq.com/unitedstates/x/261844/Corporate+Commercial+Law/The+New+Rules+For+Becoming+A+Successful+SEC+Whistleblower.

88. Supreme Court of the United States, *Digital Realty Trust, Inc. v. Somers,* February 21, 2018, https://www.supremecourt.gov/opinions/17pdf/16-1276_b0nd.pdf.

89. Dodd-Frank Wall Street Reform and Consumer Protection Act (H.R. 4173).

90. Cydney Posner, SCOTUS says whistleblowers must whistle all the way to the SEC, Cooley Pub Co, February 21, 2018, https://cooleypubco.com/2018/02/21/scotus-says-whistleblowers-must-whistle-all-the-way-to-the-sec/.

91. *Charles Matthew Erhart v. BOFI Holding, Inc., Case No. 15-cv-02287-BAS(NLS),* February 14, 2017, https://cases. justia.com/federal/district-courts/california/casdce/3:2015cv02287/486757/22/0.pdf?ts=1474967833.

92. Mark S. Schwartz, "Developing and Sustaining an Ethical Corporate Culture: The Core Elements," *Business Horizons* 56 (2013), pp. 39–50.

93. https://www.cnbc.com/2018/06/27/nearly-9-out-of-10-millennials-would-consider-a-pay-cut-to-get-this.html.

94. Matt Miller, Ex-Rite Aid VP, businessman, get years in federal prison for multimillion dollar scam, November 16, 2016, http://www.pennlive.com/news/2016/11/ex-rite_aid:vp_businessman_get.html.

95. John Carreyrou, *Bad Blood: Secrets and Lies in a Silicon Valley Startup* (NY: Vintage Books, 2020).

96. United States Department of Justice, Northern District of California, *U.S. v. , Elizabeth Holmes, et al., https://www.justice.gov/usao-ndca/us-v-elizabeth-holmes-et-al.*

97. Taylor Dunn, Victoria Thompson, and Rebecca Jarvis, Theranos whistleblowers filed complaints out of fear of patients health: 'It started to eat me up inside.' The drop out episode 4, https://abcnews.go.com/Business/theranos-whistleblowers-filed-complaints-fear-patients-health-started/story?id=610302.

98. Wikileaks, Theranos, https://en.wikipedia.org/wiki/Theranos.

99. Chris Arnold, NPR, Former Wells Fargo Employees Describe Toxic Sales Culture, Even at HQ, October 4, 2016, https://www.kqed.org/news/11115930/former-wells-fargo-employees-describe-toxic-sales-culture-even-at-hq.

100. Arnold.

101. Matt Egan, I called the Wells Fargo ethics line and was fired, September 21, 2016, http://money.cnn.com/2016/09/21/investing/wells-fargo-fired-workers-retaliation-fake-accounts/index.html.

102. Richard Bowen, Wells Fargo. Fried Again, August 17, 2017, http://www.richardmbowen.com/wells-fargo-fried-again/.

103. Egan.

104. Egan.

105. Wells Fargo, *Our Code of Ethics and Business Conduct: Living Our Vision, Values, and Goals,* https://www.08.wellsfargomedia.com/assets/pdf/about/corporate/code-of-ethics.pdf.

106. *In the Matter of TIMOTHY DALE, CPA, Respondent,* Accounting and Auditing Enforcement Release No. 4141/May 18, 2020, https://www.sec.gov/litigation/admin/2020/34-88895.pdf.

Chapter 3 Cases

Case 3-1 The Parable of the Sadhu

Bowen H. McCoy

Last year, as the first participant in the new six-month sabbatical program that Morgan Stanley has adopted, I enjoyed a rare opportunity to collect my thoughts as well as do some traveling. I spent the first three months in Nepal, walking 600 miles through 200 villages in the Himalayas and climbing some 120,000 vertical feet. My sole Western companion on the trip was an anthropologist who shed light on the cultural patterns of the villages that we passed through.

During the Nepal hike, something occurred that has had a powerful impact on my thinking about corporate ethics. Although some might argue that the experience has no relevance to business, it was a situation in which a basic ethical dilemma suddenly intruded into the lives of a group of individuals. How the group responded holds a lesson for all organizations, no matter how defined.

The Sadhu

The Nepal experience was more rugged than I had anticipated. Most commercial treks last two or three weeks and cover a quarter of the distance we traveled.

My friend Stephen, the anthropologist, and I were halfway through the 60-day Himalayan part of the trip when we reached the high point, an 18,000-foot pass over a crest that we'd have to traverse to reach the village of Muklinath, an ancient holy place for pilgrims.

Six years earlier, I had suffered pulmonary edema, an acute form of altitude sickness, at 16,500 feet in the vicinity of Everest base camp—so we were understandably concerned about what would happen at 18,000 feet. Moreover, the Himalayas were having their wettest spring in 20 years; hip-deep powder and ice had already driven us off one ridge. If we failed to cross the pass, I feared that the last half of our once-in-a-lifetime trip would be ruined.

The night before we would try the pass, we camped in a hut at 14,500 feet. In the photos taken at that camp, my face appears wan. The last village we'd passed through was a sturdy two-day walk below us, and I was tired.

During the late afternoon, four backpackers from New Zealand joined us, and we spent most of the night awake, anticipating the climb. Below, we could see the fires of two other parties, which turned out to be two Swiss couples and a Japanese hiking club.

To get over the steep part of the climb before the sun melted the steps cut in the ice, we departed at 3.30 a.m. The New Zealanders left first, followed by Stephen and myself, our porters and Sherpas, and then the Swiss. The Japanese lingered in their camp. The sky was clear, and we were confident that no spring storm would erupt that day to close the pass.

At 15,500 feet, it looked to me as if Stephen was shuffling and staggering a bit, which are symptoms of altitude sickness. (The initial stage of altitude sickness brings a headache and nausea. As the condition worsens, a climber may encounter difficult breathing, disorientation, aphasia, and paralysis.) I felt strong—my adrenaline was flowing—but I was very concerned about my ultimate ability to get across. A couple of our porters were also suffering from the height, and Pasang, our Sherpa sirdar (leader), was worried.

Just after daybreak, while we rested at 15,500 feet, one of the New Zealanders, who had gone ahead, came staggering down toward us with a body slung across his shoulders. He dumped the almost naked, barefoot body of an Indian holy man—a sadhu—at my feet. He had found the pilgrim lying on the ice, shivering and suffering from hypothermia.

I cradled the sadhu's head and laid him out on the rocks. The New Zealander was angry. He wanted to get across the pass before the bright sun melted the snow. He said, "Look, I've done what I can. You have porters and Sherpa guides. You care for him. We're going on!" He turned and went back up the mountain to join his friends.

I took a carotid pulse and found that the sadhu was still alive. We figured he had probably visited the holy shrines at Muklinath and was on his way home. It was fruitless to question why he had chosen this desperately high route instead of the safe, heavily traveled caravan route through the Kali Gandaki gorge. Or, why he was shoeless and almost naked, or how long he had been lying in the pass. The answers weren't going to solve our problem.

Stephen and the four Swiss began stripping off their outer clothing and opening their packs. The sadhu was soon clothed from head to foot. He was not able to walk, but he was very much alive. I looked down the mountain and spotted the Japanese climbers, marching up with a horse.

Without a great deal of thought, I told Stephen and Pasang that I was concerned about withstanding the heights to come and wanted to get over the pass. I took off after several of our porters who had gone ahead.

On the steep part of the ascent where, if the ice steps had given way, I would have slid down about 3,000 feet, I felt vertigo. I stopped for a breather, allowing the Swiss to catch up with me. I inquired about the sadhu and Stephen. They said that the sadhu was fine and that Stephen was just behind them. I set off again for the summit.

Stephen arrived at the summit an hour after I did. Still exhilarated by victory, I ran down the slope to congratulate him. He was suffering from altitude sickness—walking 15 steps, then stopping, walking 15 steps, then stopping. Pasang accompanied him all the way up. When I reached them, Stephen glared at me and said, "How do you feel about contributing to the death of a fellow man?"

I did not completely comprehend what he meant. "Is the sadhu dead?" I inquired.

"No," replied Stephen, "but he surely will be!"

After I had gone, followed not long after by the Swiss, Stephen had remained with the sadhu. When the Japanese had arrived, Stephen had asked to use their horse to transport the sadhu down to the hut. They had refused. He had then asked Pasang to have a group of our porters carry the sadhu. Pasang had resisted the idea, saying that the porters would have to exert all their energy to get themselves over the pass. He believed they could not carry a man down 1,000 feet to the hut, reclimb the slope, and get across safely before the snow melted. Pasang had pressed Stephen not to delay any longer.

The Sherpas had carried the sadhu down to a rock in the sun at about 15,000 feet and pointed out the hut another 500 feet below. The Japanese had given him food and drink. When they had last seen him, he was listlessly throwing rocks at the Japanese party's dog, which had frightened him.

We do not know if the sadhu lived or died.

For many of the following days and evenings, Stephen and I discussed and debated our behavior toward the sadhu. Stephen is a committed Quaker with deep moral vision. He said, "I feel that what happened with the sadhu is a good example of the breakdown between the individual ethic and the corporate ethic. No one person was willing to assume ultimate responsibility for the sadhu. Each was willing to do his bit just so long as it was not too inconvenient. When it got to be a bother, everyone just passed the buck to someone else and took off. Jesus was relevant to a more individualistic stage of society, but how do we interpret his teaching today in a world filled with large, impersonal organizations and groups?"

I defended the larger group, saying, "Look, we all cared. We all gave aid and comfort. Everyone did his bit. The New Zealander carried him down below the snow line. I took his pulse and suggested we treat him for hypothermia. You and the Swiss gave him clothing and got him warmed up. The Japanese gave him food and water. The Sherpas carried him down to the sun and pointed out the easy trail toward the hut. He was well enough to throw rocks at a dog. What more could we do?"

"You have just described the typical affluent Westerner's response to a problem. Throwing money—in this case, food and sweaters—at it, but not solving the fundamentals!" Stephen retorted.

"What would satisfy you?" I said. "Here we are, a group of New Zealanders, Swiss, Americans, and Japanese who have never met before and who are at the apex of one of the most powerful experiences of our lives. Some years the pass is so bad no one gets over it. What right does an almost naked pilgrim who chooses the wrong trail have to disrupt our lives? Even the Sherpas had no interest in risking the trip to help him beyond a certain point."

Stephen calmly rebutted, "I wonder what the Sherpas would have done if the sadhu had been a well-dressed Nepali, or what the Japanese would have done if the sadhu had been a well-dressed Asian, or what you would have done, Buzz, if the sadhu had been a well-dressed Western woman?"

"Where, in your opinion," I asked, "is the limit of our responsibility in a situation like this? We had our own well-being to worry about. Our Sherpa guides were unwilling to jeopardize us or the porters for the sadhu. No one else on the mountain was willing to commit himself beyond certain self-imposed limits."

Stephen said, "As individual Christians or people with a Western ethical tradition, we can fulfill our obligations in such a situation only if one, the sadhu dies in our care; two, the sadhu demonstrates to us that he can undertake the two-day walk down to the village; or three, we carry the sadhu for two days down to the village and persuade someone there to care for him."

"Leaving the sadhu in the sun with food and clothing—where he demonstrated hand-eye coordination by throwing a rock at a dog—comes close to fulfilling items one and two," I answered. "And it wouldn't have made sense to take him to the village where the people appeared to be far less caring than the Sherpas, so the third condition is impractical. Are you really saying that, no matter what the implications, we should, at the drop of a hat, have changed our entire plan?"

The Individual Versus the Group Ethic

Despite my arguments, I felt and continue to feel guilty about the sadhu. I had literally walked through a classic moral dilemma without fully thinking through the consequences. My excuses for my actions include a high adrenaline flow, a superordinate goal, and a once-in-a-lifetime opportunity—common factors in corporate situations, especially stressful ones.

Real moral dilemmas are ambiguous, and many of us hike right through them, unaware that they exist. When, usually after the fact, someone makes an issue of one, we tend to resent his or her bringing it up. Often, when the full import of what we have done (or not done) hits us, we dig into a defensive position from which it is very difficult to emerge. In rare circumstances, we may contemplate what we have done from inside a prison.

Had we mountaineers been free of stress caused by the effort and the high altitude, we might have treated the sadhu differently. Yet isn't stress the real test of personal and corporate values? The instant decisions that executives make under pressure reveal the most about personal and corporate character.

Among the many questions that occur to me when I ponder my experience with the sadhu are: What are the practical limits of moral imagination and vision? Is there a collective or institutional ethic that differs from the ethics of the individual? At what level of effort or commitment can one discharge one's ethical responsibilities?

Not every ethical dilemma has a right solution. Reasonable people often disagree; otherwise, there would be no dilemma. In a business context, however, it is essential that managers agree on a process for dealing with dilemmas.

Our experience with the sadhu offers an interesting parallel to business situations. An immediate response was mandatory. Failure to act was a decision in itself. Up on the mountain, we could not resign and submit our résumés to a headhunter. In contrast to philosophy, business involves action and implementation—getting things done. Managers must come up with answers based on what they see and what they allow to influence their decision-making processes. On the mountain, none of us but Stephen realized the true dimensions of the situation we were facing.

One of our problems was that, as a group, we had no process for developing a consensus. We had no sense of purpose or plan. The difficulties of dealing with the sadhu were so complex that no one person could handle them. Because the group did not have a set of preconditions that could guide its action to an acceptable resolution, we reacted instinctively as individuals. The cross-cultural nature of the group added a further layer of complexity. We had no leader with whom we could all identify and in whose purpose we believed. Only Stephen was willing to take charge, but he could not gain adequate support from the group to care for the sadhu.

Some organizations do have values that transcend the personal values of their managers. Such values, which go beyond profitability, are usually revealed when the organization is under stress. People throughout the organization generally accept its values, which, because they are not presented as a rigid list of commandments, may be somewhat ambiguous. The stories people tell, rather than printed materials, transmit the organization's conceptions of what is proper behavior.

For 20 years, I have been exposed at senior levels to a variety of corporations and organizations. It is amazing how quickly an outsider can sense the tone and style of an organization and, with that, the degree of tolerated openness and freedom to challenge management.

Organizations that do not have a heritage of mutually accepted, shared values tend to become unhinged during stress, with each individual bailing out for himself or herself. In the great takeover battles we have witnessed during past years, companies that had strong cultures drew the wagons around them and fought it out, while other companies saw executives—supported by golden parachutes—bail out of the struggles.

Because corporations and their members are interdependent, for the corporation to be strong, the members need to share a preconceived notion of correct behavior, a "business ethic," and think of it as a positive force, not a constraint.

As an investment banker, I am continually warned by well-meaning lawyers, clients, and associates to be wary of conflicts of interest. Yet if I were to run away from every difficult situation, I wouldn't be an effective investment banker. I have to feel my way through conflicts. An effective manager can't run from risk either; he or she has to confront risk. To feel "safe" in doing that, managers need the guidelines of an agreed-upon process and set of values within the organization.

After my three months in Nepal, I spent three months as an executive-in-residence at both the Stanford Business School and the University of California at Berkeley's Center for Ethics and Social Policy of the Graduate Theological Union. Those six months away from my job gave me time to assimilate 20 years of business experience. My thoughts turned often to the meaning of the leadership role in any large organization. Students at the seminary thought of themselves as antibusiness. But when I questioned them, they agreed that they distrusted all large organizations, including the church. They perceived all large organizations as impersonal and opposed to individual values and needs. Yet we all know of organizations in which people's values and beliefs are respected and their expressions encouraged. What makes the difference? Can we identify the difference and, as a result, manage more effectively?

The word *ethics* turns off many and confuses more. Yet the notions of shared values and an agreed-upon process for dealing with adversity and change—what many people mean when they talk about corporate culture—seem to be at the heart of the ethical issue. People who are in touch with their own core beliefs and the beliefs of others and who are sustained by them can be more comfortable living on the cutting edge. At times, taking a tough line or a decisive stand in a muddle of ambiguity is the only ethical thing to do. If a manager is indecisive about a problem and spends time trying to figure out the "good" thing to do, the enterprise may be lost.

Business ethics, then, has to do with the authenticity and integrity of the enterprise. To be ethical is to follow the business as well as the cultural goals of the corporation, its owners, its employees, and its customers. Those who cannot serve the corporate vision are not authentic businesspeople and, therefore, are not ethical in the business sense.

At this stage of my own business experience, I have a strong interest in organizational behavior. Sociologists are keenly studying what they call corporate stories, legends, and heroes as a way organizations have of transmitting value systems. Corporations such as Arco have even hired consultants to perform an audit of their corporate culture. In a company, a leader is a person who understands, interprets, and manages the corporate value system. Effective managers, therefore, are action-oriented people who resolve conflict, are tolerant of ambiguity, stress, and change, and have a strong sense of purpose for themselves and their organizations.

If all this is true, I wonder about the role of the professional manager who moves from company to company. How can he or she quickly absorb the values and culture of different organizations? Or is there, indeed, an art of management that is totally transportable? Assuming that such fungible managers do exist, is it proper for them to manipulate the values of others?

What would have happened had Stephen and I carried the sadhu for two days back to the village and become involved with the villagers in his care? In four trips to Nepal, my most interesting experience occurred in 1975, when I lived in a Sherpa home in the Khumbu for five days while recovering from altitude sickness. The high point of Stephen's trip was an invitation to participate in a family funeral ceremony in Manang. Neither experience had to do with climbing the high passes of the Himalayas. Why were we so reluctant to try the lower path, the ambiguous trail? Perhaps because we did not have a leader who could reveal the greater purpose of the trip to us.

Why didn't Stephen, with his moral vision, opt to take the sadhu under his personal care? The answer is partly because Stephen was hard-stressed physically himself and partly because, without some support system that encompassed our involuntary and episodic community on the mountain, it was beyond his individual capacity to do so.

I see the current interest in corporate culture and corporate value systems as a positive response to pessimism such as Stephen's about the decline of the role of the individual in large organizations. Individuals who operate from a thoughtful set of personal values provide the foundation for a corporate culture. A corporate tradition that encourages freedom of inquiry, supports personal values, and reinforces a focused sense of direction can fulfill the need to combine individuality with the prosperity and success of the group. Without such corporate support, the individual is lost.

That is the lesson of the sadhu. In a complex corporate situation, the individual requires and deserves the support of the group. When people cannot find such support in their organizations, they don't know how to act. If such support is forthcoming, a person has a stake in the success of the group and can add much to the process of establishing and maintaining a corporate culture. Management's challenge is to be sensitive to individual needs, to shape them, and to direct and focus them for the benefit of the group as a whole.

For each of us, the sadhu lives. Should we stop what we are doing and comfort him, or should we keep trudging up toward the high pass? Should I pause to help the derelict I pass on the street each night as I walk by the Yale Club en route to Grand Central Station? Am I his brother? What is the nature of our responsibility if we consider ourselves to be ethical persons? Perhaps it is to change the values of the group so that it can, with all its resources, take the other road.

Questions

1. Throughout *The Parable of the Sadhu,* Bowen McCoy refers to the breakdown between the individual and corporate ethic. Explain what he meant by that and how, if we view the hikers on the trek up the mountain in Nepal as an organization, the ethical person-organization fit applied to the decisions made on the climb.
2. Using the various ethical discussions in the first three chapters as your guide, evaluate the actions of McCoy, Stephen, and the rest of the group from an ethical perspective.
3. What role did leadership and culture play in this case?
4. What is the moral of the story of the sadhu from your perspective?

Source: Reprinted with permission from "The Parable of the Sadhu," by Bowen H. McCoy, Harvard Business Review.

Case 3-2 Rite Aid Inventory Surplus Fraud

Occupational fraud comes in many shapes and sizes. The $12.9 million dollar fraud and kickback scheme at Rite Aid is one such case.

In February 2015, Jay Findling, a New Jersey businessman, pleaded guilty to charges of conspiracy to commit wire fraud. Former vice president, Timothy Foster, pleaded guilty to making false statements to authorities. On November 16, 2016, Foster was sentenced to five years in prison and Findling, four years. Findling and Foster were ordered to jointly pay $8,034,183 in restitution. Findling also forfeited and turned over an additional $11.6 million to the government at the time he entered his guilty plea. In sentencing Foster, U.S. Middle District Judge John E. Jones III expressed his astonishment that in one instance at Rite-Aid headquarters, Foster took a multimillion dollar cash pay-off from Findling, then stuffed the money into a bag and flew home on Rite Aid's corporate jet.[94]

The charges relate to a nine-year conspiracy to defraud Rite Aid by lying to the company about the sale of surplus inventory to a company owned by Findling when it was sold to third parties for greater amounts. Findling would then kick back a portion of his profits to Foster. Foster's lawyer told Justice Jones that, even though they conned the company, the efforts of Foster and Findling still earned Rite Aid over $100 million "instead of having warehouses filled with unwanted merchandise." Assistant U.S. Attorney Kim Daniel focused on the abuse of trust by Foster and persistent lies to the feds. "The con didn't affect some faceless corporation, Daniel said, "but harmed Rite Aid's 89,000 employees and its stockholders." Findling's attorney, Kevin Buchan, characterized his client as "a good man who made a bad decision." "He succumbed to the pressure. That's why he did what he did and that's why he's here," Buchan said during sentencing.

Findling admitted he established a bank account under the name "Rite Aid Salvage Liquidation" and used it to collect the payments from the real buyers of the surplus Rite Aid inventory. After the payments were received, Findling would send lesser amounts dictated by Foster to Rite Aid for the goods, thus inducing Rite Aid to believe the inventory had been purchased by J. Finn Industries, not the real buyers. The government alleged Findling received at least $127.7 million from the real buyers of the surplus inventory but, with Foster's help, only provided $98.6 million of that amount to Rite Aid, leaving Findling approximately $29.1 million in profits from the scheme. The government also alleged that Findling kicked back approximately $5.7 million of the $29.1 million to Foster.

Assume you are the Director of Internal at Rite Aid and discover the surplus inventory scheme. Explain the steps you would take to determine whether you would blow the whistle on the scheme by applying the requirements of **Exhibit 3.15** on subordination of judgment. In that regard, answer the following questions.

Questions

1. Assume you have decided to report the fraud. What would your first step be? That is, to whom would you report the fraud and why?

2. Assume the audit committee informs you that it has decided not to report the fraud to the SEC during the current period because they don't want to raise suspicions about the quality of earnings and fraudulent activities. The committee did hold open the possibility of reporting the fraud in the next period and then putting through an error correction. How might you counter the likely reasons and rationalizations given by the audit committee for its decision?

3. In the case, Findling's attorney, Kevin Buchan, characterized his client as "a good man who made a bad decision." "He succumbed to the pressure. That's why he did what he did and that's why we're here," Buchan said during sentencing. Do you believe that the actions of Findling can best be characterized as "sometimes, good people do bad things?" Consider the six pillars of character discussed in chapter1 in answering this question.

Case 3-3 United Thermostatic Controls (a GVV case)

United Thermostatic Controls is a publicly owned company that engages in the manufacturing and marketing of residential and commercial thermostats. The thermostats are used to regulate temperature in furnaces and refrigerators. United sells its product primarily to retailers in the domestic market, with the company headquartered in Detroit. Its operations are decentralized according to geographic region. As a publicly owned company, United's common stock is listed and traded on the NYSE. The organization chart for United is presented in **Exhibit 3.1**.

EXHIBIT 1   United Thermostatic Controls Organization Chart

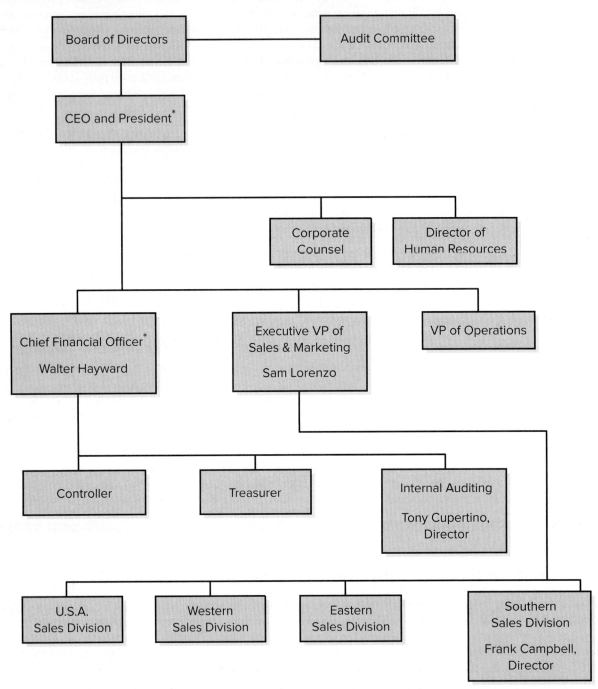

*Member of the board of directors.

Frank Campbell is the director of the Southern sales division. Worsening regional economic conditions and a reduced rate of demand for United's products have created pressures to achieve sales revenue targets set by United management nonetheless. Also, significant pressures exist within the organization for sales divisions to maximize their revenues and earnings for 2021 in anticipation of a public offering of stock early in 2022. Budgeted and actual sales revenue amounts, by division, for the first three quarters in 2021 are presented in **Exhibit 2**.

EXHIBIT 2   United Thermostatic Controls—Sales Revenue, 2021 (1st 3Qs)

Budgeted and Actual Sales Revenue First Three Quarters in 2021						
U.S.A. Sales Division				Western Sales Division		
Quarter Ended	Budget	Actual	% Var.	Budget	Actual	% Var.
March 31	$ 632,000	$ 638,000	.009%	$ 886,000	$ 898,000	.014%
June 30	640,000	642,000	.003	908,000	918,000	.011
September 30	648,000	656,000	.012	930,000	936,000	.006
Through September 30	$ 1,920,000	$ 1,936,000	.008%	$ 2,724,000	$ 2,752,000	.010%

Eastern Sales Division				Southern Sales Division		
Quarter Ended	Budget	Actual	% Var.	Budget	Actual	% Var.
March 31	$ 743,000	$ 750,000	.009%	$ 688,000	$ 680,000	(.012)%
June 30	752,000	760,000	.011	696,000	674,000	(.032)
September 30	761,000	769,000	.011	704,000	668,000	(.051)
Through September 30	$ 2,256,000	$ 2,279,000	.010%	$ 2,088,000	$ 2,022,000	(.032)%

Campbell knows that actual sales lagged even further behind budgeted sales during the first two months of the fourth quarter. He also knows that each of the other three sales divisions exceeded their budgeted sales amounts during the first three quarters in 2021. He is very concerned that the Southern division has been unable to meet or exceed budgeted sales amounts. He is particularly worried about the effect this might have on his and the division managers' bonuses and share of corporate profits.

In an attempt to improve the sales revenue of the Southern division for the fourth quarter and for the year ended December 31, 2021, Campbell reviewed purchase orders received during the latter half of November and early December to determine whether shipments could be made to customers prior to December 31. Campbell knows that sometimes orders that are received before the end of the year can be filled by December 31, thereby enabling the division to record the sales revenue during the current fiscal year. It could simply be a matter of accelerating production and shipping to increase sales revenue for the year.

Reported sales revenue of the Southern division for the fourth quarter of 2021 was $792,000. This represented an 18.6 percent increase over the actual sales revenue for the third quarter of the year. As a result of this increase, reported sales revenue for the fourth quarter exceeded the budgeted amount by $80,000, or 11.2 percent. Actual sales revenue for the year exceeded the budgeted amount for the Southern division by $14,000, or 0.5 percent. Budgeted and actual sales revenue amounts, by division, for the year ended December 31, 2021, are presented in **Exhibit 3**.

EXHIBIT 3   United Thermostatic Controls—Sales Revenue, 2021 (4 Qs)

Budgeted and Actual Sales Revenue in 2021						
U.S.A. Sales Division				Western Sales Division		
Quarter Ended	Budget	Actual	% Var.	Budget	Actual	% Var.
March 31	$ 632,000	$ 638,000	.009%	$ 886,000	$ 898,000	.014%
June 30	640,000	642,000	.003	908,000	918,000	.011

(continued)

Budgeted and Actual Sales Revenue in 2021					
September 30	648,000	656,000	.012	930,000	936,000	.006
December 31	656,000	662,000	.009	952,000	958,000	.006
2021 Totals	$ 2,576,000	$ 2,598,000	.009%	$ 3,676,000	$ 3,710,000	.009%

	Eastern Sales Division			Southern Sales Division		
Quarter Ended	Budget	Actual	% Var.	Budget	Actual	% Var.
March 31	$ 743,000	$ 750,000	.009%	$ 688,000	$ 680,000	(.012)%
June 30	752,000	760,000	.011	696,000	674,000	(.032)
September 30	761,000	769,000	.011	704,000	668,000	(.051)
December 31	770,000	778,000	.010	712,000	792,000	.112
2021 Totals	$ 3,026,000	$ 3,057,000	.010%	$ 2,800,000	$ 2,814,000	.005%

During the course of their test of controls, the internal audit staff questioned the appropriateness of recording revenue of $150,000 on two shipments made by the Southern division in the fourth quarter of the year. These shipments are described as follows:

1. United shipped thermostats to Allen Corporation on December 31, 2021, and billed Allen $85,000, even though Allen had specified a delivery date of no earlier than February 1, 2022, to take control of the product. Allen intended to use the thermostats in the heating system of a new building that would not be ready for occupancy until March 1, 2022.

2. United shipped thermostats to Bilco Corporation on December 30, 2021, in partial (one-half) fulfillment of an order that will arrive on January 2, 2022. United recorded $65,000 revenue on December 30, 2021. Bilco had previously specified that partial shipments would not be accepted. Delivery of the full shipment had been scheduled for February 1, 2022.

During their investigation, the internal auditors learned that Campbell had pressured United's accounting department to record these two shipments early to enable the Southern division to achieve its goals with respect to the company's revenue targets. The auditors were concerned about the appropriateness of recording the $150,000 revenue in 2021 in the absence of an expressed or implied agreement with the customers to accept and pay for the prematurely shipped merchandise. The auditors noted that, had the revenue from these two shipments not been recorded, the Southern division's actual sales for the fourth quarter would have been below the budgeted amount by $70,000, or 9.8 percent. Actual sales revenue for the year ended December 31, 2021, would have been below the budgeted amount by $136,000, or 4.9 percent. The revenue effect of the two shipments in question created a 5.4 percent shift in the variance between actual and budgeted sales for the year. The auditors felt that this effect was significant with respect to the division's revenue and earnings for the fourth quarter and for the year ended December 31, 2021. The auditors decided to take their concerns to Tony Cupertino, director of the internal auditing department. Cupertino is a licensed CPA.

Cupertino discussed the situation with Campbell. Campbell informed Cupertino that he had received assurances from Sam Lorenzo, executive vice president of sales and marketing, that top management would support the recording of the $150,000 revenue because of its strong desire to meet or exceed budgeted revenue and earnings amounts. Moreover, top management is very sensitive to the need to meet financial analysts' consensus earnings estimates. According to Campbell, the company is concerned that earnings must be high enough to meet analysts' expectations because any other effect might cause the stock price to go down. In fact, Lorenzo has already told Campbell that he did not see anything wrong with recording the revenue in 2021 because the merchandise had been shipped to the customers before the end of the year and the terms of shipment were FOB shipping point.

At this point, Cupertino is uncertain whether he should take his concerns to Walter Hayward, the CFO, who is also a member of the board of directors or take them directly to the audit committee. Cupertino knows that the majority of the members of the board, including those on the audit committee, have ties to the company and members of top management. Cupertino is not even certain that he should pursue the matter any further because of the financial performance pressures that exist within the organization. However, he is very concerned about his responsibilities as a CPA and obligations to work with the external auditors who will begin their audit in a few weeks. It is at this point that Cupertino learns from Campbell that the CFO of Bilco agreed to accept the partial shipment when it arrives in return for a 20 percent discount on the total price that would be paid on February 1, 2022. It seems Campbell took the initiative to help solve the revenue problem by going directly to the Bilco CFO.

Questions

1. Discuss the ethical issues in the case including how the ethical reasoning methods would address these issues.
2. Identify the stakeholders in this case and their interests.
3. Describe the ethical and professional responsibilities of Tony Cupertino.
4. Assume you are in Cupertino's position and know you have to do something about the improper accounting in the Southern sales division. Consider the following in crafting a plan how best to voice your values and take appropriate action.

- How can you get it done effectively and efficiently?
- What do you need to say, to whom, and in what sequence?
- What will the objections or pushback be? And then,
- What would you say next? What data and other information do you need to make your point and counteract the reasons and rationalizations you will likely have to address?

Case 3-4 Franklin Industries' Whistleblowing (a GVV Case)

Natalie got the call she had been waiting for over six long months. Her complaint to the human resources department of Franklin Industries had been dismissed. It was HR's conclusion that she was not retaliated against for reporting an alleged embezzlement by the Accounting Department manager. In fact, HR ruled there was no embezzlement at all. Natalie had been demoted from assistant manager of the department to staff supervisor seven months ago after informing Stuart Masters, the controller, earlier in 2021, about the embezzlement. Her blood started to boil as she thought about all the pain and agony she'd experienced these past six months without any level of satisfaction for her troubles.

Natalie Garson is a CPA who works for Franklin Industries, a publicly owned company and manufacturer of trusses and other structural components for home builders throughout the United States. Six months ago she filed a complaint with HR after discussing a sensitive matter with her best friend and coworker, Roger Harris. Natalie trusted Harris, who had six years of experience at Franklin. The essence of the discussion was that Natalie was informed by the accounting staff of what appeared to be unusual transactions between Denny King, the department manager, and an outside company no one had ever heard of before. The staff had uncovered over $5 million in payments, authorized by King, to Vic Construction. No one could find any documentation about Vic, so the staff dug deeper and discovered that the owner of Vic Construction was Victoria King. Further examination determined that Victoria King and Denny King were siblings.

Once Natalie was convinced, there was more to the situation than meets the eye, she informed the internal auditors, who investigated and found that Vic Construction made a $5 million electronic transfer to a separate business owned by Denny King. One thing leads to another, and it was determined by the internal auditors that King had funneled $5 million to Vic Construction, which, at a later date, transferred the money back to King. It was a $5 million embezzlement from Franklin Industries.

Natalie met with Roger Harris that night and told him about the HR decision that went against her. She was concerned whether the internal auditors would act now in light of that decision. She knew the culture at Franklin was "don't rock the boat." That didn't matter to her. She was always true to her values and not afraid to act when a wrongdoing had occurred. She felt particularly motivated in this case—it was personal. She felt the need to be vindicated. She hoped Roger would be supportive.

As it turned out, Roger cautioned Natalie about taking the matter any further. He had worked for Franklin a lot longer than Natalie and knew the board of directors consisted mostly of insider directors. The CEO of Franklin was also the chair of the board. It was well known in the company that whatever the CEO wanted to do, the board rubber-stamped it.

Natalie left the meeting with Roger wondering whether she was on her own. She knew she had to act but didn't know the best way to go about it. Even though Roger cautioned against going to the CEO or board, Natalie didn't dismiss that option.

Questions

Assume you are in Natalie's position. Answer the following questions.

1. What are the ethical considerations for Natalie in deciding whether to take the matter further? Where might she go and why?

2. Consider the following assuming Natalie has decided to make one last attempt to resolve the matter internally.

- What are the main arguments you are trying to counter? That is, what are the reasons and rationalizations you need to address?
- What is at stake for the key parties, including those who disagree with you?
- What levers can you use to influence those who disagree with you?
- What is your most powerful and persuasive response to the reasons and rationalizations you need to address? To whom should the argument be made? When and in what context?

Case 3-5 Theranos: A Cautionary Tale for Silicon Valley

What possessed a CEO to hype a product that didn't work and lie to financial institutions, pharmacies, the government, and the public about it? Is it hubris; plain and simple? Or, was there something nefarious going on? The case of Theranos, an once high-flyer in Silicon Valley, portrays a company run by an ambitious person who thought she could get away with just about anything. Perhaps she would have if an employee, Tyler Schultz, had not blown the whistle to a Wall Street Journal reporter in 2015.

The Wall Street Journal investigative reporter, John Carreyrou, who broke the story, wrote a book, *Bad Blood: Secrets and Lies in a Silicon Valley Startup,* that characterized what went on at Theranos as the biggest corporate fraud since Enron and a tale of ambition and hubris set amid the bold promises of Silicon Valley.[95]

Elizabeth Holmes, who dropped out of Stanford University in 2003 to start Theranos, a privately held company that would make blood tests cheaper, more convenient, and accessible to consumers. Simply by using a pin prick, blood could be analyzed quickly for diseases. Holmes believed the testing procedures would revolutionize the way diagnostics were done and aid in preventative medicine. Using a machine called the Edison, pharmacies were supposedly able to use this portable blood test from a drop of blood. However, most tests were not able to be performed from a needle prick but actually required venipuncture.

Physicians could not get information on how the tests were done. The whole process was sort of a black box, which had mysterious or unknown internal functions or mechanisms. Theranos was very secretive about the workings of the machinery and knew it did not work as intended.

Holmes duped just about everyone about the efficacy of Edison. She was able to raise hundreds of millions of dollars until Schultz blew the whistle. For 12 years, Holmes essentially ran a Ponzi scheme by attracting investment funds from primarily venture capitalists that saw it as a unique opportunity to cash in on the boom in Silicon Valley. **Exhibit 1** summarizes the facts of the case.

Holmes, the chief executive officer, and Ramesh "Sunny" Balwani, the chief operating officer, served as chairperson of the board of directors and a member of the board, respectively. A group of mostly figure-heads also served on the board including George Shultz, a former U.S. secretary of state and the grandfather of whistleblower Tyler Schultz. A majority of board members lacked the experience necessary to ensure due diligence on the part of the company.

According to a federal indictment, Holmes and Balwani defrauded doctors and patients (1) by making false claims concerning Theranos's ability to provide fast, reliable, and cheap blood tests and test results, and (2) by omitting information concerning the limits of and problems with Theranos's technologies. Allegedly, the defendants knew Theranos was not capable of consistently producing accurate and reliable results for certain blood tests. Other allegations include[96]:

- The defendants made numerous misrepresentations to potential investors about Theranos's financial condition and its future prospects, including that its patients' blood was being tested using Thermos-manufactured analyzers; when, in truth, they knew that the company had purchased and used third party, commercially available-analyzers.

- The defendants' represented to investors that Theranos would generate over $100 million in revenues and break even in 2014 and that the company was expected to generate approximately $1 billion in revenues in 2015; when, in truth, Theranos would generate only negligible or modest revenues in 2014 and 2015.

- The defendants used a combination of direct communications, marketing materials, statements to the media, financial statements, models, and other information to defraud potential investors about the company's revolutionary and proprietary analyzer, Edison. Supposedly, the machine could perform a full range of clinical tests using small blood samples drawn from a finger stick at a faster speed than previously possible and with more accurate and reliable results. Allegedly, the defendants knew that the claims about the analyzer were false. It was slower than competing devices and, in some respects, could not compete with existing, more conventional machines.

Tyler Schultz claimed to know something unethical was going on and could have major repercussions on the company. He complained to Holmes that the research results were tampered with and multiple quality control tests were failing. Shultz said the prototype of Edison only had an accuracy of 65 percent while the required accuracy results were 95 percent, adding that Theranos was knowingly misrepresenting information to its users. He told HBO in a documentary that if 100 people who had syphilis came and got tested on the Theranos devices, the company would only tell 65 of them that they had syphilis and told the other 35 that they were healthy: no need for medical intervention.

Schultz blew the whistle even though he had signed nondisclosure and confidentiality agreements. As a result, Theranos went after Schultz in court, accusing him of leaking trade secrets and violating the agreement. He and his family fought these claims spending between $400,000 and $500,000 in legal fees.

In an interview with ABC News for its 20-20 television show in May 2019, another former Theranos employee, Erika Cheung, pointed out the flawed quality controls at the company that had ignored problems with the process of analyzing blood. Cheung said she raised these issues directly with Balwani who reacted by saying, "What makes you think that we have problems? What was your training in statistics?...I'm tired of people coming in here and starting fires where there are no fires and sort of thinking that there are problems when there are no problems." Cheung realized her concerns were falling on deaf ears. She told the reporter that "This was not an environment, that is not a culture, where they really care about what consequences this might have on patients."[97]

The story of Theranos is a cautionary tale where one lie leads to another and before you know it the story snowballs out of control and coverups ensue. The culture of the company was such that it hid important information from the public, pharmacies, medical professionals, and the government. It is a classic case of the ethical slippery slope.

EXHIBIT 1   Theranos Timeline[98]

Partnerships

Between 2012 and 2015, Theranos partnered with Safeway, Walgreens, and the prestigious Cleveland Clinic, to market its product to labs and the public. The following summarizes those deals.

In 2012, Safeway invested $350 million into retrofitting 800 locations with clinics that would offer in-store blood tests. Following missed deadlines and questionable results, the deal was called off in 2015.

In 2013, Theranos partnered with Walgreens to offer in-store blood tests at more than 40 locations. Following the story in the Wall Street Journal, Walgreen's suspended plans to expand blood-testing centers in their stores. In 2016,

(continued)

Walgreens' filed a lawsuit against Theranos for breach of contract. In 2017, the original claim for damages of $140 million was settled for less than $30 million.

In March 2015, the Cleveland Clinic announced a partnership with Theranos in order to test its technology and decrease the cost of lab tests. Theranos became the lab-work provider for Pennsylvania insurers AmeriHealth Caritas and Capital BlueCross.

In July 2015, the Food and Drug Administration approved the use of the company's fingerstick blood-testing device (the Edison) for the herpes simplex virus outside a clinical laboratory setting. Theranos was awarded the 2015 Bioscience Company of the Year.

Exposure and Downfall

In October 2015, John Carreyrou of the *Wall Street Journal* reported that Theranos was using traditional blood-testing machines instead of the company's Edison devices to run its tests. Carreyrou had interviewed an employee at Theranos, Tyler Shultz, who said he attempted to bring his concerns to the attention of management to no avail. He blew the whistle by reporting the company to the New York State Department of Health.

Theranos claimed the allegations were "factually and scientifically erroneous." Walgreen's suspended plans to expand blood-testing centers in their stores. The Cleveland Clinic announced it would work to verify Theranos technology.

In January 2016, the Centers for Medicare and Medicaid Services (CMS) sent a letter to Theranos after inspecting its Newark, California lab, reporting that the facility caused "immediate jeopardy to patient health and safety" based on a test to determine the correct dose of the blood-thinning drug warfarin.

In 2016, Walgreens and Capital BlueCross announced a suspension of Theranos blood tests from the Newark lab.

In March 2016, CMS regulators announced plans to enact sanctions that included suspending Elizabeth Holmes, the chief executive officer, and Ramesh "Sunny" Balwani, vice president and chief operating officer, from owning or operating a lab for two years and CMS would revoke the Newark labs license.

By April 2016, Theranos came under criminal investigation by federal prosecutors and the SEC for allegedly misleading investors and government officials about its technology. The U.S. House of Representatives Committee on Energy and Commerce requested information on what Theranos was doing to correct its testing inaccuracies and adherence to federal guidelines.

In May 2016, Theranos announced that it had voided two years of results, representing one percent of its tests, from its Edison device.

In July 2016, Theranos announced that the CMS had revoked its license and issued sanctions including the suspension of approval to receive Medicare and Medicaid payments, and a civil monetary penalty. Theranos announced its intention to appeal the decision by regulators to revoke its license to operate the Newark lab and other sanctions.

October 2016, Theranos announced that it would close its laboratory operations and wellness centers and lay off about 40 percent of its work force to work on miniature medical testing machines.

On January 17, 2017 Theranos announced that it had laid off approximately 155 people and closed the last remaining blood-testing facility after the lab failed a second major U.S. regulatory inspection.

In April 2017, a lawsuit by Partners Investments LP alleged that Theranos had misled company directors about the practices concerning laboratory testing and that it had secretly bought lab equipment to run fake demonstrations. The company reached an undisclosed settlement.

In April 2017, Theranos reached a settlement with CMS agreeing to stay out of the blood-testing business for at least two years in exchange for reduced penalties and signed a consent decree over violations of the Arizona Consumer Fraud Act. Alleged violations included false advertisement and inaccurate blood testing.

In August 2017, Theranos announced it had reached a settlement with Walgreens.

In March 2018, the SEC charged Theranos, Holmes and Balwani in an "elaborate years-long fraud" wherein they "deceived investors into believing that its key product—a portable blood analyzer—could conduct comprehensive blood tests from finger drops of blood." Holmes reached a settlement with the SEC, which requires her to pay $500,000, forfeit 19 million shares of company stock, and be barred from having a leadership role in any public company for 10 years. Balwani did not settle with the SEC.

On June 15, 2018, Holmes and Balwani were indicted on multiple counts of wire fraud and conspiracy to commit wire fraud. According to the indictment, investors, doctors, and patients were defrauded. It alleged the defendants were aware of the unreliability and inaccuracy of their products but concealed that information. If convicted they each face a maximum fine of $250,000 and 20 years in prison. Jury selection for the Holmes trial began in August of 2021, and the trial was scheduled to start on September 8th.

In September 2018, it was announced that, with the approval of the company's board of directors and shareholders, Theranos would begin the process of corporate dissolution. The company owed at least $60 million to unsecured creditors. The move to dissolve rather than file for bankruptcy left the company with $5 million to distribute to creditors.

Questions

1. Evaluate the behavior of Elizabeth Holmes and Sunny Balwani, as officers of Theranos, from the perspective of the six pillars of character discussed in **Chapter 1**.
2. What can you conclude about the culture at Theranos and why?
3. Tyler Shultz signed a nondisclosure agreement not to divulge confidential information. Yet, he did just that in the interview with the Wall Street Journal reporter thereby violating the agreement. Analyze his actions from both a legal and ethical reasoning perspective.

Case 3-6 Blow the Whistle or Don't Blow the Whistle

John Stanton, CPA, is a seasoned accountant who left his Big-4 CPA firm Senior Manager position to become the CFO of a highly successful hundred million-dollar publicly held manufacturer of solar panels. The company wanted John's expertise in the renewable energy sector and his pedigree from working for one of the Big-4 firms. The company plans to expand its operations later in the year and is in the process of seeking a loan from a financial institution to fund the expansion. Everything went well for the first two months until the controller, Diane Hopkins, who is also a CPA, came to John with a problem. She discovered that one of her accounts payable clerks has been embezzling money from the company by processing and approving fictitious invoices from shell companies for fictitious purchases that the AP clerk had created. Diane estimated that the clerk had been able to steal approximately $250,000 over the year and a half they worked at the company. Diane and John agreed to fire the clerk immediately and did so. They also agreed that John would report the matter to the CEO, David Laskey.

John picked up the phone and called Laskey, who was also the chair of the board of directors, to give him a heads up on what had transpired. Laskey asked John to come to his office the next day to discuss the matter. At that meeting, Laskey instructed John to go no further and tell Diane to drop the matter because of the pending bank loan. John is considering his options.

Questions

1. Evaluate John's options from an ethical reasoning perspective.
2. What would it take for John to qualify as a whistleblower under Dodd-Frank? How might it be affected by the court rulings in *Digital Realty Trust, Inc. v. Somers* and *Erhart v. BofI Holdings*?
3. What would you do if you were in John's position and Laskey threatened to fire you if you take the matter any further? Why?

Case 3-7 Wells Fargo—A Toxic Sales Culture

On September 8, 2016, Wells Fargo announced it was paying $185 million in fines to Los Angeles city and federal regulators to settle allegations that its employees created millions of fake bank accounts for customers. It also agreed to pay $142 million in a national class-action lawsuit to cover fake accounts that went back to 2002 plus another $6.1

million to refund customers for unauthorized bank and credit card accounts. The impact of the Wells Fargo scandal continued well into 2020 as legal settlements with the government were drawn out, class-action lawsuits worked its way through the courts, and whistleblower retaliation lawsuits became resolved. In February 2020, the bank agreed to a $3-billion settlement with the SEC and Department of Justice over violations, which involved sales staff opening millions of bogus bank accounts for customers and others in order to meet punitive sales goals.

The problem was top management had set unrealistic sales goals that promoted aggressive sales tactics without regard for the ethics of these policies and what it meant for the public trust. Wells Fargo engaged in fraud when its employees set up fake accounts for customers, charged them for services not requested, and sold products not wanted because of aggressive cross-selling goals set by the bank. Wells Fargo pressured employees to cross-sell, offering customers with one type of product (i.e., savings or checking accounts) and then pressuring them to also buy other types of products, such as credit cards and loans. One former employee described it as a "grind house, with coworkers cracking under pressure." Another former employee reported, "If you don't meet your solutions goals you're not a team player. If you're bringing down the team then you will be fired and it will be on your permanent record."[99]

Many employees reported that company sales goals were unrealistic and incentives for compensation encouraged gaming the system. One employee said, "Everybody needs a ridiculous amount of products." The sales culture was so intense that some workers resorted to deceptive practices to make their sales goals." That completely contradicted what the former CEO, John Stumpf, said in front of a U.S. Senate Banking committee. He told committee members that "Wrongful sales practice behavior goes against everything regarding our core principles, our ethics and our culture." Stumpf said the bank never directed nor wanted employees to provide products and services to customers that they did not want.[100]

Stumpf's self-serving statement is ironic given that he presided over the massive fraud at Wells Fargo, turning a blind eye as many of his underlings sent up red flares. While the fraud was going on, he collected what was estimated at about $300 million in cash, bonuses, and stock options. The board of directors found that the compensation was excessive and clawed back about $69 million after Stumpf's dereliction of duty was revealed. Stumpf was hit with a $2.5 million penalty by the SEC. He also agreed to pay $17.5 million to other banking regulators.

Many questions can be raised as a result of the incident, including why the ethics and compliance machinery at Wells Fargo failed so miserably.

The facts of the case illustrate a company that put "profits-over-people."[101]

- 3.5 million of fake bank and credit card accounts opened in customer names.
- Improperly charged mortgage fees known as rate-lock extensions when loan approvals exceeded the 30- to 45-day period. These fees were charged even though the delay in approvals were due to the bank, not the customer.
- Set up about 528,000 unauthorized online bill paying services.
- Forced up to 570,000 borrowers into unneeded auto insurance. The cost of unneeded insurance pushed about 274,000 Wells Fargo customers into delinquency and caused nearly 25,000 wrongful vehicle repossessions.
- Illegal vehicle seizures by repossessing more than 860 vehicles of U.S. service members in violation of the Servicemembers Civil Relief Act.

How did Wells Fargo, a bank that once had a strong reputation for customer service, get to this point? Their motto was: "Our product: SERVICE. Our valued-added: FINANCIAL ADVICE. Our competitive advantage: OUR PEOPLE.

It was a failure at all levels of management, but blame was laid at the doorstep of Stumpf who was forced to resign. Under his watch, Wells violated just about every standard of ethical behavior, most of which were addressed in this chapter. For now, here is a list of the systemic failures.

- A failure of leadership.
- Creating a toxic culture.
- Ignoring employee reports of fraudulent accounts.
- Not living up to the standards in its ethics code.
- Retaliating against whistleblowers, including violations of the Sarbanes-Oxley Act.

The retaliation against Wells Fargo whistleblowers illustrates how a company's own ethics and compliance procedures are no better than the paper they are written on unless top management 'walks the talk' of ethics. Wells had an ethics hotline expressly for the purpose of reporting behavior that employees suspected as suspicious or fraudulent; then they retaliated against those employees who did just that.[102]

Bill Bado, a former Wells Fargo banker, was one of six former Wells employees who spoke to CNN about their experiences. Bado, who refused orders to open phony bank and credit accounts, called the hotline and sent an e-mail to human resources, flagging unethical sales activities as he had been instructed to do. Eight days after reporting it, Bado was terminated. The reason given was "excessive tardiness."[103]

One unnamed whistleblower, who was a former branch manager in Pomona, California, received $577,500 in back wages and damages after being fired for reporting co-workers who engaged in allegedly fraudulent activities related to the fake-account scandal by opening accounts and enrolling customers in bank products without their knowledge, consent, or disclosures.

A number of Wells Fargo employees reportedly lodged whistleblower complaints with the Occupational Safety and Health Administration (OSHA) of the U.S. Department of Labor after being fired for reporting ethics violations to the company. The Sarbanes-Oxley Act contains a provision that protects whistleblowers who have been unlawfully retaliated against. One such employee, Claudia Ponce de Leon, was reinstated by OSHA, but the bank fought the order, claiming de Leon was fired for inappropriate behavior, not reporting that colleagues were opening fake accounts in order to meet sales goals.[104] Eventually, the bank reached a settlement but the terms were kept confidential.

The culture at Wells Fargo failed at the very top of management all the way down to employees. Stumpf and others failed to set an ethical tone in the organization, didn't follow its own code of ethics, and virtually ignored employee hot line reports of what was going on. Wells' Ethics Policy stated:

"Our ethics are the sum of all the decisions each of us makes every day. We have a responsibility to always act with honesty and integrity. When we do so, we earn the trust of our customers. We have to earn that trust every day by behaving ethically, rewarding open, honest communications, and holding ourselves accountable for our decisions and actions."[105]

The saga of Wells Fargo is a company that suffered from ethical blind spots, gave in to situational pressures to meet sales goals at all costs, and functioned in a social and organizational environment that led employees to do things they otherwise would not have done, that is, set up fake accounts and charge customers for unwanted services.

Questions

1. What factors played the most important role in leading so many Wells Fargo employees to cheat the bank's customers?
2. Many employees admitted that they knew what they were doing was wrong but continued to open fraudulent accounts. Use ethical reasoning to evaluate why their actions were wrong.
3. Analyze the corporate governance failures in the Wells Fargo case.
4. Given the pressure-laden culture at Wells Fargo, if you had been in the position of bank employees what would you have done differently and why?

Case 3-8 Accountant Takes on Halliburton and Wins!

The whistleblowing aspects of this case were first discussed in the text. What follows is a more comprehensive discussion of accounting and auditing issues.

In 2005, Tony Menendez, a former Ernst & Young LLP auditor and director of technical accounting and research training for Halliburton, blew the whistle on Halliburton's accounting practices. The fight cost him nine years of his life. Just a few months later in 2005, Menendez received an e-mail from Mark McCollum, Halliburton's chief accounting officer, and a top-ranking executive at Halliburton, that also went to much of the accounting department. "The SEC has opened an inquiry into the allegations of Mr. Menendez," it read. Everyone was to retain their documents until further notice.

What happened next changed the life of Menendez and brought into question how such a large and influential company could have such a failed corporate governance system. Further, the role of the auditors, KPMG, with respect to its handling of accounting and auditing matters seemed off, and independence was an issue. **Exhibit 1** summarizes some of the relevant accounting and auditing issues in the case.

EXHIBIT 1   Issues Related to the Sarbanes-Oxley Act, SEC, and KPMG

Tony Menendez contacted Halliburton's audit committee because he believed it was in the best interest of the employees and shareholders if he made himself available to the committee in its efforts to investigate the questionable accounting and auditing practices and properly respond to the SEC. It was discovered that Halliburton did not have in place, as required by Section 301 of the Sarbanes-Oxley Act (SOX), a process for "(1) the receipt and treatment of complaints received by the issuer regarding accounting, internal controls, or auditing matters; and (2) the confidential, anonymous submission of employees of the issuer of concerns regarding questionable accounting or auditing matters."

After waiting for the company to take action to no avail, Menendez felt there was no alternative to blowing the whistle, and on November 4, 2005, he contacted the SEC and PCAOB stating in part:

"As a CPA and the Director of Technical Accounting Research and Training for Halliburton, I feel it is my duty and obligation to report information that I believe constitutes both a potential failure by a registered public accounting firm, KPMG, to properly perform an audit and the potential filing of materially misleading financial information with the SEC by Halliburton."

Two weeks later, at the agencies' request, he met with SEC enforcement staff at their Fort Worth office. On November 30, 2005, he approached members of top management of Halliburton. On February 4, 2006, Menendez provided what he believed would be a confidential report to Halliburton's audit committee, giving the company yet another opportunity for self-examination. However, on the morning of February 6, 2006, Menendez's identity was disclosed to Mark McCollum, Halliburton's chief accounting officer, and less than an hour after finding out that Menendez had reported the questionable accounting and auditing practices to the SEC, McCollum distributed information about Menendez's investigation and identity.

The disclosure was followed by a series of retaliatory actions. Halliburton management stripped Menendez of teaching and researching responsibilities, ordered subordinates to monitor and report on his activity, excluded him from meetings and accounting decisions, and ordered financial and accounting personnel to preclear any conversations about accounting issues before discussing them with Menendez.

In May 2005, Menendez filed a civil whistleblower complaint under SOX. In July 2006, Halliburton told the Department of Labor committee handling the case that KPMG had insisted that Menendez be excluded from a meeting concerning accounting for a potential joint venture arrangement called "RTA." Halliburton indicated it acceded to KPMG's demand and excluded Menendez from the meeting. SOX prohibits an employer from discriminating against an employee, contractor, or agent and from prohibiting such party from engaging in activity protected under the Act, and the SEC stated that the assertion by the company that KPMG's presence was mandatory was misleading. In fact, the SEC opined that KPMG's presence was not even advisable since KPMG was supposed to be an independent auditor in both appearance and in fact.

The RTA meeting was scheduled to determine whether or not Halliburton would be required to consolidate the proposed joint venture. Senior management explicitly stated that the division management would not receive approval to proceed unless Halliburton could both avoid consolidation and maintain control over the joint venture activities. Earlier in the development of the accounting position regarding this joint venture, KPMG told management that it would allow the company to avoid consolidation and FIN 46R's Anti-Abuse criteria on the basis that the determination required professional judgment, and indicated that KPMG would be willing to support a conclusion that Halliburton was not significantly involved in the joint venture activities, when clearly the facts and circumstances did not support such a conclusion. Menendez had vehemently objected to KPMG and management's proposed conclusion on the basis that such a position was absurd.

According to the SEC, given KPMG's previous guidance to the company regarding RTA, and its willingness to accommodate unsupportable conclusions, continued input by KPMG on RTA was inappropriate and, once again, put KPMG in the position of auditing its own recommendations and advice. In the end, the concerted failures of management and the external auditor underscored the lack of independence between company and KPMG, which was a root cause of the accounting violations Menendez fought to correct and, at last, had to report.

Nature of Halliburton's Revenue Transactions in Question

During the months following the "leaked" e-mail, Menendez waited and watched to see if Halliburton would act on his claims that the company was cooking the books. The issue was revenue recognition as discussed following.

Halliburton enters into long-term contracts with energy giants like Royal Dutch Shell or BP to find and exploit huge oil and gas fields. It sells services—the expertise of its geologists and engineers. Halliburton also builds massive and expensive machinery that its professionals use to provide those services. Then, the company charges its customers for that equipment, which has particularly high profit margins. At the crux of the matter, the company's accountants had been allowing the company to count the full value of the equipment right away as revenue, sometimes even before it had assembled the equipment. But the customers could walk away in the middle of the contracts. Menendez realized that if the equipment were damaged, Halliburton, not the customer, was on the hook.

Menendez accused Halliburton of using so-called bill-and-hold techniques that distort the timing of billions of dollars in revenue and allowed Halliburton to book product sales before they occurred.

Menendez explained Halliburton's accounting this way:

> For example, the company recognizes revenue when the goods are parked in company warehouses, rather than delivered to the customer. Typically, these goods are not even assembled and ready for the customer. Furthermore, it is unknown as to when the goods will be ultimately assembled, tested, delivered to the customer, and, finally, used by the company to perform the required oilfield services for the customer.

Based on Menendez's claims, Halliburton's accounting procedures violated generally accepted accounting principles. For companies to recognize revenue before delivery, "the risks of ownership must have passed to the buyer," the SEC's staff wrote in a 2003 accounting bulletin. There also "must be a fixed schedule for delivery of the goods" and the product "must be complete and ready for shipment" among other things.

Shortly after joining Halliburton in March 2005, Menendez said he discovered a "terribly flawed" flow chart on the company's in-house website, called the Bill and Hold Decision Tree. The flow chart, a copy of which Menendez included in his complaint, walks through what to do in a situation where a "customer has been billed for completed inventory which is being stored at a Halliburton facility."

First, it asks: Based on the contract terms, "has title passed to customer?" If the answer is no—and here's where it gets strange—the employee is asked: "Does the transaction meet all of the 'bill-and-hold' criteria for revenue recognition?" If the answer to that question is yes, the decision tree says to do this: "Recognize revenue." The decision tree didn't specify what the other criteria were.

In other words, Halliburton told employees to recognize revenue even though the company still owned the product. Ironically, the accelerated revenue for financial statement purposes led to higher income taxes paid to the IRS.

"The policy in the chart is clearly at odds with generally accepted accounting principles," said Charles Mulford, a Georgia Institute of Technology accounting professor, who reviewed the court records. "It's very clear cut. It's not gray."

According to the accounting rules, it is possible to use bill-and-hold and comply with the rules. But it's hard. The customer, not the seller, must request such treatment. The customer also must have a compelling reason for doing so. Customers rarely do.

Top Halliburton accounting executives had agreed with Menendez's analysis, including McCollum, the company's chief accounting officer. But according to Menendez, they dragged their feet on implementing a change that was certain to slow revenue growth. In an e-mail response to detailed questions, a Halliburton spokeswoman wrote, "The accounting allegations were made by Mr. Menendez almost nine years ago and were promptly reviewed by the company and the Securities and Exchange Commission. The company's accounting was appropriate and the SEC closed its investigation." This seems curious when we examine the SEC's own rules for recognition.

Hocus Pocus Accounting: Bill-and-Hold Schemes

The proper accounting for Halliburton's bill-and-hold transactions was not lost on its external auditors, KPMG. In fact, in early 2005, KPMG published an article entitled: *Bill and Hold Transactions in the Oilfield Services Industry,* which made it clear that oilfield services companies had to comply with all four criteria of SEC Staff Accounting Bulletin (SAB 101) to recognize revenue early. These include:

- Persuasive evidence of an arrangement exists.
- Delivery has occurred or services have been rendered.
- The seller's price to the buyer is fixed or determinable.
- Collectibility is reasonably assured.

KPMG went on to recognize that it would be rare for an oilfield services company to actually meet the necessary criteria. The impact to Halliburton was highlighted by KPMG's recognition that bill-and-hold transactions for oilfield services companies were "common" and "involve very large and complex products and equipment that carry significant amounts of economic value." KPMG went on to state that "perhaps no area of revenue recognition has received as much scrutiny as bill-and-hold."

Menendez's Complaint to the DOL

Menendez's allegations are part of a 54-page complaint he filed against Halliburton with a Department of Labor (DOL) administrative-law judge in Covington, Louisiana, who released the records to Menendez in response to a Freedom of Information Act request. Menendez claimed Halliburton retaliated against him in violation of the Sarbanes-Oxley Act's whistleblower provisions after he reported his concerns to the SEC and the company's audit committee.

According to a company spokesperson, Halliburton's audit committee "directed an independent investigation" and "concluded that the allegations were without merit." She declined to comment on bill-and-hold issues, and Halliburton's court filings in the case don't provide any details about its accounting practices.

Menendez filed his complaint shortly after a DOL investigator in Dallas rejected his retaliation claim. His initial claim was rejected by the court and subsequently appealed after many years, and the decision was ultimately overturned, but not until after he and his family had endured a nine-year ordeal during which time he was an outcast at Halliburton.

The Final Verdict Is in: Accountant Takes on Halliburton and Wins!

The appeals process went on for three years. In September 2011, the administrative-law appeals panel ruled. It overturned the original trial judge. After five years, Menendez had his first victory.

But it wasn't over. Halliburton appealed to the Fifth Circuit Court of Appeals. There were more legal filings, more hours of work, more money spent.

Finally, in November 2014, almost nine years after Menendez received "The E-mail," he prevailed. The appeals panel ruled that he indeed had been retaliated against for blowing the whistle, just as he had argued all along.

Because he had wanted only to be proven right, he'd asked for a token sum. The administrative-law panel, noting the importance of punishing retaliations against whistleblowers, pushed for an increase and Menendez was awarded $30,000.

To say that the outcome stunned experts is something of an understatement. "Accountant beats Halliburton!" said Thomas, the attorney and expert on whistleblower law. "The government tries to beat Halliburton and loses."

Postdecision Interview About Whistleblowing

In an interview with a reporter, Menendez offered that Halliburton had a whistleblower policy prior to this incident as required under Sarbanes-Oxley. It was required to be confidential, and although Halliburton's policy promised confidentiality, at the same time it discouraged anonymous complaints on the basis that if you didn't provide your identity, the company might not be able to properly investigate your concern. Menendez added that confidentiality was absolutely central to his case and he relied on this policy, but it was Halliburton that blatantly ignored its own policy and betrayed his trust.

He was asked how the whistleblowing policy of the SEC might be improved. He said that all too often it is almost impossible for a whistleblower to prevail and that there needs to be more protections and a more balanced playing field. "It shouldn't take nine years and hundreds of thousands of dollars to even have a remote chance of prevailing," he said.

Questions

1. Describe the inadequacies in the corporate governance system at Halliburton.

2. Consider the role of KPMG in the case with respect to the accounting and auditing issues. How did the firm's actions relate to the ethical and professional expectations for CPAs by the accounting profession?

3. The Halliburton case took place before the Dodd-Frank Financial Reform Act was adopted by Congress. Assume Dodd-Frank had been in effect and Menendez decided to inform the SEC under Dodd-Frank rather than SOX because it had been more than 180 days since the accounting violation had occurred. Given the facts of the case would Menendez have qualified for whistleblower protection? Explain.

4. Menendez objected to Halliburton's accounting for revenue on bill and hold transactions. He claims that Halliburton had violated accounting rules. What was Halliburton's motivation in recording bill and hold transactions? Did it violate accounting rules?

Case 3-9 Expense or Capitalize Research and Development Costs (a GVV Case)

Jerry Maloney, CPA has been working at Mason Pharmaceuticals for 15 years. Mason is a Fortune 1000 company whose stock trades on the New York Stock Exchange. He came to Mason after starting his career in the audit practice of PwC working on clients in the Pharmaceuticals and Medical Device manufacturing industries. Jerry loves and is very loyal to both the industry he works in and the company he works for. He believes that the drugs they manufacture save lives and he is committed to the continued success of the company. He started out as an Assistant Manager of Internal Audit at Mason, later led the internal audit division, and then moved into the Financial Reporting Department. His hard work has paid off and he was recently promoted to Senior Manager of Financial Reporting, reporting directly to the CFO. His department is responsible for preparing and ensuring the accuracy of all the required filings to the SEC and the NYSE. While his boss must certify the accuracy of the financials, the CFO relies on Jerry to ensure compliance with GAAP and that all the reporting requirements of the SEC and the NYSE are followed.

Jerry is sitting in his office reviewing a preliminary draft of the 10Q for the third quarter ended September 30, 2021. He is smiling as he reads the report as their Earnings Per Share (EPS) figures have exceeded their projected numbers for the third quarter in a row and he knows upper management will be thrilled. As he sits and contemplates what this might mean in terms of bonuses, raises, and stock valuation, Sharon Diggins, the Manager of Financial Reporting, knocks on his door. He invites her in and she explains that their staff have just found a material understatement of expenses in the draft 10Q. She explains that Research and Development Costs on a new drug to treat Colorectal Cancer had been inadvertently capitalized as direct materials inventory and they needed to reverse that entry before issuing a final 10Q with the SEC. The reversal will cause them to fall just short of their expected EPS figures.

Mason is waiting for approval of the new drug by the U.S. Food and Drug Administration (FDA) that is expected in the fourth quarter. The company expects this new drug to produce more revenue than any drug they have manufactured to date. Sharon explains that the purchasing manager had inadvertently purchased a six months' supply of the primary compound needed to produce the drug starting in the third quarter. The accounts payable clerk recorded the invoice for the compound as Direct Materials Inventory as the intent was to use the materials for the manufacture of the new drug. Under GAAP all such costs need to be expensed as Research and Development Costs up until regulatory approval is received.

Jerry is distraught over the fact that the internal audit department did not catch this error sooner. He discusses with Sharon that they will need to investigate the oversight later but right now their larger issue is getting the reports revised. He explains that convincing John Bender, the CFO, that they need to correct this error now will be difficult. Bender is also reviewing the same draft of the 10Q that Jerry has and must be delighted by the apparent results. Jerry is sure he will argue against expensing the cost of the compound. He can just imagine that at a minimum Bender will argue that following GAAP to the letter does not make sense. The intent of the purchase was to produce the drug, which they had started doing in the current quarter. He is sure Bender will state following GAAP will actually reduce the true cost of goods sold next quarter and, therefore, they should leave the cost in inventory. Besides, he will argue, regulatory approval will be forthcoming. Sharon reminds Jerry that capitalizing the costs reduces cost of goods sold in the current quarter and, consequently, overstates gross profit, a violation of GAAP. The SEC will consider it fraudulent financial and we cannot allow that to happen. She suggests that they put their GVV training to work and try to identify all the arguments that Bender will use to try and convince them to ignore this error and then prepare counter arguments. Jerry agrees and they get to work formulating their plan for discussing this matter with Bender.

Questions

1. What are the main arguments that Jerry and Sharon will need to counter? That is, what are the reasons and rationalizations they will need to address?

2. What is at stake should they not convince Bender to issue a revised 10Q?

3. What levers do Jerry and Sharon have available to them? Include in your answer a discussion of the provisions under SOX and how they might be used as a lever.

4. If they cannot convince Bender to issue the revised report, what is their next step? To whom should they report this matter to? Include other parties they might be able to involve who will support their position.

5. If they are unable to stop the draft report from being issued as is, what are their options?

Case 3-10 Cheating on Internal Training Exams at KPMG

What prompted partners at KPMG to facilitate cheating on internal training exams? In 2018, Timothy Daly, a former lead engagement partner, solicited and received questions and answers to the examination from a colleague, who was a second audit partner on one of Daly's engagements teams. After learning of KPMG's internal investigation of its audit professionals' cheating, Daly deleted text messages with his colleague in which the colleague had relayed the questions and answers to the exam, after receiving a notice from the firm requiring Daly to preserve them. Daly also made a misrepresentation to KPMG's investigators, which he subsequently self-corrected. What follows is a summary of the facts of an SEC action against Daly.[106]

The legal matter with Timothy Daly pertained to a continuing professional education online training program that qualified for CPE credit. KPMG required its auditors to pass an examination at the conclusion of each online training program. Audit professionals are given three opportunities to pass each examination. If one of KPMG's audit professionals is unable to pass after two attempts, their Performance Leader is notified. If they are unable to pass after three attempts, the consequences are more significant including: to retake the training; they are prohibited from conducting audit work until they pass the exam; and others at the firm may be notified. Audit professionals also understood that failing to pass an exam could lead to their compensation being reduced.

In the fall of 2018, KPMG required its audit staff to complete trainings and exams related to a new lease accounting standard. In late September, Daly asked Michael Bellach, the second partner on a significant KPMG engagement for which Daly was the lead engagement partner, about his progress on the lease testing. Bellach told Daly he had completed the last lease exam, and it was difficult. Bellach also told Daly he had pictures of the questions and his responses that he had taken after he failed his first attempt for his own use in preparing to retake the exam. In early October, Daly sent Bellach a text message asking for the photographs of the failed lease exam, and Bellach texted the images back to Daly.

After learning of potential cheating on internal training exams, KPMG leadership began an internal investigation. The firm's Board of Directors then formed a Special Committee led by an independent board member to oversee an investigation of this conduct.

As part of its investigation, KPMG's Office of General Counsel e-mailed an "Urgent Request" to all KPMG personnel to preserve all documents related to KPMG's training requirements or training sessions. The November 1, 2018 e-mail emphasized the importance of "strict compliance" with the document preservation order, cautioning that failure to comply could expose individuals and the firm to serious consequences. After receiving the November 1 document preservation notice, Daly deleted the text message and photos of the failed lease exam Bellach had sent him and encouraged Bellach to do the same.

In December 2018, the firm required certain audit professionals to complete a questionnaire that probed whether individuals had shared exam materials. Daly falsely answered "no" to the question of whether he had received any answers to KPMG training exams. Early the next week, Daly self-corrected by informing KPMG senior management that he had, contrary to his response to the questionnaire, received a colleague's answers to a training exam.

The SEC found that Daly willfully violated PCAOB Rule 3500T, which required Daly to comply with ethics standards, including to maintain integrity, as described in the AICPA's Code of Professional Conduct. As a result, Daly failed to comply with the meaning of Section 4C(a)(2) of the SEC Exchange Act and Rule 102(e)(1)(ii) of the Commission's Rules of Practice.

As a result of SEC's legal finding, it issued an Order requiring Daly to do the following and/or had his practice of public accounting restricted:

- Cease and desist from committing or causing any violations and any future violations of PCAOB Rule 3500T.
- Denied the privilege of appearing or practicing before the Commission as an accountant.
- After three years from May 18, 2020, the date of the legal finding, Daly may request that the Commission consider his restatement by submitting an application to resume appearing or practicing before the Commission as a preparer or reviewer, or a person responsible for the preparation or review, of any public company's financial statements that are filed with the Commission (other than as a member of an audit committee).

The SEC also found that numerous KPMG audit professionals had cheated on internal training exams during a three-year period by improperly sharing answers and manipulating test results. John Donovan, another audit professional, had received answers to the exams from subordinates on several occasions and shared answers with others. Certain employees actually lowered the pass rate for their test scores so failing scores would become passing scores. They did this through manipulation of the software program which scored the exam.

Senior partners including lead audit engagement partners who were responsible for compliance with PCAOB standards in auditing their clients' financial statements down to junior level employees were sharing the examination answers freely between themselves. They shared this information via e-mail and even sent screen shots of pages with correct answers.

The SEC Order did not state how this unethical behavior became known to the Board of Directors. It only stated, "Upon learning of the potential cheating, KPMG leadership alerted the SEC staff and began an internal investigation." The Order did specifically note that during the duration of the conduct, "Prior to the firm's investigation, no one reported sharing of exam answers to the firm's Ethics and Compliance Hotline."

The KPMG cheating on internal training exams raises many questions about how such a practice could have occurred at a Big Four CPA firm.

Questions

1. Evaluate the facts of this case from the perspective of KPMG's culture. What are the key factors that allowed the cheating on training exams to persist?
2. It could be said that senior partners that shared exam answers believed the goal of helping partners and others pass the internal training exams justified the way test questions and answers were shared and lowering the passing rate. Evaluate this statement from the perspective of "end justifies the means" ethical reasoning. How else might the firm have evaluated whether what it was doing was proper?
3. Assume you are preparing to interview for a job with KPMG. You are aware of the cheating scandal. The interview went well and you received an offer of employment. Would knowledge of the scope of the cheating scandal and the SEC's ruling in that matter change your decision to accept an offer? Why or why not?

CHAPTER 4
AICPA Code of Professional Conduct

LEARNING OBJECTIVES

After studying **Chapter 4**, you should be able to:

LO 4-1   Explain professional judgment and the CPA's obligations under the AICPA Code of Conduct.

LO 4-2   Explain how to apply the threats and safeguards approach to independence.

LO 4-3   Discuss SEC actions taken against auditors because of a lack of independence.

LO 4-4   Describe the process to resolve ethical conflicts that may cause violations of the rules.

LO 4-5   Explain how the conceptual framework works to keep in check possible violations of integrity and objectivity for CPAs in business.

LO 4-6   Explain how to apply the rules of conduct in the AICPA Code to the performance of professional services.

LO 4-7   Analyze the ethics rules for tax practice and how they are influenced by the realistic possibility standard.

LO 4-8   Describe the PCAOB independence and ethics rules.

Ethics Reflection

CPAs are expected to act in accordance with the ethical standards embodied in the AICPA Code of Professional Conduct in the performance of a variety of services, including audit, tax, and consulting. CPAs are required to follow ethical and professional standards to be members in good standing of the AICPA and to follow the regulations of their state board of accountancy to maintain their licenses.

The overriding ethical commitment of CPAs is to first and foremost serve the public interest even if it is not in the best interests of one's employer, the client, and even self-interest. Thus, egoistic methods of ethical reasoning have no place in public accounting, which emphasizes the rights of users of financial statements to receive accurate and reliable financial information and the duties of CPAs to make that happen.

The public interest requires that CPAs make sound professional judgments in the performance of professional services and to ensure that the financial statements do not contain any material misstatements, including fraud. These judgments may be influenced by cognitive biases and other factors, as was discussed in **Chapter 2**. Common problems include framing issues in a way that fails to adequately consider the ethical dimension of a problem, social and organizational pressures that create cognitive dissonance, and an ethical culture that emphasizes conformity to organizational practices rather than independent thought and ethical decision making.

The commitment to serve the public interest has eroded over the years as business and personal relationships with clients and client management increasingly create conflicts of interest that impair objective judgment and threaten the independent audit. Just imagine that a CPA trades on inside information, becomes involved in a sexual relationship with someone at the client with financial reporting responsibilities, or has become involved with client management in joint business relationships. These relationships impair independence in appearance, if not factually, and will be discussed in the chapter.

The independent audit seems to be in a downward trajectory. Some firms are now using a materiality criterion to determine whether nonaudit services provided to an affiliate entity, that would be prohibited if the parent had provided them, violate the independence requirement in audit engagements. Applying such a materiality standard can have the effect of dismissing otherwise improper relationships. The firms seem to be saying that so long as they are objective and maintain their integrity, independence concerns can be ignored.

CPAs used to earn more than 50 percent of their revenue from audit and assurance services. Today, that amount is about one-third of total revenues and, more important, advisory and consulting services bring in about the same percentage of total revenues as audit and assurance services. This is concerning because those who provide consulting services often are not CPAs and, therefore, they have not been indoctrinated into the strict ethical requirements of the AICPA Code. The culture of non-CPA providers is not the same as CPA-providers because the performance of consulting services depends on selling services in a competitive field.

Total global revenues for 2020 were $157.5 billion. Here is the breakdown of global revenue for 2020 as provided by Statista. All amounts are in billions of dollars.[1]

Firm	Audit/Assurance	Advisory/Consulting	Tax	Other
Deloitte	$15.5	$19.8	$8.7	$3.8
Ernst & Young	12.8	10.5	9.8	4.1
KPMG	11.1	11.7	6.5	N/A
PwC	17.6	14.7	10.81	N/A

Think about the following as you read the chapter: (1) How can professional judgment deal with cognitive biases that can influence ethical behavior? (2) What is the risk-based approach to deal with situations where independence, integrity, and objectivity, and adherence to other professional standards, are threatened by external relationships? (3) What are effective measures to deal with ethical conflicts that pose challenges to ethics and professionalism?

By certifying the public reports that collectively depict a corporation's financial status, the independent auditor assumes a public responsibility transcending any employment responsibility with the client. The independent public accountant performing this special function owes ultimate allegiance to the corporation's creditors and stockholders, as well as to the investing public. This "public watchdog" function demands that the accountant maintain total independence from the client at all times and requires complete fidelity to the public trust.

Source: Chief Justice Warren Burger, writing the unanimous opinion of the Supreme Court in United States v. Arthur Young & Co.

This important ruling of the U.S. Supreme Court reminds us that the independent audit provides the foundation for the existence of the accounting profession in the United States. Even though independent audits were common before the passage of the landmark legislation of the Securities Act of 1933 and the Securities Exchange Act of 1934, there is no doubt that CPAs derive their franchise as a profession from these two pieces of legislation, which require independent audits of publicly owned companies.

The Burger Court opinion emphasizes the trust that the public places in the independent auditor. The accounting profession is the only profession where one's public obligation supersedes that to a client. The medical profession recognizes the primacy of the physician's responsibility to a patient. The legal profession emphasizes the lawyer's responsibility to the client. The Public Interest Principle in the AICPA Code of Professional Conduct states (Section 53 - Article II: The Public Interest), "In discharging their professional responsibilities, members (of the AICPA) may encounter conflicting pressures from each of these groups [clients, employers . . .]. In resolving those conflicts, members should act with integrity, guided by the precept that when members fulfill their responsibility to the public, clients' and employers' interests are best served." Professional judgment and ethical reasoning enable CPAs to meet their professional obligations to resolve conflicts in a morally appropriate way when the public interest is at stake.

What is Professional Judgment in Accounting?

LO 4-1
Explain professional judgment and the CPA's obligations under the AICPA Code of Conduct.

How are ethical judgments made in accounting? The AICPA Code is the foundation for such judgments. The Code links exercising sensitive and moral judgments to professional conduct. Personal values or virtues link to ethical sensitivity and judgment. Ethical reasoning enables professional accountants to sort out consequences, evaluate rights of stakeholders, and ensure that decisions are just and fair to those who rely on the accounting profession to maintain the accuracy and reliability of financial reports.

KPMG Professional Judgment Framework

KPMG has produced a monograph intended for use as a supplement in college-level auditing and accounting courses to help students understand the components of and threats to good professional judgment. The framework has been adopted in a professional judgment resource of the Center for Audit Quality.[2]

Elevating Professional Judgment in Auditing and Accounting: The KPMG Professional Judgment Framework starts with a common definition of judgment: Judgment is the process of reaching a decision or drawing a conclusion where there are a number of possible alternative solutions.[3]

Judgment occurs in a setting of uncertainty, risk, and often conflicts of interest. We can see the link between judgment and decision making not only in Rest's model but also in the Integrated Model of Ethical Decision Making described in **Chapter 2**. The evaluation of alternatives links to ethical intent, which leads to ethical action. Professional judgment follows a similar path with pressures along the way imposed by one's supervisor, top management, or CPA firm management that might lead to compromising judgment.

The KPMG framework identifies five components of professional judgment that essentially mirror the ethical decision-making model discussed in **Chapter 2**. The components are: (1) clarify issues and objectives; (2) consider alternatives; (3) gather and evaluate information; (4) reach conclusion; and (5) articulate and document rationale. The framework recognizes that influences and biases might affect the process as could one's knowledge of professional standards.

The framework is prescriptive. In the real world we may deviate from the process because of pressures, time constraints, and limited capacity. These constraints, influences, and biases threaten good judgment. For example, let's assume on the last day of an audit you determine that copies of documents for equipment purchases were provided by the client rather than original ones. You realize that fraudulent alteration of documents can occur more readily with copies than if the documents are original. However, to ask the client to provide originals at the eleventh hour means extra time and budget pressures for the firm. Indeed, your supervisor wants to wrap up the audit at the end of the day. Since the firm has never had a problem with this client, you decide to let it go. The process then becomes altered at step three because of our biases and influences.

At the very center of the KPMG framework is *mindset*. Auditors should approach matters objectively and independently, with inquiring and incisive minds. Professional skepticism is required by auditing standards. It requires an objective attitude that includes a questioning mind and critical assessment of audit evidence. In the previous example, professional skepticism was sacrificed for expedience.

Professional skepticism is not the same as professional judgment, but it is an important component of professional judgment. It is a frame of reference to guide audit decisions and enhances ethical decision making.

As decision makers navigate through the professional judgment framework, judgment traps and tendencies can lead to bias. One common judgment trap is the tendency to want to immediately solve a problem by making a quick judgment. The auditor in the previous example may choose to shortcut the process by accepting copies of original documents rather than spending the time to convince the client of why originals are needed. This System 1 approach ignores the more deliberative System 2 side of the process that critically analyzes the reasons for and against examining additional documents to gather reliable evidence about the supportability of the expenditures.

Link between Professional Judgment and Cognitive Processes

Each of us have our own biases that may cloud decision making and alter our final choices. We may be easy going and avoid conflicts at all costs, which would not make for a very good auditor, who needs to have a questioning mind and be willing to critically assess audit data. We also need to be deliberative about our thought processes and consider both the why and the how we make decisions. Table 2.1 on cognitive biases elaborates on these issues.

Our intuitive judgments can fall prey to cognitive traps and biases that negatively influence our judgments. Three common judgment traps are groupthink, a rush to solve problems, and "judgment triggers." Groupthink finds a home in Stage 3 of Kohlberg's model. We become influenced by the expectations of the group and, consequently, we subjugate our own beliefs and thought process. We may do so to avoid conflicts or save time. In an audit, this means the team might accept copies of documents if the majority of members convince the others that the client can be trusted and the group doesn't want to bust the budget.

Judgment triggers can lead to accepting a solution to the problem before it is properly identified and evaluated. Biased judgments might be made because of judgment tendencies. KPMG identifies four common judgment tendencies that are most applicable and important for audit professionals: the availability tendency, the confirmation tendency, the overconfidence tendency, and the anchoring tendency.

The *availability tendency* may lead to judgments based on the accessibility of information rather than a deliberative analysis of how the facts of the current situation differ from prior ones. Also, an auditor may rely on past procedures in the current audit even though that approach may not be relevant to the current situation. Information that is most available to an auditor's memory may unduly influence estimates, probability assessments, and other professional judgments. The auditor in our previous example may take the easy way out and just accept the copies of documents since they already have them, rather than try to verify the existence of new equipment and match it to original documents for equipment purchases.

The tendency for decision makers to put more weight on information that is consistent with their initial beliefs or preferences is the *confirmation tendency*. The danger is an auditor may not adequately consider potentially contradictory information that could result in a valid alternative to a preliminary conclusion. The auditor trusts the client based on past experiences and is more willing to accept the copies. However, in many instances, we cannot know something to be true unless we explicitly consider how and why it may be false. Confirmation bias in auditing may occur when auditors over-rely on management's explanations for a significant difference between the auditor's expectation and management's recorded value, even when the client's explanation is inadequate.

The *overconfidence tendency* is when decision makers overestimate their own abilities to perform tasks or to make accurate diagnoses or other judgments and decisions, as may be the case when estimating outcomes or likelihoods. This may occur because of one's personal motivation or self-interest. It can lead to an inability to recognize alternative points of view or contradictory evidence. It can also affect an auditor's willingness to involve others who could provide a meaningful perspective to the analysis.

The *anchoring tendency* relates to starting from an initial numerical value and then adjusting insufficiently away from it in forming a final judgment as when the auditor becomes anchored to management's estimate. The auditor may place too much reliance on one piece of information or set of circumstances and not enough on other perspectives or data that may confirm or disconfirm a particular position or issue. The danger is the auditor uses evidence-gathering techniques from prior engagements, rather than considering objectively a fuller set of techniques.

The audit of financial statements has always required auditors to exercise their professional judgment, but the use and importance of these judgments continue to grow as the overall complexity and estimation uncertainty inherent in financial statements increase. In an effort to facilitate auditors' use of sound professional judgment, audit firms have turned to developing professional judgment frameworks, such as the one provided by KPMG, to promote a rigorous, thoughtful, and deliberate judgment process to guide making reasonable accounting judgments.[4]

Link between Professional Judgment and AICPA Code of Professional Conduct

The way in which professional judgments are made is an integral part of whether CPAs meet their ethical obligation to make objective judgments. A professional accountant should not allow bias, conflict of interest, or undue influence of others to override professional or business judgments.

The decisions auditors make to deal with judgment triggers say a lot about whether they can meet the due care standard. Competent professional service requires the exercise of sound, independent, and objective judgment in applying professional knowledge and skill in the performance of professional services.

Professional skepticism links to professional judgment through the ethical standards of independent thought, objectivity, and due care. Professional skepticism is part of the skill set auditors should have and is closely interrelated to the fundamental concepts of auditor independence and professional judgment, which contribute to audit quality.[5]

To promote the application of professional skepticism, CPA-firm management should set an appropriate tone that emphasizes a questioning mind throughout the audit and the exercise of professional skepticism in gathering and evaluating evidence.

Accountability can be thought of as the requirement to justify one's judgments to others. Absent a healthy dose of professional skepticism, it would be difficult for the auditor to justify having made judgments in accordance with the ethical standards of the accounting profession. These standards exist to protect the public interest and honor the public trust.

The auditing profession in the United States has come under periodic scrutiny from Congress during the past 40 years as a result of a series of financial frauds. In each case Congress asked: Where were the auditors? Why didn't audit firms detect and report on financial fraud? A variety of investigations studied (1) whether nonauditing services impair audit independence, (2) the need for management to report on internal controls, (3) the importance of developing techniques to prevent and detect fraud, and (4) the need to strengthen the role of the audit committee and communications between the auditor and audit committee. Each of these issues were addressed by the Sarbanes-Oxley Act, as discussed in **Chapter 3**. The Act also established the Public Company Accounting Oversight Board to inspect selected audits and report deficiencies in those audits. We discuss the PCAOB standards later.

Audit failures in companies such as Enron and WorldCom can be attributed to a lapse in professional judgment. As a result, the AICPA rules of conduct were violated because of a lack of independence and objectivity. The following discussions explain these rules, the professional judgment needed to carry them out, and the effects on ethical decision making.

AICPA Code: Independence Considerations for Members in Public Practice

LO 4-2
Explain how to apply the threats and safeguards approach to independence.

Introduction to Revised Code

On June 1, 2014, the AICPA issued a codification of the principles, rules, interpretations, and rulings in the revised AICPA Code of Professional Conduct. The most significant change is the incorporation of two broad conceptual frameworks, one for members in public practice and another for CPAs in business.[6] These conceptual frameworks incorporate a "threats and safeguards" approach and are designed to assist users in analyzing relationships and circumstances that the code does not specifically address.

A significant improvement is the section on "Ethical Conflicts" that arise from obstacles to following the appropriate course of action due to internal or external pressures and/or conflicts in applying relevant professional standards or legal standards. The ethical conflicts provision is used in combination with the conceptual framework to determine whether specific rules of conduct have been violated.

The Principles in the Code (Section 0.300) were discussed in **Chapter 1**. They are categorized as follows:

- Responsibilities (0.300.020)
- The Public Interest (0.300.030)
- Integrity (0.300.040)
- Objectivity and Independence (0.300.050)
- Due Care (0.300.060)
- Scope and Nature of Services (0.300.070)

Three important points about the applicability of the AICPA Code are as follows: (1) it applies to CPAs in the performance of all professional services except when the wording of the rule indicates otherwise; (2) it is a violation of the rules of conduct for a CPA to permit others acting on their behalf to engage in behavior that, had the CPA done so, it would have violated the rules; and (3) when differences exist between AICPA rules and those of the licensing state board of accountancy, the CPA should follow the state board's rules.

Section 1.000.010 describes a conceptual framework that applies to members in public practice and provides a foundation to evaluate whether threats to the CPA's compliance with the rules of conduct are at an acceptable level or whether safeguards should be developed to prevent a violation of the rules. Under the AICPA Code, in the absence of an interpretation of a specific rule of conduct that addresses a particular relationship or circumstance, a CPA should evaluate whether that relationship or circumstance would lead a reasonable and informed third party who is aware of the relevant information to conclude a threat exists to the CPA's compliance with the rules that is not at an acceptable level. In some circumstances no safeguards can reduce a threat to an acceptable level. For example, a CPA cannot subordinate professional judgment to others without violating the "Integrity and Objectivity" Rule.

The "Independence" Rule applies only to audited financial statements because the public (i.e., investors and creditors) rely on the independence of auditors to ensure that the financial statements are free of material misstatements. Whereas the public are the end user of audited financial statements, the client is the main beneficiary of nonaudit services so there is no direct public interest involvement, hence no independence requirement.

Conceptual Framework for AICPA Independence Standards

The conceptual framework is used to evaluate independence matters based on the application of a risk-based approach to assess whether a CPA's relationship with a client would pose an unacceptable risk. Risk is unacceptable if the relationship would compromise (or would be perceived as compromising by an informed third party knowing all the relevant information) the CPA's professional judgment when rendering an attest service to the client (i.e., audit, review, or attestation engagement). Key to that evaluation is identifying and assessing the extent to which a threat to the CPA's independence exists, and, if it does, whether it would be reasonable to expect that the threat would compromise the CPA's professional judgment and, if so, whether it can be effectively mitigated or eliminated. Under the risk-based approach, steps are taken to prevent circumstances that threaten independence from compromising the professional judgments required in the performance of an attest engagement. An attestation service is a type of assurance service wherein a CPA issues a report about the reliability of another party's assertion.

The risk-based approach involves the following steps:

1. Identifying and evaluating threats to independence.
2. Determining whether safeguards already eliminate or sufficiently mitigate identified threats and whether threats that have not yet been mitigated can be eliminated or sufficiently mitigated by safeguards.
3. If no safeguards are available to eliminate an unacceptable threat or reduce it to an acceptable level, independence would be considered impaired.

Threats to Independence

Independence in fact is defined as the state of mind that permits the performance of an attest service without being affected by influences that compromise professional judgment, thereby allowing an individual to act with integrity and professional skepticism. To *appear to be independent,* the CPA should avoid circumstances that might cause an informed third party to reasonably conclude that the integrity, objectivity, or professional skepticism of a firm or member of the audit (attest) engagement team has been compromised.

Threats to independence include a self-review threat, advocacy threat, adverse interest threat, familiarity threat, undue influence threat, financial self-interest threat, and management participation threat. A brief description of each threat follows, and **Exhibit 4.1** provides examples of each threat.

EXHIBIT 4.1   Examples of Threats to Independence

Threat	Example
Self-Review Threat	Preparing source documents used to generate the client's financial statements
Advocacy Threat	Promoting the client's securities as part of an initial public offering or representing a client in U.S. tax court
Adverse Interest Threat	Commencing, or the expressed intention to commence, litigation by either the client or the CPA against the other
Familiarity Threat	A CPA on the attest engagement team whose spouse is the client's CEO
Undue Influence Threat	A threat to replace the CPA or CPA firm because of a disagreement with the client over the application of an accounting principle
Financial Self-Interest Threat	Having a loan from the client, from an officer or director of the client, or from an individual who owns 10 percent or more of the client's outstanding equity securities
Management Participation Threat	Establishing and maintaining internal controls for the client

SELF-REVIEW THREAT

A self-review threat occurs when a CPA reviews evidence during an attest engagement that is based on his own or his firm's nonattest work. An example would be preparing source documents used to generate the client's financial statements.

ADVOCACY THREAT

An advocacy threat occurs when a CPA promotes an attest client's interests or position in such a way that objectivity may be, or may be perceived to be, compromised. These are of particular concern when performing tax services.

ADVERSE INTEREST THREAT

An adverse interest threat occurs when a CPA takes actions that are in opposition to an attest client's interests or positions.

FAMILIARITY THREAT

A familiarity threat occurs when a close relationship is formed between the CPA and an attest client or its employees, members of top management, or directors of the client entity, including individuals or entities that performed nonattest work for the client (i.e., tax or consulting services).

UNDUE INFLUENCE THREAT

An undue influence threat results from an attempt by the management of an attest client or other interested parties to coerce the CPA or exercise excessive influence over the CPA.

FINANCIAL SELF-INTEREST THREAT

A financial self-interest threat occurs when there is a potential benefit to a CPA of having a financial interest in, or from some other financial relationship with, an attest client. It goes beyond simple situations where independence would be impaired, such as directly owning shares of stock of the client or having material indirect financial interest. Financial self-interest threats can also arise from business relationships with a client or a member of management that creates a mutual self-interest.

MANAGEMENT PARTICIPATION THREAT

A management participation threat occurs when a CPA takes on the role of client management or otherwise performs management functions on behalf of an attest client.

Safeguards to Counteract Threats

Safeguards are controls that eliminate or reduce threats to independence. These range from partial to complete prohibitions of the threatening circumstance to procedures that counteract the potential influence of a threat. The nature and extent of the safeguards to be applied depend on many factors, including the size of the firm and whether the client is a public interest entity. To be effective, safeguards should eliminate the threat or reduce to an acceptable level the threat's potential to impair independence.

There are three broad categories of safeguards. The relative importance of a safeguard depends on its appropriateness in light of the facts and circumstances.

1. *Safeguards created by the profession, legislation, or regulation.*
2. *Safeguards implemented by the client.*
3. *Safeguards implemented by the firm.*

Exhibit 4.2 categorizes safeguards and provides examples of each one. It applies to the conceptual framework for independence and the Integrity and Objectivity Rule.

EXHIBIT 4.2   Examples of Safeguards in Applying the Conceptual Framework

Source of the Safeguard	Examples of Safeguards
Created by the profession, legislation, or regulation	Audit inspections by the PCAOB, threat of discipline by state board of accountancy, and continuing education requirements
Implemented by the client	A hotline to report financial statement matters of concern A tone at the top that establishes an ethical culture Corporate governance systems that support ethical behavior within the entity including and audit committee and independent board of directors Procedures to ensure compliance with laws and regulations

(continued)

Source of the Safeguard	Examples of Safeguards
Implemented by the firm	Quality control system Annual independence representations Conversations with the audit committee Procedures to ensure compliance with the AICPA rules of conduct and state board regulations

The quality control system is important because it establishes policies and procedures to provide the firm with reasonable assurance that personnel maintain independence (in fact and in appearance) in all required circumstances, perform all professional responsibilities with integrity, and maintain objectivity in discharging professional responsibilities.

A serious lapse in professional and ethical judgment brought on by a lack of quality controls occurred at KPMG when the firm hired former PCAOB staffers to obtain audit inspection information. On January 22, 2018, it was announced that a former PCAOB staffer, Brian Sweet, who was hired by KPMG in 2015, leaked confidential information about PCAOB's plans to audit the company. Most of the leaked information concerned which audit engagements the PCAOB planned to inspect, the criteria it was using to select engagements for inspection, and on what these inspections would focus. The conspiracy began when, preparing to leave the PCAOB, Sweet copied confidential information showing which audits would be reviewed. He shared the information with his new colleagues at KPMG and continued to share PCAOB information with KPMG executives through 2017 with the help of at least two other PCAOB employees. The audit partners used the inspection information to analyze and review audit workpapers relevant to the inspections and suggested revisions to avoid possible findings of deficiencies by the PCAOB. Three KPMG partners were charged with conspiracy. KPMG agreed to settle with the SEC by paying a $50 million penalty and complying with a detailed set of undertakings, including retaining an independent consultant to review and assess the firm's ethics and integrity controls and its compliance with various undertakings.

Sarbanes-Oxley Act(SOX): Nonaudit Services

Similar to AICPA and SEC rules, SOX prohibits CPAs and CPA firms from providing certain nonattest services for public company attest clients. The potential for a conflict of interest exists because of a self-review threat to independence that occurs when a CPA reviews, as part of an attest engagement, evidence that results from the CPA's own nonattest services.

Section 201 of SOX provides that the following nonattest services may not be performed for attest clients in addition to bookkeeping or other services related to the accounting records or financial statements of the audit client:

1. Financial information systems design and implementation.
2. Appraisal or valuation services, fairness opinions, or contribution-in-kind reports.
3. Actuarial services.
4. Internal audit outsourcing services.
5. Management functions or human resources.
6. Broker or dealer, investment adviser, or investment banking services.
7. Legal services and expert services unrelated to the audit.
8. Any other service that the board of directors determines, by regulation, is impermissible.

SOX allows an accounting firm to "engage in any nonaudit service, including tax services," that is not listed above, only if the activity is preapproved by the audit committee of the issuer company. The preapproval requirement is waived if the aggregate amount of all such nonaudit services provided to the issuer constitutes less than 5 percent of the total amount of revenues paid by the issuer to its auditor.

The rules do not give CPAs definitive guidance on how audit committees should determine whether a tax service is an allowable activity requiring preapproval or is a prohibited service that even preapproval cannot save other than saying that tax compliance, planning, and advice are acceptable once approved. It is generally understood that the SEC allows the provision of tax-minimization services to audit clients, except for transactions that have no business purpose other than tax avoidance (i.e., tax shelters). Tax shelters will be addressed later.

The issue of whether a CPA firm should be allowed to do permitted tax services for audit clients can be evaluated ethically from a utilitarian perspective. The question is whether the benefits of auditor-provided tax services outweigh the risks that the audit will not be performed with the level of objectivity necessary to ensure the independence standard is met. An argument to allow permitted tax services is that the insight learned from providing tax services can enhance audit effectiveness and, in turn, the client's financial reporting quality. The argument against it would be that it creates a self-review threat and could lead to an advocacy relationship between the tax accountants and audit client, which creates a threat to independence that cannot be reduced or eliminated by any safeguards.

Relationships That May Impair Independence

A variety of relationships have the potential to impair audit independence because of conflicts of interest that may arise. Some of these potential conflicts arise from financial and other relationships with an audit client or members of top management of the client, providing nonattest services for an attest client, or being employed by a former attest client.

The Independence Rule also extends to certain family members of the CPA. The detailed provisions are beyond the scope of this book, but we do want to emphasize two points to provide examples of familiarity threats to independence. First, when a CPA is part of the attest engagement team, which includes employees and contractors directly involved in an audit and those who perform concurring and second partner reviews, the rules extend to that CPA's immediate family members and close relatives. Immediate family members include the CPA's spouse, spousal equivalent, and dependents (whether or not they are related). The rules also extend to the CPA's close relatives, including parents, siblings, or nondependent children, if they hold a key position with the client (that is, one that involves direct participation in the preparation of the financial statements or a position that gives the CPA the ability to exercise influence over the contents of the financial statements). Close relatives are also subject to the Independence Rule if they own a financial interest in the client that is material to that person's net worth and of which the CPA has knowledge. The potential danger in these family relationships is that the family member's financial or employment relationship with the client might influence the perception that the CPA can be independent in fact or appearance.

Financial Relationships

The ownership of stock in a client creates a financial self-interest threat to independence. The problem with owning direct and material indirect financial interests is that these arrangements might create the impression in the mind of an outside observer that the CPA cannot make decisions without being influenced by the stock ownership, even if that is not the case for any specific CPA. Appearances matter and the perception in the mind of the public that independent, objective judgment may be compromised by the financial relationship is enough for independence to be violated.

Another example of a financial self-interest threat is when a CPA becomes involved in a loan transaction to or from a client, including home mortgage loans from financial institution clients. This type of loan is prohibited under the AICPA Code. It provides that independence is considered to be impaired if, during the period of the professional engagement, a covered member, such as a CPA on the attest engagement team or an individual in a position to influence the attest engagement team, has any loan to or from a client, any officer or director of the client, or any individual owning 10 percent or more of the client's outstanding equity securities or other ownership interests.

Examples of permitted loans include automobile loans and leases collateralized by the automobile, loans fully collateralized by cash deposits at the same financial institution (e.g., "passbook loans"), and aggregate credit card balances from credit cards and overdraft reserve accounts that are reduced to $10,000 or less on a current basis, taking into consideration the payment due and any available grace period.

One of the cases that led the SEC to require that the accounting profession tighten its independence rules when loans are received was when Jose Gomez, the lead partner of Alexander Grant (now Grant Thornton), accepted loans from an audit client during its audit of ESM Government Securities from 1977 to 1984. Over the eight-year period, ESM committed fraud and, in the process, used its leverage against Gomez from $200,000 in loans to him so he would keep silent about the fact that ESM's financial statements did not fairly present financial position and the results of operations. Top management of ESM also threatened to pull the audit from Gomez's firm if he spoke out about the fraud. Gomez compromised his integrity, and the event ruined his reputation. Ultimately, Gomez was sentenced to a 12-year prison term and served 4½ years, and the firm paid approximately $175 million in civil payments.

There are other relationships that will bring a CPA under the Independence rules, including when a partner or manager provides 10 hours or more of nonattest services to the attest client. The problem is it may appear to an outside observer that the partner or manager may be able to influence the attest work because of the significant number of hours devoted to the nonattest services.

Let's stop at this point and consider that the Independence Rule is a challenging standard for the CPA and family members to meet, and it might present some interesting dilemmas. For example, imagine that a CPA knows that his father owns a financial interest in a client entity but does not know if that interest is material to the father's net worth. Should the CPA contact the father to find out? Or, might the CPA reason that it is better not to know because the Independence Rule applies only if the CPA has knowledge of the extent of the father's financial interest in the client? From an ethical perspective, the CPA should make a good-faith effort to determine the extent of his father's financial interest in the client entity.

Business Relationships

Another case that prompted the SEC to apply pressure on the AICPA to tighten its independence rules occurred after the SEC sanctioned Ernst & Young (EY) because it was not independent in fact or appearance when it audited the financial statements of PeopleSoft for fiscal years 1994–1999. The SEC found independence violations arising from EY's business relationships with PeopleSoft while auditing the company's financial statements. These relationships created a mutuality of interests between the firm and PeopleSoft, resulting in a financial self-interest threat.

The basic facts are EY's Tax Group created a Global Expatriate Management System (EY/GEMS) as an in-house software program for assisting clients with the tax consequences of managing employees with international assignments. The EY/GEMS system was enhanced with the use of PeopleTools, a software product created by EY's audit client, PeopleSoft. A business relationship was created whereby a license to use PeopleTools was granted to EY in return for a payment to PeopleSoft of 15 percent of each licensee fee that EY received from outside customers purchasing the new software, 30 percent of each license renewal fee, and a minimum royalty of $300,000, payable in 12 quarterly payments of $25,000 each.

The licensing agreement provided that EY would make PeopleSoft a third-party beneficiary of each sublicense. PeopleSoft agreed to assist EY's efforts by providing technical assistance for a $15,000 quarterly fee. The agreement provided that EY could not distribute the derivative software to PeopleSoft's direct competitors. The agreement permitted EY to use PeopleSoft trademarks and trade names in marketing materials. PeopleSoft maintained a degree of control over the product by restricting EY's distribution rights and requiring the firm to work closely with PeopleSoft to ensure the quality of the product.

The SEC found that EY and PeopleSoft had a "symbiotic relationship," engaging in joint sales and marketing efforts and sharing considerable proprietary and confidential business information, and that EY partnered with PeopleSoft to accomplish increased sales and boost consulting revenues for EY. The findings of the SEC indicate that EY and PeopleSoft acted together to promote the product so that a reasonable investor with knowledge of all the facts would conclude that EY was closely identified in fact and appearance with its audit client.

Employment or Association with Attest Clients

It is not unusual for a CPA who has worked on an engagement for a client to be offered a position with that client. If the client has confidence in the abilities of the CPA and trusts that party, then the client may seek to hire the professional, for example, as the controller or CFO. The rules establish that independence may be impaired when a partner or professional employee leaves the firm and is subsequently employed by or associated with the client in a key position unless the following conditions are met:

- Amounts due to the former partner/professional are not material to the firm.
- The former partner/professional is not in a position to influence the accounting firm's operations or financial policies.
- The former partner/professional employee does not participate in or appear to participate in or is not associated with the firm once the relationship with the client begins.

An example of participating in the firm is continuing to consult for it or have one's name included in firm literature, which implies a relationship still exists.

Providing Nonattest Services to an Attest Client

An example of a prohibited activity under the AICPA Code is that a CPA should not perform management functions or make management decisions for an attest client. The relationship creates a management participation threat that places the CPA in the compromising position of making decisions for the client and then auditing those decisions. On the other hand, the CPA may provide advice, research materials, and recommendations to assist the client's management in performing its functions and making decisions.

Individual nonattest services may be permitted if adequate safeguards exist to mitigate potential threats to independence. However, when performing multiple services there may be unacceptable threats (i.e., management participation, self-review) to independence.

To protect against an impairment of independence, general requirements exist for the attest client when a CPA performs nonattest services, including:

- Assume all management responsibilities.
- Oversee the service, by designating an individual, preferably within senior management, who possesses suitable skill, knowledge, and/or experience.
- Evaluate the adequacy and results of the services performed.
- Accept responsibility for the results of the service.

Other requirements exist, including to clearly establish the objectives of the engagement, services to be performed, client's acceptance of its responsibilities, the CPA's responsibilities, and any limitations of the engagement.

The UK Experience

There has been a great deal of controversy in the United Kingdom about how best to restrict nonaudit services for audit clients. The UK Competition and Markets Authority, a government department in the United Kingdom, issued a report on April 18, 2019, that recommends an operational split of audit and nonaudit services. The large firms would be split into separate operating entities with respect to auditing and consultancy functions to reduce the influence of consulting practices upon auditing divisions

A study group report prepared on behalf of the UK Parliamentary Labour Party calls for a legal split between audit and nonaudit services. The group was not convinced that an operational split would go far enough, calling instead for two legally separate organizations. In essence, it calls for a structural break-up of large firms saying that it would be more effective than other options in "tackling conflicts of interest" and providing "professional skepticism needed to deliver high-quality audits."[7]

The Financial Reporting Council (FRC), the UK's accounting watchdog, told the Big 4 accounting firms to draw up plans for an operational split by separating their audit businesses by 2024. The regulator stopped short of ordering a full, structural breakup that would have required audit entities to be spun off into separate legal entities.

Companies will be required to have separate profit and loss accounts for their audit divisions, have a separate audit board, and pay auditors in line with their profits of just their division. It is in part an attempt to ensure that consultancy contract bids do not affect the quality of the audit on that company's accounts.

The United Kingdom has been trying to nudge the firms to voluntarily split off audit from nonaudit services for some time. However, the firms do not seem inclined to do so. As a result, the FRC is due to be replaced by a stronger regulator called the Audit, Reporting and Governance Authority, which is expected to have to force a break-up of the Big 4.

Mintz suggests that the SEC should examine the UK experience to assess whether a separation of audit and nonaudit services operationally would work in the United States. He points out that, "By operationally splitting audit and nonaudit services, the firms would signal that they take their obligation to be independent in fact and appearance seriously, and that they recognize the importance of avoiding conflicts of interest when both services are provided to a client. The public should expect nothing less.[8]

SEC Actions on Auditor Independence

LO 4-3

Discuss SEC actions taken against auditors because of a lack of independence.

Publicly owned companies have been obligated to follow SEC rules since the passage of the Securities Act of 1933 and the Securities and Exchange Act of 1934. The PCAOB has taken some of that responsibility away from the SEC by establishing independence rules that are then approved by the SEC.

The SEC approach to independence emphasizes independence in fact and appearance in three ways: (1) proscribing certain financial interests and business relationships with the audit client, (2) restricting the provision of certain nonauditing services to audit clients, and (3) subjecting all auditor conduct to a general standard of independence. The general standard of independence is stated as follows: "The Commission will not recognize an accountant as independent, with respect to an audit client, if the accountant is not, or a reasonable investor with knowledge of all relevant facts and circumstances would conclude that the accountant is not, capable of exercising objective and impartial judgment on all issues encompassed within the accountant's engagement."[9]

The general standard of independence is evaluated by applying four principles that are similar to the AICPA's conceptual framework and that indicate when auditor independence may be impaired by a relationship with the audit client. If a situation results in any of the following, the auditor's independence may be impaired: (1) creates a mutual or conflicting interest between an accountant and their audit client, (2) places an accountant in the position of auditing their own work, (3) results in an accountant acting as management or an employee of the audit client, or (4) places an accountant in a position of being an advocate for the audit client.

The SEC believes that these principles are "general guidance and their application may depend on particular facts and circumstances . . . [but they do] provide an appropriate framework for analyzing auditor independence issues."[10] To provide further guidance on implementing the principles, the SEC identified three basic overarching principles that underlie auditor independence: (1) an auditor cannot function in the role of management, (2) an auditor cannot audit his own work, and (3) an auditor cannot serve in an advocacy role for his client.[10]

SEC Actions against Big Four Audit Firms

The following describes actions taken by the SEC against audit firms during the past several years to provide examples of when threats to independence compromise professional judgment. The broad scope of these violations is troubling as it indicates a willingness on the part of auditors and audit firms to push the envelope on independence and make poor judgments about which relationships impair independence.

PwC's Performance of Prohibited Nonaudit Services for an Audit Client

On September 23, 2019, PricewaterhouseCoopers (PwC) agreed to pay $7.9 million to settle charges that the firm violated SEC Independence Rule 2-02 by performing prohibited nonaudit services during an audit engagement, including exercising decision-making authority in the design and implementation of software relating to an audit client's financial reporting, and engaging in management functions. The firm's actions created a self-review threat to independence. The SEC said PwC's violations occurred due to breakdowns in the auditor's quality controls, as the firm failed to review and monitor nonaudit services to make sure they were permitted. In addition, the SEC said the firm did not disclose its extended role to the Public Company Accounting Oversight Board (PCAOB).

Insider Trading at KPMG and Withdrawing Audit Opinions

On April 11, 2013, the SEC charged Scott London, the former partner in charge of KPMG's California regional audit practice, with leaking confidential information to his friend, Brian Shaw, about two audit clients—Skechers and Herbalife. Shaw, a jewelry store owner and country club friend of London, repaid London with $50,000 in cash and a Rolex watch, according to legal filings.

After federal regulators froze Shaw's investment account because of suspicious activity, the jeweler fully confessed, paid back nearly $2 million in illegally gained profits and fines to the SEC, and cooperated in the investigation against London.

London was sentenced to 14 months in a federal prison and forced to pay a $100,000 fine. He also was fired from his $900,000-a-year job as an auditor for KPMG in 2012, and the company was forced to redo several of London's prior audits. The audit opinions signed by London on Skechers and Herbalife had to be withdrawn by the firm.

EY Audit Partners Engage in Relationships with Client Personnel

On September 20, 2016, the SEC announced that EY had agreed to pay $9.3 million in total to settle charges against three of the firm's audit partners that engaged in relationships that created familiarity threats to independence. In one case, Gregory Bednar, a former senior partner on the engagement team of a public company client, "maintained an improperly close friendship" with the company's CFO, thus violating rules that ensure objectivity and impartiality during audits. Bednar reportedly spent close to $100,000 in travel and entertainment expenses between 2012 and 2015 while socializing with the CFO and his family. The firm was aware of the expenses but did nothing. Without admitting or denying the findings, Bednar and EY consented to the SEC order. The firm agreed to pay $4.975 million in monetary sanctions for the violations. Bednar agreed to a $45,000 penalty and was suspended from appearing and practicing before the SEC as an accountant for three years, but was allowed to apply for reinstatement after that time.[11]

In another case,[12] from 2012 through 2014, EY partner Pamela Hartford violated Independence Rules by having an affair with a client. Reports state she engaged in a personal relationship with Robert Brehl, the chief accounting officer of a public company that she serviced as a member of the audit engagement team. Another EY partner Michael Kamienski (the supervising partner on this engagement) became aware of facts suggesting an improper relationship between Hartford and Brehl. However, he failed to follow up on his suspicions. While Hartford and Brehl tried to keep their relationship a secret, they did attend client and EY social events. This suggests that others at both EY and the client could have been aware of the affair.

The SEC order against EY states that the firm did not have specific policies in place to inquire about personal relations with clients and client personnel. EY subsequently added specific language to engagement team members' certifications on the firm's audit work asking about their own possible relationships with client personnel and whether they are aware of any personal relationships that any other member of the engagement team might have with client personnel.

Deloitte Managers Maintain Bank Accounts with Audit Client

On February 13, 2019, the SEC announced that Deloitte Touche Tohmatsu LLC (Deloitte Japan) will pay $2 million to settle charges that it issued audit reports for an audit client at a time when dozens of its employees maintained bank accounts with the client's subsidiary. According to the SEC's order, the accounts had balances that exceeded depositary insurance limits in violation of the SEC audit independence rules. Deloitte Japan's former CEO Futomichi Amano and former reputation and risk leader and director of independence Yuji Itagaki settled related charges.

Under the SEC's rules, accountants are not considered to be independent if they maintain bank accounts with an audit client with balances greater than FDIC or similar depositary insurance limits. According to the SEC's order, Deloitte Japan knew but failed to adequately disclose that Amano maintained bank account balances with the audit client's subsidiary bank that compromised his independence. The SEC's order also found that Deloitte Japan's system of quality controls did not provide reasonable assurances that the firm and its auditors were independent from audit clients. For example, the SEC's order found that Deloitte Japan failed to adequately staff and supervise its Office of Independence and caused certain independence violations by making deposits to partners' bank accounts that exceeded the deposit insurance limits.

Insider Trading on Client Information at Deloitte

In 2010, Deloitte and Touche found itself involved in an SEC investigation of repeated insider trading by Thomas P. Flanagan, a former management advisory partner and a vice chairman at Deloitte. Flanagan traded in the securities of multiple Deloitte clients on the basis of inside information that he learned through his duties as a Deloitte partner. The inside information concerned market-moving events such as earnings results, revisions to earnings guidance, sales figures and cost-cutting, and an acquisition. Flanagan's illegal trading resulted in profits of more than $430,000.

Flanagan also tipped his son, Patrick, to certain of this material nonpublic information. Patrick then traded based on that information. Patrick's illegal trading resulted in profits of more than $57,000. The SEC charges included: (1) Between 2003 and 2008, Flanagan made 71 purchases of stock and options in the securities of Deloitte audit clients. Flanagan made 62 of these purchases in the securities of Deloitte audit clients while serving as the advisory partner on those audits; and (2) on at least nine occasions between 2005 and 2008, Flanagan traded on the basis of material nonpublic information of Deloitte clients, including Best Buy, Motorola, Sears, and Option Care.

These insider trading cases illustrate the risk to audit independence when audit engagement team members, including partners, trade on information that is not publicly available. Beyond that, the use of sensitive financial information about a client for personal reasons violates the independence requirement because it creates a financial self-interest relationship between the partner and the client.

The leaking of confidential financial information about a company to anyone prior to its public release affects the level playing field that should exist with respect to personal and business contacts of an auditor and the general public. It violates the fairness doctrine in treating equals equally, and it violates basic integrity standards. Such actions cut to the core values of integrity and trust—the foundation of the public interest obligation of CPAs.

The increase in insider trading cases is troubling. The extent of the disclosure and subsequent trades seem to have no bounds, with audit partners, tax partners, management personnel at firms, and even an unlicensed staff member all becoming embroiled in independence violations. Insider trading by the accounting professional, tips to one's broker, family members, and friends together illustrate the scope of the problem. We believe the SEC and AICPA should include these kinds of transactions as acts discreditable to the profession, as well as independence violations, to emphasize the social crime nature of these rule violations.

Emerging Issues

Loosening the Independence Rules

In October 2020, the SEC said it will focus more on auditors' objectivity and impartiality and less on their relationships with the companies they audit. The SEC said the amendments to Rule 2-01 of Regulation SX would "modernize the rules and more effectively focus the analysis on relationships that may pose threats to an auditor's objectivity and impartiality."[13] In announcing the changes, it said the SEC staff has found over the years that certain relationships and services would trigger technical violations of the independence rules and require potentially time-consuming reviews by audit committees of "nonsubstantive matters" and take time and attention from auditors, audit clients and audit committees away from other investor protection efforts.

The new rules change the auditor independence requirements to evaluate specific relationships and services that might threaten the objectivity and impartiality of auditors. In adopting the new rules, the SEC stated that the changes reflect the long-standing view that an audit by an objective, impartial and skilled professional contributes to both investor protection and investor confidence.

According to SEC chairman Jay Clayton, "These modernized auditor independence requirements will increase investor protection by focusing audit clients, audit committees, and auditors on areas that might threaten an auditor's objectivity and impartiality. They will also improve competition and audit quality by increasing the number of qualified audit firms from which an issuer can choose."

The examples discussed in this section suggest that audit firms are either ignoring or being unaware of independence requirements, at least as they pertain to whether the existence of certain personal and business relationships violates independence in appearance if not in actuality. It is troubling that the SEC may have given up in the battle to make independence the cornerstone of audit engagements and, instead, rely on objectivity and impartiality that is subject to a firm's judgment.

Materiality Determinations

One area of concern lately is when nonaudit services are performed for an entity that becomes an affiliate of the audit client. Problems arise when otherwise permissible nonaudit services are provided to a nonaudit client that becomes an affiliate of an audit client. The independence rules then apply to both clients as if they were one entity. Some firms are now using a materiality criterion to determine whether these nonaudit services provided to an affiliate entity, which would be prohibited if the parent had provided them, violate the independence requirement in audit engagements. Applying such a materiality standard can have the effect of dismissing otherwise improper relationships.

Using a materiality criterion to determine whether certain nonaudit services should be allowed opens a can of worms. Logical questions are: (1) Is independence a standard left to the individual judgment of the auditors or is it based on SEC regulations and PCAOB standards? and (2) Where do you draw the line in making materiality determinations?

We expect that the rules surrounding auditor independence will continue to evolve as more firms are found to be failing in their efforts to remain independent.

AICPA Code: Ethical Conflicts

LO 4-4
Describe the process to resolve ethical conflicts that may cause violations of the rules.

Under the AICPA Code, when evaluating whether a CPA in public practice is in compliance with the rules, a CPA should assess whether an ethical conflict exists. Ethical Conflicts (1.000.020) create challenges to ethical decision making because they present barriers to meeting the requirements of the rules of conduct. An ethical conflict may exist, for example, if a CPA in public practice suspects a fraud may have occurred, but reporting the suspected fraud would violate the confidentiality obligation. Ethical conflicts also create challenges to the Integrity and Objectivity Rule. These were discussed with respect to subordination of judgment issues in **Exhibit 3.16**. Please review that exhibit as you read through Ethical Conflicts.

Exhibit 4.3 identifies the major considerations for CPAs in assessing the risk that ethical conflicts may lead to a violation of the rules of conduct. Briefly, the CPA should consider whether any departures exist to the rules, laws, or regulations and how they will be justified in order to ensure that conflicts are resolved in a way that permits compliance with these requirements. Resolution of the conflict may call for consulting with others in the entity or others, including legal counsel. Any unresolved conflicts can lead to a violation of the rules of conduct, which, in turn, should focus the CPA's attention on any continuing relationship with the engagement team, specific assignment, client, firm, or employer.

EXHIBIT 4.3   Ethical Conflicts and Compliance with the Rules of Conduct for Members in Public Practice and Business*

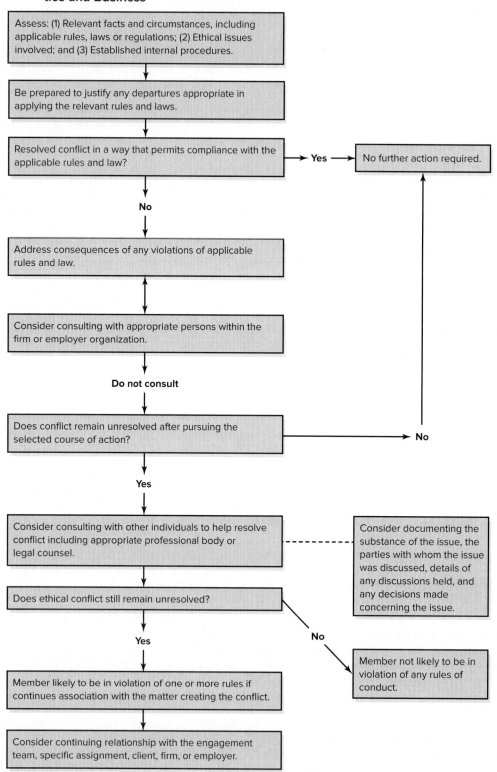

*Exhibit 4.3 was developed by author from the Ethical Conflicts provision of the revised code.

Conflicts of interest for members in public practice occur when a professional service, relationship, or specific matter creates a situation that might impair objective judgment. A conflict of interest can create threats to independence. An example of a potential conflict of interest is when a CPA accepts gifts or entertainment from a client. Threats need to be evaluated as well as the significance of any such threats and safeguards that might mitigate their effects. Such situations may create self-interest, familiarity, or undue influence threats to compliance with the rules of conduct. CPAs must be careful to ensure that acceptance of a gift doesn't impair their judgment or violate professional standards.

Accepting a form of entertainment may be acceptable if it is related to a normal course of business. For example, a CPA can go to lunch with the CFO, who pays for the meal, Typically, these kinds of outings have a business purpose involved. For example, it may be better to discuss difficult choices related to the audit away from the influences that might exist when doing so in the office.

A stricter standard exists with respect to the acceptance of gifts especially those with a quid pro quo. Let's assume your client comes to your office one day. You are the partner in charge of the audit for the client. The clients want to show their appreciation for the audit engagement team's completion of the audit one week early and under budget. They give you two tickets for yourself and your wife to use for the football game between the Kansas City Chiefs and Las Vegas Raiders. It is just a regular season game with no significance beyond that. Can you accept the gift?

If the audit has been completed, the first question is whether the acceptance of the gift might make it appear to a reasonable observer that the gift is intended to influence the audit opinion. If so, that would create an undue influence threat and compromise integrity and objectivity. Also, it could be perceived as an advance payoff for future audit opinions. The influence does not have to be immediate. Beyond that, the key issue to consider is: Would acceptance violate any laws, regulations, or firm policies? If so, acceptance would create a threat that cannot be reduced or eliminated through any safeguards. If not, consider the following:

• What is the nature, value, and intent of the gift?
• Is it more than clearly inconsequential?
• Is it reasonable in the circumstances?
• Is it standard practice to accept or reject such gifts?
• Does the client expect a "quid pro quo"?

Ethically speaking, a good way to approach the issue is to, first, apply the "feel" test. If you have an uncomfortable feeling about the relationship and think it may influence others' opinions of you, don't get involved. Second, ask whether you would be comfortable explaining why you agreed to accept the gifts if you were questioned by a superior or a newspaper reporter. Third, think about how you would feel if your decision got discussed on social media. Could you defend it? You do not want to place yourself in a position where you have to "rationalize away" accepting a gift, which is increasingly challenged as being against the rules. Finally, remember to avoid taking the first step down the ethical slippery slope by having to justify your action even though you know it is wrong.

AICPA Code: Conceptual Framework for Members in Business

LO 4-5

Explain how the conceptual framework works to keep in check possible violations of integrity and objectivity for CPAs in business.

A major improvement in the revised AICPA Code is it now includes new material for CPAs in business to evaluate whether relationships may exist between the CPA and the employing organization that create threats to compliance with the Integrity and Objectivity Rule. The conceptual framework for members in business (2.000.010) applies to integrity and objectivity, as well as other rules of conduct, but not independence, because CPAs in business do not provide attest services to clients that require complete independence. The discussion below focuses only on situations where the requirements for CPAs in business differ from those in public practice.

Similar to the guidance for CPAs in public practice, the threats and safeguards approach for CPAs in business identifies a variety of threats to compliance with the Integrity and Objectivity Rule, and other professional requirements, that create the need for safeguards to reduce the threat to an acceptable level or eliminate it. These threats and safeguards are different than those for CPAs in public practice. The examples below illustrate the differences.

Threats and Safeguards

Adverse interest threat. These threats to objectivity arise because the CPA's interests may be opposed to the interests of the employing organization. For instance, a CPA may have charged, or expressed an intention to charge, the employing organization with violations of law. The threat that arises is the result of the ethical conflict. An example would be if a CPA made a whistleblowing charge against the employer under SOX or Dodd-Frank. **Exhibit 3.16** describes the steps to be taken to avoid any subordination of judgment because of the conflict of interest.

Advocacy threat. Advocacy threats exist because a CPA may promote an employing organization's interests or position to the point that his objectivity is compromised. This would be the case if obtaining favorable financing or additional capital is dependent upon the accuracy of information included in or excluded from a prospectus, an offering, a business plan, a financing application, or a regulatory filing.

Familiarity threat. A familiarity threat arises from a long or close relationship with a person or an employing organization that causes a CPA to become too sympathetic to the latter's interests or too accepting of the person's or employing organization's product or service. Some examples include when a CPA uses an immediate family member's or a close relative's company as a supplier to the employing organization and when a CPA regularly accepts gifts or entertainment from a vendor or customer of the employing organization.

Self-interest threat. The existence of a self-interest threat means that a CPA could benefit, financially or otherwise, from an interest in or relationship with the employing organization or persons associated with the employing organization, such as when a CPA holds a financial interest in the employing organization and the value of that financial interest is directly affected by the CPA's decisions, as would be the case if the financial interest is in the form of shares or share options.

Self-review threat. A self-review threat may occur when a CPA is unable to appropriately evaluate the results of a previous judgment made or service performed or supervised by the CPA, or an individual in the employing organization, and the CPA relies on that service in forming a judgment as part of another service. An example is when performing an internal audit procedure, an internal auditor accepts work that they previously performed in a different position.

Undue influence threat. These threats occur because a CPA subordinates their judgment to that of an individual associated with the employing organization or any relevant third party due to that individual's position, reputation or expertise, aggressive or dominant personality, or attempts to coerce or exercise excessive influence over the CPA. An example is when a CPA is pressured to become associated with misleading information or to change a conclusion regarding an accounting or tax position.

The safeguards to reduce the threats to compliance with the rules for CPAs in business, or reduce them to an acceptable level, are different from those for CPAs in public practice. For CPAs in business, the safeguards are implemented by the employing organization not the firm, and client safeguards are not applicable. Notice how so many deal with corporate governance issues.

Safeguards implemented by the employing organization include:

1. A tone at the top that emphasizes a commitment to fair financial reporting and compliance with applicable laws, rules, regulations, and corporate governance policies;
2. Policies and procedures addressing ethical conduct and compliance with laws, rules, and regulations;
3. An audit committee charter, including independent audit committee members;
4. Internal policies and procedures requiring disclosure of identified interests or relationships among the employing organization, its directors or officers, vendors, suppliers, or customers;
5. Dissemination of corporate ethical compliance policies and procedures, including whistleblower hotlines, the reporting structure, dispute resolution, or similar policies to promote compliance with laws, rules, regulations, and other professional requirements;

6. Policies and procedures for implementing and monitoring ethical practices;

7. A reporting structure whereby the internal auditor does not report to the financial reporting group;

8. Policies and procedures that do not allow an internal auditor to monitor areas where the internal auditor has operational or functional responsibilities;

9. Policies for promotion, rewards, and enforcement of a culture of high ethics and integrity; and

10. Use of the third-party resources for consultation as needed on significant matters of professional judgment.

Threats to compliance with the Integrity and Objectivity Rule would not be at an acceptable level and could not be reduced to an acceptable level by the application of safeguards, and the CPA would be considered to have knowingly misrepresented facts in violation of the rule if the CPA:

• Makes, or permits or directs another party to make, materially false and misleading entries in an entity's financial statements or records;

• Fails to correct an entity's financial statements or records that are materially false and misleading when the CPA has the authority to record the entries; or

• Signs, or permits or directs another to sign, a document containing materially false and misleading information.

The Integrity and Objectivity Rule also requires the CPA in business (i.e., CFO) to be candid when dealing with the employer's external accountant and not knowingly misrepresent facts or knowingly fail to disclose material facts. This would include, for example, falsely certifying the financial statements under Section 302 of SOX.

Link between Conceptual Framework and Giving Voice to Values

The conceptual framework approach that underlies the ethical standards for CPAs in public practice and business is consistent with the thought process of the Giving Voice to Values methodology. For example, in bringing one's concerns to higher-ups in the organization, the goal should be to convince the appropriate party or parties that the position taken is the best one from both ethical and professional perspectives. In deciding what to say, how to say it, and to whom the discussion should be directed, the CPA should consider what the likely objections and pushbacks might be and how they can effectively be counteracted. Similarly, to meet one's professional responsibilities under the Integrity and Objectivity Rule, the CPA must convince others of the most ethical action.

Let's look at an example. Carl Kilgore is a CPA and the assistant controller of Linkage, Inc., a public company. He oversees the accounting for construction jobs for his company. One job has just been completed and the bill was prepared by the accounting department. Before Carl can even see it, the controller (Jack Long), who is also a CPA, drops by and tells Carl to pad the bill by 50 percent. It seems this particular client never scrutinizes the bills from Linkage, Inc. because of a long-standing relationship of trust. In fact, this is the first time to your knowledge that any such padding has occurred. What would you do if you were Carl Kilgore and why?

Application of the conceptual framework calls for discussing the threat to integrity and objectivity with his supervisor, Jack Long, and trying to convince him to eliminate the padding. This may be a futile attempt, but, still, Carl should reason out his options because he can use it to bring the matter to those above Jack, if necessary. Carl reflects on the following:

• What are the main arguments by Jack you are trying to counter?

• What is at stake for the key parties, including those who disagree with you?

• What levers can you use to influence those who disagree with you?

• What is your most effective response to the reasons and rationalizations you need to address? To whom should the argument be made? When and in what context?

Carl's an ethical guy and he doesn't want to get caught up in a fraud or cover-up so he carefully develops a game plan to counteract Jack's request to pad the bill. Carl should drive home the point that the financials will be fraudulent if Jack's request is honored. Jack should be reminded that both he and Carl have ethical responsibilities to be objective in preparing the financial statements and Carl needs to maintain his integrity in light of Jack's request to falsify the statements. Carl should also point out the potential harm to the construction company of being billed for 150 percent of the correct amount and how it may react, and possible implications for trust and the reputation of Linkage, Inc. Carl may also have the option of using a hotline to report any unresolved differences. Carl's ultimate goal is to present the most convincing case in order to avoid the need to blow the whistle externally, either to the outside auditors or the regulatory authorities. Carl's most effective tool may be to emphasize the SOX Section 302 requirements for the CFO and CEO and use them as leverage because, presumably, they would not want to commit fraud by falsely certifying the financial statements.

Rules for the Performance of Professional Services

LO 4-6

Explain how to apply the rules of conduct in the AICPA Code to the performance of professional services.

The remaining sections of the Code address ethics rules dealing with the performance of professional services for clients or one's employer. The standards for CPAs in public practice and those in business are similar with a few exceptions noted below. The rules are as follows:

- General Standards (1.300)
- Acts Discreditable (1.400)
- Fees and Other Types of Remuneration (1.500)
- Advertising and Other Forms of Solicitation (1.600)
- Confidential Information (1.700)
- Form of Organization and Name (1.800)

The conceptual framework applies to these rules in order to identify threats and safeguards when specific interpretations do not address a particular situation. If the CPA cannot demonstrate that safeguards were applied and eliminated or reduced threats to an acceptable level, then there would be a violation of the rules.

General Standards Rule

The General Standards Rule establishes requirements for competence, compliance with professional standards, and adherence to accounting principles.

Competence means having the appropriate technical qualifications to perform professional services and proper supervision and evaluation of the quality of work performed. While a reasonable care standard exists, CPAs are not expected to be infallible of knowledge or judgment.

To meet the competency standard, CPAs must be sensitive to situations when one's capabilities are limited and the conservative action may be to recommend another practitioner to perform the services. For example, a CPA or CPA firm should not undertake an audit of a school district without sufficient knowledge of generally accepted government accounting and auditing standards. Think of it this way: An accounting student who works on a group project with other students to develop a business plan might feel comfortable working on the financial plan, but presumably that student would not want to be responsible for developing the marketing plan. They would expect a marketing student to assume that responsibility.

Compliance with Standards

A variety of professional standards establish rules of conduct related to specific services including Statements on Auditing Standards (SAS), Statements on Standards for Accounting and Review Services (SSARS), Statements on Standards for Consulting Services (SSCS), Statements on Quality Control Standards (SSQS), and Statements on Standards for Tax Services (SSTS).

The Accounting Principles Rule obligates CPAs to ensure that the financial statements are prepared in accordance with GAAP and assess whether any material modifications to those statements are needed. If a CPA believes a departure from GAAP is justified to avoid misleading statements due to unusual circumstances, then the CPA can still comply with the rule by describing the departure; its approximate effects, if practicable; and the reasons why compliance with the principle would result in a misleading statement.

Acts Discreditable

Acts Discreditable covers a broad range of actions that may bring discredit to the profession. The list is long so we limit the discussion to confidential information obtained from employment, promoting or marketing professional services, returning client books and records, and removing client files or other proprietary information. As previously noted, the threats and safeguards approach is used in evaluation of ethical conflicts when interpretations do not address a particular relationship or circumstance.

Acts discreditable can include sexual harassment and discrimination as discussed below. This is because of Rule 1.400.001 in the AICPA Code (501-2–Discrimination and harassment in employment. AICPA Code of Professional Conduct) that says, "If a final determination, no longer subject to appeal, is made by a court or an administrative agency of competent jurisdiction that a member has violated any antidiscrimination laws of the United States, a state, or a municipality, including those related to sexual and other forms of harassment,"* then it is presumed the member has committed an act discreditable to the profession.

PwC Settles Lawsuit over Age Discrimination

On March 16, 2020, PwC agreed to settle a class-action lawsuit alleging age discrimination in hiring by paying out $11.625 million. The lawsuit alleged PwC refused to hire older workers for associate jobs by filling staff positions almost exclusively through college campus recruiting that was off-limits to older workers and by failing to post entry-level accountant jobs on its website. The lawsuit further alleged PwC's mandatory early retirement policy, which requires partners to retire by age 60, acts as an incentive for discrimination because older applicants present "less return" on the company's investment. These actions by PwC violated the Acts Discreditable rule.

Sexual Harassment at EY

On May 2, 2018, Jessica Casucci, a former female partner at EY, agreed to leave the firm as part of a settlement over allegations that a male senior executive sexually assaulted and harassed her. Casucci claimed that the company did nothing to help her for years, according to a complaint filed with the Equal Employment Opportunity Council (EEOC) last month.[14]

Casucci alleged that, in 2015, John Martinkat, a high-ranking partner in EY's tax division, groped and sexually harassed her in front of two other partners, who did nothing to stop Martinkat or report him to the company.

Martinkat also sent lewd texts and e-mails to Casucci, who was also a partner in the tax division, trying to get her to come to his hotel room while they were on a business trip in Orlando, Fla., according to the suit.

Casucci later reported the incidents to Karyn Twaronite, the company's head of diversity and inclusiveness officer in 2016, after she learned that another woman had been subjected to inappropriate sexual conduct, and decided she needed to take action to protect women at the company. Sexual harassment of any kind is an act discreditable to the profession.

Confidentiality of Information Gained through Employment

A confidentiality requirement exists for employees of firms that precludes disclosing confidential employer information obtained as a result of an employment relationship, such as discussions with the employer's vendors, customers, or lenders. An example where confidential information is generally protected is customer lists, target clients, costs, and marketing strategies that might afford competitive advantages. Perhaps the most dangerous situation is when an employee leaves the company, by choice or force, and decides to use confidential information for personal gain. Here, any covenants not to compete should be examined to determine restrictions and how they may affect downloading customer lists, taking client files, or using former client-related information to help start one's own practice.

Situations exist where a CPA is permitted or may be required to disclose confidential employer information under the law, such as occurs with whistleblowing disclosures when the conditions for doing so under Dodd-Frank have been met, as discussed in **Chapter 3**. Disclosure also may be required to comply with a validly issued and enforceable subpoena or summons. Other situations where disclosure is permissible include:

- Initiate a complaint to, or respond to any inquiry made by, the Professional Ethics Division, trial board of the AICPA, state CPA society, or state board of accountancy;
- Protect the CPA's professional interests in legal proceedings;
- Comply with professional standards and other ethics requirements; or
- Report potential concerns regarding questionable accounting, auditing, or other matters to the employer's confidential complaint hotline or those charged with governance.

A CPA would be considered in violation of the Acts Discreditable Rule if they disclose or use any confidential employer information acquired as a result of employment or volunteer relationships without the proper authority or specific consent of the employer or organization for whom they may work in a volunteer capacity, unless there is a legal or professional responsibility to use or disclose such information.

Promoting or Marketing Professional Services

CPAs violate the Acts Discreditable Rule if they promote or market their abilities to provide professional services or make claims about their experience or qualifications in a manner that is false, misleading, or deceptive. Promotional efforts would be false, misleading, or deceptive if they contain any claim or representation that would likely cause a reasonable person to be misled or deceived. This includes any representation about CPA licensure or any other professional certification or accreditation that is not in compliance with the requirements of the relevant licensing authority or designating body. False, misleading, or deceptive promotional efforts also violate the Advertising and Solicitation Rule.

Records Request

The records request rule is somewhat complicated and relies on basic definitions as explained below.

- *Client-provided records* are accounting or other records belonging to the client that were provided to the member [CPA] by or on behalf of the client, including hard-copy or electronic reproductions of such records.
- *Member-prepared records* are accounting or other records that the member was not specifically engaged to prepare and that are not in the client's books and records or are otherwise not available to the client, with the result that the client's financial information is incomplete. Examples include adjusting, closing, combining, or consolidating journal entries (including computations supporting such entries) and supporting schedules and documents that are proposed or prepared by the member as part of an engagement (e.g., an audit).
- *Member's work products* are deliverables as set forth in the terms of the engagement, such as tax returns.
- *Member's working papers* are all other items prepared solely for purposes of the engagement and include items prepared by the CPA, such as audit programs, analytical review schedules, and statistical sampling results and analyses.

The rules are summarized as follows.

1. Client-provided records in the custody or control of the member (CPA) should be returned to the client at the client's request.
2. Unless a member and the client have agreed to the contrary, when a client makes a request for member-prepared records, or a member's work products that are in the custody or control of the member or the member's firm and that have not previously been provided to the client, the member should respond to the client's request as follows:

a. Member-prepared records relating to a completed and issued work product should be made available to the client, except that such records may be withheld if there are fees due to the member for the specific work product.

b. Member's work products should be made available to the client, except that such work products may be withheld in any of the following circumstances:

  a. If there are fees due to the member for the specific work product.

  b. If the work product is incomplete.

  c. For purposes of complying with professional standards (for example, withholding an audit report due to outstanding audit issues).

  d. If threatened or outstanding litigation exists concerning the engagement or member's work.

Failure to File a Tax Return or Pay the Tax Liability

Accountants have a responsibility to comply with applicable federal, state, or local laws regarding the timely filing of their personal tax returns, or the timely remittance of all payroll and other taxes collected on behalf of others. The failure to do so is an act discreditable in violation of the Section 2.400.0030 of the AICPA Code.

Contingent Fees

Years ago in the accounting profession, it was a violation of the rules of conduct for a CPA to accept a contingent fee for services performed for a client or for recommending a product or service to the client. These forms of payment were thought to be "unprofessional" and could potentially compromise the CPA's professional judgment. Over the years, however, professional accountants have become more involved in performing nonattest services that do not require independence and are largely provided to satisfy the client's interest, not the public interest. Thus, there is no third-party reliance on the work of the accountant. Moreover, CPAs who provide these nonattest services to clients are now competing with non-CPAs who perform similar services and are not bound by a professional code of conduct such as the AICPA Code. The result has been a loosening of the rules to permit the acceptance of contingent fees and commissions when performing advisory-type services for a nonattest client. Certain restrictions do apply, as discussed next.

Under the rule, a CPA is prohibited from performing for a contingent fee any professional services for, or to receive such a fee from, a client for whom the CPA or CPA firm performs any of the following services: (1) an audit or review of a financial statement; (2) a compilation of a financial statement when the CPA expects, or reasonably might expect, that a third party will use the financial statement, and the compilation report does not disclose a lack of independence; (3) an examination of prospective financial information; or (4) preparation of an original or amended tax return or claim for a tax refund for a contingent fee for any client.

The danger of accepting a contingent fee for services provided to an attest client is it creates a financial self-interest threat to independence that may not be reduced or eliminated by any safeguards. Imagine if an accounting firm and audit client were to agree that the firm would receive 30 percent of any tax savings to the client resulting from tax advice provided by the firm. In this case, the fee is dependent on the outcome of the service. The fact that a government agency might challenge the amount of the client's tax savings, and thereby alter the final amount of the fee paid to the firm, heightens rather than lessens the mutuality of interest between the firm and client.

Exceptions do exist in tax practice where a contingent fee can be accepted, including: (1) if the fee is fixed by courts or other public authorities, (2) if the fee is determined based on the results of judicial proceedings or the findings of governmental agencies, (3) when filing an amended state or federal tax return claiming a tax refund based on a tax issue that is the subject of a tax case involving a different taxpayer or with respect to which the taxing authority is developing a position, or (4) when filing an amended federal or state income tax return (or refund claim) claiming a tax refund in an amount greater than the threshold for review by the Joint Committee on Internal Revenue Taxation ($1 million at March 1991) or state taxing authority.

Commissions and Referral Fees

The commission and referral fees rule is similar to that for contingent fees. Unlike a contingent fee, which is conditioned on the outcome of a service, a commission is typically paid to a CPA for recommending or referring to a client any product or service of another party, such as an investment product whereby the CPA receives a commission from the investment company if the client purchases the product. A similar arrangement exists when a CPA, for a commission, recommends or refers any product or service to be supplied by a client to another party. The restricted services identified under the contingent fees rule apply equally to the commissions rule. The same independence concerns exist because of the financial self-interest.

Imagine, for example, that a CPA is engaged to perform financial planning services for a client and to recommend a financial product or products based on the service. Now, if one of three products pays a commission to the CPA, assuming that the client purchases the product, while the other two do not, it may appear that the CPA can no longer be independent with respect to providing audit or other attest services for the client. The key point is that it doesn't matter if the CPA can, in fact, make independent decisions. The perception may be in the mind of a reasonable observer that such an independent mindset is no longer possible because of the commission arrangement. What if, for example, during the course of the audit and valuation of the investment product, the CPA discovers a flaw in the logic used to recommend the commission-based product to the client? Would the CPA disclose that fact to the client?

One requirement under the commission and referral fee rule that does not exist for contingent fees is to disclose permitted commissions and referral fees to any person or entity to whom the CPA recommends or refers a product or service to which the commission relates. In other words, the act of disclosing meets the CPA's ethical obligation under the AICPA Code. A protection beyond disclosure is that requirements for due care and adherence to the Objectivity and Integrity Rule apply in making product and service recommendations.

Advertising and Other Forms of Solicitation

The advertising and solicitations rule establishes guidelines for when and how a CPA can promote professional services or solicit clients. While advertising and solicitation are permitted, these forms of communication cannot be done in a manner that is false, misleading, or deceptive. Solicitation by the use of coercion, overreaching, or harassing conduct is prohibited under the rule.

Advertising and solicitation practices of CPAs should never cross the line as might occur if they (1) create false or unjustified expectations of favorable results; (2) imply the ability to influence any court, tribunal, regulatory agency, or similar body or official; (3) contain a representation that specific professional services in current or future periods will be performed for a stated fee, estimated fee, or fee range when it was likely at the time of the representation that such fees would be substantially increased and the prospective client was not advised of that likelihood; and (4) contain any other representations that would be likely to cause a reasonable person to misunderstand or be deceived.

Given the new ways to engage current and future clients using social media outlets, it is fair to say the AICPA rules on advertising and solicitation lack specificity. Perhaps the AICPA believes its rules provide sufficient blanket coverage on all forms of practice. In recent years, like so many professional service providers, CPAs have increasingly used the Internet and developed CPA firm Web sites. Prior to the advent of the Internet and universal access to marketing and advertising information, such information may have been in brochures or other printed material. Traditionally, such material was disseminated only by hand or mail and was not as available for general reference or scrutiny. Now, the information is available with one click, so the rules need to catch up with the technology.

Confidential Information

The general requirement to maintain client confidentiality is that a CPA should not disclose confidential client information without the specific consent of the client. Confidentiality issues can be tricky from a legal perspective so CPAs are best served when they consult with legal counsel prior to disclosing, or determining whether to disclose, confidential client information.

The rule does permit CPAs to discuss confidential client information without violating the rule in the following situations: (1) in response to a validly issued subpoena or summons, or to adhere to applicable laws and government regulations (i.e., Dodd-Frank); (2) to provide the information necessary for a review of the CPA's professional practice (inspection/quality review) under PCAOB, AICPA, state CPA society, or board of accountancy authorization; and (3) to provide the information necessary for one's defense in an investigation of the CPA in a disciplinary matter.

Client permission to discuss confidential issues generally is granted when there is a change of auditor and the successor auditor approaches the client for permission to discuss matters related to the audit with the predecessor. This step is required by generally accepted auditing standards. Of course, the client can always deny permission and cut off any such contact, in which case the successor auditor probably should run in the opposite direction of the client as quickly as possible. In other words, the proverbial "red flag" will have been raised. The CPA should be skeptical and wonder why the client may have refused permission.

Form of Organization and Name

Ethics rules apply not only to individual CPAs who are licensed by state boards but also to accounting firms and certain members of alternative practice structures, networks, and affiliate firms. The forms of organization used by CPA firms over the years have changed to recognize the importance of nonattest services to the revenue flow of firms and competition with non-CPA firms in providing such services. Years ago, CPAs had to own 100 percent of a firm's equity interests. Today, most states simply require a majority ownership in the hands of licensed CPAs.

The ownership rules now accommodate non-CPA owners who perform a variety of advisory services and want a partial ownership interest in the firm. Toffler, in her book on the demise of Arthur Andersen in the aftermath of failed audits on Enron and WorldCom,[15] laid blame on the proliferation of nonattest services at Andersen and non-CPA consultants, who operated under a less strict culture of ethical behavior than their CPA-attest colleagues. She claims that corners were cut and decisions were made that were in the interests of the client and firm, at the sacrifice of the public interest, as a result of compromises to independence and objectivity in audit services so as not to upset clients and possibly lose lucrative consulting services.

Exhibit 4.4 provides a summary of the AICPA rules to help you understand the underlying characteristics of making ethical decisions and compliance with the rules.

EXHIBIT 4.4   Characteristic Traits for Compliance with AICPA Rules of Conduct

Rule	Traits
Independence	Maintain in fact and appearance Evaluate business and financial relationships with client management/entity Make objective judgments
Objectivity	Make unbiased judgments Exercise professional skepticism
Integrity	Do not subordinate judgment Carry through ethical reason with ethical action
General Standards	Maintain competence Make decisions with due care Comply with professional standards
Acts Discreditable	Avoid relationships and actions that reflect poorly on one's character Don't engage in activities that raise questions about one's integrity
Contingent fees	Don't accept when providing audit services to a client Acceptable when providing nonaudit services only Acceptable for tax services with limitations

(continued)

Rule	Traits
Commissions/Referral Fees	Don't accept when providing audit services to a client
	Disclose to client the acceptance of such fees
Advertising and Solicitation	Don't make statements that are false, misleading, or deceptive
	Don't solicit clients in an overreaching manner or by harassment
Confidential Information	Don't disclose confidential client/employer information
	Obtain expressed approval of client to disclose
	Acceptable when required under law or to defend oneself in a legal or professional action and when disclosure is permitted by law or regulation
Form of Organization	Non-CPA ownership permitted
	CPAs must own >50% of equity interests

The Spirit of the Rules

The essence of professionalism is to follow the rules of conduct, act ethically at all times, and protect the public interest. The rules for the performance of professional services address these issues in a variety of ways. However, the rules can never cover every situation encountered, so the CPA needs to follow both the letter of the rule and the spirit of the rule. For example, the General Standards Rule calls for competence, due care, adequate planning and supervision, and gathering sufficient, relevant data. It does not directly address how to determine audit staffing and pricing. Murray points out that when charging fees, CPAs should ensure that their objectivity is not impaired by the hope of financial gain, and that such fees are proportional with the responsibilities they assume. Auditors need to be sure any threats to audit quality are met through adequate safeguards to ensure audit quality will not be adversely affected because the fee charged is insufficient to allow the necessary time and skill to be spent for this purpose.[16]

Ethics and Tax Services

LO 4-7

Analyze the ethics rules for tax practice and how they are influenced by the realistic possibility standard.

Students who graduate from college and take positions with accounting firms might end up providing tax services for a client at some time in their careers. Tax services include tax compliance, where much of the service is derived from audited financial records, tax consulting, tax planning, and tax shelters.

The AICPA explicitly recognizes the tax professional's dual obligations to the client to act as an advocate and to foster integrity in the tax system by honestly and fairly administering the tax laws. While client advocacy is an acceptable standard in tax practice, the tax accountant remains obligated to act objectively and with integrity, exercise due care, and follow the Statements on Standards for Tax Services issued by the AICPA.

In the performance of tax services for an audit client, the tax CPA is expected to consider whether any threats to independence exist that cannot be reduced or eliminated by safeguards and how such matters will be handled to avoid a violation of audit independence.

When a CPA prepares a tax return and transmits the tax return and related tax payment to a taxing authority in paper or electronic form, self-review and management participation threats to compliance with the Independence Rule may exist. In this case the CPA should apply the rules when providing nonattest services to an attest client to ensure all threats to independence have been adequately dealt with through safeguards.

Providing some tax services for audit clients can create conflicts of interest that threaten independence. Barrett points out that when auditors review the items for accrued taxes payable on the balance sheet and income tax expense on the income statement, they must reach conclusions about the validity of these amounts before they can express an opinion as to whether the financial statements fairly present the entity's financial condition and operating results in accordance with GAAP. As a result, auditors must examine the entity's tax returns and assess so-called "tax reserves" or "tax provisions" to evaluate tax expense for the current period and to determine whether any material unrecorded or undisclosed tax liabilities exist.[17] Here, a self-review threat may exist that cannot be reduced or eliminated by any safeguards.

An undue influence threat occurs if a CPA is pressured to change a conclusion regarding an accounting or a tax position. The client might seek to influence the tax position by linking it to additional attest work or consulting services.

Statements on Standards for Tax Services (SSTS)

The AICPA has issued seven Statements on Standards for Tax Services (SSTS) that explain CPAs' responsibilities to their clients and the tax systems in which they practice. The statements demonstrate a CPA's commitment to tax practice standards that balance advocacy and planning with compliance.

The statements establish required ethics rules for tax practitioners. Given the complexity of this area, we limit our discussion to the "realistic possibility" standard under *SSTS No. 1* and issues related to taking a tax position and tax planning.

SSTS No. 1—Tax Return Positions

This statement sets forth the applicable standards for CPAs when recommending tax return positions or preparing or signing tax returns (including amended returns, claims for refund, and information returns) filed with any taxing authority. The following definitions apply:

- A *tax return position* is a position reflected on a tax return on which a CPA has specifically advised a taxpayer or a position about which a CPA has knowledge of all material facts and, on the basis of those facts, has concluded whether the position is appropriate.
- A *taxpayer* is a client, a CPA's employer, or any other third-party recipient of tax services.

The statement addresses a CPA's obligation to advise a taxpayer of relevant tax return disclosure responsibilities and potential penalties. In addition to the AICPA and IRS tax regulations, various taxing authorities at the federal, state, and local levels may impose specific reporting and disclosure standards with regard to recommending tax return positions or preparing or signing a tax return. A CPA should determine and comply with the standards, if any, that are imposed by the applicable taxing authority with respect to recommending a tax return position or preparing or signing a tax return. If the applicable taxing authority has no written standards in this regard, then the following standards will apply.

A CPA should not recommend a tax return position or prepare or sign a tax return taking a position unless they have a good-faith belief that the position has at least a realistic possibility of being sustained administratively or judicially on its merits if challenged. This is known as the *realistic possibility of success* standard under *SSTS Interpretation No. 101-1*. It requires that the tax return position should not be recommended unless the position satisfies applicable reporting and disclosure standards.

Notwithstanding the previous statement, a CPA may recommend a tax return position if they conclude that there is a reasonable basis for the position and advises the taxpayer to disclose that position appropriately. An interesting aspect of the standard is the prohibition against recommending a tax return position or preparing or signing a tax return reflecting a position that the CPA knows exploits the "audit selection process of a taxing authority," or serves as a mere arguing position advanced solely to obtain leverage in a negotiation with a taxing authority. The former refers to the fact that a tax practitioner might recommend an overly aggressive position to a client hoping that the IRS does not choose to examine the client's tax return. Clearly, that would be a violation of basic ethical standards, including honesty (nondeceptiveness) and integrity.

Interpretation 1-1, Reporting and Disclosure Standards

Interpretation 1-1 states that, if the standard of the applicable taxing authority is higher than the realistic possibility of success standard, the member (CPA) should comply with the higher standard. If the applicable taxing authority's standard is lower than the realistic possibility of success, the member should comply with the realistic possibility of success standard. If the applicable taxing authority does not have written standards that apply to recommending a tax return position or preparing or signing a tax return, a CPA should not take these actions unless the CPA has a good-faith belief that the position meets the realistic possibility of success standard. However, a CPA may recommend a tax return position, or prepare or sign a tax return that reflects a position, if there is a reasonable basis for the position and the CPA, in the first case, advises the taxpayer to appropriately disclose the position, or, in the second case, the position is appropriately disclosed on the return.

The realistic possibility of success standard normally requires a one-third likelihood that the position will be sustained on its merits. The reasonable basis standard is lower than realistic possibility of success, but it is (26 CFR § 1.6662-3 - Negligence or disregard of rules or regulations.) "significantly higher than not frivolous or not patently improper and is not satisfied by a return position that is merely arguable or that is merely a colorable claim." A position normally satisfies the reasonable basis standard if it is reasonably based on one or more authorities, considering the relevance and persuasiveness of those authorities. In practice, reasonable basis normally requires at least an approximately 20 percent likelihood that the position will be upheld on its merits.

All facts and circumstances, as well as authorities relevant to the tax treatment at issue, should be considered when determining whether a reporting standard has been satisfied. The weight given to a particular authority will depend upon its relevance and persuasiveness. For example, a ruling or case with facts similar to those at issue—especially one that provides an analysis of the facts and law—carries more weight than one whose facts differ significantly. Additionally, an appellate court decision carries more weight than one of a lower court within its jurisdiction, as does a revenue ruling over a private letter ruling issued to a third party.

To determine whether required reporting and disclosure standards have been satisfied, a CPA should:

- Establish the relevant background facts;
- Consider the reasonableness of the assumptions and representations;
- Consider applicable regulations and standards regarding reliance on information and advice received from a third party;
- Apply the pertinent authorities to the relevant facts;
- Consider the business purpose and economic substance of the transaction, if relevant to its tax consequences (mere reliance on a representation that there is a business purpose or economic substance generally is insufficient);
- Consider whether the issue involves a listed or reportable transaction (or their equivalents) as defined by the applicable taxing authority; and
- Arrive at a conclusion supported by the authorities.

When engaged in tax planning, the CPA should understand the business purpose and economic substance of the transaction when relevant to the tax consequences. The business purpose for the transaction should be described, and if the business reasons are relevant to the tax consequences, it is insufficient to merely assume that a transaction is entered into for valid business reasons without specifying what those reasons are. The Caterpillar tax shelter case below illustrates how economic substance issues come into play in determining the validity of a tax position.

Examples are provided in *SSTS No. 1-1* to assist in the application of the standards to fact situations. One such example is described in **Exhibit 4.5.**

EXHIBIT 4.5   Recommending a Prior Tax Return Position

A taxpayer has engaged in a transaction that is adversely affected by a new statutory provision. Prior law supports a position favorable to the taxpayer. The taxpayer believes, and the member concurs, that the new statute is inequitable as applied to the taxpayer's situation. The statute is constitutional, clearly drafted, and unambiguous. The legislative history discussing the new statute contains general comments that do not specifically address the taxpayer's situation.

In this case, although prior law supported a favorable position for a taxpayer, if a new statutory provision now adversely affects the taxpayer, a member cannot recommend the prior return position. A position contrary to a constitutional, clear, and unambiguous statute would not satisfy the reasonable basis standard, even if appropriately disclosed.

Tax Avoidance Is Legal; Tax Evasion Is Criminal

Individuals and business owners often have more than one way to complete a taxable transaction. Tax planning evaluates various tax options to determine how to conduct business and personal transactions in order to reduce or eliminate your tax liability.[18]

Although they sound similar, "tax avoidance" and "tax evasion" are radically different. Tax avoidance lowers your tax bill by structuring your transactions so that you reap the largest tax benefits. Tax avoidance is completely legal—and extremely wise.

Tax evasion, on the other hand, is an attempt to reduce your tax liability by deceit, subterfuge, or concealment. Tax evasion is a crime.

How do you know when shrewd planning—tax avoidance—goes too far and crosses the line to become illegal tax evasion? Often the distinction turns upon whether actions were taken with fraudulent intent.

For example, engaging in accounting irregularities, such as a business's failure to keep adequate records, or a discrepancy between amounts reported on a corporation's return and amounts reported on its financial statements, generally demonstrates fraudulent intent.

Treasury Circular 230

Circular 230, *Regulations Governing Practice Before the Internal Revenue Service*, contains rules governing the recognition of attorneys, certified public accountants, enrolled agents, enrolled retirement plan agents, registered tax return preparers, and other persons representing taxpayers before the Internal Revenue Service. A detailed coverage of the rules goes beyond the scope of this chapter but two items, in particular, are worth noting.

Section 10.21 of Circular 230 requires any practitioner who knows or discovers that a client has not complied with the federal tax laws or that a client has made an error or omission on any return, document, affidavit, or other paper submitted or executed under the federal tax laws must advise the client promptly of the noncompliance, error, or omission and its consequences. However, nothing in Circular 230 requires correction of the noncompliance, error, or omission, or disengagement when the client refuses to make the correction. Ultimately, the option to correct is at the client's discretion.

The AICPA takes a similar approach in SSTS No. 6, *Knowledge of Error: Return Preparation and Administrative Proceedings*: "The member should advise the taxpayer of the error and the potential consequences, and recommend the measures to be taken." SSTS No. 6, paragraph 8, continues: "It is the taxpayer's responsibility to decide whether to correct the error. ... Although recognizing that the taxpayer may not be required by statute to correct an error by filing an amended return, a member should consider whether a taxpayer's decision not to file an amended return or otherwise correct an error may predict future behavior that might require termination of the relationship."[19]

Circular 230 forbids tax practitioners from having conflicts of interest. Specifically, it provides that a practitioner should not represent a client before the IRS if the representation involves a conflict of interest. A conflict of interest exists if:

- The representation of one client will be directly adverse to another client; or
- There is a significant risk that the representation of one or more clients will be materially limited by the practitioner's responsibilities to another client, a former client or a third person, or by a personal interest of the practitioner.

Circular 230 also provides for waiver of conflicts of interest if (1) the tax practitioner reasonably believes that they can still competently and diligently represent each client, (2) the representation is not prohibited by law, and (3) each client gives informed consent confirmed in writing at the time the conflict is known by the practitioner, but no later than 30 days. But the AICPA Code does not allow a CPA to waive a conflict of interest in a representation that requires independence under the rules.

Tax Shelters

A listed transaction is defined by the IRS as a transaction that is the same as or substantially similar to one of the types of transactions that the IRS has determined to be a tax avoidance transaction. Such actions are identified by notice, regulation, or other forms of published guidance as listed transactions. Tax avoidance transactions are sometimes labeled *tax shelters*. It is complicated, but basically the term *prohibited tax shelter transaction* means listed transactions, transactions with contractual protection, or confidential transactions.

The IRS guidelines for listed transactions identify participation in any of the following:

- A tax return reflects tax consequences or a tax strategy described in published guidance that lists the transaction.
- The CPA knows or has reason to know that tax benefits reflected on the tax return are derived directly or indirectly from such tax consequences or tax strategy.
- The client is in a type or class of individuals or entities that published guidance treats as participants in a listed transaction.

In other words, under IRS rules, any transaction that is the same or "substantially similar" to a transaction identified as a tax avoidance transaction by IRS notice, regulation, or other published guidance is a reportable transaction—it must be reported to the IRS.

KPMG Tax Shelter Case

One of the most controversial aspects of the Enron collapse was the alleged involvement of Andersen in marketing aggressive tax planning ideas that the IRS and the courts subsequently found to be abusive. After the Enron scandal, the accounting profession received a second serious blow in 2005, when KPMG settled a criminal tax case with the Department of the Treasury and the IRS for $456 million to prevent the firm's prosecution over tax shelters sold between 1996 and 2002. This is the largest criminal tax case ever filed.

The creation of tax shelter investments to help wealthy clients avoid paying taxes has been part of tax practice for many years. The difference in the KPMG case, according to the original indictment, is that tax professionals in the firm prepared false documents to deceive regulators about the true nature of the tax shelters. There appeared to be a clear intent to deceive the regulators, and that makes it fraud.

The indictment claimed that the tax shelter transactions broke the law because they involved no economic risk and were designed solely to minimize taxes. The firm had collected about $128 million in fees for generating at least $11 billion in fraudulent tax losses, and this resulted in at least $2.5 billion in tax evaded by wealthy individuals. On an annual basis, KPMG's tax department was bringing in for the firm nearly $1.2 billion of its $3.2 billion total U.S. revenue. Ultimately, the $128 million in fees were forfeited as part of the $456 million settlement.

Perhaps the most interesting aspect of the KPMG tax shelter situation is the culture that apparently existed in the firm's tax practice during the time the shelters were sold. In 1998, the firm had decided to accelerate its tax services business.

The motivation probably was the hot stock market during the 1990s and the increase in the number of wealthy taxpayers. The head of the KPMG's tax department, Jeffrey M. Stein, and its CFO, Richard Rosenthal, created an environment that treated those who didn't support the "growth at all costs" effort as not being team players. From the late 1990s, KPMG established a telemarketing center in Fort Wayne, Indiana, that cold-called potential clients from public lists of firms and companies. KPMG built an aggressive marketing team to sell tax shelters that it created with names like Blips, Flip, Opis, and SC2.

In an unusual move, the Justice Department brought a lawsuit against two former KPMG managers on 12 counts of tax evasion using illegal tax shelters. On April 1, 2009, John Larson, a former senior tax manager, was sentenced to more than 10 years and ordered to pay a fine of $6 million. Robert Plaff, a former tax partner at KPMG, was sentenced to more than eight years and fined $3 million. A third person convicted in the case, Raymond J. Ruble, a former partner at the law firm Sidley Austin, was sentenced to six years and seven months. In handing down the ruling in the U.S. District Court in Manhattan, Judge Lewis A. Kaplan stated, "These defendants knew they were on the wrong side of the line," adding later that they had cooked up "this mass-produced scheme to cheat the government out of taxes for the purposes of enriching themselves." The losses through the scheme were estimated at more than $100 million.

Caterpillar Tax Fraud Case

Tax fraud cases occur from time to time that make us sit up, take notice, and ask whether tax positions can be supported and its effect on the financial statements. The Caterpillar case described in **Exhibit 4.6** is one such case and the failure of PwC to detect and correct the fraud is troubling. A U.S. Senate subcommittee report on the tax fraud case concluded that PwC had a potential conflict of interest as Caterpillar's auditor because the firm was essentially auditing its own tax advice, a self-review threat to independence.

Tax fraud cases are not as common as financial statement fraud, but the Caterpillar case illustrates the broad scope of tax fraud and the length of time it takes to investigate tax fraud cases. An expose of the case appeared in a Bloomberg article by Bryan Gruley, David Vorecos, and Joe Deaux on June 1, 2017. What follows is a brief summary of the facts.[20]

EXHIBIT 4.6   Caterpillar Tax Fraud Case

In 2014, the U.S. Senate Permanent Subcommittee on Investigations headed by Michigan Senator Carl Levin detailed a program Caterpillar designed in 1999 with the advice of auditor PwC to use machinery part sales to shift its profits to low-tax Switzerland. The Senate investigation concluded these sales cut Caterpillar's U.S. bill by $2.4 billion between 2000 and 2012. The IRS, aided by documents provided by Caterpillar whistleblower Daniel Schlicksup, concluded in 2013 that Caterpillar had employed an "abusive" tax strategy. For years, Caterpillar accountants credited the Geneva, Switzerland office with 15 percent of the profits on parts sales, while the other 85 percent was allocated as earnings in the United States. The company paid an effective tax rate of a little less than 30 percent on those U.S. profits. Shortly thereafter, Caterpillar reorganized the Geneva operation to cut the company's tax bill so it could compete better with Komatsu Ltd. and other foreign rivals that enjoyed lower tax rates. In planning documents, PwC said, "We are effectively more than doubling the profit on parts." Essentially, Caterpillar flipped the parts profit allocation so the new Swiss entity would be credited with 85 percent of the income on those sales. The company then paid taxes on those earnings at rates ranging from 4 percent to 6 percent, as negotiated with the Swiss tax authorities.

In effect, Caterpillar removed its U.S. operations from the outbound supply chain of parts sold in foreign countries. Before the accounting change, Caterpillar in the United States bought parts from third-party suppliers and resold them in Geneva for distribution overseas. After the change, CSARL, a parts subsidiary in Switzerland, bought parts directly from the suppliers. But that was merely on paper: U.S. facilities continued to handle and manage the bulk of inventory, supplies, and manufacturing. Of its 400 or so employees, the Geneva office had about 65 people working on parts, whereas the United States had about 5,000.

Caterpillar wound up effectively keeping two sets of books. The public one attributed the bulk of parts profits to Geneva, with its slight tax rate. An internal ledger known as "accountable profits" tracked the operating income of the divisions and calculated bonuses accordingly, according to a 2014 report by the Senate Subcommittee.

(continued)

The IRS demanded $2.3 billion in back taxes and penalties. Additional investigations led to a final conclusion that Caterpillar had avoided taxes on more than $8 billion in revenue. On March 2, 2017, the federal government raided Caterpillar offices over possible tax fraud. Authorities seized documents and electronic information that could escalate a grand jury investigation into the company's tax avoidance strategies.

Resolving the tax fraud case is a complicated undertaking. Daniel Schlicksup sent memos to upper management expressing his view that there seemed to be no reason for CSARL to exist other than to lower taxes. That creates a potential problem because U.S. tax law requires a corporate structure to have clear "economic substance." In deciding tax shelter cases, the courts have mostly relied on the economic substance doctrine, which provides that transactions designed to yield tax benefits but which do not change the taxpayer's economic position independent of those benefits will not be respected. The common law doctrine normally requires the application of two separate tests—an objective test that focuses on the realistic potential of the transaction to generate a profit, and a subjective test focusing on the taxpayer's nontax business purpose in engaging in the transaction.

On March 30, 2010, the economic substance doctrine was codified in the Internal Revenue Code [IRC section 7701(o)]. It provides that, with respect to a transaction (or series of transactions) in which the common law economic substance doctrine is relevant, the transaction is treated as having economic substance only if the following tests are met:

- The transaction affects the taxpayer's economic position in a meaningful way, apart from any federal income tax effect; *and,*
- The taxpayer has a substantial purpose for engaging in the transaction, apart from any federal income tax effect.

The IRS's case against Caterpillar was still in process in 2020.

The IRS investigated Caterpillar's tax practices and concluded that the company had employed an "abusive" tax strategy and demanded $2.3 billion in back taxes and penalties. The strategy was designed to shift profits from the United States to a subsidiary in Switzerland to take advantage of that country's lower tax rate. Caterpillar's tax avoidance scheme had allegedly helped the company save more than $1 billion in taxes, according to Daniel Schlicksup, an accountant who had been with Caterpillar for 16 years. Caterpillar is vigorously fighting these charges.

Schlicksup tried to warn his bosses about the tax fraud as early as the spring of 2008. In a memo to Robin Beran, Caterpillar's Director of Taxation, Schlicksup questioned whether the Swiss strategy complied with federal case law or the requirements of the Sarbanes-Oxley Act. He also sent an e-mail to CEO Jim Owens's top underlings with the subject line "Ethics issues important to you, the Board and Cat Shareholders." In a note, he shared his concerns about the tax strategy and described a systematic effort to shut him down. "I am now an example to my colleagues, peers, and others that they made the correct choice when they chose to not report ethical issues and ignore Company Policy."[21] Attached to the e-mail was a 15-page memorandum describing how his superiors had retaliated against him for speaking out. The next morning he sent 137 pages of documents purporting to show how, with the help of its auditor, PwC, Caterpillar had devised a way to shift billions in profit to Switzerland to avoid U.S. taxes.[21]

Four months later Schlicksup was told his position was being eliminated and he was being transferred to the information technology division. He resisted because he wasn't well-versed in IT and felt less valuable to the company. He was told this was his only option. Schlicksup took the new job, and then, later that year, filed an IRS whistleblower complaint accusing Caterpillar of tax fraud and filed a complaint with the Occupational Safety and Health Administration under SOX contending his employer had retaliated against him for raising concerns about "improper and illegal conduct."

The Caterpillar case also illustrates the intersection of audited financial statements and income tax accounting.

On September 26, 2018, the United States District Court For the Northern District of Illinois Eastern Division dismissed a class-action lawsuit brought by **Société Générale** Securities Services, GMBH against Caterpillar, Inc., et al., alleging that Caterpillar made materially false and misleading statements and omitted material information regarding the substantial risk to Caterpillar's tax position and the extent of the investigation. The plaintiff had claimed that: (1) Caterpillar unlawfully used foreign subsidiaries to avoid paying billions of dollars in U.S. taxes; (2) discovery of the foregoing conduct would subject the Company to heightened regulatory scrutiny and potential criminal sanctions; and (3) as a result of the foregoing, Caterpillar's public statements were materially false and misleading at all relevant times. The Court found untenable the plaintiff's assertion that Caterpillar should have admitted a securities or tax law violation while the investigations were ongoing and the failure to do so was both a material omission and misstatement. In explaining its ruling, the Court stated that "If every investigation or executed search warrant was evidence of wrongdoing then what purpose do hearings and trials have. . .Securities laws generally do not impose such a duty upon publicly traded corporations to confess to uncharged, unadjudicated claims of wrongdoing. . ."[22]

The basis for the ruling demonstrates how difficult it is to maintain a claim for securities fraud because it must be proven that the defendant (i.e., Caterpillar) acted with the knowledge of a falsehood, the essential element in finding it violated the law. Specifically, the court ruled that: Caterpillar must have acted with the required state of mind meaning it had the intent to deceive, demonstrated by knowledge of the statement's falsity or reckless disregard of a substantial risk that the statement is false.

PCAOB Rules

> ## LO 4-8
> Describe the PCAOB independence and ethics rules.

PCAOB Ethics and Independence Standards

The reason for covering the PCAOB standards is that registered public accounting firms must comply with them in the performance of a variety of professional services. While we have mostly been discussing the AICPA Code of Professional Conduct in this chapter, those rules are only required if a CPA/CPA firm joins the Institute. They are emphasized in this chapter because most state board of accountancy rules incorporate, or refer to, the AICPA rules as being required for all licensed CPAs in those states. The following summarizes the most important PCAOB rules.

Rule 3520—Auditor Independence

Rule 3520 establishes the requirement for the accounting firm to be independent of its audit client throughout the audit and professional engagement period as a fundamental obligation of the auditor. Under Rule 3520, a registered public accounting firm or an associated person's independence obligation with respect to an audit client that is an issuer encompasses not only an obligation to satisfy the independence criteria set out in the rules and standards of the PCAOB, but also an obligation to satisfy all other independence criteria applicable to the engagement, including the independence criteria set out in the rules and regulations of the commission under the federal securities laws.

Rule 3521—Contingent Fees

Rule 3521 treats registered public accounting firms as not independent of their audit clients if the firm, or any affiliate of the firm, during the audit and professional engagement period, provides any service or product to the audit client for a contingent fee or a commission or receives from the audit client, directly or indirectly, a contingent fee or commission. This rule mirrors Rules 1.520 and 1.510 of the AICPA Code that prohibit contingent fees, commissions, and referral fees for any service provided to an attest client.

Rule 3522—Tax Transactions

Under Rule 3522, a rule that was issued in the aftermath of the tax shelter transactions, a registered public accounting firm is not independent of its audit client if the firm, or any affiliate of the firm, during the audit and professional engagement period, provides any nonauditing service to the audit client related to marketing, planning, or opining in favor of the tax treatment of either a confidential transaction or an "aggressive tax position" transaction. An aggressive tax position transaction is one that was initially recommended, directly or indirectly, by the registered public accounting firm and a significant purpose of which is tax avoidance, unless the proposed tax treatment is at least more likely than not to be allowable under applicable tax laws.

Rule 3523—Tax Services for Persons in Financial Reporting Oversight Roles

Rule 3523 treats a registered public accounting firm as not independent if the firm provides tax services to certain members of management who serve in *financial reporting oversight roles* at an audit client or to immediate family members of such persons unless any of the following apply:

1. The person is in a financial reporting oversight role at the audit client only because they serve as a member of the board of directors or similar management or governing body of the audit client.
2. The person is in a financial reporting oversight role at the audit client only because of the person's relationship to an affiliate of the entity being audited:
   a. Whose financial statements are not material to the consolidated financial statements of the entity being audited.
   b. Whose financial statements are audited by an auditor other than the firm or an associated person of the firm.
3. The person was not in a financial reporting oversight role at the audit client before a hiring, promotion, or other change in employment, and the tax services are provided pursuant to an engagement in process before the hiring, promotion, or other change in employment completed not after 180 days after the hiring or promotion event.

We are skeptical of ethics rules that build in exceptions, such as for members of the board of directors. From an ethical perspective, a practice is wrong if it violates certain standards of behavior, and it doesn't matter if the relationship with the other party is not deemed to be significant. After all, members of the board of directors at most companies today have ratcheted-up responsibilities under SOX and NYSE listing requirements. There does not appear to be a reasonable basis to exclude board members from the rule that prohibits providing tax services for persons in financial reporting oversight roles.

Rule 3524—Audit Committee Preapproval of Certain Tax Services

In connection with seeking audit committee preapproval to perform for an audit client any permissible tax service, a registered public accounting firm should do all of the following:

1. Describe, in writing, to the audit committee of the issuer:
   a. The scope of the service, the fee structure for the engagement, and any side letter or other amendment to the engagement letter, or any other agreement (whether oral, written, or otherwise) between the firm and the audit client relating to the service.
   b. Any compensation arrangement or other agreement, such as a referral agreement, a referral fee, or a fees-sharing arrangement, between the registered public accounting firm (or an affiliate of the firm) and any person (other than the audit client) with respect to the promoting, marketing, or recommending of a transaction covered by the service.
2. Discuss with the audit committee of the issuer the potential effects of the services on the independence of the firm.
3. Document the substance of its discussion with the audit committee of the issuer.

Rule 3525—Audit Committee Preapproval of Nonauditing Services Related to Internal Control over Financial Reporting

Rule 3525 provides that, when seeking audit committee preapproval to perform for an audit client any permissible nonauditing service related to internal control over financial reporting, a registered public accounting firm should describe, in writing, to the audit committee the scope of the service, discuss with the committee the potential effects of the service on the independence of the firm, and document the substance of its discussion with the audit committee of the issuer.

Rule 3526—Communication with Audit Committees Concerning Independence

Rule 3526 establishes guidelines when an accounting firm should discuss with the audit committee of the client information with respect to any relationships between the firm and the entity that might bear on auditor independence. Under the rule, a registered public accounting firm must do the following:

1. Prior to accepting an initial engagement, pursuant to the standards of the PCAOB, describe in writing, to the audit committee of the issuer, all relationships between the registered public accounting firm or any affiliates of the firm and the potential audit client or persons in financial reporting oversight roles at the potential audit client that, as of the date of the communication, may reasonably be thought to bear on independence.

2. Discuss with the audit committee the potential effects of the relationships on the independence of the firm, should it be appointed as the entity's auditor.

3. Document the substance of its discussion with the audit committee.

These requirements would also apply annually subsequent to being engaged as the auditor. An additional requirement annually is to affirm to the audit committee of the issuer of the communication that the registered public accounting firm is still independent in compliance with Rule 3520.

An important issue is whether the PCAOB has made a difference in reducing audit failures. Earlier in the chapter we discussed the significant audit deficiency rates so it would seem the PCAOB inspection process has not as yet made a notable difference in that regard, although detection may be greatly improved over the previous peer review process.

On June 1, 2017, the PCAOB adopted a new auditing standard to enhance the relevance and usefulness of the auditor's report by providing additional information to investors including a discussion of critical audit matters, which are matters that have been communicated to the audit committee, are related to accounts or disclosures that are material to the financial statements, and involve especially challenging, subjective, or complex auditor judgment.[23] More will be said about the new auditing standard in **Chapter 5**.

PCAOB Quality Control Standards

Quality controls were first addressed as a safeguard to protect against threats to independence and integrity. It is important for a CPA firm to maintain a system of quality controls to provide reasonable assurance that the internal controls are operating as intended. Exhibit 4.7 summarizes those controls under QC Section 20.

EXHIBIT 4.7   QC Section 20

System of Quality Control for a CPA Firm's Accounting and Auditing Practice

Introduction and Applicability

This section provides that a CPA firm shall have a system of quality control for its accounting and auditing practice and describes elements of quality control and other matters essential to the effective design, implementation, and maintenance of the system.

The AICPA Principles of Professional Conduct provide, among other things, that "members should practice in firms that have in place internal quality-control procedures to ensure that services are competently delivered and adequately supervised." Because of the public interest in the services provided by and the reliance placed on the objectivity and integrity of CPAs, this section provides that a CPA firm shall have a system of quality control for its accounting and auditing practice.

(continued)

Quality Control Policies and Procedures

A system of quality control is broadly defined as a process to provide the firm with reasonable assurance that its personnel comply with applicable professional standards and the firm's standards of quality. The policies and procedures designed to implement the system in one segment of a firm's practice may be the same as, different from, or interrelated with the policies and procedures designed for another segment, but the purpose of the system is the same for all segments of a firm's practice.

The quality control policies and procedures applicable to a firm's accounting and auditing practice should encompass the following elements:

1. Independence, Integrity, and Objectivity
2. Personnel Management
3. Acceptance and Continuance of Clients and Engagements
4. Engagement Performance
5. Monitoring

The elements of quality control are interrelated. For example, the maintenance of *Integrity, Objectivity,* and, where required, *Independence* requires a continuing assessment of client relationships. Similarly, the element of *Personnel Management* encompasses criteria for professional development, hiring, advancement, and assignment of the firm's personnel to engagements, which affect policies and procedures developed to meet the objectives of the quality control element of *Engagement Performance.* Similarly, policies and procedures for the quality control element of *Monitoring* are established to provide the firm with reasonable assurance that the policies and procedures related to each of the other elements of quality control are suitably designed and are being effectively applied.

Independence, Integrity, and Objectivity

Policies and procedures should be established to provide the firm with reasonable assurance that personnel maintain independence (in fact and in appearance) in all required circumstances, perform all professional responsibilities with integrity, and maintain objectivity in discharging professional responsibilities.

Independence, Integrity, and *Objectivity* are defined and more fully described in the AICPA Code of Professional Conduct.

Documentation of Compliance with Quality Control Policies and Procedures

A firm should prepare appropriate documentation to demonstrate *compliance* with its policies and procedures for the quality control system. The form and content of such documentation are a matter of judgment and depend on a number of factors, such as the size of a firm, the number of offices, the degree of authority allowed its personnel and its offices, the nature and complexity of the firm's practice, its organization, and appropriate cost-benefit considerations. Documentation should be retained for a period of time sufficient to enable those performing monitoring procedures and a peer review to evaluate the extent of the firm's compliance with its quality control policies and procedures.

PCAOB Inspections

The PCAOB conducts mandatory quality inspections of selected audits of publicly registered accounting firms. These inspections are designed to spot deficiencies in audits. Recall our discussion earlier of KPMG's hiring of former PCAOB staffers to game the system and have those staffers identify likely audit candidates for inspections by the PCAOB. It occurred, at least in part, due to a growing deficiency rate to a high of 50 percent in 2017. Since then, the rate has come down and was 29 percent in 2019.

The deficiency rates for 2019 were:[24]

Deloitte	10%
Ernst & Young	18%
KPMG	29%
PwC	30%

Some of the second-tier firms were not so lucky. BDO, the fifth largest accounting firm in the world, had a deficiency rate of 42 percent in 2019. Crowe, the eighth largest firm, had a deficiency rate of 50 percent and Marcum, one of the largest independent accounting firms, had a deficiency rate of 50 percent as well.

The audit area that gave each inspected firm the most trouble was internal controls over financial reporting followed by responses to risks of material misstatements, audit sampling, auditing accounting estimates, and audit evidence.

Former PCAOB chairman, James Doty, expressed a concern about the relatively high deficiency rates and suggested implementing rules that would increase auditors' accountability to investors and their independence from the companies they audit.

The high level of deficiencies is troubling, especially in second-tier firms. If the deficiency rates in audits investigated by the PCAOB hold true for all audits of public company clients of the Big-4 CPA firms, then we have to ask whether the pressure sometimes applied on auditors by clients seeking lucrative nonaudit services has gone too far and the need exists to split off audit from nonaudit services operationally as previously discussed.

Concluding Thoughts

Whenever a CPA must render an opinion that deals with an ethical dilemma, it must be grounded in specific, quoted, and explained rules of the profession. However, rules are sterile without the application of principles in both their making and implementation. The takeaway from the discussion in **Chapter 4** and the earlier one in **Chapter 1** with respect to ethical principles is: Always apply rules in a principled way, and always apply your principles in harmony with the rules. To avoid losing your reputation, your job, or worse, refrain from submitting (1) unprincipled work with the rationalization, "I followed the rules," or (2) work that breaks the rules with the rationalization, "I followed my *personal* principles."*

The thought process of dealing with an ethical dilemma is as simple (and as complicated) as aligning the profession's rules with ethical principles. Always remember that it's not each individual's principles that should be used but to align your principles with those in the AICPA Code and other regulations. When ethical dilemmas exist, analyze what decision should be made by using ethical reasoning methods that were discussed in **Chapter 1**. They have stood the test of time and have been used as guides to ethical decision making by philosophers over the ages. After all the various concepts, philosophies and models are discussed, the bottom line is that CPAs are bound by a deontological system requiring adherence to the AICPA rules of professional conduct.

* We wish to thank Dr. Anan Sturgess from Foothill College for her remarks that helped to form the Concluding Thoughts.

Discussion Questions

1. In our discussion of the KPMG professional judgment framework, we pointed out that biased judgments can be made because of judgment tendencies. One such tendency that was not included in the framework is self-serving bias. Explain what you think this means and how it might influence audit judgment.

2. We all know people who say, "Don't bother me with the facts. I've already made up my mind." How might such an attitude influence judgment tendencies of auditors?

3. Explain how threats to professional skepticism might influence audit judgment.

4. Explain the safeguards that can be used to reduce or eliminate threats to audit independence.

5. Do you believe the threats and safeguards approach establishes a situational or relativistic ethic? How might utilitarianism be used to evaluate the ethicality of permitting certain relationships when threats exist?

6. Can a CPA auditor be independent without being objective and impartial? Can a CPA auditor be objective and impartial without being independent? Explain your answer in the context of recent rule changes by the SEC discussed in the chapter that loosened independence requirements.

7. Is independence impaired when an auditor is hired, paid, and fired by the same corporate managers whose activities are the subject of the audit? Does it matter that in most companies the audit committee hires,

evaluates, fires (if appropriate), and determines the fees of the external auditor with minimal input from senior management?

8. When do ethical conflicts arise in the performance of professional accounting services? How should a CPA go about resolving ethical conflicts?

9. Discuss whether an ethical conflict exists in violation of the AICPA rules in each of the following situations:
   a. A senior on an audit receives a gift certificate from a client to the most expensive restaurant in town.
   b. An audit engagement partner attends a baseball game with the client who purchased the tickets.
   c. A partner in charge of the office is told by the audit client that the firm is being considered for lucrative consulting services.

10. In August 2008, EY agreed to pay more than $2.9 million to the SEC to settle charges that it violated ethics rules by co-producing a series of audio CDs with a man who was also a director at three of EY's audit clients. According to the SEC, EY collaborated with Mark C. Thompson between 2002 and 2004 to produce a series of audio CDs called *The Ernst & Young Thought Leaders Series.* Thompson served on the boards at several of EY's clients during the period when the CDs were produced. What threats to independence existed in the relationship between EY and Thompson? From an ethical perspective, would it have mattered if it were not an audit client but one for whom advisory services only were performed?

11. Explain the difference between the "realistic possibility of success" tax standard for taking a tax position under *SSTS Interpretation No. 101-1* and the "reasonable basis" standard. When should each be used?

12. Barbara Houston is a CPA with her own accounting and tax practice. One day an audit client asks her to represent him in a conference with the IRS about his prior years' tax return. It seems the IRS is claiming that the audit client owes $50,000 additional taxes. The client agrees to pay Barbara 20 percent of the amount of additional taxes saved after the conference with the IRS. What are the ethical issues of concern for Barbara under the AICPA Code and Treasury Circular 230?

13. You're struggling in your new accounting practice to tap into a potential client base. You have tried traditional advertising and marketing tools to no avail. Your friend tells you to use social media as a tool to reach potential customers. You're not sure about it. Your concern is one of ethics. The last thing you want to do is violate the ethical standards of the accounting profession. Identify the ethical issues that should be of concern to you in deciding whether and how to use social media for advertising and solicitation of new clients.

14. You have decided to leave your firm. Using the AICPA rules as a guide, answer the following questions: (1) Can you post some negative comments about your former employer on Twitter? (2) Can you call your former clients and tell them that you are leaving? (3) Can you take client files when you go?

15. Lloyd Schuman, a former senior internal auditor at Verso Corporation, learned about confidential plans that Verso, a publicly traded paper company, was going to acquire a privately held paper company, NewPage Holdings Inc. In the weeks before Verso went public with the acquisition, Schuman purchased "an unusually large" amount of Verso shares and tipped this material, nonpublic information to a close relative, who also purchased Verso shares. As soon as the deal was announced on the morning of January 6, 2014, Schuman sold all of his Verso shares, realizing more than $107,000 in profits. Schuman's relative also sold his Verso shares, realizing more than $2,500 in profits. Assume Schuman was a CPA. Were any rules of professional conduct in the AICPA Code violated? Did Schuman meet his duties to Verso? Explain.

16. Do you believe that CPAs in business should be held to the same high ethical standards as CPAs in public practice? Why or why not? Include in your discussion how those standards would apply to CPAs in business.

17. One day your ethics professor comes into class and proclaims that audit firms should be allowed to make materiality judgments when determining whether independence rules have been violated. After all, accountants make materiality judgments all the time. She suggests that a firm can maintain its objectivity and impartiality (hence its independence) in certain relationships based on a materiality exception. Do you agree with the professor's statement? Why or why not?

18. Do you agree with the proposal of the Competitions and Market Authority in the United Kingdom that the Big Four firms should be split operationally so that audit and nonaudit services are conducted in two separate divisions and profits are split based on each divisions' profits? Explain.

19. What can CPA firms do about the relatively high rate of audit deficiencies identified in PCAOB inspections of firm audits?

20. Given the discussions in this chapter about conflicts of interest in the performance of professional services and improper relationships with the clients, do you think the accounting profession is trustworthy? Why or why not?

Comprehensive Questions

1. You are a tax accountant and have just discussed a complex tax matter with your client. The client wants you to adopt a tax position that is favorable to its interests. You are not sure whether the tax position requested by the client is supportable under AICPA Statements on Standards for Tax Services. Describe the relevant standards and how you would go about determining whether the client's position can be adopted.

2. Assume you disclosed information about a client. How would you determine if you violated the Confidential Client Information rule in the AICPA Code?

3. What are the dangers of creeping commercialism in the accounting profession?

4. Internal Controls Over Financial Reporting (ICFR) is an important component in fostering confidence in a company's financial reporting, and ultimately, trust in our capital markets. Former SEC Chief Accountant Wesley Bricker (SEC Charges Four Public Companies With Longstanding ICFR Failures. SEC. 2019.) is quoted as saying, "Adequate internal controls are the first line of defense in detecting and preventing material errors or fraud in financial reporting. . . When internal control deficiencies are left unaddressed, financial reporting quality can suffer."

   Explain the concepts underlying an effective system of internal controls and its purpose in the overall financial reporting system. Include in your discussion the role of management and the external auditor in ensuring that internal controls are operating as intended.

5. A major fraud at Chinese company Luckin Coffee in 2020 has raised questions whether Chinese firms with shares listed on the New York Stock Exchange or Nasdaq should be required to undergo the same audit inspection by the PCAOB that is applied to United States listed firms. Luckin Coffee was listed in the United States but disclosed that its chief operating officer fabricated the company's 2019 sales by about 2.2 billion yuan ($310 million). As a result, the company's shares were delisted by Nasdaq and Luckin was fined $180 million.

   On December 18, 2020, President Donald Trump signed a new law to prevent Chinese companies listing stock on U.S. exchanges unless American regulators can inspect their financial audits. China's response was that it is "against politicizing securities regulation" and urged cooperation to protect investors' rights. According to a Chinese Foreign Ministry spokeswoman, Hua Chunying, the new law "will undermine the U.S. capital markets' global standing and hurt U.S. interests."

   Use ethical reasoning to analyze whether foreign company's listing shares on U.S. exchanges should be required to undergo the same rigorous audit inspections as U.S. companies.

Endnotes

1. Statista, Revenue of the Big Four Accounting/Audit Firms Worldwide by function 2019, https://www.statista.com/statistics/250935/big-four-accounting-firms-breakdown-of-revenues/.

2. https://www.thecaq.org/wp-content/uploads/2019/03/professional-judgment-resource.pdf.

3. Steven Glover and Douglas Prawitt, "Elevating Professional Judgment in Auditing and Accounting: The KPMG Professional Judgment Framework," Available at: https://www.researchgate.net/publication/258340692_Elevating_Professional_Judgment_in_Auditing_and_Accounting_The_KPMG_Professional_Judgment_Framework.

4. B. E. Christensen, S. M. Glover, and D. A. Wood, "Extreme Estimation Uncertainty in Fair Value Estimates: Implications for Audit Assurance," *Auditing: A Journal of Practice and Theory* 31, no. 1 (2012), pp. 127–146.

5. Kathy Hurtt, "Development of a Scale to Measure Professional Skepticism," *Auditing: A Journal of Theory and Practice,* May 2012, Vol. 29, No. 1, pp. 149–171.

6. Ellen Goria, "Revised AICPA Code of Ethics . . . What's the Fuss?," *Journal of Accountancy* (February 2014), pp. 42–45.

7. "Reforming the Auditing Industry," http://visar.csustan.edu/aaba/LabourPolicymaking-AuditingReforms Sec2018.pdf.

8. Steven M. Mintz, "Now is the Time to Operationally Split Audit and Nonaudit Services," *The CPA Journal* XC, no. 10/11 (October/November 2020).

9. Kueppers, Robert J. Incoming Letter. SEC, May 6, 2004.

10. SEC, *Final Rule: Revision of the Commission's Auditor Independence Requirements*, February 5, 2001, Available at: www.sec.gov/rules/final/33-7919.htm.

11. SEC, *In the Matter of Ernst & Young LLP and Gregory S. Bednar, CPA,* Accounting and Enforcement Release No. 3802, September 19, 2016, https://www.sec.gov/litigation/admin/2016/34-78872.pdf.

12. *In the Matter of Ernst & Young LLP and Robert J. Brehl, CPA, Pamela J. Hartford, CPA, and Michael T. Kamienski, CPA,* SEC Release No. 34-78873 (September 19, 2016).

13. Amendments Reflect Staff Experience Applying the Auditor Independence Framework. SEC, October, 2020.

14. Brendan Pierson, *Ernst & Young Partner Settles Complaint Over Sexual Harassment*, May 3, 2018, https://111.reuters.com/article/us-ernst-young-complaint-idUSKBN1142A.

15. Barbara Ley Toffler, *Final Accounting: Ambition, Greed, and the Fall of Arthur Andersen* (New York :Broadway Books, 2003).

16. Zowie Murray, *The Politics of Audit Pricing*, February 13, 2014, http://www.gaaaccounting.com/the-politics-of-audit-pricing/.

17. Toffler and Reingold.

18. Wolters Kluwer, https://www.bizfilings.com/toolkit/research-topics/managing-your-taxes/federal-taxes/tax-avoidance-is-legal-taxevasion-is-criminal.

19. AICPA, Statement on Standards for Tax Services No. 6, Knowledge of Error: Return Preparation and Administrative Proceedings, https://aicpa.org/content /dam/aicpa/interestareas/tax/resources/standardsethics/statementsonstandardsfortaxservices/downloadabledocuments/ssts-no.6-knowledge-of-error.pdf.

20. Bryan Gruley, David Voreacos, and Joe Deaux, "The Whistleblower Behind Caterpillar's Massive Tax Headache Could Make $600 Million," *Bloomberg News,* June 1, 2017, https://www.bloomberg.com/news/features/2017-06-01/the-whistleblower-behind-caterpillar-s-massive-tax-headache-could-make-600-million.

21. Gruley et al.

22. United States District Court For the Northern District of Illinois Eastern Division, Societe Generale, Securities Services, GMBH v. Caterpillar, Inc., et al., https://cases.justia.com/federal/district-courts/illinois/ilndce/1:2017cv01713/337299/47/0.pdf?ts=1538045132

23. PCAOB, The Auditor's Report on an Audit of Financial Statements When the Auditor Expresses an Unqualified Opinion and Related Amendments to PCAOB Standards, PCAOB Release No. 2017-001, June 1, 2017, https://pcaobus.org/Rulemaking/Docket034/2017-001-auditors-report-final-rule.pdf.

24. Jenny Lukac, New PCAOB Inspection Reports Are Here!, February 9, 2021, https://www.gaapdynamics.com/insights/blog/2021/02/09/new-pcaob-inspection-reports-are-here!/.

25. PCAOB, AU 560 Subsequent Event, https://pcaob.org/Standards/Auditng/pages/au560.aspx.

26. Peck, Emily. "She Spoke Up About Sexual Harassment At Ernst & Young And Got Caught In A Web Of Retaliation". Huffpost, Feb. 11, 2019.

27. Karyn Twaronite, the EY Global Vice Chair of Diversity & Inclusiveness.

28. EY Diversity, inclusiveness and your career. April. 17, 2020.

29. Great Place to Work. Fortune 100 Best Companies to Work For 2020.

30. PCAOB Order Instituting Disciplinary Proceedings, Making Findings and Imposing Sanctions, *In the Matter of Marcum LLP and Alfonse Gregory Giuglaino, CPA,* September 24, 2020, https://pcaobus.org/Enforcement/Decisions/Documents/105-2020-012-MARCUM-LLP.pdf.

31. In the Matter of Marcum LLP. And Alfonse Gregory Giugliano, CPA. Public Company Accounting Oversight Board, Sept. 10, 2019.

32. https://www.sec.gov/litigation/admin/2019/34-87053.pdf.

33. SEC, Accounting and Auditing Enforcement Release (AAER) No. 4084, *In the Matter of PricewaterhouseCoopers LLP,* September 23, 2019, https://www.sec.gov/litigation/admin/2019/34-87052.pdf.

Chapter 4 Cases

Case 4-1 KBC Solutions

The audit of KBC Solutions by Carlson and Smith, CPAs, was scheduled to end on February 28, 2019. However, Rick Carlson was uncertain whether it could happen. As the review partner, he had just completed going over the work paper files of the senior auditor in charge of the engagement, Grace Sloan, and had way too many questions to wrap things up by the end of the week. Rick called Grace into his office and asked her about some questionable judgments she had made. He hoped her explanations would be satisfactory and he could move on with completing the audit.

1. Why did you approve the accounting for new acquisitions of plant and equipment that were not supported by adequate underlying documentation?

2. Why did you accept the client's determinations of accrued expenses rather than make your own independent judgments?

3. How can you justify relying on last year's work papers to determine the proper allowance for uncollectibles one year later?

To say Grace was stressed out would be an understatement. This was her first engagement as a senior and she wondered whether it would be her last. Grace knew she had to make a convincing case for her judgments or suffer the consequences. She responded to each point as follows.

1. The client had problems with their systems and had to contact the vendor for a duplicate copy of the relevant invoices. She expects the copy within two days.

2. The client seemed to have a reasonable basis for those judgments so she saw no reason to delay the completion of the audit over the accrued expenses.

3. Although the confirmation rate on the receivables was slightly below expected norms, there was no reason not to accept the client's explanation for those not confirmed as being correct in amount and due date.

Grace knew her answers would not completely satisfy Rick. She did, however, believe there were extenuating circumstances she felt compelled to explain even though it might reflect negatively on her leadership abilities. She explained that the audit team pressured her to let certain matters go because they were behind schedule in the completion of the audit. She was convinced by the majority to trust the client on outstanding issues, which included the three raised by Rick.

Rick was not very happy with the explanation. He wondered about the professional judgments exercised by Grace and what her future with the firm should be.

Questions

1. Critically evaluate the judgments made by Grace as the senior by using the KPMG Professional Judgment Framework.

2. Did Grace violate any rules of conduct in the AICPA Code? Explain.

3. Does Rick have any ethical obligations in this matter? What should he do about signing off on the audit and why?

Case 4-2 Beauda Medical Center

Lance Popperson woke up in a sweat, with an anxiety attack coming on. Popperson popped two anti-anxiety pills, laid down to try and sleep for the third time that night, and thought once again about his dilemma. Popperson is an associate with the accounting firm of Hodgins and Gelman LLP. He recently discovered, through a casual conversation with Brad Snow, a friend of his on the audit staff, that one of the firm's clients managed by Snow recently received complaints that its heart monitoring equipment was malfunctioning. Cardio-Systems Monitoring, Inc. (CSM), called for a meeting of the lawyers, auditors, and top management to discuss what to do about the complaints from health care facilities that had significantly increased between the first two months of 2021 and the last two months of that year. Doctors at these facilities claimed the systems shut off for brief periods and, in one case, the hospital was unable to save a patient that went into cardiac arrest.

Popperson tossed and turned and wondered what he should do about the fact that Beauda Medical Center, his current audit client, plans to buy 20 units of Cardio-Systems' heart monitoring equipment for its brand-new medical facility in the outskirts of Beauda.

Questions

1. Assume that both Popperson and Snow are CPAs. Do you think Snow violated his confidentiality obligation under the AICPA Code by informing Popperson about the faulty equipment at CSM? Explain.

2. Apply the steps in Exhibit 4.3, Ethical Conflicts and Compliance with the Rules of Conduct, and analyze whether the relationships described in this case create a conflict of interests and, if so, what safeguards should be implemented to mitigate the threat now and in the future?

3. What, if anything, should the accounting firm do about the malfunctioning equipment at Cardio-Systems Monitoring and its ethical obligations to Beauda?

Case 4-3 Family Games, Inc. (a GVV case)

Family Games, Inc., is a privately owned company with annual sales from a variety of wholesome electronic games that are designed for use by the entire family. The company sees itself as family-oriented and with a mission to serve the public. However, during the past two years, the company reported a net loss due to cost-cutting measures that were necessary to compete with overseas manufacturers and distributors.

> "Yeah, I know all of the details weren't completed until January 2, 2022, but we agreed on the transaction on December 30, 2021. By my way of reasoning, it's a continuation transaction and the $12 million revenue belongs in the results for 2021. What's more, the goods were on the delivery truck on December 31, 2021, waiting to be shipped after the New Year."

This comment was made by Carl Land, the CFO of Family Games, to Helen Strom, the controller of Family Games, after Strom had expressed her concern that, because the lawyers did not sign off on the transaction until January 2, 2022, because of the holiday, the revenue should not be recorded in 2021. Land felt that Strom was being hyper-technical. He had seen it before from Helen and didn't like it. She needed to learn to be a team player.

> "Listen, Helen, this comes from the top," Land said. "The big boss said we need to have the $12 million recorded in the results for 2021"

> "I don't get it," Helen said to Land. "Why the pressure?"

> "The boss wants to increase his performance bonus by increasing earnings in 2021. Apparently, he lost some money in Vegas over the Christmas weekend and left a sizable IOU at the casino," Land responded.

Helen shook her head in disbelief. She didn't like the idea of operating results being manipulated based on the personal needs of the CEO. She knew that the CEO had a gambling problem. This sort of thing had happened before. The difference this time was that it had the prospect of affecting the reported results, and she was being asked to do something that she knows is wrong.

"I can't change the facts," Helen said.

"All you have to do is backdate the sales invoice to December 30, when the final agreement was reached," Land responded. "As I said before, just think of it as a revenue-continuation transaction that started in 2021 and, but for one minor technicality, should have been recorded in that year. Besides, you know we push the envelope around here."

"You're asking me to 'cook the books,'" Helen said. "I won't do it."

"I hate to play hardball with you, Helen, but the boss authorized me to tell you he will stop reimbursing you in the future for child care costs so that your kid can have a live-in nanny 24-7 unless you go along on this issue. I promise, Helen, it will be a one-time request," Land said.

Helen was surprised by the threat and dubious "one-time-event" explanation. She sat down and reflected on the fact that the reimbursement payments for her child care were $35,000, 35 percent of her annual salary. As a single working mother, Helen knew there was no other way that she could afford to pay for the full-time care needed by her autistic son.

Questions

1. Assume that Carl Land and Helen Strom are CPAs. Explain the nature of the dilemma for Helen using the AICPA Code as a guide. What steps should she take to resolve the issue?
2. Use ethical reasoning as a guide to decide what Helen should do and why.
3. Apply the Giving Voice to Values methodology and answer the following questions from the perspective of Helen Strom.

What are the main arguments you are trying to counter? That is, what are the reasons and rationalizations you need to address?

What is at stake for the key parties, including those who disagree with you?

What levers can you use to influence those who disagree with you?

What is your most powerful and persuasive response to the reasons and rationalizations you need to address? To whom should the argument be made? When and in what context?

Case 4-4 Threats to Audit Independence

Katy Carmichael, CPA, was just promoted to audit manager in the technology sector at a large public accounting firm. She started at the firm six years ago and has worked on a number of the same client audits for multiple years. She prefers being placed on same client audits year over year as she believes her knowledge about the client grows each year, resulting in a better audit. Public accounting firms tend to do this as it provides continuity between the firm and the client and often results in a more efficient (less costly) audit as well.

Katy was thrilled to learn that she would be retaining three of her prior audit clients, including what she considers her favorite client (DGS - Drako Gaming Solutions). She has friendships with those in the financial reporting area including the CFO with whom she has makes joint business investments.

The audit planning for DGS's next audit is about to begin. As is common practice with all audits, each member of the audit engagement team is asked to fill out a questionnaire about any type of relationship (personal, business, or financial) they might have (or any other member of the engagement team might have) with the client company, any of its customers, suppliers, employees, or direct family members of their employees. Katy will soon be meeting with the firm's compliance partner assigned to the DGS audit to go through the completed questionnaire. In that regard, answer the following questions.

Questions

1. Identify any potential threats to independence that exist based on the facts of the case?

2. Thinking back to the biases discussed in **Chapter 2**, what biases might the identified threat(s) make Katy more susceptible to and why?

3. Is Katy obligated to discuss her feelings about DGS with the compliance partner when they meet? If so, what should she say? Do you think the compliance partner should remove Katy from the audit? Explain.

4. The SEC seems to be adopting the position that questions about the independence of auditors and the audit engagement can be made based on a materiality criterion. The reason given is that auditors may be able to maintain their objectivity and integrity even when certain relationships exist. In other words, Katy's relationship with the CFO might be evaluated through the lens of how significant the relationship is with respect to an independent audit. What are the dangers of relying on materiality to judge independence and can reliance on objectivity and integrity be sufficient to make these judgments in Katy's situation?

Case 4-5 Han, Kang & Lee, LLC (a GVV case)

Joe Kang is an owner and audit partner of Han, Kang & Lee, LLC. As the audit of Frost Systems was reaching its concluding stages on January 15, 2022, Kang met with Kate Boller, the CFO, to discuss the inventory valuation of one of its highly valued inventory products as of the balance sheet date, December 31, 2021. She was concerned because the January 31, 2022, financial statement issuance date was coming soon. Kang told Boller that a write-down of 20 percent had to be made because the net realizable value of the inventory on December 31 was 20 percent less than the original cost recorded on its books. That meant the earnings for the year would be reduced by $2 million and the client would show a loss for the year. In a heated exchange, Boller demanded Kang use the value now estimated on January 15, 2022, which reflects a full recovery of the "proposed" 20 percent write-down. Boller reminded Kang that the financial statements could be adjusted for "subsequent events" under accounting standards and the inventory valuation matter was one such occasion. Besides, Boller said, the previous auditors had allowed her to do a similar thing.

Exhibit 1 provides an overview of the standards for recording subsequent events.

EXHIBIT 1   PCAOB Rule for Subsequent Events

The following are the rules for recognizing Subsequent Event values in accounting under the auditing standards, PCAOB AU 560.[25]

An independent auditor's report ordinarily is issued in connection with historical financial statements that purport to present financial position at a stated date and results of operations and cash flows for a period ended on that date. However, events or transactions sometimes occur subsequent to the balance-sheet date, but prior to the issuance of the financial statements, which have a material effect on the financial statements and therefore require adjustment or disclosure in the statements. These occurrences hereinafter are referred to as "subsequent events."

Two types of subsequent events require consideration by management and evaluation by the independent auditor. The first type consists of those events that provide additional evidence with respect to conditions that existed at the date of the balance sheet and affect the estimates inherent in the process of preparing financial statements. All information that becomes available prior to the issuance of the financial statements should be used by management in its evaluation of the conditions on which the estimates were based. The financial statements should be adjusted for any changes in estimates resulting from the use of such evidence.

Identifying events that require adjustment of the financial statements under the criteria stated above calls for the exercise of judgment and knowledge of the facts and circumstances. For example, a loss on an uncollectible trade account receivable as a result of a customer's deteriorating financial condition leading to bankruptcy subsequent to the balance-sheet date would be indicative of conditions existing at the balance-sheet date, thereby calling for adjustment of the financial statements before their issuance. On the other hand, a similar loss resulting from a customer's major casualty such as a fire or flood subsequent to the balance-sheet date would not be indicative of conditions existing at the balance-sheet date and adjustment of the financial statements would not be appropriate. The settlement of litigation for an amount different from the liability recorded in the accounts would require adjustment of the financial statements if the events, such as personal injury or patent infringement, that gave rise to the litigation had taken place prior to the balance-sheet date.

The second type consists of those events that provide evidence with respect to conditions that did not exist at the date of the balance sheet being reported on but arose subsequent to that date. These events should not result in adjustment of the financial statements. Some of these events, however, may be of such a nature that disclosure of them is required to keep the financial statements from being misleading. Occasionally such an event may be so significant that disclosure can best be made by supplementing the historical financial statements with pro forma financial data giving effect to the event as if it had occurred on the date of the balance sheet. It may be desirable to present pro forma statements, usually a balance sheet only, in columnar form on the face of the historical statements.

Kang was under a great deal of pressure from the other two partners of the firm to keep Boller happy. It seems the firm was about to find out if its bid to provide consulting services for Frost Systems was accepted. Kang knew that the revenue from these arrangements could turn out to be twice the audit fees. Kang called a meeting of the other partners. He was concerned that the final vote would be 2-1 to accept the client's interpretation of the accounting rules and record the inventory value estimated on January 15, 2022.

Questions

1. Did Boller apply the correct interpretation of PCAOB rules for subsequent events? Explain.
2. Assume the consulting services are permissible under SOX and the AICPA rules of conduct, explain what safeguards should exist to mitigate any threats to independence.
3. Put yourself in Kang's position. You are preparing for the meeting with the other two partners. Consider the following in crafting an outline of points you may have to respond to.

What are the main arguments you are trying to counter? That is, what are the reasons and rationalizations you need to address?

What is at stake for the key parties, including those who disagree with you?

What levers can you use to influence those who disagree with you?

What is your most powerful and persuasive response to the reasons and rationalizations you may need to address? To whom should the argument be made? When and in what context?

Case 4-6 Tax Shelters

You are a tax manager and work for a CPA firm that performs audits, advisory services, and tax planning for wealthy clients in a large Midwestern city. You just joined the tax department after five years as a tax auditor for the county government. During the first six months in tax, you found out that the firm is aggressively promoting tax shelter products to top management officials of audit clients. Basically, the company developed a product and then looked for someone in management to sell it to, rather than the more conventional method whereby an officer might approach the firm asking it to identify ways to shelter income.

The way these products work is the firm would offer an opinion letter to the taxpayer to provide cover in case the IRS questioned the reasonableness of the transaction. The opinion would say that the firm "reasonably relied on a person who is qualified to know," and that would support the contention that the opinion was not motivated out of any intention to play the audit lottery. It also would protect the taxpayer against penalties in the event the firm is not correct and does not prevail in a tax case.

As time goes on, it becomes clear that the culture of the tax department is shifting from client service to maximization of tax revenues. You become concerned when you discover the firm did not register the tax shelter products, as required under the law.

One day you are approached by the tax partner you report to and asked to participate in one of the tax shelter transactions, with the end result being you would recommend to the tax partner whether he should sign off before presenting the product to the client. You feel uncomfortable with the request based on what you have learned about these products. You make an excuse about needing to complete three engagements that are winding down and buy some time.

The first thing you do is look for completed tax shelter arrangements with clients that had been reviewed and approved by the tax quality control engagement partner. What you find makes you more suspicious about the products. Several are marked "restricted" on the cover page without any further details. You then call a friend who is a manager in the audit department and set up a time to meet and discuss your concerns.

What you learn only heightens your concerns. Your friend confided that there is a culture in the tax department where business rationality sometimes displaces professional norms, a process accelerated by a conformist culture. Your friend also confided that the audit managers and partners are jealous of their tax peers because the tax managers and partners earn almost twice what the auditors earn because of the higher level of client revenues. It was clear your friend harbors ill feelings about the whole situation.

The following week the tax partner comes back and presents you with another tax shelter opportunity for the firm and all but demands that you oversee it. He implies in a roundabout way that your participation is a rite of passage to partnership in the firm. You manage to stall and put off the final decision a few days.

Questions

1. Evaluate the ethics of the tax shelter transactions, including your concerns about the practices. Be sure to address PCAOB Rule 3522 that is discussed in the chapter.
2. Who are the stakeholders in this case, and what are your professional responsibilities to them?
3. What are the options available to you in this matter?
4. What would you do and why?

Case 4-7 Sexual Harassment at EY

When Karen Ward started at Ernst & Young in 2013, only four senior managers in her division were women. All the partners were men. This was a red flag, but she didn't see it then but soon realized that EY's lack of female leaders was no accident but the result of a hostile environment where women were demeaned, devalued, and isolated.

Ward filed a sexual discrimination complaint in late September 2018 against EY at the Equal Employment Opportunity Commission (EEOC), the federal agency that handles civil rights complaints. It was the second sex discrimination complaint filed that year against the firm, the other being Jessica Cassuci, a partner at the firm who had accused fellow partner, John Martinkat, of sexual harassment. This case is discussed in the chapter.

Ward claimed she was sexually harassed by her direct supervisor, Michael McNamara, who she said told her he liked her "great big boobs" and "nice ass" and worked to undermine her authority, stealing credit for her work.

Ward's complaint and filing with the EEOC started a complex web of retaliation. She said that for years the men in McNamara's circle undermined her work and that even after he was eventually fired, she experienced retaliation from a whole boys' club in his network, eventually losing her job and hundreds of thousands of dollars—at a minimum—in potential earnings.

Her story shows the limits of the Me Too era. Simply firing or forcing out a sexual harasser often does little to change a company's culture, as she learned. It's also a reminder that, for women, privilege can't always confer protection from sexual discrimination and harassment.

EY had repeatedly insisted that her firing had nothing to do with sexual harassment or discrimination. "Throughout her time at the firm, EY took measures to promote and support Karen," the company told the Huffington Post in a statement. "The decision to separate Karen was wholly unrelated to her gender. It was solely related to her inability to meet performance goals."[26]

Told in a series of interviews with the Post over the phone and in person at Karen's home, her story was corroborated by 22 contemporaneous e-mails, one letter and meeting notes she sent to EY executives, as well as interviews with two other former EY employees and a close friend in whom she confided in throughout the ordeal.

On a business trip early in Ward's EY tenure in 2013, McNamara texted her at 2 a.m. asking if she wanted to get a drink. She turned him down. After that, he started undercutting her authority, Ward said.

Around the same time, minutes before she was scheduled to appear on a panel at a sales conference, she said, he told her "to stand at the back with the other gals." He was referring to the administrative assistants who were in attendance. He then took her place on the stage and even used her notes. She flagged the incident to an EY partner in an e-mail reviewed by the Post.

McNamara also took credit for her work, she said, by removing her name from paperwork after deals were inked.

When Ward alerted other executives about his behavior, she was initially ignored or told to tone down her complaints, she said. One male executive told her to "be careful" because she was "being perceived as a bitch," according to her complaint.

Ward claimed that she experienced the kind of insidious sexual textbook harassment that has less to do with sex and more to do with power. Under threat, men in charge, just as she said McNamara did, may use harassment—hostile or inappropriate comments, exclusion, sexual overtures—to make a woman feel like an outsider and essentially keep her in her place.

In 2015, EY moved her away from McNamara, transferring her out of the real estate group and into the company's investment banking division.

At the time it looked like a win for Ward, and EY still sees it that way. She was promoted to partner, and she said she was told the bonuses would be better.

But the promotion glow didn't last long. After her move was announced, she got a call from Troy Jones, a sympathetic partner who worked in the same division in EY's Los Angeles office. He was distressed, she said.

He thought they were moving her because they didn't like her, she said. She complained too much, he told her in a phone call, according to her complaint. He warned her that she probably wouldn't be getting any deal referrals from her old team, and a key part of the job was the bringing in and sharing business.

"There is an issue here because you are a woman," Jones said, according to her complaint. "Women do not succeed here."

To complicate matters, a few months after Ward was transferred, McNamara was fired. EY insisted that it wasn't because of Ward and that he was let go for failing to meet revenue targets.

But his departure probably made things worse for her. "You got my guy fired," one of his former colleagues told her, according to her complaint.

McNamara was gone, in other words, but his friends hadn't forgotten him.

What came next, Ward said, was retaliation for speaking up. Jones' warning of a lack of cooperation from the team became a reality.

In her new role at EY, she grew increasingly isolated. Real estate deals were mostly getting done by her old group, which purposefully excluded her from the work, according to her EEOC complaint.

The Post reviewed e-mails sent by Ward to her supervisor and other higher-ups. She regularly communicated her concerns about being cut off from her colleagues, but her complaints went unheard.

In a phone call with her new boss, James Carter, the head of the investment banking division, she complained about the lack of cooperation and wondered aloud, "Could this be because I'm a woman?" she said.

He dismissed the idea, she said, and told her to be careful about raising the gender issue. "Don't push that rock up the hill, it will roll back on you and crush you," he told her, according to her complaint.

EY claimed in the Post interview that it had no record of Ward complaining of sexual discrimination or gender bias while she was employed at the firm. It insisted that she was promoted and transferred to her new group in order to help her do her job. And that she was fired for failing to meet her revenue goals.

The firm shared documents detailing her declining performance during her time in the investment banking group. She failed to close many deals and was repeatedly warned that she needed to turn things around, the documents showed.

Ward kept e-mails and documents too. She shared them with the Post, and they paint a more complicated picture. She clearly did complain about mistreatment by her male colleagues, though she never explicitly labeled it sexual harassment or discrimination. EY characterized these complaints as office politics. And she appears to have made significant revenue targets, including a $4.95 million deal the month before she was fired. (EY insisted that she did not play a lead role in that deal and did not deserve full credit for it.)

Ward said she tried to make the most of her new role. Without referrals for new business from her colleagues, she hustled, logging extensive travel in search of deals to bring in.

But as she started bringing in work on her own, she noticed that Carter asked her to write elaborate memos to justify her deals before he would greenlight them. Her male colleagues didn't have to jump through the same hoops, she said.

EY strongly denied this account, saying that Carter would have every incentive to make sure Ward's deals went through so she could bring in money for his group.

And throughout this time, she kept speaking up—at one point sitting down with an HR representative to complain about getting iced out by her former colleagues, according to notes reviewed by the Post.

She tried to stick it out, until August 2017, when Carter called, telling her they were shutting down her group in the banking division. She and her team were fired. He gave her time to wind down her deals. Ward's last day at EY was October 31, 2017. "I thought it would turn around," she said. "Now I see that the rock crushed me."

Casucci's claims against EY were settled privately, and the parties are bound by confidentiality requirements, leaving the truth forever unknown to the public.

Postscript

It appears EY is trying to reverse course on its diversity and inclusiveness policies. In attempting to recruit graduates to the firm, a statement appears on its website by Karyn Twaronite, the EY Global Vice Chair of Diversity & Inclusiveness: "When organizations build a culture that values all dimensions of diversity—one that provides equitable opportunities for people to grow, learn, and advance—it creates an environment where everyone thrives and were people can experience a true sense of belonging."[27]

Later on, EY addresses diversity and inclusiveness with the following statement: "At EY, you'll find a diverse and inclusive culture, where you're embraced and respected for who you are. We want you to feel like you belong here because your uniqueness helps us to stand apart. We believe we can solve the toughest challenges together by valuing our differences and teaming inclusively to build safety and trust. Diverse viewpoints are the catalysts that lead to better questions and better answers. That's when creative ideas flow, igniting innovation and inspiring more effective solutions. We welcome all people, no matter who they are or what their background. Each of us is different, and we value and respect all EY people."[28]

It's worth mentioning that EY was ranked 25th, ahead of other CPA firms, in Fortune's 100 Best Companies to Work For 2020. A statement by employees illustrates what seems to be the high esteem employees have for EY: "EY provides an incredible opportunity to learn and grow each and every day. Additionally, the culture promotes excellence, creativity, innovation, and teaming which also helps to make it a great place to work."[29]

Questions

1. Comment on diversity and inclusiveness at EY in the case of Karen Ward. Do you think the treatment of Ward by the firm illustrates a problem with the overall culture at the firm or could this be the act of a rogue partner who overstepped his bounds in the way Ward was treated?

2. Given the facts of the case, what violations of the AICPA Code of Professional Conduct are illustrated by the way Ward was treated? Explain.

3. What are the implications of the Karen Ward case, and that of Jessica Cassuci discussed in the chapter, with respect to relationships with the client?

4. Do you believe that a CPA firm such as EY can reverse course on its treatment of women and others who might feel marginalized?

Case 4-8 Marcum LLP

On September 10, 2019, the Public Company Accounting Oversight Board (PCAOB) censured Marcum LLP and Alfonse Gregory on the basis of its findings that Marcum repeatedly violated PCAOB rules and standards over the course of four years by failing to satisfy applicable independence criteria, including as set out in SEC regulations. Marcum's independence violations resulted from its conduct in connection with the firm's annual Marcum MicroCap Conference ("MicroCap Conference") from 2012 through 2015. Specifically, Marcum was not independent with respect to audits and reviews of 62 issuers that participated in the MicroCap Conference. In addition, from 2012 through 2017—including after PCAOB staff brought independence concerns to the firm's attention in 2015—Marcum failed to take sufficient steps to ensure that its system of quality control would provide reasonable assurance that the firm would identify and appropriately address potential independence issues.[30]

The MicroCap Conference was an investor conference at which smaller or emerging public companies made business presentations to audiences that included potential investors. Marcum created, organized, and hosted the conference to increase its visibility and brand in the microcap space. The success of the conference depended on companies perceiving it as a good forum to connect with potential investors, and on potential investors perceiving it as a good opportunity to find high-quality investment opportunities.

From 2012 through 2015, Marcum endeavored to establish the MicroCap Conference as an event at which the presenting companies, including dozens of Marcum's issuer audit clients, were perceived as being high-quality investment opportunities. For example, Marcum expressly touted the quality of the conference's presenting companies and told potential conference attendees, including potential investors, that the presenting companies had been selected through a vetting process. From 2012 through 2015, Marcum issued audit reports on the financial statements of its issuer audit clients that were among the presenting companies at the MicroCap Conference.

The MicroCap Conference was an important marketing event for Marcum. The firm used the event to increase its visibility in the microcap marketplace and to develop relationships with potential clients. The conference also provided a marketing opportunity for the microcap companies that presented at the conference and the firms that sponsored the conference.

The success of the MicroCap Conference depended on providing value for the participants in the conference—that is, Marcum, presenting companies, sponsors, and potential investors. Marcum understood that it could attract more conference participants, including investors, and thereby make its MicroCap Conference more attractive to presenting companies and sponsors, by building a public perception that the conference had high-quality presenting companies.

From 2012 through 2015, Marcum promoted the MicroCap Conference as an exclusive, annual showcase for microcap presenting companies that Marcum publicly described as being "highly vetted," "high-quality" investment opportunities. Many such statements were directly attributed to the Managing Partner and SEC Services Leader.

Each year, Marcum arranged for an investor relations firm to create profiles of the presenting companies. These profiles were included in the 2012 through 2015 conference books that were distributed to potential investors. The profiles included often laudatory descriptions of the presenting companies; for example, multiple Marcum audit clients were described as "leading" and "innovative" companies in the Firm's 2015 conference book.

Marcum and its personnel promoted the MicroCap Conference by distributing brochures, sending out marketing e-mails, issuing press releases, giving interviews, and posting news articles and announcements on a Marcum website dedicated to promoting the conference. In addition, Marcum sent out thousands of conference invitations to potential attendees, including fund managers and private equity investors, banks, law firms, and other service providers for micro-cap companies. The MicroCap Conference was well attended and grew in size between 2012 and 2017. For example, the conference had approximately 800 attendees in 2012 and more than 2,000 attendees by 2016.

Marcum's touting and marketing of the presenting companies extended beyond its own public statements. In 2013, for example, the firm's SEC Services Leader directed Marcum personnel to remind presenting companies of the impor-tance of issuing press releases concerning their participation in the conference. In 2014, Marcum provided the present-ing companies with a template press release that promoted the companies, promoted the conference as "a signature showcase for superior quality, under-followed public companies," and promoted Marcum as "Ranked #15 nationally."

Marcum issuer audit clients constituted a significant percentage of the presenting companies at each MicroCap Confer-ence between 2012 and 2015. They represented 18 of 64 presenting companies (28%) at the 2012 Conference, 21 of 122 (17%) at the 2013 Conference, 30 of 128 (23%) at the 2014 Conference, and 36 of 152 (24%) at the 2015 Conference. Across the four conferences, 62 separate Marcum issuer audit clients were presenting companies.

The PCAOB found that from 2012 through 2017, Marcum failed to establish policies and procedures sufficient to pro-vide the firm with reasonable assurance that: (1) it would maintain independence in all required circumstances; and (2) the policies and procedures the firm had established with respect to independence were suitably designed and were being effectively applied and monitored. Even after the firm received notice from PCAOB staff in 2015 that its conduct appeared to be inconsistent with independence requirements, the firm responded by taking certain actions, but failed to implement, apply, and monitor policies and procedures sufficient to provide reasonable assurance that it would identify and appropriately address potential independence issues in 2016 and 2017.

In early 2015, PCAOB staff notified Marcum that the Board would inspect the firm that year. In April 2015, the Board's Inspections staff issued a comment advising Marcum that it appeared the firm had failed to maintain its independence with respect to its issuer audit clients that participated in the MicroCap Conference.

After receiving the inspection comment in 2015, Marcum took certain steps to address the comment, including remov-ing certain language touting the presenting companies from future promotional materials for the conference, adding a disclaimer to portions of the MicroCap Conference website, and, in 2017, adding the following provisions to its quality control policies:

"Any public statement about a client, or any group of companies which includes a client, is prohibited without the firm's approval. Public statements would include those statements included in marketing materials, e-mail blasts or statements on websites about any Issuer audit clients or prospects, with respect to any firm-hosted or firm-sponsored conference, including the Marcum MicroCap Conference. No public statement should be made without careful con-sideration of the general standard of independence set out in Rule 2-01(b) of Regulation S-X, including consideration of the four principles in the preliminary note to Rule 2-01."[31]

After taking these steps with respect to its public touting of the presenting companies, including those that were Mar-cum issuer audit clients, the firm held its 2016 and 2017 Conferences without adequately considering other potential independence issues in relation to Marcum issuer audit clients that presented at the conference. Indeed, Marcum failed even to verify the effectiveness of the steps it took to limit its touting of presenting companies. As a result, Marcum failed to identify, evaluate, or appropriately address a number of issues concerning the 2016 and 2017 Conferences that, at the very least, raised questions about the firm's independence.

Questions

1. Describe the nature of the violations of AICPA and PCAOB rules in this case?

2. Did Marcum violate the Advertising and Solicitation Rule in the AICPA Code or the Acts Discreditable rule? Explain.

3. What should be done when a registered public accounting firm fails to follow the requirements of a PCAOB audit inspection as in the Marcum case?

Case 4-9 PwC Mischaracterizes Nonaudit Services

PwC violated SEC rule 2-02(b) of Regulation S-X and PCAOB Rule 3525 by engaging in improper professional conduct in violation of the independence rules on audit clients. This case is unique because the firm had mischaracterized certain nonaudit services as part of the audit engagement to skirt its ethical responsibilities under SEC and PCAOB rules.

In 2014, PwC performed nonaudit services for an audit client concerning Governance Risk and Compliance (GRC) software. According to AAER No. 4084, "GRC systems are used by companies to coordinate and monitor controls over financial reporting, including employee access to critical financial functions." The client "intended to use the GRC software to generate information as part of the company's control environment and to provide data to assist personnel in forming conclusions regarding the effectiveness of internal controls related to financial information systems." At the time, the GRC system was being implemented, it was intended to be subject to the internal control over financial reporting audit procedures.

As stated in AAER No. 4084, the SEC rules[32] "prohibit independent auditors from designing and implementing systems such as GRC where the software aggregates source data or generates information significant to the clients' financial statements or other financial systems as a whole. Designing, implementing, or operating systems affecting the financial statements can result in the accountant auditing his or her own work or attesting to the effectiveness of internal control systems designed or implemented by that accountant. The independence rules also prohibit an independent auditor from performing management functions."

Communications between PwC and its audit client show that the client's head of internal audit was concerned whether the firm could provide an implementation proposal and inquired about auditor independence. Brandon Sprankle, who was the partner responsible for supervising the performance of prohibited nonaudit services, violated SEC Rule 2-02 when he responded that "we are absolutely permitted to implement so there will be no issues. . .," even though he was aware that the firm's independence policies did not allow it or him to implement the GRC system.

Communications with the client show the disconnect between the client's expectations and how PwC was describing its information systems services ostensibly to skirt the requirement not to perform certain nonaudit services for audit clients. An e-mail from the then head of internal audit of the client, who objected to the description of services contained in the draft engagement letter, informed PwC that the proposed work was an implementation project that's been outsourced to the firm.

The final engagement letter described the work on the GRC project "as performing assessments and high-level recommendations" even though an internal PwC communication had characterized the engagement as a design and implementation project. **Exhibit 1** summarizes key communications over time.

EXHIBIT 1

Timeline of PwC's Design and Implementation of the Financial-Related Information System.

In seeking internal authorization to perform the nonaudit GRC work, Brandon Sprankle drafted an engagement letter for approval by PwC's Risk Assurance Independence ("RAI") group, an independence-reviewer within his business unit. In the draft engagement letter, Sprankle described the proposed services as assessing multiple areas, and providing observations and recommendations, as opposed to designing and implementing the GRC project. This description was inconsistent with Issuer A's expectation that PwC would conduct a design and implementation project as previously communicated to Sprankle.

Internal Auditor's Objections

In early June 2014, Issuer A again puts Sprankle on notice that it expected PwC to design and implement a GRC solution for Issuer A and to manage the project. After Sprankle sent the draft engagement letter, Issuer A's then-Head of Internal Audit objected to the description of the services contained in the draft engagement letter. In the e-mail, he informed Sprankle that the proposed work was an "implementation project that's been outsourced" to PwC.

(continued)

Sprankle thereafter met with the then-Head of Internal Audit, who understood from speaking with Sprankle that PwC would substantially design and implement the GRC module and would perform project management functions. At the time, PwC was continuing its audit of Issuer A for fiscal year 2014 and, due to Issuer A's prior accounting errors, performing additional audit work for fiscal years 2011 and 2012. The Head of Internal Audit was concerned that PwC would be performing internal audit-type services.

The final engagement letter for the GRC project described the work as performing assessments and high-level recommendations. However, as internal PwC communications reflect, certain PwC employees characterized the engagement as a design and implementation project. For example, in a July 2014 e-mail, a PwC manager communicated his view to Sprankle that the project involved the implementation of a financial-related information system.

In August 2014, PwC began the GRC work. To start the work, another PwC manager, who Sprankle supervised, instructed a PwC associate to prepare a design document: "I need you to immediately begin working on creating a design document for how [the GRC module] will be built for the [GRC] rules we already know about. Below are the SOD [Segregation of Duties, an internal control concept allocating duties among employees] rules we know we need to build . . . ."

Management of the Project

From August through mid-October 2014, PwC employees under Sprankle's supervision managed the project, performed substantial design work, configured the design on a nonproduction server, and provided oversight and direction for the implementation to a live environment. According to its senior manager for IT Internal Audit: Issuer A had little involvement in the assessment and design phase of the project; further, Issuer A lacked the technical expertise to configure the system; and, although Issuer A ultimately had to approve the work, Sprankle and PwC employees under his supervision exercised decision-making authority in designing and configuring the GRC module.

As the project progressed in September 2014, the PwC manager e-mailed the senior manager for IT Internal Audit at Issuer A, who had oversight of the project, and copied Sprankle, about problems with the GRC server and application that needed to be addressed before PwC could perform development work: "We identified some critical issues that need to be resolved before we can get in there and do the development."

Throughout the course of the GRC engagement, Issuer A considered PwC to be the system implementer and deferred to PwC on best practices for settings that needed to be included in the system. Further, according to the senior manager for IT Internal Audit, Issuer A allowed PwC "to make those decisions for us" and, although an Issuer A employee would technically have his hands on the keyboard, a PwC employee, under Sprankle's supervision, managed the process and directed the Issuer A employee on what actions to take.

SEC/PCAOB Rule Violations

The firm agreed to pay over $7.9 million to settle charges with the SEC that it performed prohibited nonaudit services during an audit engagement including exercising decision-making authority in the design and implementation of software relating to an audit client's financial reporting and engaging in management functions.

The firm violated PCAOB Rule 3525 by failing to describe in writing to the audit committee the scope of work, discuss the potential effects of work on independence, and document the substance of the independence discussion. These actions deprived the issuers' audit committee of information necessary to assess PwC's independence. The violations occurred due to breakdowns in PwC's independence-related quality controls, which resulted in the firm's failure to carefully review and monitor whether nonaudit services for audit clients were permissible and approved by clients' audit committee.[33]

This case illustrates a concern that in some cases audit firms are misrepresenting nonaudit services as part of the audit services to get around the rules that prohibit certain nonaudit services for audit clients. Purposely doing so misleads the users of financial statements about the independence of the client.

Questions

1. Identify any threats to independence that existed in this case. Explain how and why PwC ignored those threats to independence.
2. How would you characterize this case from the perspective of corporate governance at PwC and implementation of its own quality controls?
3. What ethical norms did PwC partner Brandon Sprankle violate?

Case 4-10 Johnson Pharmaceuticals (a GVV case)

In the first three months of 2021, Johnson Pharmaceutical's sales and earnings were declining, placing the company in financial distress. As a result, Johnson had begun the process of borrowing $1 million to stay afloat.

Around the same time, Paul Leonard, CPA, who had served as Johnson's Controller since 2004, retired from the company on March 7, 2021. After informally advising his successor (the "Successor Controller") from March 8 until April 2, Leonard was formally retained by Johnson as a consultant on April 3, 2021 to assist the Successor Controller in closing Johnson's books for the quarter ending March 31, 2021, and began receiving material, nonpublic information regarding Johnson's quarterly results and its pending impairment charge.

While in possession of material, nonpublic information, Leonard sold all of the Johnson shares he owned, and he exercised all of his stock options. This enabled Leonard to avoid losses on the stock he sold and profiting on the options he exercised by more than $100,000 in the aggregate.

Becca Lowry, the Successor Controller, who is also a CPA, found out about the sale. Not only that, she discovered that Leonard had borrowed $250,000 from a related party entity and didn't disclose it in the December 31, 2020, 10-K financial statements filed with the SEC.

Leonard was assisting Becca Lowry in closing the books. Becca wanted to approach Leonard to discuss his stock sales and borrowing. However, she didn't know how best to do so. Moreover, Becca felt beholden to Leonard for her job and training her to become the new controller.

Questions

1. What rules of conduct in the AICPA Code seem to have been violated? Explain why.
2. Put yourself in Becca's position. You are preparing for the meeting with Leonard to discuss these matters. Consider the following in crafting an outline of points you may have to respond to.
    a. What are the main arguments you are trying to counter? That is, what are the reasons and rationalizations you need to address?
    b. What is at stake for the key parties?
    c. What levers can you use to influence Leonard?
    d. What is your most powerful and persuasive response to the reasons and rationalizations you may need to address? To whom should the argument be made? When and in what context?
3. Assume you are unable to get Leonard to make things right with respect to the stock sales and borrowing, what would you do next? Why?

CHAPTER 5
Fraud in Financial Statements and Auditor Responsibilities

LEARNING OBJECTIVES

After studying **Chapter 5**, you should be able to:

LO 5-1 Distinguish between audit requirements for errors, fraud, and illegal acts.

LO 5-2 Explain the components of the Fraud Triangle and how they are integrated into AU-C 240.

LO 5-3 Describe fraud risk assessment procedures and red flags which might indicate that an individual may be committing fraud, or susceptible to it.

LO 5-4 Describe the responsibilities of the External Auditor, Board of Directors, and Company Management in regard to internal controls over financial reporting (ICFR).

LO 5-5 Explain the standards for audit reports.

LO 5-6 Identify the potential benefits and concerns over the use of Machine Based Learning systems by external and internal auditors.

Ethics Reflection

Members of the public accounting profession are generally regarded as the keepers of the public trust when it comes to the financial statements they issue audit opinions on. An audit of financial statements is intended to enhance the degree of confidence of intended users, such as lenders, creditors, and investors, and is achieved through an examination of the financial statements by an independent accountant the purpose of which is to provide reasonable assurance whether the financial statements are free of material misstatement, whether caused by error or fraud.

According to AU-C 240, Consideration of Fraud in a Financial Statement Audit, Section .05, "Due to the inherent limitations of an audit, an unavoidable risk exists that some material misstatements of the financial statements may not be detected, even though the audit is properly planned and performed in accordance with GAAS." In other words, an audit does not guaranty that financial statements actually are free of material misstatement. A large expectation gap exists between what the general public believes the purpose of an audit is and what it actually is. This gap is the result of a misunderstanding of what the term "reasonable assurance" means.

Audits utilize a sampling technique whereby they verify a small sampling of the transactions recorded by a company during a given year. That sampling is determined by an overall analysis of the company's control environment and relies on the auditors following generally accepted auditing standards (GAAS).

If the purpose of an audit was to provide absolute assurance that the financial statements being audited were free of material misstatement, then a starting point would be verifying 100 percent of the transactions recorded. Up until recently, the concept of a 100 percent transactional based audit, would have been considered not only theoretically impossible, but not cost effective. However, with the rapid technological developments in computing power and data analytics over the last decade, the entire public accounting profession appears to be moving toward 100 percent transactional-based audits.

While 100 percent transactional-based audits will hopefully help reduce the expectations gap, it cannot, by itself, guaranty that audited financials will be free of material misstatement. Unfortunately, the auditing profession has a very poor track record when it comes to performing high-quality audits. One of the many benefits of the creation of the Public Accounting Oversight Board (PCAOB) is their role as auditors of the audits conducted by public accounting firms. For the first time in the history of the profession, the actual quality of the audits conducted by members of the public accounting profession have been made public. The findings of the PCAOB surrounding audits are embarrassingly negative.

GAAP Dynamics' analysis of the PCAOB inspection reports from 2010 through 2017, found an aggregate audit deficiency rate of 35.87 percent ranging from a low of 30 percent in both 2015 and 2017 to a high of 42 percent in both 2012 and 2013.[1] The audit deficiency rates by firm varied dramatically with a low of 13 percent and a high of 73 percent. The reported deficiencies are material and indicate a high percentage of issued audit reports cannot be relied on. GAAP Dynamics reported that most deficiencies fell into the following areas:

Auditing of internal control over financial reporting	33%
Assessing and responding to risks of material misstatements	33%
Performing audit sampling procedures	15%
Auditing of accounting estimates	9%
Auditing fair value measurements and disclosures	7%

The PCAOB has expressed concern about "audit quality" and has made recommendations to the profession on ways in which they can improve the quality of the audits they conduct.

The PCAOB Quality Control (QC) Section 20 standards for the *System of Quality Control for a CPA Firm's Accounting and Auditing Practice* emphasizes that the Scope and Nature of Services Principle in the AICPA Code calls for CPAs to practice in firms that have in place internal quality control procedures to ensure that services are competently delivered and adequately supervised. A firm's system of quality control encompasses the firm's organizational structure and the policies adopted and procedures established to provide the firm with reasonable assurance of complying with professional standards.

Quality control includes the maintenance of Integrity, Objectivity, performing the audit with Professional Skepticism, Due Care, and Independence, which requires a continuing assessment of client relationships, engagement performance, and monitoring. This encompasses the values, ethics, and attitudes of auditors, which in turn are influenced by the culture of the audit firm. In addition, a new requirement for PCAOB reports is for the auditor to determine and communicate "critical audit matters." More will be said about this later in this chapter.

Both the 2018[2] and 2019[3] PCAOB reports on the inspections they conducted in these two years, made reference to not only the areas where most audit deficiencies are found, but to overall audit quality and things that the firms can do to improve it. Both reports continue to express concerns over the same areas highlighted above by GAAP Dynamics, but noted some improvement in overall audit quality.

Specifically, while overall audit deficiency rates in 2018 and 2019 did not change much, the deficiency rates for the Big 4 firms has dropped as a group, while the deficiency rates for the other firms has increased. The five-year average deficiency from 2015 through 2019 is as follows:

% of Annual Inspection Deficiencies						
Firm Type	2019	2018	2017	2016	2015	5 YR
Big 4 Average	22%	25%	31%	25%	28%	26%
Other Firms	31%	26%	32%	36%	28%	31%
Overall Average	28%	26%	32%	32%	28%	29%

(continued)

continued   Ethics Reflection

While the latest findings by the PCAOB are encouraging, the rate of audit deficiencies remains much too high. To encourage improvements in audit quality, the 2019 PCAOB[4] overview report published on October 8, 2020, highlighted the following good audit practices:

Recommendation	Description	Result
Interactive meetings/ coaching workshops	Includes entire engagement team, often tied to audit milestones	Identifying how financials might be materially misstated Identifying risks of material misstatement
Early involvement of engagement quality reviewer (EQR)	From audit planning stage forward	May result in in early identification of potential or actual audit challenges
Narrative descriptions of quality control	Firms created narratives of their quality control process or prepared process flow maps of them	Used to monitor engagement performance and enhance the audit effectiveness
Increased partner involvement in planning of audit tests and controls	Engagement team leadership held planning meetings with whole engagement team	Discussions and robust risk assessment procedures improve staff ability to analyze effectiveness of controls
Use of firm specialists during audit planning to assist in risk assessment	Early involvement of specialists during audit planning stage	Enhances the ability of auditors to more effectively identify and assess risks of material misstatement
Implementing coaching programs and refining audit tools for specific audit areas	Targeting areas where the firms have had audit deficiencies in the past	Noted improvement in the auditing of estimates at firms that implemented these programs

As you read this chapter, reflect on the following: (1) What are the auditor's responsibilities to assess the risks of material misstatement of the financial statements, whether due to error or fraud? (2) What is the fraud triangle and how does it help to identify red flags that are indicators fraud may exist? (3) What are the most common causes of financial statement fraud and how can internal controls over financial reporting and the audit firms' quality controls keep them in check? (4) What information is communicated by the audit report? (5) What potential benefits and concerns surround the use of Machine Based Learning systems in auditing?

> The true standards of audit practice are found within the auditor's character: honesty, integrity, self-control and high ethical values. The printed standards are merely guidelines for trying to make the art of auditing into a profession.
>
> *Source: Michael L. Piazza*

This quote from Michael L. Piazza, director and producer of AuditWisdom.com, harkens back to our discussion of professional ethics in **Chapter 4**. The auditing standards discussed in this chapter can make a difference and help to prevent and detect material misstatements in the financial statements if the accounting professionals who are charged with following those standards adhere to the rules of conduct in the AICPA Code and, when appropriate, PCAOB ethics and independence standards.

Fraud in Financial Statements

LO 5-1
Distinguish between audit requirements for errors, fraud, and illegal acts.

Introduction

According to the AICPA audit standard on fraud, *Consideration of Fraud in a Financial Statement Audit* (AU-C Section 240), the primary responsibility for the prevention and detection of fraud rests with both those charged with governance of the entity and management. A strong emphasis should be placed on fraud prevention, which may reduce opportunities for fraud to take place, and fraud deterrence, which could persuade individuals not to commit fraud because of the likelihood of detection and punishment.[5] As we discussed in **Chapter 3**, this involves a commitment to creating a culture of ethical behavior, tone at the top, and reinforcement through governance structures.

As discussed in the opening paragraphs of this chapter, an auditor conducting an audit in accordance with generally accepted auditing standards (GAAS) is responsible for obtaining reasonable assurance that the financial statements as a whole are free from material misstatements, whether caused by fraud or error. Due to the inherent limitations of an audit, an unavoidable risk exists that some material misstatements of the financial statements may not be detected even though the audit was conducted in accordance with those standards.[6]

The auditing profession recognizes its obligation to look for fraud by being alert to certain red flags, assessing the control environment of the organization, passing judgment on internal controls, and considering audit risk and materiality when performing an audit. However, this is a far cry from guaranteeing that fraud will be detected, especially when top management goes to great lengths to hide it from the auditors.

The expectations gap, discussed previously, takes on a different character when members of the accounting profession and finance professionals are queried on their views. On April 24, 2013, the Center for Audit Quality (CAQ) held a roundtable on the subject of the expectation gap. The participants included representatives from CAQ, the Financial Executives International (FEI), the Institute of Internal Auditors (IIA), and the National Association of Corporate Directors (NACD). The following summarizes the results of these discussions.[7]

- The vast majority of survey respondents indicated that financial executives had primary responsibility for *deterring* financial reporting fraud.

- External auditors were more likely than any other financial reporting supply chain members to suggest that boards and audit committees bore primary responsibility.

- Respondents were more likely to identify financial management as having the primary role for *detecting* fraud, but these results were not as pronounced as they were for deterrence.

- Audit committee members and internal auditors were more likely than the other two groups to place primary responsibility for fraud detection on the external auditor.

These mixed results indicate the shared responsibility of many parties in the financial reporting chain for deterring, detecting, and reporting financial statement misstatements whether due to error or fraud. Board members had confidence that management, internal audit, and external audit would be able to identify a material misstatement due to fraud. They also had a fairly high level of confidence in their own ability to identify a material misstatement, although this level of confidence was not shared by the other participants. This is somewhat surprising, given management's role in designing processes and procedures (i.e., internal controls) and monitoring their effectiveness in developing accurate and reliable financial statement information. Moreover, the CEO and CFO are both required to certify financial statements under Section 302 of SOX. The question is whether management and the board take their responsibilities seriously enough to be responsive to auditors' need for cooperation and full disclosure of information that might bear on the fair presentation of financial results.

Nature and Causes of Misstatements

Fraudulent financial reporting involves either intentional misstatements or omissions of amounts or disclosures in financial statements that are intended to deceive financial statement users. Fraudulent financial reporting generally occurs in one of three ways: (1) deception such as manipulation, falsification, or alteration of accounting records or supporting documents from which the financial statements are prepared; (2) misrepresentation in, or intentional omission from, the financial statements of events, transactions, or other significant information; and (3) intentional misapplication of accounting principles relating to measurement, recognition, classification, presentation, or disclosure. Because fraud involves an intentional act, the perpetrator of the falsehood knows, or should know, that what they propose to do is wrong. Once financial statements have been falsified, the trust relationship between an auditor and the public breaks down.

A sensitive area that should receive heightened scrutiny by auditors is accounting estimates. The financial statements contain many estimates (i.e., depreciation, uncollectible accounts, estimated warranty obligations) that require professional judgment. Biases discussed in previous chapters can lead to estimating amounts that show management's side of the story rather than conform to GAAP. Auditors must be on the lookout to identify situations where management's interpretation of the data is at odds with their own determinations.

Errors, Fraud, and Illegal Acts

Material errors, fraud, and illegal acts represent situations where the financial statements should be restated. **Exhibit 5.1** describes the auditors' obligations to detect and report each of these events. The following briefly describes the nature and effects of such acts.

EXHIBIT 5.1   Auditors' Responsibility to Detect Errors, Illegal Acts, and Fraud

	Responsible for Detection		Required to Communicate Findings	
	Material	**Immaterial**	**Material**	**Immaterial**
Errors	Yes	No	Yes (audit committee)	No
Illegal acts	Yes (direct effect)	No	Yes (audit committee)	Yes (one level above)
Fraud	Yes	No	Yes (audit committee)	Yes (by low-level employee, to one level above) (by management-level employee, to audit committee)

Errors

Errors are unintentional acts and may involve mistakes in gathering or processing data, unreasonable accounting estimates arising from oversight or misinterpretation of facts, or mistakes in the application of GAAP. Auditors are responsible for detecting errors that have a material effect on the financial statements and reporting their findings to the audit committee. An error correction is the correction of an error in previously issued financial statements. The amount is determined by calculating the cumulative effect of the error on periods prior to those presented in the financial statements. The effected asset and/or liability account(s) are adjusted with an offsetting adjustment to the opening balance of retained earnings for the current period. Financial statements should be restated for each period presented to reflect the error correction.

Fraud

Auditors should be sensitive to red flags that warn fraud is possible, if not likely. Fraud, whether fraudulent financial reporting or misappropriation of assets, involves incentive or pressure to commit fraud, a perceived opportunity to do so, and some rationalization of the act. The intentional act of fraud occurs when an individual(s) in management, those charged with governance, employees, or third parties use deception in a way that results in a material misstatement in the financial statements. In its most common form, management fraud involves top management's deceptive manipulation of financial statements.

In an "Analysis of Alleged Auditor Deficiencies in SEC Fraud Investigations: 1998–2010" conducted for the CAQ, it was determined that the failure to exercise due professional care and appropriate levels of professional skepticism resulted in auditors' inability to detect fraud. Being more attuned to the red flags that fraud may exist is an essential component of enhanced professional judgment.[8]

The intent of management determines whether the misapplication of GAAP is an error in judgment or a deliberate decision to manipulate earnings. In a court of law, it typically comes down to the credibility of the CFO and CEO who are charged with fraud. Absent a "smoking gun," the court might look for parallel actions by these top officers, such as selling their own shares of corporate stock after the fraudulent act but before it becomes public knowledge, as occurred at Enron and WorldCom.

Illegal Acts

Illegal acts are violations of laws or governmental regulations. For example, a violation of the Foreign Corrupt Practices Act (FCPA) that prohibits bribery constitutes an illegal act. Illegal acts include those attributable to the entity whose financial statements are under audit or as acts by management or employees acting on behalf of the entity. Such acts expose the company to both legal liability and public disgrace. The auditor's responsibility is to determine the proper accounting and financial reporting treatment of a violation once it has been determined that a violation has in fact occurred.

The auditor's responsibility is to detect and report misstatements resulting from illegal acts that have a direct and material effect on the determination of financial statement amounts (i.e., they require an accounting entry). The auditors' responsibility for detecting direct and material effect violations is greater than their responsibility to detect illegal acts arising from laws that only indirectly affect the client's financial statements. An example of the former would be violations of tax laws that affect accruals and the amount recognized as income tax liability for the period. Tax law would be violated, triggering an adjustment in the current period financial statements if, say, a company, for tax purposes, were to expense an item all in one year that should have been capitalized and written off over three years. Examples of items with an indirect effect on the statements include the potential violation of other laws such as the FCPA, occupational safety and health regulations, environmental protection laws, and equal employment regulations. The events are due to operational, not financial, matters and their financial statement effect is indirect, such as a possible contingent liability that should be disclosed in the notes to the financial statements.

The auditor's obligation after concluding that an illegal act has or is likely to have occurred is first to assess the impact of the actions on the financial statements, including materiality considerations. This should be done regardless of any direct or indirect effect on the statements. The auditor should consult with legal counsel and any other specialists in this regard. Illegal acts should be reported to those charged with governance such as the audit committee. Consideration should be given to whether the client has taken appropriate remedial action concerning the act. Such remedial action may include taking disciplinary actions, establishing controls to safeguard against recurrence, and, if necessary, reporting the effects of the illegal acts in the financial statements. Ordinarily, if the client does not take the remedial action deemed necessary by the auditor, then the auditor should withdraw from the engagement. This action on the part of the auditor makes clear that they will not be associated in any way with illegal activities.

The Private Securities Litigation Reform Act (PSLRA) of 1995

The Private Securities Litigation Reform Act (PSLRA) of 1995 places additional requirements upon public companies registered with the SEC and their auditors when (1) the illegal act has a material effect on the financial statements,

(2) senior management and the board of directors have not taken appropriate remedial action, and (3) the failure to take remedial action is reasonably expected to warrant departure from a standard (i.e., unmodified audit report) or to warrant resignation.

Once the auditor reports to the board that remedial action has not been taken to correct the detected illegal act, the client has one business day to inform the SEC under the requirements of Section 10A(b) of the Securities Exchange Act of 1934 ("Required Responses to Audit Discoveries"). The board should provide the auditor with a copy of the notice provided to the SEC. If, however, the client fails to report such conduct to the SEC, or the auditor fails to receive a copy of the board's notice to the SEC, then the reporting obligation falls to the auditor, who must then resign from the engagement or furnish the SEC with a copy of the audit report the following day. If the auditor resigns, they must still provide the SEC with a copy of the auditor's report within one day following the client's failure to do so.

A good example of the application of Section 10A is the litigation in the Xerox fraud. The accounting issues are discussed in **Chapter 6**; here, we look at the reporting requirements for fraud and illegal acts and whether KPMG met those standards with regard to its client Xerox.

In *SEC v. KPMG LLP, Joseph T. Boyle, Michael A. Conway, Anthony P. Dolanski, and Ronald A. Safran,* the SEC alleged, among other claims, violations of Section 10A by KPMG and four of its partners.[9] On January 29, 2003, the SEC filed an action against the firm and its partners, claiming as follows:

> "Defendants KPMG . . . and certain KPMG partners permitted Xerox Corporation to manipulate its accounting practices and fill a $3 billion "gap" between actual operating results and results reported to the investing public from 1997 through 2000. Instead of putting a stop to Xerox's fraudulent conduct, the KPMG defendants themselves engaged in fraud by falsely representing to the public that they had applied professional auditing standards to their review of Xerox's accounting, that Xerox's financial reporting was consistent with GAAP and that Xerox's reported results fairly represented the financial condition of the company . . . Section 10(A) of the Exchange Act requires a public accountant conducting an audit of a public company such as Xerox to: (1) determine whether it is likely that an illegal act occurred and, if so, (2) determine what the possible effect of the illegal act is on the financial statements of the issuer, and (3) if the illegal act is not clearly inconsequential, inform the appropriate level of management and assure that the Audit Committee of the client is adequately informed about the illegal act detected. If neither management nor the Audit Committee takes timely and appropriate remedial action in response to the auditor's report, the auditor is obliged to take further steps, including reporting the likely illegal act to the Commission."

In November 2004, KPMG reached a settlement with the SEC. KPMG consented to a finding that it violated Section 10(A) of the Securities Exchange Act of 1934; to pay disgorgement of $9,800,000, plus prejudgment interest; to pay a civil penalty of $10 million; and to implement a number of internal reforms. A final judgment against KPMG was issued on April 20, 2005.

Confidentiality Obligation

Recall that Section 1.700 of the AICPA Code of Professional Conduct prohibits CPAs from directly disclosing information to outside parties, including illegal acts, *unless the auditors have a legal duty to do so.* Compliance with the PSLRA would qualify as an exception to the bar on disclosing confidential client information, as would compliance with SOX and Dodd-Frank provisions.

A duty to notify parties outside the client may exist in each of the following circumstances:

- When the entity reports an auditor change under the appropriate securities law on Form 8-K.
- To a successor auditor when the successor makes inquiries in accordance with *Terms of Engagement* (AU-C Section 210).
- In response to a subpoena.
- To a funding agency or other specified agency in accordance with requirements for the audits of entities that receive financial assistance from a government agency.

Because potential conflicts with the auditor's ethical and legal obligations for confidentiality may be complex, the auditor should always consider consulting with legal counsel before discussing illegal acts with parties other than the client.

The Fraud Triangle and AU-C 240: Consideration of Fraud in a Financial Statement Audit

LO 5-2
Explain the components of the Fraud Triangle and how they are integrated into AU-C 240.

Donald R. Cressey, a noted criminologist, is mostly credited with coming up with the concept of a Fraud Triangle. Albrecht points out that Cressey developed a hypothesis of why people commit fraud. He found that trusted persons become trust violators when they conceive of themselves as having a financial problem that is nonsharable, are aware that this problem can be secretly resolved by violation of the position of financial trust, and are able to apply to their contacts in that situation verbalizations which enable them to adjust their conceptions of themselves as users of the entrusted funds or property.[10]

Edwin Sutherland, another criminologist, argued that persons who engage in criminal behavior have accumulated enough feelings and *rationalizations* in favor of law violation that outweigh their pro-social definitions. Criminal behavior is learned and will occur when perceived rewards for criminal behavior exceed the rewards for lawful behavior or *perceived opportunity*. So, while not directly introducing the Fraud Triangle, Sutherland did introduce the concepts of rationalizations and opportunities. It is interesting to think about how Sutherland's thesis relies on a utilitarian analysis of harms and benefits of criminal behavior.[11]

The Fraud Triangle in auditing is integrated in AU-C Section 240, Consideration for Fraud in a Financial Statement Audit. The deception that encompasses fraudulent financial reporting is depicted in **Exhibit 5.2**.[12]

Some depict the Fraud Triangle with the opportunity at the base. We prefer to show pressure at the base because we believe, absent pressure to commit fraud, it is unlikely to occur simply because a fraudster needs access to do the deed.

EXHIBIT 5.2   The Fraud Triangle

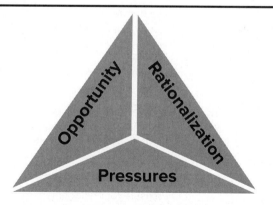

Three conditions generally are present when fraud occurs. First, management or other employees have an incentive or are under pressure, which provides the motivation for the fraud. Second, circumstances exist that provide an opportunity for a fraud to be perpetrated. Examples include the absence of, or ineffective, internal controls and management's override of internal controls. Third, those involved are able to rationalize committing a fraudulent act much like the rationalizations we discussed in the GVV methodology.

As noted in the auditing standard, some individuals possess an attitude, character, or set of ethical values that allow them to commit a dishonest act knowingly and intentionally. For the most part, this is the exception rather than the rule. However, even honest individuals can commit fraud in an environment that imposes sufficient pressure on them. The greater the incentive or pressure, the more likely that an individual will be able to rationalize the acceptability of committing fraud.[13] Two good examples previously discussed are Betty Vinson and Aaron Beam.

It is important to understand the link between elements of the Fraud Triangle and our earlier discussions about cognitive development. The disconnect between one's values and actions may be attributable to motivations and incentives to act unethically, perhaps because of a perceived gain or as a result of pressures imposed by others who might try to convince us it is a one-time request or standard practice, or to be loyal to one's supervisor or the organization. These also become rationalizations for unethical actions invoked by the perpetrator of the fraud.

Incentives/Pressures to Commit Fraud

The incentive to commit fraud typically is a self-serving one. Egoism drives the fraud in the sense that the perpetrator perceives some benefit by committing the fraud, such as a higher bonus or promotion. The fraud may be caused by internal budget pressures or financial analysts' earnings expectations that are not being met. Personal pressures also might lead to fraud if, for example, a member of top management is deep in personal debt or has a gambling or drug problem. AU-C 240 specifically identifies the incentives/pressures and potential red flags shown in **Exhibit 5.3**.[14]

EXHIBIT 5.3   Incentives/Pressures to Commit Fraud

Incentive/Pressure to Commit Fraud	Potential Red Flags to Look For
Financial stability or profitability is threatened by economic, industry, or entity operating conditions	• High degree of competition or market saturation, accompanied by declining margins • High vulnerability to rapid changes, such as changes in technology, product obsolescence, or interest rates • Significant declines in customer demand and increasing business failures in either the industry or overall economy • Operating losses suggesting going concern issues • Recurring negative cash flows from operations while reporting earnings growth • Rapid growth or unusual profitability especially compared to that of other companies in the same industry
Excessive pressure exists for management to meet the requirements or expectations of third parties	• Aggressive or unrealistic profitability or trend level expectations (whether internally or externally generated) • Need to obtain additional debt or equity financing to stay competitive • Challenges meeting exchange listing requirements or debt repayment/debt covenants • Perceived or real adverse effects of reporting poor financial results on significant pending transactions • Pressure for management to meet the expectations of legislative or oversight bodies
Available information indicates that the personal financial situation of management or those charged with governance is threatened by the entity's financial performance	• Significant financial interests in the entity • Significant portions of their compensation (for example, bonuses, stock options, and earn-out arrangements) tied to achieving aggressive targets for stock price, operating results, financial position, or cash flow • Personal guarantees of debts of the entity

Opportunity to Commit Fraud

The second side of the Fraud Triangle connects the pressure or incentive to commit fraud with the opportunity to carry out the act. Employees who have access to assets such as cash and inventory should be monitored closely through an effective system of internal controls that helps safeguard assets. Two common red flags that involve internal controls are domination of management by a single person or small group (in a nonowner-managed business) without compensating controls and when an organization has ineffective oversight over the financial reporting process and internal control by those charged with governance. AU-C 240 specifically identifies the opportunities and red flags shown in **Exhibit 5.4**.

EXHIBIT 5.4   Opportunity to Commit Fraud

Opportunity to Commit Fraud	Potential Red Flags to Look For
The nature of the industry or the entity's operations	• Related party transactions that are also significant unusual transactions • Significant transactions with related parties whose financial statements are not audited or are audited by another firm • Firms' to dictate terms or conditions to suppliers or customers that may result in inappropriate or non-arm's-length transactions • Assets, liabilities, revenues, or expenses based on significant estimates that involve subjective judgments or uncertainties • Significant or highly complex transactions or significant unusual transactions, especially those close to period end
Significant operations located or conducted across jurisdictional borders where differing business environments and regulations exist	• Use of business intermediaries for which there appears to be no clear business justification • Significant bank accounts or subsidiary or branch operations in tax-haven jurisdictions • Contractual arrangements lacking a business purpose
The monitoring of management is not effective	• Domination of management by a single person or small group • Oversight by those charged with governance over the financial reporting process and internal control • The exertion of dominant influence by or over a related party
The organizational structure is complex or unstable	• Difficulty in determining the organization or individuals that have controlling interest in the entity • Overly complex organizational structure involving unusual legal entities or managerial lines of authority • High turnover of senior management, legal counsel, or those charged with governance
Internal control components are deficient	• Inadequate monitoring of controls • High turnover rates or employment of staff in accounting, IT, or internal audit • Accounting and information systems that are not effective • Material internal control weaknesses

Rationalization for the Fraud

Fraud perpetrators typically try to explain away their actions as acceptable. For corporate executives, rationalizations to commit fraud might include thoughts such as "We need to protect our shareholders and keep the stock price high," "All companies use aggressive accounting practices," "It's for the good of the company," or "The problem is temporary and will be offset by future positive results." Other rationalizations might include "My boss doesn't pay me enough" or

"I'll pay the money back before anyone notices it's gone." The underlying motivation for the fraud in these instances may be dissatisfaction with the company and/or personal financial need. AU-C 240 identifies the attitudes or rationalizations shown in **Exhibit 5.5**.

EXHIBIT 5.5   Rationalizations/Attitudes to Justify Fraud

Rationalizations/Attitudes to Justify Fraud	Potential Red Flags to Look For
Poor Tone at the Top	• Poor communication, implementation, support, or enforcement of the entity's values or ethical standards by management • Communication of inappropriate values • Ineffective ethical standards • Known history/claims of violations of securities or other laws or regulations • Low morale among senior management • The owner-manager makes no distinction between personal and business transactions • Dispute between shareholders in a closely held entity
Management Interest in Accounting	• Nonfinancial management's excessive participation in/ preoccupation with the selection of accounting policies or the determination of estimates • Excessive interest by management in maintaining or increasing the entity's stock price or earnings trend • Commitment to analysts, creditors, and other third parties to achieve aggressive or unrealistic forecasts • Management trying to justify marginal or inappropriate accounting based on materiality • Management failing to remedy known internal control deficiencies or material weaknesses
A strained relationship between management and the current or predecessor auditor	• Frequent disputes with the current or predecessor auditor • Unreasonable demands on the auditor regarding the completion of the audit or issuance of the auditor's report • Restrictions on the auditor access to people or information • Management attempting to influence audit scope

Frisch's Restaurant: Trust but Verify

Michael Hudson, the former assistant treasurer at Frisch's Restaurant in Cincinnati that owns 95 Big Boy Restaurants in Ohio, embezzled at least $3.3 million between 2008 and 2014, during which time he gambled at the Horseshoe Casino. Hudson even occasionally sent coworkers pictures of jackpots he won.[15]

Hudson had the opportunity to commit fraud as assistant treasurer. He took advantage of his position by programming the company's payroll computer to pay himself hundreds of thousands extra annually. The company said he then hid the depleted cash by forging internal and vendor statements to show higher costs at store operations. The missing money wasn't noticed by Frisch's because they were recorded as expenses spread throughout the years and across almost all the stores. Hudson made unauthorized wire or automated transfers of funds from Frisch's bank accounts for his own benefit.

Hudson didn't seem to rationalize his actions. It appears he committed the fraud because he could do so by virtue of his position in the company, the trust placed in him by management, and, in all likelihood, the absence of effective internal controls meant he was able to get away with it for seven years.

Were there red flags that fraud was occurring at Frisch's? Company officials say no, yet the signs were there if the company looked hard enough. Consider the following:

- Hudson was helpful to others; somehow, he ended up doing some of the work for colleagues that might have exposed the theft. He built confidence to leverage the possible disclosure of the fraud by fellow employees.
- No one seemed to review the underlying documentation evidencing the fraud. A routine review of records following the fraud uncovered discrepancies when a new worker conducting an internal audit got credit card transaction records from the processing company that didn't coincide with Hudson's records.
- While Hudson didn't have a flashy car or expensive home that might have raised red flags, fellow employees knew he gambled a lot from the pictures he sent.

On September 22, 2016, Hudson pleaded guilty in federal district court in Ohio to charges of wire fraud and filing a false tax return and was sentenced to 60 months in prison, three years of supervised release, and ordered, among other things, to pay restitution to Frisch's in the amount of approximately $3.1 million. On August 4, 2017, the SEC announced fraud charges against Hudson. Among other charges, it is alleged that Hudson falsely certified to Frisch's CFO that the company's internal control over financial reporting for which he was responsible was effective. To settle the SEC's charges, Hudson agreed to the entry of a judgment imposing permanent injunctions, an officer-and-director bar, and ordering him liable for disgorgement of approximately $3.9 million, payment of which is deemed satisfied by the restitution ordered in the parallel federal criminal case. As a result of Hudson's felony conviction, he was immediately suspended from appearing and practicing before the SEC as an accountant, which includes not participating in the financial reporting or audits of public companies.

Fraud Considerations and Risk Assessment

LO 5-3

Describe fraud risk assessment procedures and red flags which might indicate that an individual may be committing fraud, or susceptible to it.

Fraud Risk Assessment

Fraud considerations in an audit require that the auditor should evaluate the risk of fraud, including the effectiveness of internal controls, and communicate with those charged with governance responsibilities about fraud. Most of the requirements of AU-C 240 call for the auditor to engage in risk assessment during the audit. Actually, the assessment of risk starts with an evaluation of evidence about the potential client before agreeing to do the audit. One important step is to communicate with the predecessor auditor to find out the reasons for the firing or the reasons for no longer servicing the client. Of particular importance is assessing the integrity of the top management and key accounting personnel. If an auditor concludes that they cannot trust management, they cannot accept the engagement. The successor auditor also should clarify with the predecessor whether there were any differences of opinion with management over the application of accounting principles and how these were handled, including the role of the audit committee.

Fraud risk assessment depends in large part on maintaining professional skepticism when evaluating the reliability of audit evidence obtained and assessing whether a material misstatement due to fraud exists. In making the assessment, of course, the auditor should not approach the audit with an attitude toward management of "You are crooks. Prove me wrong." Instead, a healthy attitude is one that informs the management in word and deed that the auditor's responsibility is to ask the tough questions, thoroughly examine relevant documentation, and probe to determine whether the organization culture promotes ethical decision making and whether there is support for financial statement amounts and disclosures.

AU-C 240 identifies the broad goals of fraud risk assessment as to (1) make inquiries of management and others within the organization to obtain their views about the risks of fraud and how they are addressed; (2) consider any unusual or unexpected relationships that have been identified in performing analytical procedures (i.e., financial statement comparisons over time and ratio analysis) in planning the audit; (3) consider whether one or more fraud risk factors exist; and (4) consider other information (i.e., interim financial results and factors associated with the acceptance of the client) that may be helpful in identifying risks of material misstatement due to fraud.

Assessing Management: Red Flags

As previously discussed, AU-C 240 states that the primary responsibility for uncovering fraud lies with the client's management team. One of the reasons that fraud can be very difficult to detect by both internal client personnel and external auditors is due to the potential of collusion by senior executives allowing them to override existing internal controls. This begs the question as to whether there are ways to identify individuals who are more likely than others to commit fraud.

Is There a Dark Triad Personality Risk?

Some evidence exists that there may be certain personality types that make it more likely fraud will occur and, if so, auditors should consider the risk that the existence of such personality types in top management may compromise the internal controls over financial reporting and lead to financial fraud.

Epstein and Ramamoorti discuss the existence of *the dark triad* deviant personalities, "whose behaviors may imply different risk profiles for audit—and financial reporting fraud—risk assessments, engagement planning, and audit execution." They suggest that "the existence and prevalence within the executive ranks of so-called dark triad personalities challenge the logic of applying the most commonly cited fraud risk models" including the Cressey Fraud Triangle. The authors identify three personality types: narcissism, Machiavellianism, and psychopathy.[16]

Kari Joseph Olsen conducted research into personality characteristics and accounting and found there is a growing prevalence of individuals with narcissistic personality tendencies, today. Narcissistic personalities can bias cognitive processing to suit a person's self-view. These persons are obsessed with power, prestige, and vanity and are mentally unable to see the destructive damage they cause to themselves and others. Olsen asks: Do narcissistic personality tendencies of the CEO influence and motivate accounting decisions? His research suggests that earnings per share is a potential avenue through which narcissistic CEOs can receive needed praise and affirmation to support their inflated sense of self-importance.[17]

Journalist Jay Ronson interviewed Al Dunlap, former CEO of Sunbeam, who was responsible for a turnaround at the company best illustrated by an increase in earnings per share (EPS) from $12.50, on the day he was hired in 1997, to a peak of $52.50 in 1998 when the board doubled his salary to $2 million. Dunlap gained the nickname "Chainsaw Al" because of his "gleeful fondness for firing people and shutting down factories." That worked at first to improve the earnings outlook, but Dunlap hit a snag once those maneuvers had all been played out. He turned to fraudulent techniques to inflate earnings including recording bogus revenue. Ronson observed that Dunlap "had a 'Grandiose sense of self-worth'—which would have been a hard one for him to deny because he was standing underneath a giant oil painting of himself." When asked about it, Dunlap said: "You've got to like yourself if you're going to be a success."[18]

Research conducted on opportunistic behavior (earnings management and fraud) in accounting choices suggests that internal motivations, specifically the emotions and the Machiavellianism personality traits, influence choices that are made.[19] Former HealthSouth CEO Richard Scrushy acted like a bully in pressuring a series of CFOs to go along with a $2.7 billion fraud undertaken by recording fake revenues on the company's books over six years and correspondingly adjusting the balance sheets and paper trails.

Epstein and Ramamoorti point out that Machiavellians are calculating and cunning and they use charm, friendliness, self-disclosure, guilt, and pressure to get what they want. Former HealthSouth CFO Aaron Beam writes that Scrushy was a charismatic leader who could get employees to follow him either through charm, encouragement, or outright intimidation.[20] In a sense, such behavior reflects an authoritarian bias as discussed in **Chapter 2**.

Dr. Alejandro Adrian LeMon suggests that psychopaths are fascinating, impressive, and charming. They are articulate and exude confidence. Oftentimes thought of as sociopaths, they are controlling and manipulative. As a co-worker, they are unethical and willing to use you for their own personal gain, even it means ruining your reputation. They are also master liars, highly successful, and use sophisticated methods to achieve their high ambitions. According to LeMon, one example of a high-profile psychopath is Jeffrey Skilling, the former president of Enron. Skilling sold shares of his company's stock while already having inside information of Enron's impending bankruptcy. He knew many families would lose their lifetime savings, their jobs, and their homes. But that did not stop him from misleading investors and his employees. In his view, he was far more important than the well-being of others. Not once did Skilling express genuine remorse or guilt for his crimes in court.[21]

Epstein and Ramamoorti state that the existence of psychopaths in corporate management suggests that auditors might find it useful to incorporate the "dark triad personality risk" factor into their risk assessments to better identify when fraud might be present. It is common for auditors to use checklists to watch out for the elements of the fraud triangle and use such indications when making decisions about audit scope.[22] We agree with the authors that auditors should consider the personality type when dealing with management. Being on the lookout for certain behavioral traits may raise red flags sooner and enable the auditors to better assess the risk of fraud because such traits may be indicators of the incentive to commit fraud. However, as the saying goes, the devil is in the details.

Tyco Fraud

In a "60 Minutes" interview, Dennis Kozlowski, the former CEO of Tyco, explained to Morley Safer that his motivation to steal from the company was to keep up with "the masters of the universe." This meant keeping up with other CEOs of large and successful companies that had pay packages in the hundreds of millions. He rationalized his actions by claiming that he wasn't doing anything different from what was done by his predecessor. In 2005, a jury found that Kozlowski and ex-CFO Marc Swartz stole about $137 million from Tyco in unauthorized compensation and made $410 million from the sale of inflated stock.

The corporate governance system at Tyco completely broke down, thereby creating the opportunity for fraud to occur and thrive. Most members of Tyco's board of directors benefited personally as a result of Tyco's practices. For example, one board member worked for a law firm that "just happened" to receive as much as $2 million in business from Tyco. This person's pay at the law firm was linked to the amount of work that he helped bring in from Tyco.

Obviously, when the fraud is perpetrated by the CEO or CFO, as was the case with Tyco, access is a given. Then it is just a matter of circumventing the controls or overriding them or, in the case of Kozlowski, enlisting the aid of others in the organization to hide what was going on.

We believe it's fair to characterize Kozlowski as having a narcissistic personality. He had an inflated view of himself and cultivated others in the company to view him the same way. Kozlowski was generous with his lieutenants because he thought they would be loyal to the boss. He was obsessed with his own self-worth, made decisions that infected the culture of the company, and failed to see how his actions were destructive, not only to himself but to Mark Swartz, board members, and the company.

LO 5-4

Describe the responsibilities of the External Auditor, Board of Directors, and Company Management in regard to internal controls over financial reporting (ICFR).

Internal Controls Over Financial Reporting

The risk that internal controls will not help prevent or detect a material misstatement in the financial statements is a critical evaluation to provide reasonable assurance that the statements are free of error or fraud. The system of internal controls and whether it operates as intended enables the auditor to gain either confidence about the internal processing of transactions, which is fine, or doubt, which the auditor should pursue.

Building on the description of the control environment in the COSO internal control framework first discussed in **Chapter 3**, the auditor should assess:

- Whether management's philosophy and operating style promote effective internal control over financial reporting;
- Whether sound integrity and ethical values, particularly of top management, are developed and understood; and
- Whether the board or audit committee understands and exercises oversight responsibility over financial reporting and internal control.

A direct relationship exists between the degree of risk that a material weakness could exist in a particular area of the company's internal control over financial reporting (ICFR) and the amount of audit attention that should be devoted to that area. In addition, the risk that a company's internal control over financial reporting will fail to prevent or detect material misstatement caused by fraud usually is higher than the risk of failure to prevent or detect error. As discussed in the ethics reflection opening this chapter, the PCAOB recommends auditors pay special attention to this area due to the high level of audit deficiencies found surrounding ICFR through their audit inspections. More simply put, the auditor should focus more of their attention on the areas of highest risk.

According to the PCAOB Staff Inspection Brief, audit deficiencies related to noncompliance with AS 2201, *An Audit of Internal Control Over Financial Reporting That is Integrated with An Audit of Financial Statements*, continue to be the most frequently identified deficiencies. The most frequent ICFR deficiencies identified related to insufficient testing of the design and operating effectiveness of selected controls, particularly with a review element. Specifically, some auditors did not evaluate the nature and/or the appropriateness of the procedures performed by management during the review, including the criteria used to identify matters for investigation and the actions taken in investigating and resolving such matters.[23]

ICFR Failures at Medicis

On September 24, 2008, Medicis announced that the Audit Committee of its Board of Directors determined that the quarterly periods in fiscal years 2003 through 2007 and the first two quarters of 2008, will need to be restated and should no longer be relied upon including EY's audit reports on the financial statements and effectiveness of ICFR for the related periods. The restatements relate to a modification in the Company's technical interpretation of GAAP relating to sales return.

Medicis restated its net revenues and diluted net income (loss) per share on Form 10/KA for the year ended December 31, 2007, as shown in **Exhibit 5.6**, including transition to calendar-year end reporting at 12/31/05. The information is taken from the PCAOB's findings as a result of its inspection of EY's audits of Medicis and other determinations.[24]

EXHIBIT 5.6   Medicis Form 10K/A (in millions) for the Year-Ended December 31, 2007

Net revenues (in millions)	Fiscal Year-Ended 12-31-2007	Fiscal Year-Ended 12-31-2006	Fiscal Year-Ended 12-31-2005	Fiscal Year-Ended 06-30-2005	Fiscal Year-Ended 06-30-2004	Fiscal Year-Ended 06-30-2003
Reported	$464.7	$349.2	$164.0	$376.9	$303.7	$247.5
Adjustment	(7.3)	44.0	1.3	(11.2)	11.5	(37.2)
Restated	$457.4	$393.2	$165.3	$365.7	$315.2	$210.3

Diluted net income (loss) per share (in dollars)	Fiscal Year-Ended 12-31-2007	Fiscal Year-Ended 12-31-2006	Fiscal Year-Ended 12-31-2005	Fiscal Year-Ended 06-30-2005	Fiscal Year-Ended 06-30-2004	Fiscal Year-Ended 06-30-2003
Reported	$1.14	($1.39)	$0.76	$1.01	$0.52	$0.84
Adjustment	(0.06)	0.51	0.03	(0.09)	0.06	(0.34)
Restated	$1.08	($0.88)	$0.79	$0.92	$0.58	$0.50

Overview of the Case

The issuance of materially misstated financial statements by Medicis Pharmaceutical Corporation for the 2003 through 2007 fiscal years and the first two quarters of 2008 illustrates what can happen when audits fail to follow PCAOB standards and auditors do not conduct an audit with due care and exercise appropriate professional skepticism. Medicis used an accounting technique not acceptable under GAAP to reserve for its product returns. The company reserved for most of its estimated product returns at the cost of replacing the product rather than the correct method based on gross sales price. Since estimated costs were below sales value, the company overstated net revenues, net income, and EPS in some years with reversal effects in others thereby creating material misstatements in most of the years reported between 2003 and 2007.

Ernst & Young

Ernst & Young and its auditors were cited by the PCAOB for deficient audits and disciplined pursuant to SOX. The auditors included: Jeffrey S. Anderson, lead engagement auditor; Robert H. Thibault, the independent review partner; Ronald Butler, Jr., a second partner supervised by Anderson; and Thomas A. Christie, also supervised by Anderson. The external auditors failed to obtain sufficient competent evidential matter to support the accounting, accepted management's representations, ignored its own internal audit quality review (AQR) of the client, thereby violating PCAOB's quality control requirements (QC Section 20), and issued unqualified audit reports that the financial statements presented fairly, in all material respects, Medicis's financial position and results of operations in conformity with GAAP in each of the periods audited. The PCAOB inspected EY's audits of Medicis in some of those years, discovered mistakes in the application of GAAP, and highlighted the deficiencies in the audits in its inspection report.

The deficiencies in EY's audit can be summarized as follows:

- Failed to follow GAAS.
- Relied on management representations rather than independently gathered audit evidence.
- Developed alternative accounting methods for the reserve for sales returns in lieu of the client doing so and didn't inform the client of the alternative.
- Failed to act on its own AQR and correct deficiencies in its audit of Medicis.
- Issued unqualified opinions when it knew there were material misstatements in the financial statements.

PCAOB Actions

The PCAOB censured EY; barred Anderson and Thibault from being associated with a registered public accounting firm; censured Butler and Christie; and imposed civil monetary penalties in the amounts of $2 million as to EY, $50,000 as to Anderson, $25,000 as to Thibault, and $25,000 as to Butler. All parties violated PCAOB rules and auditing standards related to EY's audits of the December 31, 2005, 2006, and 2007, financial statements of Medicis and in the consultation memorandum concerning Medicis' accounting for products returns stemming from EY's AQR of the December 31, 2005, Medicis audit in 2006.

The failure of EY, Anderson, and Christie to comply with PCAOB standards meant they improperly authorized the issuance of EY's audit report dated February 26, 2008, on Medicis' financial statements for the year-ended December 31, 2007, which incorrectly expressed an unqualified opinion that the financial statements presented fairly, in all material respects, Medicis' financial position and results of operations in conformity with GAAP.

Audit Committee Responsibilities for Fraud Risk Assessment

COSO's enterprise risk management framework (ERM) also discussed in Chapter 3, is designed to help an entity get where it wants to go in creating a strong internal control environment and avoid pitfalls and surprises along the way. ERM is defined as a process, effected by an entity's board of directors, management, and other personnel and applied in strategy settings and across the enterprise, designed to identify potential events that may affect the entity and to manage risk within its risk appetite. ERM adds a number of strategic issues, including objective setting by management, identification of risks and opportunities affecting achievement of an entity's objectives, and risk responses selected by management to align risk tolerance and risk appetite.

The audit committee should evaluate management's identification of fraud risks, implementation of antifraud measures, and creation of the appropriate tone at the top. Active oversight by the audit committee can help reinforce management's commitment to create a culture with "zero tolerance" for fraud. An entity's audit committee also should ensure that senior management (in particular, the CEO and CFO) implements appropriate fraud deterrence and prevention measures to better protect investors, employees, and other stakeholders. Evaluation and oversight not only helps ensure that senior management fulfills its responsibility but also can serve as a deterrent to senior management engaging in fraudulent activity (i.e., by ensuring an environment is created whereby any attempt by senior management to involve employees in committing or concealing fraud would lead promptly to reports from such employees to appropriate persons, including the audit committee).

The audit committee also plays an important role in helping those charged with governance fulfill their oversight responsibilities with respect to the entity's financial reporting process and the system of internal control. In exercising this oversight responsibility, the audit committee should consider the potential for management override of controls or other inappropriate influence over the financial reporting process. Some examples follow:

- Solicit the views of the internal auditors and independent auditors with respect to management's involvement in the financial reporting process and, in particular, the ability of management to override information processed by the entity's financial reporting system (e.g., the ability of management or others to initiate or record nonstandard journal entries).
- Consider reviewing the entity's reported information for reasonableness compared with prior or forecasted results, as well as with peers or industry averages.
- Information received in communications from the independent auditors can assist the audit committee in assessing the strength of the entity's internal control and the potential for fraudulent financial reporting.

As part of its oversight responsibilities, the audit committee should encourage management to provide a mechanism for employees to report concerns about unethical behavior, actual or suspected fraud, or violations of the entity's code of conduct or ethics policy and receive periodic reports describing the nature, status, and eventual disposition of any fraud or unethical conduct. A summary of the activity, follow-up, and disposition also should be provided to all of those charged with governance.

Auditor's Communication with Those Charged with Governance

Whenever the auditor has determined that there is evidence that fraud may exist, the matter should be brought to the attention of the appropriate level of management. AU-C 240 requires such communication even if the matter might be considered inconsequential, such as a minor misappropriation by an employee. Fraud (whether caused by senior management or other employees) that causes a material misstatement of the financial statements should be reported directly to those charged with governance. In addition, the auditor should reach an understanding with those charged with governance regarding the nature and extent of communications with them about misappropriations perpetrated by lower-level employees.

The Auditor's Communication With Those Charged With Governance (AU-C Section 260) identifies the auditor's communication responsibilities to strengthen governance:

- The auditor has access to the audit committee as necessary.
- The chair of the audit committee meets with the auditor periodically.
- The audit committee meets with the auditor without management at least annually unless prohibited by law or regulation.

Given the importance of an independent audit in detecting fraud in financial statements, the auditor should discuss with the audit committee relationships that create threats to auditor independence and the related safeguards that have been applied to eliminate or reduce those threats to an acceptable level.

Another important area for communication is about accounting estimates. Certain accounting estimates are particularly sensitive because of their significance to the financial statements and because of the possibility that future events affecting them may differ significantly from management's current judgments. In communicating with those charged with governance about the process used by management in formulating sensitive estimates, including fair value estimates, and about the basis for the auditor's conclusions regarding the reasonableness of those estimates, the auditor should consider the following:

- The nature of significant assumptions;
- The degree of subjectivity involved in the development of the assumptions; and
- The relative materiality of the items being measured to the financial statements as a whole.

If the auditor, as a result of the assessment of the risks of material misstatement, has identified such risks due to fraud that have continuing control implications, the auditor should consider whether these risks represent significant deficiencies or material weaknesses in the entity's internal control that should be communicated to management and those charged with governance. Consideration should also be given to whether the absence of or deficiencies in controls to prevent, deter, and detect fraud represent significant deficiencies or material weaknesses that should be communicated to management and those charged with governance.

Management Representations and Financial Statement Certifications

Section 302 of SOX requires certification of the financial statements by the CFO and CEO for public companies. For many years, the AICPA has required written representations as part of audit evidence gathered. One way to deal with the problem that some significant errors may not be detected, although not foolproof, is to obtain written representations (also known as management representations or client representations) to confirm certain matters and support other evidence obtained during the audit. AU-C Section 580, *Written Representations,* requires representations by the CEO, the CFO, and other appropriate officers.[25] The purpose of the representation is for management to acknowledge its responsibility for the fair presentation of financial statements, the design and implementation of programs and controls to prevent and detect fraud, whether management has knowledge of any allegations of fraud or suspected fraud affecting the entity, and whether any fraud that exists could have a material effect on the financial statements.

The representations generally include:

- A statement that the client has provided access to all known information that bears on the fair presentation of the financial statements.
- Confirmation that management has performed an assessment of the effectiveness of internal control over financial reporting based on criteria established in the Internal Control–Integrated Framework issued by COSO.
- Conclusions as to whether the company has maintained an effective ICFR.
- Disclosure of any deficiencies in the design or operation of ICFR.

Qwest Communications International Inc.

False representations occurred in one of the largest frauds back in the late 1990s and early 2000s at Qwest Communications International Inc. that certainly contributed to the SEC's inclusion of Section 302 in SOX. From at least April 1, 1999, through March 31, 2002, senior executives and others at Qwest engaged in a massive financial fraud that hid from the investing public the true source of the company's revenue and earnings growth, caused the company to fraudulently report approximately $3 billion of revenue, and facilitated the company's June 2000 merger with U.S. West. Joseph P. Nacchio, Qwest's former CEO, and the company's two former CFOs, Robert S. Woodruff and Robin R. Szeliga, directed the fraudulent scheme to carry out Nacchio's aggressive and rigid targets for revenue and earnings growth. Extreme pressure was placed on subordinate Qwest executives to meet these aggressive targets at all costs and the pressure spread throughout the company, causing a "culture of fear." For example, at a January 2001 all-employee meeting, Nacchio stated, "[T]he most important thing we do is meet our numbers. It's more important than any individual product, it's more important than any individual philosophy, it's more important than any individual cultural change we're making. We stop everything else when we don't make the numbers."[26]

The pressure on employees to meet revenue and earnings targets was intense. The opportunity to manipulate the numbers was there and carried out by top management. Qwest fraudulently and repeatedly relied on immediate revenue recognition from one-time sales of assets known as "IRUs" and certain equipment while falsely claiming to the investing public that the revenue was recurring. By hiding non-recurring revenue and making false and misleading public statements, Nacchio, Woodruff, and Szeliga fraudulently and materially misrepresented Qwest's performance and growth to the investing public.

Nacchio had consistently said that he did nothing wrong and he did not instruct anyone else to do anything wrong during his tenure at Qwest. One has to wonder why, then, did he sell $52 million worth of Qwest shares in April and May 2001 after receiving private warnings that the company would miss revenue targets? Nacchio was found guilty by the U.S. Justice Department of insider trading and received a prison sentence of six years and a $19 million fine. Nacchio's sentence was reduced by about 1 ½ years for good behavior and participation in a residential drug-treatment program.

As for Robin Szeliga, she settled with the SEC for her role in the fraud. Her mistake was signing the relevant filings with the SEC as the CFO of Qwest. Szeliga signed all of Qwest's materially false 10-Q reports filed with the SEC, and its materially false 10-K annual reports for 2000 and 2001. She signed false management representation letters to Qwest's outside auditors. She drafted and reviewed all earnings releases and spoke at financial analyst calls.

Section 302 SOX certifications from the CEO and CFO is the SEC's way to regulate management representations in light of frauds at companies such as Qwest. It's interesting to consider whether Szeliga (and Nacchio) would have falsely certified the financial statements and the design and effectiveness of disclosure controls and procedures had the SOX requirement been in effect during the fraud period.

Audit Report and Auditing Standards

LO 5-5
Explain the standards for audit reports.

Background

The free market for stocks and bonds can only exist if there is sharing of reliable financial information, strengthened by information that is transparent and unbiased. The external audit is intended to enhance the confidence that users can place on the financial statements that have been prepared by management. Since 1926 the New York Stock Exchange (NYSE) has required an auditor's report with public companies' financial statements. Then the Securities Exchange Act of 1934, which is discussed further in **Chapter 8**, required all public companies to have an independent auditor's report on annual financial statements. For both public and nonpublic entities, the auditor's report on financial statements and related disclosures provides (or disclaims) an opinion on whether the entity's financial statements and related disclosures are presented in accordance with generally accepted accounting principles in the United States (AICPA report) or based on an evaluation of the accounting principles used (PCAOB report). The PCAOB report takes a broader view because public companies with global operations may be required to follow International Financial Reporting Standards (IFRS) as well as the accounting principles in the home country.

Audit Report

The auditors' unmodified or standard report for nonpublic companies under the AICPA requirements is presented in **Exhibit 5.7**. The auditors' unqualified report for public companies under the PCAOB requirements is presented in **Exhibit 5.8**.

EXHIBIT 5.7   **Unmodified Opinion for Nonpublic Companies (SAS 134 Effective 12/15/2021, early adoption permitted)**

[Appropriate Addressee] XYZ Company

Report on the Audit of the Financial Statements[1]

Opinion

We have audited the financial statements of XYZ Company, which comprise the balance sheets as of December 31, 2021, 2020, and 2019, and the related statements of income, changes in stockholders' equity, and cash flows for the years then ended, and the related notes to the financial statements.

In our opinion, the accompanying financial statements present fairly, in all material respects, the financial position of XYZ Company as of December 31, 2021, 2020, and 2019, and the results of its operations and its cash flows for the years then ended in accordance with accounting principles generally accepted in the United States of America.

Basis for Opinion

We conducted our audits in accordance with auditing standards generally accepted in the United States of America (GAAS). Our responsibilities under those standards are further described in the Auditor's Responsibilities for the Audit of the Financial Statements section of our report. We are required to be independent of XYZ Company and to meet our other ethical responsibilities, in accordance with the relevant ethical requirements relating to our audits. We believe that the audit evidence we have obtained is sufficient and appropriate to provide a basis for our audit opinion.

Key Audit Matters [if engaged to report on them]

Key audit matters are those matters that were communicated with those charged with governance and, in our professional judgment, were of most significance in our audit of the financial statements of the current period. These matters were addressed in the context of our audit of the financial statements as a whole, and in forming our opinion thereon, and we do not provide a separate opinion on these matters.

Responsibilities of Management for the Financial Statements

Management is responsible for the preparation and fair presentation of the financial statements in accordance with accounting principles generally accepted in the United States of America, and for the design, implementation, and maintenance of internal control relevant to the preparation and fair presentation of financial statements that are free from material misstatement, whether due to fraud or error.

In preparing the financial statements, management is required to evaluate whether there are conditions or events, considered in the aggregate, that raise substantial doubt about XYZ Company's ability to continue as a going concern for [insert the time period set by the applicable financial reporting framework].

Auditor's Responsibilities for the Audit of the Financial Statements

Our objectives are to obtain reasonable assurance about whether the financial statements as a whole are free from material misstatement, whether due to fraud or error, and to issue an auditor's report that includes our opinion. Reasonable assurance is a high level of assurance but is not absolute assurance and therefore is not a guarantee that an audit conducted in accordance with GAAS will always detect a material misstatement when it exists. The risk of not detecting a material misstatement resulting from fraud is higher than for one resulting from error, as fraud may involve collusion, forgery, intentional omissions, misrepresentations, or the override of internal control. Misstatements are considered material if, individually or in the aggregate, they could reasonably be expected to influence the economic decisions of users made on the basis of these financial statements.

(continued)

In performing an audit in accordance with GAAS, we:

- Exercise professional judgment and maintain professional skepticism throughout the audit.
- Identify and assess the risks of material misstatement of the financial statements, whether due to fraud or error, and design and perform audit procedures responsive to those risks. Such procedures include examining, on a test basis, evidence regarding the amounts and disclosures in the financial statements.
- Obtain an understanding of internal control relevant to the audit in order to design audit procedures that are appropriate in the circumstances, but not for the purpose of expressing an opinion on the effectiveness of XYZ Company's internal control. Accordingly, no such opinion is expressed.[2]
- Evaluate the appropriateness of accounting policies used and the reasonableness of significant accounting estimates made by management, as well as evaluate the overall presentation of the financial statements.
- Conclude whether, in our judgment, there are conditions or events, considered in the aggregate, that raise substantial doubt about XYZ Company's ability to continue as a going concern for a reasonable period of time.

Forming an Opinion and Reporting on Financial Statements

We are required to communicate with those charged with governance regarding, among other matters, the planned scope and timing of the audit, significant audit findings, and certain internal control–related matters that we identified during the audit.

Report on Other Legal and Regulatory Requirements

[The form and content of this section of the auditor's report would vary depending on the nature of the auditor's other reporting responsibilities.]

[Signature of the auditor's firm]

[City and state where the auditor's report is issued]

[Date of the auditor's report]

[1] The subtitle "Report on the Audit of the Financial Statements" is unnecessary in circumstances in which the second subtitle, "Report on Other Legal and Regulatory Requirements," is not applicable.

[2] In circumstances in which the auditor also has a responsibility to express an opinion on the effectiveness of internal control in conjunction with the audit of the financial statements, omit the following: "but not for the purpose of expressing an opinion on the effectiveness of XYZ Company's internal control. Accordingly, no such opinion is expressed."

EXHIBIT 5.8   The Auditors' Unqualified Report Including Critical Audit Matters

Report of Independent Registered Public Accounting Firm

To the shareholders and the board of directors of ABC Company.

Opinion on the Financial Statements

We have audited the accompanying balance sheets of ABC Company (the "Company") as of December 31, 2021 and 2020, the related statements of [titles of the financial statements, e.g., income, comprehensive income, stockholders' equity, and cash flows] for each of the three years in the period ended December 31, 2021, and the related notes [and schedules] (collectively referred to as the "financial statements"). In our opinion, the financial statements present fairly, in all material respects, the financial position of the Company as of [at] December 31, 2021 and 2020, and the results of its operations and its cash flows for each of the three years in the period ended December 31, 2021, in conformity with [the applicable financial reporting framework].

Basis for Opinion

These financial statements are the responsibility of the Company's management. Our responsibility is to express an opinion on the Company's financial statements based on our audits. We are a public accounting firm registered with the Public Company Accounting Oversight Board (United States) ("PCAOB") and are required to be independent with respect to the Company in accordance with the U.S. federal securities laws and the applicable rules and regulations of the Securities Exchange Commission and the PCAOB.

We conducted our audits in accordance with the standards of the PCAOB. Those standards require that we plan and perform the audit to obtain reasonable assurance about whether the financial statements are free of material misstatement, whether due to error or fraud. Our audits included performing procedures to assess the risks of material misstatement of the financial statements, whether due to error or fraud, and performing procedures that respond to those risks. Such procedures included examining, on a test basis, evidence regarding the amounts and disclosures in the financial statements. Our audits also included evaluating the accounting principles used and significant estimates made by management, as well as evaluating the overall presentation of the financial statements. We believe that our audits provide a reasonable basis for our opinion.

Critical Audit Matters [if applicable]

The critical audit matters communicated below are matters arising from the current period audit of the financial statements that were communicated or required to be communicated to the audit committee and that: (1) relate to accounts or disclosures that are material to the financial statements and (2) involved our especially challenging, subjective, or complex judgments. The communication of critical audit matters does not alter in any way our opinion on the financial statements, taken as a whole, and we are not, by communicating the critical audit matters below, providing separate opinions on the critical audit matters or on the accounts or disclosures to which they relate.

[Include critical audit matters]

[Signature]

We have served as the Company's auditor since [year].

[City and State or Country]

[Date]

Differences exist between the unmodified report used for nonpublic companies' audits and the PCAOB unqualified audit report including:

- The PCAOB report is titled Report of Independent Registered Public Accounting Firm, and the AICPA report is titled Report on the Audit of Financial Statements.
- Reference to whether the financial statements are free of material misstatement, whether due to error or fraud, appears in the Basis for Opinion section of the PCAOB report, but in a separate section titled Auditor's Responsibility for the Audit of the Financial Statements in the AICPA report.
- The PCAOB report language specifically references the independence requirement under relevant laws and rules of the SEC and PCAOB in the Basis for Opinion Section; the AICPA report in the Basis of Opinion section references both a requirement for independence, and of meeting other ethical responsibilities, in accordance with the relevant ethical requirements relating to audits. The PCAOB report is silent as to ethics.
- The AICPA report specifically references considering the internal controls in order to design audit procedure but not to express an opinion; the PCAOB report doesn't specifically mention internal controls but addresses the role of audit procedures. The internal control report of management is required for public companies as a separate report by SOX Section 404.
- The PCAOB report that was revised on June 1, 2017, now includes a separate section on Critical Audit Matters (CAMs) that are not included in the AICPA report. However, an auditor can be hired to report on Key Audit Matters (KAMs) in conjunction with the audit of a privately held company in accordance with AU-C 701. CAMs are similar to, but not identical to KAMs.
- The PCAOB report includes a statement disclosing the year in which the auditor began serving consecutively as the company's auditor; no such statement exists in the AICPA report.

PCAOB AS 1301: Communications with Audit Committees[27]

Previously, we discussed auditor communications with those charged with governance as it pertains to AICPA standards. In this section, we address exactly what should be communicated between the registered public accounting firm and the audit committee of a public entity under PCAOB standards. The following items should be communicated to ensure the audit committee is aware of situations that may affect the auditors' evaluation of accounting and financial reporting results and problems with management in carrying out the audit.

1. *Significant accounting policies and practices.* Significant accounting policies include management's initial selection of, or changes in, significant accounting policies or the application of such policies in the current period and the effect on financial statements or disclosures of significant accounting policies in controversial areas or areas for which there is a lack of authoritative guidance, consensus, or diversity in practice.

2. *Critical accounting policies and practices.* All critical accounting policies and practices to be used should be communicated to the audit committee, including the reasons certain policies and practices are considered critical and how current and future events might affect the determination of whether certain policies are considered critical.

3. *Critical accounting estimates.* A description of the process management used to develop critical accounting estimates should be communicated, along with management's significant assumptions used in critical accounting estimates that have a high degree of subjectivity. Additional communications include any significant changes that management made to the processes used to develop critical accounting estimates or significant assumptions, a description of management's reasons for the changes, and the effects of the changes on the financial statements.

4. *Significant unusual transactions.* Significant unusual transactions include those that are outside the normal course of business for the company or that otherwise appear to be unusual due to their timing, size, or nature and the policies and practices management used to account for significant unusual transactions.

The auditor should communicate to the audit committee a variety of matters dealing with the quality of the company's financial reporting including, for example, situations in which the auditor identified bias in management's judgments about the amounts and disclosures in the financial statements. Also, the results of the auditor's evaluation of the differences between estimates best supported by the audit evidence and estimates included in the financial statements, which are individually reasonable but that indicate a possible bias on the part of the company's management.

The auditor should communicate to the audit committee any disagreements with management about matters, whether or not satisfactorily resolved, that individually or in the aggregate could be significant to the company's financial statements or the auditor's report. Disagreements with management do not include differences of opinion based on incomplete facts or preliminary information that are later resolved by the auditor obtaining additional relevant facts or information prior to the issuance of the auditor's report.

The auditor should communicate to the audit committee any significant difficulties encountered during the audit. Significant difficulties encountered during the audit include, but are not limited to:

- Significant delays by management, the unavailability of company personnel, or an unwillingness by management to provide information needed for the auditor to perform audit procedures.
- An unreasonably brief time within which to complete the audit.
- Unexpected extensive effort required by the auditor to obtain sufficient appropriate audit evidence.
- Unreasonable management restrictions encountered by the auditor on the conduct of the audit.
- Management's unwillingness to make or extend its assessment of the company's ability to continue as a going concern when requested by the auditor.

Audit committee communications are an essential part of an effective governance system and a key ingredient in creating an ethical organization environment. Open communications between the auditor and audit committee are essential to supporting the financial reporting oversight role assigned to the audit committee under SOX. The audit committee plays a critical role in resolving differences between the auditor and management and supporting the goal of a fair presentation of the financial statements and efficient and effective internal controls over financial reporting.

PCAOB AS 3101: The Auditor's Report on an Audit of Financial Statements When the Auditor Expresses an Unqualified Opinion[28]

The new PCAOB audit report went into effect for audits of fiscal years ending on or after December 15, 2017, except for the requirements related to critical audit matters (CAMs), which is effective for audits of fiscal years ending on or after June 30, 2019, for large accelerated filers and for fiscal years ending on or after December 15, 2020, for all other companies to which the requirements apply.

Critical Audit Matters

The PCAOB rule for disclosing CAMs is designed to improve audit quality. In determining whether a matter to be disclosed involved especially challenging, subjective, or complex auditor judgment, the auditor should take into account, alone or in combination, the following factors, as well as other factors specific to the audit:

- The auditor's assessment of the risks of material misstatement, including significant risks;
- The degree of auditor judgment related to areas in the financial statements that involved the application of significant judgment or estimation by management, including estimates with significant measurement uncertainty;
- The nature and timing of significant unusual transactions and the extent of audit effort and judgment related to these transactions;
- The degree of auditor subjectivity in applying audit procedures to address the matter or in evaluating the results of those procedures;
- The nature and extent of audit effort required to address the matter, including the extent of specialized skill or knowledge needed or the nature of consultations outside the engagement team regarding the matter; and
- The nature of audit evidence obtained regarding the matter.

The auditor must communicate in the auditor's report CAMs or state that none were determined to exist. However, the PCAOB has expressed that they expect at least one CAM will be identified in each audit. Deloitte's analysis of accelerated filers for the fiscal year ending June 30, 2019, found an average of 1.8 CAM's identified per audit, with the majority being related to goodwill, intangible assets, revenue, and income taxes.[29] For each CAM, the auditor should:

- Identify the CAM;
- Describe the principal considerations that led the auditor to determine that the matter is a CAM;
- Describe how the CAM was addressed in the audit; and
- Refer to the relevant financial statement accounts or disclosures that relate to the CAM.

A sample of filing reviewed by the Journal of Accountancy from 2019 concluded that CPA firms are doing a thorough job in reporting CAM's and discussing them within the audit report.[30]

Deloitte points out that management and audit committees should consider the implications of the new CAM requirements and discuss them with their auditors. Here are a few items to consider:[31]

- What matters might be included in CAMs?
- How will management and audit committees engage with the auditor as CAMs are identified and the auditor's descriptions of the CAMs are developed and finalized?
- How will the timing of auditor communications with management and the audit committee accommodate the discussion of CAMs?
- How do the auditor's statements regarding CAMs compare to management's disclosures regarding the same matters?

The reason to communicate with investors about CAMs is to inform them of key areas of the audit that might not otherwise be disclosed. As Jermakowicz et al. observe, "Reducing the level of information asymmetry between management and investors could result in more efficient capital allocation and lower the average cost of capital. ... The result should be to elevate the overall level of confidence in audited financial reports."[32]

Disclosure of Engagement Partner and Certain Other Participants in Audits

On December 15, 2015, the PCAOB adopted new rules and amendments to its auditing standards about involvement in audits. This information will be filed with the PCAOB on a new form, Auditor Reporting of Certain Audit Participants ("Form AP") and will be searchable on the PCAOB's website. The rules require disclosure of:[33]

- The name of the engagement partner;
- The names, locations, and extent of participation of other accounting firms that took part in the group audit (i.e., network firms) if their work constituted 5 percent or more of the total group audit hours; and
- The number and aggregate extent of participation of all other accounting firms that took part in the group audit whose individual participation was less than 5 percent of the total group audit hours.

This requirement brings U.S. audits into line with international standards and practices. However, one difference is the International Auditing and Assurance Standards Board (IAASB) standards requires that engagement partners physically sign the audit report with their names instead of the name of the firms, as is done in the United States. The final PCAOB standard was a compromise from the original proposal that called for having the engagement partner sign the audit report. Those who argued against it say because more than one partner is typically involved in an engagement, why single out the engagement partner to sign the report? The CAQ warned of adverse outcomes. The CAQ emphasized that engagement partners must answer to their employers, regulators, firms, audit committees, and investors already. CAQ opined that these multiple layers of accountability provide a significant incentive for engagement partners to conduct high-quality audits in accordance with professional standards.

Knowing the names of the specific partners presumably helps the SEC when it investigates registered firms for possible rule violations. We believe this is sufficient for the SEC's needs and should not be appended to the audit report itself because the audit report is issued upon the authority of the firm and not the authority of the individual engagement partner.

Audit Opinions

AICPA audit standards provide that auditors can express an unmodified/unqualified opinion, a qualified opinion, an adverse opinion, or a disclaimer. An auditor also can withdraw from the engagement under restricted circumstances. The qualified opinion, adverse opinion, or disclaimer of opinion is a "modified" opinion.

Opinion Paragraph—Unmodified or Unqualified

An auditor should give an unmodified or unqualified opinion when the financial statements "present fairly" financial position, results of operations, and cash flows. Certain situations may call for adding an additional paragraph: either an emphasis-of-matter or other-matter paragraph as defined by AU-C 706.

An emphasis-of-matter paragraph is a paragraph in the auditor's report that refers to a matter appropriately presented or disclosed in the financial statements (e.g., going concern, litigation uncertainty, subsequent events, etc.). It is added when, in the auditor's professional judgment, the item is of such importance that it is fundamental to users' understanding of the financial statements. Some emphasis-of-matter paragraphs are required by AICPA standards and others are added at the discretion of the auditor.

An other-matter paragraph is a paragraph included in the auditor's report that refers to a matter other than those presented or disclosed in the financial statements that, in the auditors' professional judgment, is relevant to users' understanding of the audit, the auditor's responsibilities, or the auditor's report (e.g., supplemental information).

An emphasis-of-matter or other-matter paragraph follows the opinion paragraph and has a section heading of "Emphasis-of-Matter" or "Other-Matter" for the AICPA report.

The PCAOB report also allows for an "emphasis paragraph" that might explain the following matters:

- Significant transactions with related parties;
- Unusually important subsequent events;
- Accounting matters, other than those involving a change in accounting principles, affecting the comparability of the financial statements with those of the preceding period;
- An uncertainty relating to the future outcome of significant litigation or regulatory actions; and
- That the entity is a component of a larger business enterprise.

Opinion Paragraph—Modified

Recall that Rule 203 of the AICPA Code of Professional Conduct precludes rendering an opinion that states that the financial statements have been prepared in accordance with GAAP, or any statement that the auditor is not aware of any material modifications that should be made to such statements or data to make them conform with GAAP, if such statements or data contain any departure from an accounting principle that has a material effect on the statements or data taken as a whole. Instead, the auditor should modify the opinion and explain the GAAP deviation.

The auditor should modify the opinion in the auditor's report when (1) the auditor concludes, based on the audit evidence obtained, the financial statements as a whole are materially misstated; or (2) the auditor is unable to obtain sufficient appropriate audit evidence to conclude that the financial statements as a whole are free from material misstatement. The circumstances when each opinion is proper are discussed next.

A qualified opinion would be appropriate when (1) the auditor, having obtained sufficient appropriate audit evidence, concludes that misstatements, individually or in the aggregate, are material but not pervasive to the financial statements; or (2) the auditor is unable to obtain sufficient appropriate audit evidence on which to base the opinion, but the auditor concludes that the possible effects on the financial statements of undetected misstatements, if any, could be material but not pervasive.

An adverse opinion is proper when the auditor, having obtained sufficient appropriate audit evidence, concludes that misstatements, individually or in the aggregate, are both material and pervasive to the financial statements. Pervasive is a term used in the context of misstatements to describe the effects on the financial statements of misstatements, if any that are undetected due to an inability to obtain sufficient appropriate audit evidence. Pervasive effects on the financial statements require professional judgment by the auditor and are not generally confined to specific elements, accounts, or items of the financial statements, but if they are, they would represent or could represent a substantial proportion of the financial statements.

A disclaimer of opinion is warranted when the auditor is unable to obtain sufficient appropriate audit evidence on which to base the opinion, and the auditor concludes that the possible effects on the financial statements of undetected misstatements, if any, could be both material and pervasive.

For modifications, the audit report should include a separate paragraph that describes the matter giving rise to the modification. This paragraph should be placed immediately before the opinion paragraph in the auditor's report and include a heading such as "Basis for Qualified Opinion," "Basis for Adverse Opinion," or "Basis for Disclaimer of Opinion" as appropriate.

Exhibit 5.9 includes a summary of various paragraphs that can be included in the standard audit report and modified opinions.

EXHIBIT 5.9   Examples of Paragraphs in the Audit Report

Type of Report/ Opinion	Management's Responsibility	Auditor's Responsibility	Opinion	Emphasis-of-Matter OR Other-Matter
Unmodified Opinion				
Emphasis-of-Matter	Standard	Standard	Standard	Description
Going Concern Issue	Standard	Standard	Standard	Description
Consistent GAAP Application	Standard	Standard	Standard	Description
Modified Opinions				
Qualified	Standard	Include departure from GAAP or scope limitation	"Except for the [GAAP departure or effects of scope limitation] . . . the financial statements present fairly . . ."	
Adverse	Standard	Include substantial reasons for adverse opinion	". . . the financial statements do not present fairly . . ."	
Disclaimer	Omitted	Omitted	Changed to indicate that an opinion cannot be expressed on the financial statements and why	

PCAOB standards require that, in certain circumstances, the auditor include explanatory language (or an explanatory paragraph) in the auditor's report that, while not affecting the auditor's opinion on the financial statements, it would shine light on certain matters that may be of concern to the users of the statements now and into the future. Here are a few examples:

- There has been a change between periods in accounting principles or in the method of their application that has a material effect on the financial statements;
- A material misstatement in previously issued financial statements has been corrected;
- Management is required to report on the company's internal controls over financial reporting, but such reporting is not required to be audited, and the auditor has not been engaged to perform an audit of management's assessment of the effectiveness of the company's internal control over financial reporting; and
- Other information in a document containing audited financial statements is materially inconsistent with information appearing in the financial statements.

Withdrawal from the Engagement

From time to time, an auditor might consider withdrawing from an engagement. Withdrawal generally is not appropriate because an auditor is hired by the client to do an audit and render an opinion, not walk away from one's obligations when the going gets tough. However, if a significant conflict exists with management or the auditor decides that management cannot be trusted, then a withdrawal may be justified. Factors that affect the auditor's conclusion include the implication of the involvement of a member of management or those charged with governance in any misconduct. Trust issues are a matter of ethics. Once pressure builds up in the auditor–client relationship and it boils over, the auditor must consider whether the breakdown in the relationship has advanced to the point that any and all information provided by the client is suspect. An auditor should not allow themselves to be in the position of questioning the client's motives with every statement made and piece of evidence gathered. Withdrawal triggers the filing of the SEC's 8-K form by management.

Limitations of the Audit Report and the Future of the Audit Profession

Limitations of the Audit Report

Three phrases in the AICPA audit report are critical to understanding the limits of the report: (1) *reasonable assurance,* (2) *material,* and (3) *present fairly.* These expressions are used to signal the reader about specific limitations of the audit report.

Reasonable Assurance

The term *reasonable* is often used in law to define a standard of behavior to decide legal issues. For example, an auditor should exercise a *reasonable* level of care (due care) to avoid charges of negligence and possible liability to the client. As discussed at the onset of this chapter, reasonable assurance is not an absolute guarantee that the financial statements are free of material misstatement. Auditors do not examine all of a company's transactions. The transactions selected for examination are determined based on materiality considerations and risk assessment. Even then, only a small percentage of transactions may be selected, often by statistical sampling techniques. Professional judgment is critical in making these determinations. Notably, increased use of data analytics could make it possible for external financial statement auditors to improve audits by testing complete sets of data.

Materiality

The concept of *materiality* recognizes that some matters are important to the fair presentation of financial statements, while others are not. The materiality concept is fundamental to the audit because the audit report states that an audit is performed to obtain reasonable assurance about whether the financial statements are free of material misstatement. Materiality judgments can be most challenging when determining whether audit adjustments are necessary.

Materiality judgments require the use of professional judgment and are based on management and auditor perceptions of the needs of a reasonable person who will rely on the financial statements. *Materiality* is defined in the glossary of Statement of Financial Accounting Concepts (SFAC) 2, Qualitative Characteristics of Accounting Information,[34] as: *The magnitude of an omission or misstatement of accounting information that, in the light of surrounding circumstances, makes it probable that the judgment of a reasonable person relying on the information would have been changed or influenced by the omission or misstatement.*

Materiality in the context of an audit reflects the auditor's judgment of the needs of users in relation to the information in the financial statements and the possible effect of misstatements on user decisions as a group. Materiality is judged by assessing whether the omissions or misstatements of items in the statements could, individually or collectively, influence the economic decisions of users taken on the basis of financial statements. Materiality depends on the size and nature of the omission or misstatement judged in the surrounding circumstances.

Typically, an auditor might use a percentage for the numerical threshold, such as 5 percent. Materiality is then judged by comparing an item in question to some amount such as total assets or net income. If the questionable item is equal to or greater than 5 percent of the comparison amount, then it is material and must be reported in the financial statements.

Assume that a company has one item in inventory that cost $400,000. The auditor believes the current market value is $381,000, or $19,000 (4.75%) below cost. Under the 5 percent rule, the item may be judged immaterial and the write-down ignored. However, what if the net income for the year is only $300,000? Then the $19,000 write-down becomes material because it equals 6.33 percent of net income.

One unintended consequence of the accounting profession's approach to materiality is that a controller—knowing the 5 percent rule is in effect—may attempt to decrease expenses or increase revenues by an amount less than 5 percent to increase earnings by an amount that will not be challenged by the auditor. It is somewhat ironic that the auditor can let the difference go unchallenged, even though it may be due to the misapplication of GAAP, simply because it is not "material" in amount. A good example is at North Face Inc., where the company engaged in barter transactions in the late 1990s. The CFO knew the materiality criteria used by the Deloitte auditors, and he structured a transaction to produce gross profit ($800,000) below the materiality amount. The auditors had recommended an adjustment for that amount, which was part of a $1.64 million revenue transaction. The auditors passed on the adjustment using material-ity as the explanation.

Staff Accounting Bulletin (SAB) 99,[35] issued by the SEC, clarifies that the exclusive use of a percentage materiality criteria to assess material misstatements in the financial statements has no basis in law and is unacceptable. The com-mission did state that the use of a percentage as a numerical threshold, such as 5 percent, may provide the basis for a preliminary assumption that, without considering all relevant circumstances, a deviation of less than the specified percentage with respect to a particular item on the registrant's financial statements is unlikely to be material. However, the SEC ruled that both qualitative and quantitative factors must be considered when assessing materiality.

Materiality is judged both by the relative amount and by the nature of the item. For example, even a small theft by the president of a company is material because it raises doubts about the trustworthiness of the president, may indicate that other misappropriations have occurred, and brings into question the tone set from the top.

The SEC lists some of the qualitative factors that may cause quantitatively small misstatements to become material in SAB 99, including:

- It arises from an item capable of precise measurement.
- It arises from an estimate and, if so, the degree of imprecision inherent in the estimate.
- It masks a change in earnings or other trends.
- It hides a failure to meet analysts' consensus expectations for the enterprise.
- It changes a loss into income or vice versa.
- It concerns a segment or other portion of the registrant's business that has been identified as playing a significant role in the registrant's operations or profitability.
- It affects the registrant's compliance with regulatory requirements.
- It affects the registrant's compliance with loan covenants or other contractual requirements.
- It has the effect of increasing management's compensation—for example, by satisfying the requirements for the award of bonuses or other forms of incentive compensation.
- It involves concealment of an unlawful transaction.

Auditors should be on the alert for these red flags, which signal that qualitatively material items may not have been recorded and disclosed in accordance with GAAP.

What Is Meant by "Present Fairly"?

Without an understanding of the term *present fairly,* the users of a financial statement would be unable to assess its reli-ability. For the purposes of our discussion about fair presentation, we will proceed with the following guideline: that the auditor's assessment of fair presentation depends on whether (1) the accounting principles selected and applied have general acceptance; (2) the accounting principles are appropriate in the circumstances; (3) the financial statements, including the related notes, are informative of matters that may affect their use, understanding, and interpretation; (4) the information presented in the statements is classified and summarized in a reasonable manner—that is, neither too detailed nor too condensed; and (5) the financial statements reflect transactions and events within a range of reason-able limits.

Present fairly is a determination made in accordance with a financial reporting framework—that is, U.S. GAAP or IFRS. Compliance with the framework includes (1) acknowledging explicitly or implicitly that, to achieve fair presentation of the financial statements, it may be necessary for management to provide disclosures beyond those specifically required by the framework; or (2) acknowledging explicitly that it may be necessary for management to depart from a requirement of the framework to achieve a fair presentation of the financial statements. Such departures are expected to be necessary only in extremely rare circumstances.

We wonder how the term *fair* in *fair presentation* relates to the traditional ethics notion of fairness as justice. Does this mean that financial statements that present fairly are just statements? We think not, because justice means, in part, to treat equals equally and unequals unequally. There is no such distinction in accounting to provide a different level of information for different user groups that might have different needs for information to assist decision making.

Outside the United States, in European and other countries that have adopted IFRS, the term *true and fair view* replaces *fair presentation.* Historically, the former is associated with a higher degree of professional judgment, while the latter is more rules-based. However, determinations of fair presentation have moved more to the professional judgment arena as standards in the United States evolve to better accord with the International Standards on Auditing (ISA). Evidence of the movement toward increased professional judgment and professional skepticism can be seen in frameworks such as the KPMG Professional Judgment Framework discussed in **Chapter 4**.

Generally Accepted Auditing Standards (GAAS)

The whole of GAAS are comprehensive and more detailed than we need to focus on for our purposes. Instead, we address matters that pertain to professional judgment and professional skepticism in keeping with one of the themes in **Chapter 4**.

An independent auditor plans, conducts, and reports the results of an audit in accordance with GAAS. *Auditing standards* provide a measure of audit quality and the objectives to be achieved in an audit. Auditing standards differ from auditing procedures because the procedures are steps taken by the auditor during the course of the audit to comply with GAAS. The application of auditing standards entails making judgments with regard to the nature of audit evidence, sufficiency, competency, and reliability. Materiality considerations also are important to assess whether the audit opinion should be modified.

The GAAS have been seen as the bedrock foundation of the auditor's obligations to conduct a proper audit. These standards address the overall responsibilities of the independent auditor and the objectives of the conduct of an audit in accordance with AU-C Section 200. The PCAOB and the AICPA both adapted these standards that are applied to audits of historical financial information, compliance audits, and audits of internal control over financial reporting.

General Responsibilities of the Independent Auditor

The general responsibilities relate to the quality of the professionals who perform the audit. These include adequate technical training and proficiency, independence in mental attitude, and due care in the performance of the audit and preparation of the report. As discussed in **Chapter 4**, to be independent means to avoid all appearances that one's judgment may be clouded by events and relationships. Due care in performing an audit requires an objective outlook on audit evidence, diligence in meeting professional responsibilities, and competence in making professional judgments, including to exercise professional skepticism.

Objectives of Audit Procedures and Evidence

Objectives of audit procedures and evidence establish the criteria for judging whether the audit has met quality requirements. The standards include adequately planning the audit work and supervising assistants so that the audit is more likely to detect a material misstatement; obtaining a sufficient understanding of the entity and its internal control, to assess the risk of material misstatement of the financial statements, whether due to error or fraud; planning effectively the nature, timing, and extent of further audit procedures; and gathering sufficient competent evidential matter through audit procedures, including inspection, observation, inquiries, and confirmations to provide a reasonable basis (support) for an opinion regarding the financial statements under audit.

Objectives of Reporting

The objectives of reporting guide auditors in rendering an audit report and in determining the degree of responsibility that the auditor is taking with respect to the expression of an opinion of the financial statements. They include determination of whether the statements have been prepared in conformity with GAAP, identification of situations where the accounting principles have not been observed consistently in the current period in relation to the preceding period, and discussion in the report of any situation identified in the footnotes to the financial statements where informative disclosures are inadequate. In each case, professional judgments are necessary to meet the requirements of these standards.

Audit Evidence

Gathering and objectively evaluating audit evidence requires the auditor to consider the competency and sufficiency of the evidence. Representations from management, while part of the evidential matter the auditor obtains, are not a substitute for the application of those auditing procedures necessary to afford a reasonable basis for an opinion regarding the financial statements under audit.

Audit risk and materiality need to be considered together in determining the nature, timing, and extent of auditing procedures and in evaluating the results of those procedures. According to AU-C Section 315, the auditor should consider audit risk and materiality both in (a) planning the audit and designing auditing procedures and (b) evaluating whether the financial statements taken as a whole are presented fairly, in all material respects, in conformity with GAAP.[36]

The auditor's response to the risks of material misstatement due to fraud involves the application of professional skepticism when gathering and evaluating audit evidence. Examples of the application of professional skepticism in response to the risks of material misstatement due to fraud are obtaining additional corroboration of management's explanations or representations concerning material matters, such as through third-party confirmation, the use of a specialist, analytical procedures, examination of documentation from independent sources, or inquiries of others within or outside the entity. The independent auditor's direct personal knowledge, obtained through physical examination, observation, computation, and inspection, is more persuasive than information obtained indirectly.

Audit procedures are specific acts performed by the auditor to gather evidence about whether specific assertions are being met. For example, the client may state that the inventory value is $1 million. That is a specific assertion. The auditor then uses the procedure of observing the physical count of inventory to assess inventory quantity and traces certain year-end purchases and sales of inventory to invoices and other documentation as part of the cutoff process to determine whether year-end transactions should be part of the inventory. Typically, the auditor also tests the pricing of the inventory to assess the application of methods such as first-in, first-out (FIFO); last-in, first-out (LIFO); and the weighted average methods. The current market value of the inventory also has to be assessed.

Audit procedures help obtain an understanding of the entity and its environment, including its internal controls, to assess the risks of material misstatements. Audit procedures also test the operating effectiveness of controls in preventing or detecting material misstatements.

Professional skepticism plays an important role in gathering audit evidence and evaluating its usefulness. Recall that the term means to have a questioning mind and make a critical assessment of audit evidence. However, these requirements are somewhat ambiguous and leave open to interpretation what constitutes appropriate levels of questioning and critical assessment and how such behavior is demonstrated and can be documented.

The PCAOB in its inspection process looks for adequate judgments and skepticism when reviewing the audit reports of registered public companies. Shortcomings in these areas may reflect audit deficiencies. The PCAOB's Observations from 2016 Inspections of Auditors of Issuers (Staff Inspection Brief) describes the three key areas with the most frequent audit deficiencies observed in the 2016 inspection cycle: assessing and responding to risks of material misstatement, auditing ICFR, and auditing accounting estimates. Audit deficiencies include the failure to design and perform audit procedures to assess fraud risks and other significant risks. The Staff Inspection Brief specifically mentions that auditors should presume that there is a fraud risk involving improper revenue recognition and evaluate the types of revenue, revenue transactions, or assertions that may give risk to such risks.[37] The failure to adequately assess the fraud risk due to improper revenue can lead to materially misstated financial statements that require reissuance or restatement.

The Future of the Auditing Profession

LO 5-6

Identify the potential benefits and concerns over the use of Machine Based Learning systems by external and internal auditors.

According to a 2020 white paper published with CPA Canada and the AICPA, the rapid evolution of the audit is being driven by technology and increases in the use of automation, analytics, and artificial intelligence.[38] As referenced in the ethics reflection at the beginning of this chapter, the technological advances of the last decade provide the ability to analyze huge sets of data and quickly identify anomalies within it. In other words, these systems are expected to revolutionize the ability of auditors to quickly identify fraud within an organization. Early stage auditing tools like IDEA, AuditBoard, TeamMate+, and others have been widely adopted by both internal and external auditors to crunch large datasets. They are just starting to integrate artificial intelligence (AI) or a subset of which, machine learning, which is where the industry is headed. The auditor currently reviews the anomalies/exceptions identified by these tools and determines a course of action.

Machine learning refers to the computer learning from the auditors clearing and classifying of the anomalies whereby the computer can get faster and better at honing in on exactly what the auditor is trying to search for. Unfortunately, should the historical data sets fed into the system for the computer to learn from have errors in it, or be skewed by incorrect assumptions or biases of those who cleared the exceptions, then the machine results will also be skewed. These systems will not replace the role of the auditor but will transform the nature of the work they do and the skillset required to perform that work. The largest of the accounting firms are investing in home grown solutions like:

- PWC's development and marketing of HALO,[39] an audit platform including journal entry analysis, and an employee expense reporting and management system which they describe as a digital intelligence and analytics platform which provides transparency into exceptions and behavioral anomalies, that supplements existing controls to detect suspicious transactions based on patterns, vendors, user profiles, and sophisticated risk scoring algorithms.
- Deloitte's[40] development and marketing of their proprietary Analytics Platform which they tout as using analytics to address fraud, waste and abuse in companies.
- KPMG's development and deployment of their own automated audit platform Clara.[41]
- EY's development and deployment of Helix,[42] their data analytics platform they use to improve audit quality and to identify areas of risk and to focus their work on those areas.

The development and use of these systems are expected to revolutionize both internal and external auditing, increasing the speed in which the work can be performed and the quality of that work as well. While larger firms like the Big Four are investing hundreds of millions of dollars into the development of these systems, smaller firms are also starting to take advantage of the off-the-shelf systems which have started to integrate machine learning into them. For example, Samantha Bowling, Audit Partner at Garbelman Winslow, CPAs, indicated that they have developed an algorithm they deploy through MindBridge to evaluate risk associated with new clients. She noted that it helps them first determine whether they should accept the client or not, and then in their development of the budget for that first-year audit as well. She said that if a potential client refuses to provide the requested data, they turn down the engagement.[43]

Both CPA Canada and the AICPA are promoting members of the profession embrace and plan for the changes that are coming. In that regard, they suggest that the profession needs to be mindful of the concerns and challenges surrounding data privacy and confidentiality, data integrity, explainability/understandability, operational management of the audit, and audit staff having the appropriate competence and capabilities. While the use of machine-based learning systems appear to have the potential to greatly enhance the quality of the audits they also pose great risk to the profession if not done in a thoughtful and ethical way.

CPA Canada and the AICPA suggest the audit profession consider the following key questions:[44]

- How do I assess the reliability of the data captured (e.g., accuracy, completeness) and method(s) of data acquisition from different systems, particularly client systems?

- What happens when clients' systems, controls, policies, or procedures change, or if a mid-year acquisition occurs that impacts overall scope?

- Do only appropriate personnel have access to modify client systems?

- If management is not able to explain or evaluate the results from an AI tool, are they able to assert that the subject matter is complete and accurate, and that internal control is effective to mitigate the risks of material misstatement?

- Similarly, if the auditor cannot explain or evaluate the results from an AI audit tool, can they conclude that they have obtained sufficient, appropriate audit evidence from the AI audit tool to form an opinion?

These newer AI-based platforms have proprietary algorithms built in them that have been developed by their creators. They are what is generally referred to as a "black-box," an unknown ingredient which magically performs the work and spits out a set of results. It is this area that should be of greatest concern to the auditing profession. Audits, whether internal or external, are grounded in the foundation of transparency. This is why the leaders of the profession are asking their members to consider the following as they start to use, create, and deploy machine-based learning systems. CPA Canada and the AICPA[45] also identify some current limitations and concerns surrounding the use of AI in auditing to be aware of:

- AI cannot work on its own. While it may transform the profession through efficiencies gained and use of new technologies and new skills, an auditor will still be required to set parameters, consider the results in relation to other evidence, and make judgments that a computer cannot make.

- AI cannot see the big picture. For example, a machine's world is restricted only to the (correct or incorrect) data to which it has access, what it has been taught, and what it has been programmed to do. It does not know the nuances of the real world and can't replace an auditor's professional judgment. Fraud or bias can happen even when transactions processed by the AI seem perfectly legitimate. Auditors need to be alert to these qualitative aspects.

- AI needs to have controls. Data integrity could be compromised if appropriate controls are not implemented and operating effectively.

- AI cannot evaluate moral or ethical concerns. For example, while AI may be able to identify fact patterns of independence infractions, it cannot effectively contextualize intent or perceptions of conflict (i.e., independence must exist in both fact and appearance). For instance, AI cannot recognize if the financial market perceives a lack of independence when the facts suggest independence does exist.

The last two statements should give us all pause as we move down this path. If we can't validate what is in the black-box, can management say that their internal controls are working? Can auditors continue to opine on the financial statements they are auditing? While AI may bring great benefits to the profession, helping to quickly uncover fraudulent transactions or schemes, the profession needs to find a way to open up the box and shed light on its inner workings if it hopes to use these systems to improve overall audit quality and maintain the public trust.

Concluding Thoughts

Financial statement fraud threatens the foundation of the financial reporting process and jeopardizes the integrity of the auditing function. Signposts that fraud may exist need to be ingrained in the DNA of auditors. Influences that might bias their approach to an audit and their evaluation of audit evidence must be controlled through an ethical approach that emphasizes objectivity, due care, and the exercise of professional skepticism.

Auditors need to be more diligent in looking for the signs that fraud may exist. The Fraud Triangle provides a valuable framework to evaluate risks of fraud and better understand how to detect it and to prevent it from occurring. Beyond that, management and the audit committee must meet their obligations to monitor ICFR and make needed adjustments as warranted. Auditors must review management's assessments and make their own determination whether internal controls are operating as intended. Audit firms need to strengthen their own quality control systems to ensure they meet quality control standards and help to identify material misstatements in the financial statements, whether due to error or fraud.

The purpose of disclosing critical audit matters is to provide audit-specific information that is useful to investors and creditors about matters that require subjective or complex auditor judgment. Addressing critical audit matters should help to improve audit quality.

Audit estimates are a problematic area. The aggressive judgments by management, such as in the Medicis Pharmaceutical case, create challenges for auditors in verifying the estimates and determining whether they contribute to improper financial reporting. Given that PCAOB inspection reports emphasize accounting estimates as frequent deficiencies, more attention is needed to this area in auditing financial statements.

As the audit profession evolves and embraces the use of machine-based learning systems, the profession needs to stay vigilant and be aware that these systems require our expertise, professional judgment and ethics. While these systems provide great potential for improving audit quality, they also provide great risk to the profession if not deployed in a carefully planned out and transparent fashion. The public trust must be maintained. Without that trust, the entire profession is at risk.

We are concerned about the quality of audits. The disclosure of CAMs may help in the long term. However, the high deficiency rates found in PCAOB inspection reports are due to other things as well, including the overreliance on management's representations. In order to meet their public interest obligation, auditors must take to heart the saying "trust but verify." That should be the mantra of a sound audit whether aided by machine-based learning systems or not. Auditors need to approach the audit with the mindset of identifying "those things that would keep them up at night" and use it to set the tone for the audit.

Discussion Questions

1. Identify and discuss the "Best Audit Practices" the PCAOB has identified as a way to improve audit quality, and reduce audit deficiencies.

2. What are the objectives of audit risk assessment, and why is it important to assess the likelihood that fraud may occur? How might the assessment influence the auditors' evaluation of ICFR?

3. Distinguish between an auditor's responsibilities to detect and report errors, illegal acts, and fraud. What role does materiality have in determining the proper reporting and disclosure of such events?

4. AU-C 240, Consideration of Fraud in a Financial Statement Audit, specifically identifies red flags the auditor should be on the lookout as for throughout the audit process (from client engagement through report issuance). Provide examples of such considerations with respect to the fraud triangle including rationalization to justify the fraud.

5. How might the existence of the dark triad personalities underlie undesirable behaviors by management and how might it influence the audit?

6. Explain the content of each section of the AICPA audit report. Evaluate the importance of each section with respect to the users of financial reports.

7. Give one example each of when an auditor might render an unmodified opinion and include either an emphasis-of-matter paragraph and/or an other-matter paragraph. What is the value of such paragraphs in the audit report?

8. Rationalization for fraud can fall under two categories: "no harm" and "no responsibility." Assume an employee is directed by management to reduce recorded expenses at year-end by insignificant amounts individually, but which are material in total. How might the employee justify her actions if questioned by the auditor with respect to no harm and no responsibility? What stage of moral development in Kohlberg's model is best illustrated by the employee's actions? Why?

9. Some criticize the accounting profession for using expressions in the audit report that seem to be building in deniability should the client commit a fraudulent act. What expressions enable the CPA to build a defense should the audit wind up in the courtroom? Do you see anything wrong with these expressions from an ethical point of view?

10. Do you think the concept of materiality is incompatible with ethical behavior? Consider in your answer how materiality judgments affect risk assessment in an audit of financial statements.

11. What is the problem with an auditor over-relying on management's representations on the financial statements?

12. Auditing standards require that a "brainstorming" session should be held at the beginning of each audit to help identify steps to assess the possibility that material misstatements/fraud in the financial statements exist. Discuss how brainstorming sessions might enhance audit judgments, professional skepticism, and decision making. Consider the groupthink dimension in your discussion.

13. What are the auditor's responsibilities to communicate information to the audit committee under PCAOB standards? If the auditor discovers that the audit committee routinely ignores such communications, especially when they are critical of management's use of GAAP in the financial statements, what step(s) might the auditor take at this point?

14. In 1995, Congress added Section 10A to the Securities Exchange Act of 1934 as part of the Private Securities Litigation Reform Act. Is it accurate to say that Congress enacted Section 10A with the intent to require auditors to blow the whistle on the fraudulent activities of their clients? Explain.

15. Explain how PCAOB inspections can lead to improvements in audit engagement quality.

16. What is the purpose of an audit firm developing a system of quality controls?

17. Do you believe the end-user cares whether the lead audit engagement partner signs their name to the report or the firm simply files Form AP with the PCAOB? Explain.

18. The modern day audit is evolving rapidly. Some fear that auditors will be replaced by artificial intelligence (AI). Is this a valid concern?

19. How do AI and machine learning systems differ from the existing data analytic auditing systems like IDEA? Include a discussion of the professions' concerns surrounding the use of AI in auditing.

20. You may know the difference between right and wrong behavior and never would consider committing fraud. But how do you maintain the highest level of professional conduct as it relates to fraudulent behaviors in others or when fraud is suspected?

Comprehensive Questions

1. Describe the types of audit deficiencies that might arise because of problems with ICFR.

2. AU-C 240 points to three conditions that enable fraud to occur. Briefly describe each condition. How does one's propensity to act ethically, as described by Rest's model of morality, influence each of the three conditions?

3. The PCAOB believes there have been improvements in audit quality during the past few years. Discuss the indicators of audit quality and why they are important to protect the public interest.

4. Mr. Arty works for Smile Accounting Firm as a senior accountant. Currently, he is doing a review of rental property compliance testing of rental receipts and expenses of the property owned by the client. He determines that the staff accountants tested only two tenants per property instead of the required three by the audit program based on materiality considerations. However, to request more information from the client would cause massive delays and the manager on the engagement is pressing hard for the information now. The manager did approach the client, who stated that she "needed the report yesterday." The manager reminds Arty that no problems were found from the testing of the two properties, in past years the work papers called for just two properties to be reviewed, the firm has never had any accounting issues with respect to the client and he is confident the testing is sufficient. Explain the relationship between the manager's explanations and the judgment tendencies discussed in Chapter 4.

5. Assume you are inspecting EY's audit of Medicis Pharmaceutical Corporation for the PCAOB. Read through the information provided about the case in the chapter and identify the factors the auditors should have taken into account in determining critical audit matters.

Endnotes

1. R. Klein, *PCAOB Inspection Results: What Do The Numbers Tell Us? Group Dynamics* (2010), https://www. gaapdynamics.com/insights/blog/2019/08/27/pcaob-inspection-results-what-do-the-numbers-tell-us/.

2. https://pcaobus.org/Inspections/Documents/Staff-Preview-2018-Inspection-Observations.pdf.

3. https://pcaobus.org/Inspections/Documents/Staff-Preview-2019-Inspection-Observations-Spotlight.pdf.

4. https://pcaobus.org/Inspections/Documents/Staff-Preview-2019-Inspection-Observations-Spotlight.pdf.

5. American Institute of Certified Public Accountants (AICPA), *Consideration of Fraud in a Financial Statement Audit* (AU-C Section 240).

6. AICPA, AU-C Section 240.

7. Center for Audit Quality (CAQ), Closing the Expectation Gap in Deterring and Detecting Financial Statement Fraud: A Roundtable Summary, October 21, 2013, http://www.thecaq.org/closing-expectation-gap-deterring-and-detecting-financial-statement-fraud-roundtable-summary.

8. *Securities and Exchange Commission v. KPMG LLP,* Joseph T. Boyle, Michael A. Conway, Anthony P. Dolanski, and Ronald A. Safaran, Civil Action No. 03-CV-0671 (DLC), Available at: www.sec.gov/litigation/complaints/comp17954.htm.

9. Mark S. Beasley, Joseph V. Carcello, Dana R. Hermanson, and Terry L. Neal, "An Analysis of Alleged Auditor Deficiencies in SEC Fraud Investigations: 1998–2010" (Center for Audit Quality, 2013).

10. W. Steve Albrecht, "Iconic Fraud Triangle Endures," *Fraud Magazine* (July–August 2014), Available at: http://www.fraud-magazine.com/article.aspx?id=4294983342.

11. Albrecht.

12. AICPA, AU-C Section 240.

13. AICPA, AU-C Section 240.

14. AICPA, AU-C Section 240.

15. Alexander Coolidge, Frisch's: Top exec stole millions, January 20, 2015, https://www.cincinnati.com/story/money/2015/01/20/frischs-top-exec-stole-millions/22038045/.

16. Barry Jay Epstein and Sridhar Ramamoorti, "Today's Fraud Risk Models Lack Personality, *The CPA Journal* (March 2016), https://www.cpajournal.com/2016/03/16/todays-fraud-risk-models-lack-personality/.

17. Kari Joseph Olsen, Kelsey Kay Dworkis, and S. Mark Young, CEO Narcissism and Accounting: A Picture of Profits, *Journal of Management Accounting Research* 26, no. 2 (Fall 2014), pp. 243–267, https://doi.org/10.2308/jmar-50638.

18. Jon Ronson, *The Psychopath Test: A Journey Through the Madness Industry* (NY: Riverview Publishing, 2011).

19. Juliana Moore and Elinor Jreige Weffort, Opportunistic Behavior in Accounting Choices: The Influence of Emotions and Personality, 2015, https://www.fea.usp.br/sites/default/files/arquivos/anexos/paper_oportunistic_behavior_in_accounting_choices_milan_et_al_2015_0.pdf.

20. Aaron Beam and Chris Warner, *HealthSouth: The Wagon to Disaster* (Fairhope, AL: Wagon Publishing, 2009).

21. Alejandro Adrian LeMon, Ph.D., Your Life Is This Dark Room and Only I Have the Key: A Closer Look into the Mind of the Psychopath, http://psychone.net/blogs/self-education/your-life-is-a-dark-room-and-i-have-the-key-a-closer-look-into-the-mind-of-the-psychopath.html.

22. Epstein and Ramamoorti.

23. PCAOB Staff Inspection Brief, Preview of Observations from 2016 Inspections of Auditors of Issuers, November 2017, https://pcaobus.org/Inspections/Documents/inspection-brief-2017-4-issuer-results.pdf.

24. PCAOB, Order Making Findings and Imposing Sanctions: In the Matter of Ernst & Young LLP, Jeffrey S. Anderson, CPA, Ronald Butler, Jr. CPA, Thomas A Christie, CPS, and Robert H. Thibault, CPA, PCAOB Release No. 105-2012-01, February 8, 2012, https://pcabus.org/Enforcement/Decisions/Documents/Ernst_Young.pdf.

25. AICPA, *Written Representations* (AU-C Section 580).

26. *In the United States District Court for the District of Colorado, SEC v. Joseph Nacchio, Robert S. Woodruff, Robin R. Szeliga, Afshin Mohebbi, Gregory Casey, James T. Kozlowski, Frank T. Noyes,* Civil Action No. 05-MK-480.

27. PCAOB, AS 1301: Communications with Audit Committees, PCAOB release No. 2012-04, December 15, 2012, https://pcaobus.org/Standards/Auditing/Pages/AS1301.aspx.

28. PCAOB, AS 3101: The Auditor's Report on an Audit of Financial Statements When the Auditor Expresses an Unqualified Opinion, PCAOB Release No. 2017-001, June 1, 2017, https://pcaobus.org/Standards/Auditing/Pages/AS3101.aspx.

29. https://www.journalofaccountancy.com/news/2019/oct/cpa-firm-reporting-critical-audit-matters-201921907.html

30. https://www.journalofaccountancy.com/news/2019/oct/cpa-firm-reporting-critical-audit-matters-201921907.html

31. Deloitte, PCAOB adopts changes to the auditor's report, *Heads Up* 24, no. 16 (June 20, 2017), https://www2.deloitte.com/us/en/pages/audit/articles/hu-pcaob-adopts-changes-to-the-auditors-report-062017.html.

32. Eva K. Jermakowicz, Barry J. Epstein, and Sridhar Ramamoorti, "CAM versus KAM—Making Judgments in Reporting Critical Audit Matters," *The CPA Journal* (February 2018), pp. 34-40.

33. PCAOB, Form AP – Auditor Reporting of Certain Audit Participants, https://pcaobus.org/Rules/Pages/Form-AP-Instructions.aspx.

34. Financial Accounting Standards Board (FASB), *Statement of Financial Accounting Standards* (Stamford, CT: FASB, November 1977).

35. SEC, Staff Accounting Bulletin 99: Materiality, Available at: https://www.sec.gov/interps/account/sab99.htm.

36. AICPA, *Understanding the Entity and its Environment and Assessing the Risks of Material Misstatement* (AU-C Section 315).

37. PCAOB Staff Inspection Brief.

38. https://www.aicpa.org/content/dam/aicpa/interestareas/frc/assuranceadvisoryservices/downloadabledocuments/the-data-driven-audit.pdf.

39. https://www.pwc.com/us/en/services/tax/tax-innovation/halo-for-employee-expenses.html.

40. https://www2.deloitte.com/us/en/pages/advisory/solutions/deloitte-analytics-platform-advisory-analytics.html.

41. https://audit.kpmg.us/kpmg-clara.html.

42. https://www.ey.com/en_us/assurance/audit-quality-report-2020/data-first.

43. https://www.journalofaccountancy.com/issues/2019/jun/artificial-intelligence-in-audit.html.

44. https://www.aicpa.org/content/dam/aicpa/interestareas/frc/assuranceadvisoryservices/downloadabledocuments/the-data-driven-audit.pdf.

45. https://www.aicpa.org/content/dam/aicpa/interestareas/frc/assuranceadvisoryservices/downloadabledocuments/the-data-driven-audit.pdf.

Chapter 5 Cases

Case 5-1 Loyalty and Fraud Reporting (a GVV case)

Assume Ethan Lester and Vick Jensen are CPAs. Ethan was seen as a "model employee" who deserved a promotion to director of accounting according to Kelly Fostermann, the CEO of Fostermann Corporation, a Maryland-based, largely privately held company that is a prominent global designer and marketer of stereophonic systems. The company has an 11-person board of directors.

Kelly considered Ethan to be an honest employee based on performance reviews and his unwillingness to accept the promotion, stating that he wasn't ready yet for the position. Kelly admired his willingness to learn and grow, not just expect a promotion. Little did she know that Ethan was committing a $50,000 fraud by embezzling cash from the company. In fact, no one seemed to catch on because Ethan was able to override internal controls. However, the external auditors were coming in and to solidify the deception, he needed the help of Vick Jensen, a close friend who was an accounting manager reporting to Ethan. Ethan could "order" Vick to cover up the fraud but hoped Vick would do so out of friendship and loyalty. Besides, Ethan knew Vick had committed his own fraud two years ago and covered it up by creating false journal entries for undocumented sales, returns, transactions, and operating expenses.

Ethan went to see Vick and explained his dilemma. He could see Vick's discomfort in hearing the news. Vick had thought he had turned the corner on being involved in fraud after he quietly paid back the $20,000 he had stolen two years ago. Here is how the conversation went.

> "Vick, I need your help. I blew it. You know Mary and I split up 10 months ago."

> "Yes," Vick said.

> "Well, I got involved with another woman who I tried to impress by buying her things. I wound up taking $50,000 from company funds."

> "Ethan, what were you thinking?"

> "Don't get all moral with me. Don't you recall your own circumstances?"

> Vick was quiet for a moment and then asked, "What do you want me to do?"

> "I need you to make some entries in the ledger to cover up the $50,000. I promise to pay it back, just as you did. You know I'm good for it."

> Vick reacted angrily, saying, "You told me to skip the bank reconciliations—that you would do them yourself. I trusted you."

> "I know. Listen, do this one favor for me, and I'll never ask you again."

> Vick grew increasingly uneasy. He told Ethan he needed to think about it . . . his relationship with the auditors was at stake.

Questions

1. Analyze the facts of the case using the Fraud Triangle. Would you characterize what Ethan Lester did as a failure of internal controls? Explain.

2. Assume Ethan sets a meeting with Vick in two days to follow-up on his request. Vick has decided not to be part of the cover-up. Use the GVV framework to help Vick prepare for the meeting. Consider the following:

   - What should Vick say to counteract Ethan's request?
   - How might Vick's intended action affect the company and the external auditors?
   - Who can Vick go to for support?

3. Assume Ethan gets upset after the meeting and decides to fire Vick. He tells Vick to leave quietly or Ethan will disclose the $20,000 fraud. What should Vick do next?

Case 5-2 ZZZZ Best[1]

The story of ZZZZ Best is one of greed and audaciousness. It is the story of a 15-year-old boy from Reseda, California, who was driven to be successful, regardless of the costs. His name is Barry Minkow. Although this case dates back over 30 years, it does serve as an example of what can happen when auditors do not look too hard to find fraud.

Minkow had high hopes to make it big—to be a millionaire very early in life. He started a carpet cleaning business in the garage of his home. Minkow realized early on that he was not going to become a millionaire cleaning other people's carpets, but that he could in the insurance restoration business. In other words, ZZZZ Best would contract to do carpet and drapery cleaning jobs after a fire or flood. Because the damage from the fire or flood probably would be covered by insurance, the customer would be eager to have the work done, and perhaps not be all that concerned with how much it would cost. The only problem with Minkow's insurance restoration idea was that it was all a fiction. Allegedly, over 80 percent of his revenue was from this work. In the process of creating the fraud, Minkow was able to dupe the auditors, Ernst & Whinney (now EY), into thinking the insurance restoration business was real. The auditors never caught on until it was too late.

How Barry Became a Fraudster

Minkow wrote a book, *Clean Sweep: A Story of Compromise, Corruption, Collapse, and Comeback,*[2] that provides some insights into the mind of a 15-year-old kid who was called a "wonder boy" on Wall Street until the bubble burst. He was trying to find a way to drum up customers for his fledgling carpet cleaning business. One day, while he was alone in his garage office, Minkow called Channel 4 in Los Angeles. He disguised his voice so he wouldn't sound like a teenager and told a producer that he had just had his carpets cleaned by the 16-year-old owner of ZZZZ Best. He sold the producer on the idea that it would be good for society to hear the success story about a high school junior running his own business. The producer bought it lock, stock, and carpet cleaner. Minkow gave the producer the phone number of ZZZZ Best and waited. It took less than five minutes for the call to come in. Minkow answered the phone and when the producer asked to speak with Mr. Barry Minkow, Minkow said, "Who may I say is calling?" Within days, a film crew was in his garage shooting ZZZZ Best at work. The story aired that night, and it was followed by more calls from radio stations and other television shows wanting to do interviews. The calls flooded in with customers demanding that Barry Minkow personally clean their carpets.

As his income increased in the spring of 1983, Minkow found it increasingly difficult to run the company without a checking account. He managed to find a banker that was so moved by his story that the banker agreed to allow an underage customer to open a checking account. Minkow used the money to buy cleaning supplies and other necessities. Even though his business was growing, Minkow ran into trouble paying back loans and interest when due.

Minkow developed a plan of action. He was tired of worrying about not having enough money. He went to his garage—where all his great ideas first began—and looked at his bank account statement, which showed that he had more money than he thought he had based on his own records. Minkow soon realized it was because some checks he had written had not been cashed by customers, so they didn't yet show up on the bank statement. Voilà! Minkow started to kite checks between two or more banks. He would write a check on one ZZZZ Best account on the last day of the reporting period and deposit it into another. The check wouldn't clear Bank #1 for at least one day so he could count the cash in both accounts (back then, checks weren't always processed in real time the way they are today).

It wasn't long thereafter that Minkow realized he could kite checks big time. Not only that, he could make the transfer of funds at the end of a month or a year and show a higher balance than really existed in Bank #1 and carry it onto the balance sheet. Because Minkow did not count the check written on his account in Bank #1 as an outstanding check, he was able to double-count.

Time to Expand the Fraud

Over time, Minkow moved on to bigger and bigger frauds, like having his trusted cohorts confirm to banks and other interested parties that ZZZZ Best was doing insurance restoration jobs. Minkow used the phony jobs and phony revenue to convince bankers to make loans to ZZZZ Best. He had cash remittance forms made up from nonexistent customers with whatever sales amount he wanted to appear on the document. He even had a co-conspirator write on the bogus remittance form, "Job well done." Minkow could then show a lot more revenue than he was really making.

Minkow's phony financial statements enabled him to borrow more and more money and expand the number of carpet cleaning outlets. However, Minkow's personal tastes had become increasingly more expensive, including purchasing a Ferrari with the borrowed funds and putting a down payment on a 5,000-square-foot home. So, the question was: How do you solve a perpetual cash flow problem? You go public! That's right, Minkow made a public offering of stock in ZZZZ Best. Of course, he owned a majority of the stock to maintain control of the company.

Minkow had made it to the big leagues. He was on Wall Street. He had investment bankers, CPAs, and attorneys all working for him–the now 19-year-old kid from Reseda, California, who had turned a mom-and-pop operation into a publicly owned corporation.

Barry Goes Public

Pressured to get a big-time CPA firm to do his audit by the underwriting firm selling his stock, Minkow hired Ernst & Whinney to perform the April 30, 1987, fiscal year-end audit. Minkow continued to be one step ahead of the auditors–that is, until the Ernst & Whinney auditors insisted on going to see an insurance restoration site. They wanted to confirm that all the business–all the revenue–that Minkow had said was coming in to ZZZZ Best was real.

The engagement partner drove to an area in Sacramento, California, where Minkow did a lot of work–supposedly. He looked for a building that seemed to be a restoration job. Why he did that isn't clear, but he identified a building that seemed to be the kind that would be a restoration job in progress.

Earlier in the week, Minkow had sent one of his cohorts to find a large building in Sacramento that appeared to be a restoration site. As luck would have it, Minkow's associate picked out the same site as had the partner later on. Minkow's cohorts found the leasing agent for the building. They convinced the agent to give them the keys so that they could show the building to some potential tenants over the weekend. Minkow's helpers went up to the site before the arrival of the partner and placed placards on the walls that indicated ZZZZ Best was the contractor for the building restoration. In fact, the building was not fully constructed at the time, but it looked as if some restoration work was going on at the site.

Minkow was able to pull it off in part due to luck and in part because the Ernst & Whinney auditors did not want to lose the ZZZZ Best account. It had become a large revenue producer for the firm, and Minkow seemed destined for greater and greater achievements. Minkow was smart and used the leverage of the auditors not wanting to lose the ZZZZ Best account as a way to complain whenever they became too curious about the insurance restoration jobs. He would even threaten to take his business from Ernst & Whinney and give it to other auditors. To get on their good side, he would wine and dine the auditors and even invite them to his house.

Minkow also took a precaution with the site visit. He had the auditors sign a confidentiality agreement that they would not make any follow-up calls to any contractors, insurance companies, the building owner, or other individuals involved in the restoration work. This prevented the auditors from corroborating the insurance restoration contracts with independent third parties.

The Fraud Starts to Unravel

It was a Los Angeles housewife who started the problems for ZZZZ Best that would eventually lead to the company's demise. Because Minkow was a well-known figure and flamboyant character, the *Los Angeles Times* did a story about the carpet cleaning business. The Los Angeles housewife read the story about Minkow and recalled that ZZZZ Best had overcharged her for services in the early years by increasing the amount of the credit card charge for its carpet cleaning services.

Minkow had gambled that most people don't check their monthly statements, so he could get away with the petty fraud. However, the housewife did notice the overcharge and complained to Minkow, and eventually he returned the overpayment. She couldn't understand why Minkow would have had to resort to such low levels back then if he was as successful as the *Times* article made him out to be. So she called the reporter to find out more, and that ultimately led to the investigation of ZZZZ Best and future stories that weren't so flattering.

Because Minkow continued to spend lavishly on himself and his possessions, he always seemed to need more and more money. It got so bad over time that he was close to defaulting on loans and had to make up stories to keep the creditors at bay, and he couldn't pay his suppliers. The complaints kept coming in, and eventually the house of cards that was ZZZZ Best came crashing down.

During the time that the fraud was unraveling, Ernst & Whinney decided to resign from the ZZZZ Best audit. It had started to doubt the veracity of Minkow and his business at ZZZZ Best. Of course, by then it mattered little because the firm had been a party to the cover-up for some time.

Legal Liability Issues

The ZZZZ Best fraud was one of the largest of its time. ZZZZ Best reportedly settled a shareholder class action lawsuit for $35 million. Ernst & Whinney was sued by a bank that had made a multimillion-dollar loan based on the financial statements for the three-month period ending July 31, 1986. The bank claimed that it had relied on the review report issued by Ernst & Whinney in granting the loan to ZZZZ Best. However, the firm had indicated in its review report that it was not issuing an opinion on the ZZZZ Best financial statements. The judge ruled that the bank was not justified in relying on the review report because Ernst & Whinney had expressly disclaimed issuing any opinion on the statements. The firm lucked out in that the judge understood that a review engagement only provides limited assurance rather than the reasonable assurance of the audit.

Barry Minkow was charged with engaging in a $100 million fraud scheme. He was sentenced to a term of 25 years.

Questions

1. Do you believe that auditors should be held liable for failing to discover fraud in situations such as ZZZZ Best, where top management goes to great lengths to fool the auditors? Explain.

2. Discuss the red flags that existed in the ZZZZ Best case and evaluate Ernst & Whinney's efforts with respect to fraud risk assessment.

3. These are selected numbers from the financial statements of ZZZZ Best for fiscal years 1985 and 1986. What calculations or analyses would you make with these numbers that might help you assess whether the financial relationships are "reasonable"?

	1985	1986
Sales	$1,240,524	$4,845,347
Cost of goods sold	576,694	2,050,779
Accounts receivable	0	693,773
Cash	30,321	87,014
Current liabilities	2,930	1,768,435
Notes payable—current	0	780,507

4. Analyze Minkow's behavior from the perspective of being a "Dark Triad Personality." Does he fit one or more of the personality types? Explain.

Case 5-3 Reauditing Financial Statements

Margaret Dairy is a CPA and the managing partner of Dairy and Cheese, a regional CPA firm located in Northwest Wisconsin. She just left a meeting with a well-respected regional credit union headquartered in her hometown. Margaret was asked whether her firm would be willing to reaudit the previous years' financial statements and, subsequently, conduct an audit of the current years' financials. This is the first time Margaret has been asked to conduct a reaudit, although she realizes it has become more common as a result of problems like Enron and WorldCom experienced. Some companies switching auditors have elected to have the new audit firm re-examine prior-period financial statements because of concerns about the quality of the earlier audit.

On her way back to the office, Margaret calls her brother Mark, who is a Senior Audit Manager at a firm in Margaret's hometown, to share her good news. She tells him that doing the audit work for the two years will increase her firm's revenue by 10 percent. Mark is taken aback by the news. The new client was a client of Mark's firm. He did not know the firm had lost the client and it might be picked up by Dairy & Cheese.

Questions

1. What issues should be of concern to Margaret in deciding whether Dairy and Cheese should accept the reaudit engagement?
2. What are Mark's ethical obligations in this matter? Should he discuss the situation with Margaret? How about bringing it up at his firm?
3. Regardless of your answer to number 2, what inquiries should Margaret make of the predecessor auditor?
4. Assume Margaret's firm discovers undetected fraud in the previous years' financial statements, what should she do?

Case 5-4 GE Multibillion Insurance Charge

On January 30, 2018, General Electric (GE) announced that it was taking an after-tax charge of $6.2 billion in the December 31, 2017 financial statements and additional cash funding of $15 billion in statutory capital contributions to its insurance subsidiary. GE also acknowledged a Securities and Exchange Commission investigation into the process leading to the sudden multibillion-dollar charge and an additional review of revenue recognition and controls over its long-term contracts. In October of 2020[1], the SEC notified GE that they may be facing a civil action for violations of securities laws surrounding their accounting for these insurance contracts. On December 9, 2020, GE agreed to a $200 million penalty to settle the matter with the SEC. While GE did not admit any wrongdoing, the SEC stated that GE misled investors and violated antifraud, accounting, and other SEC regulations.[2] When GE first announced the charge on January 16, 2018, which related to the remnants of its long-term care reinsurance portfolio, CEO John Flannery told analysts he had "underappreciated the risk in this book." [A book of business, in the context of insurance, is a database or "book" that lists all of the insurance policies the insurance company has written.][3]

GE's North America Life & Health subsidiary is a reinsurance portfolio the company held on to after mostly exiting the business between 2004 and 2006. A reinsurer buys the right to receive premiums from the primary insurers that deal directly with consumers in exchange for eventually shouldering any potential losses. Those primary insurers underwrite and administer the policies and process claims when they come in.

The majority of GE Capital's remaining insurance business, 60 percent, is related to long-term care insurance. At the time, Flannery told analysts, GE believed that a gradual runoff of existing claims—no new business has been added since 2006—would be more profitable than selling the whole business. Unfortunately, Flannery said, GE didn't anticipate the low interest rate environment, low policy lapse rates, and higher claims cost that it is seeing now.

GE warned analysts as long ago as the second quarter of 2017 that a review of its claims experience and reserves was under way, and any charge would happen in the fourth quarter. In its 2017 second-quarter filing with the SEC, GE wrote: "We have recently experienced elevated claim experience for a portion of our long-term care insurance products, which may result in a deficiency in reserves plus future premiums compared to future benefit payments. Should such a deficiency exist, we would record a charge to earnings in the second half of 2017 upon completion of this review." And in its third-quarter 2017 filing with the SEC, GE warned about the potential charge again but with more details.

"We have recently experienced elevated claim experience for a portion of our long-term care insurance contracts and are conducting a comprehensive review of premium deficiency assumptions across all insurance contracts, including a reassessment of future claim projections for long-term care contracts that will be incorporated within our annual test of future policy benefit reserves for premium deficiencies in the fourth quarter of 2017. We would record a charge to earnings for any premium deficiencies in the fourth quarter of 2017 upon completion of this review."

Accounting experts were expecting the review to result in some financial charge, but not on this scale. "The review of business always carries the risk of unexpected findings, yet the magnitude of the $6.2 billion charge is far more staggering than the $3 billion that the market anticipated," research firm Audit Analytics wrote in a note to subscribers.

At its annual meeting last November, chief financial officer Jamie Miller told shareholders that GE was likely to take a charge of more than $3 billion.

Changes in insurance claim reserves typically are disclosed in advance as changes in accounting estimates related to long-term care reserves. Companies are only required to disclose adjustments that are material. In its note, Audit Analytics wrote it looked at 30 insurance companies and found 60 changes in accounting estimates filed with the SEC for adjustment to the long-term care loss reserves filed since 2004.

The last time GE disclosed any changes in reserves even partly attributable to the long-term care reinsurance portfolio, according to Audit Analytics, was in its 2004 annual report, the same year it spun off the Genworth Financial business—another insurance company. GE wrote that liabilities, reserves, and annuity benefits were $4.5 billion higher than in 2003 and "attributable to growth in annuities, long-term care insurance, structured settlements, the effects of the weaker U.S. dollar, increases in loss reserves for policies written in prior years and 2004 U.S. hurricane-related losses."

On the call when the charge was first announced, Chief Risk Officer Ryan Zanin told analysts that a large percentage of the policyholders in their book of business were sold the policies at a very early age and are only now reaching the prime claim paying period—ages 80 and up. Therefore, approximately 40 percent of inception-to-date claims have occurred in the last two years.

A GE spokeswoman told MarketWatch: "GE has tested the adequacy of its policy reserves for the runoff insurance business every year through premium deficiency testing." In all prior years, Zanin said on the call with analysts, "these tests resulted in a positive margin, which, under GAAP, requires that original assumptions above the book remain locked." JP Morgan analyst Stephen Tusa asked GE Chief Financial Officer Jamie Miller if the company was happy with its auditor. "If these guys reviewed this stuff every year for the last several years and this is kind of a result of that, doesn't that kind of raise questions?" he asked. Flannery said that he was not planning an auditor change.

KPMG, the GE auditor for more than 100 years, is also the external auditor for Genworth Financial. A spokesman for KPMG emailed MarketWatch to say this:

"We are confident that our audits and reviews were appropriately performed in accordance with applicable professional standards, and we stand behind our work. Our client confidentiality obligations prohibit us from commenting further."

Note: In June of 2020, GE announced they would be replacing KPMG as their auditors with Deloitte. Total Audit and Tax fees charged by KPMG were $104.6 million in 2018 and $79.1 million in 2019.[4]

Questions

1. Assume you are asked as part of an audit of GE's insurance business to assess fraud risks, what would you include in your report and why?

2. At GE's annual meeting in November 2017, CFO Jamie Miller told shareholders that GE was likely to take a charge of more than $3 billion. Just 14 months later GE announced a charge of $6.2 billion. Do you believe this indicates a failure on the part of KPMG to adequately evaluate the estimates of insurance claim reserves and risk assessment, or is it reflective of a change in economic circumstances that could not have been anticipated?

3. According to the Financial Executives Research Foundation, "enhancing the effectiveness of corporate disclosures is of paramount importance to companies, investors, creditors, regulators and the capital markets at large. This has compelled many companies to take a fresh look at how effectively they 'tell their story.'"[2] Some worry that increased disclosures through different channels can be confusing and lead to "disclosure overload." What role should materiality play in determining what kinds of information should be disclosed and how frequently? What are the dangers from an audit perspective of having clients increasingly add to its disclosures, especially when estimates are involved? Did GE do the "right thing" when it warned of a $3 billion charge only to wind up taking a $6.2 billion charge?

Case 5-5 Audit Planning Gone Awry

Travis McGee, a Senior Audit Manager for a Big Four Audit, Consulting, Tax and Data Analytics organization, has just spent the last year helping the firm rollout its new Artificial Intelligence (AI)-based audit infrastructure. Travis is considered one of the most knowledgeable people in the firm surrounding the proper implementation of their new offering, Pandora. There are incredibly high hopes that Pandora will improve overall audit quality and create efficiencies in the audit practice where thin operating margins are the norm. The firm has invested over $200 million into Pandora and Travis is one of a group of senior managers who have been trained to oversee first time implementations of Pandora for the firm's audit clients.

This morning, Travis got a call from Sue, another manager who he had previously worked with and respected, who expressed concerns over statements an engagement partner she was currently working with was making about Pandora. Sue explained that she was in the process of planning the audit of a Fortune 100 client and that during a planning meeting with the engagement team, the engagement partner had stated that the firm needed to cut the budget for the audit by 20 percent or risk losing the client. The partner stated that with the rollout of Pandora, the firm should be able to substantially reduce the work needing to be done in all phases of the audit. The partner evidently spoke of Pandora as having superhuman abilities and was sure that in just a few years the need for auditor's would decrease even further. Sue asked Travis the following questions as she wanted to sit down with the engagement partner and discuss the responses with him.

Questions

1. What is the difference between Data Analytics and Artificial Intelligence-based Auditing?

2. Can AI systems replace the need for auditors? Why or why not?

3. How can AI audit platforms improve overall audit quality?

4. What risks associated with the using AI should we be aware of?

Case 5-6 EY Target of German Regulators Over Suspected Audit Deficiencies at Wirecard

In what some are suggesting is the worst financial reporting fraud since Enron, Wirecard filed for bankruptcy in June of 2020 after admitting that €1.9 billion Euros ($2.1bn U.S.) on its balance sheet (representing roughly 25% of its total assets) probably did not exist.[5]

The fraud appears to have been going on since 2015 with Wirecard recording billions of Euros of fabricated revenue. It has been reported that Wirecard used a technique known as round-tripping to accomplish this deception. Round-tripping is a process by which money and/or assets are moved between entities and end up back in the hands of the entity they originated from (completing a roundtrip). This is done to make it appear as if real economic transactions are actually taking place when they are not.

EY, Wirecard's auditor of over 10 years, has claimed responsibility for bringing the fraud to light in 2020, as a result of their 2019 audit work. When the dust finally settles, that claim may be found to be technically true, but one has to question why the fraud was not caught sooner, given both the magnitude of the fraud and the fact that questions about potential financial irregularities at Wirecard became a matter of public record as early as 2015 when the first of a series of articles was published by the Financial Times.[6]

Carmine di Sibio, Global Chairman and CEO of EY, issued a memo in 2020 to EY partners apparently written to help mitigate client fallout over this audit where he apologized for not uncovering the fraud sooner. The memo also states the following regarding EY's involvement in the Wirecard audit:

"The collusive acts of fraud at Wirecard were implemented through a highly complex criminal network designed to deceive everyone—investors, banks, supervisory authorities, investigating lawyers, and forensic auditors, as well as ourselves" and, "The public interest clearly requires that much more be done to detect fraud at its earliest stages."[7]

EY is currently under investigation by German regulators who are questioning the quality of their work on the Wirecard audit. On July 2, 2020, Kate Beioley and Amy Bell reported that "People with first-hand knowledge told the Financial Times that the auditor between 2016 and 2018 did not check directly with Singapore's OCBC Bank to confirm that the lender held large amounts of cash on behalf of Wirecard. Instead, EY relied on documents and screenshots provided by a third-party trustee and Wirecard itself."[8]

The above quote, from the Financial Times, appears to have been corroborated by an audit partner at KPMG, Alexander Geschonneck.[9] KPMG was hired to investigate the irregularities at Wirecard claimed in the Financial Times article. In speaking to German regulators, Geshconneck suggested that EY should have spotted the fraud earlier. He stated that the work that KPMG did was not rocket science, it was just work that had not been previously been performed by EY. However, EY claims that they did this work, but were fed fabricated information including fraudulent bank confirmations and noting the need for innovative techniques and processes moving forward to catch fraud of this scale.

The Financial Times article states, that in his memo, Sibio committed to making the following changes at EY as a result of what happened at Wirecard:

- Increase the amount of technology it uses to improve its audits including electronic confirmations for audit evidence and matching the company's records with those obtained by the banks.
- Increase the amount of third-party data collected during the audit.
- Increase the amount of checks it does surrounding management integrity.
- Require all EY personnel be given annual forensic accounting training.

The memo does not appear to have addressed the revenue side of the transaction, nor what work was done or should have been done to validate that revenue. In addition, some are now questioning whether EY was aware of the fraud sooner than they have indicated. On October 1, 2020, the Financial Times reported that in 2016 an internal whistleblower at EY had reported potential fraud at Wirecard and an attempt to bribe EY staff in India.[10]

Questions

1. Discuss whether you believe that EY performed its audit of Wirecard in accordance with GAAS. Identify specific requirements of GAAS in your response to support your position, referencing both risk assessment and audit procedures.
2. Discuss the changes that EY indicates they will be making to improve its audit quality as a result of what occurred at Wirecard. Do you believe these changes will make a difference in how EY conducts its audits?

Case 5-7 Diamond Foods: Accounting for Nuts[1]

Diamond Foods, based in Stockton, California, is a premium snack food and culinary nut company with diversified operations. The company had a reputation of making bold and expensive acquisitions. Due to competition within the snack food industry, Diamond developed an aggressive company culture that placed high emphasis upon performance. The company's slogan was "Bigger is better." However, without strong ethical oversight, questionable behavior started to persist at Diamond Foods in 2009. Serious allegations of fraud against top management led to a restructuring of leadership. Here is the story we dub: "Accounting for Nuts."

On November 14, 2012, Diamond Foods Inc. disclosed restated financial statements tied to an accounting scandal that reduced its earnings during the first three quarters of 2012 as it took significant charges related to improper accounting for payments to walnut growers. The restatements cut Diamond's earnings by 57 percent for FY2011, to $29.7 million, and by 46 percent for FY2010, to $23.2 million. By December 7, 2012, Diamond's share price had declined 54 percent for the year.

Diamond Foods, long-time maker of Emerald nuts and subsequent purchaser of Pop Secret popcorn (2008) and Kettle potato chips (2010), became the focus of an SEC investigation after The Wall Street Journal raised questions about the timing and accounting of Diamond's payments to walnut growers. The case focuses on the matching of costs and revenues. At the heart of the investigation was the question of whether Diamond senior management adjusted the accounting for the grower payments on purpose to increase profits for a given period.

The case arose in September 2011, when Douglas Barnhill, an accountant who is also a farmer of 75 acres of California walnut groves, got a mysterious check for nearly $46,000 from Diamond. Barnhill contacted Eric Heidman, Diamond's director of field operations, on whether the check was a final payment for his 2010 crop or prepayment for the 2011 harvest. (Diamond growers are paid in installments, with the final payment for the prior fall's crops coming late the following year.) Though it was September 2011, Barnhill was still waiting for full payment for the walnuts that he had sent Diamond in 2010. Heidman told Barnhill that the payment was for the 2010 crop, part of FY2011, but that it would be "budgeted into the next year." The problem is, under accounting rules, you cannot legitimately record in a future fiscal year an amount for a prior year's crop. That amount should have been estimated during 2010 and recorded as an expense against revenue from the sale of walnuts.

An investigation by the audit committee in February 2012 found payments of $20 million to walnut growers in August 2010 and $60 million in September 2011 that were not recorded in the correct periods. The disclosure of financial restatements in November 2012 and audit committee investigation led to the resignation of former CEO Michael Mendes, who agreed to pay a $2.74 million cash clawback and return 6,665 shares to the company. Mendes' cash clawback was deducted from his retirement payout of $5.4 million. Former CFO Steven Neil was fired on November 19, 2012, and did not receive any severance. The SEC brought a lawsuit against Diamond Foods, Mendes, and Neil. It settled with the company and Mendes on January 9, 2014. In a separate action, Neil settled charges that he had directed the effort to fraudulently underreport money paid to walnut growers by delaying the recording of payments into later fiscal periods.

As a result of the audit committee investigation and the subsequent analysis and procedures performed, the company identified material weaknesses in three areas: control environment, walnut grower accounting, and accounts payable timing recognition. The company announced efforts to remediate these areas of material weakness, including enhanced oversight and controls, leadership changes, a revised walnut cost estimation policy, and improved financial and operation reporting throughout the organization.

A number of questionable transactions took place, including unusual timing of payments to growers, a leap in profit margins, and volatile inventories and cash flows. Moreover, the company seemed to push hard on every lever to meet increasingly ambitious earnings targets and allowed top executives to pull in big bonuses, according to interviews with former Diamond employees and board members, rivals, suppliers, and consultants, in addition to reviews of public and nonpublic Diamond records.

Nick Feakins, a forensic accountant, noted the relentless climb in Diamond's profit margins, including an increase in net income as a percent of sales from 1.5 percent in FY2006 to more than 5 percent in FY2011. According to Feakins, "no competitors were improving like that; even with rising Asian demand." Reuters did a review of 11 companies listed as comparable organizations in Diamond's regulatory filings and found that only one, B&G Foods, which made multiple acquisitions, added earnings during the period.

Auditors often look at the relationship between earnings and cash flow as part of their risk assessment. At Diamond, net income growth is generally reflected in operating cash flow increases. However, the cash generation was sluggish in FY2010, when earnings were strong. Also, in September 2010, Mendes had promised EPS growth of 15 percent to 20 percent per year for the next five years. In FY2009, FY2010, and FY2011, $2.6 million of Mendes' $4.1 million in annual bonus was paid because Diamond beat its EPS goal, according to regulatory filings.

Diamond falsely disclosed its strong overall financial performance in conference calls with financial analysts. In its call for the third-quarter FY 2011, Mendes said: "Earnings per share had increased 73 percent to 52 cents, exceeding the top end of the company's guidance range. Strong operating cash flow for the period helped fund a significant increase in new product and advertising investment as EBITDA [Earnings before interest, taxes, depreciations, and amortization] of $31 million was more than double the same period in the prior year." Based on these false reports, the analysts were optimistic about future earnings and share value. They informed the investment banking groups in their firms to recommend a "buy" to their clients.

As for the role of Deloitte in the fraud, the SEC charged that Neil misled them by giving false and incomplete information to justify the unusual accounting treatment for the payments. The SEC's order against Mendes found that he should have known that Diamond's reported walnut cost was incorrect because of information he received at the time, and he omitted facts in certain representations to Deloitte about the special walnut payments. One problem was Neil did not document accounting policies or design the process for which walnut grower payments and the walnut cost estimates were determined. This was exacerbated by the fact that management did not communicate the intent of the payments effectively.

Questions

1. Use the Fraud Triangle to analyze the business and audit risks that existed at Diamond Foods during the period of its accounting fraud.

2. How would you characterize Diamond's accounting? Did they commit an error in recording walnut grower payments? Was it an illegal act? A fraudulent act? For each one, explain the reporting requirements for Deloitte assuming they were aware of the transactions.

3. What are auditors' obligations with respect to accounting estimates and judgments made by management? Explain any concerns that should have existed about these areas of the audit. Assume that Deloitte was aware of these issues. Would any of them rise to the level of a critical audit matter? Explain.

4. Do you think non-GAAP information, such as that provided to financial analysts, should be audited? Consider the value of such information to the users of financial reports in answering this question.

Case 5-8 Critical Audit Matters or Potentially Damaging Disclosure?

Ronnie Maloney, an audit partner for Forrester and Loomis, a registered public accounting firm in Boston, just received a meeting request from Jack McDuff, the chairman of the audit committee of Digital Solutions, one of his clients. The audit committee wants to discuss the draft communication the firm prepared to meet its obligations under PCAOB AS 1301. Digital Solutions, a Fortune 1000 client, has expressed concerns over the skepticism raised by the firm over accounting policies. Moreover, McDuff was worried about the impact of critical audit matters included in the draft of the December 31, 2021, audit report. He claimed that publicly disclosing the critical audit matter would muddy the waters for investors as the financial statements for the year-ended December 31, 2021, were found to fairly represent the financial condition of the company in all material respects.

Maloney is the lead engagement partner on the Digital Solutions audit. He arranges a meeting with Haley Stone, another audit partner on the engagement team, to discuss McDuff's request. They review the audit team's findings about accounting policies. It seems there was concern about a related party transaction between the CEO of Digital and a vendor whereby Digital paid about 20 percent above market price for components received from the vendor. As a result, Digital's net earnings for the year declined rather than increased, and earnings per share were $0.10 less than it would have been had the transaction been at arm's length.

As to the critical audit matters, Maloney and Stone discussed an estimate Digital made of imputed interest on a non-interest-bearing note from the same vendor for a piece of machinery that was recorded on December 30, 2021. The company used a 2 percent rate on the $400,000 five-year note and calculated the present value as $362,292. The entry recorded was:

Debit—Machinery 362,292

Debit—Discount 37,708

Credit—Note Payable 400,000

Based on an analysis of the rate Digital would incur if it borrowed funds from another source, Maloney and Stone determined that 6 percent should have been used. That would have led to the following entry:

Debit—Machinery 298,904

Debit—Discount 101,096

Credit—Note Payable 400,000

The future interest expense would be $63,388 less given the 2 percent rate, which had a material effect on future earnings. Furthermore, the difference was close to the amount of the "premium" Digital Solutions paid to the vendor for the components.

Questions

1. Given the facts of the case, what communications do you believe Forrester and Loomis should have made with the audit committee with regard to the transactions with the vendor to comply with PCAOB AS 1301?

2. How should Forrester and Loomis have determined whether to communicate the critical audit matter with the audit committee under PCAOB AS 1301?

3. Are the differences discussed in the case a matter of judgment or are there other factors at work? What concerns do you have about the audit risk and ICFR?

4. Do you believe financial statement fraud exists in this case? Explain why or why not.

Case 5-9 Weatherford International

Cast of Characters[1]

Weatherford International PLC is a multinational Irish public limited company based in Switzerland, with U.S. offices in Houston, Texas. Weatherford's shares are registered with the SEC and are listed on the NYSE. Weatherford files periodic reports, including Forms 10-K and 10-Q, with the Commission pursuant to Exchange Act Section 13(a) and related rules thereunder.

James M. Hudgins, CPA, served as Weatherford's Director of Tax from January 1999 until mid-2000, when he became Vice President of Tax, and as an Officer from February 2009 until his resignation on March 31, 2012.

Darryl S. Kitay, CPA, served as Weatherford's Tax Manager and Senior Manager from April 2004 until 2011, then as Weatherford's Tax Director through January 2013. Kitay reported to Hudgins from April 2004 until March 2012. Weatherford relieved Kitay of all supervisory responsibilities associated with Weatherford's income tax accounting in May 2012, after the filing of the Second Restatement of financial statements. Weatherford terminated Kitay's employment in July 2013.

Ernst & Young LLP was Weatherford's external auditor from 2001 to March 2013. On March 7, 2013, Weatherford's audit committee decided not to re-appoint EY.

SEC Order Against EY

On October 18, 2016, the SEC announced that EY agreed to pay more than $11.8 million to settle charges related to failed audits of Weatherford based on the auditors' failure to detect deceptive income tax accounting to inflate earnings. The EY penalty is in addition to the $140 million penalty already agreed to. The combined $152 million will be returned to investors who were harmed by the accounting fraud. The Commission also charged the EY partner who coordinated the audits, Craig Fronckiewicz, and a former tax partner who was part of the audit engagement team, Sarah Adams. Both agreed to suspensions to settle charges that they disregarded significant red flags during the audits and reviews.

The SEC's order stated that, despite placing the Weatherford audits in a high-risk category, EY's audit team repeatedly failed to detect the company's fraud until it was more than four years ongoing. The audit team was aware of post-closing adjustments that Weatherford was making to significantly lower its year-end provision for income taxes each year, but it relied on Weatherford's unsubstantiated explanations instead of performing the required audit procedures to scrutinize the company's accounting. The SEC's order also found that EY did not take effective measures to minimize known recurring problems its audit teams experienced when auditing tax accounting.[11]

Facts of the Case

Between 2007 and 2012, Weatherford, a large multinational provider of oil and natural gas equipment and services, issued false financial statements that inflated its earnings by over $900 million in violation of U.S. GAAP. Weatherford issued materially false and misleading statements about its net income, EPS, effective tax rate ("ETR"), and other key financial information. Weatherford did not have sufficient internal accounting controls to identify and properly account for its accounting of income taxes throughout the relevant period.

As a result, Weatherford was forced to restate its financial statements on three separate occasions over 18 months. The first restatement was made public on March 1, 2011, when Weatherford announced that it would restate its financial results for 2007-2010 and that a material weakness existed in its ICFR for the accounting of income taxes. That restatement, filed on March 8, 2011, reduced previously reported net income by approximately $500 million (the "First Restatement"). $461 million of the First Restatement resulted from a four-year income tax accounting fraud orchestrated by Hudgins and Kitay. Hudgins and Kitay made numerous post-closing adjustments or "plugs" to fill gaps to meet ETRs that Weatherford previously disclosed to financial analysts and the public. This deceptive intercompany tax accounting improperly inflated Weatherford's earnings and materially understated its ETR and tax expense.

The fraud created the misperception that the tax structure Weatherford designed to reduce its tax expense and ETR was far more successful than it actually was. From 2007 to 2010, Weatherford regularly promoted its favorable ETR to analysts and investors as one of its key competitive advantages, which it attributed to a superior international tax avoidance structure that Hudgins constructed at the urging of senior management.

After announcing the First Restatement, Weatherford's stock price declined nearly 11 percent in one trading day ($2.38 per share), closing at $21.14 per share on March 2, 2011. The decline eliminated over $1.7 billion from Weatherford's market capitalization.

Weatherford announced additional restatements in February 2012 and July 2012 (the "Second Restatement" and "Third Restatement," respectively). After the First Restatement, Weatherford attempted to remediate its material weakness in internal control over income tax accounting. Throughout its remediation efforts in 2011, Weatherford filed its Forms 10-Q on a timely basis and falsely reassured investors that it was performing additional reconciliations and post-closing procedures to ensure that its financial statements were fairly presented in conformity with GAAP. However, Weatherford, through Hudgins and Kitay, failed to review, assess, and quantify known income tax accounting issues that had a high risk of causing additional material misstatement as early as July 2011. When Weatherford filed its Second Restatement on March 15, 2012, Weatherford reported a $256 million drop in net income from 2007 to 2011 as a result of additional errors in its income tax accounting, and its material weakness in internal control over income tax accounting remained. At least $84 million of that drop in net income resulted from an income tax accounting GAAP violation Hudgins and Kitay knew about, but failed to assess and quantify, before Weatherford filed its third quarter financial statements.

Four months after filing the Second Restatement, Weatherford announced that it was withdrawing reliance on all previous financial statements because it had discovered additional income tax errors that reduced prior period net income by $107 million. By the time Weatherford issued its Third Restatement on December 17, 2012, Weatherford had reduced net income from prior periods by an additional $186 million, largely driven by books, records, and internal accounting controls issues identified and corrected during Weatherford's remediation efforts in 2012.

Tax Strategy

A key component of Weatherford's tax strategy was to develop a superior international tax avoidance structure that reduced Weatherford's ETR and tax expense (and increased EPS and cash flow) while providing a competitive advantage over U.S.-based peer companies. In 2002, Weatherford changed its place of incorporation from the United States to Bermuda, a 0 percent tax jurisdiction, through a process known as inversion.

Weatherford further refined its international tax structure from 2003 through 2006 by implementing a series of hybrid instruments to facilitate the movement of revenue from higher tax rate jurisdictions (i.e., Canada and the United States) to lower tax rate jurisdictions (i.e., Hungary and Luxembourg). Hybrid instruments are often used in international tax planning to achieve deductions in one, typically high tax rate, jurisdiction and shift income to another, typically low tax rate, jurisdiction. Hybrid instruments are structured to incorporate features of both debt and equity, such that the instrument typically qualifies as debt in one jurisdiction and equity in another. Payments on debt may be deducted in computing taxable income while the yields are accrued but not necessarily paid and, therefore, not calculated as taxable income. As a result, these international tax avoidance strategies reduced Weatherford's ETR from 36.3 percent in 2001 to 25.9 percent by the end of 2006.

Weatherford senior management and Hudgins understood that Weatherford's tax structure and resulting ETR added significant value and was material to analysts and investors alike. Wall Street analysts closely followed Weatherford's ETR and its effect on earnings. Each percentage point in Weatherford's ETR translated into $0.02 to $0.03 in EPS.

Weatherford's senior management knew its tax department was perpetually understaffed and overworked during the years leading up to the First Restatement. Hudgins led a tax staff that was roughly the same size as when he was hired, and Hudgins pressed his employees to work long hours to make Weatherford's tax structure extremely competitive. Weatherford and Hudgins quickly gained a reputation with the company's external auditor as a challenging and demanding client known for taking aggressive accounting positions, particularly in the area of income tax accounting.

Although Weatherford reduced its ETR by nearly 10 percent from 2001 to the end of 2006, its CFO remarked that Weatherford's ETR remained somewhat above that of other inverted peer companies in his response to an analyst's question during the year-end earnings call on January 30, 2007. Soon thereafter, Weatherford started reporting ETR results that created a false perception that its international tax structure was outperforming similarly situated competitors by a significant margin. For example, in 2008 and 2009, fueled by its deceptive income tax accounting practices, Weatherford reported pre-restatement ETRs of 17.1 percent and 6.5 percent.

In connection with fiscal years 2007 through 2010, Hudgins and Kitay engaged in fraudulent practices relating to income tax accounting that violated GAAP and made Weatherford's financial statements materially false and misleading. During each of those years, Weatherford repeatedly and publicly disclosed ETR estimates and recorded tax expenses that Hudgins and Kitay knew, or were reckless in not knowing, were fabricated. Each year, Hudgins and Kitay made or authorized unsupported post-closing adjustments to accounting data that intentionally lowered Weatherford's actual ETR and tax expense. To do so, they reversed accounting data that had been correctly input into Weatherford's consolidated tax provision from the company's accounting system, and did not notify Weatherford's accounting department why they had made such adjustments.

Hudgins and Kitay performed no work to support the adjustments, which were merely a "plug" to arrive at the lower estimated ETR and tax expense amounts. Without disclosing how they arrived at their numbers, they provided these amounts for inclusion in Weatherford's consolidated financial statements, which senior management shared with analysts and investors repeatedly during earnings calls and public financial statements. This conduct went undetected for over four fiscal years. Kitay identified the existence of the adjustments to EY each year, but, when questioned about them, Kitay made misleading and inconsistent responses to the auditors and failed to disclose the true reason for the adjustments. Kitay sometimes asked Hudgins to review his responses before providing them to EY.

The errors were finally discovered in February 2011. By that time, a "phantom income tax receivable" had increased to such dramatically disproportionate heights, over $460 million, that it defied even the unsupported explanations of Hudgins and Kitay. Shortly thereafter, Weatherford released the First Restatement in March 2011.

Results for 2007

The following summarizes the accounting and tax maneuvers for 2007. We limit the discussion to 2007 for the sake of brevity.

Throughout the first three quarters of 2007, Weatherford recorded ETR and tax expense pursuant to FIN 18, "*Accounting for Income Taxes in Interim Periods.*" FIN 18 prescribes an estimated annualized ETR approach for computing the tax provisions for the first three quarters of the year, which is based on a company's best estimate of current year ordinary income. GAAP, however, does not allow companies to use FIN 18 to calculate their year-end tax provisions.

To comply with GAAP, Weatherford was required to record ETR and tax expense at year-end pursuant to FAS 109, "*Accounting for Income Taxes.*" FAS 109 establishes standards on how companies should account for and report the effects of income taxes, including the calculation of the year-end consolidated tax provision. Tax department personnel reviewed that information, after which the tax provisions for legal entities were finalized and then combined on a region-by-region basis. The region-based tax provisions were then consolidated to arrive at a single tax provision from which current and deferred assets and liabilities, associated tax expense (or benefit), and ETR were calculated and recorded.

Shortly before Weatherford was scheduled to release its year-end financial results for 2007, however, Hudgins and Kitay discovered the year-end ETR and tax expense that had been calculated pursuant to FAS 109 far exceeded the ETR estimates and tax expense disseminated publicly to analysts and investors during the first three quarters of 2007 based on their ETR estimates. Faced with a deadline for reporting earnings, Hudgins and Kitay falsified the year-end consolidated tax provision by making an unsubstantiated manual $439.7 million post-closing "plug" adjustment to two different Weatherford Luxembourg entities. To do so, they intentionally reversed accounting data that had been correctly input to Weatherford's consolidated tax provision via the company's accounting system.[3]

The resulting plug adjustment, which Hudgins and Kitay then improperly applied a 35 percent tax rate to, allowed Weatherford to reduce its tax expense by $153.9 million for the year and to lower its ETR in line with previous ETR estimates publicly disclosed during quarterly calls with analysts.

Hudgins and Kitay took no steps to determine the necessity and accuracy of the plug adjustment, either before or after it was made. They performed no work at any time to determine whether plugging the gap was appropriate under GAAP and made no attempt to substantiate the difference between the their publicly disclosed ETR estimates and tax expenses with the FAS 109 actual results that they were witnessing. Both Hudgins and Kitay knew, or were reckless in not knowing, that they should have reviewed and substantiated the actual tax numbers after the close process, but they never did. Hudgins and Kitay made no attempt to alert Weatherford's accounting department, internal auditor, or senior management of the significant issues related to its FAS 109 actual ETR results. Nor did they notify EY of any discrepancy.

During 2007 and throughout the relevant period, Hudgins signed representation letters relied upon by Weatherford senior management and EY indicating, without exception, that the ICFR for the accounting of income taxes were effective and that the income tax accounting was completed in accordance with GAAP. These statements were false.

Phantom Income Tax Receivable

The inappropriate plug adjustments and the resulting improper tax benefits recorded from 2007 through 2010 created a $461 million debit balance to Weatherford's current income tax payable, which Respondents reclassified as an income tax receivable for reporting purposes. This improper accounting should have raised red flags long before the First Restatement.

Hudgins and Kitay made misleading statements about the true reasons for the growing tax debit balance, claiming falsely that they had made either sizeable prepayments or overpayments to foreign tax jurisdictions that they would be working to recover. For example, during the fourth quarter of 2009, Weatherford reclassified the large debit balance within the Current Income Tax Payable account to a Prepaid Other account. In response to EY inquiries about the large "Prepaid Other" debit balance, Kitay responded, "We do not believe it would be appropriate to classify these balances as receivables until such time as a claim for refund has been filed." By 2010, Hudgins was aware of the phantom receivable and told others at Weatherford that he was working to recover all overpaid amounts, although he knew there were no such overpaid amounts.

In performing its audit of Weatherford's financial statements, EY and Weatherford identified a number of additional income tax accounting errors that increased Weatherford's tax expense by tens of millions of dollars, including: (1) failure to timely accrue foreign taxes; (2) uncertain tax position accruals that were not reflected in Weatherford's consolidated tax provisions; (3) entries to prematurely reverse liabilities related to uncertain tax positions (some of which were improperly classified as current taxes payable); and (4) understatements of income tax expense related to deferred tax liability.

Material Weakness in ICFR

On or about February 15, 2011, after consideration of the errors and issues discovered and after consultation with EY, Weatherford's internal audit group concluded that there was a material weakness in internal control surrounding accounting for income taxes due to inadequate staffing and technical expertise, ineffective review and approval practices, inadequate processes to effectively reconcile income tax accounts, and inadequate controls over the preparation of Weatherford's quarterly tax provision.

After the identification of the material weakness, EY expanded the audit procedures for all income tax accounts, including a reconciliation of Weatherford's current taxes payable (and receivable) accounts. On or about February 20, 2011, a review of Weatherford's income tax receivable balance uncovered the phantom $461 million receivable which, in turn, led to the First Restatement. At no time prior to this process did Hudgins or Kitay inform anyone of the true reason they made the post-closing adjustments.

On March 1, 2011, Weatherford filed a Form 8-K with the Commission in which it made public for the first time that it would be restating its financial results for 2007–2010 and that a material weakness existed in its ICFR for the accounting of income taxes. Weatherford's stock price dropped nearly 11 percent to $21.14 on the news.

Restated Financial Statements

On March 8, 2011, Weatherford filed its First Restatement in which it restated its previously reported financial results for the years ended December 31, 2007, 2008, 2009, and the first three quarters of 2010. According to Weatherford, the First Restatement was necessary to correct "errors in [the Company's] accounting for income taxes." The following table depicts the impact the Restatement had on Weatherford's reported net income for the periods covered by the First Restatement.

Year Ended	Reported Net Income (in millions)	Restated Net Income (in millions)	% Change
2007	$1,070.6	$ 940.6	13.8%
2008	$1,393.2	$1,246.5	11.3%
2009	$ 253.8	$ 170.1	42.6%
Q1–Q3 2010	$ 78.3	$ (21.6)	462.0%

Violations

SEC Securities Act provisions prohibit any person/corporation from:

- Obtaining money or property in the offer or sale of securities by means of any untrue statement of a material fact or any omission to state a material fact necessary in order to make the statements made, in light of the circumstances under which they were made, not misleading;
- Engaging in any transaction, practice, or course of business which operates or would operate as a fraud or deceit upon the purchaser in the offer or sale of securities;

- Failing to make and keep books, records and accounts which, in reasonable detail, accurately and fairly reflect their transactions and dispositions of their assets;
- Devising and maintaining a system of internal accounting controls that doesn't sufficiently provide reasonable assurances that transactions are recorded as necessary to permit preparation of financial statements in accordance with GAAP.

Weatherford agreed to report to the SEC during a two-year term its compliance with Commission regulations and GAAP regarding its accounting for income taxes, financial reporting, and the status of any remediation, implementation, auditing, and testing of its internal accounting controls and compliance measures. Hudgins and Katay were denied the privilege of appearing and practicing before the Commission as an accountant for five years after which they could apply for reinstatement. Financial penalties included: $140 million, as to Weatherford; for Hudgins, disgorgement of $169,728, prejudgment interest of $39,339, and a civil money penalty in the amount of $125,000, for a total of $334,067 to the SEC; and for Kitay, a civil money penalty in the amount of $30,000 to the SEC.

Questions

1. Explain how pressures and incentives drove the actions taken by Hudgins and Kitay to commit financial statement fraud.
2. Describe the problems in the audit of Weatherford International by Ernst & Young.
3. Describe the deficiencies in the internal accounting systems, ICFR, and corporate governance at Weatherford. Were there any violations of the rules of conduct in the AICPA Code by Hudgins or Kitay? Explain.
4. Explain how Weatherford and Hudgins used aggressive accounting positions in the area of income tax accounting.

Case 5-10 Potential Fraud at EP Sports

Richard Lange, CPA, is a sole practitioner. The largest audit client in his office is Echo Park Sportswear (EP Sports). EP Sports is a privately owned company in South Bend, Indiana with a 12-person board of directors. Richard was hired by the audit committee of the board five years ago and is proud to have them as a client. He took an immediate liking to their CEO, Michael Walker, who is also chair of the audit committee. Michael has a gregarious personality and infectious laugh, and the rest of the company's board and management team seem to adore him.

Richard is in the process of auditing EP Sports' financial statements for the year-ended December 31, 2021. He just discovered a related-party transaction that has him worried. For one thing, the relationship has existed for the past two years, but Richard did not discover it until now. What's just as troubling is that Walker appears to have hidden it from him.

EP Sports bought a majority stake in Palladium Sportswear two years ago but still operates it as a separate entity, and since then has systematically failed to disclose to the private investors related-party transactions involving Walker. It seems that Walker is borrowing money from Palladium and is also deeply in debt to the CEO of that company, who is his brother-in-law. In addition, Palladium has hired relatives of Walker, most of whom are unqualified for their jobs, and pays them above-market salaries. All of this has been hidden from Richard.

Richard recently received an anonymous tip that EP Sports operates a secret off-balance-sheet cash account to pay cash bonuses to senior officers, travel and entertainment expenses and an apartment rental for Walker, as well as noncash gifts to local government officials to "grease the wheels" when permits need to be expedited in favor of the company. Richard has not followed-up on the tip yet because he is currently focused on the related-party transactions with Palladium Sportswear.

Richard just met with the CFO of EP Sports, Cynthia Riley, CPA to discuss these transactions. Riley explained that she had raised these issues with Walker but was instructed in no uncertain terms to leave them alone. Walker told Riley that she should just consider these transactions a part of his compensation package as the CEO, that they were common in privately held companies, and that she should focus her energies elsewhere. Riley told Richard she needed this job and wouldn't jeopardize it out of a sense of "ethics." While she did not come out and say it, Richard got the impression that Riley seemed to believe that Walker's actions were somehow justified.

Richard is back in his office and reflecting on how best to handle this situation.

Questions

1. Who are the stakeholders in this case and what are Richard's obligations to them?
2. What are related-party transactions? Why are related-party transactions a particularly sensitive area? What do you think Richard should do with respect to audit obligations for these transactions?
3. Has fraud been committed in this case? Explain. If so, what are Richard's obligations in this regard?

Motivation for Fraudulent Financial Reporting

LEARNING OBJECTIVES

After studying **Chapter 6**, you should be able to:

LO 6-1   Describe the characteristics of earnings management.

LO 6-2   Explain the purpose of providing earnings guidance and motivation for making false and misleading disclosures.

LO 6-3   Explain how an auditor might look for red flags that indicate fraud may exist in the financial statements.

LO 6-4   Explain the working of financial shenanigans and its effect on reported earnings.

LO 6-5   Describe the makeup of non-GAAP amounts and whether they distort reported earnings.

Ethics Reflection

Financial statements must be relevant and reliable. Relevance means the information being reported is meaningful. Reliability refers to the accuracy with which financial data is reported so that users know that information can be trusted.

An important quality of useful information is *representational faithfulness.* To represent the transactions and events faithfully in the financial statements, the effects of transactions and events should be reported on the basis of their economic substance instead of legal form of the transactions. For example, if a company sells an asset but is still responsible for maintaining it or has other risks of "ownership," then reporting this transaction as a sale instead of secured loan does not faithfully represent the transaction and thus would distort the effect of the transaction on reported amounts and potentially mislead the users of the statements.

Fraudulent financial reporting occurs for a variety of reasons including making the company look like it's doing better than it really is. Some companies manipulate GAAP to achieve a higher level of earnings and mislead investors and creditors about the company's current and expected future earnings. Oftentimes the motivation is to meet or exceed financial analysts' earnings projections in order to maintain or increase the company's stock price.

Companies use a variety of techniques to produce fraudulent financial reports including accelerating the reporting of revenues and delaying the reporting of expenses, oftentimes by manipulating accrual amounts. These are called *financial shenanigans.* Given the number of estimates and accounting choices to be made to produce financial reports, it is up to auditors to ensure they capture economic reality and are not manipulated by management in order to "cook the books." A skeptic might say that an unmodified (unqualified) audit opinion means the financial statements have been prepared in accordance with cooked books under GAAP.

Companies seem to look for any advantage when they report GAAP earnings results. One approach that has caught on with virtually all public companies is the reporting of non-GAAP earnings in public releases including on social media, in conference calls with investors, financial analysts, and in quarterly financial reports. In a report issued by the Center For Audit Quality, 94 percent of S&P 500 companies included at least one non-GAAP financial measure in their earnings releases in the first quarter of 2020.[1] Companies have great latitude in choosing what they report as non-GAAP metrics because FASB has not set any rules in this area even though it is in the public interest to do so.

In this chapter, we examine the motivation for producing materially misleading or fraudulent financial reports and the techniques used to do so. We also identify the red flags which signal the need for heightened professional skepticism. Auditors must act when red flags are present to ensure that fraud is detected and corrected. The Fraud Triangle discussed in **Chapter 5** provides guidance on what to look for in making that determination.

There are consequences of managing earnings to achieve a desired goal rather than to faithfully represent reality or what actually happened during the year. These are discussed in **Chapter 7** including when and how financial statements need to be reissued or restated and to inform users they no longer should rely on the original financial reports.

Here are the important questions to consider in Chapter 6: (1) What motivates fraudulent financial reporting? (2) How are financial statements manipulated to achieve a desired goal? (3) What are the red flags to look out for in spotting techniques that can lead to material misstatements of the financial statements? (4) Why do companies provide non-GAAP earnings?

> Increasingly, I have become concerned that the motivation to meet Wall Street earnings expectations may be overriding common sense business practices. Too many corporate managers, auditors, and analysts are participants in a game of nods and winks. In the zeal to satisfy consensus earnings estimates and project a smooth earnings path, wishful thinking may be winning the day over faithful representation.
>
> *Source: Arthur Levitt, former Chairman of the U.S. Securities and Exchange Commission*

This quote by former SEC chair Arthur Levitt from "The Numbers Game" links the practice of "earnings management" to an excessive zeal to project smoother earnings from year to year that casts a pall over the quality of the underlying numbers. Levitt identifies the cause as a "culture of gamesmanship" in business rooted in the emphasis on achieving short-term results such as meeting or exceeding financial analysts' earnings expectations.[2]

Warren Buffett once said, "Earnings can be as pliable as putty when a charlatan heads the company reporting them." The quote emphasizes the importance of having an ethical person at the head of a company because a CEO who practices fraud can twist earnings to make them look better than they really are, thereby deceiving the users of the financial statements.

The accounting scandals at companies such as Enron, WorldCom, and Tyco involved the use of techniques to fraudulently inflate recorded earnings in order to drive up the price of stock. Top officials then sold their shares at a considerable gain all the while thousands of employees did not, because they weren't in the know, and they lost millions of dollars of accumulated wealth in stock ownership and 401(k) plans. If the company failed, employees lost their jobs as well. The one constant in these frauds was that the use of these techniques eventually caught up with the companies because they no longer could sustain those practices. Another constant was that managers acted without due regard for their fiduciary obligations to the shareholders and in violation of securities laws. It was the old story: Managers act out of self-interest and greed; greed begets more greed. It was a classic example of egoistic behavior motivated by a sense that they would never be caught.

Companies manage earnings when they ask, "How can we best report desired results?" rather than "How can we best report economic reality (the actual results)?" Levitt attributes the practice of earnings management to the pressure on Wall Street to "make the numbers." He identifies a pattern created by earnings management whereby "companies try to meet or beat Wall Street earnings projections in order to grow market capitalization and increase the value of stock options." He notes that on the one hand auditors are under pressure to retain clients by the firm and on the other they are under pressure by management "not to stand in the way."

Characteristics of Earnings Management

LO 6-1
Describe the characteristics of earnings management.

What drives a manager to record transactions in a way that achieves a desired level of financial results even if the accounting treatment is not supportable by the facts? Is it to meet financial analysts' earnings expectations, hit overly optimistic earnings guidance, put the best face possible on the financial statements, or flat out fraud? During the era of Enron and WorldCom, earnings management occurred as a result of all of these influences and to enhance executives' performance reputation and the desire to influence the stock price, which would make stock options more valuable.

Motivation for Earnings Management

Earnings management occurs when companies artificially inflate (or deflate) their revenues, profits, or earnings per share (EPS) figures. Gaa and Dunmore point out that earnings may be managed in many different ways, but they all boil down to two basic possibilities. One is to alter the numbers already in the financial records by using discretionary accruals and other adjustments, and the other is to create or structure real transactions for the purpose of altering the reported numbers. There are also two kinds of motivations for altering the financial reports through disclosure decisions. Management may either intend to influence stakeholders' beliefs and behavior or to influence how contracts are performed.[3]

Another perspective on earnings management is to divide the techniques into two categories: operating earnings management and accounting earnings management. Operating earnings management deals with altering operating decisions to affect cash flows and net income for a period such as easing credit terms to increase sales. Accounting earnings management deals with using the flexibility in accounting standards to alter earnings numbers.[4]

Generally, the end result of earnings management is to distort the application of GAAP, thereby bringing into question the quality of earnings. The question to ask is whether the distortion is the result of appropriate decision making, given that choices exist in the application of GAAP, or if it is motivated by a conscious effort to manipulate earnings for one's advantage, which is fraud.

While some authors distinguish between earnings manipulation and earnings management, we believe earnings manipulation is a form of earnings management. For example, Hopwood et al. believe that earnings management is management's routine use of nonfraudulent accounting and economic discretion, while earnings manipulation can refer either to the legitimate or aggressive use, or fraudulent abuse, of discretion. By their reckoning, earnings management is legitimate, while earnings manipulation can be legitimate, marginally ethical, unethical, or illegal, depending on its extent.[5] The problem with this distinction is characterizing practices as ethical relies on what is a person's intent. If one intends to manipulate earnings through income smoothing or other techniques, it is unethical because it is designed to alter the earnings picture and deceive another party; if not, why engage in the practice? Recall that intent or motivation is the third factor in Rest's Model of Ethical Decision Making.

While earnings management is not necessarily the result of an intentional fraud, but the culmination of a series of aggressive interpretations of the accounting rules and aggressive operating activities, it still should be considered unethical if the primary motive for managing earnings is to deceive users of the true results of operations, portray managerial performance in the best light, and present views of earnings and liquidity not conforming with GAAP. In many cases, earnings management is carried out by otherwise honest people who are motivated to tell the company's side of the story rather than strictly adhere to GAAP. The end result is misstatement of the financial results that oftentimes builds pressure to do the same in subsequent periods. One aggressive interpretation leads to another until the quality of the financial information is in doubt.

McGregor explains earnings manipulation as follows:

> The typical case of earnings manipulation begins with a track record of success. The company or division has posted significant sales and earnings growth over recent years. [Its] stock price trades at a high price earnings multiple as the market rewards its stellar growth. Unfortunately, it is becoming more difficult for the company to maintain the sales and earnings growth that analysts have grown to expect. Sales are behind target this quarter, so management runs special incentives for its sales force to accelerate sales and uses overtime to ship out its products. It works and the firm meets expectations.
>
> The next quarter, the analyst expectations are higher. However, sales still have not picked up to the level required, so the firm provides additional incentives to its sales force, uses overtime to boost shipments but now has additional expenses to contend with (incentives and overtime), so it does not fully accrue all its consulting expenses. The following quarter rolls around and sales still haven't recovered, but the analysts keep raising the bar. This time the operating tactics are not enough, so management pressures the CFO to make the numbers. The CFO is aggressive in the interpretation of installment sales and expense accruals, and the company again meets expectations. The expectations keep rising, as does the firm's stock price. As the fourth quarter comes around, sales still are not at expectations. The CFO creates sales and under-accrues expenses all to meet expectations. The company has gone from aggressive operating practices to financial fraud.[6]

Earnings management techniques have come to be known as "financial shenanigans." Financial shenanigans are actions or omissions of information or financial structuring of transactions intended to hide or distort the real financial performance or financial condition of an entity. They range from minor deceptions to more serious misapplications of accounting principles. We discuss these techniques later in this chapter.

Income Smoothing

Arthur Levitt talks about another motivation to manage earnings: to smooth net income over time. The ideal pattern of earnings for a manager is a steady increase each year over a period of time. The results make it appear that the company is growing and doing better than it really is, and the manager should be given credit for the positive results. The market reacts by bidding up the price of the stock, and the manager is rewarded for the results by a performance bonus and stock options with a prospective value that increases over time because of income smoothing that triggers stock price increases. Levitt believes "these practices lead to erosion in the quality of earnings and, therefore, the quality of financial reporting." The notion that accounting information should represent what it purports to represent, or representational faithfulness,[7] would be distorted in these cases through adjustments up or down to net income by the use of devices such as accelerating the recognition of revenue by stuffing the distribution channels with product (i.e., channel stuffing), delaying the recognition of an expense, and creating reserve accounts such as estimated sales rebates (i.e., "cookie-jar reserves").

A classic case of the use of cookie-jar reserves to manipulate income was at HealthSouth. The SEC investigated the practice and deemed it to be fraudulent. According to the SEC, the company fraudulently reduced contractual adjustments to increase revenue by more than $2.2 billion.[8] The contractual allowances represented the amount of the healthcare billing/healthcare charges not expected to be reimbursed. During the second quarter of 1996, HealthSouth began what was to become a systematic practice of reducing contractual adjustments—that is, narrowing the gap between standard healthcare billing/healthcare charges and anticipated reimbursements—even though the applicable contractual adjustments had not actually changed and there was otherwise no support for the reductions. This practice continued without interruption in every reporting period through mid-2002. This kind of manipulation is akin to altering the allowance for doubtful accounts contra asset to accounts receivable.

One industry that routinely uses allowances to smooth net income over time is banking. Rivard et al. studied income smoothing techniques by banks and found them to be more aggressive in using loan-loss reserves as a tool of income smoothing. The provision for loan losses is a noncash accounting expense for banks. In theory, this expense represents expected future losses, which will eventually occur on loans extended during the previous period. These expenses accumulate on the bank's balance sheet in the loan-loss reserve account. When a loan is charged off, this reserve account is debited. Because banks have considerable flexibility in determining the size of the annual provision for loan losses, and because this is a noncash expense, it is an excellent tool for income smoothing. During periods of lower-than-normal earnings, the bank may understate its expected future loan loss and thus increase earnings. When profits are abnormally high, the opposite occurs. Over an extended period of time, the loan-loss reserve balance is maintained at the desired level and average earnings are unaffected. However, the variability of the earnings stream over that period is less than it would otherwise be. As the authors point out, income smoothing reduces not only earnings but also tax liabilities in high-income years, and increases them in low-income years.[9]

A fertile area for income smoothing and earnings management is through the use of discretionary accruals. *Discretionary accruals* are items that management has full control over and is able to delay or eliminate. *Nondiscretionary accruals* are items that are estimated based on changes in the fundamental economic performance of the firm, and management has no control over them. Dividing commitments into optional and non-optional confirms that total commitments are applied to offering better information for financial statements.

Unlike nondiscretionary accruals, which arise from transactions that can be considered "normal" for a firm (i.e., recording an accrual for unbilled services that have been provided), a discretionary accrual is a nonmandatory expense that is recorded within the accounting system but has yet to be realized. An example of this would be an anticipated management bonus. Discretionary accruals are those that arise from managerial discretion and are generally interpreted as indicative of managed earnings. By recognizing accruals at a "convenient" time, companies can smooth earnings and better meet or exceed analysts' earnings projections. Discretionary accrual techniques used to smooth earnings include: decreasing discretionary spending (i.e., spending on R&D or advertising) (71%); delaying starting a new project (55%); and delaying taking an accounting charge (34%).[10]

Ethical Choices

The reality in accounting is that choices must be made surrounding which methods to use to record revenues and expenses and estimations of amounts to go along.

Needles points out that the difference between an ethical and an unethical accounting choice is often merely the degree to which the choice is carried out. Needles believes the problem with many accounting judgments is that there is no clear limit beyond which a choice is obviously unethical. Thus, a perfectly routine accounting decision, such as expense estimation, may be illegal if the estimated amount is extreme, but it is perfectly ethical if it is reasonable. He provides an interesting example of how a manager might use the concept of an earnings continuum to decide whether to record the expense amount at the conservative end or aggressive end.[11]

Needles' example is based on a rather modest difference in estimate from $6,000 to $30,000 (1.0% to 5.0% of net sales). **Exhibit 6.1** shows a difference of $0.24 per share ($1.70–$1.94) or approximately 12 percent to 14 percent of EPS (assuming 100,000 shares outstanding). We recognize that judgment is an essential part of deciding when a difference is and is not material. Needles' continuum illustrates a possible basis for such judgments and how an auditor might go about deciding whether or not to accept management's position on the issue.

EXHIBIT 6.1   Where Do You Draw the Line? The Earnings Management Continuum of Ethical Financial Reporting

Questionable Conservative	Conservative	Neutral	Aggressive	Fraudulent
2a: The Earnings Management Continuum of Ethical Financial Reporting				
$1.70	$1.76	$1.82	$1.88	$1.94
Violates GAAP		Within GAAP		Violates GAAP
2b: Overly Aggressive Earnings on the Continuum				
Highly Conservative	**Overly Conservative**	**Neutral**	**Overly Aggressive**	**Fraudulent**
$1.70	$1.76	$1.82	$1.88	$1.94
Violates GAAP		Within GAAP		Violates GAAP

Acceptability of Earnings Management

There are a variety of perspectives on earnings management. Schipper defines it as a "purposeful intervention in the external reporting process, with the intent of obtaining some private gain (as opposed to, say, merely facilitating the neutral operation of the process)," as might be the case when earnings are manipulated to get the stock price up in advance of cashing in stock options.[12]

Dechow and Skinner note the difficulty of operationalizing earnings management based on the reported accounting numbers because they center on managerial intent, which is unobservable. Dechow and Skinner offer their own view that a distinction should be made between making choices in determining earnings that may comprise aggressive, but acceptable, accounting estimates and judgments, as compared to fraudulent accounting practices that are clearly intended to deceive others.[13]

Thomas E. McKee wrote a book on earnings management from the executive perspective. He defines *earnings management* as "reasonable and legal management decision making and reporting intended to achieve stable and predictable financial results." McKee believes earnings management reflects a conscious choice by management to smooth earnings over time and it does not include devices designed to "cook the books." He criticizes Schipper, Healy and Wahlen, and Dechow and Skinner for taking "unnecessarily negative view[s] of earnings management." McKee contends that a more positive definition is needed that portrays managers' motives in a positive light rather than the negative view adopted by others.[14]

Healy and Wahlen take a broader view and recognize that other financial statements may be affected by techniques used to manage earnings and they define it as "when managers use judgment in financial reporting and in structuring transactions to alter financial reports to either mislead some stakeholders about the underlying economic performance of the company, or to influence contractual outcomes that depend on reported accounting numbers."[15] They focus on management's intent to deceive the stakeholders by using accounting devices to influence reported earnings positively.

We adopt the definition by Healy and Wahlen because it allows for other financial reports to be affected as well including the balance sheet (e.g., recording accrued liabilities) and statement of cash flows (e.g., classifying an operating expense in the nonoperating cash flow category).

How Managers and Accountants Perceive Earnings Management

An early first survey of how managers view the ethics of earnings management was conducted in 1990 by Bruns and Merchant. They found that managers disagreed considerably on whether earnings management is ethically acceptable. They also found that, in general, the respondents thought manipulating earnings via operating decisions (e.g., purposefully delaying making needed repairs to a subsequent year) was more ethically acceptable than manipulation by accounting methods. The authors were disturbed by these findings. They were concerned that these practices could be misleading to users of the information and, over time, reduce the credibility of accounting numbers, thereby damaging the reputation of the accounting profession.[16]

It can be difficult to separate operating from accounting earnings management because operating decisions might be made to improperly recognize revenue before it is earned, such as the experience of Tony Menendez at Halliburton that was discussed in **Chapter 3**. In that case, the company agreed to hold product in its warehouse and not ship it until so requested by the customer (an operating decision) but still recorded the revenue right away before it was earned (an accounting decision).

Rosenzweig and Fischer followed up on the Bruns and Merchant survey in 1995 by asking accounting professionals about factors causing earnings management. Two of these factors involve accounting manipulation, and two involve operating decisions designed to influence reported earnings. The accounting factors include actions that influence earnings by changing accounting methods. Examples include recording an expense in the wrong year or changing an inventory valuation in order to influence earnings. Examples of operating decision manipulations are deferring necessary expenditures to a subsequent year or offering unusually attractive terms to customers at year-end to include next year's sales into the current year.[17]

In a 2006 survey, Akers, Giacomino, and Bellovary surveyed accounting students and practitioners about their views of earnings management. With respect to accounting practitioners, the results show that accounting manipulation is much less acceptable ethically than operating decision manipulation. This finding parallels the attitude that Bruns and Merchant found among managers.[18] Generally, the practitioners had few ethical qualms about operating decision manipulation, with scores indicating an average rating between (fully) ethical and questionable. The practitioners, however, generally felt that operating decisions that influenced expenses were somewhat more suspect than those that influenced revenues.

The five most serious infractions were (1) bury "scrap costs" in other expenses—no (operating) income effect; (2) request deferred billing from the supplier; (3) raise the return forecast (on purchases) from 22 percent to 35 percent, with actuals of 22 percent; (4) accelerate delivery to customers by 42 days; and (5) defer supply expenses by delaying recording the invoice. It is interesting to note that the most serious infraction did not even affect net income.[19] Instead, the action to bury scrap costs in other expenses shifts an operating expense into a nonoperating expense category, thereby increasing operating income, an amount on the income statement often considered to be a more important gauge of earnings than "bottom-line" net income. Other actions are clearly designed to manage earnings by either accelerating the recording of earnings or delaying the recording of operating expenses.

As to the 10 practices rated as minor infractions, the ethical significance of each is as follows: (1) reduce reserve for obsolescence to meet budget target, (2) increase reserve for obsolescence and reduce income, (3) accelerate delivery to the customer by 28 days, (4) defer expenses to meet the annual budget, (5) raise the return forecast from 22 percent to 35 percent, (6) request deferred billing from the supplier, (7) accelerate delivery to the customer by 16 days, (8) reduce reserve for obsolescence to continue work, (9) defer expenses to meet the quarterly budget, and (10) prepay expenses to reduce income by $60,000.[20]

More recently, in an article published in *Strategic Finance* in November 2018, Hamilton et al. report the results of a survey about how managers perceive the ethicality of earnings management. They asked respondents how morally right they believed earnings management to be. Managers responded on a scale of 1 to 8, where 1 = not morally right to 8 = morally right. The average response was 2.8, indicating that managers consider earnings management to be relatively immoral. A second question illustrates the role of corporate culture in earnings management. The managers were asked how acceptable earnings management was within their company's culture, with 1 = culturally unacceptable and 8 = culturally acceptable. The average response was 3.9, indicating that managers lean slightly toward perceiving earnings management as culturally unacceptable.[21] These results indicate how important setting an ethical tone at the top is to creating a culture that does not promote earnings management.

Ethics of Earnings Management

Stanga and Kelton examined investors' ethicality judgments of earnings management in a 2008 study. The authors found no significant difference in ethicality judgments between accounting methods and operating methods of earnings management. Regardless of the method, participants perceive earnings management as unethical. They also found that ethicality judgments are positively associated with investment decisions.[22]

Johnson et al. conducted a study that focused on the consequences of earnings management behavior in response to the question: Do the ends of positive organizational consequences justify the means of earnings management? The authors investigated manager evaluations of, and reactions to, a scenario in which a hypothetical employee makes a choice whether or not to engage in earnings management behavior, with consequences that are either favorable or unfavorable to the organization. The results indicated that managers may be motivated to discount the ethical impact of earnings management behavior when the consequence has a favorable impact on the organization—implying that the ends justify the means. This finding, in turn, suggests that incrementalism, or the ethical "slippery slope" of overlooking seemingly minor ethical breaches, can undermine efforts to establish a strong ethical tone throughout the organization.[23]

The authors of this book believe that the acceptability of earnings management techniques should be judged using the ethics framework established earlier in the book. Virtue ethics examines the reasons for actions taken by the decision maker as well as the action itself. As discussed under the "Acceptability of Earnings Management" section, McKee's definition is self-serving from a management perspective and does not reflect virtues such as honesty (full disclosure/transparency) and reliability (representational faithfulness). The definition also ignores the rights of shareholders and other stakeholders to receive accurate and reliable financial information year to year. McKee's explanation that earnings management is good because it creates a more stable and predictable earnings stream by smoothing net income cannot overcome the fact that a smooth net income by choice does not reflect what investors and creditors need or want to know because it masks true performance. Hopwood et al. provide cover for their view of the ethics of earnings management by stating that "the ethics issue might possibly be mitigated by clearly disclosing aggressive accounting assumptions in the financial statement disclosures."[24] We disagree with this characterization because disclosure should not be used to mask the ills of improper accounting that tests the limits of what does and does not present fairly financial position, results of operations, and cash flows. A disclosure may be nothing more than a rationalization for an unethical action with respect to earnings management, thereby closing the Fraud Triangle.

One might be able to rationalize the ethics of earnings management from an act-utilitarian perspective. Under this view, a decision about how to account for and report a financial transaction could be made by weighing the benefits to management and the company of using a particular technique (to smooth net income) versus the costs of providing potentially misleading information to the shareholders. The problem here is managers might rationalize earnings management by understating costs or overstating benefits. Under a rule-utilitarian perspective, however, financial statements should never be manipulated to put a rosier face on the financials or for personal gain regardless of any utilitarian benefits. Information provided to users must be relevant and reliable for their needs.

Earnings Guidance

LO 6-2

Explain the purpose of providing earnings guidance and motivation for making false and misleading disclosures.

Earnings guidance reflects the comments management makes about what it expects the company will do in the future. Earnings guidance is given by management to provide investors and financial analysts data that indicates expected future earnings, earnings per share, and other items. These comments are known broadly as *forward-looking statements*. They focus on sales revenues or earnings expectations in light of industry and macroeconomic trends. These comments are given for the sake of transparency and to guide investors and financial analysts in their decision making. The problem is misleading and fraudulent earnings guidance statements can be motivated by a desire to put the best spin on future performance.

The guidance may be described in a Management Discussion and Analysis (MD&A), operating and financial review, or something else. Publicly traded companies are not obligated to provide earnings guidance statements regarding future financial performance but the majority do so. The SEC can take actions against companies that provide false or misleading statements about future results.

Earnings guidance is often given in conference calls with investors and analysts and in press releases available to the public. One concern with earnings guidance statements is they represent management's subjective view of the company's future financial performance, which is exposed to uncertainties and risks. For this reason, the company's reported information is accompanied by cautions and disclaimers regarding the forward-looking statements to prevent any legal issues.

A good example of where a company provided false and misleading information in its public releases is the Cheesecake Factory. On December 4, 2020, the company settled an enforcement action by the SEC that the company had provided misleading COVID-19 related disclosures. This was the first ever enforcement action against a public company for misleading COVID-19 information. The SEC charges centered on alleged misrepresentations the company made in two press releases during the early days of the pandemic regarding how COVID-19 was impacting the company's business operations and financial condition. The SEC determined that the press releases—attached to Forms 8-K submitted to the SEC on March 23 and April 3, 2020—contained material misstatements and omissions which failed to adequately inform investors of the extent of the virus's negative impact on the company.[25]

Specifically, the SEC determined that the company's representation that its transition to a to-go/delivery restaurant model was enabling the company's restaurants to "operate sustainably at present" was misleading. In support, the SEC alleged that the statement did not disclose other information contained in internal corporate documents demonstrating that the company was excluding operational expenses from its claim of "sustainability," was losing approximately $6 million per week, and had rapidly depleting cash reserves. The SEC also noted that the company separately shared information from the internal documents with private equity investors and lenders in connection with then-ongoing fundraising efforts.

The SEC charged the company with violations of Section 13(a) and Rules 13a-11 and 12-20 of the 1934 SEC Act thereunder of its accounting and financial reporting regulations, which collectively require every issuer of a security registered with the Commission to file accurate current reports on Form 8-K that contain material information necessary to make the required statements in reports not misleading. More will be said about SEC enforcement actions in earnings management situations in **Chapter 7**.

Audit Committee Responsibilities

Audit committee oversight of forward-looking guidance is part of the board of directors' overall ongoing risk assessment process. Public companies are not required to release guidance but it has become more common since Congress passed the Private Securities Litigation Reform Act (PSLRA) in 1995. PSLRA provides a *safe harbor* when issuing forward-looking statements in SEC filings, press releases, investor presentations, and other public statements. Safe harbor statements are typically found in the fine print at the end of a corporation's press release that cautions investors not to put too much reliance on these statements because they are subject to a number of uncertainties that the company can't control and that may cause the results to differ from the statements. In particular, many estimates are made in these statements, as is common in all financial reports, and the underlying support for such estimates depend on management's interpretation of events as they are expected to transpire. Also, it is possible that such guidance is used to manage earnings and earnings per share if transactions or non-recurring adjustments are influenced by earnings pressure that increases financial reporting risks, including risk of fraud.

The audit committee should understand management's processes for (1) developing assumptions and estimates, (2) accumulating guidance information, and (3) ensuring management judgments are reasonable. The audit committee should also inquire of possible earnings management to meet the guidance.

Pull-In Sales

One technique used to meet earnings guidance is accelerating (or "pulling-in") sales from a future quarter to the present in order to close the gap between actual and forecasted revenue. Typically, this earnings management technique is triggered by offering various incentives, such as price rebates, discounted prices, and extended payment terms to entice customers to accept products in the current quarter that they would not need until next quarter. In their efforts to show earnings expectations have been met, companies that use this device mislead investors and financial analysts about the true results of quarterly earnings thereby influencing future expected earnings.

Approximately 27 percent of U.S. public companies provide quarterly earnings guidance. The SEC has been focusing on pull-in revenue in quarterly earnings guidance because of its widespread use. A survey by McKinsey indicates that when facing a quarterly earnings miss, 61 percent of companies without a self-identified long-term culture would take some action to close the gap between guided and actual earnings, with 47 percent opting to pull-in sales.

Efforts to pull-in sales from a future quarter to a current one only delays the bad news and can create a more spectacular market disappointment when, after a few quarters, there were no more future sales to cannibalize. Sunbeam Corporation learned this lesson the hard way by using the pull-in revenue technique known as "channel stuffing." Here, the company provided sales incentives, such as providing deep discounts to incentivize purchases by a customer in the current period. Normally, the customer would wait until later to buy the product but changed plans to satisfy Sunbeam. By stuffing the distribution channels in current periods, Sunbeam was borrowing from future sales to make the current sales look better than they would have been if Sunbeam had stuck with their normal sales terms.

On September 16, 2019, the SEC settled an enforcement action against Marvell Technology Group, Ltd., for its manipulation of current and future revenue in its quarterly guidance. Concerned about the adverse consequences that would result from missing its public guidance, the company developed a plan to accelerate, or pull-in, sales that had originally been scheduled for future quarters to the current quarter in order to close the gap between actual and forecasted revenue, meet publicly issued guidance, and mask declining sales. According to the enforcement action, Marvel made materially misleading public statements and omitted certain facts regarding its financial results for the fourth quarter of fiscal year 2015 and first quarter of fiscal year 2016. The SEC said that, "Marvell failed to disclose that the pull-ins reduced future sales, thereby making it exceedingly difficult for Marvell to meet its revenue guidance in future quarters, particularly in a declining market."[26]

Ethical decision making dictates that the pull-in sales technique should be discussed with the audit committee to ensure proper oversight of this and other techniques designed to manage earnings over time. External auditors should also be aware of its possible use and effects on current and future reported earnings.

Using Social Media to Report Earnings Guidance and Financial Results

Companies are required to make public information that is considered "material" to shareholders. Typically, companies will do that by filing that information with the SEC on Form 8-K, but businesses are also allowed to bypass the SEC by posting information on their websites or by issuing a press release.

In a ruling that portends changes to how companies communicate with investors, the SEC said on April 2, 2013, that postings on sites such as Facebook and Twitter are just as good as news releases and company websites as long as the companies have told investors which outlets they intend to use. The ruling permits companies to use social media channels to announce financial and other key information and post earnings information to the investing public in compliance with Regulation Fair Disclosure (Regulation FD).

The move was sparked by an investigation into a Facebook posting from Netflix Inc. Chief Executive Reed Hastings, who boasted on the social media site that the streaming-video company had exceeded 1 billion hours in a month for the first time, sending the firm's shares higher. The SEC opened the investigation in December 2012, to determine if the post had violated rules that bar companies from selectively disclosing information. The SEC did not initiate an enforcement action or allege wrongdoing by Hastings or Netflix, recognizing that there has been market uncertainty about the application of Regulation FD to social media.

"An increasing number of public companies are using social media to communicate with their shareholders and the investing public," the SEC said. "We appreciate the value and prevalence of social media channels in contemporary market communications, and the commission supports companies seeking new ways to communicate."[27]

Given the SEC's openness to using social media for company communications about financial matters, we can only observe: Students, it is a brave new world out there, and one you all should thrive in.

Red Flags

LO 6-3
Explain how an auditor might look for red flags that indicate fraud may exist in the financial statements.

A fraud risk assessment should be used by management to identify and understand the behavioral and financial indicators that certain internal control weaknesses may present a fraud risk to the organization. In **Chapter 3**, we discussed operational fraud risks and red flags that might indicate occupational fraud is present including asset misappropriation. In this section, we look at the red flags or indicators that financial fraud may exist such as intentional errors and omissions and material misstatements of the financial statements.

There are a variety of red flags that might indicate financial fraud exists. Given that choices must be made how to record underlying financial transactions, accountants and auditors should be aware of the techniques used to commit financial fraud. These are known as financial shenanigans that will be discussed in the next section.

Auditors need to be attuned to the red flags that fraud may exist because of overly aggressive accounting and outright manipulation of earnings. The following are some of the signs that trouble may lie ahead:

- Growth in the market share that seems unbelievable.
- Frequent acquisitions of businesses.
- Management growth strategy and emphasis on earnings and/or EPS.
- Reliance on income sources other than core business.
- One-time sources of income.
- Growth in revenue that doesn't line up well with changes in receivables or inventory.
- Unexpected increase in accounts receivable.
- Slowdown of inventory turnover.
- Reduction in reserves.
- Not reserving for possible future losses.
- Reduction in discretionary costs at year-end (i.e., advertising; R&D).
- Unusual increase in borrowings; short-term borrowing at year-end.
- Extension of trade payables longer than normal credit.
- Change in members of top management, especially the CFO.
- Change in auditors.
- Changes in accounting policies toward more liberal applications.

Sometimes, a forensic accountant is brought into a company or CPA firm to find suspected fraudulent activity or can be called in after the fraud has been detected to assess the magnitude of the fraudulent activity. These days we believe audit firms should have at least one forensic accountant on each audit to help identify the signs that something is amiss and prevent earnings management from getting started and catch it quickly if already underway.

Earnings Quality

Another way to spot potential fraud in the financial statements is through an assessment of earnings quality. Dichev et al. conducted a survey in 2016 that examined the views of 375 CFOs on the prevalence and identification of earnings misrepresentation. The authors were interested in identifying the characteristics of high-quality earnings. The CFOs were asked to rank specific characteristics of earnings quality. The leading indicators of quality earnings were consistent reporting choices through time and the absence of long-term estimates, both features of sustainable earnings. One participant said: "You are not trying to essentially grab earnings from the future and drag them in [to the current period] to make it look better, nor are you trying to push earnings out into the future, but you somehow reflect the underlying economics of the long-term value of this bundle of net assets that is in the firm." One key element is transparency and predictability. "Can investors anticipate what is going to happen?"[28]

One CFO pointed out that, over the long term, if earnings and cash flows are not highly linked, and if he were to consistently report a big gap between these two measures, then the market would start to wonder what is going on unless the company were in a huge growth phase. He added that if the gap between earnings and cash flows is persistently high, a significant discount in the company's stock price would be expected because, ultimately, if the cash is not being generated, then the earnings are either artificial or not a good indicator of value creation. Another CFO added that if earnings are not backed by actual cash flows, except for the very short-term, then they are not good earnings.

The assessment of earnings quality is more difficult today than ever before because companies increasingly discuss earnings information with financial analysts, on conference calls with investors, and on their websites. Auditors cannot possibly examine the information although they should act if they believe it contradicts earnings filings with the SEC. Companies now use other forms of earnings guidance, such as non-GAAP metrics, that bear on the quality of earnings. These numbers need to be carefully scrutinized to ensure they are not false or misleading or inconsistent with published information. More will be said about non-GAAP measures later in this chapter.

Financial Statement Analysis

Financial analysis can be used to identify red flags that the numbers in the financial statements may not make sense considering the relationship between selected items on the balance sheet and income statements. These relationships can be shown through comparative statements over two or more years based on reported numbers that can also be converted into percentages to enhance the analysis. These are known as common size statements. For example, assume you were given the following percentage data for 2020 and 2021.

Revenue	+20%
Inventory	+60%
Receivables	+40%

The red flag here is that generally it is more desirable to observe inventory and receivables growing at a slower (or similar) rate compared to revenue growth. After all, a company draws down inventory to meet growing sales and receivables should be collected over time. Receivables growing faster than revenue can indicate operational issues, such as lower credit standards, or aggressive accounting policies for revenue recognition, such as recording fictitious revenue. Similarly, inventory growing faster than revenue can indicate operational problems, such as improper overstatement of inventory to increase profits.

Ratios can be used to compare relationships between financial statement items or indicate trends over time. For example, the profit margin ratio is net income divided by sales. This ratio should be relatively constant over time. If fraud is committed, net income may be artificially overstated, resulting in a profit margin ratio that increases over time. It could be that improperly overstated ending inventory is the cause or expenses have been shifted from the current period to future periods indicating earnings management.

The accounts receivable turnover ratio may indicate possible fraud. The receivables turnover ratio is calculated as follows:

Net sales on Account/Average Net Receivables = Turnover

Assume the numbers are as follows:

Year Net Sales on Account/Average Net Receivables = Turnover

2020 $1 million/$500,000 = 2.00

2021 $2 million/$600,000 = 3.33

This ratio measures the number of times the receivables balance is turned over during the accounting period. In other words, the time between sales on account and the collection of funds. The increase from 2020 to 2021 may indicate fraud exists in the revenue account including recording fake revenue to "cook the books."

Here's another example:

Year Net Sales on Account/Average Net Receivables Turnover

2020 $3 million/$1 million = 3.00

2021 $4 million/$2 million = 2.00

In this case, revenue may have been recorded prematurely, such as the bill-and-hold example at Halliburton discussed in **Chapter 3**. Here, customers were being billed for product before it was shipped so that Halliburton was accelerating the recording of revenue into an earlier period and the customers may not have been required to pay back the receivable until product was shipped/delivered in a future period.

Data analytics techniques can reveal trends and metrics that would otherwise be lost in the huge volumes of information about transactions as discussed in **Chapter 5**. Data analysis can test for financial statement fraud such as anomalies in significant transactions, journal entries, and account balances. Variances uncovered by data analytics then must be investigated to determine whether they are valid, or if they actually are the result of fraudulent activities.

Green Mountain Coffee Roasters

The Green Mountain case—*Employees' Retirement System, et al. v. Green Mountain Coffee Roasters, et al.*[29]—is unusual in that the fraud occurred not only through materially misleading financial statements but through conference calls that provided false earnings guidance to shareholders and analysts. **Table 6.1** provides an overview about the company and its inventory fraud. What follows is a discussion of the content of the conference calls.

Essentially, Green Mountain knowingly misled investors through conference calls claiming to have ramped up production to meet increasing demand for its single-cup coffee brewing system while keeping inventory levels in check. Allegations in a shareholder lawsuit included that, on numerous occasions before an inventory count or audit by PwC, "bags and bags of coffee would be loaded onto trucks" that would either leave temporarily or just sit behind the facility filled with product. When employees escorted auditors through the facility, they were not permitted "beyond a point blocked off by black plastic."

Green Mountain defendants continuously reassured investors that its business was booming. For example, Green Mountain held a conference call with investors on February 2, 2011, to discuss first-quarter 2011 results. Green Mountain stated that "we remain focused on increasing production to fulfill unmet demand and achieving and maintaining optimum inventory levels." During its second-quarter conference call on May 3, 2011, Green Mountain stated "we are not building any excess inventories at all at retail." On July 27, 2011, in another conference call to discuss third-quarter results, the company stated that during the third quarter, "we got back into a place where we knew we had appropriate inventory levels." Lawrence Blanford, president, CEO, and director of the company, emphasized a need to increase production in 2012 to meet anticipated high consumer demand. When investors expressed concern about overproducing, Blanford reiterated that "we're at appropriate inventory levels."

The conference calls providing earnings guidance and other communications to the public about how well Green Mountain was doing seemed to raise red flags for some who follow such announcements. In fact, the initial class-action lawsuit that was filed in October 2011 came after a high-profile presentation by hedge fund manager David Einhorn who, in a stock bet against Green Mountain, accused the company of misleading auditors and inflating its results. Einhorn raised questions about the company's future prospects and its accounting procedures. Wall Street took notice as the stock price started to decline.

Sam Antar, a financial analyst, examined the numbers and used analytical procedures to identify warning signs that were missed. If there is inventory growth that is higher than revenue growth over extended periods of time combined with declining inventory turnover trends, this can be considered a red flag that ending inventory is inflated, thereby overstating earnings. **Table 6.1** shows the analysis.

Antar provided the numbers in Table 6.1 straight from Green Mountain's SEC filings. In September 2010, the SEC started a probe of Green Mountain's revenue accounting practices.[30]

According to Antar's analysis, Green Mountain inventory levels had been increasing much faster than revenue during a seven-quarter period in 2010–2012. Thus, the inventory turnover rate was declining, and it was taking Green Mountain longer to sell its products than in the past.

Taking the analysis further, Antar showed that by the numbers the inventory turnover was 102.04 days (to sell inventory) in the quarter ended in June 2012 versus only 72.12 days in the quarter ended in June 2011. Green Mountain claimed in SEC filings it was increasing inventory to meet holiday demand. The same explanation was given in a conference call by CFO Fran Rathke. Of course, that was just a smokescreen to hide the fraud.

The Green Mountain case is instructive because it illustrates that a company does not need to financially structure transactions and engage in a sophisticated accounting fraud, as did Enron, to pull the wool over the eyes of shareholders and auditors. A simple phone call can set the scheme in motion, as happened at Green Mountain. This raises an interesting question: Should auditors monitor conference calls with investors, analysts, and even the financial press to determine whether something is said that could be false, fraudulent, or deceptive?

Table 6.1	Green Mountain Coffee Roasters					
Fiscal Year 2012 vs. 2011 (in millions of dollars)						
Quarter Ended	Reported Revenues: Fiscal Year 2012	Reported Revenues: Fiscal Year 2011	Change	Inventory at End of Current Quarter in 2012	Inventory at End of Previous Year Comparable Quarter in 2011	Increase in Inventory
6/23/2012	$869,194	$717,210	21%	$667,005	$417,496	60%
3/24/2012	$885,052	$647,658	37%	$602,121	$300,760	100%
12/24/2011	$1,158,216	$574,148	102%	$606,679	$269,132	125%
Fiscal Year 2011 vs. 2010 (in millions of dollars)						
Quarter Ended	Reported Revenues: Fiscal Year 2011	Reported Revenues: Fiscal Year 2010	Change	Inventory at End of Current Quarter in 2011	Inventory at End of Previous Year Comparable Quarter in 2010	Increase in Inventory
9/24/2011	$711,883	$373,087	91%	$672,248	$262,478	156%
6/25/2011	$717,210	$316,583	127%	$417,496	$186,262	124%
3/26/2011	$647,658	$321,953	101%	$300,760	$109,929	174%
12/25/2010	$575,027	$345,152	67%	$269,132	$117,009	130%

Note: Revenues for the quarter ended 12/25/10 were later revised by Green Mountain Coffee from $575.027 million to $574.148 million after this blog reported discrepancies in its numbers.

Revenue Recognition

Given the prominence of revenue recognition techniques in earnings management cases, we discuss some of the criteria for determining proper revenue and provide an example of how challenging it can be.

Generally, revenue is recognized only when a specific event has occurred and the amount of revenue is measurable. The specific event addresses when revenue is realized or realizable. These decisions can be challenging because uncertainties may exist about collectability, side agreements may be made, contingencies added, and/or multiple elements may exist in a revenue transaction that need to be separately valued as discussed in the Ixia case later.

The bedrock revenue recognition principles are explained in SEC Staff Accounting Bulletin 101 (SAB 101), "Revenue Recognition in Financial Statements." The basic guidelines provide that revenue generally is realized or realizable and earned when all of the following criteria are met:[31]

1. Persuasive evidence of an arrangement exists.
2. Delivery has occurred or services have been rendered,
3. The seller's price to the buyer is fixed or determinable.
4. Collectability is reasonably assured.

Given the myriad of problems in revenue recognition and lack of consistent standards, the Financial Accounting Standards Board (FASB) issued a new revenue recognition standard, *Revenue from Contracts with Customers*. Public companies adopted the standard for their 2018 first-quarter filings with the SEC. Private companies and other entities were scheduled to implement it for fiscal years beginning after December 15, 2021. The standard is complex so we limit the discussion to the very basics here.

Under the new standard, companies under contract to provide goods or services to a customer will be required to follow a five-step process to recognize revenue:[32]

1. *Determine whether you have a contract.* Do you have a deal with a customer?
2. *Identify the performance obligations.* What are the responsibilities of each party under the contract?
3. *Determine the transaction price.* What do you expect to be owed?
4. *Allocate the transaction price.* Assign a value to the separate performance obligations.
5. *Recognize revenue (or as) performance obligations are satisfied.* When has transfer of control occurred?[33]

Multi-Element Arrangements

Vendors often provide products or services to their customers as part of a single arrangement or a series of related arrangements. These deliverables may be provided at different points in time or over different time periods. As a simple example, a vendor may enter into an arrangement with a customer to deliver and install a tangible product along with providing one year of maintenance services. In this arrangement, there are three deliverables: (1) the product, (2) installation, and (3) maintenance services. Issues often arise regarding how and whether to separate these deliverables and how to allocate the overall arrangement consideration.

A good example of the challenges faced by companies with multiple deliverables is the case of Ixia. Ixia sells network testing, visibility, and security products—hardware, software, post-contract support, and professional services—to customers in a single transaction, with none of those component products having been separately negotiated or priced. These kinds of arrangements are subject to GAAP that require Ixia to defer recognizing its software revenue from a given sale if certain criteria are not met.

In 2012, Ixia's then-CEO, Victor Alston, pushed for the company's revenue and other financial metrics to meet or exceed consensus market expectations. Discontent with the problems created by the deferral of Ixia's software revenue, Alston issued a directive to artificially split professional services onto separate purchase orders (POs) whenever they were included in any sale. Splitting POs have the false appearance that customers were buying Ixia's professional services in a stand-alone sale, and not part of a multi-element arrangement with the company's software products. It also allowed Ixia to prematurely recognize software revenue in contravention of its stated revenue recognition policy and GAAP. Following a 2014 internal investigation by its audit committee, Ixia restated its first- and second-quarter 2013 financial statements and, among other things, reversed in those periods nearly all revenue prematurely recognized because of Split POs. The audit committee further concluded that the company had not maintained effective ICFR in the first and second quarters of 2013.

Accounting for Revenue in the Cloud

On February 21, 2017, Oracle settled a lawsuit from a high-ranking accountant who claimed she was fired for threatening to blow the whistle on its illegal accounting practices. Former senior finance manager Svetlana Blackburn sued Oracle in June 2016, claiming it fired her for refusing to create false financial reports that inflated the company's revenue.

In her original complaint, Blackburn said she was ordered to add millions of dollars in unsupported revenue to financial reports for Oracle's cloud services, despite lack of billings to support those numbers. The company sought to inflate its cloud revenue with accruals not supported by evidence that those numbers would actually ever roll in. After refusing to go along with the fraud and trying to report the improprieties to superiors, Blackburn was fired. The company said she was fired due to "ongoing performance issues," not because she threatened to expose the company's allegedly fraudulent accounting practices. The settlement out of court puts the lawsuit to bed but not the difficulties in accounting for cloud revenue.

Pat Walravens, an analyst at JMP Securities stated that accounting for cloud software "can get very complex and requires judgment calls and estimates which a third party might disagree with upon further review." Accountants and analysts say that classifying software sales as cloud or traditional remains something of an art. There is some subjectivity in "is it cloud, is it traditional software?" said Steve Biskie, an auditor and co-founder of compliance consultancy

High Water Advisors. The most nebulous part of cloud accounting concerns situations where the customer buys a product that can be used partly in the cloud and partly on its own hardware. GAAP states that, in cases when use is mixed, companies should allocate the revenue between traditional, or licensed software, and cloud, or hosted software. Determining the fair value of the software license and hosting services may require the use of estimates, according to the rules. Management should consider all relevant information, such as information from the negotiation process with the vendor, in estimating the fair value of the license. That's the gray area. How can the cloud company determine how much a user uses its own hardware? Is it casual use or frequent use?[34]

Analysts report that various tricks can be used by a vendor trying to inflate its cloud figures, including:

- Lump on-premise and cloud figures together and then pretend it's all cloud;
- Give huge credit to customers moving their on-premise license value to the cloud and consider it as booked cloud sales;
- Give a cloud product for free and then extrapolate its sales value to other modules; and
- Sell a cloud subscription for a pilot population but book it as if it were for the whole company headcount.

Oracle claimed in 2015 that it made $1.5 billion from its cloud offerings. Dan Woods, chief technology officer and editor of CITO Research, claims that Oracle's cloud revenue numbers are bogus. Specifically, Woods claims that Oracle uses mechanisms such as "cloud credits" to move client revenue from traditional Oracle services to cloud computing without really achieving adoption. Frank Scavo, president of Computer Economics, said "As Oracle's traditional business in software licenses is under pressure, it needs to quickly ramp up cloud subscriptions to make up the difference. It's much easier to buy those customers than it is to grow them organically with cloud apps newly developed internally."[35] **Exhibit 6.2** summarizes the FASB standards on cloud computing arrangements.

EXHIBIT 6.2   Cloud Computing Revenue Recognition[36]

FASB issued Accounting Standards Update 2015-05, *Customer's Accounting for Fees Paid in a Cloud Computing Arrangement,* as part of its simplification initiative to reduce the diversity in practice and to reduce the costs and complexity of assessing fees paid in a cloud computing arrangement (CCA). While the new standard does not provide explicit guidance on how to account for fees paid in a CCA, it does provide guidance on which existing accounting model should be applied.

For purposes of applying the new guidance, a CCA includes software-as-a-service (SaaS) and SaaS-type services. "Hosting" refers to situations in which the end user does not take possession of the software; instead, the software resides on the vendor's or a third party's hardware, and the customer accesses the software remotely.

Under the new standard, fees paid by a customer in a CCA will be within the scope of the internal-use software guidance if both of the following criteria are met:

- The customer has the contractual right to take possession of the software at any time during the CCA period without significant penalty.
- It is feasible for the customer to run the software on its own hardware (or to contract with another party to host the software).

The standard provides some guidance on how to interpret the term "significant penalty." The ability to take delivery of the underlying software without significant cost and to use that software separately without a significant reduction in value would indicate there is not a significant penalty. Determining whether taking possession of the software will result in significant penalty will require judgment.

Arrangements that do not meet both of the criteria are considered service contracts, and separate accounting for a license will not be permitted. Arrangements that meet the criteria are considered multiple-element arrangements to purchase both a software license and a service of hosting the software. Existing guidance on internal-use software is applied to the purchased license.

Costs incurred by a customer in a CCA that includes a software license should be allocated between the license and hosting elements. The consideration should be allocated based on the relative fair value of each element. Determining the fair value of the software license and hosting service may require the use of estimates. Management should consider all relevant information, such as information from the negotiation process with the vendor, in estimating the fair value of the license. More observable inputs might be available to estimate the fair value of the hosting element.

Financial Shenanigans

LO 6-4
Explain the working of financial shenanigans and its effect on reported earnings.

Financial Statement Effects

Financial shenanigans are a colorful way to describe earnings management techniques. Howard Schilit wrote a book that has become a classic in understanding the common types of financial shenanigans. We explain the basic financial shenanigan techniques below,[37] with the number of examples in each category limited to the three most common techniques. We also use Schilit's framework to discuss earnings manipulations at two companies charged by the SEC with accounting fraud—Xerox and Lucent.

The shenanigans can be broadly classified into two types: (a) schemes that overstate revenues and profits, which are designed to enhance reported results and earnings per share, and (b) schemes that understate revenues and profits that are typically done to smooth out net income over time periods and make it appear less volatile. The company might also decide to set up reserve accounts to be shifted from one period to another based on how it wants to portray earnings in the current or future period, or set up so-called "cookie jar reserves."

1. Recording Revenue Too Soon

We have discussed this before and provided many examples where revenue is recorded before the earnings process has been completed or before an unconditional exchange has occurred. The Halliburton case discussed in Chapter 3 is a case in point where bill-and-hold transactions were used to prematurely record revenue. Other examples include:

- Recording revenue when future services remain to be provided.
- Recording revenue before shipment or before the customer's unconditional acceptance.
- Recording revenue even though the customer is not obligated to pay.

The Xerox case discussed later in this chapter illustrates how a company can move earnings into an earlier period by allocating more of the revenue in a multiyear contract to earlier years than justified given continuing servicing under the contract.

Another example is the Sunbeam Corporation previously discussed that extended the selling season for its gas grills and to boost sales in the current period by convincing retailers, including Walmart, to buy grills nearly six months before they were needed, in exchange for major price discounts or liberal return policies. Retailers agreed to purchase merchandise that they would not receive physically until six months after billing. In the meantime, the goods were shipped to a third-party warehouse and held there until the customers requested them. These bill-and-hold transactions led to recording $35 million in revenue too soon. By making deals with customers to agree to buy product sooner than they needed it, the company stuffed the distribution channels making it more difficult for the company to keep up that level of sales in future periods because the customers didn't need additional product at that time.

2. Recording Bogus Revenue

Typically, bogus revenue transactions lead to fictitious revenue. Examples include:

- Recording sales that lack economic substance.
- Recording as revenue supplier rebates that are tied to future required purchases.
- Releasing revenue that was held back improperly before a merger.

A good example of recording income that lacks economic substance is Enron that used special-purpose entities (SPEs) to mask debt while still recording the cash by having Enron sell unwanted assets to the SPEs at an inflated amount thereby creating gains that only existed on paper. More will be said about Enron later.

3. Boosting Income Using One-Time or Unsustainable Activities

The gains (and losses) from the sale of operating and investment assets that should be recorded in another (e.g., miscellaneous) income account can be classified in other ways if the intent is to boost operating income. These include:

- Boosting profits by selling undervalued assets.
- Including investment income or gains as part of operating revenue.
- Including investment income or gains as a reduction in operating expenses.

IBM used the net proceeds from the sale of an operating unit ($300 million) to lower its operating costs, rather than accounting for it as a nonrecurring, one-time gain. We consider it fraud because it is a deliberate attempt to mislead users of the financial statements into thinking that operating income is larger than it really is. Financial analysts tend to put more emphasis on operating income than net income because of the miscellaneous, non-operating items recorded below the line of operating income to get net income.

4. Shifting Current Expenses to a Later Period

A common approach to shifting expenses to a later period is by capitalizing a cost in the current period and expensing it over a period of time, rather than expensing the item completely in the current period. This was the technique used by WorldCom to inflate earnings by between $11 billion and $13 billion.

WorldCom capitalized its line costs that provided telecommunications capacity on other companies' systems rather than expense those costs as they were incurred. The effects on reported income were dramatic and illustrate how earnings management techniques can lead to reporting earnings when a loss has actually occurred. The following table illustrates just how that was done.

Table 6.2	WorldCom's Capitalization of Line Costs and Net Income Effects			
Form Filed with the SEC	Reported Line Cost Expenses	Reported Income (before Taxes and Minority Interests)	Actual Line Cost Expenses	Actual Income (before Taxes and Minority Interests)
10-Q, 3rd Q. 2000	$ 3.867 billion	$ 1.736 billion	$ 4.695 billion	$ 908 million
10-K, 2000	$ 15.462 billion	$ 7.568 billion	$ 16.697 billion	$ 6.333 billion
10-Q, 1st Q. 2001	$ 4.108 billion	$ 988 million	$ 4.879 billion	$ 217 million
10-Q, 2nd Q. 2001	$ 3.73 billion	$ 159 million	$ 4.29 billion	$ 401 million loss
10-Q, 3rd Q. 2001	$ 3.745 billion	$ 845 million	$ 4.488 billion	$ 102 million
10-K, 2001	$ 14.739 billion	$ 2.393 billion	$ 17.754 billion	$ 622 million loss
10-Q, 1st Q. 2002	$ 3.479 billion	$ 240 million	$ 4.297 billion	$ 578 million loss

5. Employing Other Techniques to Hide Expenses or Losses

The liability account is often used to manipulate earnings because when liabilities that should be recorded are not, the expenses also are understated. When liabilities are reduced improperly, the same effect on expenses occurs. The result is to overstate earnings. Some examples include:

- Failing to record expenses and related liabilities when future obligations remain.
- Releasing questionable reserves (cookie-jar reserves) into income.
- Recording revenue when cash is received, even though future obligations remain.

The recording of discretionary accruals that was previously discussed is one application of the technique. The Lucent Technologies example discussed later in this chapter illustrates a variety of these techniques.

6. Shifting Current Income to a Later Period

Some companies act to delay the recording of revenue when the amount is relatively high in a given year. In a sense, this action sets up a "rainy day" reserve that can be used to restore earnings in low-earnings years. One way to accomplish this is to create a cookie-jar reserve with the excess revenues and release it back into the income stream at a later date, when it can do more good for the bottom line. Another method is through the use of deferred revenue. Examples include:

- Deliberately overstating the allowance for uncollectible accounts, thereby understating current revenue, and adjusting the allowance downward in future years to increase revenue.
- Deferring revenue recognition on a year-end service transaction that was completed by December 31 and then transferring it to earned revenue in subsequent years.
- Deliberately overstating the estimated sales returns account and adjusting it downward in future years.

These types of transactions tend to have a smoothing effect on net income.

Another example is where the SEC went after W. R. Grace & Co. for manipulating earnings to meet Wall Street's expectations. The Commission alleged that senior Grace executives deferred reporting some 1991 and 1992 income from National Medical Care, then the main Grace health care unit. Grace assigned $10 million to $20 million of this unexpected profit to "corporate reserves," which is then used to increase the reported earnings of both the health care unit and the company between 1993 and 1995, the SEC said.[38]

The actual earnings of the unit and its parent company sometimes fell short of analysts' expectations during this period, the SEC alleged. Thus, Grace misled shareholders by reporting results buttressed by the reserves. The only problem was that Grace deferring reporting income by increasing or establishing reserves was not in conformity with GAAP. In fact, it smacks of using secret reserves to achieve a cookie-jar reserve effect and smoothing net income over time.

7. Shifting Future Expenses to the Current Period

A company might choose to accelerate discretionary expenses, such as repairs and maintenance, into the current period if the current year's revenue is relatively high in relation to expected future revenue or if future expenses are expected to be relatively high. The motivation to shift future expenses to the current period might be to smooth net income over time. This may not be illegal in this instance but certainly illustrates operating earnings management.

Sunbeam also recorded future expenses in the current period that already had a huge net loss reasoning that it might as well make the net loss larger in the current period but increasing income in future periods when it is needed more. It also helped Sunbeam to beat financial analysts' earnings expectations. This technique became known as the "big bath theory."

Examples of Shenanigans

In this section, we describe the financial shenanigans that occurred at Xerox and Lucent. We chose these companies because the techniques used to manage earnings vary from the relatively simple (recording revenue too soon) to the more exotic (using side agreements to enable customers to get out of their contracts).

The Case of Xerox

MOTIVATION FOR FRAUDULENT SCHEME OF TOP MANAGEMENT

On June 3, 2003, the SEC filed a civil fraud injunctive action in the U.S. District Court for the Southern District of New York charging six former senior executives of Xerox Corporation, including its former CEOs Paul Allaire and G. Richard Thoman and its former CFO Barry D. Romeril, with securities fraud and aiding and abetting Xerox's violations of the reporting, books and records, and internal control provisions of the federal securities laws. The complaint charged the former executives with engaging in a fraudulent scheme that lasted from 1997 to 2000 and misled investors about Xerox's earnings to "polish its reputation on Wall Street and to boost the company's stock price."[39]

The quality of the financial reports came into question as Xerox failed to disclose GAAP violations that led to acceleration in the recognition of approximately $3 billion in equipment revenues and an increase in pretax earnings by approximately $1.4 billion in Xerox's 1997–2000 financial results. The executives agreed to pay over $22 million in penalties, disgorgement, and interest without admitting or denying the SEC's allegations.

The tone at the top was one that viewed business success with meeting short-term earnings targets. Romeril directed or allowed lower-ranking defendants in Xerox's finance department at Xerox Corporate Headquarters to make accounting adjustments to results reported from operating divisions to accelerate revenues and increase earnings. These entries made are referred to as "topside" entries as they are made as part of the financial consolidation process at headquarters which enabled the corporate finance department to keep what they were doing hidden from Xerox subsidiaries. In other words, Xerox continued to record its revenue properly in each of its subsidiaries, but then intentionally adjusted those numbers during the consolidation of the results at corporate headquarters.

Also, accounting methods were used to boost earnings to meet earnings projections and predictions of outside securities analysts. Allaire and Thoman then announced these results to the public through meetings with analysts and in communications to shareholders, celebrating that Xerox was enjoying substantially greater earnings growth than the true operating results warranted.

A description of two selected fraudulent accounting devices follows.

FRAUDULENT LEASE ACCOUNTING

Xerox sold copiers and other office equipment to its customers for cash, but it more frequently entered into long-term lease agreements in which customers paid a single negotiated monthly fee in return for the equipment, service, supplies, and financing. Xerox referred to these arrangements as "bundled leases."

The leases met the criteria under *SFAS 13* to be accounted for as "sales-type" leases, whereby the fair value of the equipment leased would be recognized as income in the period the lease is delivered, less any residual value the equipment was expected to retain once the lease expired. GAAP permits the financing revenue portion of the lease to be recognized only as it is earned over the life of the lease. *SFAS 13* also specifies that the portion of the lease payments that represents the fee for repair services and copier supplies be prorated over the term of the lease, matching it against the financing income. Separating out the sales and service portions on a lease is known as "multiple deliverables" (as part of a multi-element arrangement as previously discussed).

Until the mid-1990s, Xerox followed satisfactory procedures for revenue recognition. However, the company encountered growing copier sales competition around the world and perceived a need to continue reporting record earnings. The management told KPMG that it was no longer able to reasonably assign a fair value to the equipment as it had in the past. The company abandoned the value determinations made at the lease inception for public financial reporting purposes but not for internal operating purposes and substituted a formula that management could manipulate at will.

Xerox did not test the value determinations to assess the reliability of the original method or if the new method did a better job of accurately reflecting the fair value of copier equipment.[40]

Xerox's "topside" lease accounting devices consistently increased the amount of lease revenues that Xerox recognized at the inception of the lease and reduced the amount it recognized over the life of the lease. One method was called *return on equity (ROE),* which pulled forward a portion of finance income and recognized it immediately as equipment revenue. The second, called *margin normalization,* pulled forward a portion of service income and recognized it immediately as equipment revenue. These income acceleration methods did not comply with GAAP because there was no matching of revenue with the period during which (1) financing was provided, (2) copier supplies were provided, and (3) repairs were made to the leased equipment.

"CUSHION" RESERVES

From 1997 through 2000, Xerox violated GAAP through the use of approximately $496 million of reserves to close the gap between actual results and earnings targets. Xerox had created reserves through charges to income prior to 1997. These cookie-jar reserves were released into income to make the numbers look better than they really were. The result was a smoothing of net income over time. This practice violated *SFAS 5, Accounting for Contingencies,* which allows a company to establish reserves only for identifiable, probable, and estimable risks and precludes the use of reserves, including excess reserves, for general or unknown business risks because they do not meet the accrual requirements of *SFAS 5.*

SANCTIONS BY THE SEC ON KPMG

The SEC issued a cease-and-desist order against KPMG on April 19, 2005, for its role in auditing the financial statements of Xerox from 1997 through 2000. *AAER 2234* details KPMG's consent to institute a variety of quality control measures, which included providing oversight of engagement partner changes of audit personnel and related independence issues.[41]

On February 22, 2006, the SEC announced that all four remaining KPMG staff members in the commission's action in connection with the $1.2 billion fraudulent earnings manipulation scheme by Xerox from 1997 through 2000 had agreed to settle the charges against them. Three KPMG partners agreed to permanent injunctions, payment of $400,000 in penalties, and suspensions from practice before the commission. Four partners were charged with filing materially false and misleading financial statements with the SEC and aiding and abetting Xerox's filing of false financial reports. The SEC charged that the partners knew or should have known about improper "topside adjustments" that resulted in $3 billion of the restated revenues and $1.2 billion of the restated earnings.[42] Topside entries are required to be looked at in more detail during an audit as they represent a known opportunity (red flag area) for financial shenanigans to occur. Thus, the SEC's conclusion that KPMG either knew or should have known that the financials were materially misstated.

The concurring review partner on the audit engagement team was cited because the adjustments enabled Xerox to change the allocations of revenues that it received from leasing photocopiers and other types of office equipment. The partner agreed to a censure from the SEC for failing to exercise due care and professional skepticism and adhere to GAAS.

On April 20, 2005, KPMG settled with the SEC over the financial fraud at Xerox, agreeing to pay $10 million in penalties, in addition to disgorging nearly $10 million in audit fees and paying another $2.7 million in interest.

The Case of Lucent Technologies

On May 20, 2004, the SEC charged Lucent Technologies, Inc., with securities fraud and violations of the reporting, books and records, and internal control provisions of the federal securities laws. The commission also charged current and former Lucent officers, executives, and employees with securities fraud and aiding and abetting Lucent's violations of federal securities laws. The SEC complaint alleged that Lucent fraudulently and improperly recognized approximately $1.148 billion of revenue and $470 million in pretax income during the fiscal year 2000.

The Lucent case is typical of the frauds that occurred in the late 1990s and early 2000s. The company's accounting techniques violated GAAP and were motivated by its drive to realize revenue, meet internal sales targets, and obtain sales bonuses. The internal controls were either violated or circumvented by top management. The board of directors and audit committee were either not involved or turned away from their obligations.

According to *AAER 2016*, Lucent officers improperly granted and/or failed to disclose various side agreements, credits, and other incentives (extracontractual commitments) made to induce Lucent's customers to purchase the company's products. The premature recognition of revenue occurred by "selling" $135 million in software to a customer that could choose from a software pool by September 29, 2001, and Lucent recognized $135 million in revenue in its fiscal year ending September 30, 2000. The parties reached an agreement to document separately additional elements of the software pool transaction that would give the customer more value in the form of side agreements. Top management postdated three letters documenting the side agreements with fictitious dates in October 2000. The effect of the postdated letters was to create the appearance that the side agreements were reached after September 30, 2000, and were not connected to the software pool agreement.[43] The accounting for these transactions enabled Lucent to manage earnings in a way that smoothed net income over time.

Lucent's story as a separate entity began in April 1996, when AT&T spun off the company. By 1999, operating income had reached $5.4 billion, tripling in two years. Net income had grown more than 10-fold during that time period. These remarkable increases over a relatively short period of time should have raised a red flag for KPMG, but it did not. **Exhibits 6.3** and **6.4** present the comparative amounts during the two-year period ended September 30, 1999.[44]

EXHIBIT 6.3   Lucent Technologies, Inc.: Comparative Sales and Income

Item	Sales and Income Amounts (in billions)		
	September 1999	September 1998	September 1997
Sales	$48.3	$31.8	$27.6
Operating income	5.4	2.6	1.6
Net income	4.8	1.0	0.4

EXHIBIT 6.4   Lucent Technologies, Inc.: Percentage Change in Sales and Income

	Percentage Changes in Sales and Income Amounts	
	September 1998 to September 1999	September 1997 to September 1998
Sales	52%	15%
Operating income	104	63
Net income	380	150

Schilit points out that Lucent's stock price increased from a low of about $14 per share on January 1, 1997, to a high of about $78 by September 1999. The stock price began to decline after that, to a low of about $7 per share on January 1, 2002, as the fraud unfolded.

Exhibit 6.5 takes Lucent's earnings management techniques and classifies them into Schilit's financial shenanigan categories.

EXHIBIT 6.5   Lucent Technologies, Inc.: Financial Shenanigans

Technique	Description	Shenanigan Number
Recorded revenue too soon	Lucent restated year 2000 earnings, removing $679 million of improperly included revenue.	No. 1
Boosted income with one-time gains	During fiscal 1998, Lucent recorded $558 million of pension income—over 50% of earnings for the year.	No. 3
Failed to write down impaired assets	Lucent reduced the allowance for doubtful accounts and released the previous reserves despite an increase in receivables of 32%.	No. 4
Shifted current expenses to a later period	Lucent reduced the allowance for inventory obsolescence although the inventory balance increased.	No. 4
Reduced liabilities by changing accounting assumptions	Lucent modified its accounting approach and assumptions for pensions.	No. 5
Released reserves into income	Lucent released $100 million of a previously recorded restructuring reserve, boosting operating income.	No. 5
Created new reserves from 10 acquisitions	Lucent wrote off $2.4 billion (58% of the cumulative purchase price) as an in-process R&D. This new reserve could be released into earnings later.	No. 7

The Case of Enron

The Enron case was introduced in the Introduction to Chapter 2. Here, we review the accounting techniques used by Enron used to cook the books. It's worth noting that Enron shares were worth $90.75 at their peak in August 2000 and dropped to $0.67 in January 2002. When everything was said and done, shareholders lost $64 billion. The Enron fraud caused more harm than any other and is remembered as the daddy of all the frauds that occurred in the late 1990s and early 2000s. **Exhibit 6.6** depicts the typical transaction between Enron and the SPE.

EXHIBIT 6.6   Enron Corporation's SPEs

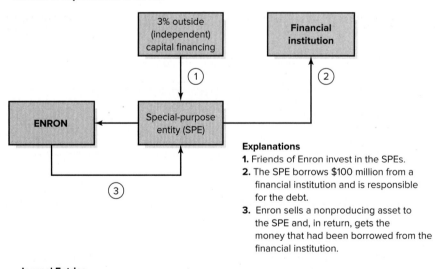

Explanations
1. Friends of Enron invest in the SPEs.
2. The SPE borrows $100 million from a financial institution and is responsible for the debt.
3. Enron sells a nonproducing asset to the SPE and, in return, gets the money that had been borrowed from the financial institution.

Journal Entries

Enron			SPE		
N/A			Cash	100m	
			Due to Bank		100M
Cash	100M		Asset	100m	
Asset (assume)	40M		Cash		100M
Gain on sale	60M				

The Enron fraud was relatively simple. The company structured financial transactions in such a way to keep partnerships that were formed to borrow funds on behalf of Enron off Enron's books. These so-called "off-balance-sheet entities" (i.e., special-purpose entity/SPE) grew in size and number over the years. For many years, Enron was successful in setting them up and borrowing funds from financial institutions through the SPEs, after which Enron would concoct a transaction with these entities to take under-performing assets from Enron in return for the cash from the borrowing. Enron padded their cash account without carrying the debt and even recorded gains on some of the transactions. The Enron example illustrates shenanigan two in that Enron recorded income from a transaction that lacked economic substance.

Non-GAAP Financial Metrics

LO 6-5

Describe the makeup of non-GAAP amounts and whether they distort reported earnings.

Non-GAAP Financial Metrics

A 2017 study by Audit Analytics that focuses on non-GAAP usage indicates that 97 percent of the Standard & Poor's (S&P) 500 used at least one non-GAAP metric in their financial statements. The findings show an increased trend over time as you can see by the **Tables 6.3** and **6.4** below.[45]

Table 6.3	Percentage Change in GAAP and Non-GAAP Metrics 2015-2017		
	2017	2016	2015
Present non-GAAP metrics	97%	96%	94%
Do not present non-GAAP metrics	3%	4%	6%

The analysis is based on annual 8-K item 2.02 fillings for the populations of S&P 500 companies *(20 companies did not file a 2.02 in 2016, 34 companies did not file in 2017)*

Table 6.4	Change in Actual Numbers Over Time 1996–2016			
Reporting Year	# of Companies Presenting Non-GAAP Metrics	# of Companies Presenting Non-GAAP Metrics	# of Companies Presenting Non-GAAP Metrics	# of Companies Presenting Non-GAAP Metrics
1996	162	113	59%	2.35
2006	331	106	76%	3.47
2016	462	19	96%	7.45

To better understand the continued growth of non-GAAP usage, Audit Analytics looked at the use of non-GAAP metrics at three different points in time for the S&P 500 companies that used non-GAAP metrics in 1996, 2006, and 2016. The trend analysis clearly demonstrates that the number of metrics per filing has increased substantially over the three years.

Most companies disclose non-GAAP financial metrics, yet little is known about the objectives of disclosing these numbers, how they are determined, management's intent in disclosing non-GAAP amounts, regulation of these disclosures, and the auditors' responsibilities. This is important because adjusting earnings from GAAP to a non-GAAP measure is subject to earnings management and it can mislead investors and analysts about the "true" earnings of a public company.

Another Audit Analytics study shown in **Exhibit 6.7** found the top five non-GAAP metrics were:[46]

- Income-related (including adjusted operating income)
- Earnings-per-share (EPS)
- Cash flow
- EBITDA
- Funds from operations

EXHIBIT 6.7   S&P 500 Companies Using a Particular Type of Non-GAAP Metric

Type of Non-GAAP Metric Used	Companies	Percentage
Income (including adjusted operating income)	363	71%
Earnings per share	366	72%
Cash flow	144	28%
EBITDA (including adjusted EBITDA)	101	20%
Fund from operations (including adjusted funds from operations)	23	5%

Source: Audit Analytics, "Trends in Non-GAAP Disclosure," Dec. 1, 2015. EBITDA= Earnings Before Interest, Taxation, Depreciation, and Amortization

SEC rules require that GAAP and non-GAAP measures be disclosed in annual reports to reconcile the numbers. **Exhibit 6.8** shows the disclosure in the 2018 annual report of Twitter.

EXHIBIT 6.8   Twitter's Reconciliation of GAAP Net Income to Adjusted EBITDA

	Year-Ended December 31,				
	2018	2017	2016	2015	2014
	(in thousands)				
Reconciliation of Net Income (Loss) to Adjusted EBITDA					
Net income (loss)	$1,205,596	($108,063)	($456,873)	($521,031)	($577,820)
Stock-based compensation expense	326,228	433,806	615,233	682,118	631,597
Depreciation and amortization expense	425,498	395,867	402,172	312,823	208,165
Interest and other expense, net	29,781	134,158	73,626	83,269	39,485
Provision (benefit) for income taxes	(782,052)	12,645	16,039	(12,274)	(531)
Restructuring charges and one-time nonrecurring gain	(4,255)	(5,427)	101,296	12,902	
Adjusted EBITDA	$1,200,796	$862,986	$751,493	$557,807	$300,896

Source: Audit Analytics, "Trends in Non-GAAP Disclosure," Dec. 1, 2015. EBITDA= Earnings Before Interest, Taxation, Depreciation, and Amortization

Former SEC Chair Mary Jo White, speaking at a corporate governance meeting in June 2016, expressed her concern that "[i]n too many cases, the non-GAAP information, which is designed to supplement the GAAP information, has become the key message to investors, crowding out and effectively supplanting the GAAP presentation."[47] Beyond that, the diverse items that have been used by companies to adjust GAAP net income to non-GAAP adjusted net income raises questions about the consistency and comparability of non-GAAP amounts. Some companies present EPS on a non-GAAP basis adding another wrinkle to the understandability issue. For example, First Energy provided the information in **Exhibit 6.9** for fiscal year 2016.

EXHIBIT 6.9   First Energy's Non-GAAP EPS

Basic Earnings (Loss) per Share (GAAP)	$(14.49)
Excluding Special Items:	
Mark-to-market adjustments:	
Pension/OPEB actuarial assumptions	0.21
Other	0.01
Merger accounting—commodity contracts	0.05
Regulatory charges	0.13
Asset impairment/Plant exit costs	16.67
Debt redemption costs	0.02
Trust securities impairment	0.03
Total Special Items	$ 17.12
Basic EPS – Operating (Non-GAAP)	**$2.63**

What is a Non-GAAP Financial Measure?

SEC Regulation G and Item 10(e) of Regulation S-K define a "non-GAAP financial measure" as a numerical measure of historical or future financial performance, financial position, or cash flows, that:

- Excludes amounts that are included in the most directly comparable measure calculated and presented in accordance with GAAP; or
- Includes amounts that are excluded from the most directly comparable measure so calculated and presented.

The SEC regulations further provide that the definition of a non-GAAP financial measure is intended to capture all measures that have the effect of depicting either:[48]

- A measure of performance that is different from that presented in the financial statements, such as income or loss before taxes, or net income or loss as calculated in accordance with GAAP; or
- A measure of liquidity that is different from cash flow or cash flow from operations computed in accordance with GAAP.

Regulation G applies to all public disclosures and is not limited to the registrant's written public filings. If a non-GAAP financial measure is made public orally, telephonically, by webcast, by broadcast, or by similar means, then the reconciliation requirements under Regulation G would exist if:[49]

- The required information (i.e., presentation and reconciliation) is provided on the registrant's website at the time the non-GAAP financial measure is made public; and
- The location of the website is made public in the same presentation in which the non-GAAP financial measure is made public.

Based on regulatory requirements, if a company takes a defined GAAP measure (such as GAAP net income) and thereafter "adjusts" for (i.e., excludes or includes) one or more expense or revenue items that are components of that GAAP measure (i.e., excluding a restructuring expense identified as "non-recurring"), then the resulting measure (i.e., "adjusted net income") is a non-GAAP financial measure. One common non-GAAP measure is EBITDA (earnings before interest, taxes, depreciation, and amortization). Other variations include EBIT, EBITA, EBITD, EBITDAR (earnings before interests, taxes, depreciation, amortization, and restructuring costs), adjusted EBITDA, and so on. A joke making the rounds is perhaps the best measure is EBBS (earnings before the bad stuff).

Requirements under Item 10(e) of SEC Regulation S-K

Item 10(e) applies to non-GAAP financial measures that are included in SEC filings. To comply with these requirements, the registrant must include the following:

- A presentation, with equal or greater prominence, of the most directly comparable financial measure or measures calculated and presented in accordance with GAAP;
- A non-GAAP measure should be presented in proximity to the GAAP measure with an appropriate balance of discussion;
- A quantitative reconciliation of the differences between the non-GAAP financial measure and the most directly comparable GAAP financial measure;
- The reconciliation should be presented with each adjustment clearly labeled and separately quantified;
- A statement disclosing why the registrant's management believes that presentation of the non-GAAP financial measure provides useful information to investors regarding the registrant's financial condition and results of operations; and
- To the extent material, a statement disclosing the additional purposes, if any, for which the registrant's management uses the non-GAAP financial measure.[50]

Item 10(e) of Regulation S-K specifically prohibits:

- Non-GAAP financial measures of liquidity that exclude charges or liabilities requiring cash settlement other than EBIT and EBITDA;
- Adjustments to non-GAAP financial measures of performance that eliminate or smooth items identified as "nonrecurring, infrequent, or unusual," when the nature of the charge or gain is such that it is reasonably likely to recur within two years or there was a similar charge or gain within the prior two years;
- The presentation of non-GAAP financial measures on the face of the registrant's financial statements prepared in accordance with GAAP or in the accompanying notes;
- The presentation of non-GAAP financial measures on the face of any pro forma financial information required to be disclosed under Regulation S-X; and
- The use of titles or descriptions of non-GAAP financial measures that are the same as, or confusingly similar to, titles or descriptions used for GAAP financial measures.

When evaluating a company's use and presentation of non-GAAP financial measures, management and the audit committee should consider the following:

- What is management's intention in disclosing non-GAAP amounts? The audit committee's responsibility is to ensure management is not attempting to manage earnings.
- How does the non-GAAP measure provide investors with useful information?
- Where should the non-GAAP amounts be disclosed (i.e., in earnings releases, conference calls with financial analysts, filings with the SEC)?
- Are there appropriate controls over the calculation of non-GAAP measures? Are these amounts presented consistently from period to period?
- Is this information designed to supplement GAAP amounts, not substitute for it?
- Have these amounts been discussed with the external auditors?

Compliance and Disclosure Interpretations

On May 17, 2016, the SEC updated its interpretive guidance on non-GAAP metrics that provides examples of potentially misleading non-GAAP measures that could violate Regulation G, including:[51]

- Presenting a performance measure that excludes normal, recurring, cash operating expenses;
- Presenting non-GAAP measures inconsistently between periods without disclosing the change and reasons for the change;
- Presenting non-GAAP measures that exclude non-recurring charges but do not exclude non-recurring gains; and
- Using individually tailored accounting principles to calculate non-GAAP earnings, for example, by presenting non-GAAP revenue that accelerates revenue recognition as though the revenue were earned sooner than for GAAP purposes.

The updated guidance also provides example disclosures that would cause a non-GAAP measure to be more prominent than the most directly comparable GAAP measure, such as:

- Omitting comparable GAAP measures from headlines of earnings releases;
- Presenting a non-GAAP measure that precedes the most directly comparable GAAP measure;
- Presenting a non-GAAP measure using a style of presentation (e.g., bold, larger font) that emphasizes non-GAAP over the comparable GAAP measures;
- Describing non-GAAP measures (e.g., record performance, exceptional) without equally prominent description of the comparable GAAP measure;
- Providing tabular disclosure of non-GAAP information without including the GAAP information in the same table or an equally prominent tabular disclosure; and
- Including unbalanced discussion and analysis of non-GAAP versus GAAP.

External Auditor Responsibilities

Professional standards require auditors only to read other information in a document containing the financial statements and accompanying audit report. There are no requirements for auditors to test non-GAAP disclosures, which are presented outside the financial statements, in earnings releases, or in the MD&A section of periodic filings. Consequently, the external auditor's opinion on the company's financial statements and, when required, the effectiveness of the company's internal controls do not cover non-GAAP measures. This raises an important question: Is there an expectation gap because users might expect that external auditors have reviewed earnings releases, or are attesting to the company's internal controls over non-GAAP measures, when they generally do not.[52]

The external auditor has no responsibility for determining whether non-GAAP financial information is properly stated. However, under PCAOB standards (AS 2710), the auditor should read the other information included in certain documents (such as annual or quarterly reports) and consider whether the information, or its manner of presentation, is materially consistent with the information appearing in the financial statements. If material inconsistencies exist, the auditor should consider whether the other information needs to be revised and communicate the matter to the client. If the other information is not revised to eliminate the material inconsistency, the auditor should communicate the material inconsistency to the audit committee and consider other actions, such as revising the audit report to include an explanatory paragraph, withholding the use of the report, and withdrawing from the engagement.[53]

Liability for Wrongful Use of Non-GAAP Financial Measures

Registrants are subject to the anti-fraud provisions of the federal securities law, in addition to the general disclosure requirement under Regulation G which provides that a registrant shall not make public a non-GAAP financial measure that, taken together with the information accompanying that measure, contains an untrue statement of material fact or omits to state a material fact necessary in order to make the presentation of the non-GAAP financial measure, in light of the circumstances under which it is presented, not misleading.[54]

Companies should ensure that the non-GAAP financial measures they use are neither misleading nor prohibited by the rules. Appropriate controls on the use of non-GAAP financial measures should be considered and established by management. Audit committees should carefully oversee and monitor the use of non-GAAP financial measures and disclosures. The audit committee should ask management to explain the usefulness of non-GAAP financial measures in the company's public disclosures. The audit committee should discuss the company's use of non-GAAP financial measures with the external auditors. A careful review by the audit committee can help save a company from legal liability for false and/or misleading non-GAAP disclosures.

Is Non-GAAP Reporting Ethical?

Do companies purposefully choose non-GAAP measures that disclose the most positive results or do they select a method that best informs investors, analysts, and other users about their "true" performance? In other words, the non-GAAP method chosen should be designed to provide information to investors that are more meaningful than GAAP in portraying not only how the company is doing but provide insight into how it might do in the future. Since adjustments to GAAP can include transitory amounts, non-recurring items, and one-time events, the result should provide better guidance on the company's performance than would occur using GAAP only. The non-GAAP measures should better reflect economic reality than GAAP amounts alone.

It's possible that some managers turn to non-GAAP reporting because they are unable to produce GAAP earnings that meet or beat earnings targets or expectations—even after engaging in earnings management. It may be difficult for an auditor to make this determination without understanding management's motivation in disclosing non-GAAP amounts and in selecting one type of non-GAAP measure versus another. External auditors need to assess motivation, look for pressures on management to disclose earnings numbers that make the company look like it's doing better than it really is, and be aware of other factors that might incentivize management to find alternative ways to present operating performance that also portray them in the most positive light.

The SEC has brought enforcement actions against companies that do not portray GAAP earnings as prominently as non-GAAP earnings. On December 26, 2018, the SEC settled with ADT Inc. over how it portrayed disclosures of non-GAAP earnings. ADT did not afford equal or greater prominence to comparable GAAP financial measures in two of its earnings releases containing non-GAAP financial measures for the fourth quarter of 2017 and fiscal year 2017. In its fiscal year 2017 earnings release and its first quarter 2018 earnings release, ADT provided non-GAAP financial measures such as EBITDA, adjusted net income, and free cash flow before special items, without giving equal or greater prominence to the comparable GAAP measures. In the headline of the fiscal 2017 earnings release, ADT presented its adjusted EBITDA for fiscal year 2017 and stated that adjusted EBITDA was up 8 percent year-over-year, without measuring ADT's net income or loss (the comparable GAAP financial measure) in the headline.[55]

Revisiting Financial Shenanigans

The improper use of non-GAAP metrics is a form of financial shenanigan and can be used to manage earnings. We believe that auditors should be required to audit these measures as part of their annual audit. The exclusion of an audit requirement for financial figures released outside of the annual report diminishes the value of the audit and provides an opportunity for fraudulent financial reporting. This is an area that needs more attention by the profession.

Now that we have completed the discussion of financial shenanigans that lead to earnings management of one kind or another, it is important to keep in mind the basics. To help you understand the essence of these matters, we have prepared the following **Exhibit 6.10**.

EXHIBIT 6.10   Analysis of Financial Shenanigans

Shenanigan	Description	Technique	Company
1	Accelerating revenue into an earlier period	Channel stuffing Bill-and-hold Multiple deliverables	Sunbeam Halliburton Xerox
2	Recording income that lacks economic substance	Special-purpose entities	Enron
3	Classifying non-operating income in the operating section	Shifting income or expense categories	IBM
4	Capitalizing costs that should be expensed	Asset misrepresentation	WorldCom
5	Reducing expenses by releasing reserves from previous charges	Cookie-jar reserves	Lucent
6	Deferring recording of current income to smooth net income over time	Shift profit to corporate reserves	W.R. Grace & Co.
7	Accelerating recording of future expenses to increase current operating loss	Big bath theory	Sunbeam

Concluding Thoughts

Earnings management is typically motivated by a desire to meet or exceed forecasted results, meet financial analysts' earnings expectations, inflate share price to make stock options more lucrative, and to enhance managerial performance. Earnings management can also occur through the use of non-GAAP measures that put the best face on the numbers even if they do not conform to GAAP.

We believe that when management manipulates earnings, the quality of such information suffers. It is hard enough for most readers of financial statements to understand the underlying accounting and financial reporting techniques used to develop the statements. When such methods are manipulated, or new ones developed to put a positive spin on company results, then there is a distortion effect that compromises the dependability of the statements. In the end it is the users who suffer the consequences of fraudulent reporting and the public interest obligation of accountants is not met.

At the end of the day, financial reporting needs to focus more on representational faithfulness, meaning that there should be a correlation or agreement between the accounting measures or descriptions in financial reports and the economic events they purport to represent. Faithful representation does not mean accurate in all respects. Free from error means there are no errors or omissions in the description of the event, and the process used to produce the reported information has been selected and applied with no errors in the process. In other words, a representation of an estimate can be faithful if the amount is described clearly and accurately as being an estimate, the nature and limitations of the estimating process are explained, and no errors have been made in selecting and applying an appropriate process for developing the estimate.

Financial shenanigans have been used for years to manage earnings by choosing how and when to report and disclose financial information. The motivation oftentimes is to smooth net income over time. These artificial maneuvers mislead investors and financial analysts about the true state of earnings in two or more years.

It's up to auditors to look for the red flags that something is not right with the reported earnings. They do this by carefully examining the structure of reported transactions and various techniques used by management to report earnings, financial position, and cash flow changes. A diligent audit entails evaluating both the form and economic substance of financial information to ensure there are no material misstatements.

As we have learned throughout this book, organizational ethics, effective ICFR, and strong corporate governance systems provide a foundation to ward off the temptation to manipulate reported results. In virtually all of the financial frauds discussed in this chapter, compromises were made in these systems in order to achieve desired results. Companies played fast and loose with the accounting rules and often were successful in deceiving the independent auditors.

The consequences of earnings management can be severe whether it affects earnings quality, results in revisions or restatements of financial statements or even in enforcement actions by the SEC. There is clearly a need for ethical leadership by management to set the proper ethical tone so that the techniques shown in **Exhibit 6.10** are not used. This will be further discussed in **Chapter 7**.

Discussion Questions

1. There is an old industry joke that if you ask an accountant what is four plus four, they will tell you it's whatever you want it to be. Explain what might be meant by this statement.

2. In Arthur Levitt's speech, referred to in the opening quote, he also said, "I fear that we are witnessing an erosion in the quality of earnings, and therefore, the quality of financial reporting. Managing may be giving way to manipulation; integrity may be losing out to illusion." Explain what you think Levitt meant by this statement. What role do financial analysts' earnings expectations play in the quality of earnings?

3. Relevance and faithful representation are the qualitative characteristics of useful information under *SFAC No. 8*.[56] How does ethical reasoning enter into making determinations about the relevance and faithful representation of financial information?

4. Evaluate the following statements from an ethical perspective:

   "Earnings management, in a narrow sense, is the behavior of management to play with the discretionary accrual component to determine high or low earnings."
   "Earnings are potentially managed because financial accounting standards will provide alternative methods."

5. Needles talks about the use of a continuum ranging from questionable or highly conservative to fraud to assess the amount to be recorded for an estimated expense. Do you believe that the choice of an overly conservative or overly aggressive amount would reflect earnings management? Explain.

6. Do you agree with Thomas McKee's conception of earnings management as applied to (a) operational earnings management and (b) accounting earnings management?

7. Comment on the statement that what a company's income statement reveals is interesting, but what it conceals is vital.

8. Maines and Wahlen[57] state in their research paper on the reliability of accounting information: "Accrual estimates require judgment and discretion, which some firms under certain incentive conditions will exploit to report non-neutral accruals estimates within GAAP. Accounting standards can enhance the information in accrual estimates by linking them to the underlying economic constructs they portray." How can accruals be used to manage non-GAAP operating earnings?

9. What is the risk of management bias for each earnings judgment and estimate? What safeguards should be in place to mitigate the risk of management bias, if any? What is the external auditor's role in this process?

10. Krispy Kreme was involved in an accounting fraud where the company reported false quarterly and annual earnings and falsely claimed that, as a result of those earnings, it had achieved what had become a prime benchmark of its historical performance; that is, reporting quarterly earnings per share that exceeded its previously announced EPS guidance by 1¢. One method used to report higher earnings was to ship two or three times more doughnuts to franchisees than ordered in order to meet monthly quotas. Would you characterize what Krispy Kreme did as earnings management? Explain.

11. What is the purpose of using financial analysis to spot earnings management?

12. Revenue recognition in the Xerox case called for determining the stand-alone selling price for each of the deliverables and using it to separate out the revenue amounts. Why do you think it is important to separate out the selling prices of each element of a bundled transaction? How do these considerations relate to what Xerox did to manage its earnings? Do you think the new revenue recognition standard will change the criteria in accounting for transactions like at Xerox?

13. Tinseltown Construction just received a $2.6 billion contract to construct a modern football stadium for the L.A. Rams and San Diego Chargers at the L.A. Sports and Entertainment District. The company estimates that it will cost $1.8 billion to construct the stadium. Explain how Tinseltown can make revenue recognition decisions each year that enable it to manage earnings over the three-year duration of the contract.

14. The SEC's new rules on posting financial information on social media sites such as Twitter means that companies can now tweet their earnings in 280 characters or less. What are the problems that may arise in using a social media platform to report key financial data, including the potential effects on shareholders and the company?

15. Discuss the revenue recognition and internal control challenges when a company uses cloud computing.

16. Schlit describes a variety of financial shenanigans. What is the purpose of using those techniques? Would you call it gimmickry? Explain.

17. In the study of earnings quality by Dichev et al.,[58] CFOs stated that "current earnings are considered to be high quality if they serve as a good guide to the long-run profits of the firm." Discuss how and why current earnings may *not* be a good barometer of the long-term profits of the firm. How do non-GAAP measures of earnings address this issue?

18. Why are non-GAAP financial measures used by many investors and analysts?

19. Explain the SEC rules and regulations applicable to the public disclosure of non-GAAP financial measures.

20. Do you agree with each of the following statements? Explain.

- EBITDA makes companies with asset-heavy balance sheets look healthier than they may actually be.
- EBITDA portrays a company's debt service ability—but only *some types of debt*.
- EBITDA isn't a determinant of cash flow *at all*.

Comprehensive Questions

1. In a recent survey of 122 public company managers with financial reporting experience, respondents were asked how morally right they believed earnings management to be. Managers responded on a scale of 1 to 8, where 1 = not morally right to 8 = morally right. The average response was 2.8, indicating that managers consider earnings management to be relatively immoral. Why do you think managers find earnings management to be relatively immoral? Use ethical reasoning to craft your answer.

2. In the same survey, managers were asked how acceptable earnings management was within their company's culture, with 1 = culturally unacceptable and 8 = culturally acceptable. The average response was 3.9, indicating that managers lean slightly toward perceiving earnings management as culturally unacceptable. Are you surprised by the findings that indicate a relative split between cultural acceptability? Explain in light of the attention we have been giving to the impact of corporate culture on ethical decision making.

3. From the first quarter of 2018 through the third quarter of 2021, Accelerator, Inc., engaged in a wide-ranging fraud designed to artificially inflate the company's reported revenue. This fraud involved Accelerator's relationship with its largest distributor and resulted in the company's misstating millions of dollars of revenue in its financial statements.

   Starting in 2018, Accelerator's sales to its distributor was gradually decreasing. As a result, during the last three quarters of the year, the company began to improperly record revenue by entering into and concealing side arrangements. The concealment of these side arrangements caused Accelerator to improperly recognize revenue representing at least 12 percent to 28 percent of its reported revenue during the relevant time period.

   Accelerator improperly recognized revenue at the time it shipped products to its distributor. This improper revenue recognition occurred because of a secret side arrangement between the company and its distributor that materially altered the terms of Accelerator's relationship with the distributor, including allowing the distributor to pay Accelerator only when it resold the products, and crediting the distributor for lost, damaged, or returned products. This side arrangement with the distributor should have prevented Accelerator from recognizing revenue at shipment.

Discuss the appropriateness of Accelerator's recognition of revenue with the distributor using the new revenue recognition standard. What would be your ethical concerns with the way the company recorded revenue from the distributor?

4. Assume you are a CPA and the CFO of a large public company. You have identified a red flag that financial impropriety may exist in the reported numbers. Would you report it to the external auditors? Should you report it to them under the rules of conduct in the AICPA Code. Why or why not?

5. Review the numbers below. Assume you are an investor. What questions would you have about the numbers and presentation?

UNAUDITED ORGANIC REVENUE GROWTH RECONCILIATION				
(in millions of dollars, except percentages)				
	Three Months Ended		Nine Months Ended	
	Revenue $	% Change	Revenue $	% Change
September 30, 2016–Revenues	$ 349,254		$ 995,343	
Organic revenue growth*	27,075	7.8%	83,556	8.4%
Impact of Non-GAAP acquisitions (dispositions), net	(3,153)	(0.9%)	36,489	3.7%
Foreign exchange impact, net	2,624	0.8%	(4,356)	(0.4%)
GAAP revenue growth	26,546	7.6%	115,689	11.6%
September 30, 2017–Revenues	$ 375,800		$ 1,111,032	

*"Organic revenue growth" and "organic revenue decline" refer to the positive or negative results, respectively, of subtracting both the foreign exchange and acquisition (disposition) components from total revenue growth. The acquisition (disposition) component is calculated by aggregating prior period revenue for any acquired businesses, less the prior period revenue of any businesses that were disposed of during the current period. The organic revenue growth (decline) component reflects the constant currency impact of (a) the change in revenue of the partner firms which the Company has held throughout each of the comparable periods presented, and (b) "non-GAAP acquisitions (dispositions), net." Non-GAAP acquisitions (dispositions), net consists of (i) for acquisitions during the current year, the revenue effect from such acquisition as if the acquisition had been owned during the equivalent period in the prior year, (ii) for acquisitions during the previous year, the revenue effect from such acquisitions as if they had been owned during that entire year (or same period as the current reportable period), taking into account their respective pre-acquisition revenues for the applicable periods, and (iii) for dispositions, the revenue effect from such disposition as if they had been disposed of during the equivalent period in the prior year.

Endnotes

1. Maria L. Murphy, How auditors can help companies with non-GAAP measures, KPIs, *Compliance Week* (October 21, 2020), https://www.complianceweek.com/accounting-and-auditing/how-auditors can-help-with-non-gaap-measures-kpis/29627.article.

2. Arthur Levitt, "The Numbers Game," Remarks made by the former SEC chairman before the NYU Center for Law and Business, September 28, 1998, Available at: https://www.sec.gov/news/speech/speecharchive/1998/spch220.txt.

3. Jim Gaa and Paul Dunmore, "The Ethics of Earnings Management," *Chartered Accountants Journal* (2007), pp. 60–62.

4. Kenneth A. Merchant, *Rewarding Results: Motivating Profit Center Managers* (Boston: Harvard Business School Press, 1989).

5. William S. Hopwood, Jay J. Leiner, and George R. Young, *Forensic Accounting and Fraud Examination* (New York: McGraw-Hill Irwin, 2012).

6. Scott McGregor, "Earnings Management Manipulation," http://webpage.pace.edu/pviswanath/notes/corpfin/earningsmanip.html

7. Financial Accounting Standards Board, "Recognition and Measurement in Financial Statements of Business Enterprises," *Statement of Financial Accounting Concepts (SFAC) No. 5* (Stamford, CT: FASB, May 1986).

8. SEC, *HealthSouth Corporation Securities Litigation,* United States District Court Northern District of Alabama Southern Division, Available at: http://securities.stanford.edu/filings-documents/1008/HRC98/200482_r03c_031500.pdf.

9. Richard J. Rivard, Eugene Bland, and Gary B. Hatfield Morris, "Income Smoothing Behavior of U.S. Banks under Revised International Capital Requirements," *International Advances in Economic Research* 9, no. 4 (November 2003), pp. 288–294.

10. Harvard Law School Forum on Corporate Guidance, SEC Cracks Down on Earnings Management, December 17, 2019, https://corpgov.law.harvard.edu/2019/12/17/sec-cracks-down-on-earnings-management/.

11. Belverd E. Needles, "Teaching Judgment and Ethics in First-year Accounting: A Good Lecture," *Trends* (June 13, 2011), https://blog.cengage.com/wp-content/uploads/2014/07/SUMMER-2011.Trends.pdf.

12. K. Schipper, "Commentary on Earnings Management," *Accounting Horizons* (December 1989), pp. 91–102.

13. P. M. Dechow and P. J. Skinner, "Earnings Management: Reconciling the Views of Accounting Academics, Practitioners, and Regulation," *Accounting Horizons* 14 (2001), pp. 235–250.

14. Thomas E. McKee, *Earnings Management: An Executive Perspective* (Mason, OH: Thompson Corporation, 2005).

15. P. M. Healy and J. M. Wahlen, "A Review of Earnings Management Literature and Its Implications for Standard Setting," *Accounting Horizons* 13 (1999), pp. 365–383.

16. William J. Bruns Jr., and Kenneth A. Merchant, "The Dangerous Morality of Managing Earnings," *Management Accounting* (August 1990), pp. 62–69.

17. K. Rosenzweig and M. Fischer, "Is Managing Earnings Ethically Acceptable?" *Management Accounting* (March 1994), pp. 44–51.

18. Michael D. Akers, Don E. Giacomino, and Jodi L. Bellovary, "Earnings Management and Its Implications: Educating the Accounting Profession," *The CPA Journal* (August 2007), pp. 33–39.

19. Akers et al.

20. Akers et al.

21. Erin L. Hamilton, Rina M. Hirsch, Uday S. Murthy, and Jason T. Rasso, "The Ethicality of Earnings Management," *Strategic Finance Magazine,* https://sfmagazine.com/post-entry/november-2018-the-ethicality-of-earnings-management/.

22. Keith G. Stanga and Andrea S. Kelton, "Ethicality and Moral Intensity of Earnings Management: Does the Method Matter?," *Research on Professional Responsibility and Ethics in Accounting* 13 (2008), pp. 19–40.

23. Eric N. Johnson, Gary Fleischman, Sean Valentine, and Kenton B. Walker, "Managers' Ethical Evaluations of Earnings Management and its Consequences," *Contemporary Accounting Research* 29, no. 3 (July 2011).

24. Hopwood et al., p. 426.

25. SEC, Administrative Proceeding File No. 3-20158, *In the Matter of The Cheesecake Factory Incorporated,* December 4, 2020.

26. SEC, Accounting and Auditing Enforcement Release No. 4076, *In the Matter of Marvell Technology Group, Ltd,* September 16, 2019.

27. Jessica Holzer and Greg Bensinger, "SEC Embraces Social Media," *The Wall Street Journal* (April 2, 2013), Available at: http://www.wsj.com/articles/SB10001424127887323611604578398862292997352.

28. Ilia Dechev, John Graham, Campbell R. Harvey, and Shiva Rajgopal, "The Misrepresentation of Earnings," *Financial Analysts Journal Journal* 72, no. 1 (2016), pp. 22–35.

29. *Employees' Retirement System, et al. v. Green Mountain Coffee Roasters, et al.,* United States Court of Appeals for the Second Circuit, July 24, 2015, Available at: http://caselaw.findlaw.com/us-2nd-circuit/1708736.html.

30. Green Mountain Coffee Roasters, Inc., *Annual Report on Form 10-K,* September 29, 2012, Available at: http://www.sec.gov/Archives/edgar/data/909954/000110465912080228/a12-21067_110k.htm.

31. SEC, Staff Accounting Bulletin: No. 101—Revenue Recognition in Financial Statements, Available at: https://www.sec.gov/interps/account/sab101.htm.

32. Kathryn Yeaton, "A New World of Revenue Recognition," *The CPA Journal* (July 2015), pp. 50–53.

33. Financial Accounting Standards Update: "Multiple-Deliverable Revenue Arrangements: A Consensus of the FASB Emerging Issues Task Force," Financial Accounting Standards Update No. 2009-13, October 2019, https://asc.fasb.org/imageRoot/62/6844362.pdf.

34. Sarah McBride, Oracle whistleblower suit raises questions over cloud accounting, *Reuters* (June 6, 2016), https://www.reuters.com/article/us-oracle-lawsuit-accounting/oracle-whistleblowers-suit-raises-questions-over-cloud-accounting-idUSKCNOYSOX1.

35. Steven J. Vaughn-Nichols, Is Oracle cooking its cloud books, *Computerworld* (June 13, 2016), https://www.computerworld.com/article/3082707/cloud-computing/is-oracle-cooking-its-cloud-books.html.

36. Financial Accounting Standards Board, Financial Accounting Series No. 2015-05, April 2015, *Customer's Accounting for Fees Paid in a Cloud Computing Arrangement*, http://www.fasb.org/jsp/FASB/Document_C/DocumentPage?cid=1176165941746&acceptedDisclaimer=true.

37. Howard M. Schilit, Jeremy Perler, and Yoni Engelhart, *Financial Shenanigans: How to Detect Accounting Gimmicks and Fraud in Financial Reports,* 4th ed. (New York: McGraw-Hill, 2018).

38. *W. R. Grace & Co.*

39. SEC, Litigation Release No. 18174, *Securities and Exchange Commission v. Paul A. Allaire, G. Richard Thoman, Barry D. Romeril, Philip D. Fishbach, Daniel S. Marchibroda, and Gregory B. Tayler,* June 5, 2003, *Accounting and Auditing Enforcement Release No. 1796,* Available at: https://www.sec.gov/litigation/litreleases/lr18174.htm.

40. SEC, Litigation Release No. 17645, *Accounting and Auditing Enforcement Release No. 1542, Securities and Exchange Commission v. Xerox Corporation,* Civil Action No. 02-CV-2780 (DLC) (S.D.N.Y.), April 11, 2002.

41. SEC, *In the Matter of KPMG LLP, Accounting and Auditing Enforcement Release No. 2234,* April 19, 2005, Available at: www.sec.gov/litigation/admin/34-51574.pdf.

42. SEC, Litigation Release No. 19573, *Accounting and Auditing Enforcement Release No. 2379, SEC v. KPMG LLP et al.,* Civil Action No. 03-CV 0671 (DLC) (S.D.N.Y.), February 22, 2006.

43. SEC, Litigation Release No. 18715, *Accounting and Auditing Enforcement Release No. 2016, Securities and Exchange Commission v. Lucent Technologies, Inc., Nina Aversano, Jay Carter, A. Leslie Dorn, William Plunkett, John Bratten, Deborah Harris, Charles Elliott, Vanessa Petrini, Michelle Hayes-Bullock, and David Ackerman,* Civil Action No. 04-2315 (WHW) (D.N.J.), filed May 17, 2004, Available at: www.sec.gov/litigation/litreleases/lr18715.htm.

44. SEC, *Accounting and Auditing Enforcement Release No. 2380, In the Matter of Thomas J. Yoho, CPA, Respondent,* Administrative Proceeding File No. 3-12215, February 22, 2006.

45. Jessica McKeon, *Long-Term Trends in Non-GAAP Disclosures: A Three-Year Overview* (October 10, 2017), https://blog.auditanalytics.com/long-term-treninon-gaap-disclsoures-a-three-year-overview/.

46. Jian Zhang, "Learning from the Current Research on Non-GAAP Financial Measures," *The CPA Journal* (July 2019), pp. 36–44.

47. Mary Jo White, Keynote Address, International Corporate Governance Network Annual Conference: Focusing the Lens of Disclosure to Set the Path Forward on Board Diversity, Non-GAAP, and Sustainability, June 2016, https://www.sec.gov/news/speech/chair-white-icgn-speech.html.

48. SEC Release No. 33-8145, Proposed Rule: Conditions for Use of Non-GAAP Financial Measures (November 4, 2002), https://www.sec.gov/rules/proposed/33-8145.htm, and SEC Release No. 33-8176, Final Rule: Conditions for the Use of Non-GAAP Financial Measures (January 22, 2004), https://www.sec.gov/rules/final/33-8176.htm.

49. Cornell Law School Legal Information Institute, 17 CFR 244.100 – General Rules Regarding Disclosure of Non-GAAP Financial Measures, https://www.law.cornell.edu/cfr/text/17/244.100.

50. SEC, Regulation S-K, Item 10(e)(1)(i), https://www.sec.gov/divisions/corpfin/ecfrlinks.shtml.

51. PwC, SEC Updates Interpretive Guidance on Non-GAAP financial Measures, May 19, 2016. https://www.pwc.com/us/en/cfodirect/publications/in-brief/sec-non-gaap-financial-measures.html. These interpretations were updated in 2017: SEC, Non-GAAP Financial Measures, October 17, 2016, https://www.sec.gov/divisions/corpfin/guidance/nongaapinterp.htm.

52. BKD, Non-GAAP Financial Measures, https://www.bkd.com/docs/pdf/Non-GAAP-Financial-Measures.pdf.dit report.

53. PCAOB, AS 2710: Other Information in Documents Containing Audited Financial Statements, https://pcaobus.org/Standards/Auditing/Pages/AS2710.aspx.

54. SEC, Regulation G, Rule 102; 17 CFR 244.100(b), https://www.sec.gov/rules/final/33-8176.htm.

55. SEC, Accounting and Auditing Enforcement Release No. 4009/December 26, 2018, *In the Matter of ADT Inc.*, https:/www.sec.gov/litigation/admin/2018/34-84956.pdf.

56. FASB, *Statement of Financial Accounting Concepts No. 8, Conceptual Framework for Financial Reporting—Chapter 1,* The Objective of General Purpose Financial Reporting, *and Chapter 3*, Qualitative Characteristics of Useful Financial Information (a replacement of FASB Concepts Statements No. 1 and No. 2), September 2010, Available at http://www.fasb.org/cs/BlobServer?blobkey=id&blobwhere=1175822892635&blobheader=application%2Fpdf&blobcol=urldata&blobtable=MungoBlobs.

57. Laureen A. Maines and James M. Wahlen, "*The Nature of Accounting Information Reliability: Inferences from Archival and Experimental Research*" (November 3, 2003), Available at: http://repository.binus.ac.id/content/m0034/m003421831.pdf.

58. Ilia D. Dichev, John R. Graham, Campbell R. Harvey, and Shivaram Rajgopal, The Misrepresentation of Earnings, *Financial Analysts Journal* (August 10, 2015), Forthcoming. Available at SSRN: http://ssrn.com/abstract=2376408 or http://dx.doi.org/10.2139/ssrn.2376408.

Chapter 6 Cases

Case 6-1 Winners & Losers, Inc.

Winners & Losers, Inc. (WLI) is a Nevada corporation with its principal place of business in Las Vegas. Its business model is to provide electronic sports betting in conjunction with a new law that legalized it in Nevada. The company's shares are registered with the SEC.

It is not against Federal law to gamble on the Internet or place bets on sporting events as an individual. Some states have laws against online gambling, but they are, literally, never enforced. If an individual places bets and does not act as a bookie and accepts wagers, then that party has nothing to worry about from a legal perspective. Moreover, Nevada recently legalized mobile and Internet sports betting throughout the state.

Overview

WLI made improper adjustments to its accrual for bonuses and accounting for stock compensation that enabled it to meet or exceed financial analysts' earnings projections from the second quarter of 2021 through the fourth quarter of the year. It reported earnings per share (EPS) that did not accurately reflect the company's underlying performance. During these three consecutive financial quarters, WLI's then-Corporate Controller, Bonnie Buyers, CPA, directed or otherwise caused her subordinates to book unsupported, manual accounting adjustments to WLI's management bonus accruals and stock-based compensation. These adjustments did not comply with generally accepted accounting principles (GAAP) and artificially inflated WLI's income and EPS, which resulted in the company's meeting or beating consensus estimates for EPS and showing earnings growth. WLI's then-Chief Financial Officer (CFO), Kathy Sellers, also caused Buyers to direct entries in two quarters that lacked support and did not comply with GAAP. Buyers and Sellers were able to direct or cause the improper adjustments because WLI failed to have sufficient accounting controls or procedures in place to prevent unsupported, manual, period-end, journal entries.

The adjustments were also material to WLI's financial statements and caused the company to make false disclosures in public filings, press releases, and earnings calls about its actual EPS results, its earnings growth, and its pattern of meeting or beating consensus analyst estimates. Had Buyers (controller) and Sellers (CFO) ensured the financial statements complied with GAAP, WLI's reported earnings would have been more volatile than reported.

Second Quarter of 2021

In Q2 2021, WLI reported EPS of $0.33 and its earnings release stated that it had "finished with earnings per share that tied our all-time record." In truth, WLI did not achieve record EPS in Q2 2021 because it understated its actual expenses for management bonuses by $1.58 million, which in turn inflated its pretax income by 5 percent and its EPS by $0.02.

WLI paid nondiscretionary management bonuses based on the achievement of established targets for operating income before incentives ("OIBI") and cash flow. If WLI met the stated "goal" for those targets, management would receive 100 percent of their bonus potential. If WLI exceeded the goal, management would receive up to a maximum, 150 percent, of their bonus potential depending on the amount by which the goal was exceeded.

At the time that Buyers improperly reduced the bonus accrual, WLI's best estimate was that annual bonuses at levels greater than 100 percent would be paid. The reduction in the accrual, however, caused WLI's accrual level to fall far below the 100 percent level, during the closing process for the second quarter, when WLI was on track to report an all-time record EPS of $0.33.

Third Quarter of 2021

In Q3 2021, WLI publicly reported that it had met consensus estimates for EPS of $0.31, reflecting a continued pattern of meeting or beating analyst estimates for two consecutive quarters. In truth, Buyers had directed unsupported accounting entries and otherwise understated expenses, which inflated WLI's pretax income by 12 percent, or a total of over $3.12 million. Rather than report a meet of consensus EPS estimates, WLI should have reported a $0.04 miss. The improper entries in Q3 2021 concerned WLI's stock-based compensation and management bonus.

Fourth Quarter of 2021

In Q4 2021, WLI reported a quarterly EPS of $0.28 and an annual EPS of $1.10, which represented a record for WLI and a $0.02 beat of consensus estimates for the year. While the quarter's EPS was a $0.01 miss of the consensus, it was just enough to allow WLI to report a $0.02 beat of estimates for the year, and the company's earnings release highlighted that the "fourth quarter rounded out a phenomenal year in which WLI posted all-time records for net income and earnings per share." In truth, however, WLI's results were artificially inflated by Buyer's adjustments to the Consultant's bonus and the management bonus.

In total, Buyer's improper adjustments and Seller's failure to ensure the bonus accruals were accurate caused Buyers to overstate income by a total of $1.63 million, or 7 percent of the quarter's pretax income. In reality, WLI should have reported EPS of $0.26 for the quarter and $1.08 for the year, which inflated pretax income by 8 percent for the year, or $1.7 million of pretax income.

Exhibit 1 summarizes the effects of improperly recording the bonus accrual, stock compensation expense, and consultant's bonus during the three quarters of 2021 and for the year.

EXHIBIT 1   Summary of Misstated Bonus Accrual and Stock Compensation Expense for 2021

		Q2 2021		Inflated Amounts	
Consensus EPS	Reported EPS	Correct EPS	EPS[1]	Pretax Income	
$0.28	$0.33	$0.31	$0.02	$1.58 million (5%)	
		Q3 2021			
Consensus EPS	Reported EPS	Correct EPS	EPS	Pretax Income	
$0.31	$0.31	$0.27	$0.04	$3.12 million (12%)	
		Q4 2021			
Consensus EPS	Reported EPS	Correct EPS	EPS	Pretax Income	
$0.28	$0.28	$0.27	$0.01	$1.63 million (7%)	
		For 2021			
Consensus EPS[2]	Reported EPS	Correct EPS	EPS	Pretax Income	
$1.08	$1.10	$1.08	$0.02	$1.70 million (8%)	

[1] EPS = Reported EPS - Correct EPS
[2] Q1 2021 numbers not shown because there was no manipulation of EPS

WLI Lacked Accurate Books and Records and Sufficient Internal Accounting Controls

These adjustments to WLI's expenses, which inflated EPS quarter after quarter, were made in part because WLI lacked sufficient internal accounting controls over (a) significant recurring accruals subject to management estimate including incentives and stock-based compensation, (b) journal entries, and (c) period-end adjustments made during the closing process. WLI did not require, for example, corporate-level accounting entries to have supporting documentation, and corporate finance staff regularly recorded manual adjustments with nothing more than an e-mail or oral directive. In addition, Buyer's direct reports did not analyze or consider the propriety of the entries he directed, and WLI's Internal Audit function did not perform procedures sufficient to ensure adjustments directed by Sellers and Buyers had support and complied with GAAP.

As a result, WLI's internal accounting controls were not designed or maintained to provide reasonable assurance that WLI's financial statements would be presented in conformity with GAAP. WLI's books, records, and accounts also did not accurately and fairly reflect, in reasonable detail, the company's transactions.

Questions

1. Do you believe electronic sports betting should be legalized in all states? Use ethical reasoning to support your point of view.

2. Internal accountants and auditors play a critical role in ensuring the financial statements present fairly financial position, net income, and cash flows. Describe the deficiencies in these systems at WLI.

3. Publicly owned companies are not required to have their forward-looking statements audited including earnings guidance, although auditors should make sure statements are not made that conflict with the numbers and other disclosures in the financial statements. Do you believe auditors should be required to audit forward-looking statements and earnings releases? Why or why not?

4. Assume you are a CPA and one of the subordinates who booked unsupported adjustments to bonus accruals, stock compensation expense, and consultant's bonus for 2021. Explain your ethical obligations under the AICPA Code and the steps you should have taken in lieu of going along with Bonnie Buyer's directions.

Case 6-2 Solutions Network, Inc. (a GVV case)

"We can't recognize revenue immediately, Paul, since we agreed to buy similar software from DSS," Sarah Young stated.

"That's ridiculous," Paul Henley replied. "Get your head out of the sand, Sarah, before it's too late."

Sarah Young is the controller for Solutions Network, Inc., a publicly owned company headquartered in Sunnyvale, California. Solutions Network has an audit committee with three members of the board of directors that are independent of management. Sarah is meeting with Paul Henley, the CFO of the company on January 7, 2019, to discuss the accounting for a software systems transaction with Data Systems Solutions (DSS) prior to the company's audit for the year ended December 31, 2018. Both Young and Henley are CPAs.

Young has excluded the amount in contention from revenue and net income for 2018, but Henley wants the amount to be included in the 2018 results. Without it, Solutions Network would not meet earnings expectations. Henley tells Young that the order came from the top to record the revenue on December 28, 2018, the day the transaction with DSS was finalized. Young points out that Solutions Network ordered essentially the same software from DSS to be shipped and delivered early in 2019. Therefore, according to Young, Solutions Network should delay revenue recognition on this "swap" transaction until that time. Henley argues against Sarah's position, stating that title had passed from the company to DSS on December 31, 2018, when the software product was shipped FOB shipping point.

Background

Solutions Network, Inc., became a publicly owned company on March 15, 2014, following a successful initial public offering (IPO). Solutions Network built up a loyal clientele in the three years prior to the IPO by establishing close working relationships with technology leaders, including IBM, Apple, and Dell Computer. The company designs and engineers systems software to function seamlessly with minimal user interface. There are several companies that provide similar products and consulting services, and DSS is one. However, DSS operates in a larger market providing IT services management products that coordinate the entire business infrastructure into a single system.

Solutions Network grew very rapidly during the past five years, although sales slowed down a bit in 2018. The revenue and earnings streams during those years are as follows:

Year	Revenues (millions)	Net Income (millions)
2013	$148.0	$11.9
2014	175.8	13.2
2015	202.2	15.0
2016	229.8	16.1
2017	267.5	17.3
2018 (projected)	$262.5	$16.8

The Transaction

On December 28, 2018, Solutions Network offered to sell its Internet infrastructure software to DSS for its internal use. In return, DSS agreed to ship similar software 30 days later to Solutions Network for that company's internal use. The companies had conducted several transactions with each other during the previous five years, and while DSS initially balked at the transaction because it provided no value added to the company, it did not want to upset one of the fastest-growing software companies in the industry. Moreover, Solutions Network might be able to help identify future customers for DSS's IT service management products.

The $15 million of revenue would increase net income by $1.0 million. For Solutions Network, the revenue from the transaction would be enough to enable the company to meet targeted goals, and the higher level of income would provide extra bonus money at year-end for Young, Henley, and Ed Fralen, the CEO.

Accounting Considerations

In her discussions with Henley, Young points out that the auditors will arrive on January 15, 2019; therefore, the company should be certain of the appropriateness of its accounting before that time. After all, says Young, "the auditors rely on us to record transactions properly as part of their audit expectations." At this point Henley reacts angrily and tells Young she can pack her bags and go if she doesn't support the company in its revenue recognition of the DSS transaction. Young is taken aback. Henley seems unusually agitated. Perhaps he was under a lot more pressure to "meet the numbers" than she anticipated. To defuse the matter, Young makes an excuse to end the meeting prematurely and asks if they could meet on Monday morning, after the weekend. Henley agrees.

Over the weekend, Sarah Young calls her best friend, Shannon McCollough, for advice. Shannon is a controller at another company and Sarah would often commensurate with Shannon over their mutual experiences. Shannon suggests that Sarah should explain to Paul Henley exactly what her ethical obligations are in the matter. Shannon thinks it might make a difference because Paul is a CPA as well.

After the discussion with Shannon, Sarah considers whether she is being too firm in her position. On the one hand, she knows that regardless of the passage of title to DSS on December 31, 2018, the transaction is linked to Solutions Network's agreement to take the DSS product 30 days later. While she doesn't anticipate any problems in that regard, Sarah is uncomfortable with the recording of revenue on December 31 because DSS did not complete its portion of the agreement by that date. She has her doubts whether the auditors would sanction the accounting treatment.

On the other hand, Sarah is also concerned about the fact that another transaction occurred during the previous year that she questioned but, in the end, went along with Paul's accounting for this transaction. On December 28, 2017, Solutions Network sold a major system for $20 million to Laramie Systems but executed a side agreement with Laramie on that date which gave Laramie the right to return the product for any reason within 30 days. Even though Solutions Network recorded the revenue in 2017 and Sarah felt uneasy about it, she did not object because Laramie did not return the product; her acceptance was motivated by the delay in the external audit until after the 30-day period had expired. Now, however, Sarah is concerned that a pattern may be developing.

Questions

1. What are the main arguments Sarah is trying to counter? That is, what are the reasons and rationalizations she needs to address in deciding how to handle the meeting with Paul Henley?

2. What is at stake for the key parties in this case? What are Sarah's ethical obligations to them?

3. Should Sarah's decision on revenue recognition in 2017 influence how she handles the DSS transaction? Explain.

4. Should Sarah follow Shannon's advice? What if she does and Paul Henley does not back off? What additional levers can she use to strengthen her position?

5. What is the most powerful and persuasive response to the reasons and rationalizations Sarah needs to address? To whom should the argument be made? When and in what context?

6. What should Sarah do next if all parties at Solutions Network support Paul Henley's position and flat out tell Sarah to be a team player?

Case 6-3 Allergan: Mind the GAAP

Exhibit 1 presents the fourth quarter press release of Allergan. Allergan is a global pharmaceutical company and a leader in a new industry model—Growth Pharma. Allergan's product lines include Botox, Juvederm, Latisse, Namenda, and Restasis. **Exhibit 2** presents the reconciliation from GAAP to non-GAAP income that was included with the release.

Over the years, Allergan has had many disagreements with the SEC about the presentation of non-GAAP metrics in their financial reports and press releases. Allergan's responses to SEC staff comments have been to emphasize that its performance measures "are useful to both management and investors in assessing current performance and future operations." Moreover, Allergan contended in its response that "analysts for our industry group base their third-party consensus estimates on non-GAAP earnings per share metrics."

Review **Exhibit 1** and answer the following questions.

1. Do you believe Allergan's financial information in its press release is useful? Why or why not?

2. Do you believe this kind of information should be subject to audit procedures? If so, what procedures should be used? If not, why not?

3. Do you believe the financial and non-financial information provided by Allergan in its press release is veiled attempt at earnings management? Explain.

Review **Exhibit 2** at the end of the case and answer the following questions.

4. Does the reconciliation shed light on the usefulness and understandability of the non-GAAP numbers? Explain.

5. Look at each item included in the reconciliation and briefly discuss whether you think each one should or should not be included in a reconciliation from GAAP to non-GAAP.

Allergan Reports Solid Finish to 2017 with 12 Percent Increase in Fourth-Quarter GAAP Net Revenues to $4.3 Billion:

*   Q4 2017 GAAP Continuing Operations Income Per Share of $9.97; Q4 Non-GAAP Performance Net Income Per Share of $4.86

*   Q4 2017 GAAP Operating Loss from Continuing Operations of $90.5 Million; Q4 Non-GAAP Adjusted Operating Income from Continuing Operations of $2.17 Billion

*   Q4 2017 GAAP Revenue Growth Versus Prior Year Quarter Powered by BOTOX®, JUVÉDERM® Collection, ALLODERM®, CoolSculpting®, and Launch Products

EXHIBIT 1   Allergan Earnings Release

(unaudited; $ in millions, except per share amounts)	Q4 '17	Q4 '16	Q3 '17	Q4 '17 v Q4 '16	Q4 '17 v Q3 '17	Year Ended December 31, 2017	Year Ended December 31, 2016	2017 v 2016
Total net revenues	$ 4,326.10	$ 3,864.30	$ 4,034.30	12.0%	7.2%	$ 15,940.70	$ 14,570.60	9.4%
Operating (Loss)	$ (90.50)	$ 900.00	$ (4,022.30)	-89.9%	-97.8%	$ (5,921.20)	$ (1,825.50)	224.4%
Diluted EPS—Continuing Operations	$ 9.97	$ (0.31)	$ (12.05)	n.m.	-182.7%	$ (11.99)	$ (3.17)	278.2%
SG&A Expense	$ 1,266.80	$ 1,276.80	$ 1,169.70	-0.8%	8.3%	$ 5,016.70	$ 4,740.30	5.8%
R&D Expense	$ 408.20	$ 913.30	$ 442.60	-55.3%	-7.8%	$ 2,100.10	$ 2,575.70	-18.5%
Continuing Operations Tax Rate	n.m.	96.4%	29.3%	n.m.	n.m.	64.2%	67.0%	-2.8%
Non-GAAP Adjusted Operating Income	$ 2,174.30	$ 1,868.70	$ 1,968.20	16.4%	10.5%	$ 7,647.50	$ 7,245.30	5.6%
Non-GAAP Performance Net Income Per Share	$ 4.86	$ 3.90	$ 4.15	24.6%	17.1%	$ 16.35	$ 13.51	21.0%
Non-GAAP Adjusted EBITDA	$ 2,284.50	$ 1,975.70	$ 2,051.70	15.6%	11.3%	$ 8,097.60	$ 7,628.70	6.1%
Non-GAAP SG&A Expense	$ 1,132.80	$ 1,067.00	$ 1,099.60	6.2%	3.0%	$ 4,554.80	$ 4,081.70	11.6%
Non-GAAP R&D Expense	$ 405.70	$ 425.90	$ 405.30	-4.7%	0.1%	$ 1,598.80	$ 1,433.80	11.5%
Non-GAAP Continuing Operations Tax Rate	11.4%	10.4%	13.1%	1.0%	-1.7%	12.6%	8.9%	3.7%

** Excludes the reclassification of revenues of ($80.0) million in the 12 months ended December 31, 2016, related to the portion of Allergan product revenues sold by our former Anda Distribution Business into discontinued operations.

EXHIBIT 2   Allergan PLC Reconciliation Table

	Three Months Ended December 31,		Twelve Months Ended December 31,	
(Unaudited; in millions except per share amounts)	2017	2016	2017	2016
GAAP to Non-GAAP Performance net income calculation				
GAAP income/(loss) from continuing operations attributable to shareholders	$3,506.6	$ (41.9)	$(3,722.6)	$ (941.1)
Adjusted for:				
Amortization	$1,922.2	$ 1,638.50	$ 7,197.1	$ 6,470.4
Acquisition, divestiture, and licensing charges[1]	$ 108.4	$ 800.40	$ 4,083.4	$ 1,593.6
Accretion and fair-value adjustments to contingent consideration	$ (81.6)	$ (143.50)	$ (133.2)	$ (64.2)
Impairment/asset sales and related costs	$ 238.5	$ 456.00	$5,380.0	$ 748.9
Non-recurring losses/(gains)	$ 16.2	$ (9.50)	$ 210.1	$ 8.9
Non-acquisition restructurings, including Global Supply Chain initiatives	$ 113.6		$ 208.4	
Legal settlements	$ 22.2	$ 17.30	$ 96.5	$ 117.3
Income taxes on items above and other discrete income tax adjustments	$(4,137.8)	$(1,242.20)	$(7,508.8)	$(2,432.2)
Non-GAAP performance net income attributable to shareholders	$1,708.3	$ 1,475.1	$ 5,810.9	$ 5,501.6
Diluted earnings per share				
Diluted income/(loss) per share from continuing operations attributable to shareholders—GAAP	$ 9.97	$ (0.12)	$ (11.15)	$ (2.45)
Non-GAAP performance net income per share attributable to shareholders	$ 4.86	$ 3.90	$ 16.35	$ 13.51
Basic weighted average ordinary shares outstanding	331.3	356.8	333.8	384.9
Effect of dilutive securities:				
Dilutive shares	20.3	21.8	21.6	22.3
Dilutive weighted average ordinary shares outstanding	351.6	378.6	355.4	407.2

(1) Includes stock-based compensation primarily due to the Zeltiq, Allergan and Forest acquisitions as well as the valuation accounting impact in interest expense net.

- Full-Year 2017 GAAP Net Revenues of $15.94 Billion
- Full-Year 2017 GAAP Continuing Operations Loss Per Share of $11.99; Full-Year Non-GAAP Performance Net Income Per Share of $16.35
- Company Continues to Advance R&D Pipeline Beyond Six "Star" Programs
- Provides Full-Year 2018 Guidance and First Quarter 2018 GAAP Net Revenue and Non-GAAP Performance Net Income Per Share Guidance

Dublin, Ireland – February 6, 2018 – Allergan plc (NYSE: AGN) today reported its fourth-quarter and full-year 2017 continuing operations performance.

Continuing on from the earnings release, the total fourth-quarter net revenues were $4.33 billion, a 12.0 percent increase from the prior year quarter, driven by BOTOX® Cosmetic, BOTOX® Therapeutic, JUVÉDERM® Collection,

ALLODERM®, CoolSculpting®, and new products, including VRAYLAR™, NAMZARIC®, and VIBERZI®. The increase was partially offset by lower revenues from products losing patent exclusivity, and the continuing decline in ACZONE® and NAMENDA XR®. For the full year 2017, Allergan reported total net revenues of $15.94 billion, a 9.4 percent increase versus the prior year, driven by continued strong growth across key therapeutic areas and key products, and the addition of Regenerative Medicine products and CoolSculpting®.

"2017 was a pivotal year for Allergan and we delivered solid results. We powered strong revenue growth of our top products and in each of our regions. We acquired, integrated, and grew two new businesses and continued to advance our R&D pipeline. Allergan also continued to execute our capital deployment plan by completing a $15 billion share repurchase program, instituting a dividend and paying down debt in 2017," said Brent Saunders, Chairman and CEO of Allergan. "I believe that Allergan has a strong future and I am especially proud of our Allergan colleagues who continue to be Bold for Life by delivering treatments that make a difference for patients around the world."

Fourth-Quarter 2017 Performance

GAAP operating loss from continuing operations in the fourth-quarter 2017 was $90.5 million, including the impact of amortization, in-process research and development (R&D) impairments and charges associated with the December 2017 restructuring program announced on January 3, 2018. Non-GAAP adjusted operating income from continuing operations in the fourth quarter of 2017 was $2.17 billion, an increase of 16.4 percent versus the prior year quarter. Cash flow from operations for the fourth quarter of 2017 increased to approximately $2.05 billion.

Full-Year 2017 Performance

GAAP operating loss from continuing operations for the full year 2017 was $5.92 billion, compared with $1.83 billion in 2016 primarily due to impairment charges recognized in the third quarter of 2017 of $3.2 billion related to RESTA-SIS® and $646.0 million related to ACZONE®. Non-GAAP adjusted operating income from continuing operations for the full-year 2017 was $7.65 billion, an increase of 5.6 percent versus prior year. GAAP cash flow from operations for the full year of 2017 increased to approximately $5.87 billion, compared to $1.45 billion in 2016, which was negatively impacted by cash taxes paid in connection with the gain recognized on the businesses sold to Teva Pharmaceuticals Industries, Ltd ("Teva").

Operating Expenses

Total GAAP Selling, General and Administrative (SG&A) Expense was $1.27 billion for the fourth-quarter 2017, compared to $1.28 billion in the prior year quarter. Included within GAAP SG&A in the fourth-quarter and full-year 2017 were charges related to the December 2017 restructuring program of $80.0 million. Total non-GAAP SG&A expense increased to $1.13 billion for the fourth-quarter 2017, compared to $1.07 billion in the prior year period, primarily due to costs associated with the addition of the Regenerative Medicine and CoolSculpting® businesses. GAAP R&D investment for the fourth quarter of 2017 was $408.2 million, compared to $913.3 million in the fourth quarter of 2016. Non-GAAP R&D investment for the fourth quarter 2017 was $405.7 million, a decrease of 4.7 percent over the prior year quarter, due to reprioritization of R&D programs and tight expense management.

Asset Sales & Impairments, Net and In-Process R&D Impairments

The Company recorded impairment charges of $238.5 million and $456.0 million in the three months ended December 31, 2017 and 2016, respectively. The Company excludes asset sales and impairments, net and in-process research and development impairments from its non-GAAP performance net income attributable to shareholders as well as Adjusted EBITDA and Adjusted Operating Income.

Amortization, Other Income (Expense) Net, Tax and Capitalization

Amortization expense from continuing operations for the fourth-quarter 2017 was $1.92 billion, compared to $1.64 billion in the fourth quarter of 2016.

The Company's GAAP continuing operations tax rate benefit in the fourth quarter of 2017 was primarily attributable to discrete income tax benefits recognized as a result of the Tax Cuts and Jobs Act ("TCJA"). The Company's non-GAAP adjusted continuing operations tax rate was 11.4 percent in the fourth-quarter 2017. As of December 31, 2017, Allergan had cash and marketable securities of $6.45 billion and outstanding indebtedness of $30.1 billion.

Provisional Estimates of the Impact of U.S. Tax Reform

Allergan recorded a net provisional benefit of approximately $2.8 billion related to the TCJA. This amount includes a $730 million provisional expense representing the U.S. tax payable on deemed repatriated earnings of non-U.S. subsidiaries offset by a $3.5 billion net reduction of U.S. deferred tax liabilities due to the lower enacted U.S. tax rate and the change in assertion regarding permanently reinvested earnings as a result of the transition to a territorial tax system. These provisional estimates are based on the Company's initial analysis and current interpretation of the legislation. Given the complexity of the TCJA, anticipated guidance from the U.S. Treasury, and the potential for additional guidance from the Securities and Exchange Commission or the Financial Accounting Standards Board, these estimates may be adjusted during 2018.

Discontinued Operations and Continuing Operations

As a result of the divestiture of the Company's generics business and the divestiture of the Company's Anda Distribution business in 2016, the financial results of those businesses have been reclassified to discontinued operations for all periods presented in our consolidated financial statements up through the date of the divestitures.

Included within (loss) from discontinued operations for the three months ended December 31, 2017, was a charge to settle certain Teva-related matters, net of tax of $387.4 million.

Included in segment revenues in the 12 months ended December 31, 2016, are product sales that were sold by the Anda Distribution business once the Anda Distribution business had sold the product to a third-party customer. These sales are included in segment results and are excluded from total continuing operations revenues through a reduction to Corporate revenues. Cost of sales for these products in discontinued operations is equal to our average third-party cost of sales for third-party branded products distributed by Anda Distribution.

Case 6-4 The Potential Darkside of Using Non-GAAP Metrics (a GVV case)

The CFO, King Bernard, of Blackswan Petfood, a large publicly traded manufacturer of organic gourmet dog and cat food, is getting ready for the quarterly conference call with major investors and financial analysts in two days. The King has been reviewing a draft of the quarterly financial statements for the fourth quarter ending September 30, 2018, and working with his financial team on how best to present the numbers in the conference call. During the current quarter, the company had two material transactions which to him appear to unfairly distort the financial condition of the company in the GAAP numbers provided by Debbie Doberman, the senior manager in charge of financial reporting. The first relates to a loss of $2 million due to a massive tsunami that wiped out their manufacturing facilities in Chihuahua, Mexico. This amount was included in Additional Income/Expense Items. The second item relates to a loss of $1 million from the disposal of their Red Rooster product line of gourmet chicken feed that was discontinued.

The income statement currently reads as follows:

Blackswan Pet Food Income Statement September 30, 2018	(in millions of dollars)
Sales	$ 458,543
Cost of Goods Sold	$ (257,678)
Gross Profit	$ 200,865
Selling and Administrative	$ (123,738)
Depreciation and Amortization	$ (25,324)
Non-Recurring Items	$ (25,000)
Other Operating Items	$ (13,435)
Operating Income	$ 13,368
Additional Income/Expense Items	$ (2,456)
Earnings before Interest and Tax	$ 10,912
Interest Expense	$ (3,478)
Earnings before Tax	$ 7,434
Income Tax	$ 1,918
Net Income before Discontinued Operations	$ 5,516
Discontinued Operations (net of tax)	$ (7,500)
Net Income (loss)	$ (1,984)
Earnings (loss) per share	(0.20)

Loyal Doge, the newest member of the CFO's financial team (and recent college graduate), suggests that they provide the analysts with a number of GAAP and non-GAAP metrics. He double majored in accounting and marketing to obtain the required 150 credits to sit for the CPA exam. He said he learned in his strategic marketing class that a lot of companies are now using non-GAAP metrics to "better" explain their financial results and provide more useful information to users of the financial reports. He also noted that the recent change to GAAP which eliminated the concept of Extraordinary Items was just bad accounting and he believed that alone was reason enough to create some metrics of their own. King Bernard thought his idea made a lot of sense as he, too, was wondering why the costs related to the tsunami should be included in operating income.

The group discussed providing the analysts with the following measures.

- Earnings before Interest Tax, Depreciation, Tax and Amortization (EBITDA),
- Earnings before Discontinued Operations,
- Earnings before Extraordinary Items, and
- Recurring Earnings which would exclude both the discontinued operation and extraordinary item.

Whichever number(s) were to be presented would be net of tax, and an EPS number would be calculated as well. In addition, they discussed highlighting these new measures in the financials presented on their website. The group had a very animated discussion, and excitement continued to build as they realized that, through the use of these new metrics, they could paint a much better picture of the operating results of the company.

"Dilly, Dilly," Loyal Doge said expressively. He was excitedly talking about using multiple colors, large fonts, and the bolding of non-GAAP numbers in the quarterly financials when Debbie Doberman decided to speak up. Since it was 5 p.m., the group decided to stop for the day and meet at 8 a.m. the following morning at which time they would address Debbie's concerns.

Assume you are in Debbie's place. You are a CPA, MBA, and CFE. You have purposefully been silent up until now to first gather all the facts, hear everyone's opinion, and then provide guidance on what is and is not acceptable with respect to non-GAAP disclosures. Consider the following in developing a game plan for what to say when you address the group tomorrow.

Questions

1. What are the main arguments that you will need to counter? That is, what are the reasons and rationalizations you will need to address?

2. What is at stake should you not convince King Bernard to follow the SEC guidelines on the use of non-GAAP metrics? Include both short- and long-term potential consequences in your answer.

3. What levers do you have available? Include in your answer a discussion of the specific rules and guidelines for the use of non-GAAP metrics.

4. If you cannot convince the King to follow the guidelines for using non-GAAP metrics, what is your next step?

5. If the earnings call goes forward and the non-GAAP measures are prominently highlighted as Loyal Doge suggests, what are your options then?

Case 6-5 Harrison Industries

It's no fun accepting a position for your dream job and then red flags are raised that make you wonder about the culture of the company. Those are the thoughts of Donna Mason on January 18, 2022, as she prepares for a meeting with her accounting supervisor, Cheryl Miles. Mason graduated summa cum laude from State University one year ago and recently passed the CPA Exam. She is working as a staff accountant at Harrison Industries in Provo, Utah. Mason is one of three staff accountants. She reports to Cheryl Miles who, in turn, reports to Kelly Lang, the chief accounting officer. Lang reports to the CEO, Ken Harrison, and the third generation of owner-CEOs of the privately held company. Harrison is also the chair of the board of directors, which has five of nine independent members.

Mason's concern is that on January 15, 2022, she was approached by Miles and told to record an accrual for unpaid severance payments of $5 million to be included in the December 31, 2021, financial statements. When questioned, Miles told Mason that the company had exceeded projected earnings in 2021 but knew 2022 was going to be a down year. Mason still expressed her concern because it was an unusually high amount. Miles looked for another reason for the accrual and told Mason that the company planned to shut down the home appliance division in 2022 and the severance payments would be significant. This was the first Mason heard about a shutdown of any division, and she found it strange because the company's operating income in all divisions had set record levels in fiscal year 2021. Moreover, the severance amounts are five times the annual payroll of the division.

The numbers below show the operating income levels and accruals for 2019 through 2021:

	12/31/2019	12/31/2020	12/31/2021
Operating income	$10 million	$12 million	$20 million (pre-adjusting entries)
Accrued bonus and severance	$ 1 million	$ 1.2 million	???

Mason took a firm stance at first and told Miles she needed some documentation to record the accrued severance liability. Miles instructed Mason to record the entry, that it wasn't her job to question orders. Miles made it clear in no uncertain terms that questioning directions from one's supervisor was a basis for termination. This occurred on January 15, 2022.

Mason knew she had three days before the next meeting with Miles to consider her options. The first step she took was to contact her mentor, Steve Hahn, who explained the culture of the company is to go along to get along. Hahn quickly added that it was a rare occurrence for an employee to be asked to go along with something not right, so he advised Mason to do what Miles had asked. He seemed to be saying that if Miles asked her to record the severance payments, then it must be supportable.

Mason did a lot of independent checking of the company's computer files between January 15 and January 18, 2022 and found no evidence of a planned shutdown of the division. In fact, the division's income had risen on average by 5 percent a year for three straight years. The income level for 2021 was the highest—8 percent. It exceeded projections by 3 percent.

Mason is trying to build a strategy to convince Miles of why the severance accrual is not justified. She realizes that Miles could be under orders from Kelly Lang and/or Ken Harrison. She wonders whether it would be wise to approach them about her concerns. After all, they interviewed Mason for the accounting position and ultimately made the decision to offer her the job. Mason felt good about working for them and Harrison Industries because she thought organizational values and ethics were high, as is Mason's. Now, she's not so sure.

Questions

1. Discuss how the accrual of these expenses might be used to manage earnings.
2. What is at stake for the key parties? What are Mason's ethical obligations to them?
3. Explain the rationalizations given by Miles to Mason and how it should affect the way Mason handles the matter.
4. What should Mason do any why?

Case 6-6 TierOne Bank

It took a long time, but in 2014 the Securities and Exchange Commission finally acted and held auditors responsible for the fraud that occurred in banks during the financial recession. Surprisingly to some, the TierOne bank case explained below was the nation's first case brought by federal securities regulators against auditors of a company that went down in the multibillion-dollar financial crisis and real estate meltdown. Federal banking authorities had brought a handful of cases against auditors, but the SEC hadn't brought one until TierOne.

TierOne Corporation, a holding company for TierOne Bank, had $3 billion in assets when it collapsed in 2010. The facts of the case are drawn from the initial decision reached by the SEC, *In the Matter of John J. Aesoph, CPA, and Darren M. Bennett, CPA,* unless otherwise noted.[1] Aesoph and Bennett were the KPMG auditors of TierOne.

TierOne was a regional bank headquartered in Lincoln, Nebraska, that originated and purchased loans, and loan participation interests, with its primary market area in Nebraska, Iowa, and Kansas. From 2002 to 2005, TierOne opened or acquired nine loan production offices (LPO) in Arizona, Colorado, Florida, Minnesota, Nevada, and North Carolina, the main purpose of which was to originate construction and land-development loans. Over time, TierOne increased its portfolio in these high-risk loans. By September 2008, TierOne closed the LPOs in the wake of real estate market deterioration. By year-end 2008, TierOne had a total net loan portfolio of approximately $2.8 billion, with a quarter of its loans concentrated in the LPO states. In October 2008, TierOne's regulator, the Office of Thrift Supervision (OTS), issued a report following its June 2008 examination of the bank, in which it downgraded TierOne's bank rating, criticized management and loan practices, and found that the bank had collateral-dependent loans either without appraisals or with unsupported or stale appraisals. The bank was closed by OTS in 2010. TierOne Corp. filed for bankruptcy three weeks later.

TierOne Management

The SEC alleged in the indictment that TierOne's executives hid loan losses as OTS repeatedly requested information. On December 10, 2014, Gilbert Lundstrom, the former chief executive officer of TierOne, was indicted for hiding the condition of the bank from regulators, investors, and auditors. Allegedly, Lundstrom conspired with others to hide the bank's problems as losses mounted on its loan portfolio. "Lundstrom is essentially charged with having two sets of books, with the books shown to regulators concealing tens of millions of dollars in delinquent loans," said Christy L. Romero, special inspector general for the U.S. Troubled Asset Relief Program, established during the financial meltdown.[2]

The trigger for the fraudulent activities by TierOne management was that TierOne's core capital ratio had fallen below the 8.5 percent minimum threshold mandated by the OTS. Lundstrom and others caused the bank to issue false statements that it met or exceeded the ratio.

Lundstrom knew that the bank needed to increase its reserves to cover loan losses and didn't report this, according to the indictment. Lundstrom, in 2012, settled a lawsuit brought by the SEC claiming he understated TierOne's loan losses and losses on real estate repossessed by the bank so that the bank would appear to meet its mandated regulatory capital requirements. Lundstrom, who didn't admit the allegations when settling, agreed to pay $500,921 in penalties.

Another former TierOne executive, Don Langford, the bank's chief credit officer, pleaded guilty for his role in what prosecutors called a scheme to defraud shareholders and regulators. Langford played a major role in developing an internal estimate of losses embedded in TierOne's loan portfolio, but did not disclose that estimate to auditors or regulators. Langford's initial analysis indicated the bank needed an additional $65 million in loan loss reserves; a refined analysis, entitled the "Best/Worst Case Scenario," showed losses ranging from a "best case" of $36 million to a "worst case" of $114 million. Langford did not share any of this analysis with the bank's accounting staff or external auditors.

As the value of properties declined and defaults increased during 2008 and 2009, Lundstrom and others directed TierOne employees to forgo ordering new appraisals even when the old ones were stale or no longer accurate. In some cases, when appraisals were made and came in at lower values than recorded by TierOne, the new appraisals were rejected at the direction of Lundstrom and other bank executives. They also restructured loan terms to disguise the borrowers' inability to make timely interest and principal payments. As a result, Lundstrom and others were allegedly able to hide millions of dollars in losses from regulators and investors.

KPMG

KPMG LLP (KPMG) audited TierOne's 2008 financial statements. In March 2009, KPMG issued an unqualified audit opinion on TierOne's consolidated financial statements and effectiveness of its internal controls over financial reporting as of year-end 2008; certified that the audit was conducted in accordance with PCAOB standards that required KPMG to plan and perform the audit to obtain reasonable assurance whether the financial statements were free of material misstatement; and opined that the financial statements reflected in TierOne's year-end 2008 Form 10-K presented fairly, in all material respects, the financial position of TierOne and the results of its operations and cash flows, in conformity with U.S. generally accepted accounting principles (GAAP).

Subsequently, TierOne recorded $120 million in losses relating to its loan portfolio after obtaining updated appraisals. In April 2010, when KPMG learned that TierOne had failed to disclose the document created by Langford showing an internal analysis of varying estimates of additional loan-loss reserves higher than what had been disclosed during the audit, the firm resigned and withdrew its audit opinion. Citing risk of material misstatement, KPMG had also warned the audit committee that TierOne's financials were not to be relied upon by investors. The two items cited in the report to the audit committee were: (1) TierOne's year-end 2008 financial statements contained "material misstatements related to certain out-of-period adjustments for loan loss reserves," and (2) TierOne's internal controls could not be relied on "due to a material weakness in internal control over financial reporting related to the material misstatements."

Aesoph and Bennett were charged with improper professional conduct in connection with the December 31, 2008, year-end audit of TierOne's financial statements. They failed to comply with Public Company Accounting Oversight Board (PCAOB) auditing standards because they failed to subject TierOne's loan-loss estimates—one of the highest risk areas of a bank audit—to appropriate scrutiny. The SEC also said the pair "failed to obtain sufficient competent evidential matter to support their audit conclusions, and failed to exercise due professional care and appropriate professional skepticism."

According to the SEC's order instituting administrative proceedings against Aesoph and Bennett, they "rubber stamped" TierOne's accounting for loan losses. The auditors failed to comply with professional auditing standards in their substantive audit procedures over the bank's valuation of loan losses resulting from impaired loans. They relied principally on stale appraisals and management's uncorroborated representations of current value despite evidence that management's estimates were biased and inconsistent with independent market data rather than make an independent analysis of loan value and collectability.[3]

As for the internal controls, the SEC said that the controls over the allowance for loans and lease losses identified and tested by the auditing engagement team did not effectively test management's use of stale and inadequate appraisals to value the collateral underlying the bank's troubled loan portfolio. For example, the auditors identified TierOne's Asset Classification Committee as a key control. But there was no reference in the audit workpapers to whether or how the committee assessed the value of the collateral underlying individual loans evaluated for impairment, and the committee did not generate or review written documentation to support management's assumptions. Given the complete lack of documentation, Aesoph and Bennett had insufficient evidence from which to conclude that the bank's internal controls for valuation of collateral were effective. Robert Khuzami, director of the SEC's Division of Enforcement, said, "Aesoph and Bennett merely rubber-stamped TierOne's collateral value estimates and ignored the red flags surrounding the bank's troubled real estate loans."[4]

In 2016, Aesoph and Bennett appealed the original decision of the Administrative Law Judge that suspended them from practicing before the SEC for a term of one year and a term of six months, respectively. The SEC cross-appealed, asking for a three- and two-year term, respectively, after which time they could apply for reinstatement. In his appeal, Bennett took issue with statements made by the SEC that, he claimed, suggested that the auditors should be responsible for "auditing" each of TierOne's loan-loss reserve estimates, whereas under PCAOB standards "[t]he auditor is responsible for evaluating the reasonableness of accounting estimates made by management in the context of the financial statements taken as a whole." The SEC, however, contended that in order to evaluate the reasonableness of the estimates in the context of the financial statements taken as whole, they were required to evaluate those estimates on a loan-by-loan basis. In the end, the SEC cross-appeal won the day based on evidence provided that the two KPMG auditors violated PCAOB auditing standards in three specific areas with respect to the loan-loss reserves: (1) their audit of the effectiveness of ICFR, (2) their substantive audit test work over the account, and (3) their post-audit procedures following the discovery of new appraisals in 2009.[5]

Questions

1. Was TierOne's accounting for the loan-loss reserve indicative of "managed earnings"? How would you make that determination?
2. What is the purpose of the auditor's assessment of ICFR? Describe the deficiencies in KPMG's audit work in that regard?
3. Would you conclude from the facts of this case that TierOne's fraud caused KPMG's auditing standards violations? Explain.
4. Which rules of conduct in the AICPA Code were violated by KPMG auditors? Be specific.

Case 6-7 Non-GAAP Metric Disclosure by General Electric: Value Added, Red Herring, or Red Flag?

According to an October 16, 2017, article by Richard Clough of Bloomberg News,[1] General Electric reported earnings per share of $0.28, $0.13, $0.19, and $0.15 for the quarter ending September 30, 2017, on an earnings call. Yes, you read that correctly, GE reported four different earnings per share figures for the same quarter. The numbers represent profit that includes or excludes certain items, such as pension costs and discontinued operations. For example, GE referred to one of these measures as "industrial operating plus verticals earnings per share" rather than simply "adjusted," "core," or "non-GAAP earnings per share" as is common place at most companies.[2] GE is not alone in the use of both GAAP and non-GAAP metrics they include in their financial reporting. However, according to Bloomberg, GE is only one of 21 S&P 500 companies to use more than one earnings per share figure.

Fast forward to the fourth quarter of 2017 and the fiscal year 2017, and we see a different picture in the MD&A. These results are presented in **Exhibit 1**. Notice there are five measures of GAAP and five non-GAAP metrics. The numbers have declined from the third quarter in large part due to insurance adjustments. Beyond that, the descriptions do not seem to match up. To say this is confusing would be an understatement.

EXHIBIT 1   General Electric Financial Metrics

(Dollars in millions; except per-share amounts) 31-12-2018	Fourth Quarter Results			Total Year Results		
	2017	2016	Year on Year	2017	2016	Year on Year
GAAP Metrics						
Continuing Operations EPS	$ (1.15)	$ 0.39	U	$ (0.68)	$ 1.00	U
Net Earnings EPS	$ (1.13)	$ 0.39	U	$ (0.72)	$ 0.89	U
Total Revenues	$ 31,402	$ 33,088	−5.0%	$ 1,22,092	$ 1,23,693	−1%
Industrial Margin	1.1%	12.0%	(1090) bps	5.7%	11.4%	(570) bps
GE CFOA	$ 6,990	$ 11,618	−40%	$ 11,040	$ 29,960	−63%
Non-GAAP Metrics						
Industrial Operating + Verticals EPS	$ (1.23)	$ 0.46	U	$ (0.45)	$ 1.49	U
Industrial Segment Organic Revenues	$ 28,712	$ 30,503	−6%	$ 1,09,430	$ 1,09,296	0%
Industrial Operating Profit/(Loss)[c]	$ 3,526	$ 5,226	−33%	$ 13,868	$ 15,558	−11%
Industrial Operating Profit/(Loss) Margin[b]	11.2%	16.8%	(560) bps	12.1%	14.0%	(190) bps
Adjusted Industrial CFOA[a]	$ 7,757	$ 8,242	−6%	$ 9,698	$ 11,610	−16%

bps = book value per share

CFOA = cash flow from operating activities

a) Excluding deal taxes and GE Pension Plan funding, and with BHGE on a dividend basis

b) Excludes impact of acquisition and disposition activity in industrial segments

c) Excludes non-operating pension, gains/(losses) and restructuring & other

Back in July 2017, the SEC sent a comment letter to GE[3] in regard to their improper use of non-GAAP metrics and inconsistencies in their description and application of them. Per Tomi Kilgore's October 27, 2017, Market Watch article, the SEC letter identified "16 items in its 10-K filing were listed as being potentially misleading to investors, with half the items mentioning the reporting of numbers that were inconsistent with generally accepted accounting principles (GAAP)."[4]

GE's response letter to the SEC seems to confuse matters even more. For example, the SEC asked: "We note your discussion regarding the $0.5 billion increase in industrial earnings. Explain to us how you determined industrial earnings and whether it is a non-GAAP measure. Tell us how the measure differs from industrial profit, the GAAP measure presented [in your report]." GE's response was: "With regard to how industrial earnings and industrial profits differ, industrial earnings is an after-tax measure that reflects an adjustment for earnings/losses attributable to noncontrolling interests, while industrial profit is a pretax measure."

This is the second time the SEC has called out GE for their use of non-GAAP metrics, as they sent them a series of letters on this topic during 2016 as well. However, GE is not being singled out as the only company who perhaps stretches the limit of their usage. In both 2016 and 2017, the SEC sent more comment letters regarding the use of non-GAAP measures than on any other topic (with 429 letters to 223 registrants in 2016 or 16.75% and 656 letters to 311 registrants in 2017 or 28.34% of all SEC comment letters sent).[5] The growing use of non-GAAP metrics is also of concern to the PCAOB, who are actively researching their use and questioning whether the current standards should require auditors to perform specific testing of non-GAAP metrics contained in public filings and even those used on earnings calls and other types of releases.[6]

Per Bloomberg, the use of non-GAAP metrics has increased from just 58 percent of publicly traded companies to virtually all of them in just 20 years. However, Bloomberg suggests that the use of this many metrics by GE has made their financials more confusing, resulting in investors shying away from GE and negatively impacting their market price per share. The Bloomberg article quotes an executive from Westwood Holdings who has been decreasing the size of a major stake in GE as saying, "GE somewhere along the line lost the benefit of the doubt that the non-GAAP adjusted EPS number was a good reflection of what they were earning." A look at GE's stock performance in relation to the overall market showing a steady decline supports this contention with their stock currently trading at close to its lowest level since the 2009 market crash. As of February 16, 2018, GE was trading at around $15 dollars per share, which was 50 percent of what it was trading at the same date in 2017, while the rest of the market was up over 18 percent during that same period.

It is also worth noting that, in late 2017, GE's CFO Jeff Bornstein left the company after 28 years working in various positions within GE. GE's CEO and incoming new CFO pledged to make life easier for investors, and reporters, not only by narrowing the focus of its businesses, but also by making its earnings reports simpler and more transparent. However, on January 24, 2018, Jamie Miller, the new CFO, announced that the SEC is now investigating GE's revenue recognition and controls for insurance contracts just days after the companies surprise announcement that they would be taking a $6.2 billion loss from insurance claims and beefing up insurance contract reserves by $15 billion.[7] It would appear the troubles for GE are far from over and perhaps suggests that the use of non-GAAP metrics could be red flag that there is trouble on the horizon. Matt Egan of CNN Money, on January 24, 2018, quotes Scott Davis, the head analyst at Melius Research, regarding GE as stating, "we can't be certain that prior management misled investors, but we certainly believe there were ethical lapses that deserve attention."[8]

Questions

1. Consider the costs/harms and benefits of disclosing non-GAAP financial numbers. What value, if any, do you see in the use of non-GAAP metrics?
2. What responsibilities do auditors currently have related to the use of non-GAAP measures by their attest clients? What responsibilities do you think they should have? Be specific.
3. Do you believe that GE is attempting to manage earnings by disclosing five different non-GAAP measures? Explain.
4. If you were a financial analyst looking at GE's metrics in **Exhibit 1**, what questions would you ask and why?

Case 6-8 BMW's Sales Reporting Practices

The SEC bought an action against BMW NA for inaccurate disclosures of its retail vehicle sales volume in the United States. In order to close the gap between actual retail sales volume and internal retail sales targets, and in an effort to publicly maintain a leading position relative to other premium automotive companies, BMW's domestic subsidiary, BMW NA, engaged in an effort to increase the number of publicly reported retail vehicle sales in the U.S. BMW NA used practices that had the effect of inaccurately reporting its U.S. retail vehicle sales volume (a non-financial metric). The company also used reserves to adjust period sales revenue as needed.

The SEC's order found that BMW AG, BMW NA, and BMW US Capital (hereinafter referred to as BMW) violated antifraud provisions of Sections 17(a)(2) and (3) of the Securities Act of 1933. Although BMW didn't admit nor deny anything, it agreed to pay the $18 million fine and completely stop violating the provisions.

Sales Volume

From January 2015 through March 2017, BMW used its demonstrator and service loaner programs to boost reported retail sales volume and meet internal targets, resulting in demonstrator and loaner vehicles accounting for over one quarter of BMW NA's reported retail sales in this period. BMW offered independently owned BMW auto dealers' financial incentives to designate (or "punch") vehicles as demonstrators (i.e., vehicles used for test drives, showroom displays, or other marketing purposes) or service loaners, so that those vehicles would be counted by BMW as retail sales, even though the dealers had not sold the vehicles to customers.

This was done without regard to whether dealers had a legitimate business need for additional demonstrators and service loaners, or whether the dealers put those vehicles to use as demonstrators or service loaners. BMW engaged in this conduct toward the end of a given month, often on the last day, when it became apparent that BMW would be unable to meet its internal retail sales volume target through additional sales to dealerships' customers. Faced with these shortfalls, BMA used end-of-month practices that improperly increased reported retail sales and created a misleading impression of BMW's sales performance in the U.S. market, despite internal concerns about these practices.

Excess Reserves

From 2015 through 2019, BMW maintained an excess reserve of unreported retail vehicle sales that it used when necessary to meet internal targets in a given month, without proper regard to when the underlying retail sales actually occurred. BMW referred to these unreported retail sales as the "bank," and managed the bank to keep a supply of unreported retail sales available when needed to meet internal retail sales targets. BMW relied on a reserve of unreported car sales that it used to meet its sales targets between 2015 and 2019—using them regardless of when the sales took place in order to shore up low-sales months. It also falsely designated some of its vehicles as sold when they had not yet been sold. The company even adjusted its sales reporting calendar in 2015 and 2017 to meet targets and/or bank excess sales for future use.

The use of the bank was part of BMW's ongoing planning. In months when BMW expected retail sales to be slow because of seasonal variation, such as January and February, BMW built into its planning assumptions the use of banked retail sales. In addition, when BMW anticipated difficulty achieving its internal retail sales targets for a month, it used banked retail sales as a cushion to effectively reduce the targets for that month. For instance, in January 2015, BMW management explained that they were following "the original plan . . . to use 1,200 units from the bank" to help achieve the target, and that "[a]ny shortfall to the January target will be taken from the planned March Bank."

The use of the bank was planned and approved by BMW management. For instance, in September 2016, BMW management discussed that the forecasted number of retail sales for that month "includes bank withdrawal of 2,325." BMW publicly reported 25,389 retail sales for September 2016, which included these 2,325 banked retail sales. For October 2016, BMW reported retail sales of 24,017 BMW brand vehicles, after a BMW executive decided to "[p]ick a number slightly above 24k and bank the rest."

Internal Audit

BMW's Internal Audit group detected two of the retail sales reporting practices being used by the company and recommended that the practices be discontinued, but BMW failed to implement these recommendations in a timely manner.

In May 2015, Internal Audit determined that BMW was using demonstrators and loaners to accelerate reporting of retail vehicle sales. Internal Audit further determined that the Specialty 8 demonstrator program was used to "fine tune monthly retail figures" and that demonstrators typically remained with dealers at the time they were reported as retail sales.

In response to Internal Audit's findings, BMW management responded that the use of Specialty 8 demonstrators was "the most efficient instrument to meet sales targets." Internal Audit recommended limiting what percentage of overall retail sales could consist of demonstrators and service loaners, and carefully monitoring the use of these categories. However, BMW failed to promptly implement changes to address Internal Audit's concerns. Six months later, in November 2015, Internal Audit determined that the company had failed to take sufficient measures to avoid "unjustified retail reporting" and that dealer inventory of Specialty 8 demonstrators had actually increased.

Starting in March 2015, Internal Audit also repeatedly identified and objected to BMW's use of the "bank." Internal Audit noted that the company's use of the bank was tied to "meeting requested monthly or quarterly targets." Internal Audit cautioned that these "[r]etail sales reporting inaccuracies lead to an inappropriate assessment of sales performance and may result in unsustainable marketing and sales business practices," and recommended that BMW cease using the bank. Over the next few years, Internal Audit repeatedly warned about the use of the bank, but BMW did not discontinue the practice until 2020.

BMW management also discussed the use of the bank with BMW AG personnel. In at least one instance, BMW AG told BMW NA that it could bank retail sales from the prior year because BMW AG had already achieved its internal targets without those additional retail sales.

Questions

1. What was the motivation of BMW in developing the two practices discussed in the case? Did its practices adhere to the concept of representational faithfulness? Explain.

2. Would you consider the practice of falsifying unit sales volume a financial shenanigan? How about the use of excessive reserves to affect reported numbers for sales revenue? Explain.

3. Consider the role of the internal auditors in identifying the improper financial reporting practices. Did they meet their ethical obligations in dealing with those matters? What else could they have done?

Case 6-9 The North Face, Inc.

The North Face, Inc. (North Face) is an American outdoor product company specializing in outerwear, fleece, coats, shirts, footwear, and equipment such as backpacks, tents, and sleeping bags. North Face sells clothing and equipment lines catered toward wilderness chic, climbers, mountaineers, skiers, snowboarders, hikers, and endurance athletes. The company sponsors professional athletes from the worlds of running, climbing, skiing, and snowboarding.

North Face is located in Alameda, California, along with an affiliated company, JanSport. These two companies manufacture about half of all small backpacks sold in the United States. Both companies are owned by VF Corporation, an American apparel corporation.

The North Face brand was established in 1968 in San Francisco. Following years of success built on sales to a high-end customer base, in the 1990s North Face was forced to compete with mass-market brands sold by the major discount retailers. It was at that point the company engaged in accounting shenanigans that led to it being acquired by VF Corporation.

Barter Transactions[1]

Consumer demand for North Face products was steadily growing by the mid-1980s, and the higher levels of demand for production were causing the manufacturing facilities to be overburdened. Pressure existed to maintain the level of production that was required. As North Face continued to grow in sales throughout the 1980s and into the 1990s, the management team set aggressive sales goals. In the mid-1990s, the team established the goal of reaching $1 billion in annual sales by the year 2003. The pressure prompted Christopher Crawford, the company's chief financial officer (CFO), and Todd Katz, the vice president of sales, to negotiate a large transaction with a barter company and then proceed to improperly account for it in the financial statements.[1]

North Face entered into two major barter transactions in 1997 and 1998. The barter company North Face dealt with typically bought excess inventory in exchange for trade credits. The trade credits could be redeemed by North Face only through the barter company, and most often the trade credits were used to purchase advertising, printing, or travel services.

North Face began negotiating a potential barter transaction in early December 1997. The basic terms were that the barter company would purchase $7.8 million of excess inventory North Face had on hand. In exchange for that inventory, North Face would receive $7.8 million of trade credits that were redeemable only through the barter company.

Before North Face finalized the barter transaction, Crawford asked Deloitte & Touche, North Face's external auditors, for advice on how to account for a barter sale. The auditors provided Crawford with the accounting literature describing GAAP relating to non-monetary exchanges. That literature generally precludes companies from recognizing revenue on barter transactions when the only consideration received by the seller is trade credits.

What Crawford did next highlights one of the many ways a company can structure a transaction to manage earnings and achieve the financial results desired rather than report what should be recorded as revenue under GAAP.

Crawford structured the transaction to recognize profit on the trade credits. First, he required the barter company to pay a portion of the purchase price in cash. Crawford agreed that North Face would guarantee that the barter company would receive at least a 60 percent recovery of the total purchase price when it resold the product. In exchange for the guarantee, the barter company agreed to pay approximately 50 percent of the total purchase price in cash and the rest in trade credits. This guarantee took the form of an oral side agreement that was not disclosed to the auditors.

Second, Crawford split the transaction into two parts on two days before the year-end December 31, 1997. One part of the transaction was to be recorded in the fourth quarter of 1997, the other to be recorded in the first quarter of 1998. Crawford structured the two parts of the barter sale so that all of the cash consideration and a portion of the trade credits would be received in the fourth quarter of 1997. The barter credit portion of the fourth-quarter transaction was structured to allow profit recognition for the barter credits despite the objections of the auditors. The consideration for the 1998 first-quarter transaction consisted solely of trade credits.

On December 29, 1997, North Face recorded a $5.15 million sale to the barter company. The barter company paid $3.51 million in cash and issued $1.64 million in trade credits. North Face recognized its full normal profit margin on the sale. Just 10 days later on January 8, 1998, North Face recorded another sale to the barter company, this time for $2.65 million in trade credits, with no cash consideration. North Face received only trade credits from the barter company for this final portion of the $7.8 million total transaction. Again, North Face recognized its full normal profit margin on the sale.

Materiality Issues

Crawford was a CPA and knew all about the materiality criteria that auditors use to judge whether they will accept a client's accounting for a disputed transaction. He committed the fraud because he saw internal control weaknesses and believed no one would notice. Crawford realized that if he made sure the portion of the barter transaction recorded during the fourth quarter of fiscal 1997 was below a certain amount, the auditors would not look at it. He also believed that Deloitte & Touche would not challenge the profit recognized on the $3.51 million portion of the barter transaction because of the cash payment.

Crawford also realized that Deloitte would maintain that no profit should be recorded on the $1.64 million balance of the December 29, 1997, transaction with the barter company for which North Face would be paid exclusively in trade credits. However, Crawford was aware of the materiality thresholds that Deloitte had established for North Face's key financial statement items during the fiscal 1997 audit. He knew that the profit margin of approximately $800,000 on the $1.64 million portion of the December 1997 transaction fell slightly below Deloitte's materiality threshold for North Face's collective gross profit. As a result, he believed that Deloitte would propose an adjustment to reverse the $1.64 million transaction but ultimately "pass" on that proposed adjustment since it had an immaterial impact on North Face's financial statements. As Crawford expected, Deloitte proposed a year-end adjusting entry to reverse the $1.64 million transaction but then passed on that adjustment during the wrap-up phase of the audit.

In early January 1998, North Face recorded the remaining $2.65 million portion of the $7.8 million barter transaction. Crawford instructed North Face's accountants to record the full amount of profit margin on this portion of the sale despite being aware that accounting treatment was not consistent with the authoritative literature. Crawford did not inform the Deloitte auditors of the $2.65 million portion of the barter transaction until after the 1997 audit was completed.

The barter company ultimately sold only a nominal amount of the $7.8 million of excess inventory that it purchased from North Face. As a result, in early 1999, North Face reacquired that inventory from the barter company.

Audit Considerations

The auditors did not learn of the January 8, 1998, transaction until March 1998. Thus, when the auditors made the materiality judgment for the fourth-quarter transaction, they were unaware that a second transaction had taken place and unaware that Crawford had recognized full margin on the second barter transaction.

In mid-1998 through 1999, the North Face sales force was actively trying to resell the product purchased by the barter company because the barter company was unable to sell any significant portion of the inventory. North Face finally decided, in January and February 1999, to repurchase the remaining inventory from the barter company. Crawford negotiated the repurchase price of $690,000 for the remaining inventory.

Crawford did not disclose the repurchase to the 1998 audit engagement team, even though the audit was not complete at the time of the repurchase.

During the first week of March 1999, the auditors asked for additional information about the barter transaction to complete the 1998 audit. In response to this request, Crawford continued to mislead the auditors by failing to disclose that the product had been repurchased, that there was a guarantee, that the 1997 and 1998 transactions were linked, and that the company sales force had negotiated almost all of the orders received by the barter company.

Crawford did not disclose any of this information until he learned that the auditors were about to fax a confirmation letter to the barter company that specifically asked if any of the product had been returned or repurchased. Crawford then called the chair of North Face's audit committee to explain that he had withheld information from the auditors. A meeting was scheduled for later that day for Crawford to make "full disclosure" to the auditors about the barter transactions.

Even at the "full disclosure" meeting with the auditors, Crawford was not completely truthful. He did finally disclose the repurchase and the link between the 1997 and 1998 transactions. He did not, however, disclose that there was a guarantee, nor did he disclose that the company's employees had negotiated most of the orders for the product.

Deloitte & Touche

Richard Fiedelman was the Deloitte advisory partner assigned to the North Face audit engagement. Pete Vanstraten was the audit engagement partner for the 1997 North Face audit. Vanstraten was also the individual who proposed the adjusting entry near the end of the 1997 audit to reverse the $1.64 million barter transaction that North Face had recorded in the final few days of fiscal 1997. Vanstraten proposed the adjustment because he was aware that the GAAP rules generally preclude companies from recognizing revenue on barter transactions when the only consideration received by the seller is trade credits. Vanstraten was also the individual who "passed" on that adjustment after determining that it did not have a material impact on North Face's 1997 financial statements. Fiedelman reviewed and approved those decisions by Vanstraten.

Shortly after the completion of the 1997 North Face audit, Vanstraten transferred from the office that serviced North Face. In May 1998, Will Borden was appointed the new audit engagement partner for North Face. In the two months before Borden was appointed the North Face audit engagement partner, Richard Fiedelman functioned in that role.

Fiedelman supervised the review of North Face's financial statements for the first quarter of fiscal 1998, which ended on March 31, 1998. While completing that review, Fiedelman became aware of the $2.65 million portion of the $7.8 million barter transaction that Crawford had instructed his subordinates to record in early January 1998. Fiedelman did not challenge North Face's decision to record its normal profit margin on the January 1998 "sale" to the barter company. As a result, North Face's gross profit for the first quarter of 1998 was overstated by more than $1.3 million, an amount that was material to the company's first-quarter financial statements. In fact, without the profit margin on the $2.65 million transaction, North Face would have reported a net loss for the first quarter of fiscal 1998 rather than the modest net income it actually reported that period.

In the fall of 1998, Borden began planning the 1998 North Face audit. An important element of that planning process was reviewing the 1997 audit workpapers. While reviewing those workpapers, Borden discovered the audit adjustment that Vanstraten had proposed during the prior year audit to reverse the $1.64 million barter transaction. When Borden brought this matter to Fiedelman's attention, Fiedelman maintained that the proposed audit adjustment should not have been included in the prior year workpapers since the 1997 audit team had *not* concluded that North Face could *not* record the $1.64 million transaction with the barter company. Fiedelman insisted that, despite the proposed audit adjustment in the 1997 audit workpapers, Vanstraten had concluded that it was permissible for North Face to record the transaction and recognize the $800,000 of profit margin on the transaction in December 1997.

Borden accepted Fiedelman's assertion that North Face was entitled to recognize profit on a sales transaction in which the only consideration received by the company was trade credits. Borden also relied on this assertion during the 1998 audit. As a result, Borden and the other members of the 1998 audit team did not propose an adjusting entry to require North Face to reverse the $2.65 million sale recorded by the company in January 1998.

After convincing Borden that the prior year workpapers misrepresented the decision that Vanstraten had made regarding the $1.64 million barter transaction, Fiedelman began the process of documenting this revised conclusion in the 1997 working papers that related to the already issued financial statements for 1997. The SEC had concluded in its investigation that Deloitte personnel prepared a new summary memorandum and proposed adjustments schedule reflecting the revised conclusion about profit recognition and replaced the original 1997 working papers with these newly created working papers.

SEC Actions against Crawford

In the SEC action against Crawford and Katz, the SEC charged that Crawford tried to conceal the true nature of the improperly reported transactions from North Face's accountants and auditors. He made, directly or indirectly, material misrepresentations and omissions to the auditors in an attempt to hide his misconduct. Katz also made, directly or indirectly, material misrepresentations and omissions to the accountants and auditors in an attempt to hide his misconduct.[2]

The commission charged that Crawford committed a fraud because his actions violated Section 10(b) of the Exchange Act of 1934, in that he knew or was reckless in not knowing that (1) it was a violation of GAAP to record full margin on the trade credit portion of the sale, and (2) that the auditors would consider the amount of the non-GAAP fourth-quarter profit recognition immaterial and would not insist on any adjusting entry for correction.

A second charge was that Crawford aided and abetted violations of Section 13(a) of the Exchange Act that requires every issuer of a registered security to file reports with the SEC that accurately reflect the issuer's financial performance and provide other information to the public.

A third charge dealt with record-keeping and alleged violations of Section 13(b) in that the Exchange Act requires each issuer of registered securities to make and keep books, records, and accounts that, in reasonable detail, accurately and fairly reflect the business of the issuer and to devise and maintain a system of internal controls sufficient to provide reasonable assurances that, among other things, transactions are recorded as necessary to permit preparation of financial statements and to maintain the accountability of accounts.

The SEC asked the U.S. District Court of the Northern District of California to enter a judgment:

- Permanently enjoining Crawford and the vice president of sales, Katz, from violating Sections 10(b) and 13(b)(5) of the Exchange Act;
- Ordering Crawford to provide a complete accounting for and to disgorge the unjust enrichment he realized, plus prejudgment interest thereon;
- Ordering Crawford and Katz to pay civil monetary penalties pursuant to Section 21(d)(3) of the Exchange Act; and
- Prohibiting Crawford and Katz from acting as an officer or director of a public company pursuant to Section 21(d)(2) of the Exchange Act.

Crawford agreed to the terms in a settlement with the SEC that included his suspension from appearing or practicing before the commission as an accountant for at least five years, after which time he could apply to the commission for reinstatement.

Questions

1. Use the fraud triangle to analyze the red flags that existed in the case and the role and responsibilities of the auditors at Deloitte & Touche. Assume the Deloitte auditors had confronted Crawford about the impropriety of accounting for barter transactions. What reasons and rationalizations do you think would have been provided by Crawford?

2. Why do auditors have a responsibility to assess the key decisions made by management? Which decisions in this case should the auditors have scrutinized more carefully?

3. Should materiality considerations have entered into the auditors' decisions whether to accept North Face's accounting? Does it matter that earnings management was the motivation for the accounting?

4. Comment on the quality of the audit performed by Deloitte.

Case 6-10 Beazer Homes

Beazer Homes is a home-building company headquartered in Atlanta, Georgia. Its stock is listed on the New York Stock Exchange. Beazer is required to file Form 10-Q and Form 10-K, as well as an 8-K form when certain changes occur, such as restating financial statements.

As a homebuilder, Beazer often builds "model homes" for prospective homebuyers to tour while the remainder of a neighborhood and its future homes are under construction. As one of the last homes to be sold, model homes often may not be sold to a homebuyer for years, and thus may not provide a homebuilder with revenue and income on their sale until years after construction.

What follows is a description of the SEC's agreement in *SEC v. Michael T. Rand* to resolve charges that Beazer engaged in fraudulent accounting that led to material noncompliance with federal securities laws by improperly inflating Beazer's income by reducing or eliminating previously established artificial reserves and improperly recognizing sales revenue and income in sale-leaseback transactions involving its model homes.[1]

Sale-Leaseback Scheme

Under its sales-leaseback program, Beazer sold its model homes to investors, typically at a discounted price, thereby permitting it to recognize revenue and income from the sales. Under the "leaseback" portion of the transaction, Beazer leased back from the investor/buyer the same model homes, which Beazer could then use to show prospective home buyers.

In December 2005, the chief accounting officer, Michael T. Rand, CPA, entered into a secret side-agreement with one or more GMAC Model Home Finance personnel under which: (a) Beazer would "sell" the model homes and recognize revenue and income from such sales, (b) the homes would be leased back to Beazer for its use, but (c) Beazer would secretly receive a share of any profits from any subsequent sale of the model homes to a third party at the end of the leases. Under GAAP, a seller is not permitted to recognize revenue and income from a sale in a sale-leaseback transaction if the seller retains a continuing interest in the property after it has been sold. Beazer's continuing and secret interest in a share of any profits from the ultimate sale of the models was such a continuing interest.

What follows is a table showing model homes sold and improper pretax income recognized from the sale-leaseback transactions in violation of GAAP.

Overstated Pretax Income from Sale-Leaseback Transactions		
Quarter Ended	# Homes Sold	Overstated Pretax Income
December 31, 2005	90	$8.0 million
March 31, 2006	79	$4.2 million
June 30, 2006	37	$1.6 million
September 30, 2006	140	$8.3 million

Cookie-Jar Reserves

Prior to 2006, Rand and other Beazer employees engaged in an accounting scheme involving "cookie-jar accounting." Specifically, Rand improperly decreased Beazer's income by artificially establishing, increasing, and/or maintaining future anticipated expenses or "reserves." He executed this strategy by manipulating, among other accounts, Beazer's land development and house reserve accounts.

In fiscal year 2006, when Beazer was in jeopardy of not meeting analysts' expectations, Rand eliminated certain unnecessary excess reserves that had been built up, thereby improperly boosting Beazer's pretax income by over $27.5 million. Beazer's arbitrary elimination of reserves to boost income resulted in financial statements that were not compiled in accordance with GAAP.

Land Inventory Accounting

As part of its home building and sale operations, Beazer purchased parcels of land upon which it constructed houses to form subdivisions. Beazer recorded the acquired land, along with costs for the common development of the parcel, such as sewer systems and streets, as an asset on Beazer's balance sheet in the land inventory accounts. As subdivisions were built, Beazer allocated the costs accumulated in the land inventory accounts to individual home lots, which were then offered for sale. When the home sale was recorded in Beazer's books, all associated homebuilding costs, including allocated costs recorded in the land inventory accounts, were expensed as a cost of the sale with a corresponding reduction or credit in the land inventory account.

Because Beazer sold houses within a subdivision as the development of that subdivision progressed, the land inventory expense recorded for any particular house sale was necessarily an estimate. The setting of inventory credits was done by each division based on estimates of costs to acquire, develop, and complete subdivisions plus an added amount for contingencies. Once established, divisions needed approval from Rand, who reviewed the reserves on a monthly basis, to make adjustments.

As additional houses in a subdivision were sold, the land inventory account continued to be decreased (credited) by amounts representing the land acquisition and development costs allocated to each individual house. If costs had been allocated properly, then, shortly after the final house in a development had been sold, the balance in the land inventory account should have been at or near zero.

What follows is a table showing the overstatement in land inventory costs between 2001 and 2005.

Overstatement of Land Inventory Costs			
	Quarter 1	Quarter 2	Quarter 3	Quarter 4
2001	$ 1,455,000	$ 584,000	$ 1,322,000	$ 2,571,000
2002	$ 1,827,000	$ 2,761,000	$ 1,270,000	$ 2,586,000
2003	$ 2,440,000	$ 1,422,000	$ 1,086,000	N/A
2004	$ 3,996,000	$ 4,253,000	$ 5,963,000	$ 2,227,000
2005	$ 3,388,000	$ 4,443,000	$ 5,122,000	$ 4,469,000

In order to reduce its first quarter 2002 earnings, which had exceeded analysts' EPS expectations, Rand fraudulently increased the land inventory expense recorded for homes sold during the quarter.

On January 8, 2002, after the end of the first quarter, Rand e-mailed a target earnings amount to the relevant financial personnel in numerous Beazer divisions with instructions not to exceed the target by a certain amount. The distributed target for each division was less than each division's previously expected quarterly results. Rand advised the divisions to review their land inventory accounts in order to increase expenses and reduce earnings. In one particular e-mail, Rand instructed the Florida division to provide "more than adequate land allocations in communities closing out this year" as a means to reduce its earnings.

On January 10, 2002, Rand, via e-mails, directed certain divisions to, "[s]et aside all the reserves you reasonably can . . . the quarter is too high." This was followed by a series of e-mails in which Rand specified the amounts by which certain divisions should increase their reserves, along with targets for their EBIT (earnings before interest and taxes). The divisions substantially carried out his directions, and Rand was able to reduce Beazer's quarterly EPS from $2.60 to $2.47 a share, which exceeded analysts' consensus of $2.00 per share. In total, Beazer recorded approximately $1.827 million in excess land inventory costs for that quarter, or approximately 8 percent of its reported net income.

By increasing land inventory expenses, Rand caused Beazer to understate its net income by a total of $56 million ($33 million after tax effect; approximately 5% of reported net income) between 2000 and 2005. Beginning in the first quarter of 2006, Rand began to reverse the reserves existing in the land inventory accounts, which increased then-current period earnings. The credit balances in land inventory accounts were debited (i.e., zeroed out), and a cost of sales expense credited (i.e., reduced). These reversals improperly reduced expenses and increased Beazer's earnings. During all four quarters of 2006, Rand caused Beazer to release these land inventory reserves, boosting then-current period earnings by approximately $100,000 in the first quarter of 2006, approximately $301,000 in the second quarter of 2006, approximately $14,278,000 in the third quarter of 2006, and approximately $10,816,000 in the fourth quarter of 2006.

Manipulation of "House Cost-to-Complete" Reserves

Under its accounting policies, Beazer recorded revenue and profit on the sale of a house after the close of the sale of that house to a homebuyer. In the journal entries to record the sale, Beazer typically reserved a portion of its profit earned on the house. This reserve, called a "house cost-to-complete" reserve, was established to cover any unknown expenses that Beazer might incur on the sold house after the close, such as minor repairs or final cosmetic touch-ups. Although the amount of this reserve varied by region, it was typically $1,000 to $4,000 per house.

Beazer's policy was to reverse any unused portion of the house cost-to-complete reserve within four to nine months after the close, taking any unused portion into income at that time. As specified below, in various quarters between 2000 and 2005, Rand over-reserved house cost-to-complete expenses. Rand then took steps to maintain these reserves beyond the typical four to nine months and until increased earnings were required in future periods.

The following table shows the over-expensing of the cost-to-complete expense from 2000 to 2005.

Over-Expensing of the Cost-to-Complete Expense				
Year	**Quarter 1**	**Quarter 2**	**Quarter 3**	**Quarter 4**
2000	N/A	$ 610,000	$ 5,000	$ 2,288,000
2001	$ 1,138,000	$ 543,000	N/A	N/A
2002	$ 2,184,000	$ 813,000	N/A	N/A
2003	$ 1,380,000	N/A	N/A	N/A
2004	$ 1,057,000	N/A	$ 1,137,000	$ 2,051,000
2005	N/A	$ 805,000	$ 1,427,000	N/A

Beginning in 2006, Beazer began reversing some of the excess cost-to-complete reserves that it had previously recorded. As a result of Rand's directives, Beazer reduced its cost of sales expense by approximately $1.5 million by reducing the cost-to-complete reserve to zero on a number of houses. The following shows the amount of reversal of excess cost-to-complete reserves as earnings of the period that were previously recorded fraudulently.

Reversal of Excess Cost-to-Complete Reserves		
Year	Quarter Ended	Amount of Reversal
2006	March 31	$183,000
2006	September 30	$2,130,000
2006	December 31	$209,000
2007	March 31	$1,549,000

Additionally, at Rand's instruction, certain Beazer divisions, in order to report more income, failed to establish a house cost-to-complete reserve on house sales closing during the quarter. Beazer's Las Vegas division failed to record any cost-to-complete reserve for approximately 85 houses sold during December 2005. This resulted in an improper recognition, in violation of GAAP, of more than $200,000 of income for the period. All totaled, the additional income due to cost-to-complete reserve accounting added approximately $0.03 to Beazer's EPS.

Press Release

During the first quarter of fiscal year 2006, December 31, 2005, Beazer's stock price reached an all-time high of $82.03. The price was artificially inflated as a result of Beazer's false and misleading financial statements. On January 19, 2006, Beazer issued a press release titled "Beazer Homes Reports First Quarter 2006 EPS of $2.00, up 27%; Company expects Diluted EPS to Meet or Exceed $10.50 for Fiscal Year 2006." The company announced first quarter results as follows:

- Net income of $89.9 million, or $2.00 per diluted share (up 29% and 27.4%, respectively)
- Home closings: 3,829 (up 7.1%)
- Total revenues: $1.11 billion (up 21.3%)
- Operating income margin: 12.6 percent (up 40 basis points)
- New orders: 3,872 homes (up 9.2%), sales value $1.13 billion (up 11.3%)
- Backlog at 12/31/05: 9,276 homes (up 10.1%), sales value $2.78 billion (up 18.3%).

A statement released attributed Beazer's positive financial results to the success of Beazer's Profitable Growth Strategy: "These results illustrate the effectiveness of our Profitable Growth Strategy aimed at achieving greater profitability by optimizing efficiencies, *selectively increasing market penetration,* and leveraging our national brand."

Deloitte & Touche

Beazer's auditor, Deloitte & Touche, specifically advised Rand via e-mail that Beazer's appreciation rights in the homes represented a continuing interest that, pursuant to GAAP, precluded Beazer from recognizing revenue when the homes were sold to GMAC. In an attempt to circumvent GAAP, and to deceive Deloitte, Rand caused the final, written versions of the sale-leaseback agreements to omit any reference to Beazer's continuing profit participation. Rand then directed, by e-mail, his subordinates to record revenue at the time the model homes were initially sold to the GMAC investor pools. Rand provided Deloitte with copies of the sale-leaseback agreements that intentionally omitted the provisions relating to the continuing profit participation by Beazer. Rand also failed to disclose the side agreements to Deloitte.

Additionally, on January 18, 2006, Rand provided to Deloitte a memo that specifically stated Beazer would not "participate in the appreciation" of the leased assets (model homes). Based on Rand's concealment and misrepresentations, Deloitte agreed that immediate revenue recognition was proper.

As reported by *CFO Magazine* and summarized in the following paragraphs,[2] a class-action lawsuit filed against Deloitte was settled on May 7, 2009. The agreement said that the audit firm should have considered the homebuilder's "make the numbers" culture to be a red flag as the housing market tanked. Deloitte agreed to pay investors of Beazer Homes nearly $1 million to settle the claim.

The investors had accused Beazer of managing earnings, recognizing revenue earlier than allowed under generally accepted accounting principles, improperly accounting for sale-leaseback transactions, creating "cookie-jar" reserves, and not recording land and goodwill impairment charges at the proper time.

The investors accused Deloitte of turning "a blind eye" to the myriad of "red flags" that should have alerted the firm to potential GAAP violations. These warning signs included the "excessive pressure" employees were under to meet their higher-ups' sales goals, tight competition in Beazer's market, and weak internal controls. Accusing the auditor of "severe recklessness," the shareholders alleged, for example, that Deloitte should have noticed that Beazer was likely overdue in recording impairments on its land assets, as the real estate market began to decline, among the other alleged accounting violations.

"Deloitte either knowingly ignored or recklessly disregarded Beazer's wide-ranging material control deficiencies and material weaknesses during the class period," according to the shareholders' complaint. "For example, Deloitte was specifically aware that financial periods were regularly held open or re-opened because it had access to Beazer's detailed financial and accounting information via, among other means, access to Beazer's JD Edwards software."

In the Beazer settlement, Deloitte denied all liability and settled to avoid the expense and uncertainty of continued litigation, according to a spokeswoman.

Restatements of Financial Statements

Due to Beazer's material noncompliance with the financial reporting requirements of the federal securities laws, Beazer was required to issue accounting restatements. On May 12, 2008, Beazer filed accounting restatements for the fiscal year 2006. In various reports filed that day, Beazer restated its financial statements for fiscal 2006 and each of the first three quarters of fiscal 2006. Beazer admitted to the improper accounting with the following statement:

> During the course of the investigation, the Audit Committee discovered accounting and financial reporting errors and/or irregularities that required restatement resulting primarily from: (1) inappropriate accumulation of reserves and/or accrued liabilities associated with land development and house costs ("Inventory Reserves"), and (2) inaccurate revenue recognition with respect to certain model home sale-leaseback transactions.

In the filings, Beazer further acknowledged material weaknesses in its internal control over financial reporting "specifically related to the application of GAAP in accounting for certain estimates involving significant management judgments."

As set forth in those filings, Beazer acknowledged that its material weaknesses had several impacts on the Company's financial reporting, including "[i]nappropriate reserves and other accrued liabilities [being] recorded relating to land development costs, house construction costs and warranty accruals" and "[t]he accounting for certain model home sale and leaseback agreements [being] not in compliance with GAAP. . . [as the] Company's arrangement for certain sale and leaseback transactions."

Those filings went on to state that Beazer had "terminated our former Chief Accounting Officer who we believe may have caused, or allowed to cause, the internal control breakdown"; and that Beazer "believe[d] his termination has addressed concerns about the internal control deficiencies that we believe he caused or permitted to occur."

In July 2009, a federal bill of information was filed in U.S. District Court charging Beazer with, among other things, participation in the conspiracy and securities fraud with Rand. Beazer accepted responsibility for those charges and, in a deferred prosecution agreement, agreed to pay restitution of $50 million. Rand was indicted by a federal grand jury in August 2010.

On July 18, 2014, a federal jury convicted Rand of conspiracy and obstruction of justice charges stemming from the federal investigation into the seven-year accounting fraud and related conspiracy at Beazer. On April 30, 2015, U.S. District Judge Robert J. Conrad Jr. sentenced Rand to 120 months in prison and to three years of supervised release on conspiracy and obstruction of justice charges in connection with the investigation.[3]

A statement released by the U.S. Attorney's Office quotes John A. Strong, the special agent in charge for the Charlotte Division of the FBI:

The U.S. Attorney's Office is committed to safeguarding the integrity of our financial markets from corporate executives like Rand, who put profits ahead of duty. Rand's actions breached his obligation to the investors and the public and jeopardized the stability of the housing industry. Today's verdict should send a clear message that corporate fraud, in this case cooking the books, will not be tolerated and you engage in such frauds at the risk of your freedom.[4]

Questions

1. Did Deloitte do an adequate job of evaluating the internal control environment at Beazer? Be specific.

2. Describe each of the financial shenanigans used by Beazer and how they manipulated earnings.

3. What do you believe should be done about companies like Beazer that engage in financial statement fraud for a period of time and issue false and misleading press releases during that time? Is it in the public interest to require external auditors to test this kind of information for accuracy and reliability? Explain by addressing the costs and benefits of such a requirement.

4. Assume you were hired to analyze the information in this case and write a two- to three-page report on your findings. Discuss each element of the fraud and why Beazer, Rand, and/or Deloitte violated ethical and professional standards.

Consequences of Earnings Management: The Need for Ethical Leadership in Accounting

LEARNING OBJECTIVES

After studying **Chapter 7** you should be able to:

LO 7-1   Describe the characteristics of financial statement restatements.
LO 7-2   Explain how errors in accounting and reporting can trigger restatements.
LO 7-3   Explain how restatements due to operational issues occur.
LO 7-4   Explain how corporate governance systems influence earnings management.
LO 7-5   Describe the characteristics of ethical leadership.
LO 7-6   Discuss how various leader types influence earnings management.
LO 7-7   Explain how ethical leadership in accounting might positively influence whether earnings management occurs.

Ethics Reflection

As we learned in Chapter 6, companies use earnings management to smooth out fluctuations in earnings and present more consistent earnings each month, quarter, or year. Management might react to a lower level of earnings when compared to internal estimates or financial analysts' earnings expectations. They feel pressured to manage earnings by using overly aggressive accounting techniques or financial shenanigans. These actions distort the quality of earnings and make it more difficult for investors and creditors to make informed decisions.

Akers et al. observe that "where management does not try to manipulate earnings, there is a positive effect on earnings quality. The earnings data is more reliable because management is not influencing or manipulating earnings by changing accounting methods, recognizing one-time items, deferring expenses, or accelerating revenues to bring about desired short-term earnings results."[1] This doesn't mean that the absence of earnings management guarantees high earnings quality because some information or events that affect future earnings may not be disclosed in the financial statements.

Earnings management reduces the usefulness of reported results because it artificially smooths net income over time thereby making valid comparisons questionable from period to period. Earnings management that occurs due to financial misrepresentations may lead to restating the financial statements if fraud exists.

Audit Analytics defines corporate restatements as "errors due to unintentional misapplication of U.S. GAAP" and corporate financial frauds as "intentional manipulation of financial data or misappropriation of assets."

Financial reporting quality indicators (i.e., the determination and detection of restatements or frauds) were examined using Audit Analytics data for 2019.[2] According to the Audit Analytics report, material misstatements discovered through the audit or otherwise determined after the financial statements have been issued may require the reissuance or revision of prior years' financial statements. These are known as *Reissuance Restatements or Revision Restatements* of the financial statements. Reissuance restatements, sometimes referred to as "Big R" restatements, address a material error that calls for the reissuance of past financial statements. Alternatively, revision restatements,

(continued)

continued   Ethics Reflection

or "little r" restatements, deal with immaterial misstatements, or adjustments made in the normal course of business. Because revision restatements are less severe, they are generally not looked at as a sign of poor reporting. According to Audit Analytics, some would argue that the disclosure of revision restatements shows a level of transparency and honesty by the filer.

Financial statement restatements include both revision restatements and reissuance restatements. SEC Form 8-K shows a total of 484 restatements of financial statements in 2019. The disclosures of reissuance restatements, as part of overall restatements, have been declining from 2007 through 2019. Some important findings in the 2019 report include:[3]

- The total of 484 restatements in 2019, including both revisions and reissuances, is the lowest amount during the 19 years analyzed;
- Revision restatements totaled roughly 80 percent of all restatements in 2019;
- In 2019, 57 percent of restatements had no impact on income statements;
- There were only 32 reissuance restatements filed in 2019 with an 8-K;
- The average number of days restated dropped for the third consecutive year, averaging around 451 days in 2019;
- The average number of issues per restatement dropped for the second year in a row, averaging around 1.5 issues per restatement in 2019.

It is encouraging to see a decline in reissuance restatements of the total amount of restatements. However, we are not convinced the good news will last forever as past history indicates that these things run in cycles. We are also concerned about non-GAAP disclosures that may need to be revised down the line depending on how the standard-setting bodies decide to deal with these issues given almost every company now discloses such metrics.

As for revision restatements, their number for 2019 represents a 15-year low of 334, the lowest number since the disclosure requirement came into effect. However, the percentage of revision restatements of the total restatements is high—79 percent in 2019. One question we have that has not been answered to our satisfaction is whether companies are shifting reissuance restatements to the revision category because they are then categorized as having a less severe impact on earnings.

Financial statement restatements might demonstrate a weakness in the internal controls over financial reporting and in corporate governance. They also implicate ethical leadership because corporate governance failings can trigger revisions or reissuances and may be attributable to a lack of ethics from the top—that is, CFO and CEO. This is true when the restatements are due to fraud rather than an honest error. These restatements raise questions about the role of ethical leadership as a driver of what can only be described as a poorly functioning corporate culture.

Here are the important questions to consider in Chapter 7: (1) What is the difference between reissuance restatements and revision restatements of the financial statements? (2) How can earnings management lead to regulatory actions and why? (3) How can corporate governance reduce or even eliminate earnings management? (4) What is the role of ethical leadership and ethical leaders in keeping earnings management in check?

> "To thine own self be true, and it must follow, as the night the day, thou canst not then be false to any man [or woman]."
>
> Source: a quote from Shakespeare's Hamlet

We chose this quote from Shakespeare's Hamlet because it crystallizes the need to be honest with oneself and maintain integrity, two essential characteristics of an ethical leader. Absent these characteristics, there is little reason for subordinates to follow the lead of those in the organization charged with corporate governance. This is why we conclude this chapter with a discussion of ethical leadership, the heart and soul of good corporate governance.

Characteristics of Financial Statement Restatements

LO 7-1

Describe the characteristics of financial statement restatements.

When financial statements are revised, the reason generally is because of errors in previously issued financial statements including: (1) accounting errors; (2) noncompliance with GAAP; and (3) fraud and misrepresentation. A materiality test is done to determine if the amount requires restatement. If so, the purpose is to advise statement users of erroneous information in previously released statements and provide corrected documents.

To be considered material, the amount in question would lead those receiving the financial statements to come to an inaccurate conclusion about the reliability and usefulness of the originally issued financial statements. In other words, the amount is large enough to influence decision making. Accounting rules require restatements only for items that are material.

Drilling down into financial restatements that were discussed in the Introduction, Fatima Alali and Sophia I-Ling Wang reviewed the Audit Analytics data from 2000 to 2014 and found that Big R restatements are typically accompanied by filing amended financial restatements for the periods affected. The audit opinion is also revised to reflect the restatements. The users of financial statements are alerted not to rely on the originally issued financials because of the error or fraud. The authors point out that there is an increasing trend of filing restatements without first announcing them to the public, mainly because the determination of the exact day previously issued financial statements should no longer be relied upon is subject to the discretion of the companies and their auditors.[4] This seems to be a rationalization for failing to be transparent and can put the public at a disadvantage, especially investors. The authors found the 2002 implementation of SOX 404 that requires management to issue a report on their internal controls over financial reporting led to an initial spike in Big R restatements which subsequently declined.[5] The good news is the rate has remained relatively steady for the last nine years.

Even though restatements have declined, there is at least one issue of concern, which is the number of "stealth restatements." The SEC requires companies to disclose within four business days a determination that past financial statements should no longer be relied on. This disclosure must appear in an 8-K report. The SEC defines a stealth restatement as one that is disclosed only in periodic reports and not in the 8-K or amended periodic report such as a 10-K/A or 10-Q/A.

A recent study of restatements shows that many companies are turning away from announcing restatements in Form 8-K and have avoided amending previously issued financial statements for the periods affected. Companies are instead revising the affected numbers for the previous periods and showing them in subsequent quarterly or annual reports (little "r" restatements).[6] The problem is by not including it in an 8-K filing, the restatement does not get publicly disclosed and may mislead users into thinking nothing important has happened that would warrant restatement. It is ethically problematic to bury restatements in quarterly and annual reports rather than to have a separate filing with the SEC in the 8-K.

What about immaterial amounts? Generally, these do not require either revision or reissuance of the financial statements. Instead, adjustments are made to current period financial reporting amounts. These are known as out-of-period adjustments. For example, let's say a company while preparing the quarter 2 financial statements for 2022 discovers that its inventory balance for quarter 1 was overstated by $200,000, an immaterial amount. The company can recognize the $200,000 charge in the current period rather than going back and restating the quarter 1 financial results.[7]

One consequence of having restatements is that material misstatements caused by accounting irregularities may cast doubt on management's integrity and expose the company to regulatory scrutiny or litigation. It is up to the audit committee to ensure that these restatements are properly disclosed and relevant adjustments to the financial statements are made. The audit committee should also discuss these matters with the external auditors.

It is interesting to see which issues tend to be corrected by means of restatements (i.e., revision or reissuance) and which lean more toward adjustments made in the normal course of business (i.e., out-of-period adjustments). The following data is provided by the Audit Analytics report.[8]

2019 Top Five Most Common Issues Cited in Restatements

1. Revenue recognition **(16.7%)**
2. Cash flow statement classification errors **(16.1%)**
3. Securities—debt, quasi-debt, warrants, and equity **(15.3%)**
4. Taxes **(13.0%)**
5. Liabilities **(12.2%)**

2019 Top Five Most Common Issues Cited in Adjustments

1. Taxes **(22.3%)**
2. Revenue recognition **(16.3%)**
3. Expense recording **(9.9%)**
4. Inventory **(9.9%)**
5. Value/diminution of PPE intangibles or fixed assets **(7.4%)**

Audit Analytics concludes that "irrespective of the scale of the error correction and the issues contributing to the errors, both restatements and adjustments negatively impact the financial reporting of a company. Even immaterial errors in financial reporting may predict future material weaknesses and errors in financial statements."

Investors and creditors need to know about these changes because they bear on their decisions making needs. Financial analysts rely on the accuracy of the financial data so they too have a need to know. The users have a right to know about these restatements and accountants have an ethical duty to make it so. In particular, accountants have a duty to inform the users that certain errors may exist in previously issued financial statements (revisions) and in some cases (reissuance) and that the investors and creditors should not rely on the originally issued financial statements or the audit report when reissuances exist. **Exhibit 7.1** depicts the financial reporting process when revision and reissuance is required or out of period adjustments are made.

Summary Reporting of Accounting Restatements

On July 16, 2015, Hertz Global Holdings, Inc., (Hertz) announced that it had filed its annual report on Form 10-K for the fiscal year ending December 31, 2014, which includes the restated results for 2012 and 2013 as well as selected unaudited restated financial information for 2011. In addition, the company had filed its quarterly report on Form 10-Q for the period ending March 31, 2015.

As discussed in the Form 10-K filed with the SEC, Hertz identified accounting misstatements for the years 2011 through 2013. The following information in **Exhibit 7.2** summarizes the impact of misstatements identified.[9]

EXHIBIT 7.1   Financial Statement Restatements

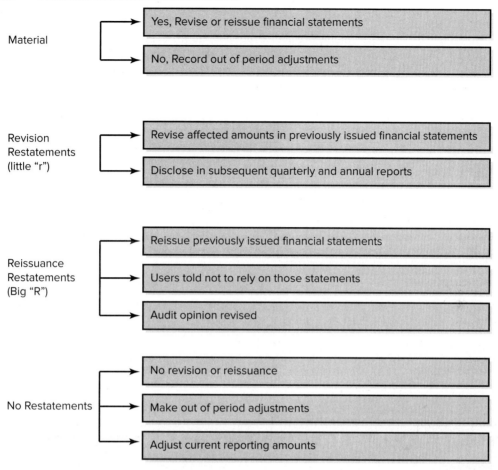

EXHIBIT 7.2   Hertz Impact of Misstatements

(In millions)	Year Ended December 31, (Unaudited) Increase/(Decrease)*		
	2011	2012	2013
As originally filed			
GAAP pretax income	$324	$451	$663
GAAP net income attributable to Hertz	$176	$243	$346
Misstatements previously disclosed and included in the originally filed 10-K/A**			
GAAP pretax income	$(19)	$ (9)	N/A
GAAP net income attributable to Hertz	$(12)	$ (4)	N/A
Additional misstatements identified			
GAAP pretax income	$(54)	$(81)	$(72)
GAAP net income attributable to Hertz	$(19)	$(58)	$(51)

(continued)

(In millions)	Year Ended December 31, (Unaudited) Increase/(Decrease)*		
Cumulative misstatements (Misstatements previously revised in 10-K/A plus additional errors identified)*			
GAAP pretax income	$(73)	$(90)	$(72)
GAAP net income attributable to Hertz	$(31)	$(62)	$(51)
Cumulative misstatements as a %			
GAAP pretax income	(23)%	(20)%	(11)%
GAAP net income attributable to Hertz	(18)%	(26)%	(15)%

*Increase/Decrease associated with misstatements and impact to GAAP pretax and GAAP net income.

**Amounts recorded as a revision in the 2013 Form 10-K/A.

***In addition, $114 and $87 in errors reducing GAAP pretax income and GAAP net income, respectively, related to periods prior to 2011 were recorded as a cumulative adjustment to opening retained earnings for 2011. Of these amounts, $7 and $5 GAAP pretax and GAAP net income, respectively, were recorded in the 2013 Form 10-K/A as a revision.

The Form 10-K contained audited restated financial information for 2012 and 2013, audited financial information for 2014, and unaudited restated selected financial information for 2011. The Form 10-K also contained quarterly information for the quarters in 2013, as restated, and 2014. The Form 10-Q contained quarterly information for the first quarter of 2015.

The company noted that the filing of its Form 10-K cures the filing deficiency notice from the New York Stock Exchange (NYSE) as reported on March 24, 2015, and brings Hertz back into compliance with the NYSE listing requirements.

Restatements Due to Errors in Accounting and Reporting

LO 7-2
Explain how errors in accounting and reporting can trigger restatements.

An analysis of causes of restatement due to errors in accounting and reporting was made by Turner and Weirich. Results from their study with respect to the kinds of accounting errors that trigger restatements are particularly relevant to the discussion of earnings management. **Exhibit 7.3** presents these results.[10]

EXHIBIT 7.3   Accounting Errors That Trigger Financial Statement Restatements

Category	Cause of Restatements
Revenue recognition	Improper revenue recognition, including questionable items and misreported revenue
Expense recognition	Improper expense recognition, including period of recognition, incorrect amounts; includes improper lease accounting
Misclassification	Improper classification on income statement, balance sheet, or cash flow statement; includes non-operating revenue in the operating category; cash outflow from operating activities in investment activities

Category	Cause of Restatements
Equity	Improper accounting for EPS; stock-based compensation plans, options, warrants, and convertibles
Other comprehensive income (OCI)	Improper accounting for OCI transactions, including unrealized gains and losses on investments in debt and equity securities, derivatives, and pension-liability adjustments
Capital assets	Improper accounting for asset impairments; asset-placed-in-service dates and depreciation
Inventory	Improper accounting for valuation of inventory, including market adjustments and obsolescence
Reserves/ allowances	Improper accounting for bad debt reserves on accounts receivable, reserves for inventory, and provision for loan losses
Liabilities/ contingencies	Improper estimation of liability claims, loss contingencies, litigation matters, commitments, and certain accruals

A good example of a company needing to correct an error due to switching from non-GAAP to GAAP occurred at Cubic Corporation, with its "development contracts." Cubic announced on August 1, 2012, that the audit committee of the company's board of directors, after consultation with Ernst & Young, its independent auditor, determined that Cubic's financial statements for the fiscal years ending September 30, 2011, 2010, and 2009; the quarters ended March 31, 2012, and December 31, 2011; and each of the prior quarters of 2011 and 2010 could no longer be relied upon as complying with GAAP. Accordingly, Cubic informed the SEC that it would restate the financial statements.[11] **Exhibit 7.4** provides additional information on how the Cubic restatements were identified and reported.

EXHIBIT 7.4   Cubic Corporation Restatement of Financial Statements (August 1, 2012)[12]

The Audit Committee's decision to restate these financial statements follows a recommendation by management that revenues in these previously issued financial statements should be adjusted due to errors in calculating revenues on certain long-term fixed-price development type contracts ("development contracts") and on certain long-term service contracts with non-U.S. Government customers ("service contracts").

Preliminary indications from the company's evaluation are that the changes described below will result in an increase in revenues and net income cumulatively over the period of the restatement and an increase in retained earnings as of March 31, 2012. Cubic Corporation is continuing to evaluate the total amount of the adjustments and the specific impact on each period covered by the restatement, which may result in an increase or decrease in previously reported amounts for individual periods.

Cubic has historically recognized sales and profits for development contracts using the cost-to-cost percentage-of-completion method of accounting, modified by a formulary adjustment. Under the cost-to-cost percentage-of-completion method of accounting, sales and profits are based on the ratio of costs incurred to estimated total costs at completion. Cubic has consistently applied a formulary adjustment to the percentage completion calculation for development contracts that had the effect of deferring a portion of the indicated revenue and profits on such contracts until later in the contract performance period.

Cubic believed that this methodology was an acceptable variation of the cost-to-cost percentage-of-completion method as described in Accounting Standards Codification ("ASC") 605-35. The company now believes that generally accepted accounting principles do not support the practice of using a formulary calculation to defer a portion of the indicated revenue and profits on such contracts. Instead, Cubic believes that sales and profits should have been recognized based on the ratio of costs incurred to estimated total costs at completion, without using a formulary adjustment. The company is in the process of evaluating the differences resulting from this change but has not yet completed this evaluation.

While evaluating its revenue recognition for development contracts, Cubic also evaluated its long-standing practice of using the cost-to-cost percentage-of-completion method to recognize revenues for many of its service contracts. Under the accounting literature the cost-to-cost percentage of completion method is acceptable for U.S. Government contracts but not for contracts with other governmental customers, whether domestic or foreign.

Errors in accounting and financial reporting that affect earnings are corrected through a prior period adjustment to retained earnings. The importance of such adjustments to users of the statements depends on materiality issues. In the context of potentially faulty financial statements, however, the process by which materiality is determined is complex and can be lengthy. Depending on the timing of the discovery of the error and its magnitude, this event can lead to negative effects with respect to share value.

It is important to note the trend that both FASB and the SEC want accountants and auditors to follow: the application of professional judgment in making materiality decisions. We agree and reiterate that the application of professional judgment entails an ethical approach to decision making. The qualities of an ethical auditor of objectivity, integrity, due care, and professional skepticism are critical components of that judgment. The shift to more professional judgments should be accompanied by better training for auditors in the area of ethical decision making. We would like to see the SEC address this issue.

Restatements Due to Operational Issues

LO 7-3

Explain how restatements due to operational issues occur.

Operational issues can also trigger restatements. In both the Kraft and MagnaChip examples discussed below, management engaged in earnings management resulting in subsequent restatements.

On May 6, 2019, Kraft Heinz Co. disclosed that it would restate its financial statements due to faulty procurement practices. This is an example where the timing of expense recognition triggered the restatement rather than error corrections in the accounting and reporting.

Heinz said that it will restate nearly three years of financial results due to employee misconduct in its procurement department that caused it to understate the cost of products sold by $181 million.[13]

The processed-foods giant conducted an internal investigation of its procurement function after receiving a subpoena from the U.S. Securities and Exchange Commission in October 2018 related to agreements with its suppliers.

In a regulatory filing, Kraft said the investigation showed "several employees in the procurement area engaged in misconduct" that qualitatively affected its financial reporting for 2016, 2017, and the first three quarters of 2018.

"As a result of the findings from the company's investigation ... the company has recorded adjustments to correct prior period misstatements that increase the total cost of products sold in prior financial periods," the filing said.

According to Kraft, the misstatements "principally relate to the incorrect timing of when certain cost and rebate elements associated with complex supplier contracts and arrangements were initially recognized, and once corrected for, the company expects to recognize corresponding decreases to costs of products sold in future financial periods." The adjustments to financial statements totaled about $208 million, of which approximately $27 million was recorded in the fourth-quarter 2018 cost of products sold, leaving a cumulative net misstatement of $181 million.

Kraft also disclosed it had received an additional subpoena from the SEC related to its assessment of goodwill and intangible asset impairments. The company's own review, it said, had identified misstatements resulting in an increase of approximately $13 million from the previously disclosed $15.4 billion goodwill impairment loss in the fourth quarter of 2018.

Kraft said that "The findings from the investigation did not identify any misconduct by any member of the senior management team." We're skeptical of this statement because misconduct in its procurement department is unlikely to occur without someone in top management knowing about it. At the least, the internal controls failed in this case. Without admitting to any wrong-doing, the case was settled on September 3, 2021, when Kraft agreed to pay $62 million to resolve the matter.

Kraft shareholders have sued the company for fraud alleging that Kraft had inappropriate accounting policies, procedures, and internal controls over financial reporting. In August of 2021, a federal judge ruled that this class action can proceed to trial.

MagnaChip Semiconductor, Ltd

The MagnaChip Semiconductor fraud illustrates how much can go wrong when management seeks to manage earnings through revenue recognition transactions, internal controls are overridden, and the auditors are kept out of the loop.

The financial shenanigans used by MagnaChip to commit fraud and their motivations included:

Channel stuffing. Accelerating the recording of revenue into earlier periods by recording revenue on sales of incomplete or unshipped products.

Pull-in sales practices. Offering distributors undisclosed concessions through side agreements to incentivize them to order products earlier than wanted or needed in order to hit revenue targets.

Delaying the recording of obsolete inventory. The company also delayed recording obsolete inventory to manipulate its reported gross margin. It also helped the company to hit its earnings targets.

Additional details are included in **Exhibit 7.5**.[14]

EXHIBIT 7.5   Accounting Fraud at MagnaChip Semiconductor

MagnaChip Semiconductor, Ltd., designs and manufactures analog and mixed-signal semiconductor products for consumer, computing, communication, industrial, automotive, and Internet applications. The company offers display solutions for a range of flat-panel display sizes used in LCD televisions, LCD monitors, notebooks, tablet PCs, public information displays, and other applications.

MagnaChip Semiconductor Corporation is a Delaware corporation headquartered in Luxembourg with the majority of its operations in South Korea. It maintains a U.S. sales subsidiary in Cupertino, California. MagnaChip's stock is listed on the New York Stock Exchange. MagnaChip Korea engaged in a variety of transactions to accelerate the recording of revenue into earlier periods through channel stuffing arrangements, recording revenue on sales of incomplete or unshipped products, and delaying recording obsolete inventory to manipulate its reported gross margin. The underlying motivation for the fraud was to hit earnings targets and was carried out through aggressive action directed by or in response to pressure from the former CFO, Margaret Sakai.

MagnaChip stated in its public filings that it recognized revenue on a "sell-in" basis under GAAP (i.e., when it sold and shipped the product to a distributor, not when the distributor sold and shipped the product to an end customer). This revenue recognition treatment for sales to distributors is consistent with GAAP only when the aforementioned revenue recognition requirements are met.

The revenue recognition criteria in MagnaChip's quarterly and annual filings during the relevant period was signed off by Sakai. The filings stated that it utilized these criteria to recognize revenue "upon shipment, upon delivery of the product at the customer's location or upon customer acceptance . . . when the risks and rewards of ownership have passed to the customer" and that, outside of warranty obligations and contractual terms, its sales contracts "do not include any other post-shipment obligations that could have an impact on revenue recognition." Those statements were later determined to have been materially false and misleading because MagnaChip recognized substantial revenue even when the disclosed criteria were not met.

Contrary to the disclosures in its public filings, as well as to its written policies, from late 2011 through the third quarter of 2013, certain MagnaChip employees engaged in what they called a "pull-in" sales practice whereby they offered distributors undisclosed concessions via side agreements to incentivize them to order products earlier than wanted or needed so that MagnaChip would hit revenue targets. The concessions included payment term extensions, credit limit increases, unlimited return and stock rotation rights on unsold inventory, and price protection. As a result of the concessions, MagnaChip improperly recognized revenue on certain transactions that did not meet the requirements of GAAP.

Although the "pull-in" sales practice was known to numerous individuals throughout MagnaChip's Korean management structure, Sakai, as CFO of MagnaChip, approved payment term extensions and credit limit increases for certain of the improper pull-in sales, failed to correct the improper accounting treatment of other pull-in sales, and understood how they would impact MagnaChip's reported revenue. Sakai signed MagnaChip's financial statements disclosing the

(continued)

company's revenue recognition policy and GAAP requirements. She also represented to MagnaChip's auditors in management representation letters that MagnaChip had not entered into any side agreements, and certified MagnaChip's public filings. Sakai either knew or was reckless in not knowing that the concessions and side agreements precluded revenue recognition under GAAP and violated MagnaChip's disclosed revenue recognition policy. Further, Sakai either knew or was reckless in not knowing that the Company engaged in these practices solely to meet revenue targets.

MagnaChip also improperly recognized revenue on "sales" of non existent or unfinished products in order to meet revenue targets. In 2011, some MagnaChip Korean sales employees met with some manufacturing employees to express concern about their ability to meet the sales targets set by senior management because manufacturing could not keep up. After that meeting, certain of MagnaChip's manufacturing employees in Korea began circumventing the Company's accounting controls and falsified books and records to create entries that made it appear that products that had not yet begun production or were still in production had been completed, shipped, and billed to customers. MagnaChip then recognized revenue on the sales of those unfinished products. In so doing, MagnaChip violated GAAP because it recognized revenue on purported sales of products that had not yet completed manufacturing and therefore had not yet shipped or been delivered, and the risk of loss had not transferred to the purchaser.

MagnaChip also had material weaknesses in its internal controls concerning revenue recognition. As such, MagnaChip violated SEC regulation Section 15(d) that provides:

> Every issuer which has a class of securities pursuant to Section 15(d) shall –
>
> A. Make and keep books, records, and accounts, which, in reasonable detail, accurately and fairly reflect the transactions and dispositions of the assets of the issuer; and
>
> B. Devise and maintain a system of internal accounting controls sufficient to provide reasonable assurances that –
>
>   i.   transactions are executed in accordance with management's general or specific authorization;
>
>   ii. transactions are recorded as necessary (a) to permit preparation of financial statements in conformity with generally accepted accounting principles or any other criteria applicable to such statements, and (b) to maintain accountability for assets;
>
>   iii. access to assets is permitted only in accordance with management's general or specific authorization; and
>
>   iv. the recorded accountability for assets is compared with the existing assets at reasonable intervals and appropriate action is taken with respect to any differences.

Defendants also certified the accuracy of the financial statements under SOX Section 302. However, that certification was false.

Two control deficiencies were reported by the independent registered public accounting firm that concluded represented a material weakness in MagnaChip's internal control over financial reporting. These included not having a sufficient number of financial personnel with the requisite financial accounting experience and that the Company's controls over non-routine transactions were not effective to ensure that accounting considerations are identified and appropriately recorded.

The actions of MagnaChip's CFO, Margaret Sakai, and/or the company willfully violated a variety of SEC rules. Here is a description of all those violations as they pertain to the financial statements and internal controls.

Rule 10(b) of the Exchange Act and Rule 10b-5, in connection with the purchase or sale of securities, prohibit (1) employing any device, scheme, or artifice to defraud; (2) making any material misrepresentation or omission; or (3) engaging in any transaction, practice, or course of business that operates as a fraud or deceit upon any person.

Rule 12b-20 requires that the required financial reports must contain any material information necessary to make the required statements made in the reports not misleading.

Rule 13a-14 requires that the principal financial officer of an issuer sign a certification that the issuer's Forms 10-Q and 10-K fairly presented, in all material respects, the financial condition and results of operations of the company.

Rule 13(b)(2)(A) requires issuers of securities registered pursuant to Section 12 of the Exchange Act to make and keep books, records, and accounts, which, in reasonable detail, accurately and fairly reflect their transactions and dispositions of their assets.

Rule 13(b)(2)(B) requires issuers of securities registered pursuant to Section 12 of the Exchange Act to, among other things, devise and maintain a system of internal accounting controls sufficient to provide reasonable assurances that transactions are recorded as necessary to permit preparation of financial statements in accordance with generally accepted accounting principles.

Rule 13(b)(5) prohibits any person from knowingly circumventing or knowingly failing to implement a system of internal accounting controls or knowingly falsifying books, records, or accounts described in Section 13(b)(2) of the Exchange Act.

Rule 13b2-1 prohibits any person from directly or indirectly falsifying any books and records subject to Section 13(b)(2)(A) of the Exchange Act.

Rule 13b2-2 promulgated under the Exchange Act prohibits any director or officer of an issuer from directly or indirectly making, or causing to be made, or omitting to state or causing another person to omit to state, a materially false or misleading statement or any material fact necessary in order to make statements made, in light of the circumstances under which such statements were made, not misleading, to an accountant in connection with any audit, review or examination of the financial statements of the issuer, or the preparation or filing of any document or report required to be filed with the Commission.

The MagnaChip case illustrates how things can go so wrong, so quickly, when a top official (i.e., the CFO) directs a fraud and creates a pressure-laden culture to meet earnings targets. MagnaChip's misconduct was pervasive, from senior employees like Sakai down to manufacturing plant employees and employees in other departments. By late 2013, both Magna's outside auditors (Samil PricewaterhouseCoopers) and its audit committee suspected something was wrong. In March 2014, the audit committee disclosed its investigation to investors, and, in 2015, the company restated revenues for 2011, 2012, and most of 2013. The SEC began its investigation shortly thereafter and settled in June 2017 by imposing a $3 million fine against MagnaChip, deferred another $3 million in penalties, that it may impose in the future if the company has more trouble. Sakai must pay $135,000 in personal penalties, cannot appear before the SEC again as an accountant, and cannot serve as a director or officer of a U.S.-listed company ever again.

SEC Clawback for Accounting Violations

Recall that in **Chapter 3** we discussed clawback provisions, which are SEC regulations designed to ensure that company executives don't manipulate financial information to maximize earnings linked to their compensation payments. Clawback provisions kick in when such events occur requiring executives to pay back bonuses they received if the incentive was based on a performance benchmark that later turned out to be an incorrect number.

Based on her research on whether firms conceal material misstatements by reporting revisions rather than restatements, Rachel Thompson found that managers that are subject to clawback provisions are significantly more likely to revise rather than restate financial statements compared with managers who are not subject to clawbacks. Specifically, Thompson found that firms with clawback provisions are over 2.5 times more likely to report material misstatements as revisions compared with firms without clawback provisions (70.1% and 26.8%, respectively). Thompson observed based on her findings that in the presence of clawback provisions managers are more likely to use discretion afforded by the materiality rules to correct misstatements through revisions instead of restatements. She concluded that this was "an unintended consequence of clawbacks, namely that clawback provisions deter the filing of restatements upon a misstatement discovery." [15]

SOX section 304 provides a reimbursement remedy against CEOs and CFOs when the issuer of financial statements has restated its financial statements as a result of misconduct. The misconduct does not have to have been committed directly by the CEO or CFO. Instead, the triggering event is misconduct by the issuer, acting through any of its officers, agents, or employees.

In 2007, the first clawback claim was successful and the executive involved had to return approximately $600 million in cash and stock options. More recently, the SEC settled charges against the former CEO and CFO of WageWorks, Inc., alleging that they made false and misleading statements and omissions, including to the company's outside audit firm, that led to improper revenue recognition and ultimately resulted in a financial restatement. The settlements with both former executives included reimbursement of incentive-based compensation under SOX 304.[16]

SOX 304 provides that, if

> "an issuer is required to prepare an accounting restatement due to the material noncompliance of the issuer, as a result of misconduct, with any financial reporting requirement under the securities laws, the chief executive officer and the chief financial officer of the issuer shall reimburse the issuer for—
>
> (1) any bonus or incentive-based or equity-based compensation received by that person from the issuer during the 12-month period following the first public issuance or filing with the Commission (whichever first occurs) of the financial document embodying such financial reporting requirement; and
>
> (2) any profits realized from the sale of securities of the issuer during that 12-month period."

In 2011, the SEC ratcheted up the stakes when it announced another settlement to recover bonus compensation and stock sale profits from a CFO under SOX 304, even though there were no charges of personal misconduct by the CFO.

In 2016, a court ruled for the first time that Section 304 did provide for a disgorgement remedy against CEOs and CFOs when the issuer restated its financial statements as a result of misconduct, even if the CEO and CFO were not alleged to have engaged in the misconduct themselves.

As a result of this ruling, the courts supported the SEC's broader view that under SOX, the CEO and CFO are required to take "affirmative steps to prevent fraudulent accounting schemes from occurring on their watch," and, if they receive substantial incentive compensation and stock sale profits while their company is misleading investors and committing accounting fraud, those amounts should be forfeited.[17]

Corporate Governance and Earnings Management

LO 7-4
Explain how corporate governance systems influence earnings management.

A financial restatement is perhaps the most significant indication of an accounting failure. Inability to provide reliable financial statements may shake investor confidence and raise concerns about a company's overall health. Moreover, a material restatement caused by an accounting irregularity may cast doubt on management integrity and expose the company to regulatory scrutiny or litigation. Indeed, extensive prior academic research has documented notable, negative stock returns before and around the dates that restatements are announced.[18]

Companies that engage in earnings management raise questions about the role of corporate governance. How is it that managers, the board of directors, and audit committee failed to identify and stop earnings management? What was their role in managing opportunistic behavior of managers who use various financial shenanigan techniques to make the company look better than it really is? What role did the internal controls over financial reporting play in keeping earnings management at bay? What are the implications of earnings management for ethical leadership? These are a few of the questions to be asked when evaluating the consequences of earnings management.

The discussion in **Chapter 6** about earnings management and its consequences in **Chapter 7** raise questions about the lack of a strong corporate governance system. The purpose of this section is to discuss the relationships and gain a better understanding why and how earnings management occurs.

We begin by reviewing the agency theory. Recall that managers act as the agents of the shareholders who expect management to act in shareholders' best interests. For many shareholders, this means to maximize profits, increase the value of stock holdings, and facilitate stock options. The perceived pressures applied on management to serve shareholder needs can lead to earnings management. For example, it is better to smooth net income over time than have wide fluctuations in the stream of earnings. Shareholders like predictability so managers may feel pressured to engage in techniques that aid in those decision-making needs. Moreover, investors and financial analysts need reliable financial information so they can predict future earnings. Earnings management techniques compromise the quality of earnings.

Chi Keung Man observes that good corporate governance can reduce or even eliminate the extent of earnings management. He looks at the role of internal corporate governance in allowing earnings management to persist. He studied corporate governance systems and found that better corporate governance can use the internal control system to control opportunistic earnings management.[19]

An interesting perspective is board independence can reduce earnings management because independent directors do not pursue self-interests such as executive compensation or partake in the misappropriation of assets. They do not bend to pressure from shareholders to meet or beat expectations of firm performance. Independent directors recognize the need to maintain a good personal reputation in the eyes of the public. Board independence can also prevent managers' abuse of power. More importantly, shareholders can control the appointment and replacement of independent directors so that an incentive exists to maintain their independence from management.

Based on his literature review, Chi found that managers are likely to cover their opportunistic behavior by managing earnings. Thus, the audit committee can actively monitor the quality of work done by internal auditors and can choose better external auditors to improve the quality of financial statements. Maintaining good internal control effectiveness can reduce earnings management and improve financial information. Song and Windham argue that limitations on the audit committee's ability can affect its monitoring of financial accounting quality. Thus, audit committee structure is an important corporate governance mechanism.[20]

The failure of corporate governance systems can be attributed to: (1) management override of internal controls; (2) not setting an ethical tone at the top; (3) creating a pressure-laden culture that emphasizes egoistic goals; (4) lack of an independent audit committee; and (5) lack of ethical leadership. We now turn our attention to ethical leadership failings and a lack of ethical leaders, two factors that corrupt corporate governance and can lead to earnings management.

What Is Ethical Leadership?

LO 7-5

Describe the characteristics of ethical leadership.

There are consequences of earnings management for ethical leadership. In the aftermath of SEC investigations, the Commission shined light on failures of ethical leadership that allowed fraudulent financial statements to go forward.

There are a variety of definitions of ethical leadership. The Center for Ethical Leadership defines it as "knowing your core values and having the courage to live them in all parts of your life in the service of the common good."[21] We like this definition because it points to core values (i.e., virtues) and courage (i.e., integrity) as integral parts of serving the common good (i.e., public interest).

According to the Harvard Business Review, ethical leaders will not overlook wrongdoing, even in cases when doing so may benefit their businesses. Showing integrity and doing what's right are at the core of being an ethical leader. Ethical leaders set an example for the rest of the company.[22] This squares with our discussions in this book about the ethical tone at the top.

One characteristic of ethical leadership is to influence others. Yukl emphasized the importance of influence when identifying a leader: "Leadership is the process of influencing others to understand and agree about what needs to be done and how to do it, and the process of facilitating individual and collective efforts to accomplish shared objectives."[23] Dhar and Mishra point out that leadership has been defined in terms of individual traits, leader behavior, interaction patterns, role relationships, followers' perceptions, influence over followers, influence on task goals, and influence on organizational culture.

Traits of Ethical Leaders

The ethical leader understands that positive relationships built on respect, openness, and trust are critical to creating an ethical organization environment. The underlying principles of ethical leadership are: integrity, honesty, fairness, justice, responsibility, accountability, and empathy. Copeland links these values to leader effectiveness, ethical leadership behavior, and transformational leadership. She believes that ethical leaders will be highly effective at getting subordinates to follow their lead if they incorporate these characteristic traits of behavior into their decision making.[24] Ethical leaders, therefore, establish an environment of honesty and trust that subordinates will want to follow making it less likely that earnings will be managed for egoistic reasons.

Leaders lead by example. They set an ethical tone at the top. They lead with an attitude of "Do what I say as well as what I do." Ciulla argues that what is distinctive of leadership is the concept of vision: "Visions are not simple goals, but rather ways of seeing the future that implicitly or explicitly entail some notion of the good."[25]

The Ethics and Compliance Initiative (ECI) points out research has consistently shown that:[26]

- Ethical leadership is a critical factor driving down ethics and compliance risk;
- Leaders have a "rosier" view of the state of workplace integrity and often have more positive beliefs than employees further down the chain of command; and
- The quality of the relationship between supervisors and employees goes a long way in determining whether employees report workplace integrity issues to management.

According to research conducted by Brown et al., most employees look outside themselves to significant others for ethical guidance. Therefore, in the workplace, leaders should be a central source of such guidance. The ethical dimension of leadership represents a small component that falls within the core of inspiring, stimulating, and visionary leader behaviors that make up transformational and charismatic leadership. The authors developed a measure of ethical leadership known as the "ethical leadership scale," which includes several behavioral characteristics of ethical leaders:[27]

- Talk about the importance of workplace integrity and doing the right thing.
- Set a good example.
- Do not blame others when things go wrong.
- Support employees' efforts to do the right thing.
- Hold themselves and others accountable for violating the organization's code of conduct.
- Give positive feedback for acting with integrity.
- Keep their promises and commitments.

Organizations suffer when leadership does not set an ethical tone at the top. The employees may be ethical, but acting ethically requires an ethical leader who supports such behavior, not a leader blinded by ambition or greed as occurred in so many of the financial failures of the early 2000s.

Lawton and Paez developed a framework for ethical leadership built on three interlocking questions: First, who are leaders and what are their characteristics? Second, how do ethical leaders do what they do? Third, why do leaders do as they do and what are the outcomes of ethical leadership?[28] The authors suggest that the three factors will not necessarily form discrete areas of ethics. For example, auditors need to be virtuous and exhibit the characteristics of honesty, integrity, objectivity, and professional skepticism. These traits are also essential in auditors' relations with clients because they enable professional judgment and ethical decision making in client relationships. They also facilitate the kind of probing audits and targeted inquiries of management that should be conducted selflessly and in the public interest, not that of the client or even self-interest.

Lawton and Paez believe that virtues cannot be separated from the context within which they are practiced. This is certainly true of accounting professionals and the accounting profession. They also opine that different virtues will be appropriate to the different roles that leaders play. We agree that context is important. As leaders within their firms, partners must exhibit moral imagination through ethical perception of what it means to be ethical, professional, and successful. In dealing with conflicts in relationships with clients, auditors should demonstrate courage and moral judgment. Here, ethical judgment and ethical decision-making skills become critically important in finding a solution to ethical dilemmas as we have discussed throughout the book.

Ethical leadership entails building an environment where those in the organization feel comfortable in talking to others to share perspectives of the importance of finding an ethical solution to problems. Internal accountants and auditors may possess ethical values, but it will mean nothing unless a supportive organization exists to help develop the courage to put those values into action. Voicing one's values when conflicts exist creates challenges that can be exacerbated by an indifferent leader and culture that operates by rationalizing unethical actions. Pressures imposed by top management to go along with financial wrongdoing under the guise of "It is expected practice around here" or "You need to be a team player" challenges a protagonist who must counter those reasons and give voice to one's values. As Patrick Kelly observes, "Ethical leaders must consistently make correct moral decisions, even under challenging circumstances."[29]

In a recent study, Copeland examined ethical leadership and its impact on leader effectiveness for leaders in large regional accounting firms. She collected data on leadership attributes. Copeland found that there was a significant relationship between ethical leadership behaviors and leaders who were evaluated by their subordinates as more effective. Her analysis shows that ethical and transformational leadership make incremental independent contributions in explaining leader effectiveness. Ethical leadership was a significant predictor of leader effectiveness over and above transformational leadership, the number of years a subject has worked for a leader, the number of years the subject has worked for the organization, and the subordinates gender. Copeland concluded that a need exists for individuals to be ethical and to emerge as ethical leaders in the accounting profession.[30]

A distinguishing characteristic of many of the accounting frauds discussed in this book is that short-term factors were allowed to compromise long-term ethical decision making in the interest of creating the illusion that earnings were strong and sustainable. CFOs and CEOs acted based on non-ethical values, such as enhancing share prices and creating personal wealth. Those on the front line "held their nose" and carried out unethical orders that led to managed earnings. "Leaders" such as Jeff Skilling at Enron, Bernie Ebbers at WorldCom, and Dennis Kozlowski at Tyco created hands-off environments that sent the message "all is well" while the companies were collapsing around them.

Building a reputation for ethical leadership means to enable ethics and values to shine through the fog of beating the competition and meeting financial projections. During the accounting scandals, the mantra was to meet or beat analysts' earnings expectations. All kinds of financial shenanigans were used to accomplish the goal, as explained in **Chapter 6**. Some companies even turned to customized earnings per share calculations, like GE, to project the image of exceeding expectations.

Values-Driven Leadership

The starting point of a values-driven organization is the individual leader. A leader needs to connect with organizational values. Leaders must ask what they stand for and why. Leaders must consider why others would want to follow them. The goal is to get in touch with what motivates one's actions and how best to motivate those in the organization who look to the leader for direction.

We should think about values-based leadership in connection with the GVV approach to decision making. As we learned in **Chapter 2**, GVV addresses how to respond to ethical conflicts in the workplace. Rather than the usual focus on ethical analysis, GVV focuses on ethical implementation and asks the question: What would I say and do if I were going to act on my values? Ethical organizations encourage employees to voice their values. Ethical leaders know that if employees feel comfortable speaking up about matters of concern in a supportive environment, then problems will not fester and the likelihood of whistleblowing activity is lessened.

Consider the following situation: Amy is an auditor at Black and White, LLP, a mid-sized accounting firm in New York City. Amy has identified what may be a major fraud at a client entity. It seems the client engaged in a "sell-through" product agreement whereby an apparent sale to another party included a side agreement that obligated that party to resell the merchandise prior to paying for the "acquisition." Thus, a contingency existed that should have delayed the recording of the sales revenue but did not. Amy has already spoken to Pat, the audit manager, who instructed her to leave the transaction alone. It seems the amount involved was not material, according to Pat. Moreover, it seems the client has exerted a great deal of pressure on the firm to go along with its accounting because the revenue involved is sufficient to change a loss for the year into a profit.

Amy is disappointed in Pat and what may be the firm's position on the matter. She knows the firm has a core set of values that do not square with the intended accounting. One such accounting value is how materiality is applied. Changing a loss to a profit is material in and of itself. It seems as though Amy may be facing an instance of organizational dissidence in that the way in which she expected the organization to act is not the way that it did act. She wants to find a way to give voice to her values but is not sure how to go about it. What are the key issues for Amy to consider? What road should she take?

Values-based leadership cuts both ways. Amy may be disappointed in the firm's leadership, but if she envisions herself as a leader (or potential leader), then she wants to demonstrate leadership instincts in deciding how to handle the matter. Perhaps she can influence the actions of the firm if she is successful in voicing her values using the GVV framework.

- What are the shared values that should drive my actions?
- With whom do I need to speak to enable voicing my values?
- What do I need to say to most effectively give importance to my values?
- What are the likely objections or pushback I should expect? And, then,
- What should I say next?

As we have discussed many times before, Amy should evaluate the reasons and rationalization she needs to address. One may be that the leader(s) in the firm she decides to approach may "play the loyalty card" or insist that they "keep the client happy." This is where the dissidence becomes a factor in Amy's decision.

Once Amy decides on a course of action, she needs to ask herself: What if I don't act and voice my values? How will I feel about myself? Would I be proud for others to know about it, including family members? What will happen if I do nothing and get blamed for inaction down the road? How will I feel if I do nothing and the organization implodes?

Ethical Leadership Competence

Ethical Leadership Competence refers to the ability to handle all kinds of moral problems that may arise in an organization. It means to develop the problem-solving and decision-making skills to make difficult decisions. Leaders might try to deal with a moral problem in an automatic way, essentially using their authority for the basis of decision making. However, this System 1 approach is fraught with danger because the interests of all stakeholders may not be adequately considered, subtle moral issues may go unnoticed, and expediency is emphasized instead of thought and deliberation. What is needed is to develop the competency to reason through ethical conflicts in a systematic way. There is no shortcut to making ethical decisions. It requires judgment and reflection on what the right thing to do is.

Thornton identifies five levels of ethical competence: personal, interpersonal, organizational, professional, and societal.[31] On a personal level, accounting professionals should internalize the values of the profession, including objectivity, integrity, diligence, and duty to society. Auditors are part of a larger social environment within the organization that may lead to pressures to conform with organizational expectations. The influence of organizational systems and ethics can create ethical dissonance. Auditors should identify the source of the dissonance and seek out ways to bring ethical expectations more in line with ethical behavior.

Auditors have a professional role to play in their organizations. They work in teams so how they deal with others (i.e., showing respect, fair-mindedness) is a critical component of ethical competence. As members of an accounting firm, auditors should follow the ethics codes and expectations of their organizations, but they should never compromise their professional identity.

Kelly and Earley developed three measures called *The Ethical Leadership Scales,* which provide a measure of personal ethical competence, ethical leadership, and ethical organization. We have found the scales useful in teaching ethical leadership because they enable students to self-evaluate their leadership skills. Beginning with the understanding that effective ethical leadership depends on personal ethical competence, the *Ethical Competence Scale* provides a measuring stick of whether one's values consistently direct behavior. Questions to ask yourself include: Are you reliable and dependable? Are you willing to admit mistakes? Are you true to your word? Are you worthy of confidence? Do you keep promises and commitments?[32] Ethical reflection is the key to ethical competence.

The *Ethical Leadership Scale* fits nicely with GVV methodology. It engages participants in reflecting on specific leadership qualities that can support voicing one's beliefs when conflicts exist in an organization and when interacting with others in organizational relationships. In discussing the usefulness of the Scales, Kelly and Earley point out that techniques of role-playing, simulation, and scenario writing can be used to enhance the experience.

The perception that followers have of managers in an organization, whether they are viewed as ethical leaders, depends on whether they are seen as moral persons and moral managers. Being a moral person is not enough to encourage ethical behavior of followers because of the distance between both parties. Moral managers gain legitimacy only if employees believe they are principled and caring, and say what they will do and do what they say.

Consistency in words and actions underlies ethical leadership. Followers must be comfortable that, if they follow the ethical path, they will be rewarded for doing so. In most of the companies that we have discussed in this book, the opposite was the case. Still, there are ethical organizations out there and leaders truly committed to doing the right thing.

When people face a moral problem, they sometimes have great difficulties in not confusing moral goals, values, feelings, and emotions with the problem-solving and decision-making processes and the methods adopted for the solution of the problem. By now you know these skills can be learned but require practice, commitment, reflection, and a continuous cycle of re-examining whether you need to adjust your thinking to match the ethical demands of a situation. We suggest that a worthwhile goal is to strive to eliminate any cognitive dissonance so that your behaviors match your values and beliefs. Ethical leaders possess the competencies to influence ethical behavior in a positive direction.

Trust-Based Organizations

As we have discussed throughout the book, the culture of an organization says a lot about whether it tolerates inappropriate behavior. Ethical failings at Enron, WorldCom, HealthSouth, and others, occurred because the organization tolerated fraudulent behaviors and even motivated them such as Enron's "rank and yank" policy that determined which employees would be fired based on the ratings of other employees.

Trust-based organizations build relationships and promote responsible behavior at all levels of the organization. It establishes a culture that says: "Do what I say and what I do," rather than "Do what I say not what I do." It engenders feelings of respect for others in the organization and builds ethical leaders. Such an organization establishes an ethical tone at the top and directs others in a way that is consistent with sound organizational values and in compliance with rules and regulations.

Types of Leaders

LO 7-6
Discuss how various leader types influence earnings management.

It is important to understand the way in which leaders lead because, in accounting, the influence of leaders on the ethical decision-making process makes a difference whether the core values of the profession are followed and how they drive behavior.

Authentic Leaders

Authentic leaders are focused on building long-term shareholder value, not in just beating quarterly estimates. Authentic leaders are individuals "who are deeply aware of how they think and behave and are perceived by others as being aware of their own and others' values/moral perspectives, knowledge, and strengths; aware of the context in which they operate; and are confident, optimistic, resilient, courageous, and of high moral character. Authentic leaders acknowledge the ethical responsibilities of their roles, can recognize and evaluate ethical issues, and take moral actions that are thoroughly grounded in their beliefs and values."[33]

Authentic leaders hold altruistic values and are concerned with achieving a common good for the group or organization for which they are responsible. Authentic leadership produces a number of positive ethical effects in followers that significantly influence the creation of an ethical organizational environment and help to promote values-based decision making. Followers are likely to emulate the example of authentic leaders who set a high ethical standard. They are empowered to make ethical choices on their own without the input of the leader. They become moral agents of the organization.

Transformational Leadership

The need for good leaders to be ethical in their leadership is embedded within definitions of transformational leaders. Transformational leadership is defined as a leadership approach that causes change in individuals and social systems. In its ideal form, it creates valuable and positive change in the followers with the end goal of developing followers into leaders. Enacted in its authentic form, transformational leadership enhances the motivation, morale, and performance of followers through a variety of mechanisms. These include connecting the follower's sense of identity and self to the mission and the collective identity of the organization; being a role model for followers that inspires them; challenging followers to take greater ownership for their work; and understanding the strengths and weaknesses of followers, so the leader can align followers with tasks that optimize their performance.[34]

Transformational leadership is more effective than transactional leadership, where the appeal is to more selfish concerns. An appeal to social values thus encourages people to collaborate rather than working as individuals. Transformational leadership is an ongoing process rather than the discrete exchanges of the transactional approach.

A transformational leader is one who is able to influence major change in the attitudes of subordinates and inspire and empower them to support and commit to the organizational mission.[35] Transformational leaders raise the bar by appealing to higher ideals and values of followers. In doing so, they may model the values themselves and use appealing methods to attract people to the values and to the leader.

In her study of leadership in the accounting profession, Copeland found that ethical leadership is essential in creating an ethical culture. According to Copeland: "Transformational leaders are able to influence followers to make personal sacrifices, commit to organizational objectives, and achieve higher outcomes organizationally than originally envisioned." She gives as an example a tax partner who may be able to encourage subordinates to work hard, sacrifice their personal time, challenge them intellectually and professionally, and lead their group to better outcomes when compared to a non-transformational leader. Her study supports the development of ethical leaders as ethical leadership enhances leadership effectiveness over and above the contribution of transformational leadership behaviors. She concludes that: "Organizations that want to develop the most effective leaders should train and develop their leaders to be both ethical and transformational."[36]

Followership/Servant Leadership

The flip side of leadership is followership. First introduced by Hollander and Webb, the term *followership* is characterized as an independent relationship in which the leader's perceived legitimacy can affect the degree to which followers allow themselves to be influenced.[37] This early work emphasizes the reciprocal relationship in which followers play an active role not only by receiving but also exerting influence.

Servant leadership advocates a perspective that leaders have a responsibility to serve their followers by helping them achieve and improve by modeling leaders' ethical values, attitudes, and behaviors that influence organizational outcomes through the fulfillment of followers' needs. The basic premise of servant leadership is leaders should put the needs of followers before their own needs. Servant leaders use collaboration and persuasion to influence followers rather than coercion and control. They understand their stewardship role and are accountable for their actions. Servant leadership helps to create an ethical, trusting organizational climate.

Trust is a key component in developing successful relationships between leaders and followers. A trusting relationship is built on shared values, respect, open communication, and accountability. Trevino et al.'s pillars of ethical leadership are the relevant behaviors that leaders can employ to demonstrate integrity to followers and build trust. The pillars are antecedents to trust and include role-modeling through visible action, the use of rewards and discipline, and communicating about ethics and values.[38]

Followership, servant leaders, and authenticity all share one common characteristic: *leader ethicality.* De Cremer and Tenbrunsel define leader ethicality as the intention to demonstrate normatively appropriate conduct and to create an environment within which others will be encouraged to act ethically and discouraged from acting unethically. Demonstrating normatively appropriate conduct is in part determined by follower perceptions; thus, leader intent is important. Moreover, this definition takes into consideration the importance of moral perspectives and underscores the notion that ethical behavior is to some extent defined by how it is construed within the context of social prescriptions.[39] In accounting, the social contract with the public is the context within which leaders model ethical behavior to nourish the perception that the accounting profession is an ethical profession with norms and values.

The social perception of a leader's legitimacy may play an important role in determining how the leader's morally relevant actions are interpreted and the influence leaders have on followers. The social context created by followers' normative expectations is a significant determinant of leader legitimacy, and violations of such expectations can cast doubt on the leader's position, authority, status, and influence. Imagine, for example, if a controller was pressured by the CFO, who paid no regard to the ethical standards of the profession but allowed personal goals to influence professional values. The followers would be less likely to embrace the actions of such a leader.

De Cremer and Tenbrunsel posit that, due to the socially construed nature of leader legitimacy, leaders are vulnerable to follower judgments. Leaders may gain legitimacy from followers when they allow themselves to receive follower influence and behave in accordance with followers' normative expectations.[40] It stands to reason that, if leadership is important to performance, followership must have something to do with it too. Organizational dissidence is best controlled when both parties strive for high ethics in their behavior and decision making.

Exhibit 7.6 summarizes the characteristics of good leaders.

EXHIBIT 7.6   Leadership Characteristics

Types of Leaders	Characteristics
Authentic	Moral awareness
	Ability to evaluate ethical issues
	Emphasis on the common good
	Promote values-based decision making
Transformational	Develop followers into leaders
	Enhance motivation, morale, and performance
	Influence attitudes of subordinates
	Improve and empower followers to support organizational mission
Followership/Leadership	Serve followers by modeling ethical values, attitudes, and servant behaviors
	Put the needs of followers ahead of their own
	Rely on collaboration and persuasion to influence followers
	Understand their stewardship role

Social Learning Theory

Social learning theory has been used to understand how leaders influence followers more generally. Social learning theory holds that individuals look to role models in the work context and model or imitate their behavior. Modeling is acknowledged to be one of the most powerful means for transmitting values, attitudes, and behaviors. Employees learn what to do, as well as what not to do, by observing their leaders' behavior and its consequences. Leaders become role models by virtue of their assigned role, their status and success in the organization, and their power to affect the behavior and outcomes of followers.[41] Through social learning, people may adopt ethical behaviors, as evidenced by the impact of ethical leadership[42] or antisocial behaviors.[43]

Leaders who engage in unethical behaviors create a context supporting what Kemper calls "parallel deviance," meaning that employees observe and are likely to imitate the inappropriate conduct.[44] If leaders are observed "cooking the books," or enriching themselves at the expense of others, as did Skilling, Ebbers, and Kozlowski, followers learn that such behavior is expected. If leaders are rewarded for unethical conduct, the lesson for followers becomes particularly strong, and we might expect them to emulate such behavior, especially if no consequences exist for wrongful actions.

The social learning approach suggests a mostly instrumental understanding of what drives unethical behavior in organizations. It argues that, because of leaders' authority role and the power to reward and punish, employees will pay attention to and mimic leaders' behavior, and they will do what is rewarded and avoid doing what is punished in the organization. The rewards and punishments need not be direct but also can be learned by observing how others in the organization are rewarded and disciplined.

A good example of antisocial behavior in what might be called a game of corporate survivor was at Enron where a policy nicknamed "rank and yank" had employees give one another annual ratings, with the bottom 15 percent being fired. Every year, all employees were rated from 1 (best) to 5 (worst). The more money you made for the company, the better your rating. Skilling was fond of saying that money was the only thing that motivated people. Skilling mandated that between 10 percent and 15 percent of the employees had to be rated as 5s. And to get a rating of 5 meant that you were fired.

Ethical Skills of Leaders in Accounting Firms

The results of the study by Krohmer and Noel of ethical skills of the Big Four CPA firms show strong similarities in ethical skills management among those firms. They have similar organizations, almost identical values, and similar required competencies or in-firm day-to-day management. Ethical skills are defined by auditors as the capacity to rigorously apply rules and procedures. It is first of all a matter of keeping a professional distance from the client, which restricts auditors from holding shares with the firm's clients, accepting gifts, or having personal or business relationships with clients that violate independence and mask the need for objective decision making. The Big Four have quality control systems to monitor compliance with the rules. Professional confidentiality is also a predominant aspect of auditors' ethical skills. Auditors must not divulge confidential client information unless exceptions apply. Auditors must not use such information for personal gain.[45]

The study shows ethics are primarily personal skills. Character traits, such as integrity, perseverance, humility, and the ability to be objective, were mentioned by the auditors as being necessary to conduct a quality audit. As some auditors mentioned, it is always possible to lie or pretend. What distinguishes auditors, therefore, are their values. One senior auditor talked of the following case: "For example, you find an error and it's a pain, because it's going to waste your time. It's your sense of ethics that makes you sort out the error anyway. And on every level you are confronted with this type of problem. For me, ethics means having a professional conscience. You have to act like a professional. You are there to represent your company. So your behavior could tarnish your employer's image. It's not only your reputation at stake, but the profession you represent." Krohmer and Noel concluded from their study that the perceived image auditors have of their employer and the respect they have for them come into play as a factor capable of reinforcing auditors' ethical behavior.[46]

Leadership Failures in the Accounting Profession

True leaders set an ethical tone at the top. There are times when the opposite occurs. The following discussion is taken from a PBS interview with Joseph Berardino, former worldwide CEO of Andersen, on May 1, 2002. Berardino was asked about the controversial decision to remove Carl Bass from oversight of the Enron audit. Bass was an Andersen partner at the Professional Standards Group—sometimes referred to as "The Keeper of the Holy Grail," an internal team of accounting experts that reviewed and passed judgment on tricky accounting issues facing local offices. Bass documented a conflict over how Enron should account for the sale of options owned by one of the partnerships managed by Andrew S. Fastow.

In the PBS interview, Berardino was asked about memos sent by Bass from 1999 to 2001 that said there was no substance to the partnerships that Enron was setting up off-books, Berardino claimed ignorance of the memos. When the PBS reporter probed further, perhaps out of disbelief, Berardino responded testily.

> Well, it didn't come to me. I've not read those memos. I've heard about them. There were disagreements. At the end of the day, what has happened is, if you look at the restatements that we agreed to on Enron, there were two restatements of some $500 million of earnings over a five-year period. In one instance, representing about 80 percent of that restatement. Frankly, we didn't have all the facts. Whether it was withheld from us purposefully or not, we didn't have all the facts. In the second instance—roughly 20 percent of the restatement—we did have the facts, and we made a bad judgment call. . . . At the end of October, when we reviewed the transaction, we realized our people had the information they needed to make a judgment call and they made the wrong call.

This is an astounding statement by the chairman of the once largest CPA firm in the world. Perhaps it is an extreme example of bad leadership; perhaps a one-time lapse in ethical judgment. We doubt it. Instead, it reflects ethical blindness toward what is the real mission of conducting an audit and who it serves. This statement is indicative of a culture that the most important goal was to keep the client happy at all costs. It was a failure of ethical leadership. Andersen violated the social contract with shareholders, investors, and the public at large.

Berardino established a culture at Andersen that can best be characterized as "see no evil, hear no evil, and speak no evil." One could hardly claim that he was an authentic leader who encouraged followers to follow the ethical path in auditing Enron. In fact, his inability or unwillingness to perceive the ethical issues in the Enron audit and their moral intensity opened the door to antisocial behaviors by audit personnel.

Ethical Leadership in the Accounting Profession

LO 7-7

Explain how ethical leadership in accounting might positively influence whether earnings management occurs.

At an organizational level, ethical leaders build trust through actions and relationships with others. They set the tone that the value system is more important than producing numbers. In an interview with *Fraud Magazine,* Sherron Watkins characterizes the leadership of Ken Lay at Enron as follows:

> Ken Lay was setting the wrong tone. He was in effect letting his managers know that once you get to the executive suite, the company's assets are there for you to move around to yourself or your family. In some perverse way, Andy Fastow . . . could justify his behavior, saying to himself, "Well, my creative off-balance-sheet deals are helping Enron meet its financial statement goals. Why can't I just take a million here and there for myself as a 'structuring fee,' just like Lay has been taking a little Enron money and transferring it to his sister for all these years?"[47]

Watkins followed up by saying the CEO "must have pristine ethics if there is to be any hope of ethical behavior from the employees." She also suggested that CEOs must have a zero tolerance policy for ethically challenged employees, otherwise the internal control system will eventually be worthless.[48]

Ethical Leadership and Audit Firms

The ethical environment within an accounting firm is created through espoused values and management practices. The culture of the firm results from leadership style and may be the most important deterrent to unethical behavior.[49] Authentic (partner) leaders gain the confidence of audit staff and managers and create a foundation for ethical decision making.

We can learn a great deal about ethical leadership and organizational culture in audit firms from research studies. Morris gathered data from 120 practicing senior auditors representing the Big Four firms, other international firms, large regional firms, and local firms. Participants were asked to indicate the frequency of selected dysfunctional behavior among audit seniors. Morris hypothesized that perceptions of authentic leadership are negatively related to the frequency of dysfunctional audit behaviors. The behaviors identified include under-reporting of time worked on an engagement, premature sign-off on audit procedures, and other dysfunctional behaviors.[50]

The results indicate that a typical audit senior at these firms more frequently under-reports time than prematurely signing off on audit work. The results also indicate there was a significant negative correlation between all measures of authentic leadership and dysfunctional audit behaviors with few exceptions. With respect to ethical culture, there was a negative relationship between the audit seniors' perceptions of their firms as ethical, and instances of dysfunctional audit behavior. The findings support the mediation of perceptions of authenticity in leaders on the auditors' perception of ethical firm culture and on auditors' instances of dysfunctional behavior. The results seem to indicate that ethical leaders have influence over the employee's perception of the ethical content of a firm's organizational culture.[51]

The takeaway from the Morris study is that authentic leaders can help to promote an ethical culture and reduce the instances of dysfunctional auditor behavior. Authentic leaders seek to eliminate ethical dissonance. As we discussed in **Chapter 2**, ethical (authentic) leaders commit to a high person-organization fit where organizational ethics are high and the culture promotes high individual ethics (High-High). Any other combination may jeopardize ethical decision making and sacrifice the public trust in the audit profession—at least in that instance.

Consider what might have happened at Andersen if Joseph Berardino were an authentic leader who placed ethical values ahead of non-ethical values. The culture within the firm would have been quite different. The message sent would have been that the red flags raised by Carl Bass about accounting for the off-balance-sheet partnerships had to be dealt with, not swept under the rug. Perhaps Berardino's biggest fault was in not balancing processing of information; instead, the negative aspects of what was happening at Enron were shoved in the background and hidden from view.

Studies have shown a disconnect exists between the perceptions of organizational ethics between higher and lower levels of an organization. Employees at higher levels perceive organizational ethics at a higher level.[52] In accounting, Bobek et al. found a disconnect exists between tax partners and nonpartner tax practitioners with respect to perceptions of organizational ethics when they described a self-identified ethical dilemma. On average, they found tax partners rated the ethical environments of their firms as stronger than nonpartner tax practitioners, especially with respect to firm leadership. While tax partners were more likely to describe an actual ethical dilemma than nontax practitioners, the group who described a dilemma rated the ethical environment as weaker, and this discrepancy was more pronounced for nontax practitioners.[53] This raises a question whether the ethical expectations of tax professionals are being met by their firms.

In a later study, Bobek et al. probed the reasons for the difference in perceptions of tax partners and nonpartner tax practitioners. They found that, when nonpartners believe they have a meaningful role in shaping and maintaining the ethical environment of their firms and/or have strong organizational fit with the firm, they are more likely to perceive the ethical environment as strong and perceive it similarly to firm leaders. They also found that, among firm leaders (i.e., tax partners), the sense of having a stronger public interest responsibility and a higher frequency of receiving mentoring are both associated with stronger perceptions of the ethical environment.[54]

Recall that in **Chapter 2**, and as we have discussed so far in this chapter, we discussed the relationship between organizational fit and ethical culture. It is not surprising that a strong (ethical) fit positively influences perceptions of an ethical culture. Beyond that, an important issue is what steps a firm can take to provide a meaningful role to nonpartners in shaping the ethical environment of their firm. Studies indicate that the weakest part of the ethical environment appears to be outcomes (e.g., rewards and sanctions) and "explicitly rewarding (and punishing) ethical (unethical) behavior is a tangible way to encourage nonleaders to participate in maintaining a strong ethical environment for the firm."[55]

Ethical Leadership and the Internal Audit Function

Internal auditors operate within the culture of an organization and their behavior is heavily influenced by whether ethical leadership exists. Some studies have looked at whether executive leadership can influence ethical behavior within the internal audit group. For example, when deciding whether to record a questionable journal entry (i.e., any entry for which a reasonable business case can be made for either recording it or not recording it), auditors may take their cue from executive management's behavior, especially if such behavior is the social norm and has been rewarded in the past.[56] In addition, a high-quality internal audit function can reinforce the tone at the top and provide guidance for decision makers by monitoring internal control and management's actions. For instance, accountants may hesitate to record a questionable entry if they know that internal audit is likely to detect inappropriate financial reporting practices.

In another study, Arel et al. studied the impact of ethical leadership, the internal audit function, and moral intensity on a decision to record a questionable entry. The authors found that the joint influence of ethical leadership and internal audit quality on accountants' willingness to book a questionable accrual entry is fully mediated by participants' perception of the moral intensity of the issue. Specifically, a strong internal audit function and weak ethical leadership combined to alter accountants' perception of the moral intensity of the issue. As a result, accounting professionals who perceive greater moral intensity associated with the controller's request to record a questionable entry are less willing to book the questionable entry.[57] We can also conclude that a lesser moral intensity might lead to recording questionable entries and managing earnings.

The Arel study also found that a strong internal audit function may cause accountants to question the appropriateness and ethicalness of an undocumented journal entry when combined with weak ethical leadership. Conversely, a weak internal audit function removes the most important internal control to help prevent and detect financial statement fraud. A case in point is at HealthSouth. Maron Webster, a former internal auditor at HealthSouth, testified that CEO Richard Scrushy had fired him in 1989 after he questioned accounting at a company operation in Miami. Webster said he raised concerns about improperly booked receivables and was told by Scrushy that "we're under certain pressures to make certain numbers. We have an obligation to stockholders and shareholders."[58]

Former chief internal auditor Teresa Rubio Sanders, who was hired by Scrushy in 1990 and quit in late 1999, testified that her office wasn't allowed to see the general ledger, where previous testimony showed a $2.7 billion earnings over-statement occurred from 1996 through 2002. Under questioning from defense lawyer Jim Parkman, Sanders testified she never complained to HealthSouth directors about the lack of access to corporate records. She also said she rarely met with directors or the audit committee.[59] Her lack of concern for the welfare of the company or its shareholders speaks volumes about the importance of ethical leadership to the internal audit function. Internal auditors, like Sanders, who bury their head in the sand while fraud occurs not only fail in their ethical leadership role but make it more difficult for the external auditors to uncover what is still hidden under the surface.

Ethical leadership positively influences ethical decision making and can keep earnings management in check. Prawitt et al. discovered from their study of earnings management that a quality internal audit function is associated with moderation in the level of earnings management using abnormal accruals and the propensity to meet or beat analysts' earnings forecasts as proxies.[60]

The Prawitt study examined leaders at large regional CPA firms to determine the impact of an accounting firm on ethical leadership behaviors. They found that ethical leadership behaviors contribute to the effectiveness of leaders and the ethical conduct of subordinates. Their study also suggests that transformational leaders are able to influence followers to make personal sacrifices, commit to organizational objectives, and achieve higher outcomes organizationally. They also found that developing ethical leadership skills in ethical leaders also makes a significant contribution to explaining leadership effectiveness over and above the contribution of transformational leadership behaviors.[61]

Culture and Ethical Leadership in Accounting

Accountants and auditors are less likely to report financial wrongdoing if they perceive that past attempts by others in the organization to blow the whistle internally lead to retaliation against the reporter. According to Mesmer-Magnus and Viswesvaran, organizational employees have three options to address an unsatisfactory situation faced within an organization: (1) exit the organization; (2) voice discontent (i.e., blow the whistle); or (3) remain silent.[62] Employees with greater organizational commitment may prefer voicing discontent to exiting. Near and Miceli suggest that internal reporters will demonstrate high levels of firm loyalty in their initial decision to report.[63] However, absent ethical leadership and support for the reporter, it's less likely voicing discontent will occur.

Sims and Keenan studied organizational and interpersonal values as predictors of external whistleblowing. They found employees were more likely to engage in external whistleblowing if they had the support of their supervisor or they perceived that company policies suggested that such behavior was acceptable. The study also reported that external whistleblowing channels would be used only if would-be whistleblowers believed internal whistleblowing would be ineffective. The desire to use internal channels to report wrongdoing puts the ball in the court of companies to develop ethical systems to facilitate such reporting.[64] Ethical dissonance can be avoided by cultivating high organizational ethics and high individual ethics. Ethical leaders play a critical role in setting the tone for whistleblowers that reports of alleged improper financial reporting will be taken seriously and reporters will not be retaliated against for reporting the wrongdoing.

It is worth reflecting back to our discussion in **Chapter 3** of whistleblower reporting mechanisms as shown in **Exhibit 3.13**. Having an ethics hotline was an important internal control in making sure questionable accounting that may reflect improper earnings management gets reported to one's direct supervisor and that reports can be made without retaliation. This is not likely to occur unless ethical leadership exists and, if leaders skirt the ethical issues, then the consequences of earnings management can be severe including violating SEC regulations.

Brennan and Kelly studied some of the factors that influence propensity or willingness to blow the whistle among trainee auditors. The factors studied included audit firm organizational structures, personal characteristics of whistle-blowers, and situational variables. The authors found that formal structures for whistleblowing and internal (versus external) reporting channels increase the likelihood of the subjects' reporting of an ethical violation by an audit partner. Their findings indicate that audit firms should examine their structures for reporting suspected or actual wrongdoing and, where necessary, improve such structures by encouraging staff to voice their concerns internally. A key issue is whether the firms have in place a system of quality controls to report internally. This is important because the respondents showed a reluctance to report externally. Brennan and Kelly's results have potentially significant implications for whether auditors use external reporting mechanisms, such as those of Dodd-Frank, if internal reporting has not resolved the differences between the auditor and firm management.[65]

Whistleblowing can be perceived as an effective response to an organization's failure to establish accountability mechanisms internally no doubt due in large part by the failure of ethical leadership. For auditors, the act of whistleblowing is internally required when differences exist on accounting issues with management because of their compliance obligations. External auditors have a similar obligation and additional reporting requirements to the SEC under Section 10(A) of the Securities Exchange Act of 1934.

Ethical leadership is a critical component in providing a supportive environment for whistleblowers to come forward. When leaders model ethical behavior, whistleblowers feel more confident in reporting wrongdoing. However, when leaders discourage whistleblowing, the opposite effect occurs. A good example is that of Aaron Beam, a former CFO at HealthSouth, that was first discussed in **Chapter 2**.

The $2.8 billion HealthSouth fraud involved recording fake revenues on the company's books from 1996 through 2012 and correspondingly adjusting the balance sheets and paper trails. Methods included overestimating insurance reimbursements, manipulating fixed-asset accounts, improperly booking capital expenses, and overbooking reserve accounts.

Beam allowed the CEO, Richard Scrushy, to bully him into manipulating financial reports to reflect the numbers Scrushy promised investors. During a meeting in 1996, Beam told Scrushy they would have to finally report a bad quarter. Scrushy said no, and they devised a way to hide the earnings shortfall. An ethical leader would have argued against such actions pointing out that the manipulation of earnings harms the public interest. An ethical leader would have found a way to voice their values and at least attempt to influence Scrushy's actions. Beam failed in both regards. "I should have had the courage to stand up and say, 'No, we can't cross this line,'" Beam said. Scrushy promised to deny everything if Beam reported the fraud and accused Beam of not being a team player.[66]

According to the testimony of former CFOs Beam, Smith, Michael D. Martin, William T. Owens, and Malcolm McVay, each one realized the error of his ways, but most felt helpless to blow the whistle or even leave the company. Scrushy "managed greatly by fear and intimidation," according to Owens, who served as HealthSouth's third CFO from 2000 to 2001. Second CFO Martin testified that he tried to quit at least three times during his 1997 to 2000 tenure. "[Scrushy] said, 'Martin, you can't quit. You'll be the fall guy.'"

The following points highlight when auditors are more likely to report wrongdoing: (1) superiors and top management do not place obstacles in their way; (2) the reporter has a high commitment to the organization and/or colleagues; (3) the issue has high moral intensity; (4) ethical dissonance is not present; and (5) the reporter perceives the organization provides reliable outlets (i.e., hotline) to report wrongdoing and retaliation will not occur.

As we end the discussion of ethical leadership in the accounting profession, let's not forget that there are those in the accounting profession who still reported financial wrongdoing even though the company created obstacles. The examples of Cynthia Cooper at WorldCom and Tony Menendez at Halliburton come to mind. They were willing to put everything on the line to correct the financial misstatements even in the face of pressure from superiors to stay silent. They stand as heroes in the accounting profession and embody the leadership qualities students should aspire to develop.

Concluding Thoughts

Financial Statement Restatements occur because some companies push the envelope with respect to reporting earnings. As we learned in **Chapter 6**, aggressive accounting techniques (i.e., financial shenanigans) have been used to manage earnings and make the company look better from quarter to quarter and year to year. In some cases, it was discovered later that these techniques were inappropriate and may even have been fraudulent. The result can be to revise or reissue financial statements and inform investors and creditors that the clean audit opinion has been revised.

Earnings management occurs in large part because of failures in corporate governance and ethical leadership. The accounting profession needs to pay more attention to how ethical leaders can be developed and the characteristic traits of behavior that should be ingrained in ethical leaders.

In order to avoid SEC lawsuits for improper financial reporting, companies must tighten their corporate governance system and build ethical leaders. Ethical leaders can set the tone for subordinates who then become followers in the organization. To build ethical leaders, the organization must commit to doing the right thing at every turn.

As the Copeland study shows, ethical and transformational leadership behaviors make independent and significant contributions to explaining leader effectiveness in accounting. It all comes down to ethical behavior and setting an ethical tone at the top to build an ethical culture and do the kinds of things that will help the company to avoid SEC investigations and legal liability, the topic of **Chapter 8**.

Discussion Questions

<u>Financial Statement Restatements</u>

1. What are financial statement restatements?
2. When should financial statements be restated?
3. Assume the auditor has determined that prior financial statements need to be restated. What disclosures and other information should be communicated to shareholders, investors, and creditors about this matter?
4. Distinguish between big R and little r restatements. What is required of management and the external auditors when such events occur?
5. Explain how errors in accounting and reporting can trigger restatements.
6. Explain how restatements due to operational issues can trigger restatements.
7. Explain how the quality of corporate governance, risk management, and compliance systems are critical in controlling financial restatement risk within organizations.
8. Rule 10b-5 is a regulation created under the Securities and Exchange Act of 1934 that targets securities fraud. Explain how the provision is applied in determining whether fraud has occurred including when earnings management is the underlying motivation for the fraud.
9. Safety-Kleen issued a major financial restatement in 2001. The next year, the company restated (reduced) previously reported net income by $534 million for the period 1997–1999. PwC withdrew its financial statement audit reports for those years. Do you believe that financial restatements and withdrawing an audit report are *prima facie* (acceptable) indicators that a failed audit has occurred? Explain.
10. When financial results aren't what they seemed to be—and a company is forced to issue material financial restatements—should it be required to develop policies to clawback incentive pay and bonuses that were awarded to senior managers on the basis of rosier outcomes? Use ethical reasoning to support your point of view.

<u>Ethical Leadership</u>

11. Distinguish between authentic leadership, transformational leadership, and servant leadership. Are all necessary to change individuals and social systems within an organization?
12. Identify three reasons why there may be ethical leadership failures and explain why failed leadership occurs.

13. In well-governed companies, a sense of accountability and ethical leadership create a culture that places organizational ethics above all else. What role does organizational culture play in preventing financial shenanigans from being used to manage earnings?

14. Values-driven leadership as envisioned in the Giving Voice to Values technique poses the following question: Once I know what is right, how do I get it done and get it done effectively? Discuss how an authentic leader would go about addressing this question.

15. Why do you think studies show that no single factor has a bigger impact on the ethicality of a firm's culture than the personal examples set by firm leaders?

16. Describe the role of professional judgment in ethical leadership as it pertains to accountants and auditors and the link to their moral role in society.

17. How might an accounting firm influence whether nontax practitioners view a contentious issue with a client as having been handled ethically?

18. Explain how the circumstances under each of the following might reflect failed leadership by auditors and the audit firm:

   - Under-reporting of time on an engagement
   - Premature sign-off on audit procedures
   - Accepting weak client explanations for accounting

19. Assume you are asked in an interview: Give me one word that describes you best? Then, explain why it is important in effective leadership. What would you say?

20. It has been said that "Businesses don't fail—Leaders do." Explain what this means.

Comprehensive Questions

1. How does organizational dissonance influence ethical leadership and decision making?

2. Auditors are supposed to "sniff out" fraud. How can being an effective leader help in this regard?

3. Bruns and Merchant found that managers did not agree on the types of earnings management activities that are acceptable. Refer to the definitions of earnings management in **Chapter 6**. Explain how leadership traits influence how managers might perceive the acceptability of earnings management.

4. According to Linda Thornton, ethical leadership failures can be caused by different types of problems that may worsen. Some of these problems are caused by individuals and others may be embedded in the organizational culture. Discuss the individual and organizational factors that can lead to ethical failures.

5. How does the nature of the internal audit function, strength of ethical leadership, and level of moral intensity influence whether an auditor will record questionable and undocumented journal entries?

Endnotes

1. Michael D. Akers, Don E. Giacomino, and Jodi L. Bellovary, "Earnings Management and Its Implications: Educating the Accounting Profession, *The CPA Journal* (August 2007), http://atchives.cpajournal.com/2007/807/essentials/p64.htm.

2. *2019 Financial Restatements: A Nineteen Year Comparison* (July 2020), https://www.auditanalytics.com/audit-analytics-reports?categories%5B%5D-Financial%20Restatements.

3. Audit Analytics, *2019 Financial Restatements Review* (July 28, 2020), http://blog.auditanalytics.com/2019-financial-restatements-review/.

4. Fatima Alali and Sophia I-Ling Wang, "Characteristics of Financial Restatements and Frauds: An Analysis of Corporate Reporting Quality from 2004–2014," *The CPA Journal* (November 2017), https://www.cpajournal.com/2017/11/20/characteristics-financial-restatements-frauds/.

5. Alali and I-Ling Wang.

6. Alali and I-Ling Wang.

7. Audit Analytics, Derryck Coleman, The Rise of Out of Period Adjustments, September 16, 2014, https://blog. audit analytics.com/the-rise-of-out-of-period-adjustments/.

8. Audit Analytics.

9. PR Newswire, *"Hertz Completes Financial Restatement; Provides 2015 Business Outlook"* (July 16, 2015), http:// www.stockhouse.com/news/press-releases/205/07/16/hertz-completes-financial-restatement-provides-2015-business-outlook.

10. Lynn E. Turner and Thomas R. Weirich, "A Closer Look at Financial Statement Restatements: Analyzing the Reasons Behind the Trend," *The CPA Journal* (December 2006), pp. 33–39.

11. https://www.businesswire.com/news/home/201402100006450/en/Cubic-Corporation-Restate-Financial-Statements.

12. Cubic Corp, *"Cubic Corporation to Restate Financial Statements,"* Company Press Release (August 1, 2012), https://www.cubic.com/hews-events/news/cubic-corporation-restate-financial-statements.

13. CFO, Kraft Heinz to Restate Results for Nearly 3 Years, May 6, 2019, CFO, Kraft Heinz to Restate Results for Nearly 3 Years, May 6, 2019, https://www.cfo.com/financial-reporting-2/2029/05/kraft-heinz-to-restate-results-for-nearly-3-years/.

14. United States District Court Northern District of California, *Keith Thomas and Richard Hayes v. MagnaChip Semiconductor Corp., et al.* (October 1, 2014), http://securities.stanford.edu/filings-documents/1051/MSC00_01/2014101_r01c_a4CV01160.pdf.

15. Rachel Thompson, *Do Firms Conceal Material Misstatements by Reporting Revisions Rather than Restatements?* (October 15, 2019), https://clsbluesky.law.columbia.edu/2019/10/15/do-firms-conceal-material-misstatements-by-reporting-revisions-rather-than-restatements/.

16. Cydney Poser, SEC Enforces a Clawback for Accounting Violations, February 4, 2001, https://cooleypubco.com/2021/02/04/sec-enforces-clawback/.

17. SEC Enforces a Clawback for Accounting Violations, https://cooleypubco.com/2021/02/04/sec-enforces-clawback/.

18. Investors Overreact to Restatements in the Short Term, February 6, 2019, https://www.cfo.com/accounting-accounting-tax-2019/02investors-overreact-to-restatements-in-the-short-term/.

19. Chi Keung Man, "Corporate Governance and Earnings Management: A Survey of Literature," *Journal of Applied Business Research* 29, no. 2 (February 2013), pp. 391–418.

20. Chi Keung Man.

21. The Workplace Coach, The Importance of Ethical Leadership, March 6, 2013, https://bit.ly/3rsFB7P.

22. Max H. Bazerman, A New Model for Ethical Leadership, https://hbr.org/2020/09/a-new-model-for-ethical-leadership.

23. Gary Yukl, *Leadership in Organizations,* 8th ed. (London, England: Pearson Education, 2012).

24. Mary Kay Copeland, "The Importance of Ethics and Ethical leadership in the Accounting Profession," *Research in Professional Responsibility and Ethics in Accounting* 19 (2015), pp. 61–98.

25. Joanne Ciulla, "The State of Leadership Ethics and the Work that Lies Before Us," *Business Ethics: A European Review* 14, no. 4 (2005), pp. 323–335.

26. ECI, Executive Summary: Ethical Leadership Around the World, https://higherlogicdownload.s3.amazonaws.com/THEECOA/11f760b1-56e0-43c6-85da-03df2ce2b5ac/UploadedImages/research/EthicalLeadership-ExecutiveSummary.pdf.

27. Michael Brown, Linda Klebe Trevino, and David A. Harrison, "Ethical Leadership: A Social Learning Perspective for Construct Development and Testing," *Organizational Behavior and Human Decision Processes* 97, no. 2 (July 2005), pp. 117–134.

28. Alan Lawton and Iliana Paez, "Developing a Framework for Ethical Leadership," *Journal of Business Ethics* 130 (2015), pp. 639–649.

29. Patrick Kelly, "Developing Ethical Leader for the Accounting Profession," *The CPA Journal* (March 2017), https://www.cpajournal.com/2017/03/20/developing-ethical-leaders-accounting-profession/.

30. Mary Kay Copeland, "The Importance of Ethics and Ethical leadership in the Accounting Profession," *Research in Professional Responsibility and Ethics in Accounting* 19 (2015), pp. 61–98.

31. Linda Fisher Thornton, *7 Lenses: Learning the Principles and Practices of Ethical Leadership*, (Richmond, VA: Leading in Context LLC, 2013).

32. Patrick T. Kelly and Christine E. Earley, "Ethical Leaders in Accounting," in Anthony H. Catanach Jr. and Dorothy Feldmann (eds.), *Advances in Accounting Education: Teaching and Curriculum Innovations, Vol. 12* (Bingley, U.K.: Emerald, 2011), pp. 53–76.

33. Bruce J. Avolio and William L. Gardner, "Authentic Leadership Development: Getting to the Root of Positive Forms of Leadership," *The Leadership Quarterly* 16 (2005), pp. 315–338.

34. James MacGregor Burns, *Leadership* (New York, NY: Harper & Row, 1978).

35. Gary Yukl, *Leadership in Organizations*, 8th ed. (London, England: Pearson Education, 2012).

36. Copeland, p. 90.

37. Edwin P. Hollander and Wilse B. Webb, "Leadership, Followership, and Friendship," *The Journal of Abnormal and Social Psychology* 50, no. 2 (1955), pp. 163–167.

38. Linda Klebe Trevino, Laura Pincus Hartman, and Michael Brown, "Moral Person and Moral Manager: How Executives Develop a Reputation for Ethical Leadership," *California Management Review*, Vol. 42, Issue 4 (Summer 2000), pp. 128-142.

39. David De Cremer and Ann E. Tenbrunsel, *Behavioral Business Ethics* (New York, NY: Taylor & Francis Group LLC, 2012).

40. De Cremer and Tenbrunsel, pp. 84–88.

41. Trevino et al.

42. Michael Brown, Linda Klebe Trevino, and David A. Harrison, "Ethical Leadership: A Social Learning Perspective for Construct Development and Testing," *Organizational Behavior and Human Decision Processes* 97, no. 2 (July 2005), pp. 117–134.

43. Sandra L. Robinson and Anne M. O'Leary-Kelly, "Monkey See, Monkey Do: The Influence of Work Groups on the Antisocial Behavior of Employees," *The Academy of Management Journal* 41, no. 6 (December 1998), pp. 658–672.

44. Theodore D. Kemper, "Representative Roles and the Legitimization of Deviance," *Social Problems* 13 (1966), pp. 288–298.

45. Cathy Krohmer and Christine Noel, Responsible Leadership for Audit Quality: How Do the Big Four Manage the personal Ethics of Their Employees, https://allsh.univ-amu-fr-sites/allsh.univ-amu.fr/files/responsible_leadership_for_corporate_responsibility.pdf.

46. Cathy Krohmer and Christine Noel.

47. Dick Carozza, "Interview with Sherron Watkins: Constant Warning," *Fraud Magazine* (January/February 2007), Available at: http://www.fraud-magazine.com/article.aspx?id=583.

48. Carozza.

49. Patricia Casey Douglas, Ronald A. Davidson, and Bill N. Schwartz, "The Effect of Organizational Culture and Ethical Orientation on Accountants' Ethical Judgments," *Journal of Business Ethics* 34 (2001), pp. 101–121.

50. Jan Taylor Morris, "The Impact of Authentic Leadership and Ethical Firm Culture on Auditor Behavior," *Journal of Behavioral Studies in Business* 7 (September 2014), pp. 1–32.

51. Morris.

52. See, for example, Linda Klebe Trevino, Gary R. Weaver, and Michael E. Brown, "It's Lovely at the Top: Hierarchical Levels, Identities, and Perceptions of Organizational Ethics," *Business Ethics Quarterly* 18, no. 2 (2008), pp. 233-252; and Jill M. D'Aquila, "Financial Accountants' Perceptions of Management's Ethical Standards," *Journal of Business Ethics* 31, no. 3 (June 2001), pp. 233-244.

53. Donna D. Bobek, Amy M. Hageman, and Robin R. Radtke, "The Ethical Environment of Tax Professionals: Partner and Non-Partner Perceptions and Experiences," *Journal of Business Ethics* 92 (2010), pp. 637–654.

54. Donna D. Bobek, Amy M. Hageman, and Robin R. Radtke, "The Influence of Roles and Organizational Fit on Accounting Professionals' Perceptions of Their Firms' Ethical Environment," *Journal of Business Ethics* 126 (2015b), pp. 125–141.

55. Donna D. Bobek and Robin R. Radtke, "An Experiential Investigation of the Ethical Environment of Tax Professionals," *Journal of American Tax Association* 29, no. 2 (2007), pp. 63–84.

56. David M. Mayer, Maribeth Kuenzi, Rebcca Greenbaum, Mary Bardes, and Rommel (Bombie) Salvador, "How Does Ethical Leadership Flow? Test of a Trickle-Down Model," *Organizational Behavior and Human Decision Processes* 108 (2009), pp. 1–13.

57. Barbara Arel, Cathy A. Beaudoin, and Anna M. Cianci, "The Impact of Ethical Leadership and Internal Audit Function, and Moral Intensity on a Financial Reporting Decision," *Journal of Business Ethics* 109, no. 3 (2012), pp. 351–366.

58. *The New York Times,* "Fifth Chief Financial Officer at HealthSouth to Admit Fraud," April 25, 2003, Available at: http://www.nytimes.com/2003/04/25/business/fifth-chief-financial-officer-at-healthsouth-to-admit-fraud.html.

59. *SEC v. HealthSouth Corporation and Richard Scrushy, Defendants,* United States District Court for the Southern Division of Alabama, 261 F. Supp. 2d 1298 (May 7, 2003), Available at: http://law.justia.com/cases/federal/district-courts/FSupp2/261/1298/2515723/.

60. Douglas F. Prawitt, Jason L. Smith, and David A. Wood, "Internal Audit Quality and Earnings Management, *The Accounting Review* 84, no. 4 (2009), pp. 1255–1280.

61. Prawitt et al., p. 90.

62. Jessica R. Mesmer-Magnus and Chockalingam Viswesvaran, "Whistleblowing in Organizations: An Examination of Correlates of Whistleblowing Intentions, Actions, and Retaliation," *Journal of Business Ethics* 62, no. 3 (2005), pp. 277–297.

63. Janet P. Near and Marcia P. Miceli, "Organizational Dissidence: The Case of Whistle-blowing," *Journal of Business Ethics,* Vol. 4, No. 1 (1985), pp. 1–16.

64. Randi L. Sims and John P. Keenan, "Predictors of External Whistleblowing: Organizational and Intrapersonal Variables," *Journal of Business Ethics* 17 (1998), pp. 411–421.

65. N. Brennan and J. Kelley, "A Study of Whistleblowing among Trainee Auditors," *The British Accounting Review* 39 (2007), pp. 61–87.

66. Alix Stuart, "Keeping Secrets: How Five CEOs Cooked the Books at HealthSouth," *CFO Magazine* (June 1, 2005), http://ww2.cfo.com/human-capital-careers/2005/06/keeping-secrets/.

Chapter 7 Cases

Case 7-1 Should the Financial Statements be Reissued or Revised?

You just became the new external auditor of a large public company that carries freight throughout the world. You just began to audit the 2021 financial statements and have come across a transaction that occurred in 2020 that would materially change the reported results for calendar years 2020 and 2021. The transaction in question is the reporting of the cost of a new, expensive truck as an expense for the year rather than as a capitalized asset to be depreciated over the useful life of the truck. It seems the company had a high earnings level in 2020 and thought that year could better absorb the full cost of the new truck as an expense rather than a capitalized amount with future depreciation charges that would affect 10 years of earnings. There was no question that the treatment caused the 2020 and 2021 financial statements to be materially misstated.

Upon further examination, you notice that the company had not revised or restated the financial statements for 2020, and its financial statements for 2021 continue to show the effects of the error. You are trying to determine whether the financial statements for 2020 previously issued should be restated or reissued in advance of a meeting with the company's chief financial officer and what the effects might be on the 2021 statements.

Questions

1. Describe the circumstances under which financial statements should be revised and reissued as opposed to restated. What would be the consequences of such restatements? Which treatment would you recommend to the CFO given that the misstated amount is material and why?
2. What are some of the possible consequences for the company of the error and resulting material misstatements of the financial statements?
3. Under what circumstances might the SEC seek to clawback executive compensation?

Case 7-2 PPP Loans: Free Money at a Cost (a GVV case)

Meredith Merriweather, CPA is the CFO of Trego Bikes and Trikes (TBT), a manufacturer of Bicycles ranging from tricycles to high-end racing bikes. The company has good market penetration and has seen a very stable demand for its bikes over the last few years. TBT sells its products to retailers across the United States, who in turn sell the bikes to the end user.

In late January of 2020, TBT's management team started to worry about the potential impact that COVID-19 would have on the business. While there had not been any decrease in orders of their bikes as of yet, they were still concerned and met weekly to discuss the latest news surrounding the impact that the pandemic was having on other businesses. Like other businesses, they modified their operations to include social distancing of their employees and required all employees to use masks while at work. As a result, they expected to be able to maintain the normal production schedule for their products.

In March of 2020, the U.S. Congress passed the Coronavirus Aid, Relief and Economic Security (CARES) Act. That act included the creation of a $669 billion business loan program implemented by the Small Business Administration (SBA). The Paycheck Protection Program (PPP) was created to help small businesses that were struggling due to the pandemic. The PPP program allowed entities to apply for low-interest private loans to pay for their payroll, payroll-related costs, interest, rent, and utilities. Each qualifying business could apply for a loan equal to 2.5 times their average monthly payroll costs. By keeping the number of employees and payroll dollars stable over the period the loan proceeds were used, the loan would be forgiven.

The CEO of TBT asked Meredith to research the PPP program and see if the company would qualify for a loan. Meredith thought this was a great idea thinking, a forgivable loan, who would have ever thought that possible. How great! She called her banker, got the application, and gathered all the required data together. Based on her calculation, Meredith determined that TBT would qualify for a $1.8 million loan. The only caveat to obtaining the loan was a requirement for the borrower to certify that "current economic uncertainty makes this loan request necessary to support the ongoing operations of the applicant."[1] At that point in the year TBT sales were still strong, but all the members of the management team were very concerned that they would subsequently drop off and other debt would be hard to come by. There was a huge amount of uncertainty surrounding how the pandemic would affect them. No other guidance was provided by the SBA as to what current "economic uncertainty" actually meant. The banker told Meredith that TBT qualified from the banks read of the SBA's loan guidance.

Meredith relayed the good news to the CEO along with the information on the certification requirement. The CEO authorized her to apply for the loan right away as the media was reporting that available PPP funds were likely to run out quickly. TBT's application was processed by the bank quickly and the loan was funded on April 20th of 2020.

On April 23, 2020, the SBA issued additional guidance surrounding the certification of loan need. This guidance indicated that companies making this certification needed to take into account both their current business activity and liquidity. This new guidance was not very informative and upon the review of both TBT's management team and that of their bank, neither entity was concerned that it somehow would make TBT ineligible for the loan. The SBA subsequently stated that they would be auditing all loans in excess of $2 million partially to ensure the economic need of the loan. While not specifically stated, any loan made in an amount less than $2 million would be assumed to have met the economic need threshold.

TBT made sure to keep track of how the funds were spent and made sure to spend those specific funds for TBT payroll, payroll-related costs, interest, rent, and utilities as required by the provisions of the PPP loan. The SBA started accepting loan forgiveness applications in August. By that time, TBT was projecting that 2020 might end up being their best year ever. Demand for their products started to swell in May and continued to increase every month since. TBT ended up needing to hire more personnel to try and keep up with demand. Moreover, sale of bikes continued to increase in 2020 as many folks had lost their job and had free time to ride and exercising outdoors was one of the activities permitted during the shutdowns due to the spread of the coronavirus.

Meredith was uncertain about what to do. By all accounts TBT had met the PPP loan requirements and she firmly believed that they also qualified for loan forgiveness under the terms of the program. However, she felt a little guilty about asking to have the loan forgiven, as in hindsight TBT had not really needed the loan. She wasn't sure that asking for loan forgiveness was the right thing to do.

Meredith spoke to the banker about her concerns, and the banker stated that the loan did not require any testing of any sort, or proof that the company's concerns over economic uncertainty at the time the loan was funded actually resulted in a negative economic event. The banker assured her that TBT could apply for loan forgiveness and that the SBA would approve it. The forgiveness application focuses solely on how PPP funds are spent (verifying they were spent on qualifying expenses). It does not ask anything regarding the need for the loan.

Questions

1. As the CFO of TBT, Meredith was aware of her leadership obligations and the opportunity to positively influence the accounting function starting with the controller through the entry-level accounting staff. What would she do to be a transformational leader in that regard?

2. Assume Meredith decides to ask for a meeting with the CEO to discuss the matter of applying for loan forgiveness. Before doing so, she sits down and reflects on the values that should guide her actions. Discuss how Meredith might go about influencing the actions of TBT.

3. Describe the reasons and rationalizations Meredith is likely to hear from the CEO to apply for loan forgiveness and how Meredith might respond to them.

4. What levers can Meredith use to counteract the opposing viewpoint of the CEO?

Case 7-3 Managing Earnings and Putting Ethical Leadership to the Test

Jeremy Strong, CPA was recently hired as the new CFO of Imageware Consolidated (IC), a small publicly owned company. This is Jeremy's first job outside of public accounting, leaving Deloitte after 10 years, where he rose in the ranks to senior audit and assurance manager. IC is a rapidly growing and trend setting company in the sportswear industry. They are being compared to an early-stage Nike or Under Armour and Jeremy is excited by the prospect of working for a company that appears to have tremendous growth potential.

During Jeremy's recruitment, he was told by the CEO, that the old CFO was forced to retire for health reasons. The CEO stated that IC really needed someone who would hit the ground running. Specifically, the CEO said that IC needed someone to step into this role who had a firm grasp of SEC reporting requirements and was comfortable speaking with all the various stakeholder groups including industry analysts who were following the company closely.

One of Jeremy's first tasks was to prepare for an earnings-call where he would be introduced as the new CFO. He had just one week to prepare for that call. Jeremy spent that first week in meetings with IC's Controller, Samantha (Sam) Bee, CPA, and other executives who provided him with reams and reams of financial and operational data to help bring him up to speed and prepare him for the call.

In one discussion with Sam, Jeremy was told that the company has been able to meet or exceed the analysts' consensus EPS estimates every quarter since going public two and a half years ago. She explained that the company relies heavily on a continuous flow of financial data (actual and forecasted) from the financial reporting group that she oversees. Sam explained that their expertise in forecasting provides the company with an early warning system of sorts that has enabled the sales and marketing department to make very sound operational decisions quarter after quarter, resulting in their ability to meet or beat analysts expectations. The hairs on the back of Jeremy's neck rose a little as he listened to what Sam was telling him.

In response, Jeremy asked Sam to explain what she meant by operational decisions. Sam stated that while there has been a steady increase in demand for their products year over year, there are seasonal swings and other trends that can impact monthly and quarterly sales demand in the sportswear industry. She explained that the sales and marketing department have the authority to use a variety of techniques to entice IC's customers to purchase their products (earlier then they would have otherwise) including things like rebates, discounts, free products, and even extended payment terms.

Jeremy then asked Sam whether these practices had been disclosed publicly. Without realizing it he held his breath as we waited for her response.

Questions

1. Explain how the sales and marketing incentives used by IC represent earnings management. In your response explain why Jeremy asked about disclosure of these practices.
2. The case states that the hair on the back of Jeremy's neck rose during a discussion with IC's Controller when he learned about the first of several red flags outlined in the case. Identify and discuss at least three actual and two potential red flags at IC.
3. What additional questions should Jeremy ask to help him assess the ethical culture within the organization?

Case 7-4 Monsanto Company Roundup

Overview of the Case

Monsanto is an agricultural seed and chemical company that manufactures and sells glyphosate, an herbicide, under the trade name "Roundup." Roundup historically was one of Monsanto's most profitable products, and the company sells it to both retailers and distributors. After the patent expired in 2000, competition from generic products began to erode Monsanto's profit margins. By fiscal year 2009, generic competitors were undercutting Monsanto's prices in the United States and Canada by more than 70 percent. Monsanto was losing share in these markets as customers—concerned they could not profitably sell high-priced Roundup—shifted their purchases to generic brands. By the end of fiscal 2009, Monsanto had lost more than half of its share of the glyphosate market (dropping from 55% market share to less than 25%).

During fiscal years ended August 31 of 2009, 2010, and 2011, Monsanto improperly accounted for millions of dollars of rebates offered to Roundup distributors and retailers in the United States and Canada to incentivize them to purchase Roundup. Monsanto also improperly accounted for rebate payments to Roundup customers in Canada, France, and Germany as selling, general, and administrative expenses ("SG&A") rather than rebates, which boosted Roundup gross profit in those countries. Monsanto did not have sufficient internal accounting controls to identify and properly account for rebate payments promised to customers.

As a result, Monsanto materially misstated its consolidated earnings and its revenues and earnings for its Roundup business lines in its periodic reports filed with the SEC for fiscal years 2009, 2010, and 2011. As a result of the improper accounting, Monsanto met consensus earnings-per-share analyst estimates for fiscal year 2009.

On November 14, 2011, Monsanto restated its 2009 and 2010 annual reports on Form 10-K and its 2011 quarterly reports on Form 10-Q (collectively "the Restatement").

As a result of the action of Monsanto and top managers, the company violated reporting provisions of Securities and Exchange Acts, the books and records provisions, and the internal accounting control provisions of Exchange Act Section 13(b)(2)(B).

Monsanto agreed to pay an $80 million penalty and retain an independent consultant to settle charges that it violated accounting rules and misstated company earnings as it pertained to its flagship product Roundup. Three accounting and sales executives also agreed to pay penalties to settle charges against them.

Cast of Characters

Sara M. Brunnquell was the External Reporting Lead at Monsanto from April 2009 through October 2015. In that capacity, she reported to the Controller of Monsanto. Brunnquell was a CPA during the time of the accounting fraud.

Jonathan W. Nienas was the U.S. Strategic Account Lead for the Roundup Division from September 1, 2009, until he retired in January 2014.

Anthony P. Hartke held the title of U.S. Business Analyst in the Roundup Division from July 2008 to August 2010. He was a CPA during the time of the accounting fraud.

Accounting Standards

The accounting standards governing Monsanto's rebate programs is set forth in FASB Emerging Issues Task Force ("EITF") Issue No. 01-9, "Accounting for Consideration Given by a Vendor to a Customer (Including a Reseller of the Vendor's Products)," codified as ASC 605-50.[1] Specifically, Issue 6 of EITF 01-9 (ASC 605-50-25-7) requires a vendor like Monsanto to recognize a rebate obligation as a reduction of revenue based on a systematic or rational allocation of the cost of honoring the rebate offer to each underlying transaction that results in progress by the customer towards earning the rebate. Issue 4 of EITF 01-9 (ASC 605-50-25-3) requires a vendor to recognize the cost of certain sales incentives at the later of either the date at which the related revenue is recognized or the date at which the sales incentive is offered.

Issue 1 of EITF 01-9 (ASC 605-50-45-1) addresses the circumstances in which a vendor may record payments to customers as a cost or expense [e.g., under the selling, general, and administrative (SG&A) accounting classification] rather than as a reduction of revenue. EITF 01-9 (ASC 605-50-45-1) requires a vendor like Monsanto to recognize payments to customers to perform services on its behalf (and which provide an identifiable benefit to the vendor) as a reduction of revenue for the amount of the payments that exceeds the estimated fair value of the services rendered. If the services provided by customers do not provide a benefit to the vendor, it should recognize the total amount as a reduction of revenue.

Summary of the Facts

The SEC investigation found that Monsanto had insufficient internal accounting controls to properly account for millions of dollars in rebates offered to retailers and distributers of Roundup after generic competition had undercut Monsanto's prices and resulted in a significant loss of market share for the company. Monsanto booked substantial amounts of revenue resulting from sales incentivized by the rebate programs, but failed to recognize all of the related program costs at the same time. Therefore, Monsanto materially misstated its consolidated earnings in corporate filings during a three-year period.

According to the SEC's order instituting a settled administrative proceeding against Monsanto and three executives:[2]

- Monsanto's sales force began telling U.S. retailers in 2009 that if they "maximized" their Roundup purchases in the fourth quarter they could participate in a new rebate program in 2010.
- Hartke developed and Brunnquell approved talking points for Monsanto's sales force to use when encouraging retailers to take advantage of the new rebate program and purchase significant amounts of Roundup in the fourth quarter of the company's 2009 fiscal year. Approximately one-third of its U.S. sales of Roundup for the year occurred during that quarter.
- Brunnquell and Hartke knew, or should have known, that the sales force used this new rebate program to incentivize sales in 2009, and Generally Accepted Accounting Principles (GAAP) required the company to record in 2009 a portion of Monsanto's costs related to the rebate program. But Monsanto improperly delayed recording these costs until 2010.
- Monsanto also offered rebates to distributors who met agreed-upon volume targets. However, late in the fiscal year, Monsanto reversed approximately $57.3 million of rebate costs that had been accrued under these agreements because certain distributors did not achieve their volume targets (at the urging of Monsanto).
- Monsanto then created a new rebate program to allow distributors to "earn back" the rebates they failed to attain in 2009 by meeting new targets in 2010.
- Under this new program, Monsanto paid $44.5 million in rebates to its two largest distributors as part of side agreements arranged by Nienas, in which they were promised late in fiscal year 2009 that they would be paid the maximum rebate amounts regardless of target performance.
- Because the side agreements were reached in 2009, Monsanto was required under GAAP to record these rebates in 2009. But the company improperly deferred recording the rebate costs until 2010.
- Monsanto repeated the program the following year and improperly accounted for $48 million in rebate costs in 2011 that should have been recorded in 2010.
- Monsanto also improperly accounted for more than $56 million in rebates in 2010 and 2011 in Canada, France, and Germany. They were booked as SG&A expenses rather than rebates, which boosted gross profits from Roundup in those countries.

Scott W. Friestad, Associate Director in the SEC's Division of Enforcement, said, "Monsanto devised rebate programs that elevated form over substance, which led to the booking of substantial amounts of revenue without the recognition of associated costs. Public companies need to have robust systems in place to ensure that all of their transactions are recognized in the correct reporting period."

Monsanto consented to the SEC's order without admitting or denying the findings that it violated Sections 17(a)(2) and 17(a)(3) of the Securities Act of 1933; the reporting provisions of Section 13(a) of the Securities Exchange Act of 1934 and underlying rules 12b-20, 13a-1, 13a-11, and 13a-13; the books-and-records provisions of Exchange Act Section 13(b)(2)(A); and the internal accounting control provisions of Exchange Act Section 13(b)(2)(B).

Brunnquell, Hartke, and Nienas also consented to the order without admitting or denying the findings that they violated Rule 13b2-1 and caused Monsanto's violations of various provisions. Nienas also was found to have violated Exchange Act Section 13(b)(5). Brunnquell, Nienas, and Hartke must pay penalties of $55,000, $50,000, and $30,000, respectively, and Brunnquell and Hartke agreed to be suspended from appearing and practicing before the SEC as an accountant, which includes not participating in the financial reporting or audits of public companies. The SEC's order permits Brunnquell to apply for reinstatement after two years, and Hartke is permitted to apply for reinstatement after one year.

The SEC's investigation found no personal misconduct by Monsanto CEO Hugh Grant and former CFO Carl Casale, who reimbursed the company $3,165,852 and $728,843, respectively, for cash bonuses and certain stock awards they received during the period when the company committed accounting violations. Therefore, it wasn't necessary for the SEC to pursue a clawback action under Section 304 of the Sarbanes-Oxley Act.

Ethics and Compliance Requirements

In determining to accept Monsanto's Offer, the Commission considered remedial acts undertaken/to be undertaken by Monsanto.[3]

- Retain a qualified independent ethics and compliance consultant to conduct an ethics and compliance program assessment of Monsanto's Crop Protection business. The Consultant shall also have expertise in, or retain someone with expertise in, internal accounting controls and public company financial reporting as well as vendor rebate and market funding programs.
- Analyze whether the components of Monsanto's ethics and compliance program for its Crop Protection business have been implemented successfully and are having the desired effects. The Consultant will determine whether the culture is supportive of ethical and compliant conduct, including strong, explicit, and visible support and commitment by the Board and senior management.
- In discharging this undertaking, the Consultant shall evaluate and assess the effectiveness of the internal accounting controls and financial reporting policies and procedures with respect to Monsanto's rebate and market funding programs for its Crop Protection business, including but not limited to:
  - Assess whether Monsanto's internal accounting controls with respect to Monsanto's rebate and market funding programs for its Crop Protection business are sufficient to provide reasonable assurances that the company is maintaining fair and accurate books, records, and accounts, with particular emphasis on whether they are designed to address the integrity of its revenue accounting and ensure consistent accuracy and integrity given the global nature of Monsanto's business; and
  - Determine whether Monsanto has specific accounting and financial reporting controls and procedures sufficient to ensure that all rebate and/or market funding programs for its Crop Protection business comply with applicable accounting rules and policies.
  - Provide a report to Commission staff and Monsanto's General Counsel and Chief Ethics and Compliance Officer regarding the Consultant's findings and recommendations.

Whistleblower

On August 30, 2016, the SEC announced the award of more than $22 million to an anonymous whistleblower whose detailed tip and extensive assistance helped the agency stop the well-hidden fraud at Monsanto, where the whistleblower worked. At the time, the $22 million-plus award was the second-largest total the SEC had awarded to a whistleblower under the Dodd-Frank Financial Reform Act.[4]

The whistleblower's attorney, Stuart Meissner, shed light on the role of the external auditors Deloitte, in speaking on behalf of the whistleblower, in an interview with "Corporate Crime Reporter."[5] Meissner raised concerns about the role of outside auditors.

We hope the agency will probe Monsanto's outside auditor Deloitte for the role we believe it played in enabling the company to overstate earnings and issue misleading financial statements—not only once, but twice. There was an initial misstatement by Monsanto and a subsequent restatement—the restatement is actually the bigger issue of the two in my view," Meissner said. When auditors are allowed to audit their own mistakes, it is difficult for them to be independent and objective. And when independence is impaired, the professional skepticism needed to recognize and flush out improprieties by management is not present. Professional skepticism of the auditor is the last line of defense for a management team that may have a clear bias in reporting positive results. To this day, Monsanto investors still do not have accurate financial statements for the periods involved in the case. I do not believe that investors have been able to reasonably access the performance of the company, including whether or not Monsanto hit the mid-teen percentage growth targets management committed to in 2010. If a true independent auditor not associated with the financials had been appointed to audit the restated financials, I believe there would be a higher likelihood that investors would know the true performance of the company and be in a better position to make fully informed decisions.

Questions

1. What is the underlying accounting and financial reporting concept at issue as described in EITF Issue No. 01-9 with respect to the way Monsanto accounted for customer rebates? Explain in your own words how Monsanto's accounting led to materially misstated financial statements.

2. Given that Monsanto was under great pressure from competitors that sold generic brands similar to Roundup, would you characterize the Monsanto situation as a business failure, an accounting failure, and/or an audit failure? Explain.

3. Of what value are the ethics and compliance requirements agreed to by Monsanto? Do you believe all companies that experience financial fraud should be required to institute such changes? Can such requirements change the culture of a global company such as Monsanto?

Case 7-5 Kraft Heinz

The Kraft Heinz Co. case was discussed in the chapter. To refresh your memory, on May 6, 2019, Kraft Heinz disclosed that it would restate its financial statements due to faulty procurement practices. The financial statements for 2016, 2017, and the first three quarters of 2018 were misstated because of inappropriate timing of the recognition of when certain cost and rebate elements associated with supplier contracts were initially recorded and then recognized through corresponding decreases to costs of products sold in future financial periods. The Form 8-K Report was filed with the SEC on May 2, 2019, pursuant to Items 2.02 and 4.02 of the Securities Exchange Act of 1934. The information in **Exhibit 1** is taken from the Report.[1]

Due to the findings above, the company said it would not be able to timely file its quarterly report for the period ended March 30, 2018.

EXHIBIT 1   Non-Reliance on Previously Issued Financial Statements or a Related Audit Report or Completed Interim Review[36]

On May 2, 2019, the Company, in consultation with the Audit Committee of its Board of Directors, reached a determination that the Company's consolidated financial statements and related disclosures for the years ended December 30, 2017, and December 31, 2016, included in its Annual Reports on Form 10-K, and for each of the quarterly and year-to-date periods in 2017 and the quarterly and year-to-date periods for the nine months ended September 29, 2018, should no longer be relied upon because of certain misstatements contained in those financial statements.

The Company does not believe that such misstatements constitute a quantitatively material misstatement to any individual period presented in the Company's prior annual or interim financial statements, but due to the qualitative nature of the matters identified in the investigation, including the number of years over which the misconduct occurred and the number of transactions, suppliers, and procurement employees involved, the Company has determined that it is appropriate to correct the misstatements in the Company's previously issued financial statements through restating such financial statements.

As previously disclosed in the Company's press release as furnished with its Current Report on Form 8-K filed on February 21, 2019 (the "Earnings Release"), the Company received a subpoena in October 2018 from the SEC related to the Company's procurement area, more specifically the Company's accounting policies, procedures, and internal controls related to its procurement function, including, but not limited to, agreements, side agreements, and changes or modifications to its agreements with its suppliers. Following receipt of this subpoena, the Company, together with external counsel and forensic accountants, and under the oversight of the Audit Committee, initiated an investigation into the procurement area, which is now substantially complete.

As a result of the findings from the Company's investigation, which identified that several employees in the procurement area engaged in misconduct, the Company has recorded adjustments to correct prior period misstatements that increase the total cost of products sold in prior financial periods, which the Company does not believe constitute a quantitatively material misstatement to any individual period. These misstatements principally relate to the incorrect timing of when certain cost and rebate elements associated with complex supplier contracts and arrangements were initially recognized, and once corrected for, the Company expects to recognize corresponding decreases to costs of products sold in future financial periods.

The findings from the investigation did not identify any misconduct by any member of the senior management team. Additionally, the Company has implemented and continues to implement certain remedial actions, including employee personnel actions and certain improvements to its internal controls, to mitigate the likelihood of this occurring in the future. The Company also continues to cooperate fully with the SEC.

In connection with the internal investigation described above, the Company also conducted a comprehensive review of significant supplier contracts to identify other potential misstatements in the timing of the recognition of supplier rebates, incentive payments, and pricing arrangements. The review identified additional misstatements, which may or may not have resulted from the misconduct noted above, primarily related to certain supplier contracts and arrangements where the allocation of value of all or a portion of rebates and up-front payments to contractual elements in the current period should have been deferred and recognized over an applicable contractual period.

These misstatements will be corrected for in the same manner as those noted above. The Company corrected these misstatements to defer the up-front consideration from suppliers when the retention or receipt of that consideration was contingent upon future events and to correctly recognize the consideration as a reduction of cost of products sold over the terms of the arrangements with the suppliers. The misstatements arising from the contract review relate to the timing of recognizing certain cost and rebate elements, and the Company thus expects to recognize corresponding decreases to costs of products sold in future financial periods.

The Company's investigation and review described above identified required adjustments of approximately $208 million, of which approximately $27 million was recorded in the previously furnished fourth-quarter 2018 cost of products sold. As a result, the cumulative net misstatements to the previously furnished or reported annual and interim financial statements were approximately $181 million, which, when reflected over the relevant periods, resulted in misstatements that are not quantitatively material to any prior year or quarter, but would have been significant to the fourth quarter of 2018 if corrected in that period. The impact of these corrections to previously reported financial statements is an increase to cost of products sold of approximately $25 million in 2015, $26 million in 2016, and $100 million in 2017. The impact to the previously furnished financial statements in 2018 is an increase in cost of products sold of approximately $30 million. These misstatements were also not quantitatively material to any quarter, with the largest correction being a $38 million increase to cost of products sold in the third quarter of 2017.

In addition, the Company evaluated other elements of these complex supplier contracts and arrangements, including the classification of leases embedded in supplier arrangements as capital or operating. As a result of the review, the Company identified certain arrangements that were improperly classified as embedded capital leases. The correction of this error did not impact previously reported 2017 net income and resulted in a decrease to previously furnished 2018 net loss of approximately $2 million. The correction reduced previously reported 2017 Adjusted EBITDA by approximately $2 million and previously furnished 2018 Adjusted EBITDA by approximately $33 million. The Company will also correct for these misstatements in connection with the restatement.

The effect of the restatements in prior periods on both Adjusted EBITDA and Adjusted EPS is expected to be less than two percent in each year and less than four percent in each quarter. The misstatements also had less than 1 percent impact on total assets or total liabilities at December 30, 2017.

Exhibit 2 shows the preliminary estimated impact of misstatements for supplier rebates, capital leases, impairments, and other misstatements described in **Exhibit 1**. The tables illustrate the impact to net income/(loss), Adjusted EBITDA, diluted earnings per share ("diluted EPS"), and Adjusted EPS for 2016 and 2017 as compared to the previously reported financial statements as well as the impact of these metrics for 2018 as compared to the previously furnished financial statements in the Earnings Release issued on February 21, 2019. These misstatements and illustrated restated numbers are preliminary, unaudited, and subject to further change in connection with the completion of the Company's Annual Report on Form 10-K for the fiscal year ended December 29, 2018.

EXHIBIT 2   Effects of Misstatements on Reported Net Income

The preliminary unaudited increase (decrease) in net income (loss) for the misstatements for fiscal years 2016 to 2018 is expected to be as follows (in millions)

	Net Income/(Loss) as Previously Reported or Furnished	Estimates of Misstatements (Unaudited)	Net Income/(Loss) as Restated (Unaudited)	% Change
2016 as reported	$3,642	$(20)	$3,622	(0.5%)
2017 as reported	10,990	(69)	10,921	(0.6%)
2018 as furnished	(10,292)	27	(10,265)	0.3%

Fiscal 2016 and 2017 values are as reported in the Company's 2017 Annual Report on Form 10-K filed on February 16, 2018. Fiscal 2018 values are unaudited and as furnished in the Earnings Release issued on February 21, 2019.

The preliminary unaudited increase (decrease) in Adjusted EBITDA for the misstatements for fiscal years 2016 to 2018 is expected to be as follows (in millions)

	Adjusted EBITDA as Previously Reported or Furnished	Estimate of Misstatements (Unaudited)	Adjusted EBITDA as Restated (Unaudited)	% Change
2016 as reported	$7,778	$(54)	$7,724	(0.7%)
2017 as reported	7,930	(120)	7,810	(1.5%)
2018 as furnished	7,084	(70)	7,014	(1.0%)

Fiscal 2016 and 2017 values are as reported in the Company's 2017 Annual Report on Form 10-K filed on February 16, 2018. Fiscal 2018 values are unaudited and as furnished in the Earnings Release issued on February 21, 2019.

The preliminary unaudited increase (decrease) in diluted EPS for the misstatements for fiscal years 2016 to 2018 is expected to be as follows:

	Diluted EPS as Previously Reported or Furnished	Estimate of Misstatements (Unaudited)	Adjusted EPS as Restated (Unaudited)	% Change
2016 as reported	$2.81	$(0.01)	$2.80	(0.4%)
2017 as reported	8.95	(0.05)	8.90	(0.6%)
2018 as furnished	(8.39)	0.02	(8.37)	0.02%

Fiscal 2016 and 2017 values are as reported in the Company's 2017 Annual Report on Form 10-K filed on February 16, 2018. Fiscal 2018 values are unaudited and as furnished in the Earnings Release issued on February 21, 2019.

The preliminary unaudited increase (decrease) in Adjusted EPS for the misstatements for fiscal years 2016 to 2018 is expected to be as follows:

	Adjusted EPS as Previously Reported or Furnished	Estimate of Misstatements (Unaudited)	Adjusted EPS as Restated (Unaudited)	% Change
2016 as reported	$3.33	$(0.01)	$3.32	(0.3%)
2017 as reported	3.55	(0.06)	3.49	(1.7%)
2018 as furnished	3.53	(0.03)	3.50	(0.8%)

Fiscal 2016 and 2017 values are as reported in the Company's 2017 Annual Report on Form 10-K filed on February 16, 2018. Fiscal 2018 values are unaudited and as furnished in the Earnings Release issued on February 21, 2019.

SEC Issues Two Subpoenas

In February 2019, buried in a press release announcing its 2018 Quarter 4 results, the company stated that it had received a subpoena from the SEC associated with an investigation into the company's procurement area. It said the SEC was investigating its "accounting policies, procedures, and internal controls related to its procurement function, including, but not limited to, agreements, side agreements, and changes or modifications to its agreements with its vendors." At that time Kraft Heinz said it was recording a $25 million increase to costs of products sold as an out of period correction as the Company determined the amounts were immaterial to the fourth quarter of 2018.[2]

In the most recent SEC filing, the company also said it has received a second subpoena associated with its assessment of goodwill and intangible asset impairments, and that this subpoena also included document requests related to the procurement area.

"The Company is taking action to improve our policies and procedures and will continue to strengthen our internal financial controls," said Michael Mullen senior vice president of corporate affairs at Kraft Heinz. "The findings from the investigation did not identify any misconduct by any member of the senior management team. We are pleased to report that the investigation is now substantially complete."

Questions

1. Given the discussion in the chapter about reporting restatements of the financial statements to the SEC, explain why Kraft did not follow all the rules in reporting the numbers in Exhibit 2.

2. Comment on how the company addressed operational issues in its Form 8-K. What role did they play in deciding to restate the financial statements?

3. Are there any conclusions you can draw about the cause of misstatements at Kraft Heinz during the affected periods with respect to ethical leadership? Explain.

Case 7-6 New Leadership at General Electric

On June 12, 2017, GE announced that 30-year GE veteran and current President and CEO of GE Healthcare John Flannery would be replacing Jeff Immelt as CEO of the company as of August 1, 2017. Immelt had been the CEO for 16 years, taking over that role from the iconic Jack Welch. GE stated that the announcement was the culmination of a six-year succession planning process for the company's top spot. Flannery started at GE in 1987 fresh out of Wharton

Business School's MBA program and has worked in many positions, including successfully turning around the failing health care division of the company. The Company's CFO Jeff Bornstein was named Vice Chairman. Bornstein was one of three other final candidates considered for the CEO position. Barclays' analyst, Scott Davis, observed that Jeff Immelt has been criticized for his inability to connect with investors, and now many are expecting "fairly dramatic changes" under Flannery.

In a statement from the company, Immelt was quoted as saying he was supportive of his successor: "John is the right person to lead GE today. He has broad experience across multiple businesses, cycles, and geographies. He has a track record of success and led one of our most essential businesses," Immelt said. "Most important are his strong leadership traits—good judgment, resilience, a learner, team builder, and a tough-minded individual and competitor. He will be trusted by investors, our customers and the GE team."

GE's Market Cap at $153.6 Billion, while greater than 93 percent of the rest of the companies in the S&P 500, has dropped $240 billion in the last 10 years. Analysts at Seeking Alpha issued a statement saying that: "General Electric has gotten absolutely crushed over the last two days, falling 15 percent from $20.50 down to $17.50. GE's peak of the current bull market for the S&P 500 came on July 20th of last year (2016), but since then it's down 47 percent. Even more shocking is that at $17.50, GE's share price is trading at the same level it was at 20 years ago in early 1997. Of course, there have been dividends paid, but it's not a good look for a company when share price is unchanged on a 20-year basis."

On the GE July 21, 2017, second-quarter earnings call with financial analysts and investors, Flannery stated that, while he does not officially start his new role as CEO until August 1, he was already underway conducting a "deep dive" into all the business areas within GE.[5] He stated, "In addition to the business reviews, I want to repeat the process I used in healthcare to really get out and listen to what people are thinking, good and bad about the Company. I always start with customers and employees, but it's also important to get the view of our government partners and especially our investors." His plan was to take his first 90 days in his role to develop a new strategic plan for the company with the intent to report back to the investors in regard to that plan in November. The rest of this earnings call was handled by the current CEO Immelt and CFO Bornstein and was relatively optimistic as to earnings for the year and into the future.

On the October 20, 2017, third-quarter earnings call with investors, Flannery led the call with Bornstein as CFO and Bornstein's successor Jamie Miller who would be taking over as CFO on November 1. Flannery kicked off the call by stating, "While the company has many areas of strength, it's also clear from our current results that we need to make some major changes with urgency and a depth of purpose. Our results are unacceptable, to say the least. He went on to say that his review of the company has been, and continues to be, exhaustive. The team and I have performed deep dives on all aspects of the Company," and left no stone unturned. "We are evaluating our business [structure], corporate [systems], our culture, how decisions are made, how we think about goals and accountability, how we incentivize people, how we prioritize investments in the segments; and at the overall Company level, including global research, digital and additive. We have also reviewed our operating processes, our team, capital allocation and how we communicate to investors. Everything is on the table, and there have been no sacred cows." One of those changes was that Jeff Bornstein would be leaving the company and not be the new vice chairman.

While stating he would give more details on the November call, he further stated that "We are driving sweeping change and moving with speed and purpose. I'm focusing on the culture of the Company. Our culture needs to be driven by mutual candor and intense execution, and the accountability that must come with that. We have announced changes in our team at the highest levels of the Company. In addition to changes in our culture and our team, I will also share more with you in November on our capital allocation methods, changes we are making to analytics and metrics, and process improvements. In particular, these changes will be focused on improving the cash generation of the Company. We have to manage the Company for cash and profitability in addition to growth."

On the November 17, 2017 call, Flannery led an Investor Update to provide a detailed analysis of his "deep dive" into the business and his plans for the company. He reiterated, "that the current operating results were unacceptable" and "the management team is completely devoted to doing what it takes to correct that." He went on to say, "going forward, we really just have to focus on how we can create the most value and portfolio of assets that we have for our owners and we're going to do that with a very dispassionate eye, very critical analytical dispassionate eye. The GE of the future is going to be a more focused industrial company, it will leverage a lot of really game changing capabilities in digital in Additive in industrial research, culture of the company much more open, much more transparent, much more connected. And at the end of the day, we really exist to deliver outcomes for the customers, performance for the owners and have an environment where our employees are motivated by, excited by, rewarded for delivering on those two things."

Only time will tell whether Flannery is able to turn GE around and deliver on these promises.

Questions

1. What are the characteristic traits of a good leader?
2. Describe the characteristic traits of leadership at GE. How would you describe Flannery's leadership style?
3. Do you believe that leadership style and connection with employees can influence operating systems? Explain.
4. Scott Davis criticized Immelt's tenure as CEO and observed: "Jack Welch brought much needed energy and charisma to the CEO job and streamlined the bureaucracy." Can a leader's personal qualities be directly responsible for a higher level of earnings? Explain.

Case 7-7 Krispy Kreme Doughnuts Inc.

On March 4, 2009, the SEC reached an agreement with Krispy Kreme Doughnuts, Inc., and issued a cease-and-desist order to settle charges that the company fraudulently inflated or otherwise misrepresented its earnings for the fourth quarter of its FY2003 and each quarter of FY2004. By its improper accounting, Krispy Kreme avoided lowering its earnings guidance and improperly reported earnings per share (EPS) for that time period; these amounts exceeded its previously announced EPS guidance by 1 cent.

The primary transactions described in this case are "round-trip" transactions. In each case, Krispy Kreme paid money to a franchisee with the understanding that the franchisee would pay the money back to Krispy Kreme in a prearranged manner that would allow the company to record additional pretax income in an amount roughly equal to the funds originally paid to the franchisee.

There were three round-trip transactions cited in the SEC consent agreement. The first occurred in June 2003, which was during the second quarter of FY2004. In connection with the reacquisition of a franchise in Texas, Krispy Kreme increased the price that it paid for the franchise by $800,000 (i.e., from $65,000,000 to $65,800,000) in return for the franchisee purchasing from Krispy Kreme certain doughnut-making equipment. On the day of the closing, Krispy Kreme debited the franchise's bank account for $744,000, which was the aggregate list price of the equipment. The additional revenue boosted Krispy Kreme's quarterly net income by approximately $365,000 after taxes.

The second transaction occurred at the end of October 2003, four days from the closing of Krispy Kreme's third quarter of FY2004, in connection with the reacquisition of a franchise in Michigan. Krispy Kreme agreed to increase the price that it paid for the franchise by $535,463, and it recorded the transaction on its books and records as if it had been reimbursed for two amounts that had been in dispute with the Michigan franchisee. This overstated Krispy Kreme's net income in the third quarter by approximately $310,000 after taxes.

The third transaction occurred in January 2004, in the fourth quarter of FY2004. It involved the reacquisition of the remaining interests in a franchise in California. Krispy Kreme owned a majority interest in the California franchise and, beginning in or about October 2003, initiated negotiations with the remaining interest holders for acquisition of their interests. During the negotiations, Krispy Kreme demanded payment of a "management fee" in consideration of Krispy Kreme's handling of the management duties since October 2003. Krispy Kreme proposed that the former franchise manager receive a distribution from his capital account, which he could then pay back to Krispy Kreme as a management fee. No adjustment would be made to the purchase price for his interest in the California franchise to reflect this distribution. As a result, the former franchise manager would receive the full value for his franchise interest, including his capital account, plus an additional amount, provided that he paid back that amount as the management fee. Krispy Kreme, acting through the California franchise, made a distribution to the former franchise manager in the amount of $597,415, which was immediately transferred back to Krispy Kreme as payment of the management fee. The company booked this fee, thereby overstating net income in the fourth quarter by approximately $361,000.

Additional accounting irregularities were unearthed in testimony by a former sales manager at a Krispy Kreme outlet in Ohio, who said a regional manager ordered that retail store customers be sent double orders on the last Friday and Saturday of FY2004, explaining "that Krispy Kreme wanted to boost the sales for the fiscal year in order to meet Wall Street projections." The manager explained that the doughnuts would be returned for credit the following week—once FY2005 was under way. Apparently, it was common practice for Krispy Kreme to accelerate shipments at year end to inflate revenues by stuffing the channels with extra product, a practice known as "channel stuffing."

Some could argue that Krispy Kreme's auditors—PwC—should have noticed a pattern of large shipments at the end of the year with corresponding credits the following fiscal year during the course of their audit. Typical audit procedures would be to confirm with Krispy Kreme's customers their purchases. In addition, monthly variations analysis should have led someone to question the spike in doughnut shipments at the end of the fiscal year. However, PwC did not report such irregularities or modify its audit report.

In May 2005, Krispy Kreme disclosed disappointing earnings for the first quarter of FY2005 and lowered its future earnings guidance. Subsequently, as a result of the transactions already described, as well as the discovery of other accounting errors, on January 4, 2005, Krispy Kreme announced that it would restate its financial statements for 2003 and 2004. The restatement reduced net income for those years by $2,420,000 and $8,524,000, respectively.

In August 2005, a special committee of the company's board issued a report to the SEC following an internal investigation of the fraud at Krispy Kreme. The report states that every Krispy Kreme employee or franchisee who was interviewed "repeatedly and firmly" denied deliberately scheming to distort the company's earnings or being given orders to do so; yet, in carefully nuanced language, the Krispy Kreme investigators hinted at the possibility of a willful cooking of the books. "The number, nature, and timing of the accounting errors strongly suggest that they resulted from an intent to manage earnings," the report said. "Further, CEO Scott Livengood and COO John Tate failed to establish proper financial controls, and the company's earnings may have been manipulated to please Wall Street." The committee also criticized the company's board of directors, which it said was "overly deferential in its relationship with Livengood and failed to adequately oversee management decisions."

Krispy Kreme materially misstated its earnings in its financial statements filed with the SEC between the fourth quarter of FY2003 and the fourth quarter of FY2004. In each of these quarters, Krispy Kreme falsely reported that it had achieved earnings equal to its EPS guidance plus 1 cent in the fourth quarter of FY2003 through the third quarter of FY2004 or, in the case of the fourth quarter of FY2004, earnings that met its EPS guidance.

On March 4, 2009, the SEC reached agreement with three former top Krispy Kreme officials, including one-time chair, CEO, and president Scott Livengood. Livengood, former COO John Tate, and CFO Randy Casstevens all agreed to pay more than $783,000 for violating accounting laws and fraud in connection with their management of the company.

Livengood was found in violation of fraud, reporting provisions, and false certification regulations. Tate was found in violation of fraud, reporting provisions, record keeping, and internal controls rules. Casstevens was found in violation of fraud, reporting provisions, record keeping, internal controls, and false certification rules. Livengood's settlement required him to pay about $542,000, which included $467,000 of what the SEC considered as the "disgorgement of ill-gotten gains and prejudgment interest" and $75,000 in civil penalties. Tate's settlement required him to return $96,549 and pay $50,000 in civil penalties, while Casstevens had to return $68,964 and pay $25,000 in civil penalties. Krispy Kreme itself was not required to pay a civil penalty because of its cooperation with the SEC in the case.

SEC Charges against PricewaterhouseCoopers[2]

In a lawsuit brought on behalf of the Eastside Investors group against Krispy Kreme Doughnuts, Inc., members of management, and PricewaterhouseCoopers, a variety of the fraud charges leveled against the company were extended to the alleged deficient audit by PwC. These charges were settled and reflect the following findings.

PwC provided independent audit services and rendered audit opinions on Krispy Kreme's FY2003 and FY2004 financial statements. The firm also provided significant consulting, tax, and due diligence services. Of the total fees received during this period, 66 percent (FY2003) and 61 percent (FY2004) were for nonaudit services. The lawsuit alleged that PwC was highly motivated not to allow any auditing disagreements with Krispy Kreme management to interfere with its nonaudit services.

PwC was charged with a variety of failures in conducting its audit of Krispy Kreme. These include: (1) failure to obtain relevant evidential matter whether it appears to corroborate or contradict the assertions in the financial statements; (2) failure to act on violations of GAAP rules with respect to accounting for franchise rights and the company's relationship with its franchisees; and (3) ignoring numerous red flags that indicated risks that should have been factored into the audit and in questioning of management. These include:

- Unusually rapid growth, especially compared to other companies in the industry;
- Excessive concern by management to maintain or increase earnings and share prices;
- Domination of management by a single person or small group without compensating controls such as effective oversight by the board of directors or audit committee;
- Unduly aggressive financial targets and expectations for operating personnel set by management; and
- Significant related-party transactions not in the ordinary course of business or with related entities not audited or audited by another firm.

The legal action against PwC referenced Rule 10b-5 of the Securities Exchange Act of 1934 in charging the firm with making untrue statements of material fact and failing to state material facts necessary to make Krispy Kreme's financial statements not misleading. The company wound up restating its statements for the FY2003 through FY2004 period.

Questions

1. How was mismanagement at Krispy Kreme reflective of leadership failure?
2. Describe the financial shenanigans used by Krispy Kreme. In this regard, is earnings management always a sign of failed leadership?
3. PwC had been Krispy Kreme's auditor since 1992. How can a firm's length of service influence audit decisions? What biases may creep up over time? Does it seem this occurred at PwC?
4. One of the reasons behind Krispy Kreme's financial shenanigans was its failure to meet earnings guidance. How might earnings guidance and the choice of non-GAAP measures reflect a particular style of leadership?

Case 7-8 Sunbeam Corporation

One of the earliest frauds during the late 1990s and early 2000s was at Sunbeam. The SEC alleged in its charges against Sunbeam that top management engaged in a scheme to fraudulently misrepresent Sunbeam's operating results in connection with a purported "turnaround" of the company. When Sunbeam's turnaround was exposed as a sham, the stock price plummeted, causing investors billions of dollars in losses. The defendants in the action included Sunbeam's former CEO and chair Albert J. Dunlap, former principal financial officer Russell A. Kersh, former controller Robert J. Gluck, former vice presidents Donald R. Uzzi and Lee B. Griffith, and Arthur Andersen LLP partner Phillip Harlow.

The SEC complaint described several questionable management decisions and fraudulent actions that led to the manipulation of financial statement amounts in the company's 1996 year-end results, quarterly and year-end 1997 results, and the first quarter of 1998. The fraud was enabled by weak or nonexistent internal controls, inadequate or nonexistent board of directors and audit committee oversight, and the failure of the Andersen auditor to follow GAAS. The following is an excerpt from the SEC's *AAER 1393,* issued on May 15, 2001:

From the last quarter of 1996 until June 1998, Sunbeam Corporation's senior management created the illusion of a successful restructuring of Sunbeam in order to inflate its stock price and thus improve its value as an acquisition target. To this end, management employed numerous improper earnings management techniques to falsify the Company's results and conceal its deteriorating financial condition. Specifically, senior management created $35 million in improper restructuring reserves and other "cookie-jar" reserves as part of a year-end 1996 restructuring, which were reversed into income the following year. Also, in 1997, Sunbeam's management engaged in guaranteed sales, improper "bill-and-hold" sales, and other fraudulent practices. At year-end 1997, at least $62 million of Sunbeam's reported income of $189 million came from accounting fraud. The undisclosed or inadequately disclosed acceleration of sales through "channel-stuffing" also materially distorted the Company's reported results of operations and contributed to the inaccurate picture of a successful turnaround.

A brief summary of the case follows.

Chainsaw Al

Al Dunlap, a turnaround specialist who had gained the nickname "Chainsaw Al" for his reputation of cutting companies to the bone, was hired by Sunbeam's board in July 1996 to restructure the financially ailing company. He promised a rapid turnaround, thereby raising expectations in the marketplace. The fraudulent actions helped raise the market price to a high of $52 in 1997. Following the disclosure of the fraud in the first quarter of 1998, the price of Sunbeam shares dropped by 25 percent, to $34.63. The price continued to decline as the board of directors investigated the fraud and fired Dunlap and the CFO. An extensive restatement of earnings from the fourth quarter of 1996 through the first quarter of 1998 eliminated half of the reported 1997 profits. On February 6, 2001, Sunbeam filed for Chapter 11 bankruptcy protection in U.S. Bankruptcy Court.

Accounting Issues

Cookie-Jar Reserves

The illegal conduct began in late 1996, with the creation of cookie-jar reserves that were used to inflate income in 1997. Sunbeam then engaged in fraudulent revenue transactions that inflated the company's record-setting earnings of $189 million by at least $60 million in 1997. The transactions were designed to create the impression that Sunbeam was experiencing significant revenue growth, thereby further misleading the investors and financial markets.

Sunbeam took a total restructuring charge of $337.6 million at year-end 1996. However, management padded this charge with at least $35 million in improper restructuring and other reserves and accruals, excessive write-downs, and prematurely recognized expenses that materially distorted the Company's reported results of operations for fiscal year 1996 and would materially distort its reported results of operations in all quarters of fiscal year 1997, as these improper reserves were drawn into income.

The most substantial contribution to Sunbeam's improper reserves came from $18.7 million in 1996 restructuring costs that management knew or was reckless in not knowing were not in conformity with generally accepted accounting principles. Sunbeam also created a $12 million litigation reserve against its potential liability for an environmental remediation. However, this reserve amount was not established in conformity with GAAP and improperly overstated Sunbeam's probable liability in that matter by at least $6 million.

Channel Stuffing

Eager to extend the selling season for its gas grills and to boost sales in 1996, CEO Dunlap's "turnaround year," the company tried to convince retailers to buy grills nearly six months before they were needed, in exchange for major discounts. Retailers agreed to purchase merchandise that they would not receive physically until six months after billing. In the meantime, the goods were shipped to a third-party warehouse and held there until the customers requested them. These bill-and-hold transactions led to recording $35 million in revenue too soon. However, the auditors (Andersen) reviewed the documents and reversed $29 million.

In 1997, the company failed to disclose that Sunbeam's 1997 revenue growth was partly achieved at the expense of future results. The company had offered discounts and other inducements to customers to sell merchandise immediately that otherwise would have been sold in later periods, a practice referred to as "channel stuffing." The resulting revenue shift threatened to suppress Sunbeam's future results of operations.

Sunbeam either didn't realize or totally ignored the fact that, by stuffing the channels with product to make one year look better, the company had to continue to find outlets for their product in advance of when it was desired by customers. In other words, it created a balloon effect, in that the same amount or more accelerated amount of revenue was needed year after year. Ultimately, Sunbeam (and its customers) just couldn't keep up, and there was no way to fix the numbers.

Sunbeam's Shenanigans

Exhibit 1 presents an analysis of Sunbeam's accounting with respect to Schilit's financial shenanigans.

EXHIBIT 1   Sunbeam Corporation's Aggressive Accounting Techniques

Technique	Example	Shenanigan Number
Recorded bogus revenue	Bill-and-hold sales	2
Released questionable reserves into income	Cookie-jar reserves	5
Inflated special charges	Litigation reserve	7

Red Flags

Schilit points to several red flags that existed at Sunbeam but either went undetected or were ignored by Andersen, including the following:

1. *Excessive charges recorded shortly after Dunlap arrived.* The theory is that an incoming CEO will create cookie-jar reserves by overstating expenses, even though it reduces earnings for the first year, based on the belief that increases in future earnings through the release of the reserves or other techniques make it appear that the CEO has turned the company around, as evidenced by turning losses into profits. Some companies might take it to an extreme and pile on losses by creating reserves in a loss year, believing that it doesn't matter whether you show a $1.2 million loss for the year or a $1.8 million loss ($0.6 million reserve). This is known as "big-bath accounting."

2. *Reserve amounts reduced after initial overstatement.* Fluctuations in the reserve amount should have raised a red flag because they evidenced earnings management as initially record reserves were restored into net income.

3. *Receivables grew much faster than sales.* A simple ratio of the increase in receivables to the increase in revenues should have provided another warning signal. Schilit provides the following for Sunbeam's operational performance in **Exhibit 2** that should have created doubts in the minds of the auditors about the accuracy of reported revenue amounts in relation to the collectability of receivables, as indicated by the significantly larger percentage increase in receivables compared to revenues.

EXHIBIT 2   Sunbeam Corporation's Operational Performance

Operational Performance			
	9 months 9/97 ($ in millions)	9 months 9/96 ($ in millions)	% Change
Revenue	$830.1	$715.4	16%
Gross profit	231.1	123.1	86%
Operating revenue	132.6	4.0	3,215%
Receivables	309.1	194.6	59%
Inventory	290.9	330.2	12%
Cash flow from operations	(60.8)	(18.8)	N/A

4. *Accrual earnings increased much faster than cash from operating activities.* While Sunbeam made $189 million in 1997, its cash flow from operating activities was a negative $60.8 million. This is a $250 million difference that should raise a red flag, even under a cursory analytical review about the quality of recorded receivables. Accrual earnings and cash flow from operating activity amounts are not expected to be equal, but the differential in these amounts at Sunbeam seems to defy logic. Financial analysts tend to rely on the cash figure because of the inherent unreliability of the estimates and judgments that go into determining accrual earnings.

Quality of Earnings

No one transaction more than the following illustrates questions about the quality of earnings at Sunbeam. Sunbeam owned a lot of spare parts that were used to fix its blenders and grills when they broke. Those parts were stored in the warehouse of a company called EPI Printers, which sent the parts out as needed. To inflate profits, Sunbeam approached EPI at the end of December 1997, to sell its parts for $11 million (and book a $5 million profit). EPI balked, stating that the parts were worth only $2 million, but Sunbeam found a way around that. EPI was persuaded to sign an "agreement to agree" to buy the parts for $11 million, with a clause letting EPI walk away in January 1998. In fact, the parts were never sold, but the profit was posted anyway.

Along came Phillip E. Harlow, the Arthur Andersen managing partner in charge of the Sunbeam audit. He concluded the profit was not allowed under GAAP. Sunbeam agreed to cut it by $3 million but would go no further. Harlow could have said that if such a spurious profit were included, he would not sign off on the audit. But he took a different tack. He decided that the remaining profit was not material. Since the audit opinion says the financial statements "present fairly, in all material respects" the company's financial position, he could sign off on them. The part that was not presented fairly was not material. And so, it did not matter.

Dunlap Tries to Quiet the Markets . . . and the Board

Paine Webber, Inc., analyst Andrew Shore had been following Sunbeam since the day Dunlap was hired. As an analyst, Shore's job was to make educated guesses about investing clients' money in stocks. Thus, he had been scrutinizing Sunbeam's financial statements every quarter and considered Sunbeam's reported levels of inventory for certain items to be unusual for the time of year. For example, he noted massive increases in the sales of electric blankets in the third quarter of 1997, although they usually sell well in the fourth quarter. He also observed that sales of grills were high in the fourth quarter, which is an unusual time of year for grills to be sold and noted that accounts receivable were high. On April 3, 1998, just hours before Sunbeam announced a first-quarter loss of $44.6 million, Shore downgraded his assessment of the stock. By the end of the day, Sunbeam's stock prices had fallen 25 percent.

Dunlap continued to run Sunbeam as if nothing had happened. On May 11, 1998, he tried to reassure 200 major investors and Wall Street analysts that the first-quarter loss would not be repeated and that Sunbeam would post increased earnings in the second quarter. It didn't work. The press continued to report on Sunbeams' bill-and-hold strategy and the accounting practices that Dunlap had allegedly used to artificially inflate revenues and profits.

Dunlap called an unscheduled board meeting to address the reported charges on June 9, 1998. Harlow assured the board that the company's 1997 numbers were in compliance with accounting standards and firmly stood by the firm's audit of Sunbeam's financial statements. As the meeting progressed the board directly asked Sunbeam if the company would make its projected second-quarter earnings. His response that sales were soft concerned the board. A comprehensive review was ordered and eventually Dunlap was fired after the directors said they had "lost confidence" in his leadership. Sunbeam employees reportedly cheered the move openly when it was announced.

Settlement with Andersen

Harlow authorized unqualified audit opinions on Sunbeam's 1996 and 1997 financial statements although he was aware of many of the company's accounting improprieties and disclosure failures. These opinions were false and misleading in that, among other things, they incorrectly stated that Andersen had conducted an audit in accordance with generally accepted auditing standards, and that the company's financial statements fairly represented Sunbeam's results and were prepared in accordance with generally accepted accounting principles. In 2002, the SEC resolved a legal action against

Andersen when a federal judge approved a $141 million settlement in the case. Andersen agreed to pay $110 million to resolve the claims without admitting fault or liability. In the end, losses to Sunbeam shareholders amounted to about $4.4 billion, with job losses of about 1,700.

Questions

1. Explain the accounting techniques used by Sunbeam to manage its earnings.

2. How did pressures for financial performance contribute to Sunbeam's culture, where quarterly sales were manipulated to influence investors? To what extent do you believe the Andersen auditors should have considered the resulting culture in planning and executing its audit?

3. Why is it important for auditors to use analytical comparisons such as the ratios in the Sunbeam case to evaluate possible red flags that may indicate additional auditing is required? How does making such calculations enable auditors to meet their ethical obligations?

Case 7-9 KPMG Tax Shelter Scandal

In **Chapter 4**, we discussed the artificial tax shelter arrangements developed by KPMG LLP for wealthy clients that led to the settlement of a legal action with the Department of Treasury and the Internal Revenue Service. On August 29, 2005, KPMG admitted to criminal wrongdoing and agreed to pay $456 million in fines, restitution, and penalties as part of an agreement to defer prosecution of the firm. In addition, nine members of the firm were criminally indicted for their role in relation to the design, marketing, and implementation of fraudulent tax shelters.

In the largest criminal tax case ever filed, KPMG admitted it engaged in a fraud that generated at least $11 billion in phony tax losses, which, according to court papers, cost the United States at least $2.5 billion in evaded taxes. In addition to KPMG's former deputy chairman, the individuals indicted included two former heads of KPMG's tax practice and a former tax partner in the New York City office of a prominent national law firm.

The facts of the tax shelter arrangement are complicated, so we have condensed them for purposes of this case and present them in **Exhibit 1**.

EXHIBIT 1   Summary of Tax Shelter Transactions Developed by KPMG[1]

KPMG developed tax shelters to generate losses of $11.2 billion for 601 wealthy clients that enabled them to avoid paying $2.5 billion in income taxes. KPMG mainly used four methods to help the wealthy clients avoid their tax liabilities or tax charges on capital gains. The shelters implemented were the Foreign Leveraged Investment Program (FLIP), Offshore Portfolio Investment Strategy (OPIS), Bond Linked Issue Premium Structure (BLIPS), and Short Option Strategy (SOS/SC 2). These shelters were designed to artificially create substantial phony capital losses through the use of an entity created in the Cayman Islands (a tax haven) for the purpose of the tax shelter transactions. The client purportedly entered into an investment transaction with the Cayman entity by purchasing purported warrants or entering into a purported swap. The Cayman entity then made a prearranged series of purported investments, including the purchase from either Bank A, which at the time was a KPMG audit client, Bank D, or both using money purportedly loaned by Bank A or Bank D, followed by redemptions of those stock purchases by the pertinent bank. The purported investments were devised to eliminate economic risk to the client beyond the cost to develop the tax shelters.

In the implementation of FLIP and OPIS, KPMG issued misleading opinion letters with assistance from its co-conspirators. The opinion letters were misleading because KPMG knew that the tax positions taken were more likely than not to prevail against the IRS, and the opinion letters and other documents used to implement FLIP and OPIS were false and fraudulent in a number of ways. For instance, the opinion letters began by falsely stating that the client requested KPMG's opinion regarding the U.S. federal income tax consequences of certain investment portfolio transactions, while the real fact is that the conspirators targeted wealthy clients based on the clients' large taxable gains and offered to generate phony tax losses to eliminate income tax on that gain as well as to provide a "more likely than not" opinion letter.

(continued)

The "more likely than not" opinion letters provided an ambiguous and confusing view of the tax shelters to the users, but it brought an income of $50,000 to KPMG for each such opinion letter. In addition to that, the opinion letter continued by falsely stating that the investment strategy was based on the expectation that a leveraged position in the foreign bank securities would provide the investor with the opportunity for capital appreciation, when in fact the strategy was based on the expected tax benefits promised by certain conspirators in the tax frauds.

Back in **Chapter 4** we discussed the "realistic possibility of success" standard in taking tax positions under the Statements on Standards for Tax Services of the AICPA. This is a high standard to meet. Generally, there would need to be a 70–80 percent of prevailing if a tax position were challenged by the IRS. The "more likely than not" standard appears in Treasury Circular 230, which covers rules of conduct for those who practice before the IRS, including CPAs, attorneys, and enrolled agents. A tax preparer who fails to comply with Circular 230 will likely be subject to penalties and possibly other sanctions if she advises a client to take a position on a tax return or a document that does not meet the applicable tax reporting standard.

The three standards for tax positions in Treasury Circular 230, ranked from lowest to highest, are reasonable basis, substantial authority, and more likely than not. A description of each of these standards appears in **Exhibit 2**.

EXHIBIT 2   Circular 230 Tax Positions and Compliance Standards[2]

Reasonable basis: Reasonable basis is the minimum standard for all tax advice and for preparation of all tax returns and other required tax documents to avoid a penalty under Section 6694 for the underpayment of taxes. If a return position is reasonably based on at least one relevant and persuasive tax authority cited, the return position will generally satisfy this standard.

Substantial authority: Substantial authority for the tax treatment of an item exists only if the weight of the tax authorities (Internal Revenue Code, Treasury regulations, court cases, etc.) supporting the treatment is substantial in relation to the weight of authorities supporting contrary treatment. All authorities relevant to the tax treatment of an item, including the authorities contrary to the treatment, are taken into account in determining whether substantial authority exists. This standard may be measured as a greater than 40 percent likelihood of being sustained on its merits.

More likely than not: More likely than not is "the standard that is met when there is a greater than 50 percent likelihood of the position being upheld." This is the standard for tax shelters under Section 6694 and reportable transactions.

KPMG admitted that its personnel took specific, deliberate steps to conceal the existence of the shelters from the IRS by, among other things, failing to register the shelters with the IRS as required by law, fraudulently concealing the shelter losses and income on tax returns, and attempting to hide the shelters using sham attorney-client privilege claims.

The information and indictment alleged that top leadership at KPMG made the decision to approve and participate in shelters; issue KPMG opinion letters despite significant warnings from KPMG tax experts and others throughout the development of the shelters; and, at critical junctures, that the shelters were close to frivolous and would not withstand IRS scrutiny, that the representations required to be made by the wealthy individuals were not credible, and the consequences of going forward with the shelters—as well as failing to register them—could include criminal investigation, among other things.

As we noted in **Chapter 4**, an unusual aspect of the case is the culture that apparently existed in KPMG's tax practice during the time the shelters were sold, which was to aggressively market tax shelter arrangements targeting wealthy clients by approaching them with the deals rather than the clients coming to KPMG. Back in the late 1990s, the stock market was booming, and the firm sought to take advantage of the increasing number of wealthy clients by accelerating its tax-services business. The head of KPMG's tax department at the time, Jeffrey M. Stein, and its CFO, Richard Rosenthal, created an environment that treated those who didn't support the "growth at all costs" effort as not being team players.

Once it became clear that the firm faced imminent criminal indictment over its tax shelters, KPMG turned to its head of human resources, Timothy Flynn, to somehow persuade the government not to indict. He knew that criminal charges against the firm would probably kill it, as they did Arthur Andersen after the Enron scandal.

For years, KPMG had stoutly denied any impropriety, calling its tax advice legal. But Flynn took a gamble and met with Justice Department officials to acknowledge that KPMG had engaged in wrongdoing. He got no promises in return, and the admission could have sunk the firm. Instead, it provided flexibility to the prosecutors, who were aware that the collapse of one of only four remaining accounting giants could harm the financial markets. Two months later, the government gave KPMG a deferred-prosecution deal, holding off indicting if KPMG paid a $456 million penalty and met other conditions.

The agreement between KPMG and the IRS required permanent restrictions on KPMG's tax practice, including the termination of two practice areas, one of which provided tax advice to wealthy individuals, and permanent adherence to higher tax practice standards regarding the issuance of certain tax opinions and the preparation of tax returns. In addition, the agreement banned KPMG's involvement with any prepackaged tax products and restricted KPMG's acceptance of fees not based on hourly rates. The agreement also required KPMG to implement and maintain an effective compliance and ethics program; to install an independent, government-appointed monitor to oversee KPMG's compliance with the deferred prosecution agreement for a three-year period; and its full and truthful cooperation in the pending criminal investigation, including the voluntary provision of information and documents.

Questions

1. Describe the link between the tax culture at KPMG and leadership. Do you believe there is a direct correlation between dysfunctional tax decisions and culture?
2. How can tax positions taken reflect leadership style?
3. Describe the relationship between the tax shelters developed by KPMG and management of the tax practice at the firm.
4. What's wrong with a CPA firm, such as KPMG, aggressively seeking to establish tax shelters for wealthy clients? Did KPMG's role in this regard reflect a failure of leadership or a failure of judgment? Explain.

Case 7-10 Theranos: Accounting for Bad Blood

Introduction

The story of Theranos, a company that sought to make blood tests cheaper, is a cautionary tale for Silicon Valley about what can happen when a company fails to develop internal control systems or overrides them, and when the CEO creates a psychological climate built on fear. The facts of this case were first discussed in Case 3-5 back in **Chapter 3**. A review of those facts follows. We then turn to the accounting and fraud issues that led to the demise of the company and legal proceedings that continue to this day.

The leadership-style of Elizabeth Holmes, the CEO, created an environment of don't go against the boss. She was backed up by Ramesh "Sunny" Balwani, the chief operating officer, who railed against anyone in the organization seeking to get the word out about the problems with the blood testing process and that it did not work as intended. Along the way, the company blocked would-be whistleblowers and one, Tyler Schultz, voiced his concerns about the product to the media.

The Theranos case shows what can happen when corporate governance barely exists and there are no independent directors or an audit committee to provide checks and balances on top management behavior. It also illustrates the lengths that a company can go to deceive business partners, patients, and doctors who rely on their blood-testing equipment to produce cheaper and quicker results. In the end, it is a story of a hard-charging CEO with ethical blind spots who was motivated by greed and hubris.

Case Overview

In 2003, Elizabeth Holmes dropped out of Stanford University to start Theranos, a privately held company that would make blood tests cheaper, more convenient, and accessible to consumers. Simply by using a pin prick, she claimed blood could be analyzed quickly for diseases. Holmes believed the testing procedures were a revolution in the way diagnostics were done and would revolutionize preventative medicine. Using a machine called the Edison, pharmacies were able to use this portable blood test from a drop of blood. Unfortunately, the reports generated by the machine were not accurate. Most tests could not be accurately performed with a needle prick but required a venipuncture.

Physicians could not get information on how the tests were done. The whole process was sort of a black box, which had mysterious or unknown internal functions or mechanisms. Theranos was very secretive about the workings of the machinery and knew it did not work as intended.

Holmes duped just about everyone about the efficacy of Edison. She was able to raise hundreds of millions of dollars until an employee, Tyler Schultz, blew the whistle. For 12 years, Holmes essentially ran a Ponzi scheme by attracting investment funds from primarily venture capitalists that saw it as a unique opportunity to cash in on the boom in Silicon Valley.

Tyler Shultz, whose job involved checking the accuracy of the blood analysis results in the company's Edison machines, claimed he knew right away that the devices did not work as advertised. Shultz said: "Right off the bat, you could tell that this thing does not do hundreds of tests from a single drop of blood. This device can only run one test at a time. So, if you came in and ordered 300 tests, even if those tests could be run on the Theranos platform, you'd have to run them on 300 different devices."[1]

Schultz blew the whistle on the fraud at Theranos. In an interview with the Markkula Center for Applied Ethics, he commented on how corporate culture contributed to the Theranos failure. He described responses to concerns he expressed as retaliatory. He was seen as not being a team player and even a troublemaker.[2]

As far as its corporate governance systems were concerned, Elizabeth Holmes, the chief executive officer, and Ramesh "Sunny" Balwani, the chief operating officer, served as chairperson of the board of directors and a member of the board, respectively. A group of mostly figure-heads also served on the board including George Shultz, a former U.S. secretary of state and the grandfather of whistleblower Tyler Schultz. A majority of board members lacked the experience necessary to ensure due diligence on the part of the company.

The majority of the board members were not qualified with respect to knowledge of how financial information should be disclosed and lacked experience in dealing with products and services like Theranos. Holmes controlled the board so she controlled the information flow.

Chronology of Events

Partnerships

Between 2012 and 2015, Theranos partnered with Safeway, Walgreens, and the prestigious Cleveland Clinic, to market its product to labs and the public. The following summarizes those deals.

In 2012, Safeway invested $350 million into retrofitting 800 locations with clinics that would offer in-store blood tests. Following missed deadlines and questionable results, the deal was called off in 2015.

In 2013, Theranos partnered with Walgreens to offer in-store blood tests at more than 40 locations. Following a story in the Wall Street Journal by John Carreyrou that was critical of the claims of the company, Walgreen's suspended plans to expand blood-testing centers in their stores. In 2016, Walgreens' filed a lawsuit against Theranos for breach of contract. In 2017, the original claim for damages of $140 million was settled for less than $30 million.[3]

In March 2015, the Cleveland Clinic announced a partnership with Theranos in order to test its technology and decrease the cost of lab tests. Theranos became the lab-work provider for Pennsylvania insurers AmeriHealth Caritas and Capital BlueCross.

In July 2015, the Food and Drug Administration approved the use of the company's fingerstick blood testing device (the Edison) for the herpes simplex virus outside a clinical laboratory setting. Theranos was awarded the 2015 Bioscience Company of the Year.

Exposure and Downfall

In his Wall Street Journal article, Carreyrou revealed that Theranos was using traditional blood testing machines instead of the company's Edison devices to run its tests. Carreyrou, who had interviewed Tyler Shultz, the Theranos whistleblower, said he attempted to bring his concerns to the attention of management to no avail. He blew the whistle by reporting the company to the New York State Department of Health.

Theranos claimed the allegations were "factually and scientifically erroneous." Walgreen's suspended plans to expand blood-testing centers in their stores. The Cleveland Clinic announced it would work to verify Theranos technology.

In January 2016, the Centers for Medicare and Medicaid Services (CMS) sent a letter to Theranos after inspecting its Newark, California lab, reporting that the facility caused "immediate jeopardy to patient health and safety" based on a test to determine the correct dose of the blood-thinning drug warfarin.

In 2016, Walgreens and Capital BlueCross announced a suspension of Theranos blood tests from the Newark lab.

In March 2016, CMS regulators announced plans to enact sanctions that included suspending Elizabeth Holmes, the chief executive officer, and Ramesh "Sunny" Balwani, vice president and chief operating officer, from owning or operating a lab for two years and CMS would revoke the Newark labs license.

By April 2016, Theranos came under criminal investigation by federal prosecutors and the SEC for allegedly misleading investors and government officials about its technology. The U.S. House of Representatives Committee on Energy and Commerce requested information on what Theranos was doing to correct its testing inaccuracies and adherence to federal guidelines.

Company Response

In May 2016, Theranos announced that it had voided two years of results, representing one percent of its tests, from its Edison device.

In July 2016, Theranos announced that the CMS had revoked its license and issued sanctions including the suspension of approval to receive Medicare and Medicaid payments, and a civil monetary penalty. Theranos announced its intention to appeal the decision by regulators to revoke its license to operate the Newark lab and other sanctions.

On October 2016, Theranos announced that it would close its laboratory operations and wellness centers and lay off about 40 percent of its work force to work on miniature medical testing machines.

On January 17, 2017, Theranos announced that it had laid off approximately 155 people and closed the last remaining blood-testing facility after the lab failed a second major U.S. regulatory inspection.

Legal Actions

Theranos defrauded investors, who lost nearly $1 billion. The company was accused of defrauding doctors and patients as well by providing inadequate test results that could have resulted in improper treatment and prescription decisions.

What happened at Theranos was more than corporate fraud. The actions of the company compromised public health and safety. Normally, we might look to the company's code of ethics for guidance as to what went wrong. However, it did not appear that the company had a code of ethics. One thing is clear. There was a lack of ethics and integrity starting at the top of the company's corporate governance system. The culture at the top was to ignore the warnings signs that the blood testing system did not work. The company pursued growth at all costs and made false and misleading statements to cover up the deficiencies in the product.

Legal Settlements

Continuing with the timeline, Theranos settled several legal actions as it wound down the business as follows.

In April 2017, a lawsuit by Partners Investments LP alleged that Theranos had misled company directors about the practices concerning laboratory testing and that it had secretly bought lab equipment to run fake demonstrations. The company reached an undisclosed settlement.

In April 2017, Theranos reached a settlement with CMS agreeing to stay out of the blood-testing business for at least two years in exchange for reduced penalties and signed a consent decree over violations of the Arizona Consumer Fraud Act. Alleged violations included false advertisement and inaccurate blood testing. Also, Walgreens and Capital BlueCross announced a suspension of Theranos blood tests from the Newark lab.

In August 2017, Theranos announced it had reached a settlement with Walgreens.

In March 2018, the SEC charged Theranos, Holmes, and Balwani in an "elaborate years-long fraud" wherein they "deceived investors into believing that its key product—a portable blood analyzer—could conduct comprehensive blood tests from finger drops of blood." Holmes reached a settlement with the SEC, which requires her to pay $500,000 forfeit 19 million shares of company stock and be barred from having a leadership role in any public company for 10 years. Balwani did not settle with the SEC.

On June 15, 2018, Holmes and Balwani were indicted on multiple counts of wire fraud and conspiracy to commit wire fraud. According to the indictment, investors, doctors, and patients were defrauded. The indictment alleged that the defendants were aware of the unreliability and inaccuracy of their products but concealed that information. If convicted they each face a maximum fine of $250,000 and 20 years in prison. As mentioned in Case 3-5, the trial of Elizabeth Holmes began on August 31, 2021, with jury selection. The key issue is whether fraud was committed by Holmes in the development and distribution of Theranos's blood-testing technology. The trial was slated to last 13 weeks or longer.

In September 2018, it was announced that, with the approval of the company's board of directors and shareholders, Theranos would begin the process of corporate dissolution. The company owed at least $60 million to unsecured creditors. The move to dissolve rather than file for bankruptcy left the company with $5 million to distribute to creditors.

Corporate Culture

Elizabeth Holmes told John Carreyrou in the interview that she did not start out to perpetrate a con, she just had a vision and lost sight of right and wrong as she pursued a goal to become a billionaire. In other words, she had ethical blind spots because she was immersed in pursuing her own self-interest to the detriment of doctors, business partners, and patients.

Holmes did not tell the board of directors about the problems with the testing equipment and the challenges faced by the company in financing its continued operations. Holmes sought out board members that had accomplished resumes but that did not mean they were experts in matters faced by Theranos or that they would challenge Holmes's decisions. They did not understand the intricacies of blood testing. They did not know enough to question her decisions. In that regard, they were not independent of Holmes and, in all likelihood, were reluctant to ask probing questions once it became known the company was in trouble.

The company also stifled dissent as when one of its employees, Erika Cheung, told Sunny Balwani about the flawed quality controls at the company that had ignored problems with the process of analyzing blood. As further described below, Balwani basically told Cheung to mind her own business.

Fraudulent Reporting of Operating Results

According to the federal indictment, Holmes and Balwani defrauded doctors and patients (1) by making false claims concerning Theranos's ability to provide fast, reliable, and cheap blood tests and test results, and (2) by omitting information concerning the limits of and problems with Theranos's technologies. Allegedly, the defendants knew Theranos was not capable of consistently producing accurate and reliable results for certain blood tests. Other allegations include:[4]

- The defendants made numerous misrepresentations to potential investors about Theranos's financial condition and its future prospects, including that its patients' blood was being tested using Thermos-manufactured analyzers; when, in truth, they knew that the company had purchased and used third party, commercially available analyzers.

- The defendants' represented to investors that Theranos would generate over $100 million in revenues and break even in 2014 and that the company was expected to generate approximately $1 billion in revenues in 2015; when, in truth, Theranos would generate only negligible or modest revenues in 2014 and 2015.

- The defendants used a combination of direct communications, marketing materials, statements to the media, financial statements, models, and other information to defraud potential investors about the company's revolutionary and proprietary analyzer, Edison. Supposedly, the machine could perform a full range of clinical tests using small blood samples drawn from a finger stick at a faster speed than previously possible and with more accurate and reliable results. Allegedly, the defendants knew that the claims about the analyzer were false. It was slower than competing devices and, in some respects, could not compete with existing, more conventional machines.

Whistleblowing

Tyler Schultz claimed to know something unethical was going on that could have major repercussions on the company. He complained to Holmes that the research results were tampered with and multiple quality control tests were failing. Shultz said the prototype of Edison only had an accuracy of 65 percent while the required accuracy results were 95 percent, adding that Theranos was knowingly misrepresenting information to its users. He told HBO in a documentary that if a hundred people who had syphilis came and got tested on the Theranos devices, the company would only tell 65 of them that they had syphilis and told the other 35 that they were healthy: no need for medical intervention.

Schultz's whistleblowing came with costs. He had signed non-disclosure and confidentiality agreements. Theranos went after Shultz in court, claiming he was revealing trade secrets and forcing his parents to spend between $400,000 and $500,000 on his defense.

In an interview with ABC News for its 20-20 television show in May 2019, Erika Cheung, pointed out the flawed quality controls at the company that had ignored problems with the process of analyzing blood. Cheung said she raised these issues directly with Balwani who reacted by saying, "What makes you think that we have problems? What was your training in statistics?...I'm tired of people coming in here and starting fires where there are no fires and sort of thinking that there are problems when there are no problems." Cheung realized her concerns were falling on deaf ears. She told the reporter that "This was not an environment, that is not a culture, where they really care about what consequences this might have on patients."[5]

Financial Reporting and Audit Problems

An independent investigative journalist, Francine McKenna, wrote an article for MarketWatch that analyzed the operating and financial reporting environment at Theranos. The article outlines the financial reporting issues related to the Theranos fraud.[6]

The operating deficiencies described above and false reporting to partners masked the fact that Theranos was bleeding cash. In December 2017, Holmes was forced to mortgage all of Theranos's assets to Fortress Investment Group in return for a desperately needed $100 million loan. The terms of the loan agreement included the requirement to finally produce audited financial statements, something that had not been attempted since at least 2009, according to Philippe Poux, Theranos's last chief financial officer.

Poux stepped up the process of preparing financial statements for the calendar year 2017 that could eventually be audited. The goal of the 2017 audit was to get a clean opinion on Theranos's financials—that is, the auditors' "reasonable assurance" that the numbers did not include a material misstatement due to error or fraud.

Theranos closed a deal in December 2017 to borrow $100 million from Fortress Investment Group and it became Theranos's most important creditor. The deal gave Fortress a lien on all of Theranos's assets, including its portfolio of patents.

One additional covenant was a requirement to get an independent auditor's opinion on its 2017 financial statements by June 2018. Fortress released $65 million when the deal closed, with the rest contingent on achieving certain milestones, as well as the audit. In an interview with MarketWatch, Poux said that: "We would have been in default of the Fortress agreement if a clean opinion was not delivered by that date."

As Poux and his staff finalized the financial statements, significant adjustments had to be made for additional expenses, in particular legal expenses, incurred after December 31, 2017. Poux told MarketWatch that it became painfully obvious the company's cash-burn rate would outstrip the funds available.

The external auditors began work on the audit in April 2018. To avoid the auditor's "going concern" warning, Theranos needed to prove it would have enough cash to support itself for 12 months from the date of the audit report, which was expected to be in June 2018. The problem was the auditors discovered that Theranos did not have sufficient cash to survive long enough to secure regulatory approval for its blood testing product.

Holmes unsuccessfully solicited additional financial support from investors in April 2018. Her effort to sell the company that spring also failed. Achieving the Fortress milestones—and securing more funds—before the cash was depleted was essential.

Fraud Charges

On March 14, 2018, the SEC filed charges against Theranos, Holmes, and Balwani for fraud. The SEC's suit alleged that the company had "never told" Walgreens it was having problems successfully developing a proprietary analyzer that was capable of conducting a comprehensive set of blood tests from drops of blood drawn from a finger. Instead, Theranos was actually testing some blood on modified third-party analyzers.

Theranos and Holmes settled the SEC's fraud charges immediately. Holmes agreed to a settlement that stripped her of voting control of Theranos, banned her from being an officer or director of any public company for 10 years and required her to pay a $500,000 penalty. Balwani, who had become the company's president in 2009 after guaranteeing a line of credit for Holmes, is still fighting the allegations.

On June 15, 2018, federal prosecutors filed criminal charges against Holmes and Balwani, alleging they had defrauded investors out of hundreds of millions of dollars and also defrauded doctors and patients.

To add to its fraud problems, Poux and David Taylor, who became Theranos's CEO shortly after Holmes was indicted, had been signing what Poux called "certificates of compliance" on a monthly set of financial statements presented to the board.

In the end, the auditors knew that even if Theranos had received the remaining $35 million in funding from Fortress by the summer of 2018, the company would not have had enough cash to support itself for 12 months, according to the auditor's opinion on the company's 2017 financial statements. The auditors had no choice but to issue a going concern alert.

In the aftermath of legal proceedings against Holmes and Balwani, payments by the company of legal fees incurred by them and other former executives and directors had stopped.

The story of Theranos is a cautionary tale where one lie leads to another and before you know it the story snowballs out of control and coverups ensue. Theranos is an example of how the ethical slippery slope works. The culture of the company was such that it hid important information from the public, pharmacies, medical professionals, and the government. This was allowed to occur in large part because of the lack of ethical leadership by Elizabeth Holmes and Sunny Balwani.

Questions

1. Describe the corporate culture failures at Theranos that enabled the fraud to occur.
2. What were the consequences of the fraudulent accounting and financial reporting at Theranos?
3. What kind of leadership existed at Theranos? What was Holmes' leadership style? How did this contribute to the problems at Theranos and, ultimately, its downfall?

CHAPTER 8
Auditors' Legal Liabilities and Defenses

LEARNING OBJECTIVES

After studying **Chapter 8**, you should be able to:

LO 8-1   Describe common-law rulings and auditors' legal liabilities to clients and third parties.
LO 8-2   Explain auditor defenses to negligence, negligent misrepresentation, and fraud.
LO 8-3   Explain the basis for auditors' statutory legal liability.
LO 8-4   Explain the provisions of the PSLRA.
LO 8-5   Discuss auditors' legal liabilities under SOX.
LO 8-6   Explain the provisions of the FCPA.

Ethics Reflection

Is the auditor a watchdog or a bloodhound? This question has been asked frequently to assess the legal liability of auditors. For many years, the answer has been that the auditor is a watchdog. An auditor is not expected to be a detective, at least in the view of the audit profession. The public sometimes has a different view in that auditors are expected to disclose material misstatements in the financial statements including fraud and, when they don't, legal liability may ensue.

As discussed in Chapter 5, the environment of auditor liability has changed over the years and expanded to include a stronger obligation to approach the audit with professional skepticism. Auditors cannot simply accept the word of management but must ask probing questions to satisfy themselves that the audit conforms to generally accepted auditing standards. This is necessary for auditors to provide reasonable assurance that the financial statements are free of material misstatements whether due to error or fraud.

Auditors are expected to conduct an audit with due care in order to defend against claims of negligence and fraud. Simply stated, due care is based on a *prudent person* concept, which means to exercise a level of care that a reasonable person with knowledge of all the facts would do. Due care generally implies four things:

1. The auditor must be competent as indicated by possessing the requisite skills to evaluate the financial transactions.

2. The auditor has a duty to employ such skill with reasonable care and due diligence.

3. The auditor must undertake tasks with good faith and integrity.

4. The auditor may be liable for negligence, bad faith, or dishonesty, but not for mere errors in judgment, which is not the same as dishonesty, so long as they acted in good faith.

Auditors are liable to clients in which they have a contractual relationship called *privity*. Auditors also may be liable to third parties that rely on the financial statements for decision making assuming there is an established relationship between the auditor and third party. These standards are complex and will be discussed later in the chapter.

(continued)

continued   Ethics Reflection

The conditions necessary for a third party to prevail in a lawsuit against auditors for fraudulent misrepresentation include:

1. A representation was made.

2. The representation was false.

3. The representation, when made, was either known to be false, a legal standard called *scienter,* or made recklessly without knowledge of its truth.

4. The third party did, in fact, rely on the representation.

5. The third party suffered damages as a result of relying on the representation.

According to the ethics standards of the accounting profession, auditors are expected to look for fraud risks and the fraud triangle helps in that regard.

There are times during traditional audits when the auditors have the opportunity to detect fraud. But there are two questions that must be asked to establish legal liability:

1. Could the auditors have detected the fraud?

2. Should the auditors have detected fraud?

Think about the following as you read this chapter: (1) What are the professional and ethical requirements for auditors to avoid legal liability to clients and third parties? (2) What legal actions can be taken against auditors? (3) What are auditor defenses to fraud? (4) What are additional legal obligations under SOX, the Private Securities Litigation Reform Act, and the Foreign Corrupt Practices Act?

> Accountants must be prepared to compensate all foreseeable victims whose economic losses are proximately caused by the accountants' negligent statements.
>
> *Source: U.S. Supreme Court Justice Benjamin Cardozo*

In the above statement from the case, *Ultramares Corporation v Touche 174 N.E. 441 (1932),* Justice Benjamin Cardozza created the first common-law legal liability standard for auditors, known as the privity/near privity rule. This standard would ultimately be accompanied by others that addressed third-party liability as more and more lawsuits were filed against auditors for negligence/gross negligence and fraud.

In 1924, the auditors of Touche Niven provided an unqualified audit certificate to Fred Stern & Company, having failed to discover that management had falsified entries to overstate accounts receivable. The auditors knew the accounts, when certified, would be used to raise money. Ultramares Corporation lent Stern and Company money. Stern declared bankruptcy in 1925. Ultramares sued Touche Niven for the amount of the Stern debt, declaring that a careful audit would have shown Stern to be insolvent. The fraud claim against Touche was dismissed by the court of first instance for the plaintiff's failure to present evidence to the court that it had deliberately been misled by Touche or indeed that the defendant had knowingly covered up the irregularity in Fred Stern's audited accounts. Although the audit was initially found to have been negligent, the negligence claim was also dismissed when a verdict of $186,000 was returned by the jury. The judge set the negligence finding aside based on the doctrine of privity (i.e., auditors' have a contractual relationship with the client only), which protects auditors from third-party lawsuits. An intermediate appellate court reinstated the negligent verdict. The case went to the New York Court of Appeals where Judge Cardozza held that the claim in negligence failed on the ground that the auditors owed the plaintiff no duty of care, there being no sufficiently proximate relationship. He said no "to a liability in an indeterminate amount for an indeterminate time to an indeterminate class."

Given the complexity of issues in legal liabilities and defenses, we summarize that portion of the chapter in **Exhibit 8.1**. You can use it to refer back to the standards as you read through the chapter.

EXHIBIT 8.1   Auditors' Legal Liabilities and Defenses

Legal Liability	Defenses	
To Clients	**General**	**Specific**
Negligence	Exercised due care	Client suffered no damages
	Followed GAAS	Damages due to another event
To Third Parties	**General**	**Specific**
Negligence	Exercised due care	No duty to third party, or
	Followed GAAS	Third party was negligent, or
		Third party did not suffer a loss, or
		Loss caused by another event
Fraud	Exercised due care	No knowledge representation was untrue
	Followed GAAS	No intent to deceive (Scienter)
	Representation not false	Third party did not rely on representation
	Representation not material	Third party did not suffer damages
		Damages due to another event

Legal Liabilities of Auditors: An Overview

LO 8-1

Describe common-law rulings and auditors' legal liabilities to clients and third parties.

Zoe-Vonna Palmrose, a former professor at the University of Southern California and now at the University of Washington, identifies the four general stages in an audit-related dispute: (1) the occurrence of events that result in losses for users of the financial statements; (2) the investigation by plaintiff attorneys before filing, to link the user losses with allegations of material omissions or misstatements of financial statements; (3) the legal process, which commences with the filing of the lawsuit; and (4) the final resolution of the dispute.[1] The first stage comes about as a result of some loss-generating event, including client bankruptcy, fraudulent financial reporting, and the misappropriation of assets.

Auditors can be sued by clients, investors, creditors, and the government for failure to perform services adequately and in accordance with the profession's ethics standards. Auditors can be held liable under two classes of law: (1) common law and (2) statutory law. Common-law liability evolves from legal opinions issued by judges in deciding a case. These opinions become legal principles that set a precedent and guide judges in deciding similar cases in the future. Statutory law reflects legislation passed at the state or federal level that establishes certain courses of conduct that must be adhered to by covered parties.[2] **Exhibit 8.2** summarizes the types of liability and auditors' actions that result in liability.

EXHIBIT 8.2   Summary of Types of Liability and Auditors' Actions Resulting in Liability

Types of Liability	Auditors' Actions Resulting in Liability
Common law—clients	Breach of contract (privity relationship)
	Negligence
	Gross negligence/constructive fraud
	Fraud
Common law—third parties	Negligence
	Gross negligence/constructive fraud
	Fraud
Federal statutory law—civil liability	Negligence
	Gross negligence/constructive fraud
	Fraud
Federal statutory law—criminal liability	Willful violation of federal statutes

Source: William F. Messier Jr., Steven M. Glover, and Douglas F. Prawitt, *Auditing and Assurance Services: A Systematic Approach* (New York: McGraw-Hill Irwin, 2012), p. 664.

There are four basic theories of liabilities which, depending on the type of lawsuit, can render a defendant liable for injuries they cause.[3]

1. *Intent* (also called willfulness) means the person acted with the intent to cause harm.

2. *Recklessness* means the person knew (or should have known) that their actions were likely to cause harm.

3. *Negligence* means that the person acted in violation of a duty to someone else, with the breach of that duty causing harm to someone else.

4. *Strict liability* is reserved for certain specific situations where someone can be held liable for harm they cause no matter what their mental state was.

Common-Law Liability

Common-law liability requires the auditor to perform professional services with due care. Evidence of having exercised due care exists if the auditor can demonstrate having performed services with the same degree of skill and judgment possessed by others in the profession. Typically, an auditor would cite adherence to generally accepted auditing standards (GAAS) as evidence of having exercised due care in conducting the audit. Due care includes exercising the degree of professional skepticism expected in the audit of financial statements.

Tort actions (for wrongdoings other than breach of contract) cover other civil complaints (e.g., fraud, deceit, and injury) arising from auditors' failure to exercise the appropriate level of professional care, sometimes referred to as substantiated performance. Clients or users of financial statements can bring tort actions against auditors.[4]

Lawsuits for damages under common law usually result when someone suffers a financial loss after relying on financial statements later found to be materially misstated. Plaintiffs in legal actions involving auditors, such as clients or third-party users of financial statements, generally assert all possible causes of action, including breach of contract, tort, deceit, fraud, and anything else that may be relevant to the claim. These cases are often referred to as "audit failures" in the financial press.

Liability to Clients—Privity Relationship

An accountant has a contractual obligation to the client that creates a *privity relationship*. Breach of contract is a claim that accounting and auditing services were not performed in a way consistent with the terms of a contract. Although auditors may have contractual relationships with third parties, cases involving breach of contract are brought most frequently against auditors by their clients.[5] Privity does not necessarily mean only clients. Third-party beneficiaries that are named in the contract also have a contractual relationship/privity. When privity exists, plaintiffs must demonstrate all of the following:[6]

1. They suffered an economic loss.
2. Auditors did not perform in accordance with the terms of the contract, thereby breaching that contract.
3. Auditors failed to exercise the appropriate level of professional care related to tort actions.
4. The breach of contract or failure to exercise the appropriate level of care caused the loss.

In addition to breach of contract, auditors may be liable to clients for tort liability that ranges from simple, ordinary negligence to the more serious case of fraud. It's worth noting the similarity between the claim that the auditor failed to exercise due care or the standard of care that other accountants would have done in similar situations and the universality perspective of Rights Theory. In other words: What would other accountants have done in similar situations (for similar reasons)?

Legal liability exists along a continuum of ordinary negligence to outright fraud—the intentional act to deceive another party. In between, an auditor might be held liable for gross negligence or constructive fraud that represents an extreme or reckless departure from professional standards of care.

Professional Negligence

Professional negligence is the liability theory most often referred to as an "accounting malpractice" claim. The elements of a professional negligence action against an accountant are similar to those present in any other type of negligence lawsuit. They are:[7]

- *Duty*—the accountant must have owed the plaintiff a duty to use reasonable care in delivering accounting services.
- *Breach of Duty*—the plaintiff must show that the accountant failed to use that degree of skill and learning normally possessed and used by public accountants in good standing in a similar practice and under like circumstances.
- *Damage*—the plaintiff must show that they suffered damage as a direct result of the accountant's breach of duty. In the words of one court, "no hurt, no tort."
- *Causation*—a causal nexus between the asserted breach and damages, such as a business driven into bankruptcy because it went into debt in reliance on overstated financial statements.

Defending Audit-Malpractice Cases

Contributory negligence of the client can be regarded as a defense to the liability of the accountant for malpractice. However, it has to be proved that the negligence of the client has proximately contributed to the accountant's failure to perform. Some courts have ruled that accountants are not immune from the consequences of their own negligence because their clients have conducted the business negligently. In *National Surety Corp. v. Lybrand,* the plaintiff sued its auditors for failing to detect embezzlement by a company employee. The auditors asserted they were not liable—even if they were negligent—because the client's claim was barred by its contributory negligence; failing to supervise the embezzler or by failing to follow its established internal controls. To avoid this harsh result, the court held that accountants should not be able to escape liability altogether by virtue of their client's negligence, and thus the client's negligence "is a defense only when it has contributed to the accountant's failure to perform their contract and to report the truth."[8]

In *Shapiro v. Glekel,* the accounting firm failed to detect and report inaccuracies in certain financial statements of the client during the course of an audit. The court observed that knowledge of the financial condition of the corporation by the president and board chairman will not constitute contributory negligence precluding the accountant's liability. Accountants cannot be allowed to avoid liability resulting from their own negligence except upon a showing of substantial negligence or fault by the client. The court did observe that if the doctrine of contributory negligence is repudiated, an accounting firm is entitled to assert the defense of *comparative negligence* in malpractice action instituted against the firm by a client.[9]

The comparative negligence rule replaced the harsh all-or-nothing approach of contributory negligence with a formula based upon allocation of fault. The change from contributory negligence to comparative fault did not totally immunize defendants from liability if the plaintiff was the slightest bit negligent. Courts now allow accountants to assert a comparative negligence defense and have affirmed the jury's apportionment of damages between the accountants and the corporation if, for example, the corporation allowed an embezzlement to occur by failing to use reasonable care in the operation of the business.

But in some jurisdictions, auditors must contend with the *audit-interference rule.* The audit-interference rule may restrict the type of client conduct that counts for purposes of apportioning fault. In jurisdictions adopting this rule, an auditor may only assert a comparative-fault defense where it can establish that the client's negligence "interfered with" the auditor's performance of its duties.

In recent years, many juries have determined that the principle of contributory negligence led to unfair results, and have therefore ignored the rule. As a result, most states in the United States have abolished the contributory negligence defense, in favor of a comparative negligence test. Comparative negligence recognizes the fact that a plaintiff had some culpability in the incident, and assigns relative percentages of negligence by the parties in order to determine the amount of damages that should be awarded to the injured party. The bottom line is any negligence by a client, whether or not it directly interferes with the accountant's performance of its duties, can reduce the client's recovery.

Recklessness

Recklessness involves conduct that is short of actual intent to cause harm, but greater than simple negligence. Unlike negligence—which occurs when a person unknowingly takes a risk that they should have been aware of—recklessness means to knowingly take a risk. It may seem that recklessness and negligence are the same. The difference is that negligence simply involves acting in a careless manner, while recklessness involves a person taking a risk while knowing their actions may cause harm to another.

Recklessness is a state of mind that is determined both subjectively and objectively. There are two types of reckless behavior. The first looks at what the actor knew or is believed to have been thinking when the act occurred (subjective test). The second considers what a reasonable person would have thought in the defendant's position (objective test). In both situations, the issue depends on conscious awareness, or whether the person knew (or should have known) their actions may cause harm to another.[10]

Negligent Misrepresentation

Negligent misrepresentation occurs when an accountant gives false information to a third party with respect to financial statement information. A liability exists when the accountant knows the person who will rely on the statement and knows the purpose of relying. In other words, the trigger events include that,

- The accountant had knowledge that the third party will rely on the information, or had knowledge that the client for whom the audit report was prepared intended to supply the information to a third party who will rely on such information, and

- The third party justifiably relied upon the information in its decision concerning the transaction involved or one substantially similar to it.

When an independent accountant audits the financial statements of a corporation, then the auditor is liable for negligent misrepresentation to those third parties who reasonably and foreseeably relied on the audited financial statements.

Auditor liability for negligent misrepresentation does not require proof that the audit was intended to influence the particular plaintiff. A complaint for negligent misrepresentation is sufficient if it alleges the audit was intended to influence the particular classes of person to which the plaintiff belongs.

However, an action by a third party against an auditor for negligent misrepresentation must be based on representations of an existing fact. Mere expressions of opinion about a future fact or event, or event representations of future performance cannot be made as negligent misrepresentations.

Exhibit 8.3 compares accountants' liability for negligence and recklessness.

EXHIBIT 8.3   Accountants' Liability for Negligence and Recklessness

NEGLIGENCE	RECKLESSNESS
Negligence refers to the failure to take proper and reasonable care, causing injury or loss to another person	Recklessness is the state of mind where a person deliberately pursues a course of action while consciously disregarding any risks stemming from such action
An individual not aware of the risk involved, but should have known what risks are	An individual is aware of the risk involved
Carries a lesser liability than recklessness	Carries a greater liability than negligence

Liability to Third Parties

Near-Privity Relationship

While the *Ultramares* decision established a strict privity standard, a number of subsequent court decisions in other states moved away from this standard over time. Following years of broadening the auditor's liability to third parties to include those that were "foreseen" and "reasonably foreseeable" (which we will discuss shortly), in a 1985 decision, the court seemed to move the pendulum back in favor of limiting the liability of accountants to third parties based on the privity standard. The New York Court of Appeals expanded the privity standard in the case of *Credit Alliance v. Arthur Andersen & Co.*[11] to include a *near-privity relationship* between third parties and the accountant. In the case, Credit Alliance was the principal lender to the client and demonstrated that Andersen had known Credit Alliance was relying on the client's financial statements prior to extending credit. The court also ruled that there had been direct communication between the lender and the auditor regarding the client.

The *Credit Alliance* case establishes the following tests that must be satisfied for holding auditors liable for negligence to third parties: (1) knowledge by the accountant that the financial statements are to be used for a particular purpose; (2) the intention of the third party to rely on those statements; and (3) some action by the accountant linking them to the third party that provides evidence of the accountant's understanding of intended reliance. The 1992 New York Court of Appeals decision in *Security Pacific Business Credit, Inc. v. Peat Marwick Main & Co.*[12] sharpens the last criterion in its determination that the third party must be known to the auditor, who directly conveys the audited report to the third party or acts to induce reliance on the report.

Actually Foreseen Third Parties

The "middle ground" approach followed by the vast majority of states (and federal courts located within those states) expands the class of third parties that are allowed to sue successfully an auditor for negligence beyond near-privity to a person or limited group of persons whose reliance is (*actually*) *foreseen,* even if the specific person or group is unknown to the auditor.[13]

The courts have deviated from the *Ultramares* principle through a variety of decisions. For example, a federal district court in Rhode Island decided a case in 1968, *Rusch Factors, Inc. v. Levin,*[14] that held an accountant liable for negligence to a third party that was not in privity of contract. In that case, Rusch Factors had requested financial statements prior to granting a loan. Levin audited the statements, which showed the company to be solvent when it was actually insolvent. After the company went into receivership, Rusch Factors sued, and the court ruled that the *Ultramares* doctrine was inappropriate. In its decision, the court relied heavily on the *Restatement (Second) of the Law of Torts.*

Restatement (Second) of the Law of Torts

The Restatement (Second) of the Law of Torts approach, sometimes known as Restatement 552,[15] expands accountants' legal liability exposure for negligence beyond those with near privity to a small group of persons and classes who are or *should be* foreseen by the auditor as relying on the financial information. This is known as the *foreseen third-party* concept because even though there is no privity relationship, the accountant knew that that party or those parties would rely on the financial statements for a specified transaction.

Section 552 states: "The liability . . . is limited to loss (a) suffered by the person or one of the persons for whose benefit and guidance they intend to supply the information, or knows that the recipient [client] intends to supply it; and (b) through reliance upon it in a transaction which they intend the information to influence, or knows that the recipient so intends." For example, assume that a client asks an accountant to prepare financial statements and the accountant knows that those statements will be used to request a loan from one or more financial institutions. The accountant may not know the specific bank to be approached, but does know the purpose for which the statements will be used. Thus, the third parties as a class of potential users can be foreseen.

A majority of states now use the modified privity requirement imposed by Section 552 of the *Restatement (Second) of the Law of Torts.* The *Restatement* modifies the traditional rule of privity by allowing nonclients to sue accountants for negligent misrepresentation, provided that they belong to a "limited group" and provided that the accountant had actual knowledge that their professional opinion would be supplied to that group. In some state court decisions, a less restrictive interpretation of Section 552 has been made. For example, a 1986 decision by the Texas Court of Appeals in *Blue Bell, Inc. v. Peat, Marwick, Mitchell & Co.* (now KPMG) held that if an accountant preparing audited statements knows or should know that such statements will be relied upon, the accountant may be held liable for negligent misrepresentation.[16]

Reasonably Foreseeable Third Parties

A third judicial approach to third-party liability expands the legal liability of accountants well beyond *Ultramares.* The *reasonably foreseeable third-party* approach results from a 1983 decision by the New Jersey Supreme Court in *Rosenblum, Inc. v. Adler.*[17] In that case, the Rosenblum family agreed to sell its retail catalog showroom business to Giant Stores, a corporation operating discount department stores, in exchange for Giant common stock. The Rosenblums relied on Giant's 1971 and 1972 financial statements, which had been audited by Touche. When the statements were found to be fraudulent and the stock was deemed worthless, the investors sued Touche. The lower courts did not allow Rosenblums' claims against Touche on the grounds that the plaintiffs did not meet either the *Ultramares* privity test or the *Restatement* standard. The case was taken to the New Jersey Supreme Court, and it overturned the lower courts' decision, ruling that auditors can be held liable for ordinary negligence to all *reasonably foreseeable third parties* who are recipients of the financial statements for routine business purposes. In finding for Rosenblum on certain motions, the Court held, "Independent auditors have a duty of care to all persons whom the auditor should reasonably foresee as recipients of the statements from the company for proper business purposes, provided that the recipients rely on those financial statements. It is well recognized that audited financial statements are made for the use of third parties who have no direct relationship with the auditor. Auditors have responsibility not only to the client who pays the fee but also to investors, creditors, and others who rely on the audited financial statements."

Another important case that followed this approach was *Citizens State Bank v. Timm, Schmidt, & Company.*[18] In this case, the bank sued the public accounting firm after relying on financial statements for one of its debtors that had been audited by Timm. The Wisconsin court used a number of reasons for extending auditors' liability beyond privity. The following quote from the case demonstrates the court's rather liberal leanings with respect to auditor legal liability to third parties: "If relying third parties, such as creditors, are not allowed to recover, the cost of credit to the general public will increase because creditors will either have to absorb the cost of bad loans made in reliance on faulty information or hire independent accountants to verify the information received."

Since 1987, no state high court has adopted this foreseeability approach to accountants' legal liability, while a large number have approved or adopted one of the narrower standards.[19] For example, in its 1992 ruling in *Bily v. Arthur Young,* the California Supreme Court expressly rejected the foreseeability approach in favor of the *Rusch Factors* or *Restatement* standard. The court gave a number of reasons for rejecting the *Rosenblum* foreseeability approach, including that the foreseeability rule exposes auditors to potential liability in excess of their proportionate share and the sophisticated plaintiffs have other ways to protect themselves from the risk of inaccurate financial statements (e.g., they can negotiate improved terms or hire their own auditor).[20]

However, in its 2003 ruling in *Murphy v. BDO Seidman, LLP*, the California Court of Appeals ruled that "grapevine plaintiffs," who alleged indirect reliance based on what others (e.g., stockholders and stockbrokers) told them about the financial statements, had legal claims for ordinary negligence against the auditors so long as the auditor would have reasonably foreseen that stockholders or stockbrokers would tell other people of the content of the financial statements and that the other people would rely upon the misrepresentations in purchasing the corporate stock. The court ruled that nothing in the *Bily* decision precludes indirect reliance.[21]

The *Murphy* ruling seems to stretch auditors' legal liability to third parties beyond reasonable bounds. Imagine, for example, that you are watching Jim Cramer's television show "Mad Money" on CNBC, and Cramer recommends a stock that you then purchase online. Shortly thereafter, news breaks of an accounting fraud. You sue the auditors based on your belief that the auditors should have known the public would buy the stock after Cramer recommended it. It makes little sense to conclude that a plaintiff may be successful in a lawsuit against the auditors based on a claim of ordinary negligence in this situation, given that auditors cannot control every use of audit information.

The conflicting common-law rulings can be confusing in trying to apply legal precedent to current court cases. To assist students, we have developed a summary in **Exhibit 8.4** of the primary legal issues and guiding principles addressed in important court cases in deciding the auditor's liability to third parties.

EXHIBIT 8.4   Auditor Legal Liability to Third Parties

Legal Approach	Case	Legal Principle	Legal Liability to Third Parties
Ultramares	*Ultramares v. Touche*	Privity	Possibly gross negligence that constitutes (constructive) fraud
Near-privity relationship	*Credit Alliance*	Three-pronged approach: knowledge of accountant that the statements will be used for a particular purpose; intention of third party to rely on those statements; some action by third party that provides evidence of the accountant's understanding of intended reliance	Ordinary negligence
Restatement (Second) of the Law of Torts	*Rusch Factors*	Foreseen third-party users	Ordinary negligence beyond near-privity
Foreseeable third party	*Rosenblum*	Reasonably foreseeable third-party users	Ordinary negligence with reliance on the statements

Common-Law Liability For Fraud

Common-law liability for fraud is available to third parties in any jurisdiction. The plaintiff (third party) must prove (1) a false representation by the accountant, (2) knowledge or belief by the accountant that the representation was false, (3) that the accountant intended to induce the third party to rely on false representation, (4) that the third party relied on the false representation, and (5) that the third party suffered damages.[22]

A common-law fraud case that explains these requirements is *Pacific Mutual Life Insurance v.* Ernst & Young.[23] In late 1986 and early 1987, Arthur Young & Company (now Ernst & Young), audited the financial statements of RepublicBank Corporation "Republic-Bank") for the year ending December 31, 1986. Following the audit, Ernst & Young issued a report stating it had conducted the audit in accordance with generally accepted auditing standards and, in its opinion, the financial statements "fairly presented" the financial position of RepublicBank as of December 31, 1986. This information was disseminated in January 1987. The facts of this case are summarized in **Exhibit 8.5**.

EXHIBIT 8.5   Pacific Mutual Life Insurance v. Ernst & Young

Subsequent to the audit of the financial statements of Republic Bank, Ernst & Young consented to having its audit report included in certain documents filed with the SEC. Those documents, which included a joint proxy statement and prospectus, discussed in significant detail the terms of a potential merger between RepublicBank and Interfirst Bank. The documents indicated, among other things, that Republic-Bank's 1986 year-end financial statements had been examined by Ernst & Young, and those financial statements were being incorporated into the documents "in reliance upon (Ernst & Young's) report and upon the authority of such firm as experts in auditing and accounting." Shortly thereafter, in June 1987, the merger between the two banks occurred and the new entity, First RepublicBank Corporation ("First Republic"), assumed responsibility for Interfirst's existing debts.

Shortly after the merger, Pacific Mutual Life Insurance (Pacific), an insurance company based in Newport Beach, California, purchased nearly $8 million worth of "non-investment grade debt securities" previously issued by Interfirst (the "Interfirst notes"). The notes were scheduled to mature on October 1, 1989. However, shortly after Pacific purchased the notes, First Republic publicly disclosed that it was experiencing serious financial problems with its real estate portfolio. Not long thereafter, First Republic filed for bankruptcy. This, according to Pacific, rendered the Interfirst notes "effectively worthless."

After First Republic filed for bankruptcy, Pacific sued Ernst & Young as well as a number of other entities. In its petition, Pacific alleged, among other things, that (1) Ernst & Young's 1986 audit report of RepublicBank was "materially false and misleading," (2) Ernst & Young "knew" at the time it issued the report that it had not reviewed RepublicBank's financial statements "in accordance with generally accepted auditing standards," and (3) Ernst & Young had "seriously breached the applicable auditor's standard of independence."

Sometime later, Ernst & Young filed a motion for summary judgment on Pacific's claims. In the motion, Ernst & Young argued it was entitled to judgment as a matter of law because (1) it did not make any material misrepresentations regarding the Interfirst notes; (2) Pacific did not actually, nor justifiably, rely on any statements or representations made by Ernst & Young; (3) Ernst & Young did not know its representations were false, nor did it act recklessly with respect to the truth or falsity of the representations; (4) Ernst & Young did not intend for Pacific to rely on its representations; and (5) Ernst & Young did not owe any duty to Pacific.

In March and April 1997, Pacific filed a cross-motion for partial summary judgment on the issue of Ernst & Young's intent and a response to Ernst & Young's motion, contending (among other things) that Ernst & Young's motion failed to address Pacific's cause of action for "aiding and abetting" the commission of fraud by others. Ernst & Young responded to the latter point by filing special exceptions in the trial court. Thereafter, on April 17, 1997, the trial court granted Ernst & Young's summary judgment motion. Several weeks later, the court denied Pacific's cross-motion as moot. Pacific then appealed the trial court opinion.

The trial judge agreed with Ernst & Young's stated defenses to common law liability for fraud. Summary judgment was granted to Ernst & Young. On appeal, Pacific contended that this ruling was an error. After reviewing the record in the appeal, the court reversed the opinion and ruled that Ernst & Young should be held legally liable.

In reaching the decision, the court of appeals rejected Ernst & Young's argument that summary judgment was proper because Ernst & Young made no representations at all regarding Interfirst or the condition of the Interfirst notes. The allegations made by Pacific did not turn on whether Ernst & Young made misrepresentations about the condition of Interfirst or the notes originally issued by Interfirst; instead, they focus on whether Ernst & Young made any material misrepresentations about Republic Bank and its financial condition. Because Pacific's claims were not premised on any alleged misrepresentation regarding Interfirst or the Interfirst notes, the court concluded Ernst & Young's argument based on the absence of any such representations lacked merit.

The court also rejected the suggestion in Ernst & Young's brief that the alleged misrepresentations were not material because no reasonable investor would have relied on a report of RepublicBank's 1986 year-end financial condition in making the decision to purchase the Interfirst notes. Evidence was provided by experts that convinced the court otherwise.

Ernst & Young had argued its judgments were proper because (1) to prevail on the fraud claim, Pacific was required to show Ernst & Young specifically intended for Pacific to rely on the representations made in the 1986 audit report when making its decision to purchase the Interfirst notes; and (2) no such showing could be made in this case. Ernst & Young made a similar argument on appeal. In response, Pacific argued that summary judgment was improper on this point because Pacific was only required to show (1) Ernst & Young intended that a particular class of persons rely on its representations, and (2) Pacific was a member of that class. After reviewing the record in this cause as well as applicable law, the court agreed with Pacific.

Statutory Law Liability for Fraud

To establish liability for fraud under Section 10(b) of the Securities Act, a plaintiff must show that:

- The defendant made a material misstatement or omission;
- The misstatement or omission was made with an intent to deceive, manipulate or defraud (i.e., *scienter*);
- There is a connection between the misrepresentation or omission and the plaintiff's purchase or sale of a security;
- The plaintiff relied on the misstatement or omission;
- The plaintiff suffered economic loss; and
- There is a casual connection between the material misrepresentation or omission and the plaintiff's loss.

Courts have held that *scienter* or fraudulent intent may be established by proof that the accountant acted with knowledge of the false representation. However, liability for fraud is not limited to cases where the auditor was knowingly deceitful. Some courts have interpreted gross negligence or constructive fraud as an instance of fraud. An important case in this area is *State Street Trust Co. v. Ernst.*[24] In this case, the auditors issued an unqualified opinion on their client's financial statements, knowing that State Street Trust Company was making a loan based on those financial statements. A month later, the auditors sent a letter to the client indicating that receivables had been overstated. The auditors, however, did not communicate this information to State Street, and the client subsequently went bankrupt. The New York court ruled that the auditor's actions appeared to be grossly negligent and that "reckless disregard of consequences may take the place of deliberate intention." In such cases, while fraudulent intent may not be present, the court "constructs" fraud due to the grossness of the negligence.[25]

In *Phar-Mor v. Coopers & Lybrand,* (now PricewaterhouseCoopers) the auditors were found guilty of fraud under both common and statutory law, even though the plaintiffs acknowledged that the auditors had no intent to deceive. Instead, the plaintiff successfully argued reckless disregard for the truth which gives rise to an inference of fraud. An important part of this ruling is that plaintiffs who are barred from suing for ordinary negligence because they lack a privity relationship or are not foreseen users can choose to sue the auditor for fraud because to find an auditor guilty of fraud, the plaintiffs need only prove gross negligence.[26]

In more recent cases, the court ruled in *Houbigant, Inc. v. Deloitte & Touche LLP*[27] and *Reisman v. KPMG Peat Marwick LLP*[28] that for an auditor to be found guilty of fraud, the plaintiffs must prove only that the auditor was aware that its misrepresentations might reasonably be relied upon by the plaintiff, not that the auditor intended to induce the detrimental reliance. The court referred to recent audit failures in its *Houbigant* decision: "It should be sufficient that the complaint contains some rational basis for inferring that the alleged misrepresentation was knowingly made. Indeed, to require anything beyond that would be particularly undesirable at this time, when it has been widely acknowledged that our society is experiencing a proliferation of frauds perpetrated by officers of large corporations . . . unchecked by the 'impartial' auditors they hired."[29]

An example of a successful lawsuit brought by the SEC for the failure of an auditor to detect fraud is the audit of mortgage loan originator, Taylor, Bean & Whitaker (TBW) Mortgage Corp. by Deloitte. Deloitte served as TBW's external auditor between 2002 and 2008 until the mortgage broker's collapse in 2009. TBW's collapse was linked with its acquisition of a majority stake in ColonialBancGroup, which also folded in 2009 after wide-ranging fraud dating back to 2002 was uncovered, including collusion between high ranking individuals at TBW and Colonial Bank.

TBW allegedly sold fictitious loans insured by the Federal Housing Administration during the mortgage collapse that triggered the 2008-2009 financial recession. The U.S. Department of Justice claimed TBW's financial statements failed to reflect its severe financial distress and knowingly deviated from applicable auditing standards. Deloitte, therefore, allegedly failed to detect TBW's fraudulent conduct and materially false and misleading financial statements. Furthermore, the Justice Department claimed that Deloitte's failure to detect misconduct enabled TBW's improper behavior to continue and thus contributed to its collapse. Deloitte came to a settlement with the Department on March 2, 2018, agreeing to pay $149.5, which makes no determination of liability.[30]

Liability for Fraudulent Misrepresentation

Section 531 of the Restatement Second of Torts discusses the imposition of liability for fraudulent misrepresentations. That section states: One who makes a fraudulent misrepresentation is subject to liability to the persons or class of persons whom they intend or has reason to expect to act or to refrain from action in reliance upon the misrepresentation, for monetary loss suffered by them through their justifiable reliance in the type of transaction in which they intend or has reason to expect their conduct to be influenced. Under Section 531, a person has "reason to expect" that the result will follow or would govern his conduct upon the assumption that it will do so. Stated otherwise, the maker of a misrepresentation is liable if they have information that would lead a reasonable man to conclude that "an especial likelihood" exists that it will reach certain persons and will influence their conduct.

Section 531 makes it clear that liability for fraudulent misrepresentations may be imposed even when the maker of the misrepresentation does not know the identity of the person whom the misrepresentation will reach. In that regard, the maker may have reason to expect that their misrepresentation will reach any of a class of persons, although they do not know the identity of the person whom it will reach or indeed of any individual in the class. . . . The class may include a rather large group, such as potential sellers, buyers, creditors, lenders or investors, or others who may be expected to enter into dealings in reliance upon the misrepresentation.

One who makes a fraudulent misrepresentation intending or with reason to expect that more than one person or class of persons will be induced to rely on it, or that there will be action or inaction in more than one transaction or type of transaction, is subject to liability for monetary loss to any one of such persons justifiably relying upon the misrepresentation in any one or more of such transactions.

"Reason to Expect" versus "Should Have Known" Standard

In the Pacific case previously discussed, the plaintiff presented a significant amount of summary judgment evidence indicating that Ernst & Young had "reason to expect" that (1) its representations regarding the 1986 year-end audit would reach a certain class of persons (i.e., investors), and (2) members of that class would act in reliance on those representations.

The court reviewed the evidence and concluded (1) it raises a fact issue on whether Ernst & Young had "reason to expect" that Pacific would rely on its representations regarding the RepublicBank audit when making its decision to purchase the Interfirst notes, and (2) summary judgment on this ground was therefore improper. Although Ernst & Young presented summary judgment evidence indicating it did *not* intend for Pacific to rely on the 1986 year-end audit, other evidence in the summary judgment record suggests otherwise and a fact issue therefore remained on this point. Accordingly, the court concluded the trial judge erred in granting summary judgment on this ground.

In reaching the decision, the court rejected Ernst & Young's reliance on the court's opinion in *Blue Bell* that was previously discussed. In that case, Peat Marwick (now KPMG) audited the financial statements of Myers Department Store ("Myers") for the fiscal year ending February 1, 1981, and forwarded 70 copies of its audit report to Myers following completion of the audit. Thereafter, Myers furnished a copy of the report to Blue Bell, a clothing manufacturer with whom a Myers subsidiary had done business in the past. Based on that report, Blue Bell agreed to extend a substantial amount of credit to the Myers subsidiary. Thereafter, Myers filed for bankruptcy, and Blue Bell ultimately sued Peat Marwick for fraud and negligent misrepresentation in connection with the 1981 audit.

The trial court granted summary judgment in favor of Peat Marwick on all of the claims asserted, and Blue Bell appealed. On appeal, the appeals court reversed the trial court's grant of summary judgment on the negligent misrepresentation claim but affirmed summary judgment on Blue Bell's fraud claim. In reaching the decision, the court noted that while evidence that Peat Marwick *should have known* that Blue Bell would rely on its misrepresentations may have been sufficient to sustain Blue Bell's negligent misrepresentation claim, it was not sufficient to overcome summary judgment on the fraud claim. Because Blue Bell provided no summary judgment evidence tending to show Peat Marwick *intended* to induce Blue Bell's reliance, the court concluded summary judgment on the fraud claim was proper.

The court found that *Blue Bell* was distinguishable from *Pacific Mutual* reasoning in that its decision in *Blue Bell* stated only that a "should have known" standard is not applicable to fraud claims. However, unlike the plaintiff in *Blue Bell,* the plaintiff in *Pacific Mutual* did not argue that liability should be imposed because Ernst & Young "should have known" the plaintiff would rely on the representations. Rather, Pacific argued that liability should be imposed because the requirements of Section 531 of the Restatement had been met. The decision in *Blue Bell* said nothing about the applicability of Section 531 to fraud claims or whether Section 531's *reason to expect* standard is sufficient to establish the "intent to induce reliance" element of a fraud cause of action. Reason to expect requires possession of affirmative knowledge while "should have known" implies a lack of knowledge that should have been possessed. Thus, the decision in *Blue Bell* did not foreclose the possibility that having a reason to expect standard certain would suffice to support a fraud claim.

Given the complexity of the "should have known" and "reason to expect" standards, **Exhibit 8.6** presents the key determinants whether fraud exists.

EXHIBIT 8.6   Legal Standards in Fraud Cases

Case	Standard	Interpretation	Applicability in Fraud Cases
Blue Bell	Should have known	Implies a lack of knowledge that auditors should have possessed	No
Pacific Mutual Life	Reason to expect	Possession of affirmative knowledge	Yes

Income Tax Fraud versus Tax Negligence

Accountants' legal liability extends to actions of personal tax fraud and negligence as well as permitting and/or enabling the tax fraud of a client. Accountants need to know about tax fraud and tax negligence whether on the part of a client or themselves. Income tax fraud is the willful attempt to evade tax law or defraud the IRS. Tax fraud occurs when a person or company does any of the following:

- Intentionally fails to file an income tax return
- Willfully fails to pay taxes due
- Intentionally fails to report all income received
- Makes fraudulent or false claims in preparing the tax return
- Prepares and files a false return.

When careless errors occur, if signs of fraud are absent, the IRS will usually assume that it was an honest mistake rather than a willful evasion of the tax code. In this circumstance, the mistake is typically attributable to negligence. Although unintentional, the IRS may still fine the taxpayer a penalty of 20 percent of the underpayment.

Whether as a result of client behavior or that of an accountant, the IRS can usually distinguish when an error is the result of negligence or the willful evasion of the tax law. The IRS looks for common types of suspicious and fraudulent activity, such as:

- Overstatement of deductions and exemptions
- Falsification of documents
- Concealment or transfer of income
- Keeping two sets of financial ledgers
- Falsifying personal expenses as business expenses
- Using a false Social Security number
- Claiming an exemption for a nonexistent dependent, such as a child
- Willfully underreporting income.

Actions of accountants that are judged to be tax fraud can be deemed an act discreditable to the profession in violation of the rules of conduct in the AICPA Code of Professional Conduct. These actions are in many respects the most egregious violation of ethical standards that rely on honesty and integrity. A valid question to ask is how can we expect an accountant to identify and act on fraud of a client when they can't even monitor their personal behavior?

Auditor Defenses to Negligence and Fraud

LO 8-2

Explain auditor defenses to negligence, negligent misrepresentation, and fraud

Auditor Defenses to Negligence

Lawsuits against auditors for negligence typically claim that the auditor failed to use due care, failed to follow GAAS, and failed to identify a material misstatement. The due care defense is based on the *prudent person* concept. This defense implies four things:

1. The auditor possessed the requisite skills to evaluate accounting entries.
2. The auditor employed such skill with reasonable care and diligence.
3. The auditor undertook their task(s) with good faith and integrity.
4. While the auditor may be liable for negligence, the auditor is not liable for errors in judgment.

The auditor's defense against third-party lawsuits for negligence that claim the auditor did not detect a misstatement or fraud requires proof that (1) the auditor did not have a duty to the third party, (2) the third party was negligent, (3) the auditor's work was performed in accordance with professional standards, (4) the third party did not suffer a loss, (5) any loss to the third party was caused by other events, or (6) the claim is invalid because the statute of limitations has expired.[31] Here are examples of the various defenses that an auditor can use:

1. Auditors can defend a common-law action by presenting arguments and evidence to rebut third-party plaintiffs' claims and evidence. Once a plaintiff has demonstrated an economic loss and materially misstated financial statements, defenses available to auditors against third parties include the following:[32] (1) the third party lacked standing to sue in a particular jurisdiction, as would be the case when bringing a lawsuit for ordinary negligence; and (2) the appropriate relationship between the auditor and third party did not exist (i.e., a privity relationship).
2. The third party's loss was due to events other than the financial statements and auditors' examination, as might be the case if poor business practices or stock market declines caused the loss.

3. Auditors' work was performed in accordance with GAAS, which is generally interpreted to mean that auditors were not negligent (ordinary negligence).

In summary, in order for a third party or a client to successfully sue an auditor under negligence, it is not sufficient to just come up with some evidence and file a court case. The auditor must have failed to exercise due care and follow GAAS. The plaintiff must prove the following four criteria that are depicted in **Exhibit 8.7**.

EXHIBIT 8.7   Auditor Liability for Negligence[33]

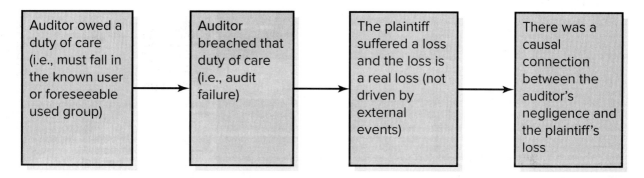

| Auditor owed a duty of care (i.e., must fall in the known user or foreseeable used group) | → | Auditor breached that duty of care (i.e., audit failure) | → | The plaintiff suffered a loss and the loss is a real loss (not driven by external events) | → | There was a causal connection between the auditor's negligence and the plaintiff's loss |

Auditor Defenses to Negligent Misrepresentation

A Texas Supreme Court decision in 2010 in the case of *Grant Thornton LLP v. Prospect High Income Fund, et al.* has strengthened defenses available to auditors brought by third parties for negligent misrepresentation and fraud. The Court overruled what had been a broader standard for establishing liability in negligent misrepresentations when financial failings of their clients exist. The ruling also sets new limitations on "holder" claims, wherein investors contend that they were put at a disadvantage because they held securities based on an auditor's report that they otherwise would have sold.[34]

In *Prospect,* the Texas Supreme Court expressly rejected the standard set forth in *Blue Bell* in favor of the stricter standard set forth in the 1999 decision of *McCamish, Martin, Brown & Loeffler v. F. E. Appling Interests* (a lawyer case). In doing so, it stated: "*McCamish* has served as a guidepost for our courts of appeals in analyzing the tort of negligent misrepresentation, in contrast to earlier decisions applying a broader standard."[35] The only case the Supreme Court cited as applying the rejected broader standard was *Blue Bell.*

The significance of adopting *McCamish* for auditors and others is that it applies a strict standard for determining who can assert a negligent misrepresentation claim—a plaintiff must be "a known person" who relied upon the auditor's representations for "a known purpose." The importance of this limitation is apparent from the court's first holding—the Cayman Fund's claims were all dismissed because it was merely a potential public investor with no prior connections to either Grant Thornton or the issuer of the bonds. "[P]redicating scope of liability on [the auditor's] general knowledge that investors may purchase bonds would 'eviscerate the Restatement rule in favor of a *de facto* foreseeability approach—an approach [we] have refused to embrace.'"

Courts in Texas and other states have allowed negligent misrepresentation claims against auditors and others by persons who should not have been considered to be within the "limited group" that the authors of the Restatement of Torts intended to be able to sue. Adopting the *McCamish* standard of a "known person for a known purpose" to identify proper plaintiffs should reduce litigation against auditors, particularly by potential public investors. Requiring even a known person to have direct communication with a defendant to assert a claim that a misrepresentation caused the plaintiff to hold onto an investment should eliminate additional claims against accountants and others in litigation. Equally important for both fraud and negligent misrepresentation defense is the finding that a plaintiff who knows the financial condition of a company cannot assert reliance upon an auditor's opinion as the basis of its damages.[36]

The good news for accountants and other defendants is that this ruling sets forth a strong defense to the otherwise difficult-to-defend claim that "if I had known, I would have sold or taken other action to protect myself." Up until now, defendants have had little ability to defend holder claims because there is rarely any proof other than the plaintiff's testimony of what they did not do or would have done. *Prospect* significantly closes that door.

Auditor Defenses to Fraud

The audit client holds primary responsibility for the prevention and detection of fraud, so blame cannot be placed automatically or solely on the auditor. The auditor should be liable only if inadequacies in their audit resulted in failure to detect the fraud. Primarily, it will depend on whether failure to detect the fraud was due to shortcomings in the auditor's work. The absence of deficiencies in the audit provides a defense to fraud.

An auditor's role is to form an opinion about whether the financial reports as a whole are free from material misstatements including fraud. The auditing standards issued by the AICPA and PCAOB provide the requirements for the conduct of an audit, which is intended to provide reasonable but not absolute assurance that the final reports are accurate and reliable. It is not a guarantee. In essence, according to Claire Grayson a policy advisor on audit and assurance, "the auditor should be liable only if inadequacies in their audit resulted in the failure to detect fraud."

Fraud requires an intent to deceive another party or scienter. In such cases, the auditor acted with knowledge of a false representation. Unlike negligence where the auditor might have made a careless statement, fraud requires the belief that representation was false. Fraudulent intent means a representation was made with reckless indifference to the truth or falsity.

An auditors' defense against fraud begins with the claim that due care has been exercised and the auditor followed GAAS. Beyond that, the auditor must show that,

1. The representation in question was not false,
2. The representation in question was not material,
3. The auditor did not know the representation was untrue,
4. There was no intent to deceive,
5. The third party did not rely on the representation, and
6. The third party did not suffer any damages.

You may want to refer back to **Exhibit 8.1** for a summary of accountants' legal liabilities and defenses.

Consideration of Fraud in a Financial Statement Audit

In order to avoid statutory liability for fraud discussed in the next section, the auditor must demonstrate that they carefully considered fraud risks in the financial statement audit. These were first discussed in **Chapter 5**. We summarize them below.

It is important for auditors to meet professional standards with respect to the consideration of fraud in a financial statement audit. Doing so provides a defense to allegations of fraud. Recall from our discussions in **Chapter 5** that *fraud* is an intentional act that results in a material misstatement in financial statements that are the subject of an audit. Two types of misstatements are relevant to the auditor's consideration of fraud—misstatements arising from fraudulent financial reporting and misstatements arising from misappropriation of assets. We discussed both types of fraud in **Chapter 3** and summarize the requirements in **Exhibit 8.8**.

Fraudulent financial reporting may occur because management representatives rationalize the appropriateness of a material misstatement, for example, as an aggressive rather than indefensible interpretation of complex accounting rules, or as a temporary misstatement of financial statements, including interim statements, expected to be corrected later when operational results improve.

Misappropriation of assets may be accompanied by false or misleading records or documents, possibly created by circumventing controls. In this chapter, we are mainly concerned with actions that cause the financial statements not to be fairly presented, in all material respects, in conformity with GAAP.

EXHIBIT 8.8   Auditor Responsibility to Detect Fraud[37]

Misstatements arising from fraudulent financial reporting

These are intentional misstatements or omissions of amounts or disclosures in financial statements designed to deceive financial statement users where the effect causes the financial statements not to be presented, in all material respects, in conformity with GAAS. Fraudulent financial reporting may be accomplished by the following:

- Manipulation, falsification, or alteration of accounting records or supporting documents from which financial statements are prepared;
- Misrepresentation in or intentional omission from the financial statements of events, transactions, or other significant information;
- Intentional misapplication of accounting principles relating to amounts, classification, manner of presentation, or disclosure.

Misstatements arising from misappropriation of assets

These are referred to as occupational fraud in Chapter 3. They involve the theft of an entity's assets where the effect of the theft causes the financial statements not to be presented, in all material respects, in conformity with GAAP. Misappropriation of assets can be accomplished in various ways, including embezzling receipts, stealing assets, or causing an entity to pay for goods or services that have not been received.

Recall from our discussion of the fraud triangle in **Chapter 5** that three conditions generally are present when fraud occurs. A brief summary of those conditions is presented in **Exhibit 8.9**.

EXHIBIT 8.9   Detecting Fraudulent Reporting Using the Fraud Triangle

There are three factors to consider in detecting fraud in financial statements. These are summarized below.

Pressure or incentive

This may occur when management or other employees have an *incentive* or are under *pressure*, which provides a reason to commit fraud.

Opportunity to commit fraud

Circumstances may exist that enable the fraud to occur including the absence of internal controls, ineffective controls, or the ability of management to override controls—that provide an *opportunity* for a fraud to be perpetrated.

Rationalizing the fraud

Those involved in the fraud are able to *rationalize* committing a fraudulent act such as the need to carry out the wishes of top management to make the financial statements look better. They may also express a concern that if they exposed the fraud, the result may be retaliation by top management including the possibility of a loss of job.

Some individuals possess an *attitude*, character, or set of ethical values that allow them to commit a dishonest act knowingly and intentionally. However, even otherwise honest individuals can commit fraud in an environment that imposes sufficient pressure on them. The greater the incentive or pressure, the more likely an individual will be able to rationalize the acceptability of committing fraud.

Typically, management and employees engaged in fraud will take steps to conceal the fraud from the auditors and others within and outside the organization. Doing so opens the door to legal liability for fraud under the Securities Exchange Act of 1934. Fraud may be concealed by withholding evidence or misrepresenting information in response to inquiries or by falsifying documentation. For example, management that engages in fraudulent financial reporting might alter shipping documents. Employees or members of management who misappropriate cash might try to conceal their thefts by forging signatures or falsifying electronic approvals on disbursement authorizations. An audit conducted in accordance with GAAS rarely involves the authentication of such documentation, nor are auditors trained as or expected to be experts in such authentication. In addition, an auditor may not discover the existence of a modification of documentation through a side agreement that management or a third party has not disclosed.

Fraud also may be concealed through collusion among management, employees, or third parties. Collusion may cause the auditor who has properly performed the audit to conclude that evidence provided is persuasive when it is, in fact, false. For example, through collusion, false evidence that controls have been operating effectively may be presented to the auditor, or consistent misleading explanations may be given to the auditor by more than one individual within the entity to explain an unexpected result of an analytical procedure. As another example, the auditor may receive a false confirmation from a third party that is in collusion with management.

The auditor has a responsibility to plan and perform the audit to obtain reasonable assurance about whether the financial statements are free of material misstatement, whether caused by fraud or error. However, absolute assurance is not attainable and thus even a carefully planned and performed audit may not detect a material misstatement resulting from fraud. A material misstatement may not be detected because of the nature of audit evidence or because the characteristics of fraud as discussed above may cause the auditor to rely unknowingly on audit evidence that appears to be valid, but is, in fact, false and fraudulent. Furthermore, audit procedures that are effective for detecting an error may be ineffective for detecting fraud.

In summary, for auditors to assert a valid defense to fraud, they must prove that due care had been exercised in the conduct of the audit and that they have considered the risk that material misstatements in the financial statements exist in order to provide reasonable assurance that the audit is free of material misstatements that might otherwise lead to legal liability for fraud.

Statutory Liability

LO 8-3

Explain the basis for auditors' statutory legal liability.

As explained briefly in **Chapter 7**, auditors may have legal liability under the Securities Act of 1933 and the Securities Exchange Act of 1934. These statutory liabilities may lead to convictions for crimes, provided their conduct was "willful."

The term "willful" and its application in criminal securities law cases often is influenced by the context of the situation. Section 32(a) of the Securities Exchange Act of 1934 provides that any person who "willfully" violates any provision of the Act can be charged with a crime, while Section 15(b)(4) authorizes the SEC to seek civil administrative penalties against any person who "willfully" violates certain provisions of the securities laws.

Securities Act of 1933

The Securities Act of 1933 regulates the disclosure of material facts in a registration statement for a new public offering of securities (i.e., IPO). A registration statement contains information and documents that must be filed with the SEC, such as capital structure, description of management and the business enterprise, and financial statements certified by independent public accountants. Companies must file registration statements (S-1, S-2, and S-3 forms) and prospectuses that contain financial statements that have been audited by an independent CPA. Accountants who assist in the preparation of the registration statement are civilly liable if the registration statement (1) contains untrue statements of material facts, (2) omits material facts required by statute or regulation, or (3) omits information that if not given makes the facts stated misleading.[38]

Section 11 of the Securities Act of 1933 imposes a liability on issuer companies and others, including auditors, for losses suffered by third parties when false or misleading information is included in a registration statement. Any purchaser of securities may sue: The purchaser generally must prove that (1) the specific security was offered through the registration statements, (2) damages were incurred, and (3) there was a material misstatement or omission in the financial statements included in the registration statement. The plaintiff need not prove reliance on the financial statements unless the purchase took place after one year of the offering.

If items (2) and (3) are proven, it is a *prima facie* case (sufficient to win against the CPA unless rebutted) and shifts the burden of proof to the accountant, who may escape liability by proving the following: (1) after reasonable investigation, the CPA concludes that there is a reasonable basis to believe that the financial statements were true and there was no material misstatement (the materiality defense); (2) a "reasonable investigation" was conducted (the due diligence defense); (3) the plaintiff knew that the financial statements were incorrect when the investment was made (the knowledge of falsehood defense); or (4) the loss was due to factors other than the material misstatement or omission (the lack of causation defense).

Materiality Defense

An accountant might argue that the false or misleading information is not material and thus should not have had an impact on the purchaser's decision-making process. The SEC and the courts have attempted to define materiality in this context. The term *material* describes the kind of information that an average prudent investor would want to have so that he can make an intelligent, informed decision whether or not to buy the security. A material fact is one that, if correctly stated or disclosed, would have deterred or tended to deter the average prudent investor from purchasing the securities in question. The term does not cover minor inaccuracies or errors in matters of no interest to investors. Facts that tend to deter a person from purchasing a security are those that have an important bearing upon the nature or condition of the issuing corporation or its business.[39]

Due Diligence Defense

To establish a due diligence defense under Section 11, the defendant must prove that a reasonable investigation of the financial statements of the issuer and controlling persons was conducted. As a result, there was no reason to believe any of the information in the registration statement or prospectus was false or misleading. To determine whether a reasonable investigation has been made, the law provides that the standard of *reasonableness* is that required of a prudent person in the management of their own property. The burden of proof is on the defendant, and the test is as of the time the registration became effective. The due diligence defense, in effect, requires proof that a party was not guilty of fraud or negligence.[40]

Section 11 Liability Under Securities Act of 1933

A major opinion of the U.S. Supreme Court on March 24, 2015, in *Omnicare, Inc. v. Laborers District Council Construction Industry Pension Fund* changes the legal landscape with respect to when an issuer of financial statements may be held liable under Section 11 of the Securities Act of 1933 for statements of opinion made in a registration statement. The Court vacated and remanded the Sixth Circuit's 2013 decision holding that a Section 11 plaintiff need only allege that an opinion in a registration statement was "objectively false," notwithstanding the company's understanding when the statement was made. The Supreme Court ruled a statement of opinion in a registration statement may not support Section 11 liability merely because it is "ultimately found incorrect." Addressing Section 11's alleged misstatements of facts, the Supreme Court held that "liability under Section 11's false-statement provision would follow . . . not only if the speaker did not hold the belief they professed but also if the supporting facts they supplied were untrue." The Court held that with respect to potential misstatement liability under Section 11, "a sincere statement of pure opinion is not an 'untrue statement of material fact,' regardless whether an investor can ultimately prove the belief wrong."

The Court further held that an issuer may be liable under Section 11 for omitting material facts about the inquiry into or knowledge concerning a statement of opinion if those facts "conflict" with what a reasonable investor would "understand an opinion statement to convey" with respect to "how the speaker has formed the opinion" or "the speaker's basis for holding that view." The Court clarified that an issuer need not disclose every fact "cutting the other way" against an opinion because "[r]easonable investors understand that opinions sometimes rest on a weighing of competing facts."

The essence of the *Omnicare* opinion can be summarized as follows:

- An investor cannot state a claim by alleging only that an opinion was wrong; the complaint must also call into question the issuer's basis for offering the opinion;
- Statements of opinion are actionable under Section 11 of the Securities Act of 1933 as false or misleading only if the issuer of the opinion held a subjective belief inconsistent with the opinion; and
- A Section 11 plaintiff must identify particular and material facts about an inquiry the issuer did or did not conduct or the knowledge it did or did not have whose omission makes the opinion statement questioned misleading to a reasonable person reading the statement fairly and in context.

In summary, the Court emphasized that Section 11 "does not allow investors to second-guess inherently subjective and uncertain assessments." Even if wrong, a genuinely held statement of pure opinion, therefore, cannot be an untrue statement of material fact. It is worth noting that the essence of this statement is motivation. In rendering an opinion, so long as the issuer believes the statement to be true, allegations of legal liability under Section 11 will not survive.

Section 11 Liability Standard for Auditors

In analyzing the *Omnicare* ruling with respect to auditors' opinions, Griggs, Mixter, and Rissier, writing for Bloomberg BNA, point to three statements in the audit report that can be examined using the *Omnicare* framework.[41]

- The auditor's "opinion" that "the financial statements . . . present fairly, in all material respects, the [consolidated] financial position of [the company at the identified balance sheet dates], and the [consolidated] results of [its] operations and [its] consolidated cash flows for [each of the three years in the period] ended in conformity with [U.S. generally accepted accounting principles ['GAAP']]";
- The auditor's statement that audits were conducted "in accordance with [the standards of the [PCAOB]]"; and
- The auditor's belief that the audits "provide a reasonable basis for [the] opinion."

According to the authors, under *Omnicare,* an auditor can be held liable under Section 11 for its audit opinion in only three circumstances: (1) if the auditor does not actually hold the opinion; (2) the opinion contains an embedded statement of fact that is misleading; or (3) if the opinion omits a fact that makes the opinion misleading to the ordinary investor. A material omission claim would require the plaintiff "to identify actual and material steps taken or not taken by [the defendant auditor] in its audit or knowledge it did or did not have in the formation of the opinion" rather than simply "claiming that any reasonable audit would have uncovered a material fact whose omission renders the opinion misleading to a reasonable person reading the statement fairly and in context."

The authors conclude their analysis by stating that Omnicare labels auditors' statements as opinions, which seems appropriate. Labeling or forming a statement as an opinion expresses uncertainty. Although a plaintiff could later prove that opinion erroneous, the words in the audit report "[We] believe" themselves admit to this possibility, thus precluding liability for an untrue statement of fact. Statements of fact express certainty; statements of opinion do not.

It remains to be seen what long-term effect the Section 11 liability standard will have on auditors under the Securities Act of 1934, especially Section 10 and Rule 10b-5, that pertain to annual and quarterly report filings in Forms 10-K and 10-Q.

Section 11 Auditors' "Opinion" Statements

In their review of SEC Section 11 regulations with respect to registration statements, Douglas and Rowe point out that independent auditors and CPA firms have long been the target of plaintiffs' attorneys seeking to impose liability under federal securities laws. However, changes in these standards mean auditors may have a new shield to deflect frivolous claims. Recently, courts in a growing number of jurisdictions have required that plaintiffs asserting a Section 11 claim under the Securities Act of 1933 must plead both objective and subjective falsity to properly allege a misstated "opinion" statement with respect to financial-statement line items.[42]

Section 11 of the Securities Act provides a cause of action to investors who can prove that a registration statement "contained an untrue statement of a material fact or omitted to state a material fact required to be stated therein or necessary to make the statements therein not misleading."[43] Those potentially liable under Section 11 include every person who signed the registration statement, every director or partner of the issuer at the time of the filing, every underwriter, and, as relevant here, every accountant who consented to being named as having prepared or certified any part of the registration statement. Independent auditors who consent to being named as having prepared financial statements that are later included in a registration statement are frequent targets under Section 11.

Only recently have courts considered whether financial-statement line items constitute an opinion for purposes of Section 11 pleading, and, thus, whether an accountant's representation regarding its "opinion" can lead to Section 11 liability. At least two courts have now held that certain financial-statement line items are "opinions" such that a plaintiff must allege that the financial-statement account was objectively and subjectively false.

In *Fait v. Regions Financial Corp.,* the Second Circuit addressed whether goodwill and the loan-loss reserve were balance sheet "opinions." As to goodwill, the court recognized that "[e]stimates of goodwill depend on management's determination of the 'fair value' of the assets acquired and liabilities assumed, which are not matters of objective fact." Likewise, the Second Circuit found that a loan-loss reserve is similarly subject to the opinion of the accountant and registrant. That is, "loan-loss reserves reflect management's opinion or judgment about what, if any, portion of amounts due on the loans ultimately might not be collectible." Because both determinations were "inherently subjective," the Second Circuit held that matters of opinion are actionable only if the statements "misstate the opinions or belief held, or, in the case of statements of reasons, the actual motivation for the speaker's actions, *and* they are false or misleading with respect to the underlying subject matter they address."[44]

A similar issue existed in *MHC Mutual Conversion Fund, L.P. v. United W. Bancorp, Inc.* There, the plaintiffs alleged that United Western Bancorp's registration statement materially misstated the value of certain collateralized mortgage obligations and mortgage-backed securities. Specifically, the plaintiffs alleged that United Western Bancorp failed to recognize timely as much as $69 million in other-than-temporary impairment (OTTI), which improperly inflated the value of the underlying securities. The court ruled that the OTTI account balance constituted an opinion. In so doing, the court reasoned, all impairment analysis requires the issuer to determine an asset's fair value, which itself takes into account such subjective indicia as "market forces, market trends, and buyers' whims," and it also observed that the issuer must subjectively assess its "expectation" as to whether it will recover the security's amortized cost.[45]

Ultimately, a significant number of financial-statement accounts and decisions require some degree of subjective input. If *Fait* and *MHC Mutual* are to serve as any guide, plaintiffs pursuing a Section 11 claim against the registrant's auditors must now plead that any material misstatement to such an account is both subjectively and objectively false.

Securities Exchange Act of 1934

The Securities Exchange Act of 1934 regulates the ongoing reporting by companies whose securities are listed and traded on stock exchanges. The Act requires ongoing filing of quarterly (10-Q) and annual (10-K) reports and the periodic filing of an 8-K form whenever a significant event takes place affecting the entity, such as a change in auditors. Entities having total assets of $10 million or more and 500 or more stockholders are required to register under the Securities Exchange Act. The form and content of 10-K and 10-Q filings are governed by the SEC through Regulation S-X (which covers annual and interim financial statements) and Regulation S-K (which covers other supplementary disclosures).[46]

In addition to these two regulations, auditors must be familiar with Financial Reporting Releases (FRRs), which express new rules and policies about disclosure, and Staff Accounting Bulletins (SABs), which provide unofficial, but important, interpretations of Regulations S-X and S-K. Taken together, these four pronouncements provide the authoritative literature for information that must be filed with the SEC.[47]

Section 18 of the Act imposes liability on any person who makes a material false or misleading statement in documents filed with the SEC. The auditor's liability can be limited if the auditor can show that he "acted in good faith and had no knowledge that such statement was false or misleading." However, a number of cases have limited the auditor's good-faith defense when the auditor's action has been judged to be grossly negligent.[48]

The liability of auditors under the act often centers on Section 10 and Rule 10b-5. These provisions make it unlawful for a CPA to (1) employ any device, scheme, or artifice to defraud; (2) make an untrue statement of material fact or omit a material fact necessary in order to make the statement made, in the light of the circumstances under which they were made, not misleading; or (3) engage in any act, practice, or course of business to commit fraud or deceit in connection with the purchase or sale of the security.[49]

Once a plaintiff has established the ability to sue under Rule 10b-5, the following elements must be proved: (1) a material, factual misrepresentation or omission; (2) reliance by the plaintiff on the financial statements; (3) damages suffered as a result of reliance on the financial statements; and (4) the intent to deceive, manipulate, or defraud.[50]

A common technique used to implicate accountants in claims of violation of Rule 10b-5 is a claim of aiding and abetting the violation of others. Rule 10b-5 reaches not only those persons who actually made a material misstatement, but also those persons who aid and abet such a violation. It has become routine in cases involving accounting firms for plaintiffs to plead both a direct violation by the firm of the statute and rule, and that the firm aided and abetted the violation of others. Most lower courts have recognized that a claim can be stated for aiding and abetting a violation of federal securities laws when the plaintiff establishes that a violation was committed by some other defendant and a party had knowledge of the violation and took some action in furtherance of the violation. The most aggressive use of the aiding and abetting doctrine has been the claim that the failure of the accountants to blow the whistle on their client during the course of performing services constituted aiding and abetting the violation of others.

A valid defense for auditors against claims of aiding and abetting a fraud is any violation of Section 10(b) was attributable to some other defendant and that party had knowledge of the violation and took some action in furtherance of the violation. The plaintiff must establish that she actually relied on the financial statements, which then becomes a valid defense for auditors if reliance cannot be proven.

There are several defenses the auditor might use against the claim of aiding and abetting including:

1. There was no causal connection between the alleged deficiencies in the audits and the financial problems that ultimately resulted in the failure of the company.

2. The company failed because of market forces and management deficiencies, not because the financial statements were false and misleading.

3. A defense also exists if the auditor can show that she did not intend for the third party to rely on a material misstatement so there was no scienter.

Reliance by Plaintiff

The first element can include materially misleading information or the omission of material information. Reliance cannot be established if the damages or loss suffered by the plaintiff would have occurred regardless of whether the audited financial statements were misstated. A good example of the failure to establish direct causation between the audited financial statements, reliance thereon, and damages to the plaintiff is the court ruling in *Maxwell v. KPMG LLP*. In this case, the court ruled that even if the other elements necessary to sue under Rule 10b-5 could be established, Maxwell's alleged reliance on the audited financial statements of an acquiring entity was irrelevant, as the business model of that entity was bound to fail because of the dot.com collapse, and thus Maxwell's harm was not caused by KPMG's audit.[51]

This ruling stands as an example of non-accounting events that are the proximate cause of a failed business being given more weight than audited statements. The necessary conditions for the demise of the audit client (Whittman-Hart) were, first, its decision to buy US Web, and, second, the precipitate decline of the dot.com business. The decision to buy US Web was not influenced by KPMG's approving Whittman-Hart's accounting decisions, and neither were the dot.com troubles. US Web's agreement to be bought may have been influenced by KPMG's advice to Whittman-Hart, but that is irrelevant because US Web was doomed by the coming collapse of its market and thus was not harmed by the advice.

Intent to Deceive or Defraud

Under Rule 10b-5, auditor liability is linked to the intent to deceive, manipulate, or defraud. It is not enough to assert the failure to exercise the appropriate level of care to cause liability. The *Louisiana School Employees'* case that appears in **Exhibit 8.10** illustrates the stringent requirements for plaintiffs to successfully bring securities fraud cases against auditors. What follows is a brief discussion of key facts in the case.

EXHIBIT 8.10   Louisiana School Employees' Retirement System v. Ernst & Young

Pleading Scienter Against an Outside Auditor

The Sixth Circuit Court of Appeals addressed the liability of an outside auditor named as a primary violator in a securities fraud action in *Louisiana School Employees' Retirement System v. Ernst & Young, LLP.*[52] There, the Circuit Court held that a plaintiff "may survive a motion to dismiss only by pleading with particularity facts that give rise to a strong inference that the defendant acted with knowledge or conscious disregard of the fraud being committed . . ." as to a defendant. However, "[t]he standard of recklessness is more stringent when the defendant is an outside auditor."

The case is based on the acquisition by Accredo Health, Inc., of a division of Gentiva Health Services, Inc. The deal closed in June 2002. EY issued an unqualified audit opinion on Accredo's 2002 fiscal year financial results. Prior to closing, EY participated in due diligence. According to the complaint, the audit firm learned that nearly $58.5 million of the receivables in one division were uncollectible. EY also recognized that the allowance for doubtful accounts was understated, resulting in revenue being materially overstated.

In May 2003, Accredo issued a press release stating that it was writing off the $58.5 million of accounts receivable acquired from Gentiva. In its Form 10-Q for the third quarter of 2003, the company noted that if the collection rates had been evaluated based on data as of January 1, 2003, the charge would have been recorded as of that date. Plaintiffs claim this statement was made to avoid a restatement. The company terminated EY and filed a malpractice suit against the firm, alleging violations of the antifraud provisions of the federal securities laws. The district court dismissed the complaint, finding that scienter had not been adequately pleaded as required by the Private Securities Litigation Reform Act (PSLRA) and the Supreme Court's decision in *Tellabs, Inc. v. Makor Issuers & Rights, Ltd.,* 551 U.S. 308 (2007).[53]

The Sixth Circuit affirmed the dismissal. The Court began by noting that the PSLRA requires a securities law plaintiff to state with particularity both the facts constituting the alleged violation of Section 10(b) and those establishing scienter. As *Tellabs* holds, the "strong inference" standard of the PSLRA was intended to "raise the bar" for pleading scienter. While reckless conduct will suffice, when the case is against an outside auditor, more is required. In that instance, "the complaint must identify specific, highly suspicious facts and circumstances available to the auditor at the time of the audit and allege that these facts were ignored, either deliberatively or recklessly." Those well-pleaded facts must give rise to a strong inference of scienter. In addition, a comparative analysis must be done regarding possible competing inferences.

The plaintiffs failed to adequately plead scienter. Pleading accounting irregularities or a failure to comply with GAAP is, by itself, insufficient. Central to plaintiffs' allegations is a claim that EY failed to adhere to proper professional standards. This keyed to a claim that its testing of the receivables was deficient because the firm used "old and stale" data. Even if true, this type of allegation does not constitute securities fraud, the Court noted.

Plaintiffs' claim was not bolstered by its assertion that the audit firm missed "red flags." To create a strong inference of scienter from such a claim, the factual allegations must demonstrate an "egregious refusal to see the obvious, or to investigate the doubtful." Typically, courts look for multiple, obvious red flags before drawing an inference of scienter. In this regard, the plaintiffs pointed only to a series of facts which support conflicting inferences or that are not supported by facts demonstrating that the audit firm was aware of it.

Likewise, the magnitude of the error does not support a finding of scienter, as plaintiffs claim. In this regard the court held, "[w]e decline to follow the cases that hold that the magnitude of the financial fraud contributes to an inference of scienter on the part of the defendant . . . Allowing such an inference would eviscerate the principle that accounting errors alone cannot support a finding of scienter." The Court opinion states "such a claim is little more than hindsight, speculation, and conjecture."

Finally, the allegations regarding motive do not save the complaint. Plaintiffs accuse EY of committing fraud because of a promise of future professional fees. It is beyond dispute that the firm earned substantial fees from the company. There is no allegation, however, that the fees from Accredo were more significant than those from other clients. There are no facts in the complaint demonstrating that EY's motive to retain Accredo as a client was any different than its general desire to retain business. Overall, plaintiffs' claims are little more than the classic fraud by hindsight case.

Courts impose very difficult and, some would argue, unreasonably high barriers to imposing federal securities liability upon accountants and auditors. In *Louisiana School Employees' Retirement System v. Ernst & Young,*[54] the Sixth Circuit Court of Appeals affirmed the dismissal of a securities fraud complaint against EY finding that the recklessness necessary to establish auditor liability under the federal securities laws is conduct "akin to conscious disregard [that] is highly unreasonable [and] an extreme departure from standards of ordinary care" such that "any reasonable man would have known it." The Sixth Circuit imposed an even higher burden on plaintiffs attempting to plead securities fraud against an auditor, stating that "[t]he standard for recklessness is more stringent when the defendant is an outside auditor . . . and [proof of] recklessness [for an auditor defendant] requires a mental state so culpable that it approximates an actual intent to aid in the fraud being perpetrated by the audited company." In evaluating an auditor's application of accounting principles, the Sixth Circuit also held that, to establish scienter on the part of an auditor, a complaint must plead much more than misapplication of accounting principles. Specifically, the Sixth Circuit held that a plaintiff must prove that (1) the accounting practices were so deficient that the audit amounted to "no audit at all;" (2) an egregious refusal to see the obvious or investigate the doubtful; or (3) the accounting judgments made amounted to decisions that no reasonable accountant would have made under the same circumstances.[55]

Private Securities Litigation Reform Act (PSLRA)

LO 8-4

Explain the provisions of the PSLRA.

The Private Securities Litigation Reform Act (PSLRA) of 1995 amends the Securities Exchange Act of 1934 by adding Section 10A, "Audit Requirements," which specified that each independent auditor of an issuer under the Act must include "Procedures designed to provide reasonable assurance of detecting illegal acts that would have a direct and material effect on the determination of financial statements amounts." The Act also includes in federal law the auditor's responsibility to detect fraud and requires auditors to promptly notify the audit committee and board of directors of illegal acts. Recall that we had discussed the reporting requirements of illegal acts in **Chapter 5**.

Proportionate Liability

The attempts to reform auditor liability in the United States focused on the argument that the tort system was out of control, partly as a consequence of the 1933 Securities Act, which placed auditors under a joint-and-several liability regime and made them, not the plaintiffs, carry the burden of proof. The accounting profession had fought over time to effectuate this change because of what the profession perceived to be frivolous lawsuits that included the auditors as defendants primarily because the plaintiffs counted on out-of-court settlement by the auditors who had "deep pockets"; auditors also carry large amounts of professional liability insurance for such matters. The senior partners in the large firms argued that SEC Rule 10-b permits class-action claims against companies and auditors where share prices have fallen. Because there is no provision in U.S. law for recovery of costs by successful defendants, auditors felt compelled to settle even meritless legal claims in order to avoid high costs of litigation. Prior to enactment of the PSLRA, the average claim in 1991 was $85 million; the average settlement was $2.6 million, with legal costs of $3.5 million. The audit firms claimed that legal costs represented nine percent of their revenues in 1991.[56]

The PSLRA changes the legal liability standard of auditors from joint-and-several liability to proportionate liability. The Act adopts proportionate liability for all unknowing securities violations under the Exchange Act. (It adopts the same rule for non-officer directors under Section 11 of the Securities Act.) This provision is particularly important for underwriters, venture capital firms, outside directors, accounting firms, and others pulled into securities cases as deep-pocketed defendants. Plaintiffs will no longer have the hammer of joint-and-several liability to coerce peripheral defendants into settlements because the risk to those defendants of defending the action is unacceptable and they fear being charged with the entire responsibility for the fraud rather than only their share of it. Only those whom the trier of fact finds to have committed "knowing" securities fraud—that is, had actual knowledge that (1) a statement was false and/or that an omission led to a misleading statement and (2) investors were reasonably likely to rely on the misrepresentation or omission—will suffer joint-and-several liability.

One of the most influential (and confusing) cases involving application of the PSLRA was *Tellabs, Inc. v Makor Issues & Rights*. Several plaintiffs brought a class action securities fraud lawsuit against Tellabs, a manufacturer of equipment for fiber optic cable networks. The plaintiffs alleged that Tellabs had misrepresented the strength of its products and earnings in order to conceal the declining value of the company's stock. The District Court dismissed the complaints. The court held that the plaintiff's allegations were too vague to establish a "strong inference" of scienter on the part of Tellabs.[57]

On appeal, the U.S. Court of Appeals for the Seventh Circuit reversed one of the lower court's dismissals. The Court of Appeals ruled that a plaintiff need only allege "acts from which, if true, a reasonable person could infer that the defendant acted with the required intent." The Court of Appeals decided to consider only the plausibility of the inference of a guilty mental state and not any competing inferences of an innocent mental state. This decision was due in part to the Court's concern that weighing competing inferences was more properly the task of a jury. The Appeals Court ruling conflicted with those of other Courts of Appeals, which required plaintiffs to show that the inference of scienter supported by the alleged facts was more plausible than any competing inference of innocent intent.

The case went to the U.S. Supreme Court, where Justice Ruth Bader Ginsburg wrote the opinion for the Court, which held that the Seventh Circuit's more relaxed standard was not strong enough to comport with Congress' intent in PSLRA to limit securities fraud litigation. "The strength of an inference cannot be decided in a vacuum. The inquiry is inherently comparative [. . .]," the Court ruled. A court must consider each plausible inference of intent, both fraudulent and nonfraudulent, and then decide whether a reasonable person would consider the guilty inference "at least as strong as any opposing inference."[58]

Establishing Scienter

Application of the PSLRA seems to rely as much on scienter after the passage of the Act as it did before. The key is for plaintiffs to establish a degree of recklessness sufficient to establish knowledge of the falsehood. Additionally, courts have sided with auditors, in some instances, when they successfully assert the fraud was hidden from them by management or when internal controls are overridden by management. A good example is the ruling in Doral Financial Corporation against PwC, which is summarized in **Exhibit 8.11**.

EXHIBIT 8.11   PricewaterhouseCoopers Escapes Liability in Doral Litigation[59]

In a 2010 decision with potential implications for securities fraud claims against accounting firms, the U.S. Court of Appeals for the Second Circuit upheld a lower court's dismissal of securities fraud claims by shareholders of Doral Financial Corporation (Doral) against Doral's auditor, PwC. The litigation arose after Doral, a financial services company that engages in mortgage and commercial banking, restated its financial statements for the years 2000 through 2004. The restatements showed that Doral had overstated its pretax income by $920 million and understated its debt by $3.3 billion.

The plaintiffs alleged that Doral engaged in at least two substantial frauds involving the securitization of mortgages. First, the plaintiffs claimed that Doral engaged in "side deals and oral agreements" that essentially turned the "sales" of the securities into secured borrowings, resulting in the overstatement of earnings and an understatement of debt. Second, the plaintiffs claimed that Doral improperly valued the interest-only strips (IO Strips) that it retained as part of the securitizations by using "manufactured" assumptions to conceal losses in its IO Strip portfolio. With respect to PwC, the plaintiffs claimed that the firm's audit reports and its report on Doral's internal controls were materially false and allowed Doral to conceal and perpetuate its frauds. On this basis, the plaintiffs claimed that PwC, like Doral, violated Section 10(b) of the Securities and Exchange Act of 1934 and Rule 10b-5 thereunder.

Judge Jed Rakoff of the U.S. District Court for the Southern District of New York had dismissed the claims against PwC in 2009, holding that the plaintiffs failed to allege the requisite scienter under the PSLRA. In a summary order issued on September 3, 2009, the Second Circuit agreed. Citing the U.S. Supreme Court's 2007 decision in *Tellabs, Inc. v. Makor Issues & Rights, Ltd.,* the Second Circuit noted that, under the PSLRA, a plaintiff must "state with particularity facts giving rise to a strong inference" of scienter, or an intent to "deceive, manipulate, or defraud." The inference of scienter must be such that a reasonable person would deem it "cogent and at least as compelling as any opposing inference one could draw" from the same alleged facts. The Second Circuit opinion states that this burden could be

(continued)

met by alleging facts showing that the defendant had "both motive and opportunity to commit the fraud," or constituting "strong circumstantial evidence of conscious misbehavior or recklessness." However, in determining whether the alleged facts were sufficient to raise a "strong inference" of scienter, the Court was required to "take into account plausible opposing inferences," even if neither party had raised them.

The Seventh Circuit acknowledged that the plaintiffs raised "numerous allegations of carelessness" by PwC, but concluded that the allegations failed to create a strong inference of recklessness. The plaintiffs alleged, for instance, that PwC recklessly failed to uncover the side agreements that altered the terms of the mortgage sales. However, the plaintiffs also alleged that the side agreements were a "tightly-held secret," known only to a few individuals within Doral's management. The court therefore held that it was more plausible that PwC failed to discover the side deals because Doral's management hid them from PwC.

The Seventh Circuit also held that PwC's failure to identify problems with Doral's system of internal controls was insufficient to establish recklessness. It noted that the plaintiffs had alleged that Doral overrode several of its internal controls, which further undermined any inference of recklessness by PwC.

The Court ruled that "the PSLRA requires . . . more than mere plausibility." Because the "competing inference" that Doral deceived PwC was stronger than the inference that PwC was reckless, it was proper to dismiss the claims. Indeed, it is not uncommon for securities fraud claims to allege that the individuals within a company who perpetuated an alleged fraud took steps to conceal their actions and ignored or circumvented the company's system of internal controls. Following the Court's rationale, allegations of this nature would give rise to a strong "competing inference" that the auditor, like the plaintiffs themselves, was a victim of the fraud, and therefore should not be held liable for it.

It should be noted that the competing inference prevailed even though, as the District Circuit had stated, the plaintiffs alleged that PwC personnel were "regularly present" at Doral and had "unlimited access" to information regarding its operations and that PwC violated GAAP and GAAS in conducting its audits. The District Court held that these allegations were insufficient to establish scienter unless accompanied by some evidence of "corresponding fraudulent intent." The same was true of the plaintiff's allegations that PwC had a financial incentive to ignore the fraud because it collected over $6 million in fees from Doral and provided nonaudit services to Doral during the relevant period.

In effect, these court decisions require allegations of facts rising to the level of deliberate or willful ignorance of misconduct (if not conscious knowledge or active participation) in order to hold an auditor liable under Section 10(b) and Rule 10b-5. Indeed, the District Court framed the issue in these terms when it discussed and dismissed allegations based on information allegedly provided by a former Doral internal auditor that PwC personnel attended meetings of the Doral Audit Committee at which questions about the company's internal controls were raised: "At most, [the former internal auditor's] information may raise an inference the PwC was negligent in not following up on such discussions, but it certainly does not show the conscious turning away from the true facts required for recklessness."

We believe not much has changed, in reality, with respect to auditors' legal liability and what we are experiencing is different interpretations by different courts in somewhat different circumstances. The intent standard still should provide the legal basis, at least for fraud determination.

SOX and Auditor Legal Liabilities

LO 8-5

Discuss auditors' legal liabilities under SOX.

Major developments in auditor liability have occurred as a result of the Sarbanes-Oxley Act. SOX was passed to increase the transparency of financial reporting by enhancing corporate disclosure and governance practices and to foster an ethical climate.[60] SOX increases auditor liability to third parties by specifying or expanding the scope of third parties to whom an auditor owes a duty of care. SOX also increases auditor liability to third parties because it requires accounting firms to review and assess management's report on internal controls and issue its own report.

Section 404. *Internal Control over Financial Reporting*

Traditionally, because auditors had no duty to disclose control weaknesses or their effects on substantive audit testing in the audit report, courts deemed control irregularities immaterial for deciding auditors' liability under Section 11 of the Securities Exchange Act of 1933. The case of *Monroe v. Hughes* (1991) illustrates the current law.[61] In that case, the auditor found internal control irregularities, conferred with management, and expanded the scope of its financial audit by performing more elaborate substantive testing. The auditor issued an unqualified audit report, but did not disclose the control irregularities in the audit report. In the following year, the auditor found significant deterioration in internal controls and was unable to issue an unqualified financial statement opinion for that year. The client collapsed and investors sued the auditor under Section 11, claiming that the auditor should have disclosed in its audit opinion the internal control irregularities it discovered. The *Monroe* court (and others facing similar questions) rejected the investors' argument, citing Section 11's due diligence defense, negligence standard, and observing that good faith compliance with GAAS discharges an auditor's professional obligation to act with reasonable care. No legal or accounting authority required auditors to disclose control irregularities.[62]

Under PCAOB AS 2201, the auditor must form an opinion on the ICFR and either prepare a separate report on such matters or include the assessment in the auditor's report. Since the assessment of ICFR is required under Section 404 of SOX, the auditor may be held legally liable for deficiencies in the audit of ICFR much like the deficiencies in applying GAAS and material misstatements in the financial statements.

Important Definitions

A *deficiency* in internal control over financial reporting exists when the design or operation of a control does not allow management or employees, in the normal course of performing their assigned functions, to prevent or detect misstatements on a timely basis.

A *material weakness* is a deficiency, or a combination of deficiencies, in internal control over financial reporting, such that there is a *reasonable possibility* that a material misstatement of the company's annual or interim financial statements will not be prevented or detected on a timely basis.

A *significant deficiency* is a deficiency, or a combination of deficiencies, in internal control over financial reporting that is less severe than a material weakness, yet important enough to merit attention by those responsible for oversight of the company's financial reporting.

Section 11 and 10(b) Liability and Attesting to Management's Assessment of ICFR

The auditors' assessment of management's assertions about ICFR and related audit of internal controls are intended, in part, to create an early warning system to alert financial statement users to material weaknesses in ICFR that may impair an issuer's ability to prepare reliable financial statements in current- and future-accounting periods.[63]

Cunningham et al. believe that PCAOB AS 2 (superseded by AS 2201) is likely to change the legal landscape for auditors. If auditors conclude that internal controls are effective when they are not, the situation is much like that occurring when they inappropriately conclude that financial statements are fair and conform to GAAP. The authors explore auditors' potential legal liability under Section 11 of the Securities Act. The authors suggest that, given the standards established in AS 2201, it seems reasonable to assume that a court might find an auditor culpable for failing to disclose a material weakness in internal controls. Thus, auditors would have incentives when providing ICFR opinions to disclose discovered weaknesses and to err on the side of characterizing control deficiencies as material when they could alternatively be described instead as significant deficiencies not requiring disclosure. The problem, as the authors see it, is even though this incentive appears to be consistent with AS 2201's early warning system objectives, it may create false positive signals, which ultimately may render the adverse opinion less meaningful or result in lower pricing by the market of public offerings. Additionally, a definition of a material weakness in this way sets a low threshold that even some well-managed companies are likely to get caught up by the negative ICFR.[64]

Under Section 3 of the Securities Exchange Act of 1934, a violation of the Act or any rule of the PCAOB shall be treated for all purposes in the same manner as a violation of the Exchange Act of 1934. Looking at Section 10(b) of the Act, Cunningham et al. suggest that to the extent auditor behavior is influenced by applicable legal liability risks, Section 10(b)'s incentives could bias auditors' decisions to resolve uncertain cases as significant deficiencies rather than material weaknesses. This is because most courts apply a bright-line rule that an auditor must make a false or misleading statement to the public to be liable under section 10(b).[65]

Section 302. *Corporate Responsibility for Financial Reports*

Section 302 requires the certification of periodic reports filed with the SEC by the CEO and CFO of public companies. The certification states that "based on the officer's knowledge, the report does not contain any untrue statement of a material fact or omit to state a material fact necessary in order to make the statements, in light of the circumstances under which such statements were made, not misleading."

The certifications aim to prevent fraudulent financial disclosures by emphasizing the CEO's and CFO's personal accountability for integrity in financial reporting. As a result, CEOs and CFOs are exposed to personal civil and criminal liability if they sign false certificates for SEC registrants, which includes falsely certifying corporate financial reports and reports on internal controls.

The early cases set the tone for SEC's expectations with respect to Section 302 certifications. The first reported case was *Higginbotham v. Baxter Int'l.* in 2005. The plaintiffs argued that the 302 certifications concerning the adequacy of the company's internal controls were false, and accordingly, the court could infer that Section 10(b)'s scienter requirement was met as to the individuals signing those certifications. The *Higginbotham* court rejected this argument because plaintiffs provided "no specific allegations as to what the deficiencies in the controls were, nor [did they provide] any specific allegations as to [the certifying executives'] awareness of those deficiencies."[66] The ruling does not mean that a false statement with regard to internal controls is not an actionable offense. Instead, the conclusion to be drawn is that claims of scienter require more than just an assertion; specific proof of such knowledge must exist.

The next such case was *In re Lattice Semiconductor Corp.* In *Lattice Semiconductor,* plaintiffs alleged a series of accounting errors that resulted in materially misstated financial statements. In this case, plaintiffs argued that false 302 certifications raised a strong inference that the CEO and CFO were, at a minimum, deliberately reckless, thereby satisfying Section 10(b)'s scienter requirement. Defendants responded by arguing that if "these certifications raised a strong inference of *scienter,* every corporate officer who signed a certification for a Form 10-Q or 10-K filing that was later found to be incorrect would be subject to a securities fraud action."[67]

The *Lattice Semiconductor* court sided with plaintiffs, holding that the 302 certifications in that case did, in fact, give rise to an inference of scienter "because they provide evidence either that defendants knew about the improper journal entries and unreported sales credits that led to the over-reporting of revenues (because of the internal controls they said existed) or, alternatively, knew that the controls they attested to were inadequate."

Soon after *Lattice Semiconductor,* the court in *In re WatchGuard Secs. Litig.* considered allegedly false 302 certifications in the context of a private Section 10(b) action. In *WatchGuard,* plaintiffs alleged that the defendant company had made material misstatements about interest expenses and revenue recognition in its financial statements. Plaintiffs also contended that WatchGuard's quarterly 302 certifications were themselves actionable misstatements on which they could base a Section 10(b) and Rule 10b-5 claim. Plaintiffs also argued that the certifications demonstrated scienter under the "deliberate recklessness" standard because the certifying individual defendants either knew about WatchGuard's revenue recognition problems or were "deliberately reckless in not obtaining the information or conducting the investigations described in their certifications prior to publishing the false financial statements."[68]

The *WatchGuard* court rejected plaintiffs' arguments, holding that the individual defendants' 302 certifications were, by themselves, inadequate to support a strong inference of scienter. In so holding, the court stressed that the failure of plaintiffs to plead scienter adequately is what doomed their 302 argument. "In a case like this one, however, where the court finds no strong inference that any defendant was at least deliberately reckless in issuing corporate earnings statements, the court has no basis for a strong inference that the Sarbanes-Oxley certifications were culpably false."[69]

It is safe to say the courts are still finding their way with respect to legal liability issues and alleged violations of SOX under Section 302. However, based upon the reported private securities cases thus far, it appears that that Section 302 certifications that turn out to be inaccurate do not give rise to independent private claims under the securities laws, nor do they appear to alter the fundamental standards that are applied in Section 10(b) actions. Rather, they are viewed by courts in the overall context of a case and bear on civil liability only when other pleaded facts create a strong inference of scienter against the 302 certifier.[70]

As discussed in **Chapter 3**, most major corporations have implemented internal compliance systems that make it very difficult to show that the CEO or CFO knowingly signed a false certification. One reason is multiple layers of subcertification are put in place, requiring lower-level officials to attest to the accuracy of financial reports all the way up the chain of command to the CEO and CFO. The subcertifications provide cover for CEOs and CFOs from false certification charges. To prove SOX charges, prosecutors have to show that top officials signed off on financial reports they knew to be false. The subcertifications make it much tougher to prove since CEOs and CFOs can claim they relied on the attestations of their underlings.

Foreign Corrupt Practices Act (FCPA)

LO 8-6
Explain the provisions of the FCPA.

In addition to SOX, other laws have influenced audit procedures, legal liability, requirements for internal controls over financial reporting, and ethics requirements under the due care principle. The law with the greatest effect in the United States is the Foreign Corrupt Practices Act (FCPA).

The FCPA establishes standards for the acceptability of payments made by U.S. multinational entities or their agent to foreign government officials. The act was motivated when, during the period of 1960 to 1977, the SEC cited 527 companies for bribes and other dubious payments that were made to win foreign contracts. Lockheed Corporation was one of the companies caught in this scandal. It was determined that Lockheed had made about $55 million in illegal payments to foreign governments and officials. One such payment, $1.7 million to Japanese premier Kukuei Tanaka, led to his resignation in disgrace in 1974.

The FCPA makes it a crime to offer or provide payments to officials of foreign governments, political candidates, or political parties for the purpose of obtaining or retaining business. It applies to all U.S. corporations, whether they are publicly or privately held, and to foreign companies filing with the SEC. The U.S. Department of Justice (DOJ) is responsible for all criminal enforcement and for civil enforcement of the antibribery provisions with respect to domestic entities and foreign companies and nationals. The SEC is responsible for civil enforcement of the antibribery provisions with respect to registrants.

Under the FCPA, a corporation that violates the law can be fined up to $2 million, while its officers who directly participated in violations of the act or had "reason to know" of such violations can be fined up to $100,000, imprisoned for up to five years, or both. The act also prohibits corporations from indemnifying directors, officers, employees, or agents for fines. FCPA does not prohibit "grease payments" (i.e., *permissible facilitating payments*) to foreign government employees whose duties are primarily ministerial or clerical because such payments are sometimes required to persuade recipients to perform their normal duties.[71]

As a result of the criticisms of the antibribery provisions of the 1977 FCPA, Congress amended the act as part of the Omnibus Trade and Competitiveness Act of 1988 to clarify when a payment is prohibited, as follows:[72]

1. A payment is defined as illegal if it is intended to influence a foreign official to act in a way that is incompatible with the official's legal duty.

2. The "reason to know" standard is replaced by a "knowing" standard, so that criminal liability for illegal payments to third parties applies to individuals who "knowingly" engage in or tolerate illegal payments under the act.

3. The definition of "grease" payments is expanded to include payments to any foreign official that facilitates or expedites securing the performance of a routine governmental action.

4. Examples of acceptable payments include (1) obtaining permits, licenses, and the official documents to qualify a person to do business in a foreign country; (2) processing governmental papers, such as visas or work orders; (3) providing police protection, mail pickup, and delivery, or scheduling inspections associated with contract performance or inspections related to the transit of goods across country; (4) providing telephone service, power, and water, unloading and loading cargo, or protecting perishable product or commodities from deterioration; and (5) performing actions of a similar nature.

The Two Affirmative Defenses under the FCPA

The FCPA provides two circumstances where a payment or promise of value to a foreign public official may qualify as an "affirmative defense":

The "local law" defense, under which the defendant must establish that "the payment, gift, offer, or promise of anything of value that was made, was lawful under the written laws and regulations of the foreign official's, political party's, party official's, or candidate's country."

The reasonable and *bona fide* expenditures defense, under which the defendant must show that the "the payment, gift, offer, or promise of anything of value that was made, was a reasonable and bona fide expenditure, such as travel and lodging expenses, incurred by or on behalf of a foreign official, party, party official, or candidate" and that the payment was directly related to either "the promotion, demonstration, or explanation of products or services" or "the execution or performance of a contract with a foreign government or agency thereof."

The SEC has clarified that when relying on the local law defense, the law or regulation, the defendant is relying upon must have been a "written" law at the time of the relevant conduct. Local practices, customs, and other unwritten policies do not qualify for the local law affirmative defense. When Congress created the local law defense in 1988, they sought "to make clear that the absence of written laws in a foreign official's country would not by itself be sufficient to satisfy this defense." Thus, the fact that bribes may not be prosecuted under local law is insufficient to establish the defense.

In a speech on compliance on March 3, 2015, Andrew Ceresney, SEC's Director of the Division of Enforcement, pointed out that the best way for a company to avoid FCPA violations is to have a robust FCPA compliance program that includes compliance personnel, extensive policies and procedures, training, vendor reviews, due diligence on third-party agents, expense controls, escalation of red flags, and internal audits to review compliance.[73] An effective compliance program also includes performing risk assessments and monitoring internal controls over financial reporting.

Internal Accounting Control Requirements

The FCPA requires all SEC registrants to maintain internal accounting controls to ensure that all transactions are authorized by management and recorded properly. The Act requires public company issuers to maintain adequate books and records that, in reasonable detail, accurately and fairly reflect an issuer's transactions and disposition of assets. In addition, public companies must maintain internal controls to ensure transparency in the financial condition of the company, the relevant risk to the company, and the transactions conducted by the company.

Under Section 13(b)(2)(B) of the Securities Exchange Act of 1934, registrants must devise and maintain a system of internal accounting controls sufficient to provide reasonable assurances that transactions are recorded as necessary to permit preparation of financial statements in conformity with GAAP or any other criteria applicable to such statements. To meet these standards, the following needs to be demonstrated:

1. Transactions are executed in accordance with management's general or specific authorization;

2. Transactions are recorded as necessary (1) to permit preparation of financial statements in conformity with generally accepted accounting principles or any other criteria applicable to such statements and (2) to maintain accountability for assets;

3. Access to assets is permitted only in accordance with management's general or specific authorization; and

4. The recorded accountability for assets is compared with the existing assets at reasonable intervals and appropriate action is taken with respect to any differences.

In **Chapter 3,** we examined the whistleblower case of Tony Menendez against Halliburton. Now, we look at an FCPA enforcement action against Halliburton for internal control failures in its business relationships in Angola. On July 27, 2017, the SEC charged Halliburton Company with violating the books and records and internal accounting controls provisions of the FCPA while selecting and making payments to a local company in Angola in the course of winning lucrative oilfield services contracts. **Exhibit 8.12** summarizes the facts of the case.

EXHIBIT 8.12   FCPA and Halliburton

According to the SEC's order,[74] officials at Angola's state oil company Sonangol advised Halliburton management in 2008 that it was required to partner with more local Angolan-owned businesses to satisfy local content regulations for foreign firms operating in Angola. Halliburton assigned then vice president Jeannot Lorenz with leading these efforts. When a new round of oil company projects came up for bid, Lorenz began a lengthy effort to retain a local Angolan company owned by a former Halliburton employee who was a friend and neighbor of the Sonangol official who would ultimately approve the award of the contracts. It took three attempts, but Halliburton ultimately outsourced more than $13 million worth of business to the local Angolan company.

There were multiple issues in the enforcement action around internal controls, their effectiveness (or lack thereof), and management override of internal controls. The SEC's order found that Halliburton entered into contracts with the local Angolan company that were intended to meet local content requirements rather than the stated scope of work. Lorenz violated Halliburton's internal accounting controls by starting with the local Angolan company and then backing into a list of contract services rather than first determining the services and then selecting an appropriate supplier. Lorenz also failed to conduct competitive bidding or substantiate the need for a single source of supply, and he circumvented an internal accounting control that required contracts of more than $10,000 in countries like Angola with high corruption risks to be reviewed and approved by a special committee within Halliburton. The company eventually paid $3.705 million to the local Angolan firm, and Sonangol approved the award of seven lucrative subcontracts to Halliburton.

Without admitting or denying the findings, Halliburton and Lorenz consented to the order requiring them to cease and desist from committing or causing any violations or any future violations of the books and records and internal accounting controls provisions of the FCPA. Halliburton agreed to pay $14 million in disgorgement plus $1.2 million in prejudgment interest and a $14 million penalty. Halliburton was required to retain an independent compliance consultant to review and evaluate its anti-corruption policies and procedures, particularly in regard to local content obligations for business operations in Africa.

FCPA violations are troubling because they result from bribery of foreign government officials or agents of the government. If bribery occurs in a company, we can only wonder what other ethical transgressions exist. Halliburton is a case in point. It is rare that a company violates a law, oftentimes very blatantly, and toes the line in other areas of operations. The violations always reflect a failure of the corporate governance system and unethical tone at the top. As for the auditors, we have to wonder how they can miss FCPA violations given the heightened ethical requirements when operating in the global arena where different cultures establish different standards of ethical conduct.

Concluding Thoughts

Auditors are liable to clients and third parties for failing to conduct an audit in accordance with generally accepted auditing standards, SOX requirements under 302 and 404, the rules of conduct under the AICPA Code, and SEC regulations.

Auditor liability under common law tends to focus on whether auditors' actions breached the privity relationship, were conducted in a negligent manner, and whether fraud existed because auditors did not properly assess whether there were material misstatements in the financial statements.

Auditors are liable for fraud when they (1) make misrepresentations in the financial statements; (2) the misrepresentations are made to induce third parties to rely on those statements; (3) the third parties did rely on the misrepresentations; and (4) such reliance was the proximate cause of suffering a loss. The key element in fraud is the intent to deceive another party; fraud does not occur by accident.

The history of litigation against auditors indicates that the most important standards to protect auditors from legal liability are exercising due care in the performance of professional services, including professional skepticism; properly assessing whether the internal controls are operating as intended; and conducting an audit in accordance with GAAS. These requirements are necessary to determine whether material misstatements of the financial statements are present thereby making it impossible for auditors to provide reasonable assurance that the financial statements are free of fraud.

The importance of properly assessing ICFR under Section 404 cannot be overstated. Audit firms and auditors must do everything in their power to ensure that deficiencies are identified and determined to be either significant or material. Legal actions against auditors can take place when they fail to properly assess internal controls and management's assessment of ICFR is deficient.

As discussed in **Chapter 4** and expanded upon in **Chapter 5**, audit inspection reports issued by the PCAOB for 2019 show an alarming rate of deficiencies: Deloitte 10 percent, Ernst & Young 18 percent, KPMG 29 percent and PwC 30 percent. Given the independence concerns raised in that chapter, we wonder whether the Big 4 have lost their way and no longer can serve the public interest.

Finally, students should realize that there are significant links between prior discussions and auditors' legal liabilities and defenses including when:

(1) Auditors fail to maintain an adequate system of internal controls and when corporate governance systems fail to identify and correct for material deficiencies in internal controls (discussed in **Chapter 3**).

(2) Auditors fail to conduct an audit with due care and in accordance with GAAS (discussed in **Chapter 4**).

(3) Auditors fail to put into place adequate systems to detect and correct fraud in the financial statements; using the Fraud Triangle for guidance is required (discussed in **Chapter 5**).

(4) Auditors permit clients to engage in transactions that are motivated by earnings management using techniques that materially misstate financial statements (discussed in **Chapter 6**).

Discussion Questions

1. Distinguish between the legal standards of negligence and recklessness.
2. Distinguish between the legal standards of gross negligence and fraud.
3. Under what circumstances might an auditor be held legally liable for negligent representation versus a fraudulent misrepresentation based on court rulings discussed in the chapter? Include in your discussion the tests for reliance on misrepresentations.
4. During a particularly stimulating lecture by your accounting ethics professor on accountants' legal liabilities, the following question was posed: Assume you are a CPA and have just been sued by a third party for your failure to conduct a proper audit. What are your defenses to allegations of negligence? What about defenses to allegations of fraud?
5. Distinguish between common-law liability and statutory liability for auditors. What is the basis for the difference in liability?
6. Is there a difference between an error in financial statements, fraud, and negligence from a reasonable care perspective? Give examples of each in your response. How would each event affect accountants' legal liability?
7. Distinguish between the legal concepts of actually foreseen third-party users and reasonably foreseeable third-party users. How does each concept establish a basis for an auditor's legal liability to third parties?

8. Describe the possible entities that may sue an auditor and the possible reasons for a lawsuit.

9. What is the *comparative negligence* defense? When can it shield auditors from legal liability for their actions?

10. What must a plaintiff assert in a Section 11 claim under the Securities Act of 1933 to properly allege an "opinion" statement is materially misleading? When might certain financial statement items constitute "opinions"?

11. What are the legal requirements for a third party to sue an auditor under Section 10 and Rule 10b-5 of the Securities Exchange Act of 1934? How do these requirements relate to the *Louisiana School Employees* decision?

12. Explain the defenses available to auditors in plaintiff claims of "aiding and abetting" of fraud in violation of Section 10b-5 of the Securities Exchange Act of 1934.

13. Valley View Manufacturing Inc. sought a $500,000 loan from First National Bank. First National insisted that audited financial statements be submitted before it would extend credit. Valley View agreed to do so, and an audit was performed by an independent CPA who submitted his report to Valley View. First National, upon reviewing the audited statements, decided to extend the credit desired. Certain ratios used by First National in reaching its decision were extremely positive, indicating a strong cash flow. It was subsequently learned that the CPA, despite the exercise of reasonable care, had failed to discover a sophisticated embezzlement scheme by Valley View's chief accountant. Under these circumstances, what liability might the CPA have?

14. Danny Boy, a local CPA who owns a tax practice, is being investigated by the IRS for the preparation of false income tax returns for a client. The IRS alleges that the individual taxpayer/client used a substantial amount of his company's funds for personal expenses, including payments for his personal car, car insurance, country club dues, and personal credit card charges. The IRS alleges that these personal expenses were used to reduce business taxable income so that the income taxes were underpaid by a significant amount. During its audit, the IRS found a schedule in Danny Boy's workpapers that supported the false income of the client. Assuming the IRS concludes the allegations are true, is Danny guilty of tax fraud? Could he successfully claim to have exercised due care and any fraud is that of the client alone? Explain with regard to what the IRS has to show to prove the tax fraud.

15. Do you believe the standard for liability under the PSLRA better protects auditors from legal liability than the standards which existed before the Act was adopted by Congress? Explain.

16. How has the Sarbanes-Oxley Act affected the legal liability of accountants and auditors?

17. Assume a U.S. company operates overseas and is approached by foreign governments officials with a request to provide family members with student internships with the company. The company does business in that country with foreign customers and is negotiating for a contract with one such customer to provide services. Under what circumstances might such a request violate the FCPA?

18. How does auditors' meeting public interest obligations relate to avoiding legal liability?

19. Has the accounting profession created a situation in which the auditors' ethical behavior is impaired by their professional obligations? How does the profession's view of such obligations relate to how courts tend to view the legal liability of auditors?

20. Explain how the intent requirement of the legal principle of *scienter* relates to ethical standards of behavior discussed in previous chapters.

Comprehensive Questions

1. Answer each of the following questions from the perspective of an auditors' liability to a third party. In each case, discuss whether the bank has a legitimate cause of action against the auditor and the legal principle that supports such an action.[75]

   (a) A client retains a CPA firm to audit the financial statements required by a bank as a condition to extending a loan to the client. The auditor knows the bank is the client's principal lender and is aware of the bank's reliance on the financial statements, particularly the valuation of accounts receivable. The bank and auditor have direct oral and written communication during the lending period and have met to discuss the client's financial statements.

After the audit report is issued, the bank discovers that the client's accounts receivable were overstated. The client subsequently goes bankrupt and defaults on the loan. The bank alleges that the auditor failed to communicate about the inadequacy of the client's internal recordkeeping.

(b) A client is negotiating a loan with a bank requiring audited financial statements. The client hires a CPA firm, explaining that the purpose of the audit is to negotiate a loan. The firm audits those financial statements. Subsequent to issuing the financial statements the client goes bankrupt mainly because the inventory was overvalued. In reality, the inventory was worthless. The auditor failed to point this out in the financial statements.

(c) A CPA audits a company and issues an opinion that the financial statements fairly represent the financial condition of the entity. A bank made loans to the client after receiving the audited financial statements. The financial statements contained numerous errors, and the client subsequently defaulted on the loans.

2. Explain the legal basis for a cause of action against an auditor. What are the defenses available to the auditor to rebut such charges? How does adherence to the ethical standards of the accounting profession relate to these defenses?

3. What do you believe would be required for an auditor to successfully assert the fraud of a client's managers as a defense against the company's charges of breach of contract, failure to exercise due care, and failure to uncover fraud?

4. Consider the practice of making "facilitating payments" to foreign officials and others as part of doing business abroad in the context of the following statement: International companies are confronted with a variety of decisions that create ethical dilemmas for the decision makers. "Right-wrong" and "just-unjust" derive their meaning and true value from the attitudes of a given culture. Some ethical standards are culture-specific, and we should not be surprised to find that an act that is considered quite ethical in one culture may be looked upon with disregard in another. How do cultural factors influence the acceptability of making facilitating payments in a country? Use rights theory and justice reasoning to analyze the ethics of allowing facilitating payments such as under the FCPA.

5. Nixon and Co., CPAs, issued an unmodified opinion on the 2021 financial statements of Madison Corp. These financial statements were included in Madison's annual report and Form 10-K filed with the SEC. Nixon did not detect material misstatements in the financial statements as a result of negligence in the performance of the audit. Based upon the financial statements, Harry purchased stock in Madison. Shortly thereafter, Madison became insolvent, causing the price of the stock to decline drastically. Harry has commenced legal action against Nixon for damages based upon Section 10(b) and Rule 10b-5 of the Securities Exchange Act of 1934. What would be Nixon's best defense to such an action? Explain.

Endnotes

1. Zoe-Vonna Palmrose, *Empirical Research in Auditor Litigation: Considerations and Data, Studies in Accounting Research No. 33* (Sarasota, FL: American Accounting Association, 1999).

2. William F. Messier Jr., Steven M. Glover, and Douglas F. Prawitt, *Auditing and Assurance Services: A Systematic Approach* (New York: McGraw-Hill Irwin, 2012).

3. Find Law, Recklessness, http://injury.findlaw.com/accident-injury-law/recklessness.html.

4. Timothy J. Louwers, Robert J. Ramsay, David H. Sinason, Jerry R. Strawser, and Jay C. Thibodeau, *Auditing and Assurance Services* (New York: McGraw-Hill Irwin, 2013).

5. Louwers et al., pp. 640–642.

6. Louwers et al., pp. 637–638.

7. *In Re Gouiran Holdings, Inc.,* 165 B.R. 104 (E.D.N.Y. 1994), *U.S. District Court for the Eastern District of New York* (February 10, 1994), https://law.justia.com/cases/federal/district-courts/BR/165/104/1942863/.

8. Steven P. Garmisa, *Supreme Court Debates Defense in Claims Against Service Providers* (January 19, 2004), http://www.hoeyfarina.com/supreme-court-debates-defense-claims-against-service-providers.

9. *Shapiro v. Glekel,* US District Court for the Southern District of New York, *380 F. Supp. 1053 (S.D.N.Y. 1974),* https://law.justia.com/cases/federal/district-courts/FSupp/380/1053/1457899/.

10. Find Law, Recklessness.

11. *Credit Alliance v. Arthur Andersen & Co.,* 483 N.E. 2d 100 (N.Y. 1985).

12. *Security Pacific Business Credit v. Peat Marwick Main & Co.,* 165 A.D.2d 622 (N.Y. App. Div. 1991), Available at: https://casetext.com/case/security-pacific-v-peat-marwick.

13. Messier et al., pp. 692–693.

14. *Rusch Factors, Inc. v. Levin,* 284. F.Supp. 85, 91.

15. *Restatement (Second) of the Law of Torts,* Section 552A–E (1997), www.tomwbell.com/NetLaw/Ch05/R2nd Torts.html.

16. *Blue Bell, Inc. v. Peat, Marwick, Mitchell & Co.,* 715 S.W. 2d 408 (Dallas 1986).

17. *Rosenblum, Inc. v. Adler,* 93 N.J. 324 (1983).

18. *Citizens State Bank v. Timm, Schmidt & Co.* (1983), Available at: https://law.justia.com/cases/wisconsin/supreme-court/1983/81-801-9.html.

19. Dan M. Goldwasser and Thomas Arnold, *Accountants' Liability* (New York: Practising Law Institute, 2009).

20. *Bily v. Arthur Young,* 834 P. 2d 745 (Cal. 1992).

21. Richard Mann and Barry Roberts, *Essentials of Business Law and the Legal Environment* (Boston, MA: Cengage Learning, 2015).

22. Messier et al., p. 705.

23. Court of Appeals of Texas, Dalla, *Pacific Mutual Life Insurance v Ernst & Young* (January 28, 2000), https://www.leagle.com/decision/20008081Osw3d7981749.

24. *State Street Trust Co. v. Ernst,* Court of Appeals, N.Y. (1938), 278 N.Y. 104. 15 N.E.2d 416.

25. Messier et al., p. 705.

26. *Phar-Mor v. Coopers & Lybrand,* Available at: www.cases.justia.com/us-court-of-appeals/F3/22/1228/579478/.

27. Supreme Court, New York County, *Water St. Leasehold LLC v Deloitte & Touche, Llp,* Available at: http://law.justia.com/cases/new-york/other-courts/2004/2004-51260.html.

28. *Howard Reisman & others vs. KPMG Peat Marwick LLP,* 57 Mass. App. Ct. 100, April 10, 2002–January 15, 2003, November 24, 2003, Available at: http://masscases.com/cases/app/57/57massappct100.html.

29. *Houbigant, Inc. v. Deloitte & Touche LLP.*

30. CFO Magazine, *Deloitte to Pay $149M Over TBW Loan Fraud* (March 1, 2018), https://www.cfo.com/fraud/2018/03/deloitte-pay-149m-tbw-loan-fraud/.

31. Louwers et al., pp. 641–642.

32. Louwers et al., pp. 642–643.

33. Corporate Finance Institute, *What is Legal Liability of Auditors?,* https://corporatefinanceinstitute.com/resources/knowledge/accounting/legal-liability-of-auditors/#.

34. *Grant Thornton LLP v. Prospect High Income Fund, et al.* (July 2, 2010), Available at: http://www.txcourts.gov/media/819887/OpinionsFY2010.pdf.

35. Supreme Court of Texas, *McCamish, Martin, Brown & Loeffler v. F.E. Appling Interests,* No. 97-0970 (April 29, 1999), http://caselaw.findlaw.com/tx-supreme-court/1164179.html.

36. Wilson Elser Moskowitz Edelman & Decker LLP, *Texas Supreme Court Clarifies Law Regarding Auditors' Liability to Third Parties* (September 2010), https://www.wilsonelser.com/news_and_insights/insights/992-texas_supreme_court_clarifies_law_regarding.

37. AICPA, AU Section 316, Consideration of Fraud in a Financial Statement Audit.

38. Securities Exchange Act of 1934, Title 15 of the U.S. Code.

39. O. Lee Reed, Marisa Anne Pagnattaro, Daniel R. Cahoy, Peter J. Shedd, and Jere W. Morehead, *The Legal and Regulatory Environment of Business* (New York: McGraw-Hill Irwin, 2013).

40. Reed et al.

41. Linda Griggs, Christian Mixter, and Warren Rissier, A Matter of Opinion: Parsing the Independent Auditor's Report in the Context of Omnicare, *Bloomberg BNA*, https://www.morganlewis.com/-/media/files/publication/outside-publication/article/bna-a-matter-of-opinion-29jan16.ashx?la=en&hash=1E12AEC2D41F132D001B324F8A4ECDDA58F3CCF1.

42. Dana S. Douglas and Michael Rowe, Section 11 and Auditors' "Opinion" Statements, American Bar Association Section on Litigation: Professional Services Liability, http://apps.americanbar.org/litigation/committees/professional/articles/spring2013-0513-section-11-auditors-opinion-statements.html.

43. Cornell Law School Legal Information Institute, *15 U.S. Code § 77k - Civil liabilities on account of false registration statement*, https://www.law.cornell.edu/uscode/text/15/77k.

44. Leagle, *Fait v. Regions Financial Corp.*, 655 F.3d 105 (2011), https://www.leagle.com/decision/infco20110823108.

45. *MHC Mutual Conversion Fund v. United Western Bancorp, Inc.,* United States Court of Appeals, Tenth Circuit, No. 13-1016, http://caselaw.findlaw.com/us-10th-circuit/1674400.html.

46. Securities Exchange Act of 1934, Title 15 of the U.S. Code.

47. Louwers et al., p. 648.

48. Messier et al., p. 709.

49. Messier et al., p. 709.

50. Securities Exchange Act of 1934.

51. Jean Braucher (Editor), John Kidwell (Editor), William C. Whitford (Editor), *Revisiting the Contracts Scholarship of Stewart Macaulay: On the Empirical and the Lyrical (International Studies in the Theory of Private Law)* (Oxford: UK, Hart Publishing, 2013).

52. *Louisiana School Employees Retirement System v. Ernst & Young, LLP.*

53. United States Supreme Court, *Tellabs, Inc., et al. v. Makor Issues & Rights, Ltd., et al.,* No. 06-484, Decided June 21, 2007, https://supreme.justia.com/cases/federal/us/551/308/.

54. United States Court of Appeals Sixth Circuit *Louisiana School Employees Retirement System v. Ernst & Young, LLP,* No. 08-6194, December 22, 2010, http://caselaw.findlaw.com/us-6th-circuit/1538932.html.

55. *SFMS Securities Law Bulletin* (Fall 2010), https://www.sfmslaw.com/News-Events/Quarterly-Securities-Law-Bulletin/securities-bulletin-2010-11.pdf.

56. HR 3763: Sarbanes-Oxley Act in full, Available at: www.sec.gov/about/laws/soa2002.pdf.

57. U.S. Court of Appeals for the Seventh Circuit, Tellabs Inc. v. Makor Issues & Rights, Docket No. 06-484, Available at: http://www.oyez.org/cases/2000-2009/2006/2006_06_484.

58. U.S. Supreme Court, Tellabs Inc. v. Makor Issues & Rights, Ltd. et al., Available at: http://www.oyez.org/cases/2000-2009/2006/2006_06_484.

59. American Bar Association, "*Second Circuit Affirms Dismissal of Securities Fraud Claims Against PricewaterhouseCoopers in Doral Litigation,*" Available at: https://apps.americanbar.org/litigation/committees/professional/casenotes/0110_doral.html.

60. Lawrence A. Cunningham, Stephen Kwaku, and Arnold Wright, "The Sarbanes-Oxley Act: Legal Implications and Research Opportunities," *Research in Accounting Regulation* 19 (2006).

61. *Monroe v. Hughes,* 860 F. Supp. 733 (1991), Available at: http://law.justia.com/cases/federal/district-courts/FSupp/860/733/2159100/.

62. Cunningham et al.

63. PCAOB, AS 2201: An Audit of Internal Control Over Financial Reporting That Is Integrated with An Audit of Financial Statements, PCAOB Release No. 2007-005A, Fiscal years ending on or after November 15, 2007, https://pcaobus.org/Standards/Auditing/Pages/AS2201.aspx.

64. Lawrence A. Cunningham, Stephen Kwaku Asare, and Arnold Wright, "The Sarbanes-Oxley Act: Legal Implications and Research Opportunities," GW Law Scholarly Commons 2006, http://lawdigitalcommons.bc.edu/cgi/viewcontent.cgi?article=1191&context=lsfp.

65. Cunningham et al.

66. *Higginbotham v. Baxter Int'l.,* 2005 WL 1272271 (N.D. Ill. May 25, 2005).

67. *In re Lattice Semiconductor Corp. Secs. Litig.,* 2006 U.S. Dist. LEXIS 262 (January 3, 2006 Dist. Ore.).

68. *In re WatchGuard Secs. Litig.,* 2006 U.S. Dist. LEXIS 272717 (W.D.Wash., April 21, 2006).

69. *In re WatchGuard Secs. Litig.*

70. Timothy P. Harkness, Celiza P. Bragança, and John Bessonnette, *Minding Your 302s: Assessing Potential Civil, Administrative, and Criminal Liability for False Financial Statement Certifications,* Available at: www.pli.edu/emktg/compliance_coun/Minding_302s_CC_34.pdf.

71. *United States v. Richard Scrushy,* Available at: www.justice.gov/archive/dag/cftf/chargingdocs/scrushy indictment.pdf.

72. Richard D. Ramsey and A. F. Alkhafaji, "The 1977 Foreign Corrupt Practices Act and the 1988 Omnibus Trade Bill," *Management Decision* 29, no. 6, pp. 22–39.

73. Andrew Ceresny, "FCPA, Disclosure, and Internal Controls Issues Arising in the Pharmaceutical Industry," Remarks at CBI's Pharmaceutical Compliance Congress, Washington, D.C. (March 3, 2015), Available at: http://www.sec.gov/news/speech/2015-spch030315ajc.html.

74. SEC, *In the Matter of Halliburton Company and Jeannot Lorenz,* Accounting and Auditing Enforcement Release No. 3884 (July 27, 2017), https://www.sec.gov/litigation/admin/2017/34-81222.pdf.

75. Stanley Sterna, Esq., Defensing third-party audit claims, April 30, 2013, *Journal of Accountancy,* https://www.journalofaccountancy.com/issues/2013/may/20137570.html.

Chapter 8 Cases

Case 8-1 Your Tax Client

Your tax client, Steve Michaels, told you that his former accountant who prepared his annual tax returns made errors that resulted in him suffering more than $100,000 in losses. Apparently, the errors involved adjustments to his income for a loss resulting from his sale of a property that had greatly diminished in value. Michaels alleged that the former accountant incorrectly advised him that his income was too high to deduct the loss on the property. You confirmed that Michaels overpaid his taxes to the IRS and he did not receive a tax refund that otherwise would have been received.

Questions

Based on the facts of the case, answer the following:

1. Did the former accountant violate any of the rules of conduct in the AICPA Code of Professional Conduct? Be specific.
2. Describe the legal standards of negligence and recklessness. Explain whether the former accountant violated one and/or the other standard.
3. Describe the legal standards of negligence and gross negligence. Explain whether the former accountant violated one and/or the other standard.
4. Discuss whether there any defenses the former accountant can assert to avoid legal liability.

Case 8-2 Joker & Wild LLC

Joker & Wild LLC has just been sued by its audit client, Canasta, Inc., claiming the audit failed to be conducted in accordance with generally accepted auditing standards, lacked the requisite care expected in an audit, and failed to point out that internal controls were not working as intended. The facts of the case are that the auditors failed to find the accounting manager's misappropriation of assets when he stole inventory and then improperly, knowingly, wrote down inventory for market declines.

Current market values of inventory were not provided to the auditors despite numerous requests for this information. The auditors relied on management's representations about these values, which understated inventory by 10 percent. The plaintiff client brought the suit against the CPA firm claiming negligence, asserting the firm's failure to find the vice president's misappropriations of inventory and false valuations damaged the company by prematurely recognizing losses and then causing large reversals in the subsequent fiscal year when the inventory was sold for 15 percent above the original cost. The defendant CPA firm sought to blame the client, claiming Canasta did not cooperate on the audit and the vice president overrode internal controls.

Questions

1. Are the auditors guilty of malpractice? Explain.
2. What defenses are available to Joker & Wild in this case? Explain what they must prove to successfully assert these defenses.
3. Assume you are not aware of state laws on auditor legal liability. What legal concepts might a court of law use to resolve the lawsuit?
4. Do you believe the auditors should be held legally liable? Why or why not?

Case 8-3 QSGI, Inc.

Overview of the Case[1]

QSGI, Inc., is in the business of purchasing, refurbishing, selling, and servicing used computer equipment, parts, and mainframes. During its 2008 fiscal year (FY) and continuing up to its filing for Chapter 11 bankruptcy on July 2, 2009 (the "relevant period"), Mark Sherman was the CEO and chairman of the board of directors. The SEC alleged that Sherman was aware of deficiencies in and the circumvention of internal controls for inventory and the resulting falsification of the Company's books and records. The SEC alleged that Sherman withheld this information from the Company's external auditors in connection with their audit of the financial statements for the FY 2008 and review of the financial statements for the quarter ended March 31, 2009, and made affirmative material misrepresentations and statements that were materially misleading as a result of his omission of information in management representation letters to the auditors about the design, maintenance, and operation of internal controls. It was further alleged that Sherman signed a Form 10-K and Form 10-K/A for the 2008 fiscal year, each containing a management's report on ICFR as required by Section 404 of SOX and Exchange Act Rule 13a-15(c), which falsely represented that he, in his capacity as CEO, had participated in assessing the effectiveness of the ICFR. Sherman also signed certifications required under Section 302 of SOX and Rule 13a-14 of the Exchange Act included in filings with the SEC falsely representing that he had evaluated ICFR and, based on this evaluation, disclosed all significant deficiencies to the auditors. The certifications were attached to the 2008 Forms 10-K and 10-K/A, and to the first-quarter 2009 Form 10-Q filed with the Commission, which Sherman also signed.

Facts of the Case

Leading up to its bankruptcy in 2009, QSGI experienced recurring inventory control problems. Throughout the relevant period, Company personnel: (1) shipped certain inventory out to customers without making the appropriate entries and (2) removed items from physical inventory without reducing inventory on the Company's books. Company personnel removed component parts from the physical inventory for such parts without recording the parts removed and occasionally stripped component parts from operating systems without recording the parts removed. As a result, the Company's books and records incorrectly reflected certain components in inventory and operating systems as intact systems. These component parts were then sold by the Company or used for the Company's maintenance services. These internal control problems resulted in the falsification of QSGI's books and records relating to its inventory.

QSGI's efforts to introduce new controls during FY 2008 largely failed. The Company failed to design procedures taking into consideration the control environment, including the qualifications and experience level of persons employed to handle accounting. Controls were mostly ignored during FY 2008 and well into FY 2009. For example, sales and warehouse personnel often failed to document their removal of items from inventory or, to the extent they did prepare paperwork, accounting personnel often failed to process the paperwork and to adjust inventory in the company's financial reporting system. The Company's attempts to monitor compliance on an ongoing basis were also inadequate. Company personnel regularly circumvented controls.

During the relevant period, Sherman knew of ongoing deficiencies in and the circumvention of internal controls relating to inventory. As an example, in the final days of FY 2008, QSGI senior management, including Sherman, openly communicated among themselves about the failed implementation, including training in, and circumvention of, controls introduced into operations earlier in the year. Management agreed that corrective action was needed which, given the timing, could not be undertaken until 2009. Based on further communications, management, including Sherman, was aware that the problems continued through the Company filing for bankruptcy in July 2009.

Sherman's False Representations in Management's Report on ICFR and Critical Accounting Policies

At no time during the relevant period did Sherman disclose, or direct anyone to disclose, to QSGI's external auditors the foregoing inventory issues and the resulting falsification of QSGI's books and records. To the contrary, in the management representation letters to the auditors, Sherman made affirmative misrepresentations and made statements that were misleading as a result of his omitting material facts which were necessary in order to make the statements made not misleading. He represented to the auditors that either there were no significant deficiencies or that he had disclosed to the auditors all such deficiencies. At the conclusion of FY 2008, he provided yet another representation letter in connection with the auditor's audit of the FY 2008 financial statements in which he acknowledged his responsibility for establishing and maintaining ICFR. Omitted from the letter was any reference to the existence, or his disclosure to the auditors, of significant deficiencies. In the management representation letter relating to the auditors' review of the first-quarter 2009 financial statements, Sherman affirmatively misrepresented that he had disclosed to the auditors all significant deficiencies.

QSGI's Form 10-K for FY 2008 included a Company management's report on ICFR, as required by Section 404 of SOX and Exchange Rule 13a-15(c). A management's report on ICFR was also included in a Form 10-K/A for FY 2008. These management reports falsely represented that QSGI's management, with the participation of CEO Sherman, had evaluated ICFR using the criteria set forth by COSO Internal Control–Integrated Framework (see **Chapter 3**). In fact, Sherman did not participate as CEO, did not participate in the referenced evaluation, and was unfamiliar with the referenced framework.

The discussion on critical accounting policies in QSGI's Form 10-K for FY 2008 falsely stated that "[m]anagement continually monitors its inventory valuation. . ., closely monitors and analyzes inventory for potential obsolescence and slow-moving items on an item-by-item basis. Sherman knew, or was reckless in not knowing, that these statements were materially false and misleading because he knew that the Company did not closely monitor inventory in the manner described because the Company lacked the necessary resources. Sherman signed the 2008 Form 10-K and 10-K/A. He was the sole signing officer for the 10-K/A.

Sherman's False SOX Certifications

Pursuant to SOX Section 302 and Exchange Act Rule 13a-14, Sherman signed certifications attached to the financial statements that said, based on his and the other certifying officer's (CFO) "most recent evaluation of [ICFR]," they had disclosed to QSGI's external auditors all significant deficiencies, "in the design or operation of [ICFR] which are reasonably likely to adversely affect [QSGI's] ability to record, process, summarize and report financial information." Omitted from the certification attached to the Form 10-K, but included in the certification attached to the Form 10-Q, were Sherman's certifications to the effect that the other certifying officer and he: (1) had been responsible for establishing and maintaining ICFR and designing, or supervising others in the design of, ICFR and (2) had designed, or caused to be designed, such ICFR. These certifications were false because Sherman had not participated in or evaluated ICFR and did not make referenced disclosures to the external auditors.

Findings

The SEC found that Sherman violated various Sections of the Exchange Act dealing with proper financial statements and certifications under SOX. Sherman was ordered to cease and desist from committing or causing any future violations of the Act, prohibited for five years from acting as an officer or director of any issuer of stock, and pay a civil money penalty of $7,500.

Questions

1. Assume that a third party(ies) is considering whether to sue the external auditors of QSGI. What could they allege in their lawsuit and why?

2. Assuming a third party(ies) files the lawsuit, what defenses could the external auditors use to rebut the charges?

3. Did SOX fail to protect investors and other users of QSGI's financial statements? Explain.

Case 8-4 *Anjoorian et al.*: Third-Party Liability

In the 2007 case of *Paul V. Anjoorian v. Arnold Kilberg & Co., Arnold Kilberg, and Pascarella & Trench,* the Rhode Island Superior Court ruled that a shareholder can sue a company's outside accounting firm for alleged negligence in the preparation of the company's financial statements even though the accountant argued it had no duty of care to third parties like the shareholder with whom it never engaged in a direct financial transaction. Judge Michael A. Silverstein disagreed, saying an accountant owes a duty to any individual or group of people who are meant to benefit from or be influenced by the information the accountant provides. Silverstein relied on the *Restatement (Second) of the Law of Torts:* "The Restatement approach strikes the appropriate balance between compensating victims of malpractice and limiting the scope of potential liability for those who certify financial statements. While it remains to be proved that [the firm] actually did foresee that [its] financial statements would be used by the shareholders [in the manner alleged], the absence of a particular financial transaction does not preclude the finding of a duty in this case."[1]

The facts of the case are described in **Exhibit 1**.

EXHIBIT 1   *Anjoorian et al.:* Third-Party Liability

Facts of the Case

The defendants Pascarella and Trench, general partners of the accounting firm Pascarella & Trench (P&T), asked the court for summary judgment in their favor with respect to plaintiff Anjoorian's claim that P&T committed malpractice in the preparation of financial statements and that the plaintiff (Anjoorian) suffered pecuniary harm as a result.

Anjoorian formerly owned 50 percent of the issued shares of Fairway Capital Corporation (FCC), a Rhode Island corporation. The other 50 percent of the shares were held by the three children of Arnold Kilberg. Kilberg himself owned no stock in the corporation, but he served as the day-to-day manager of the company. FCC was in the business of making and servicing equity loans to small businesses under the regulation of the U.S. Small Business Administration (SBA), and was capitalized by loans from the SBA and a $1.26 million investment by Anjoorian.

Beginning in 1990, P&T provided accounting services to FCC. The firm audited FCC's annual financial statements following the close of each calendar year between 1990 and 1994. In its representation letter (similar to the current Section 302 requirement under SOX), P&T stated that FCC was "responsible for the fair presentation in the financial statements of financial position." P&T's responsibility was to perform an audit in accordance with GAAS and to "express an opinion on the financial statements" based on the firm's audit. The first page of each financial statement contained the auditor's opinion that "the financial statements referred to above present fairly, in all material respects, the financial position of FCC in conformity with generally accepted accounting principles." Each report is addressed to "The Board of Directors and Shareholders." The 1990–1994 statements indicate that "it is management's opinion that all accounts presented on the balance sheet are collectible." In addition, the 1991–1994 statements indicate that "all loans are fully collateralized" according to the board of directors.

On March 2, 1994, Anjoorian filed a complaint and motion for a temporary restraining order seeking the dissolution of FCC on various grounds. P&T was not a party to that suit. As a result of that action, the three Kilberg children exercised their right to purchase the plaintiff's shares of the corporation. The court appointed an appraiser to determine the value of Anjoorian's shares, which the other shareholders would have to pay. The bulk of FCC's assets comprised its right to receive payment for the loans that it had made. The appraiser determined that the value of the corporation was $2,395,000, plus a payroll adjustment of $102,000, and minus a "loss reserve" adjustment to account for the fact that 10 of FCC's 30 outstanding loans were delinquent. The loss reserve adjustment reduced the total appraised value of the corporation by $878,234. Consequently, Anjoorian's 50 percent interest in the corporation was reduced accordingly by $439,117. He ultimately received a judgment for $809,382.85 against the other shareholders in exchange for the buyout of his shares.

In 1997, Anjoorian brought the lawsuit against Kilberg, Kilberg's company, and P&T. He claimed that P&T was negligent in preparing the annual financial statements for FCC because it did not include an accurate loan-loss reserve in the statements. Anjoorian argued that he relied on the financial statements prepared by the defendants, and that if the

(continued)

statements had included a loan-loss reserve, he would have sought dissolution of the corporation much earlier than 1994, when his shares would have been more valuable. Anjoorian submitted an appraisal suggesting that the appropriate loan-loss reserve figure would have been much less—and, therefore, his share value much higher—in the years 1990 and 1991. He alleged that he lost over $300,000 in share value between 1990 and March 2, 1994. Nine years later, the defendants moved for summary judgment on the grounds that P&T owed no duty to Anjoorian as a shareholder.

Accountants' Liabilities to Third Parties

Silverstein observed that while the question of accountant liability to third parties was unsettled in Rhode Island, the Rhode Island Supreme Court had identified three competing interpretations. The first interpretation was the "foreseeability test," under which an auditor has a duty to all foreseeable recipients of information he provides. "This rule gives little weight to the concern for limiting the potential liability for accountants and is not widely adopted," Silverstein noted.

The second interpretation, the judge continued, was the "privity test," requiring a contractual relationship to exist between an accountant or auditor and another party.

Finally, the *Restatement* test, found in §522 of the *Restatement (Second) of Torts,* states an accountant who does not exercise reasonable care "is only liable to intended persons or classes of persons, and only for intended transactions or substantially similar transactions," said Silverstein. "[This approach] applies not only [to] specific persons and transactions contemplated by the accountant, but also specific classes of persons and transactions." Silverstein settled on the *Restatement* rule.[2]

Applying the rule, Silverstein denied summary judgment for the accounting firm, concluding there was a genuine issue of material fact on whether the accounting firm could be liable. "This court would have no difficulty finding a duty in this case, in the absence of a specific financial transaction, if it can be shown that [the defendant] intended the shareholders to rely on the financial statements for the purpose of evaluating the financial health of the company, and therefore, their investment in the company," wrote Silverstein.[3]

Case Analysis

The court found that the addressing of the reports to the shareholders, while not conclusive, is a strong indication that P&T intended the shareholders to rely upon them. Therefore, the court concluded that genuine issues of fact exist as to whether P&T intended for Anjoorian to rely on these financial statements. Perhaps the court would have reached a different conclusion for a widely held public corporation with a potentially unlimited number of shareholders whose identities change regularly. Here, however, FCC was a close corporation with only four shareholders, giving greater significance to the fact that the financial statements were addressed "to the shareholders."

The defendants also argued that, in order to find a duty to third parties, an accountant must have contemplated a specific transaction for which the financial statement would be used and that no such transaction was contemplated here.[4] The court found this argument unconvincing, stating that the case is unusual in that the alleged malpractice did not arise from a specific financial transaction. The typical case involves a person whose reliance on a defective financial statement induces the person to advance credit or invest new equity into the corporation.[5] When the investment is lost, or the loan unpaid, the person sues the accountant. In this case, however, Anjoorian had already invested his capital in the corporation when P&T was hired, and he alleged that he used the financial statements as a tool to evaluate the value of that investment. The alleged malpractice did not result in his advancing new value to the corporation and then losing his investment, but instead resulted in Anjoorian failing to withdraw his capital from the corporation while its value was higher.

The court opined that it would have no difficulty finding a duty in this case, in the absence of a specific financial transaction, if it could be shown that P&T intended the shareholders to rely on the financial statements for the purpose of evaluating the financial health of the company and, therefore, their investment in the company. In this case, the "particular transaction" contemplated by the *Restatement* relates to the purpose for which the financial statements would be used—the shareholders' decision whether to withdraw capital or not. While it remains to be proved that P&T actually did foresee that its financial statements would be used by the shareholders in this manner, the absence of a particular financial transaction does not preclude the finding of a duty in this case. Because the value of the shareholders' investment was limited to the amounts reflected in the company balance sheets, any loss from malpractice was an insurable risk for which accounting professionals can plan.[6]

The defendants argued that the plaintiff's theory of damages was speculative and against public policy. Anjoorian based his damage claims on the assertion that he relied on four annual audited financial statements to evaluate the status of his $1.26 million investment in FCC. Because the statements failed to include a loan-loss reserve figure, he argued that the statements overstated the value of the corporation at the end of each year from 1990 to 1993. When Anjoorian sought dissolution in 1994, the value he obtained for his shares was significantly less than his expectation. He contended that if he had accurate financial information, he would have liquidated his investment earlier when his shares were more valuable. At issue was the existence and amount of the loan-loss reserve. An appraiser of the value of the corporation in the dissolution action determined that the inclusion of a loan-loss reserve in the financial statements was proper, and that created a genuine issue as to whether a breach of the duty of care occurred. The defendant had questioned the computation of the loan-loss reserve but the court disagreed. (A detailed analysis of the amount of loan-loss reserve has been omitted.)

Questions

1. Analyze the potential for legal liability of P&T under each of the four basic theories of liabilities discussed in **Chapter 7**.
2. Were the auditors guilty of professional negligence? Explain.
3. Judge Silverstein relied on the *Restatement (Second) of the Law of Torts* for his ruling. Assume he had relied on the "near-privity relationship" ruling in *Credit Alliance,* and evaluate the legal liability of the auditors using that standard.
4. The defendants argued in the case that, in order to find a duty to third parties, an accountant must have contemplated a specific transaction for which the financial statement would be used and that no such transaction was contemplated here. Do you agree with this statement from the perspective of auditors' third-party liability? Why or why not?

Case 8-5 *Vertical Pharmaceuticals Inc. et al. v. Deloitte & Touche LLP[1]*

On December 13, 2012, Vertical Pharmaceuticals Inc. and an affiliated company sued Deloitte & Touche LLP in New Jersey state court for alleged accountant malpractice, claiming the firm's false accusations of fraudulent conduct scrapped Trigen Laboratories (TLI) plans to acquire Vertical for more than $50 million.

Vertical is a privately owned company that sells niche prescription drugs geared toward women's health and pain management. TLI, a public company, sells and markets generic drugs. Deloitte was auditing the 2011 financial statements of Vertical and TLI, which are owned by the same three partners, when it abruptly suspended that review because of supposedly troubling items that two whistleblowers brought to the firm's attention, according to the complaint, which was filed November 21 in Morris County Superior Court.

Deloitte insisted that Vertical hire independent counsel and conduct an internal investigation with a forensic audit, the complaint said. Vertical agreed to those steps, but Deloitte eventually notified Vertical that it was resigning rather than finishing its work, according to the complaint.

"As a forensic audit later discovered—no money was being pilfered from the company. No partner was stealing money from another. No improper conduct was taking place," the complaint said.

The revelation that Deloitte resigned from the 2011 audit and the allegations of potential criminal conduct and financial improprieties that the auditor passed on to the audit committee left the acquisition for dead, the complaint said. The public company found another pharmaceutical company to acquire.

The deal would have helped rapidly grow Vertical's business and established a revenue stream for the company of more than $500 million, the complaint contended. "Deloitte knew the deal would be final once the 2011 audit was completed. Without Deloitte's interference in concocting a series of false, negligent statements regarding Vertical's financials, the 2011 audit would have been issued and the deal completed."

Vertical has asked for $200 million or more in damages on multiple counts, including accounting malpractice and breach of fiduciary duty. Deloitte also demanded and received $120,000 for all of its invoiced services before resigning, according to the complaint, which seeks back those funds as well.

Deloitte's allegedly slanted statements involved accusations that Vertical was pilfering company funds through two LLCs, inappropriately paying company employees through car allowances, committing fraud by having an owner's father as tax auditor, and paying an owner's wife off the books, according to the complaint.

The firm also falsely claimed Vertical's books were in terrible shape and that its management was unreliable, the complaint said. "A subsequent forensic audit initially to assuage Deloitte was ultimately completed . . . which found: None of these items had merit nor did they consider any resolution items justified to engender Deloitte's resignation; that Deloitte was well aware of the nature prior to its supposed whistleblower disclosures of the items; and that many of these items were in the process of being resolved based on advice provided by Deloitte as early as May 2011," the complaint said.

Questions

1. Do you believe Deloitte & Touche breached its fiduciary duty to Vertical Pharmaceuticals in this case? Explain.
2. Do you believe Deloitte was guilty of malpractice as alleged by Vertical? Why or why not?
3. Could Vertical have sustained a claim that Deloitte acted recklessly in prematurely withdrawing from the engagement? Be sure to address the legal requirements to make a case that recklessness occurred by the auditor.
4. When should an auditor withdraw from an engagement? Do you believe Deloitte was justified in resigning from the Vertical Pharmaceuticals engagement? Do you believe Deloitte acted ethically in this regard?

Case 8-6 *Kay & Lee, LLP*

Kay & Lee LLP was retained as the auditor for Holligan Industries to audit the financial statements required by prospective banks as a prerequisite to extending a loan to the client. The auditor knows whichever bank lends money to the client is likely to rely on the audited statements.

After the audit report is issued, the bank that ultimately made the loan discovers that the client's inventory and accounts receivable were overstated. The client subsequently went bankrupt and defaulted on the loan. The bank alleged that the auditor failed to communicate about the inadequacy of the client's internal recordkeeping and inventory control. Moreover, the bank claims that the auditors were grossly negligent in not discovering the overvaluation of inventory and accounts receivable.

The auditors asserted that there was no way for them to know that the client included in the inventory account $1 million of merchandise in transit to a customer on December 31, 2021. The shipping terms were unclear so the auditors accepted management's representations in that regard. As for the receivables, the auditors claimed the client falsified confirmations by sending them to a post office address, retrieving them, and then confirming the stated balances.

Questions

1. What would the bank have to prove to successfully bring a lawsuit against Kay & Lee?
2. What defenses might the auditors use to rebut any charges made about their (deficient) audit?
3. Critically evaluate the auditors' statements about the inventory and receivables with respect to generally accepted auditing standards and the firm's ethical responsibilities.

Case 8-7 Alexion

Overview

Alexion is a global biopharmaceutical company with shares of its stock traded on the Nasdaq Stock Market in the United States. The company develops and sells drugs for patients with life-threatening rare and ultra-rare diseases. Alexion began commercial sales of its first drug, Soliris, in 2007.[1]

From 2010 to 2015, Alexion's subsidiary in Turkey made payments to foreign officials in order to influence them to provide favorable regulatory treatment for Alexion's primary drug, Soliris, and to approve Soliris prescriptions for individual patients. In connection with these improper payments, false books and records were maintained by Alexion's subsidiaries in Turkey and Russia. Alexion had insufficient internal accounting controls to detect and prevent these payments and to provide reasonable assurances that these transactions were recorded accurately in the books and records of these subsidiaries, which were consolidated into Alexion's books and records. The payments continued through 2015 due to Alexion's inadequate internal accounting controls and the lack of an effective anti-corruption compliance program. As a result, Alexion was unjustly enriched by over $14 million. There were no written laws making such payments legal under the written laws of Turkey.

Improper Payments

Alexion began selling Soliris through Turkey's named patient sales ("NPS") program in 2009. Under Turkish law, each patient's application to begin Soliris therapy required review and approval by health care providers ("HCPs") appointed to serve on commissions in Turkey's Ministry of Health, separate approvals to pay for the prescription, and recurring approvals to continue the patient on Soliris therapy. Alexion Turkey paid HCPs employed at state-owned health care institutions for services, including research and educational events.

Alexion initially struggled to get these approvals for Soliris. In January 2010, a senior Ministry of Health official suggested to an Alexion Turkey regional account manager that, to obtain more patient approvals, Alexion Turkey may need to make payments to government officials. Thereafter, Alexion Turkey hired a consultant ("Consultant") to assist Alexion Turkey with the patient approval process. The Consultant was hired in significant part due to the Consultant's connections to top Ministry of Health officials.

From 2010 to 2015, Alexion Turkey paid the Consultant over $1.3 million, consisting of consulting fees and purported expense reimbursements. The Consultant passed a portion of these funds on to Turkish government officials, in the form of cash, meals, or gifts, to secure favorable treatment for Soliris. As a result of these payments, Alexion Turkey not only secured approvals for patient prescriptions, but also received confidential information and advance feedback from government officials on regulatory submissions. Alexion Turkey recorded these improper payments inaccurately, claiming them as legitimate expenses.

Two Alexion Turkey managers made some of the payments to the Consultant by asking a third-party vendor to pay the Consultant and provide falsified invoices for reimbursement to Alexion Turkey. Certain Alexion Turkey employees recorded these payments inaccurately in Alexion Turkey's books and records. Further, an Alexion Turkey manager directed that the description of the Consultant's claimed expenses should be written in pencil. The use of pencil would allow the description of the expenses to be easily changed or concealed.

Alexion Turkey failed to require that the Consultant provide sufficient documentation of expenses or services provided in return for the payments. From 2010 to 2015, the Consultant provided little or no explanation for many expenses and failed to provide independent documentation for most of the purported expenses. Expense documentation that was submitted often sought reimbursement for large, vague expenses [e.g., categorized only as ("other expense")]. Even so, expense documentation associated with some of the payments indicates that the funds were for the benefit of government officials (e.g., noting first names of known government officials on submitted expense reports or notes attached thereto).

In addition to paying government officials through the Consultant, from 2012 to 2015, Alexion Turkey managers paid over $100,000 to or at the request of HCPs serving on Ministry of Health commissions. These HCPs were responsible for approving or denying patient prescriptions for Soliris and had influence over key regulatory matters, such as treatment guidelines and reimbursement criteria. Alexion Turkey paid these HCPs to influence them to approve patient prescriptions and support regulatory actions favorable to Soliris. These payments were recorded inaccurately in Alexion Turkey's books and records as honoraria and grants.

For example, from 2012 to 2014, Alexion Turkey paid over $15,000 to or at the request of an HCP who Alexion Turkey senior management recognized was "the decision maker for the reimbursement criteria" and the decision maker for the approval of patient prescriptions for Soliris. Alexion Turkey began paying the HCP once the HCP assumed responsibility for approving or denying patient prescriptions. Alexion Turkey made these payments to improperly influence the HCP to make decisions that would favor Alexion, including approving patient prescriptions for Soliris.

SEC Action

As a result of the conduct described above, Alexion violated Section 13(b)(2)(A) of the Exchange Act, which requires issuers to make and keep books, records, and accounts which, in reasonable detail, accurately and fairly reflect their transactions and dispositions of the assets of the issuer. As a result of the conduct described above, Alexion violated Section 13(b)(2)(B) of the Exchange Act, which requires issuers to devise and maintain a system of internal accounting controls sufficient to provide reasonable assurances that:

1. Transactions are executed in accordance with management's general or specific authorization;
2. Transactions are recorded as necessary:

    (a) to permit preparation of financial statements in conformity with generally accepted accounting principles or any other criteria applicable to such statements, and

    (b) to maintain accountability for assets;

3. Access to assets is permitted only in accordance with management's general or specific authorization; and
4. The recorded accountability for assets is compared with the existing assets at reasonable intervals and appropriate action is taken with respect to any differences.

As a result of the conduct described above, Alexion violated Section 13(b)(2)(A) of the Exchange Act because its books and records did not accurately reflect certain expenses and payments, including improper payments to foreign officials and third parties. Alexion violated Section 13(b)(2)(B) of the Exchange Act by failing to devise and maintain sufficient internal accounting controls over the payments to foreign officials and third parties.

Questions

1. Explain why the corporate governance systems and internal controls failed at Alexion.
2. How would you evaluate the role of top management in enabling the fraud including its compliance systems?
3. Alexion contended that their payments to foreign government officials were required to do business in Turkey. Alexion claimed this was a customary business practice. From an ethical perspective, should multinationals play by the rules in the United States or those of foreign countries? Use ethical reasoning to answer this question and consider the rules of conduct in the AICPA Code of Professional Conduct.

Case 8-8 Disclosing Material Weaknesses in ICFR or Protecting the Firm from Litigation? (A GVV case)

Billy Muldoon, CPA and CFO, just finished reading a preliminary draft of his company's annual audit report from Local CPAs, LLC. He was concerned that the CPA firm plans to issue a qualified audit report because it had concluded that the company had a material weakness in their internal controls over financial reporting. Billy was concerned that such a disclosure might result in a large drop in the market price of the company's stock. Included with the draft of the report was the following note of explanation from the partner in charge of the engagement as to how Local CPAs had reached this conclusion:

Dear Billy,

As you know, we perform an integrated audit which combines our testing of the adequacy of internal controls with our performance of our normal audit procedures. This process starts during our audit planning process with the review of managements' assertions surrounding the adequacy of internal controls, including those surrounding financial reporting. Unfortunately, as we conducted our work we discovered a series of deficiencies, which individually are immaterial. Taken together, we believe these significant deficiencies represent a more than remote likelihood that a material misstatement could occur and not be prevented or detected. Therefore, in accordance with Section 404 of SOX and PCAOB AS 2201, the deficiencies need to be disclosed as material in the audit report. We are also concerned that other internal control weaknesses could provide indirect evidence of managerial ability because the design and implementation of internal controls is a primary management responsibility.

Once you have had a chance to review, please feel free to reach out to me to discuss.

Identified Weaknesses:

- We found inadequate segregation of duties over access to your sales information system controls.
- We found several instances of transactions on the general ledger which were not also recorded in the appropriate subsidiary ledger: These transactions were not material individually or in aggregate.
- We found that timely reconciliations of certain intercompany transaction accounts were not being performed: The individual transactions were material on an individual basis and only impacted balance sheet accounts.
- We found insufficient procedures to qualitatively assess whether the fair value of a reporting unit is less than its carrying value in order to assess goodwill impairment.

Billy immediately shot off an email to the partner requesting a meeting stating he vehemently disagreed with his analysis. He further stated that he thought Local CPAs was intentionally misclassifying these items as material weaknesses over fear of potential legal liability.

Questions

1. What are the main arguments that the partner from Local CPAs will need to counter when he meets with Billy? That is, what are the reasons and rationalizations he should expect to hear from Billy as to why a material weakness in the ICFR does not exist?
2. What is at stake for both Billy and Local CPAs should the partner be unable to convince Billy to accept the material weakness disclosure? Consider the requirements of certification under SOX 302 in your response in addition to those of SOX 404. Address the potential liability to both Local CPAs and Billy's company for failure to follow AS 2201.
3. What levers does the partner have? Where can he go to for support?
4. Assume Billy suggests the opinion on ICFR be changed from material to significant. Should the Local CPAs partner go along? What is at stake for Local CPAs, Billy, and the company of characterizing the deficiency as significant if it is, in fact, material?

Case 8-9 Miller Energy Resources, Inc.

On August 15, 2017, the SEC completed an Administrative Hearing process initiated by a PCAOB investigation of KPMG, LLP and one of their audit partners John Riordan, CPA[1] for conducting a materially deficient audit of Miller Energy Resources Inc. KPMG became the successor auditor of Miller for fiscal 2011. Miller was charged with accounting fraud in 2015.

Among other things, the SEC found that KPMG and Riordan:

- failed to properly assess the risks associated with accepting Miller Energy as a client and to properly staff the audit;
- failed to adequately address the audit team's lack of industry experience resulting in a lack of planning, supervision, due care, and professional skepticism;
- failed to obtain sufficient competent evidence to assess the impact of the opening balance of the Alaska Assets on Miller Energy's current year financial statements;
- failed to adequately assess whether Miller Energy's valuation of the Alaska Assets conformed with GAAP (Miller inaccurately revalued an asset costing $4.5 million at $480 million);
- did not obtain sufficient competent evidence regarding the assumptions on which Miller Energy's valuation of the Alaska Assets was based; and
- failed to take reasonable steps to assess Miller Energy's recorded value of $110 million for certain fixed assets included in the Alaska acquisition.

In a class-action lawsuit against one-half dozen former executives of Miller, the plaintiffs charged that Miller overlooked the overvaluation of certain oil and gas interests that the company had purchased in Alaska the previous year. According to the lawsuit, David M. Hall, who served as chief operating officer, understated the cost to run the oil field. Also, it charged that the former CFO, Paul W., Boyd, and Hall, provided expense projections that were, in many cases, significantly lower than expenses recorded by the previous owners of the field. For example, the lawsuit claims internal documents maintained by Hall indicated that the cost to drill a new well was roughly $13 million, however he told the engineering firm preparing reports used to determine the value of the company that the costs to drill at the field was only $4.6 million per well. Additional understatements were made.

As a result of the above, in addition to agreeing to pay $6.2 million in penalties to settle SEC charges that it failed to properly audit Miller Energy, KPMG agreed to complete a firm wide review and evaluation "of the sufficiency and adequacy of their quality controls, including their policies and procedures for audits and interim reviews" of specific items identified by the SEC. KPMG also had to hire and bear the cost of having an independent consultant evaluate the adequacy of KPMG's internal policies and procedures to ensure compliance with all relevant commission regulations and PCAOB standards. In addition, KPMG must certify they have implemented the recommendations of the consultant and then certify the adequacy of their controls at the end of 2018 and 2019, as well.

Questions

1. Analyze the facts of the case with respect to the AICPA Code and explain any perceived deviation from ethical standards.
2. Assume Miller Energy is considering bringing a lawsuit against KPMG for malpractice. What would it have to demonstrate to be successful? What defenses are available to KPMG to counteract the malpractice claim?
3. Assume investors in Miller Energy met to discuss whether to bring a class-action lawsuit against KPMG. On what basis might they bring the lawsuit?
4. Assume Miller Energy negotiated a $10 million loan with a financial institution during 2015. Subsequent to the SEC's finding of accounting fraud in 2015, the financial institution brought a lawsuit against KPMG for negligence. What judicial approaches might be used to decide the case?

Case 8-10 Biotechnologies

Helen Roberts is reviewing two transactions recorded by her client, Biotechnologies (Biotech), as part of her accounting firm's annual audit of the client for the December 31, 2021, financial statements. She knows Biotech is under pressure to maximize revenues for the year and reverse three years of losses. The reported revenue on its financial statements is $2.2 million. The amount of revenue from two transactions being reviewed is $1.0 million. Biotech lost $2.0 million during the last two years. If the revenue can be recorded at the $2.2 million level, Biotech would cover the losses for the past two years and be profitable for 2021.

Biotechnologies develops vaccines for infectious diseases like COVID-19. The company was formed following the outbreak of the virus. While it's not working on a vaccine for COVID, the company hopes to develop therapeutics to fight similar infections in the future. Biotech went public in 2019 and its stock is listed on Nasdaq.

Helen Roberts is one of five partners in the firm of Morton & Best, LLC. Even though Biotech is its only public client, the firm is obligated to register with the PCAOB.

The fees earned from Biotech make up one-third of the firm's total revenue from fees. As a result, it's an important client for the firm.

Accounting Transactions

Sales to Distributor 1 on December 27, 2021

On December 27, 2021, Biotech sent Distributor 1 revised terms of a deal between Biotech and the Distributor. Under the revised terms, in order for the Distributor to receive a product they ordered and wanted, it would have to place an order for another product in inventory so that Biotech is able to record the $600,000 revenue on that product in 2021. Biotech expects the distributor to place the 600,000 order for this product that could be shipped by December 31, 2021.

The arrangement with Distributor 1 was developed because Biotech could not ship the specific product ordered by the Distributor by year-end as desired by the Distributor. That is why Biotech identified products in its inventory that it could ship by year-end so that it could record the revenue in 2021. Even though the Distributor didn't order or want that product, it agreed to go through with the arrangement because Biotech's agreement included a provision that the Distributor could return the unwanted product in the first quarter of 2022 and replace it with the product desired. The purchase order was changed to reflect the new arrangement.

Sales to Distributor 2 on December 30, 2021

An order for the purchase of $400,000 product of Biotech on December 1, 2021 by Distributor 2 contained the terms of payment as net 30 days or due by December 31, 2021. The product was to be shipped on December 20, 2021. Distributor 2 informed Biotech that because it was a start-up company, it wouldn't be able to pay by that date and maybe for at least 60 days thereafter. Biotech then came up with an arrangement whereby Distributor 2 could return the product anytime during the 60-day period, with no questions asked, and be credited for its account payable. Distributor 2 agreed to buy the product based on these terms and Biotech recorded the $400,000 as revenue on December 20, 2021, the shipping date.

Biotech's Arguments for Recording the Revenue in Fiscal-Year End December 31, 2021

The CFO of Biotech explained why revenue should be recorded on the sale of product to both distributors as follows. Revenue from the product shipped to Distributor 1 by year-end could be recognized on the shipping date. The fact that the Distributor could return it next year was nothing new. The sale of any product to a customer could be returned after purchase.

The product shipped to Distributor 2 occurred on December 20, 2021, before year-end, so revenue could be recorded on that date. The sale of any product to a customer could be returned after purchase. The fact that the return would be credited with no questions asked was standard company policy.

Helen Roberts is preparing to meet with the CFO of Biotech to discuss these transactions and the way revenue has been recognized. Answer the following questions to help her prepare for the meeting.

Questions

1. Analyze the transactions with both distributors with respect to revenue recognition and how the CFO explained the position of Biotech. Was revenue recognized properly under GAAP? Why or why not?

2. How would you characterize the motivation of Biotech for the way it recorded the transactions? What was the effect on the way earnings were recorded?

3. How would you explain Biotech's responsibilities under SOX? Be specific.

4. Assume Roberts is attempting to determine the firm's possible liability for recklessness or fraud depending on whether it accepts the client's explanations. How might she go about the analysis?

Major Cases

The following cases can serve as detailed reviews of major issues discussed in the text. The cases vary in length to provide flexibility for instructors. The longer ones (Logitech International, Cendant Corporation, and Vivendi Universal) are ideal for final projects. Kiley Nolan's Ethical Dilemma can be used to review the Giving Voice to Values methodology. The Colonial Bank case is one of the most important cases affecting the accounting profession in the past few years. It was the biggest bank failure of 2009. The Luckin Coffee case is current and deals with a Chinese company with stock listed on NASDAQ. Five major cases from the third and fourth editions have been removed from the text and are accessible in the Instructor's Resources: Adelphia Communications, Cumberland Lumber, Parmalat, Royal Ahold N.V., and Waste Management.

Major Case 1: Colonial Bank

- Auditor responsibility when client management commits fraud
- Auditors' inability to understand underlying cause of fraud: accounting for mortgage securitizations
- Reliance on work of outsourced internal audit and internal control issues
- Application of AICPA Code and auditing standards

Major Case 2: Logitech International

- Application of lower cost or market valuations to inventory
- Corporate governance failures
- Application of AICPA Code and auditing standards
- Ethical dilemma for staff accountant: Application of Sarbanes-Oxley and Dodd-Frank

Major Case 3: Kiley Nolan's Ethical Dilemma (a GVV case)

- Inability to meet loan covenant amounts
- Application of FASB revenue recognition standard, *Revenue from Contracts with Customers*
- Ethical reasoning and cognitive development
- Whistleblowing

Major Case 4: Cendant Corporation

- Income smoothing
- Application of the Fraud Triangle
- Professional judgment/AICPA Code
- Trust in relationship between client and auditor

Major Case 5: Vivendi Universal

- Ethical leadership
- Role of internal controls and ethical corporate culture
- Financial disclosure fraud
- Earnings releases, EBITDA, and earnings management

Major Case 6: Luckin Coffee

- Fabricated transactions and earnings management
- Red flags
- Corporate governance failures
- Ethical reasoning

Major Case 1

Colonial Bank

Case Overview

On January 2, 2018, U.S. District Court Judge Barbara Rothstein ruled that PricewaterhouseCoopers (PwC) negligently failed to uncover a $2.3 billion fraud scheme between PwC audit client Colonial Bank and Taylor, Bean & Whitaker. Colonial Bank is now in receivership under Federal Deposit Insurance Corporation (FDIC) rules. Taylor Bean is a bankrupt mortgage lender. PwC already paid an undisclosed amount in 2016 to settle related claims by Taylor Bean's trustee.[1] The decision in the case means it now moves into a damages phase, where the FDIC is seeking as much as $2.1 billion.

The collapse of Colonial Bank, which had $25 billion in assets and $20 billion in deposits, was the biggest bank failure of 2009. The FDIC estimates Colonial's failure will ultimately cost its insurance fund $5 billion, making it one of the most expensive bank failures in U.S. history. The lawsuit against PwC was the first of its kind filed against an accounting firm in the aftermath of the financial recession. On August 12, 2012, some former Colonial Bank directors and officers agreed to settle the securities class action lawsuit against them for the bank's collapse. The settlement did not include PwC.

While Judge Rothstein held PwC liable for negligence, it rejected similar claims by the bankruptcy trustee for Colonial BancGroup because the bank itself was responsible for the fraud. That professional negligence claim was barred by the *in pari delicto* doctrine and the audit interference rule. Latin for "in equal fault," *in pari delicto* means, if the fault of the fraud is more or less equal between two or more parties (i.e., Colonial Bank and PwC), neither party can claim breach of the contract by the other. The audit interference rule holds that an auditor may assert a comparative-fault defense where it can establish that the client's negligence "interfered with" the auditor's performance of its duties, as in the Colonial Bank case.

In her opinion, Judge Rothstein emphasized that PwC had relied on the chief architect of the fraud, Taylor Bean chair Lee Farkas, to verify key information about the collateral underlying a Colonial credit facility for Taylor Bean. PwC signed off on Colonial's audit without ever understanding the underlying accounting event, which was based on phantom mortgage securitizations. PwC allowed Colonial to account for certain types of mortgages from Taylor Bean as sales rather than as loans from Colonial to Taylor Bean that were secured by mortgages.

Judge Rothstein ruled PwC was guilty of professional negligence. It rapped the firm for following "illogical dates" and to check whether an entire class of loans—nearly 20 percent of its mortgage lending warehouse—existed. She also cited testimony from a PwC partner in an earlier, related case that "our audit procedures were not designed to detect fraud."

PwC gave the bank's parent, Colonial BancGroup, a clean audit opinion for years before it was disclosed that substantial portions of Colonial's loans to Taylor Bean were secured against assets that did not exist. In the malpractice case, Judge Rothstein agreed with the FDIC that PwC failed to meet professional accounting standards in its audits of Colonial. "PwC did not design its audits to detect fraud and PwC's failure to do so constitutes a violation of the auditing standards," Rothstein ruled.[2]

PwC Defense of Audit

PwC, in its defense, said it was duped by Farkas, who skimmed millions of dollars from Colonial to buy a private jet, vintage cars, and a vacation home. Rothstein had ruled that Colonial executives lied to PwC's auditors, circumvented internal controls by "recycling" mortgage data, and even created wire transfers to trick PwC into believing Taylor Bean's collateral mortgages had been paid off.

---

1. Alison Frankel, At heart of FDIC's win v. PwC, an unsettled theory, *Reuters*, January 2, 2018, https://www.reuters.com/article/us-otc-fdic/at-heart-of-fdics-win-v-pwc-an-unsettled-theory-idUSKBN1ER1U1.

2. Matthew Heller, PwC Found Liable for $2B Colonial Bank Fraud, cfo.com, January 2, 2018, http://ww2.cfo.com/fraud/2018/01/pwc-found-liable-2b-colonial-bank-fraud/.

PwC put its own spin on the verdict by stating that the court's ruling recognized that in addition to those Colonial Bank employees who perpetrated the fraud, numerous other employees at Colonial BancGroup actively and substantially interfered with their audit. But Rothstein faulted PwC for failing to inspect or even request to inspect the underlying documents for some Taylor Bean mortgages. "PwC argues that even if it had attempted to inspect the underlying loan documents, it would not have uncovered the fraud because the fraudsters would simply have created fake documents. This, of course, is something that we will never know."[3]

Elizabeth Tanis, PwC's lead trial counsel said, "As the professional audit standards make clear, even a properly-designed and executed audit may not detect fraud, especially in instances when there is collusion, fabrication of documents, and the override of controls, as there was at Colonial Bank."

PwC has maintained in court documents that its responsibility is to follow accounting principles—which might not necessarily detect fraud.

A rather unusual aspect to the claim that PwC did not follow appropriate professional standards is the allegation that PwC did not understand the nature and scope of the transactions. After a PwC auditor who was supposed to make sense of the transactions gave up, saying they were "above his pay grade," PwC assigned a college-graduate intern to evaluate the nearly $600 million asset. Rothstein was distinctly harsh about PwC's failings. Basing Colonial's certification on Farkas' account of Taylor Bean's collateral was "quintessentially the same as asking the fox to report on the condition of the hen house." She added that expecting an intern to decipher a loan facility beyond the expertise of a senior auditor was a "truly astonishing" departure from PwC's mandate.[4]

Internal Audit and ICFR

Colonial Bank had outsourced internal audit to another accounting firm, Crowe Horwath. PwC was required to review Crowe's work product, and it did so. Crowe, however, never identified or performed any evaluation of internal controls specifically relating to the credit facility, and there was no documentation suggesting otherwise. Nonetheless, PwC concluded that internal controls for Colonial's Treasury operation (including the credit facility) were effective and could be relied upon by PwC to reduce its substantive audit procedures. PwC reached this conclusion in the absence of any evidence that Crowe (or anyone else) had tested any internal controls for the credit facility.[5]

Digging deeper, PwC knew that Colonial's Treasury and Securities Purchased Under Agreements to Resell (which included $51.5 billion in credit facility financing for Taylor Bean at December 31, 2007) was a "Significant Process" for which it would test controls. During the actual audit, however, PwC excluded the credit facility entirely from the key controls that it tested despite the credit facility significant account balance and distinct class of transactions that called for transaction-specific controls.

PwC did not perform any walkthrough, skipping this crucial step because key controls were not identified by Crowe, and/or PwC did not properly assess the inherent risks regarding the existence and validity of credit facility assets. PwC instead decided that it would rely on Crowe to perform all walkthroughs.

The FDIC's claims against Crowe Horwath, who acted under a consulting contract as Colonial's internal audit department, were unusual. PwC's workpapers gave FDIC a glimpse into PwC's opinion of the quality of Crowe's work. Regardless of what PwC thought, the FDIC believed that PwC did not do enough to compensate for any failings or verify the assertions about internal controls Crowe made on behalf of Colonial management.[6]

The FDIC asserted gross negligence by Crowe. Allegedly, there was concealment and collusion to perpetrate a fraud within the bank and from outside sources. Crowe was held to the AICPA's standards for consulting work which, while stringent as the AICPA Code of Professional Conduct standards, do not carry the force of law that the Sarbanes-Oxley

---

3. Matthew Heller.
4. Allison Frankel.
5. Francine McKenna, A Tale of Two Lawsuits – PricewaterhouseCoopers and Colonial Bank, forbes.com, November 10, 2012, https://www.forbes.com/sites/francinemckenna/2012/11/10/a-tale-of-two-lawsuits-pricewaterhousecoopers-and-colonial-bank/#435a.
6. Francine McKenna.

Act and the PCAOB auditing standards do. The FDIC also maintained that Crowe should have followed the professional standards promulgated by the Institute of Internal Auditors. Would an internal audit function staffed by Colonial employees instead of an outside consultant have been sued under the same circumstances? On April 4, 2018, the FDIC settled its claims of professional malpractice and breach of contract against Crowe, disclosing that Crowe will make a $60 million payment to the FDIC.

On March 15, 2019, the FDIC announced that it had reached a $335 million settlement of the negligence action the agency had brought against PwC in connection with the accounting firm's audit work for Colonial Bank. The curious thing about this settlement is that it represents only a little more than half of the amount that a federal district court judge awarded the FDIC as damages in a July 2018 order in the case.

The Colonial ruling marks the first time an auditor has been held liable for fraud in many years. Lawyers who defended auditors were outraged by the ruling, calling it "an aggressive interpretation," "extremely disturbing," and a "one-off decision that will be reversed upon appeal." They are particularly upset that the case ever went to trial. In most auditing failure cases, companies are barred from suing their auditors for failing to detect fraud if—as happened at Colonial—their employees actively participated in the malfeasance. But in this case, the bank went bankrupt, and the FDIC sued to recover money for taxpayers. Courts around the country are split on whether the government can do that, and Judge Rothstein opted to let the FDIC sue. Attorney Michael Dell argued that the Colonial decision would fundamentally change the nature of auditing: "Audit firms would effectively be insurers for the wrongdoing of their clients." If the ruling stands, some lawyers believe investors will find it easier to hold auditors accountable in future corporate fraud cases.[7]

Questions

1. Which rules of conduct in the AICPA Code of Professional Conduct were violated by PwC? Explain.
2. Which PCAOB auditing standards were violated by PwC? Explain why those violations occurred and whether PwC should be held responsible.
3. Attorney Michael Dell argued that the Colonial Bank ruling would effectively hold audit firms liable for the wrongdoing of their clients. Is that the way you read the facts of the case and Judge Rothstein's ruling? Is there anything wrong with holding auditors responsible for the wrongdoing of their clients when client employees actively participate in the malfeasance? Explain.
4. When should auditors disclose critical audit matters (CAMs)? Assume the Colonial Bank case occurred subsequent to the effective dates of the new auditing standard on disclosing CAMs. Which disclosures should PwC have included in the audit report of Colonial Bank?

Major Case 2

Logitech International

Logitech International S.A. (LOGI) is incorporated in Switzerland and has substantial operations in the United States. LOGI is primarily involved in manufacturing and selling peripherals for computers and electronic devices. Its shares are listed on both the Nasdaq Global Select Market, under the trading symbol LOGI, and the SIX Swiss Exchange, under the trading symbol LOGN. The company maintains an executive office and its Americas region headquarters in Newark, California. LOGI's common stock is registered with the Securities Exchange Commission (SEC) pursuant to the Exchange Act of 1933.

In the fourth quarter of 2010, LOGI released the Revue, a TV set-top box designed to integrate cable/satellite TV with internet content. The Revue Google search bar was designed to find any desired content from any provider and project that content to the TV screen. The Revue was manufactured by contract manufacturers, not LOGI itself. In the arrangement with the contract manufacturers, the company authorized the manufacturers to purchase about $11 million of parts before production of the Revue began. LOGI was gearing up for high sales during the 2010 holiday season.[1]

---

7. Brooke Masters, PwC's Failure to Spot Colonial Fraud Spells Trouble for Auditors, January 5, 2018, https://www.ft.com/content/c2cc45d6-f1f6-11e7-b220-857e26d1aca4

Overview of the Case

During the 2010 holiday season, sales of Revue were much less than LOGI anticipated. In the fourth quarter of 2010, 165,000 Revues were sold, far less than the 350,000 units the company expected to sell. The Revue's high price, the blocking of content from Hulu, CBS, and ABC, and numerous software bugs doomed the Revue to be discontinued less than one year after its arrival. LOGI had millions of dollars invested in excess inventory of Revue component parts.

Despite knowing that the component parts in inventory would not be used in manufacturing other LOGI parts and that the market value of those components was minimal, the lower-of-cost-or-market (LCM) inventory write-down that the company did make fell far short of the actual decline in market value.

In 2016, the SEC alleged that some of LOGI's executives and accounting staff committed accounting fraud. LOGI paid a fine of $7.5 million to settle with the SEC over this improper inventory accounting and two other accounting issues. Individuals from the company including the former CFO paid fines of $25,000–$50,000.[2]

In a separate filing, the SEC brought a case against Erik K. Bardman, former Senior Vice President of Finance, and Jennifer F. Wolf, CPA, Chief Financial Officer (CFO) and Acting Controller of LOGI. The SEC filing details facts about Revue, that it was projected to be a significant percentage of LOGI's sales revenue, and that it represented a new strategic direction for the company—but the product failed to live up to expectations. Its sales were 70 percent lower than internal projections by the fourth quarter of the 2011 fiscal year (March 31, 2011). Compounding the poor sales performance of Revue, in March 2011, LOGI lowered its forecast of operating income to $140–$150 million, causing an immediate 16 percent drop in the company's share price. Given the shortfall, senior management, including Bardman and Wolf, were under substantial pressure to meet the lowered guidance. Rather than ensure that Logitech accurately account for its problems, Bardman and Wolf engaged in a scheme to materially inflate the operating income that the company reported to its investors in a late April 2011 earnings release and in its annual report, or Form 10-K, filed with the SEC on May 27, 2011, for the fiscal year ended March 31, 2011.

By this time, LOGI had 163,000 units of Revue in storage in the United States that the company had not sold, and it had halted production of additional units in light of the poor sales performance. LOGI's current price for the product at that time—$299—was more than double the price of competing products and part of the reason Revue was not selling. Indeed, by at least May 19, 2011, Bardman knew that the company's Chief Executive Officer had been evaluating whether to "shut [Revue] down now."

Through their scheme, Bardman and Wolf concealed the extent of these problems by, among other forms of misconduct: (1) improperly calculating Revue's inventory valuation reserves by falsely assuming that Logitech would build excess component parts it was trying to sell into finished units of Revue; (2) misrepresenting to LOGI's independent auditor that the Company's excess component parts would be used in production and the company's future plans for Revue; and (3) misrepresenting to the independent auditor the proper amount of LOGI's write-down of finished goods inventory by failing to incorporate probable future pricing adjustments. As a result of this misconduct, LOGI overstated its fiscal 2011 operating income by $30.7 million (over 27%).

In addition, in a letter to LOGI's independent auditors dated May 27, 2011, Bardman and Wolf falsely represented that the company's accounting was compliant with GAAP. These representations, demanded by and relied upon by Logitech's independent auditors, were designed to ensure that the company's accounting was done in accordance with accepted standards and did not mislead the investing public. Bardman misled the company's independent auditors regarding the extent of Logitech's problems with Revue. He signed and certified the accuracy of Logitech's 2011 financial statements, thereby misleading investors as to these same misstatements and omissions. At the time, Bardman knew, was reckless in not knowing, or should have known that the financial statements he was certifying were materially false or misleading.

Bardman and Wolf violated rules related to the antifraud provisions of the Securities Act of 1933 and Section 10(b) and Rule 10b-5 of the Securities Exchange Act of 1934. They violated the internal controls and books and records

---

1. Wendy Tietz, What could a Logitech staff accountant have done if he/she knew that the CFO and controller failed to writedown the discontinued Revue parts inventory? *Accounting in the Headlines*, May 25, 2017, https://accountingintheheadlines.com/2017/05/25/what-could-a-logitech-staff-accountant-have-done-if-heshe-knew-that-the-cfo-and-controller-failed-to-write-down-the-discontinued-revue-parts-inventory/.

2. *In the Matter of Logitech International, S.A., Michael Doktorczyk and Sherralyn Bolles, CPA,* Accounting and Enforcement Release No. 3765, April 19, 2016, https://www.sec.gov/litigation/admin/2016/34-77644.pdf.

provisions of Section 13(b)(5) of the Exchange Act and aided and abetted Logitech's violations of the antifraud, reporting, books and records, and internal controls provisions. The two also violated the lying to accountants' provision of the Act. Bardman violated the certification provision of the Exchange Act and the clawback provision of the Sarbanes-Oxley Act of 2002.

The SEC sought injunctive relief, including an officer and director bar, disgorgement of ill-gotten gains, prejudgment interest, civil penalties, and other appropriate and necessary equitable relief from Bardman and Wolf. In addition, the Commission sought an order requiring Bardman to forfeit any bonus, incentive-based compensation, or stock sales profits received during the relevant period. The case against Bardman and Wolf was unresolved at the time of writing.

The following is a summary of the accounting issues in this case.[3]

Accounting for Revue Product/Components

From the outset, Revue sales were significantly below LOGI's internal forecasts. By late November 2010, sales and finance personnel, including senior executives, were addressing whether the market price of $299 should be cut. LOGI's CFO at the time and its acting controller were aware that LOGI might have to evaluate taking a "lower of cost or market" (LCM) charge if the value of Revue inventory was impaired.

Under GAAP, the Company was required to value its inventory at the lower of the inventory's cost or market value. Specifically, if the market value of a company's inventory (generally calculated for finished goods as the estimated selling prices in the ordinary course of business, less reasonably predictable costs of completion, disposal, and transportation) is less than its cost, then the company must write-down the inventory value in its financial statements.

On or around December 7, 2010, because of high inventory levels and weak sales, LOGI directed the contract manufacturer to stop manufacturing Revue, including halting all work in progress. LOGI also instructed the manufacturer not to ship over 26,000 finished Revue units. Further, because the manufacturer, at LOGI's direction, had purchased parts for future manufacturing, LOGI was liable for approximately $11 million of excess components.

At the end of the third quarter of fiscal year 2011 (December 31, 2010), Revue sales were only 40 percent of LOGI's forecasts for that product. As part of its financial closing process, LOGI performed an LCM analysis of the Revue finished goods inventory and concluded that no adjustment, or write-down, was required.

On or around January 5, 2011, LOGI's Senior Vice-President (SVP) of Operations informed several executives that he intended to "dispose of the components" awaiting assembly by the manufacturer in light of Revue's "current trajectory." Shortly thereafter, the SVP-Operations instructed the VP of Global Sourcing/Supplier Management (VP-Global Sourcing) to "sell all of the components we could."

Later in January 2011, LOGI management informed the Board of Directors about the poor sales of Revue and about management's future plans for the product, including a plan to lower the retail price of Revue to $249 in the first quarter of 2012 and to $199 in the third quarter. Management did not inform its independent auditor of this pricing plan strategy.

On January 27, 2011, LOGI issued its third-quarter 2011 earnings release, reporting strong results, increasing its guidance for annual revenue for fiscal year-end March 31, 2011, and affirming its guidance for annual operating income in a range of $170–$180 million.

During LOGI's fourth-quarter fiscal 2011, Revue sales continued to be far below projections. For all of quarter four, despite regular discounting and promotions, Revue sales were 30 percent of internal product forecasts. By quarter end, retailers were selling fewer than 1,000 Revue units per week.

At the end of the fourth quarter 2011, LOGI had over 163,000 units of Revue finished inventory in its U.S. distribution centers, with another 52,000 finished and work-in-progress units in Asia. Based on the sales rate for that quarter, LOGI had over a year's supply of Revue. At the quarter-end sales rate to retailers, LOGI had over three years of inventory.

---

3. *Securities and Exchange Commission v. Erik K. Bardman and Jennifer F. Wolf* Complaint Demand for Jury Trial April 18, 2016, https://www.sec.gov/litigation/complaints/2016/comp-pr2016-74.pdf.

In mid-March 2011, an accountant in LOGI's Regional Finance area asked LOGI's VP-Global Sourcing about financial risk for the Revue product and the number of units that could be built from on-hand components. The VP-Global Sourcing informed her that there was no plan to use the components and that Global Sourcing was attempting to sell whatever could be sold. He also noted: "If we need to scrap [work-in-progress] and components, we should assume a recoverable value of zero."

On or around March 23, 2011, a LOGI Finance employee sent Wolf a summary of potential excess and obsolete inventory for contract manufacturers in preparation for a meeting the next day to discuss required accounting adjustments for the year-end financials. The summary highlighted a total potential excess inventory of $19.4 million for Revue units and components that "should be reserved."

On March 31, 2011, LOGI announced that, for reasons unrelated to Revue, it would miss the guidance it had provided to the market two months earlier. LOGI lowered the previous guidance for operating income by $30 million (to a range of $140–$150 million). Internally, the CEO characterized the guidance miss as a "disaster" and informed his executive team, including Barden and Wolf, that management's credibility with the market was damaged.

For its fiscal year 2011 year-end financial close process, LOGI initially prepared an LCM analysis indicating that no LCM adjustment was required for Revue finished goods inventory. The company's independent auditor arranged separate meetings with Barden and Wolf to discuss the importance of the assumptions in the LCM analysis. In the meetings, the independent auditor stressed the need to consider future pricing assumptions and strategies. Within days, LOGI revised the LCM analysis and, based on a planned price cut to $249 in the first quarter of 2012, recorded a $2.2 million adjustment. However, in the revised analysis, LOGI did not account for the planned third quarter of 2012 price cut to $199, nor did LOGI consider the excess component inventory.

After receiving the revised LCM with the $2.2 million adjustment, the independent auditor noted the roughly $11 million of excess component inventory and informed Barden and Wolf that LOGI was also required to evaluate and, if necessary, record an adjustment for the component inventory.

LOGI's Regional Finance accountant resisted adjusting for the component inventory. When the independent auditor persisted, Regional Finance again emailed the VP-Global Sourcing, notifying him there was "heated discussion" with the independent auditor about Revue and asking him to determine the number of Revue units that could be built from the component inventory.

The VP-Global Sourcing, who was responsible for managing the component inventory liability, informed Regional Finance and Wolf that production had been stopped for months and that he did not "see a chance that we are ever going to build [the components] into units." He wrote that a build-out of components was a "far-fetched scenario that has never been formulated."

On the next day (April 18, 2011), Wolf received a detailed list of the excess components. Less than an hour later, she sent a spreadsheet containing an LCM component analysis to the independent auditor, calculating an adjustment of $1.1 million, based on a hypothetical build-out of 79,000 additional finished units of Revue. Wolf ignored the fact (communicated to her two days earlier) that LOGI had been actively attempting to sell all of the components, with only limited success and below cost. Instead, she based the Company's accounting on the implausible scenario.

On or around April 18, 2011, after forwarding the component LCM analysis spreadsheet to the independent auditor, Wolf met with members of the independent audit team. At that meeting, Wolf discussed LOGI's plans to use the $11 million of excess components to build 79,000 finished Revue units. She also represented that LOGI could use excess components (beyond what was needed to make 79,000 Revue units) to manufacture even more Revue units. These representations were false.

During the week of April 18, 2011, Barden and Wolf met with senior members of the independent audit team, where they confirmed the assumptions used in the LCM analyses, and represented that LOGI was committed to the Revue product for the long-term and was going to build at least 79,000 additional units using excess components. These representations were false.

At the time the representations were made, Barden and Wolf knew or were reckless in not knowing that LOGI had no plan to produce additional units of Revue. They knew or were reckless in not knowing that the contract manufacturer had not shipped any Revue units since late November 2010 and had stopped production in early December 2010. In fact, they knew or were reckless in not knowing that LOGI had no timetable for re-starting production or even for completing the work-in-progress units and, for months, had been attempting to sell excess component inventory at substantial discounts.

On or around May 27, 2011, Barden and Wolf signed a management representation letter to the independent audit firm. The letter contained material misrepresentations concerning the valuation of inventory and the LCM analysis for Revue inventory. Specifically, with respect to the Revue LCM analysis, the letter represented that "we considered future pricing adjustments/discounts which are probable of occurring." This representation was false because the LCM analysis did not consider the planned price drop to $199 in the third quarter of 2012 or other discounting or promotions that would likely be required to sell the excess finished goods inventory. The company acknowledged the falsehood in its November 2014 restatement of financial statements.

On May 27, 2011, LOGI filed its Form 10-K with the SEC. Wolf signed the Form 10-K as the Company's CFO and Principal Accounting Officer. LOGI reported operating income of $142.7 million, which was within the lowered range of $140–$150 million that LOGI had communicated to investors on March 31, 2011.

On November 14, 2014, LOGI restated its financial results for fiscal years 2011 and 2012 because of errors in the timing of the Revue-related inventory write-downs. At the time it initially filed its fiscal 2011 financial statements, LOGI overstated its operating income by $30.7 million (27%). If LOGI had properly accounted for Revue-related inventory in May 2011, it would have reported operating income of approximately $112 million, far below the lowered guidance of $140–$150 million.

Questions

1. Analyze any weaknesses in the internal control systems and how it affected the work of the external auditors.
2. Did the external auditors meet their ethical obligations? Should external auditors be expected to find fraud when they are deliberately misled by members of top management?
3. There is no indication that LOGI staff accountants knew of the improper inventory accounting during 2010–2011. However, assume that one LOGI staff accountant, who is a CPA, did know about it. What steps should the staff accountant have taken once aware of the inventory issue? Be sure to explain each of the steps and why they would be taken.
4. Notwithstanding your answer to #3, assume the staff accountant decides to blow the whistle on the improper inventory accounting to the SEC. What protections are available to the staff accountant under the (a) Sarbanes-Oxley Act and (b) Dodd-Frank Financial Reform Act? Are there any conditions for these protections?

Major Case 3

Kiley Nolan's Ethical Dilemma (a GVV Case)

South City Electronics is involved in printed circuit board assembly (PCBA), dealing with the assembly of complex electronic system processes. The equipment is sold to a variety of customers throughout the United States and abroad. The electronics company, based in the city of South San Francisco, is publicly owned. Josh Goldberg is the chief executive officer of the company. David Levin is the chief financial officer.

It's March 30, 2022, and Kiley Nolan, controller for South City Electronics, has just gotten off the phone with her supervisor, David Levin, who reiterated the points he made in a face-to-face meeting with her earlier that day—that the company would be in default on a $10 million loan if its cash flow and earnings for the quarter ended March 31, 2022, did not meet set goals in the loan agreement.

At that date, the company's cash flow was $920,000 and the earnings were $460,000. These are $380,000 and $240,000, respectively, below prescribed levels. Gilmore knew her boss wanted her to agree to immediate revenue treatment for the transaction described below to overcome the problem.

The Transaction

South City transferred title to equipment sold to Victor Systems on March 29, 2022, the date of delivery on a $1.6 million sale. The arrangement allowed for the transfer of title upon delivery to Victor's site, as had occurred. However, customer-specific acceptance provisions permit the customer to return the equipment unless the equipment satisfies certain performance tests. South City cannot demonstrate that, at the time of delivery, the equipment already met all the criteria and specifications in the customer-specific acceptance provisions. The arrangement also called for the vendor to perform the installation. South City also provides technical support for the installation and use of the equipment going forward.

Kiley is agonizing about what she should do. She believes it would be wrong to record the transaction as revenue in the first quarter of 2022 under GAAP and FASB's revenue recognition standard, *Revenue from Contracts with Customers* that went into effect for annual reporting periods beginning after December 15, 2019, and interim reporting periods within annual reporting periods beginning after December 15, 2020. However, she is under a great deal of pressure to do so. Levin, her boss, took the position that the conditions under which the customer intends to operate the equipment were replicated in pre-shipment testing. Kiley knew, however, that the performance of the equipment, once installed and operated at the customer's facility, may reasonably be different from that tested prior to shipment.

Meeting between Kiley and Levin

Kiley and Levin's face-to-face meeting earlier in the day featured an acrimonious dispute over whether to record the $1.6 million as revenue for the quarter ended March 31, 2022. Here's how the meeting went.

"Kiley, we have fallen below debt covenant requirements," Levin said. "The only option is to record the sale to Victor Systems now. Besides, I believe the revenue recognition rules allow us to do so."

Kiley disagreed and said: "The accounting rules are quite clear on this matter," Kiley said. "We can't recognize the revenue, given the terms of the sale, because the performance of tests at our end may result in a different outcome once it is installed and tested."

"I understand your concerns, Kiley, but we expect you to support the company's position on this matter," Levin responded. "We disagree with how you have defined the performance obligations and responsibilities. The equipment passed all pre-shipment tests with flying colors."

"You're using an aggressive accounting interpretation that may have passed muster before the FASB's revenue recognition standard went into effect but doesn't anymore," Kiley responded.

"You're being hyper-technical," Levin responded. "We can't afford such a luxury given our precarious position."

"You and I both know," said Kiley, "that we can't just pick and choose how to apply accounting standards. As CPAs, we need to follow both the letter of the new standard and the spirit of it."

Levin became visibly upset. "Now wait a minute. This is an operating decision made by me, not an accounting decision. The accounting should reflect my operating decision. You'd better get on board."

Kiley hesitated to answer. She wasn't sure what to say next. She decided to buy some time to develop a game plan to counter Levin's position. Levin and Kiley decided to meet the next day to put this matter to bed.

Questions

1. Review the requirements for revenue recognition in **Chapter 6**. Do you believe Kiley interpreted the rules correctly? Be specific.
2. What motivated Nolan and the company to stand steadfastly to the position that revenue should be recognized on March 29, 2022? What are the likely consequences of the actions if the company records the $1.6 million revenue for the quarter ended March 31, 2022?
3. Use ethical reasoning to evaluate the appropriateness of Levin's position.

4. Assume you are in Kiley Nolan's position. Answer the following questions as you prepare for the meeting with Levin tomorrow.

   - What are the main arguments you are trying to counter?
   - What is at stake for the key parties?
   - What levers can you use to influence Levin?
   - What is your most powerful and persuasive response to the reasons and rationalizations you need to address?

5. Assume the meeting concludes and Kiley has failed to change Levin's mind. In fact, he insists Kiley get on board. What should Kiley do next and why?

6. Regardless of your answer to #5, assume Levin takes it upon himself to record the $1.6 million revenue as of March 31, 2022. Should Kiley go to the SEC and blow the whistle on financial wrongdoing? Would it be appropriate to do so under the Sarbanes-Oxley Act and/or the Dodd-Frank Financial Reform Act? If so, under what conditions should she report her concerns? Explain.

Major Case 4

Cendant Corporation[1]

The Merger of HFS and CUC

HFS Incorporated (HFS) was principally a controller of franchise brand names in the hotel, real estate brokerage, and car rental businesses, including Avis, Ramada Inn, Days Inn, and Century 21. Comp-U-Card (CUC) was principally engaged in membership-based consumer services such as auto, dining, shopping, and travel "clubs." Both securities were traded on the NYSE. Cendant Corporation was created through the December 17, 1997, merger of HFS and CUC. Cendant provided certain membership-based and Internet-related consumer services and controlled franchise brand names in the hotel, residential real estate brokerage, car rental, and tax preparation businesses.

Overview of the Scheme

The Cendant fraud was the largest of its kind until the late 1990s and early 2000s. Beginning in at least 1985, certain members of CUC's senior management implemented a scheme designed to ensure that CUC always met the financial results anticipated by Wall Street analysts. The CUC senior managers used a variety of means to achieve their goals, including:

- Manipulating recognition of the company's membership sales revenue to accelerate the recording of revenue.
- Improperly using two liability accounts related to membership sales that resulted from commission payments.
- Consistently maintaining inadequate balances in the liability accounts, and, on occasion, reversing the accounts directly into operating income.

With respect to the last item, to hide the inadequate balances, senior management periodically kept certain membership sales transactions off the books. In what was the most significant category quantitatively, the CUC senior managers intentionally overstated merger and purchase reserves and subsequently reversed those reserves directly into operating expenses and revenues. CUC senior management improperly wrote off assets—including assets that were unimpaired—and improperly charged the write-offs against the company's merger reserves. By manipulating the timing of the write-offs and by improperly determining the nature of the charges incurred, the CUC senior managers used the

---

1. The information for this case comes from a variety of litigation releases on the SEC Web site, including www.sec.gov/litigation/admin/34-42935.htm (June 14, 2000); www.sec.gov/litigation/admin/34-42934.htm (June 14, 2000); www.sec.gov/litigation/admin/34-42933.htm (June 14, 2000); www.sec.gov/litigation/litreleases/lr16587.htm (June 14, 2000); and www.sec.gov/litigation/complaints/comp18102.htm (April 24, 2003).

write-offs to inflate operating income. As the scheme progressed over the course of several years, larger and larger year-end adjustments were required to show smooth net income over time. The scheme added more than $500 million to pretax operating income during the fiscal years ended January 31, 1996; January 31, 1997; and December 31, 1997.

SEC Filings against CUC and Its Officers

SEC complaints filed on June 14, 2000, alleged violations of the federal securities laws by four former accounting officials, including Cosmo Corigliano, CFO of CUC; Anne M. Pember, CUC controller; Casper Sabatino, vice president of accounting and financial reporting; and Kevin Kearney, director of financial reporting. The allegations against Corigliano included his role as one of the CUC senior officers who helped engineer the fraud, and he maintained a schedule that management used to track the progress of their fraud. Corigliano regularly directed CUC financial reporting managers to make unsupported alterations to the company's quarterly and annual financial results. The commission alleged that Corigliano profited from his own wrongdoing by selling CUC securities and a large number of Cendant securities at inflated prices while the fraud he helped engineer was under way and undisclosed.

The commission alleged that Pember was the CUC officer most responsible for implementing directives received from Corigliano in furtherance of the fraud, including implementing directives that inflated Cendant's annual income by more than $100 million, primarily through improper use of the company's reserves. According to the SEC, Pember profited from her own wrongdoing by selling CUC and Cendant stock at inflated prices while the fraud she helped implement was under way and undisclosed.

Sabatino and Kearney, without admitting or denying the commission's allegations, consented to the entry of final judgments settling the commission's action against them. The commission's complaint alleged that Sabatino was the CUC officer most responsible for directing lower-level CUC financial reporting managers to make alterations to the company's quarterly financial results.

In the first of the three separate administrative orders, the commission found that Steven Speaks, the former controller of CUC's largest division, made or instructed others to make journal entries that effectuated much of the January 1998 income inflation directed by Pember. In a second, separate administrative order, the commission found that Mary Sattler Polverari, a former CUC supervisor of financial reporting, at the direction of Sabatino and Kearney, regularly and knowingly made unsupported alterations to CUC's quarterly financial results.

In a third administrative order, the commission found that Paul Hiznay, a former accounting manager at CUC's largest division, aided and abetted violations of the periodic reporting provisions of the federal securities laws by making unsupported journal entries that Pember had directed. Hiznay consented to the issuance of the commission's order to cease and desist from future violations of the provisions.

In a fourth and separate administrative order, the commission found that Cendant violated the periodic reporting, corporate record-keeping, and internal controls provisions of the federal securities laws, in connection with the CUC fraud. Among other things, the company's books, records, and accounts had been falsely altered, and materially false periodic reports had been filed with the commission, as a result of the long-running fraud at CUC. Simultaneous with the institution of the administrative proceeding, and without admitting or denying the findings contained therein, Cendant consented to the issuance of the commission order, which ordered Cendant to cease and desist from future violations of the provisions.

On February 28, 2001, the SEC filed a civil enforcement action in the U.S. District Court for the District of New Jersey against Walter A. Forbes, the former chair of the board of directors at CUC, and E. Kirk Shelton, the former vice chair, alleging that they directed a massive financial fraud while selling millions of dollars' worth of the company's common stock. For the period 1995–1997 alone, pretax operating income reported to the public by CUC was inflated by an aggregate amount of over $500 million. Specific allegations included:

- Forbes, CUC's chair and CEO, directed the fraud from its beginnings in 1985. From at least 1991 on, Shelton, CUC's president and COO, joined Forbes in directing the scheme.
- Forbes and Shelton reviewed and managed schedules listing fraudulent adjustments to be made to CUC's quarterly and annual financial statements. CUC senior management used the adjustments to pump up income and earnings artificially, defrauding investors by creating the illusion of a company that had ever-increasing earnings and making millions for themselves along the way.

- Forbes and Shelton undertook a program of mergers and acquisitions on behalf of CUC in order to generate inflated merger and purchase reserves at CUC to be used in connection with the fraud. Forbes and Shelton sought out HFS as a merger partner because they believed that the reserves that would be created would be big enough to bury the fraud. To entice HFS management into the merger, Forbes and Shelton inflated CUC's earnings and earnings projections.

- Forbes and Shelton profited from their own wrongdoing by selling CUC and Cendant securities at inflated prices while the fraud they had directed was under way and undisclosed. The sales brought Forbes and Shelton millions of dollars in ill-gotten gains.

- After the Cendant merger, Forbes served as Cendant's board chair until his resignation in July 1998. At the time of the merger, Shelton became a Cendant director and vice chair. Shelton resigned from Cendant in April 1998.

Specific Accounting Techniques Used to Manage Earnings

MAKING UNSUPPORTED POSTCLOSING ENTRIES

In early 1997, at the direction of senior management, Hiznay approved a series of entries reversing the commissions payable liability account into revenue at CUC. The company paid commissions to certain institutions on sales of CUC membership products sold through those institutions. Accordingly, at the time that it recorded revenue from those sales, CUC created a liability to cover the payable obligation of its commissions. CUC senior management used false schedules and other devices to support their understating of the payable liability of the commissions and to avoid the impact that would have resulted if the liability had been properly calculated. Furthermore, in connection with the January 31, 1997, fiscal year-end, senior management used this liability account by directing postclosing entries that moved amounts from the liability directly into revenue.[2]

In February 1997, Hiznay received a schedule from the CUC controller setting forth the amounts, effective backdates, and accounts for a series of postclosing entries that reduced the commission's payable account by $9.12 million and offsetting that reduction by increases to CUC revenue accounts. Hiznay approved the unsupported entries and had his staff enter them. They all carried effective dates spread retroactively over prior months. The entries reversed the liability account directly into revenues, a treatment that, under the circumstances, was not in accordance with GAAP.

KEEPING REJECTS AND CANCELLATIONS OFF-BOOKS: ESTABLISHING RESERVES

During his time at CUC, Hiznay inherited, but then supervised, a long-standing practice of keeping membership sales cancellations and rejects off CUC's books during part of each fiscal year. Certain CUC membership products were processed through various financial institutions that billed their members' credit cards for new sales and charges related to the various membership products. When CUC recorded membership sales revenue from such a sale, it would allocate a percentage of the recorded revenue to cover estimated cancellations of the specific membership product being sold, as well as allocating a percentage to cover estimated rejects and chargebacks.[3] CUC used these percentage allocations to establish a membership cancellation reserve.

Over the years, CUC senior management had developed a policy of keeping rejects and cancellations off the general ledger during the last three months of each fiscal year. Instead, during that quarter, the rejects and cancellations appeared only on cash account bank reconciliations compiled by the company's accounting personnel. The senior managers then directed the booking of those rejects and cancellations against the membership cancellation reserve in the first three months of the next fiscal year. Because rejects and cancellations were not recorded against the membership cancellation reserve during the final three months of the fiscal year, the policy allowed CUC to hide the fact that the reserve was understated dramatically at each fiscal year-end. At its January 31, 1997 fiscal year-end, the balance in

---

2. *Postclosing journal entries* means entries that are made after a reporting period has ended, but before the financial statements for the period have been filed, and that have effective dates spread retroactively over prior weeks or months.

3. Rejects resulted when the credit card to be charged was over its limit, closed, or reported as lost or stolen. Chargebacks resulted when a credit card holder disputed specific charges related to a particular membership program.

the CUC membership cancellation reserve was $29 million; CUC accounting personnel were holding $100 million in rejects and $22 million in cancellations off the books. Failing to book cancellations and rejects at each fiscal year-end also had the effect of overstating the company's cash position on its year-end balance sheet.

Accounting and Auditing Issues

Kenneth Wilchfort and Marc Rabinowitz were partners at Ernst & Young (EY), which was responsible for audit and accounting advisory services provided to CUC and Cendant. During the relevant periods, CUC and Cendant made materially false statements to the defendants and EY about the company's true financial results and its accounting policies. CUC and Cendant made these false statements to mislead the defendants and EY into believing that the company's financial statements conformed to GAAP. For example, as late as March 1998, senior Cendant management had discussed plans to use over $100 million of the Cendant reserve fraudulently to create fictitious 1998 income, which was also concealed from the defendants and EY. CUC and Cendant made materially false statements to the defendants and EY that were included in the management representation letters and signed by senior members of CUC's and Cendant's management. The statements concerned, among other things, the creation and utilization of merger-related reserves, the adequacy of the reserve established for membership cancellations, the collectability of rejected credit card billings, and income attributable to the month of January 1997.[4]

The written representations for the calendar year 1997 falsely stated that the company's financial statements were fairly presented in conformity with GAAP and that the company had made available to EY all relevant financial records and related data. Those written representations were materially false because the financial statements did not conform to GAAP, and, as discussed further, the company's management concealed material information from the defendants and EY.

In addition to providing the defendants and EY with false written representations, CUC and Cendant also adopted procedures to hide its income-inflation scheme from the defendants and EY. Some of the procedures that CUC and Cendant employed to conceal its fraudulent scheme included (1) backdating accounting entries; (2) making accounting entries in small amounts and/or in accounts or subsidiaries the company believed would receive less attention from EY; (3) in some instances, ensuring that fraudulent accounting entries did not affect schedules already provided to EY; (4) withholding financial information and schedules to ensure that EY would not detect the company's accounting fraud; (5) ensuring that the company's financial results did not show unusual trends that might draw attention to its fraud; and (6) using senior management to instruct middle- and lower-level personnel to make fraudulent entries. Notwithstanding CUC and Cendant's repeated deception, defendants improperly failed to detect the fraud. They were aware of numerous practices by CUC and Cendant indicating that the financial statements did not conform to GAAP, and, as a consequence, they had a duty to withhold their unqualified opinion and take appropriate additional steps.

Improper Establishment and Use of Merger Reserves

The company completed a series of significant mergers and acquisitions and accounted for the majority of them using the pooling-of-interests method of accounting.[5] In connection with this merger and acquisition activity, company management purportedly planned to restructure its operations. GAAP permits that certain anticipated costs may be recorded as liabilities (or reserves) prior to their incurrence under certain conditions. However, here, CUC and Cendant routinely overstated the restructuring charges and the resultant reserves and would then use the reserves to offset normal operating costs—an improper earnings management scheme. The company's improper reversal of merger and acquisition–related restructuring reserves resulted in an overstatement of operating income by $217 million.

The EY auditors provided accounting advice and auditing services to CUC and Cendant in connection with the establishment and use of restructuring reserves. The auditors excessively relied on management representations concerning the appropriateness of the reserves and performed little substantive testing, despite evidence that the reserves were established and utilized improperly.

---

4. Available at: www.sec.gov/litigation/complaints/comp18102.htm.

5. *Statement of Financial Accounting Standards (SFAS) 141, Business Combinations*, which eliminated the pooling methods for business combinations. The purchase method now must be used for all acquisitions.

One example of auditor failures with reserve accounting is the Cendant reserve. Cendant recorded over $500 million in merger, integration, asset impairment, and restructuring charges for the CUC-side costs purportedly associated with the merger of HFS and CUC. The company recorded a significant portion of this amount for the purpose of manipulating its earnings for December 31, 1997, and subsequent periods, and, in fact, Cendant had plans, which it did not disclose to defendants and EY, to use a material amount of the reserve to inflate income artificially in subsequent periods.

In the course of providing accounting and auditing services, the auditors failed to recognize evidence that the company's establishment and use of the Cendant reserve did not conform to GAAP. For example, CUC and Cendant provided EY with contradictory drafts of schedules when EY requested support for the establishment of the Cendant reserve. The company prepared and revised these various schedules, at least in part as a result of questions raised and information provided by the defendants. The schedules were inconsistent with regard to the nature and amount of the individual components of the reserve (i.e., component categories were added, deleted, and changed as the process progressed). While the component categories changed over time, the total amount of the reserve never changed materially. Despite this evidence, the auditors did not obtain adequate analyses, documentation, or support for changes that they observed in the various revisions of the schedules submitted to support the establishment of the reserves. Instead, they relied excessively on frequently changing management representations.

The company planned to use much of the excess Cendant reserve to increase operating results in future periods improperly. During the year ended December 31, 1997, the company wrote off $104 million of assets that it characterized as impaired as a result of the merger. Despite the size and timing of the write-off, the defendants never obtained adequate evidence that the assets were impaired as a result of the merger and, therefore, properly included in the Cendant reserve. In fact, most of the assets were not impaired as a result of the merger.

Cash Balance from the Membership Cancellation Reserve

CUC and Cendant also inflated income by manipulating their membership cancellation reserve and reported cash balance. Customers usually paid for membership products by charging them on credit cards. The company recorded an increase in revenue and cash when it charged the members' credit card. Each month, issuers of members' credit cards rejected a significant amount of such charges. The issuers would deduct the amounts of the rejects from their payments to CUC and Cendant. CUC and Cendant falsely claimed to EY auditors that when it resubmitted the rejects to the banks for payment, it ultimately collected almost all of them within three months. CUC and Cendant further falsely claimed that, for the few rejects that were not collected after three months, it then recorded them as a reduction in cash and a decrease to the cancellation reserve. The cancellation reserve accounted for members who canceled during their membership period and were entitled to a refund of at least a portion of the membership fee, as well as members who joined and were billed, but never paid for their memberships.

At the end of each fiscal year, the company failed to record three months of rejects (i.e., it did not reduce its cash and decrease its cancellation reserve for these rejects). CUC and Cendant falsely claimed to the defendants and EY that it did not record rejects for the final three months of the year because it purportedly would collect most of the rejects within three months of initial rejection. According to CUC and Cendant, the three months of withheld rejects created a temporary difference at year-end between the cash balances reflected in the company's general ledger and its bank statements. The rejects were clearly specified on reconciliations of the company's numerous bank accounts, at least some of which were provided to EY and retained in its workpapers. CUC and Cendant falsely claimed to the defendants and EY that the difference between the general ledger balance and bank statement balance did not reflect an overstatement of cash and understatement in the cancellation reserve since it collected most rejects. In fact, the majority of rejects were not collected. By not recording rejects and cancellations against the membership cancellation reserve during the final three months of each fiscal year, CUC and Cendant dramatically understated the reserve at each fiscal year-end and overstated its cash position. CUC and Cendant thus avoided the expense charges needed to bring the cancellation reserve balance up to its proper amount and the entries necessary to record CUC and Cendant's actual cash balances.

The rejects, cancellation reserve balance, and overstatement of income amounts for the period 1996 to 1997 are as follows:

Date	($ in millions)		
	Rejects	Cancellation Reserve Balance	Understated Reserve/Overstated Income
01/31/96	$ 72	$37	$35
01/31/97	$100	$29	$28
12/31/97	$137	$37	$37

The EY defendants did not adequately test the collectability of these rejects and the adequacy of the cancellation reserve and instead relied primarily on management representations concerning the company's successful collection history and inconsistent statements concerning the purported impossibility of substantively testing these representations.

Membership Cancellation Rates

The company also overstated its operating results by manipulating its cancellation reserve. The cancellation reserve accounted for members who canceled during their membership period. A large determinant of the liability associated with cancellations was CUC and Cendant's estimates of the cancellation rates. During the audits, CUC and Cendant intentionally provided EY with false estimates that were lower than the actual estimated cancellation rates. This resulted in a significant understatement of the cancellation reserve liability and an overstatement of income. To justify its understated cancellation reserve, CUC and Cendant provided to EY small, nonrepresentative samples of cancellations that understated the actual cancellation rates. The defendants allowed the company to choose the samples. EY did not test whether the samples provided were representative of the actual cancellations for the entire membership population.

Audit Opinion

EY issued audit reports containing unqualified (i.e., unmodified) audit opinions on, and conducted quarterly reviews of, the company's financial statements that, as already stated, did not conform to GAAP. The Securities Exchange Act requires every issuer of a registered security to file reports with the commission that accurately reflect the issuer's financial performance and provide other information to the public. For the foregoing reason, the firm aided and abetted violations of the securities laws.

Legal Issues

SEC SETTLEMENTS

Between Hiznay's arrival at CUC in July 1995 and the discovery of the fraudulent scheme by Cendant management in April 1998, CUC and Cendant filed false and misleading annual reports with the commission that misrepresented their financial results, overstating operating income and earnings and failing to disclose that the financial results were falsely represented.

The commission's complaint alleged that Sabatino, by his actions in furtherance of the fraud, violated, or aided and abetted violations of, the anti-fraud, periodic reporting, corporate record-keeping, internal controls, and lying to auditors provisions of the federal securities laws. Sabatino consented to entry of a final judgment that enjoined him from future violations of those provisions and permanently barred him from acting as an officer or director of a public company.

Kearney consented to entry of a final judgment that enjoined him from future violations of those provisions, ordered him to pay disgorgement of $32,443 in ill-gotten gains (plus prejudgment interest of $8,234), and ordered him to pay a civil money penalty of $35,000. Kearney also agreed to the issuance of a commission administrative order that barred him from practicing before the commission as an accountant, with the right to reapply after five years.

Corigliano, Pember, and Sabatino each pleaded guilty to charges pursuant to plea agreements between those three individuals and the SEC. Pursuant to his agreement, Corigliano pleaded guilty to a charge of wire fraud, conspiracy to commit mail fraud, and causing false statements to be made in documents filed with the commission, including signing

CUC's periodic reports filed with the commission and making materially false statements to CUC's auditors. Pember pleaded guilty to a charge of conspiracy to commit mail fraud and wire fraud. Sabatino, pursuant to his agreement, pleaded guilty to a charge of aiding and abetting wire fraud.

In another administrative order, the commission found that Hiznay aided and abetted violations of the periodic reporting provisions of the federal securities laws in connection with actions that he took at the direction of his superiors at CUC. Among other things, the commission alleged that Hiznay made unsupported journal entries that Pember had directed. Additional orders were entered against lower-level employees.

The commission found that Cendant violated the periodic reporting, corporate record-keeping, and internal controls provisions of the federal securities laws in connection with the CUC fraud in that the company's books, records, and accounts had been falsely altered, and materially false periodic reports had been filed with the SEC.

On December 29, 2009, the SEC announced a final judgment against Forbes, the former chair of Cendant, arising out of his conduct in the Cendant fraud.[6] The commission alleged that Forbes orchestrated an earnings management scheme at CUC to inflate the company's quarterly and annual financial results improperly during the period 1995 to 1997. CUC's operating income was inflated improperly by an aggregate amount exceeding $500 million.

The final judgment against Forbes, to which he consented without admitting or denying the commission's allegations, enjoined him from violating relevant sections of the securities laws and barred him from serving as an officer or director of a public company.

CLASS-ACTION LAWSUITS

A class-action suit by stockholders against Cendant and its auditors, led by the largest pension funds, alleged that stockholders paid more for Cendant stock than they would have had they known the truth about CUC's income. The lawsuit ended in a record $3.2 billion settlement. Details of the settlement follow.

By December 1999, a landmark $2.85 billion settlement with Cendant was announced that far surpassed the recoveries in any other securities law class action case in history. Until the settlements reached in the WorldCom case in 2005, this stood as the largest recovery in a securities class action case by far and clearly set the standard in the field. In addition to the cash payment by Cendant, which was backed by a letter of credit that the company secured to protect the class, the Cendant settlement included two other very important features. First, the settlement provided that if Cendant or the former HFS officers and directors were successful in obtaining a net recovery in their continuing litigation against EY, the class would receive half of any such net recovery. As it turned out, that litigation lasted another seven years—until the end of 2007—when Cendant and EY settled their claims against each other in exchange for a payment by EY to Cendant of nearly $300 million. Based on the provision in the Cendant settlement agreement and certain further litigation and a court order, in December 2008, the class received another $132 million. This brought the total recovered from the Cendant settlement to $2.982 billion.

Second, Cendant was required to institute significant corporate governance changes that were far-reaching and unprecedented in securities class action litigation. Indeed, these changes included many of the corporate governance structural changes that would later be included within the Sarbanes-Oxley Act of 2002 (SOX). They included the following:

- The board's audit, nominating, and compensation committees would be comprised entirely of independent directors (according to stringent definitions, endorsed by the institutional investment community, of what constituted an independent director).
- The majority of the board would be independent within two years following final approval of the settlement.
- Cendant would take the steps necessary to provide that, subject to amendment of the certificate of incorporation declassifying the board of directors by vote of the required supermajority of shareholders, all directors would be elected annually.
- No employee stock option could be "repriced" following its grant without an affirmative vote of shareholders, except when such repricings were necessary to take into account corporate transactions such as stock dividends, stock splits, recapitalization, a merger, or distributions.

---

6. *Securities and Exchange Commission v. Walter A. Forbes et al.*, District Court N.J., filed February 28, 2001.

The Settlement with EY

On December 17, 1999, it was announced that EY had agreed to settle the claims of the class for $335 million. This recovery was and remains today as the largest amount ever paid by an accounting firm in a securities class action case. The recovery from EY was significant because it held an outside auditing firm responsible in cases of corporate accounting fraud. The claims against EY were based on EY's "clean" (i.e., unmodified) audit and review opinions for three sets of annual financial statements, and seven quarterly financial statements, between 1995 and 1997.

The district court approved the settlements and plan of allocation in August 2000, paving the way for Cendant and EY to fund the settlements. Approximately one year later, in August 2001, the settlements and plan of allocation were affirmed on appeal by the U.S. Third Circuit Court of Appeals. And in March 2002, the U.S. Supreme Court determined that it would not hear any further appeals in the case.

Questions

1. Cendant manipulated the timing of write-offs and improperly determined charges in an attempt to smooth net income. Is income smoothing an ethical practice? Are there circumstances where it might be considered ethical and others where it would not? What motivated Cendant to engage in income smoothing practices in this case?

2. Analyze the actions taken by the company and its management from the perspective of the Fraud Triangle.

3. Describe the role of professional judgment in the audits by EY. Did the firm meet its ethical obligations under the AICPA Code? Did it adhere to all appropriate auditing standards?

4. Trust is a basic element in the relationship between auditor and client. Explain how and why trust broke down in the Cendant case, including shortcomings in corporate governance.

5. Do you believe auditors should be expected to discover fraud when a client goes to great lengths, as did Cendant, to withhold evidence from the auditors and mask the true financial effects of transactions? Explain.

Major Case 5

Vivendi Universal

"Some of my management decisions turned wrong, but fraud? Never, never, never." This statement was made by the former CEO of Vivendi Universal, Jean-Marie Messier, as he took the stand on November 20, 2009, for a civil class-action lawsuit brought against him, Vivendi Universal, and the former CFO, Guillaume Hannezo. The class-action suit accused the company of hiding Vivendi's true financial condition before a $46 billion three-way merger with Seagram Company and Canal Plus. The case was brought against Vivendi, Messier, and Hannezo after it was discovered that the firm was in a liquidity crisis and would have problems repaying its outstanding debt and operating expenses (contrary to the press releases by Messier, Hannezo, and other senior executives that the firm had "excellent" and "strong" liquidity); that it participated in earnings management to achieve earnings goals; and that it had failed to disclose debt obligations regarding two of the company's subsidiaries.[1] The jury decided not to hold either Messier or Hannezo legally liable because "scienter" (i.e., knowledge of the falsehood) could not be proven. In other words, the court decided it could not be shown that the two officers acted with the intent to deceive other parties.

The stock price of the firm dropped 89 percent, from $111 on October 31, 2000, to $13 on August 16, 2002, over the period of fraudulent reporting and press releases to the media.

As you read the case, consider whether Messier was accurate in his belief that fraud was not committed and whether this was an ethics failure.

---

1. *SEC v. Vivendi Universal, S.A., Jean-Marie Messier, and Guillaume Hannezo*, United States District Court Southern District of New York, December 23, 2003. Available at: https://www.sec.gov/litigation/complaints/comp18523.htm.

Background

Vivendi is a French international media giant, rivaling Time Warner Inc., that spent $77 billion on acquisitions, including the world's largest music company, Universal Music Group (UMG). Messier took the firm to new heights through mergers and acquisitions that came with a large amount of debt.

In December 2000, Vivendi acquired Canal Plus and Seagram, which included Universal Studios and its related companies, and became known as Vivendi Universal. At the time, it was one of Europe's largest companies in terms of assets and revenues, with holdings in the United States that included Universal Studios Group, UMG, and USA Networks Inc. These acquisitions cost Vivendi cash, stock, and assumed debt of over $60 billion and increased the debt associated with Vivendi's Media & Communications division from approximately $4.32 billion at the beginning of 2000 to over $30.25 billion in 2002.

In July 2002, Messier and Hannezo resigned from their positions as CEO and CFO, respectively, and new management disclosed that the company was experiencing a liquidity crisis that was a very different picture than the previous management had painted of the financial condition of Vivendi Universal. This was due to senior executives using four different methods to conceal Vivendi Universal's financial problems:

- Issuing false press releases stating that the liquidity of the company was "strong" and "excellent" after the release of the 2001 financial statements to the public.
- Using aggressive accounting principles and adjustments to increase EBITDA and meet ambitious earnings targets.
- Failing to disclose the existence of various commitments and contingencies.
- Failing to disclose part of its investment in a transaction to acquire shares of Telco, a Polish telecommunications holding company.

Earnings Releases/EBITDA

On March 5, 2002, Vivendi issued earnings releases for 2001, which were approved by Messier, Hannezo, and other senior executives, that their Media & Communications business had produced $7.25 billion in EBITDA and just over $2.88 billion in operating free cash flow. These earnings were materially misleading and falsely represented Vivendi's financial situation because, due to legal restrictions, Vivendi was unable unilaterally to access the earnings and cash flow of two of its most profitable subsidiaries, Cegetel and Maroc Telecom, which accounted for 30 percent of Vivendi's EBITDA and almost half of its cash flow. This contributed to Vivendi's cash flow actually being "zero or negative," making it difficult for Vivendi to meet its debt and cash obligations. Furthermore, Vivendi declared $1.44 per share dividend because of its excellent operations for the past year, but Vivendi borrowed against credit facilities to pay the dividend, which cost more than $1.87 billion after French corporate taxes on dividends. Throughout the following months before Messier's and Hannezo's resignations, senior executives continued to lie to the public about the strength of Vivendi as a company.

In December 2000, Vivendi and Messier predicted a 35 percent EBITDA growth for 2001 and 2002, and, in order to reach that target, Vivendi used earnings management and aggressive accounting practices to overstate its EBITDA. In June 2001, Vivendi made improper adjustments to increase EBITDA by almost $85 million, or 5 percent of the total EBITDA of $1.61 billion that Vivendi reported. Senior executives did this mainly by restructuring Cegetel's allowance for bad debts. Cegetel, a Vivendi subsidiary whose financial statements were consolidated with Vivendi's, took a lower provision for bad debts in the period and caused the bad debts expense to be $64.83 million less than it would have been under historical methodology, which in turn increased earnings by the same amount. Furthermore, after the third quarter of 2001, Vivendi adjusted earnings of UMG by at least $14.77 million or approximately 4 percent of UMG's total EBITDA of $360.15 million for that quarter. At that level, UMG would have been able to show EBITDA growth of approximately 6 percent versus the same period in 2000 and to outperform its rivals in the music business. It did this by prematurely recognizing revenue of $4.32 million and temporarily reducing the corporate overhead charges by $10.08 million.

Financial Commitments

Vivendi failed to disclose in its financial statements commitments regarding Cegetel and Maroc Telecom that would have shown Vivendi's potential inability to meet its cash needs and obligations. It was also worried that, if it disclosed this information, companies that publish independent credit opinions would have declined to maintain their credit rating of Vivendi. In August 2001, Vivendi entered into an undisclosed current account borrowing with Cegetel for $749.11 million and continued to grow to over $1.44 billion at certain periods of time. Vivendi maintained cash pooling agreements with most of its subsidiaries, but the current account with Cegetel operated much like a loan, with a due date of the balance at December 31, 2001 (which was later pushed back to July 31, 2002), and there was a clause in the agreement that provided Cegetel with the ability to demand immediate reimbursement at any time during the loan period. If this information would have been disclosed, it would have shown that Vivendi would have trouble repaying its obligations.

Regarding Maroc Telecom, in December 2000, Vivendi purchased 35 percent of the Moroccan government–owned telecommunications operator of fixed line and mobile telephone and Internet services for $3.39 billion. In February 2001, Vivendi and the Moroccan government entered into a side agreement that required Vivendi to purchase an additional 16 percent of Maroc Telecom's shares in February 2002 for approximately $1.58 billion. Vivendi did this in order to gain control of Maroc Telecom and consolidate its financial statements with Vivendi's own because Maroc carried little debt and generated substantial EBITDA. By not disclosing this information on the financial statements, Vivendi's financial information for 2001 was materially false and misleading.

Stakeholder Interests

The major stakeholders in the Vivendi case include (1) the investors, creditors, and shareholders of the company and its subsidiaries—by not providing reliable financial information, Vivendi misled these groups into lending credit and cash and investing in a company that was not as strong as it seemed; (2) the subsidiaries of Vivendi and their customers—by struggling with debt and liquidity, Vivendi borrowed cash from the numerous subsidiaries all over the globe, jeopardizing their operations; (3) the governments of these countries—because some of Vivendi's companies were government owned (such as the Moroccan company Maroc Telecom), and these governments have to regulate the fraud and crimes that Vivendi committed; and (4) Vivendi, Messier, Hannezo, and other senior management and employees—Messier was putting his future, the employees of Vivendi, and the company itself in jeopardy by making loose and risky decisions involving the sanctity of the firm.

SEC Actions Under Section 1103 of SOX

Section 1103 of SOX provides that:

> Whenever, during the course of a lawful investigation involving possible violations of the Federal securities laws by an issuer of publicly traded securities or any of its directors, officers, partners, controlling persons, agents, or employees, it shall appear to the Commission that it is likely that the issuer will make extraordinary payments (whether compensation or otherwise) to any of the foregoing persons, the Commission may petition a Federal district court for a temporary order requiring the issuer to escrow, subject to court supervision, those payments in an interest-bearing account for 45 days. In the Fair Funds provisions of SOX, Congress gave the SEC increased authority to distribute ill-gotten gains and civil money penalties to harmed investors. These distributions reflect the continued efforts and increased capacity of the commission to repay injured investors, regardless of their physical location and their currency of choice.

Based on these provisions, Messier was required to relinquish his claim to a severance package of about $29.4 million, which includes back pay and bonuses for the first half of 2002, and to pay a civil money penalty of $1 million and disgorgement of $1. Hannezo was required to disgorge $148,149 and to pay a penalty of $120,000.

On August 11, 2008, the SEC announced the distribution of more than $48 million to more than 12,000 investors who were victims of fraudulent financial reporting by Vivendi Universal. Investors receiving checks resided in the United States and 15 other countries. More than half bought their Vivendi stock on foreign exchanges and received their Fair Fund distribution in euros.

Failure of Ethical Leadership

In his analysis of the fraud at Vivendi, Soltani points to failures in ethical practice, corporate governance, and leadership as the root cause of the failure at Vivendi. He characterizes the actions of Messier as motivated by egoism, using one's authoritative position to influence others to ignore ethical practices, failure to set an ethical tone at the top, and failed corporate governance. What follows is an analysis of the points he makes in dissecting the fraud.[2]

- Use of company funds for personal benefit, including to enhance lifestyle choices.
- Failure to conceptualize core values and ethical standards in the company.
- Lack of internal control mechanisms to prevent and detect fraud.
- Ineffective control environment to prevent and detect fraud.
- Excessive risk taking.
- Opportunistic behavior.
- False earnings announcements.
- Aggressive earnings management.
- Use of loopholes in financial reporting standards to alter numbers as far as possible to achieve a desired goal.
- Lapses in accountability.
- Inability of external auditors to exercise their functions in an independent manner and detect material misstatements and fraudulent financial reporting.

It is clear that the culture at Vivendi enabled the fraud to occur and prevented the company from dealing with the crisis as it unfolded.

Questions

1. What is the role of internal controls in facilitating ethical behavior in an organization? Briefly describe the problems with internal controls at Vivendi with respect to its relationships with Cegetel and Maroc Telecom.

2. Why are disclosures in financial statements important? Why were they important in the relationship between Vivendi and Cegetel and Maroc Telecom? Is there such a thing as disclosure fraud? Explain.

3. Why do financial analysts look at measures such as EBITDA and operating free cash flow to evaluate financial results? How do these measures differ from GAAP earnings? Do you believe auditors should be held responsible for auditing such information?

4. Is using earnings management and aggressive accounting in EBITDA calculations just as serious as doing the same with the financial statements prepared under GAAP? Explain.

5. Analyze the appropriateness of the provisions in Section 1103 of SOX from an ethical reasoning perspective.

Major Case 6

Luckin Coffee

The speedy rise and then fall of China-based company Luckin Coffee Inc. shows what can happen when a company is driven by fraudulent behavior that goes unchecked. It also demonstrates why strong corporate governance systems are essential to ensure that material misstatements of the financial statements are detected and reported.

---

2. Bahram Soltani, "The Anatomy of Corporate Fraud: A Comparative Analysis of High Profile American and European Corporate Scandals," *Journal of Business Ethics*, Vol. 120 (2014), pp. 251–274.

Overview

Luckin is a retail coffee provider incorporated in the Cayman Islands with its principal place of business in the Siming District, Xiamen, Fujian, China. The company was touted as the next Starbucks. The company's shares were traded on the U.S. stock exchange, NASDAQ, through its trading of American Depositary Shares ("ADS").

ADS refer to shares in foreign companies that are held by U.S. depository banks and can be traded in the United States, including on major exchanges. ADS are meant to facilitate trading of the shares. Listing on a major exchange in the United States generally requires the same level of reporting as that done by domestic companies, as well as adherence to GAAP. ADSs allow foreign companies access to a wider investor base and the world's most sophisticated financial marketplace. The main drawback of ADS for investors is that there is some currency risk, even though they are denominated in U.S. dollars.

Luckin made an initial public offering of ADS in the United States on May 17, 2019, raising approximately $600 million. In the prospectus, Luckin disclosed that the company's total revenues were $125 million for the year-end 2018 and $71.3 million for the quarter ending March 31, 2019. Luckin acknowledged that it had incurred significant operating losses since its inception and that it may continue to be unprofitable if it could not sustain its historical growth rate.

Luckin made statements in its IPO that hyped the financial results including "strong growth since inception." Various news reports characterized its results as "staggering" and "super-charged" occurring at a "break-neck speed." According to news reports, several rounds of private fundraising had already rapidly escalated Luckin's pre-IPO valuation from $1 million in July 2018 to $2.2 billion in November 2018, to $2.9 billion in April 2019. Its May 2019 IPO priced at $17 per ADS valued the company at $3.9 billion.

On its first day of trading, Luckin's shares rose as high as $25 per ADS. By mid-June 2019, a number of analysts recognized that the company did not anticipate break-even profitability in the near term but focused on Luckin's extraordinary revenue growth trajectory. The only problem was that it used fraudulent revenue recognition techniques to achieve such a growth rate.

On April 2, 2020, Luckin acknowledged its fabricated sales, as well as fabricated transactions that substantially inflated Luckin's costs and expenses. Luckin warned investors that they should no longer rely upon its 2019 quarterly reports or its fourth-quarter earnings guidance. When Luckin's fraud was revealed the price of its ADS plummeted by more than 75 percent, from a closing price of $26.20 per ADS on April 1, 2020, to $6.40 per ADS on April 2, 2020. On July 13, 2020, the NASDAQ delisted Luckin's ADS from the exchange.

Luckin's fraudulent practices, including but not limited to its fabricated sales transactions and its false statements regarding revenue, income, and expenses, deceived investors about the true financial performance of the company, in particular, its rapid growth, and violated the anti-fraud and other provisions of the U.S. federal securities laws.

The amounts discussed below are approximations because they have been converted from the Chinese currency called Renminbi to U.S. dollars.

Fabricated Transactions

Chief among Luckin's fraudulent revenue was fabricated coupon sales transactions for the purpose of artificially inflating its revenue and growth. These transactions were carried out by certain Luckin employees, including senior officers and directors who directed and carried out three separate fraudulent schemes to fabricate coupon sales and associated revenue. Luckin and certain of its employees knew or were reckless in not knowing that by fabricating coupon sales and associated revenues and income, the company was providing investors with materially false and misleading information about the company's financial results. This practice operated as a fraud on or deceit of Luckin investors.

As an example of the fraudulent transactions, Luckin fabricated coupon sales and redemptions by purported individual customers. Beginning in April 2019, Luckin employees and others transferred money from individual bank accounts—controlled by Luckin employees and their family members, as well as employees of two entities associated with certain officers and directors of Luckin (i.e., related entities)—to WeChat and Alipay accounts associated with mobile phone numbers those individuals controlled. The transferred funds were then used to purchase coupons on Luckin's app. Luckin, through the actions of its employees, then created fake customer orders to "redeem" the coupons, although real orders were never placed and the coupons were never actually redeemed. Luckin recognized the fabricated revenue. In one scheme Luckin fabricated sales of several million dollars.

Luckin carried out similar schemes using Luckin personnel or employees of the two related entities and another with third-party shell companies—purported intermediary agents that would resell coupons to fictitious individual customers.

Luckin maintained a database to track its business operations, including coupons sales and redemptions and customer orders. To carry out these schemes, certain employees created a second database that included both legitimate coupon sales, redemptions, and customer orders as well as fabricated coupon sales, redemptions, and customer orders. Essentially, the company was keeping two sets of books, one real and the other fabricated.

The employees then switched the source data for certain reports—reports used by Luckin's Finance Department for bookkeeping and financial reporting purposes. The Finance Department had access only to the fabricated database so could not distinguish the legitimate from the fabricated transactions. As a result, the Finance Department incorporated the fabricated transactions into Luckin's publicly disclosed financial statements.

An April 2019 e-mail from an employee of one of the related entities to certain Luckin officers confirmed that "the original reports/forms in the system are all unseeable," and that those reports included the cost carryover and income reports. In total, Luckin fabricated transactions and revenues totaling approximately $311 million from April 2019 through at least January 2020.

While fabricating coupon sales, Luckin returned funds to the funding sources both directly through bank transfers and indirectly through fabricated expense payments to vendors. For example, Luckin made payments to 13 purported suppliers of raw materials that did not provide any materials to the company, overpaid two providers of human resources (outsourcing) services, and paid delivery fees to three companies that did not provide any services to Luckin. Nevertheless, Luckin reported these payments as business-related expenses in its publicly disclosed financial statements.

In total, Luckin fabricated costs and expenses totaling approximately $196 million in 2019, which inflated its costs and expenses by more than 20 percent.

Luckin's fabricated costs and expenses allowed for funds to be returned, in part, to the funding sources, which were controlled by or associated with Luckin employees and employees of related companies. The employees increased costs to make those costs consistent with its increased, inflated revenue. In March and April 2020, Luckin continued returning money to the funding sources through direct bank transfers, and certain vendors refunded fabricated and inflated expenses to Luckin. Certain Luckin officers were kept apprised of the progress of the schemes as indicated in two e-mails in October 2019 to Luckin officers writing that "the same-store revenue can maintain a growth rate of more than 35 percent, but its credibility will be questioned..." and "suppliers will notice the abnormality [in Luckin's growth] because we don't purchase that much."

In advance of Luckin's first earnings release as a public company, analysts expected quarterly revenues of approximately $133 million. By contrast, Luckin's revenue for the entire fiscal year of 2018 was $125 million.

SEC Action

On August 14, 2019, Luckin furnished to the SEC a Form 6-K disclosing its earnings for the second quarter ending June 30, 2019. In its 6-K, Luckin reported that its net revenues for the second quarter were $132 million. Total net revenues from products sold were reportedly approximately $126 million, an increase of 698 percent over the same quarter in 2018. Luckin highlighted this astronomical growth on a same-day earnings call. Luckin's reported total net revenues for the second quarter of 2019 were overstated by more than 27 percent. Despite Luckin's substantial revenue growth, analyst reports generally characterized the results as "in line" with expectations. Luckin's stock declined moderately, closing at $20.68 per ADS the following day.

The company's expenses were also overstated in this period because of fraudulent expense transactions created to return funds and create the appearance that expenses were consistent with reported revenue. Luckin's reported total operating expenses of approximately $233 million were overstated by approximately $22 million, or approximately 9 percent.

Because Luckin materially misstated its total revenues and expenses in the second quarter of 2019, it also materially understated its net loss in this period. The company reported a loss of approximately $99 million, which was understated by approximately $14 million, or approximately 15 percent. Fabricated revenue and expense transactions continued through the fourth quarter of 2019 but are not discussed here in the interest of brevity.

The SEC charged Luckin with defrauding investors by misstating its revenue, expenses, and net operating loss to appear to be more profitable and growing faster than it actually was, and to meet the company's earnings estimates. Specifically, the SEC had charged that Luckin violated Section 10(b) of the Securities Exchange Act of 1934 and Rule 10b-5 "by using any means of instrumentality of interstate commerce, or of the mails, or any facility of any national securities exchange, in connection with the purchase or sale of any security: (a) to employ any device, scheme, or artifice; (b) to make any untrue statement of a material fact or to omit to state a material fact necessary in order to make statements made, in the light of the circumstances under which they were made, not misleading; or (c) to engage in any act, practice, or course of business which operates or would operate as a fraud or deceit upon any person."[1]

Luckin reached an agreement to settle legal charges on February 4, 2021. It agreed to pay a $180 million penalty to settle the accounting fraud charges. The company filed for bankruptcy in the United States less than a year after it admitted that millions of dollars in sales had been fabricated.

In its filing, Luckin said the move will help it financially restructure itself and strengthen its balance sheet. According to a press release, the bankruptcy won't "materially impact" Luckin's day-to-day operations and its roughly 3,600 cafes will remain open.

The filing also reveals that Luckin's former chief operating officer Jian Lu and several of his direct reports "had engaged in certain misconduct, including fabricating certain transactions" beginning in 2019 amounting to about $310 million. Lu and CEO Jenny Zhiya Qian were both fired in May 2020. Months later its stock was delisted.

Ernst & Young

Ernst & Young Hua Ming LLP, the auditor for Luckin Coffee, said it had no responsibility for the company's 2019 financial statements and what it called the company's fraudulent misconduct. EY said it did not issue an audit report on the Luckin's 2019 earnings statement and so was not liable for the company's financial fraud. EY claimed to bear no liability based on an on-site investigation by China's finance ministry, the audit firm said in an official statement posted on WeChat.

EY stressed that Luckin's fraudulent practices began in April 2019, and it spotted an anomaly in Luckin's 2019 financial statement late in January 2020. EY promptly brought in its anti-fraud team, which later found that some managers had inflated earnings between the second and fourth quarters of 2019 with bogus transactions. The determination led to Luckin's disclosure of the fraud.

That discovery eventually prompted Luckin to issue a public announcement about the fraud. Luckin filed a notice with the U.S. SEC on April 2, 2020, admitting that it had falsified roughly $300 million worth of transactions between the second and fourth quarters of 2019. The company said that the incident started from "certain issues" identified during the audit of the consolidated financial statements for the year ended December 31, 2019. This makes it seem as though EY may have prompted Luckin's admission.

Questions

1. What was the motivation of Luckin in developing fraudulent transactions and fraudulent accounting? Was it indicative of earnings management? Explain.
2. Discuss the red flags that something was amiss at Luckin.
3. What role did corporate governance play in the fraud?
4. Use ethical reasoning to analyze what the motivation of Luckin might have been in carrying out the fraudulent transactions.

---

1. *Securities Exchange Commission v. Luckin Coffee, Inc.* Civil Action No. 1:20-cv-10631, February 4, 2021, https://law.justia.com/cases/federal/district-courts/new-york/nysdce/1:2020cv10631/550751/14/.

Name Index

Note: Page numbers followed by n indicate notes.

A

Abbasi, R. Umar, 55
Adams, Sarah, 275
Aesoph, John J., 329–331
Akers, Michael D., 288
Alali, Fatima, 347
Albrecht, W. Steve, 118
Allaire, Paul, 301
Almeder, Robert F., 71
Alston, Victor, 296
Amano, Futomichi, 188
Andersen, Arthur, 3, 46, 77, 100, 199, 204, 387, 389–391, 393, 405
Anderson, Jeffrey S., 243
Antar, Sam, 294
Arel, Barbara, 366
Aristotle, 4, 11, 15, 20
Armstrong, Lance, 14
Armstrong, Mary Beth, 62
Asch, Solomon, 52

B

Bado, Bill, 167
Balwani, Ramesh, 393–398
Balwani, Sunny, 162–165
Bardman, Erik K., 453–456
Barnhill, Douglas, 273
Barr, Rosanne, 11
Bashant, Cynthia, 144, 145
Bass, Carl E., 364, 366
Bazerman, Max H., 49, 50, 55
Beam, Aaron, 53, 54, 60, 63, 80, 235, 240, 368
Beam, Jimmy, 92
Bednar, Gregory, 187
Bee, Samantha, 376
Beioley, Kate, 272
Bell, Amy, 272
Bellach, Michael, 172, 173
Bellovary, Jodi L., 288
Bender, John, 171, 172
Bennett, Darren M., 329–331
Bentham, Jeremy, 15, 18

Beran, Robin, 206
Berardino, Joseph F., 364–366
Bernard, King, 326, 327
Blackburn, Svetlana, 296
Blake, Todd, 37
Blanford, Lawrence, 294
Bloom, Kyle, 28, 29
Bobek, Donna D., 366
Boller, Kate, 218
Boo, El'fred H. Y., 69
Borden, Will, 337, 338
Bornstein, Jeff, 333, 384
Bowling, Samantha, 259
Boxill, Jeanette M., 10
Boyd, Paul W., 446
Boyle, Joseph T., 234
Brehl, Robert, 187
Brennan, N., 368
Brown, Michael, 358
Brunnquell, Sara M., 377–379
Bruns, William J., 287, 288
Buchan, Kevin, 157
Buffett, Warren, 2, 283
Burchard, Mary Jo, 69
Burger, Warren, 175
Butler, Ronald Jr., 243

C

Campbell, Frank, 158–161
Camus, Albert, 113
Cardozzo, Benjamin, 400
Carlson, Rick, 215
Carmichael, Katy, 217
Carreyrou, John, 162, 164, 394–396
Carter, James, 222
Casale, Carl, 379
Casstevens, Randy, 386
Casucci, Jessica, 195
Ceresney, Andrew, 428
Cheung, Erika, 163, 396, 397
Chi Keung Man, 357
Christie, Thomas A., 243

Ciulla, Joanne, 358
Clayton, Jay, 189
Clough, Richard, 331
Conrad, Robert J., 343
Conway, Michael A., 234
Conyers, John Jr., 95
Cooper, Cynthia, 3, 30, 58, 70, 76, 77, 100, 101, 131, 368
Copeland, James E. Jr., 24
Copeland, Mary Kay, 359, 362, 369
Corigliano, Cosmo, 459, 463
Crain, William, 59
Cramer, Jim, 407
Crawford, Christopher, 335–338
Cressey, Donald R., 235
Cummings, Edward, 129
Cunningham, Lawrence A., 425, 426
Cupertino, Tony, 158, 160, 161

D

Dairy, Margaret, 268–269
Daly, Timothy, 172, 173
Daniel, Kim, 157
Daniels, Jackson, 92
Davis, Larry, 74, 75, 77–80
Davis, Michael, 136
Davis, Naeem, 55
Davis, Scott, 333, 384
De Cremer, David, 127, 362, 363
De Tocqueville, Alexis, 16, 17
Deaux, Joe, 205, 206
Dechow, P. M., 287
Dell, Michael, 452
Di Sibio, Carmine, 272
Diane, Blake, 37
Dichev, Ilia, 292
Diggins, Sharon, 171, 172
Disraeli, Benjamin, 7
Doberman, Debbie, 326, 327
Dobson, J., 46
Doge, Loyal, 327
Dolanski, Anthony P., 234

Donovan, John, 173
Doty, James, 211
Douglas, Dana S., 418
Duncan, David, 52
Dunlap, Albert J., 240, 387, 388

E

Earley, Christine E., 360
Ebbers, Bernie, 3, 100, 101, 359, 363
Egan, Matt, 333
Einhorn, David, 294
Emerson, Ralph Waldo, 64
Epstein, Barry J., 240, 241
Erhart, Charles Matthew, 144
Everson, Miles, 133

F

Farrow, Ronan, 94
Fastow, Andrew S., 364
Fastow, Andy, 46, 47, 52, 110, 111, 365
Feakins, Nick, 273
Ferrell, Linda, 117
Ferrell, O. C., 67, 70, 117
Festinger, Leon, 54
Fiedelman, Richard, 337, 338
Findling, Jay, 156-157
Fischer, M., 287
Flanagan, Thomas P., 188
Flannery, John, 269, 270, 383-385
Fletcher, Joseph, 23
Flynn, Timothy, 393
Forbes, Walter A., 459-460, 464
Foster, Timothy, 156
Fostermann, Kelly, 265
Fowler, Susan, 66-67
Frank, Anne, 24
Frankel, Alison, 450n1, 451n4
Frankel, Allison, 129
Franken, Al, 55, 95
Freeman, R. Edward, 125
Friedman, Milton, 125
Friestad, Scott W., 378
Fronckiewicz, Craig, 275
Fuld, Richard S. Jr., 122

G

Gaa, James C., 5
Gabhart, David R. L., 71
Garson, Natalie, 161-162
Gentile, Mary, 76

Gentile, M. C., 77
Gerstner, Louis V., 103
Geschonneck, Alexander, 272
Giacomino, Don E., 288
Giannulli, Mossimo, 37
Giles, Ed, 38-39
Gilmore, Madison, 456
Gino, Francesca, 55
Ginsburg, Ruth Bader, 143, 423
Gioia, Dennis, 127
Glover, Steven M., 402
Gluck, Robert J., 387
Goldberg, Josh, 456
Gomez, Jose, 184
Grace, W. R., 300
Grant, Hugh, 379
Griffith, Lee B., 387
Griggs, Linda, 418
Gruley, Bryan, 205

H

Hahn, Steve, 328
Hall, David M., 446
Hamilton, Erin L., 288
Hamilton, V. Lee, 69
Han, Ki-Suck, 55
Hannezo, Guillaume, 465-467
Harlow, Phillip, 387, 390
Harris, Roger, 161-162
Harrison, John, 41
Harrison, Ken, 328, 329
Hart, Kevin, 11
Hartford, Pamela, 187
Hartke, Anthony P., 377-379
Hartman, Laura P., 125
Hastings, Reed, 291
Hayward, Walter, 158, 160
Healy, P. M., 287
Heidman, Eric, 273
Heinel, Donna, 37
Heller, Matthew, 450n2, 451n3
Hemingway, Ernest, 23
Henley, Paul, 320-322
Hernandez, Gloria, 41
Hiltebeitel, Kenneth M., 68
Hirth, Robert B. Jr., 133
Hiznay, Paul, 459, 460, 463
Holder, Eric, 67
Hollander, Edwin P., 362
Holmes, Elizabeth, 162, 164, 165, 393-398
Homer, Julia, 100

Hopkins, Diane, 165
Hopwood, William S., 284, 289
Hudgins, James M., 275-280
Hudson, Michael, 238-239
Huffman, Felicity, 37
Humber, James M., 71

I

Immelt, Jeff, 383, 384
Itagaki, Yuji, 188

J

Jennings, Marianne, 110-112
Jensen, Michael C., 118
Jensen, Vick, 265
Jermakowicz, Eva K., 252
Johnson, Craig E., 61, 64, 72
Johnson, Eric N., 288
Jones, Barbara, 3
Jones, Jack, 73-75, 78, 79
Jones, John E., 156
Jones, Paul, 74, 75, 77-80
Jones, Scott K., 68
Josephson, Michael, 11, 13
Judd, Ashley, 94
Jung, Carl, 22

K

Kahneman, Daniel, 49, 53
Kalanick, Travis, 67
Kamienski, Michael, 187
Kang, Joe, 218-219
Kant, Immanuel, 15, 19, 20, 58
Kantor, Jodi, 94
Kaplan, Lewis A., 205
Kastiel, Kobi, 139
Katz, David K., 100
Katz, Todd, 335, 338
Kearney, Kevin, 459, 463
Keenan, John P., 367
Kelly, Patrick T., 359, 360, 368
Kelman, Herbert, 69
Kelton, Andrea S., 288
Kemper, Theodore D., 288, 363
Keon, Thomas L., 70
Kersh, Russell A., 387
Khuzami, Robert, 331
Kidder, Rushworth, 48, 72
Kilberg, Arnold, 439
Kilgore, Carl, 193

King, Denny, 161
King, Victoria, 161
Kitay, Darryl S., 275–280
Koh, Hian Chye, 69
Kohlberg, Lawrence, 56, 58, 59, 61, 78
Kozlowski, Dennis, 104, 110, 111, 241, 359, 363
Krohmer, Cathy, 364
Kueppers, Robert J., 186
Kumar, Sanjay, 112

L

Land, Carl, 216–217
Lang, Kelly, 328, 329
Lange, Richard, 280
Langford, Don, 330
Larson, John, 205
Laskey, David, 165
Lauer, Matt, 55, 95
Laughlin, Lori, 37
Lawton, Alan, 358
Lay, Ken, 46–47, 118, 365
LeMon, Alejandro Adrian, 241
Leonard, Paul, 227
Leroy, James, 43–44
Lester, Ethan, 265
Levin, Carl, 205
Levin, David, 456, 457
Levitt, Arthur, 283, 285
Lewis, C. S., 54
Libby, Theresa, 61, 62
Livengood, Scott, 386
London, Scott, 187
Long, Jack, 193
Lorenz, Jeannot, 429
Lorenzo, Sam, 158, 160
Loucks, Kristi, 80
Lowe, Kevin, 42
Lowry, Becca, 227
Lundstrom, Gilbert, 329, 330

M

MacDonald, Chris, 123
MacFarlane, Seth, 94
MacIntyre, Alasdair, 21
Mackey, John, 124
Madoff, Bernie, 8, 54
Maloney, Jerry, 171
Maloney, Ronnie, 274
Markowicz, Sammie, 96–97
Martin, Michael D., 368

Martinkat, John, 195, 220, 221
Mason, Donna, 328, 329
Masters, Brooke, 452n7
Matousek, Mark, 52
Maxwell, Morris, 119, 120
McClam, Erin, 101
McCollough, Shannon, 321
McCollum, Mark, 137, 138, 167–169
McCoy, Bowen H., 152
McDuff, Jack, 274
McGee, Travis, 271
McGregor, Scott, 285
McKee, Thomas E., 287–289
McKenna, Francine, 134, 397, 451n5, 451n6
McNamara, Michael, 220, 221
McVay, Malcolm, 368
Meckling, William H., 118
Meissner, Stuart, 379, 380
Mendes, Michael, 273, 274
Menendez, Anthony, 137–139, 145
Menendez, Tony, 138, 167–170, 287, 368, 429
Merchant, Kenneth A., 287, 288
Merriweather, Meredith, 374–375
Mesmer-Magnus, Jessica R., 367
Messick, David M., 49, 50
Messier, Jean-Marie, 465, 465n1
Messier, William F. Jr., 402
Miceli, Marcia P., 135, 136, 367
Michaels, Steve, 436
Milano, Alyssa, 94
Miles, Cheryl, 328. 329
Milgram, Stanley, 52
Mill, John Stuart, 15, 18
Miller, Jamie, 270, 333, 384
Miller, W. F., 77
Milton, Irv, 95, 97
Minkow, Barry, 266–268
Mintz, Steven M., 2, 10, 103, 186
Mixter, Christian, 418
Morris, Jan Taylor, 365
Morse, Gene, 3
Muldoon, Billy, 444–445
Mulford, Charles, 169
Mullen, Michael, 383
Murray, Zowie, 200
Musk, Elon, 119
Myers, David, 100

N

Nacchio, Joseph P., 245, 246
Near, Janet P., 135, 136, 367

Needles, Belverd E., 286
Neil, Steven, 273, 274
Nienas, Jonathan W., 377–379
Noel, Christine, 364

O

Obama, Barack, 119
Olsen, Kari Joseph, 240
O'Neil, Cathy, 66
Owens, Jim, 206
Owens, William T., 368

P

Padilla, Art, 69
Paez, Iliana, 358
Palmrose, Zoe-Vonna, 401
Pandit, Vikram, 120
Parkman, Jim, 367
Peck, Emily, 221
Pember, Anne M., 459, 463, 464
Piazza, Michael L., 230
Pincoff, Edmund L., 13
Pishevar, Shervin, 67
Plaff, Robert, 205
Plato, 4, 15, 21
Plotkin, Ann, 95, 97
Polverari, Mary Sattler, 459
Ponemon, L., 71
Popperson, Lance, 216
Poux, Philippe, 397, 398
Prawitt, Douglas F., 367, 402

R

Rabinowitz, Marc, 461
Rakoff, Jed, 423
Ramamoorti, Sridhar, 240, 241
Rand, Ayn, 16–18
Rand, Michael T., 339–343
Rathke, Fran, 294
Rawls, John, 16, 20, 59
Regas, Susan, 38–39
Rest, James, 15, 60, 61
Rezaee, Zabihollah, 115
Rick, William, 37
Riddell, Mark, 37
Rigas, John, 112
Riley, Cynthia, 280
Riordan, John, 445, 446
Rissier, Warren, 418
Rivard, Richard J., 285

Roberts, Helen, 446, 447
Romeril, Barry D., 301
Romero, Christy L., 329
Ronson, Jay, 240
Roosevelt, Eleanor, 13
Rose, Charlie, 95
Rose, Madison, 28, 29
Rosenthal, Jason, 141
Rosenthal, Richard, 205, 392
Rosenzweig, K., 287
Rothstein, Barbara, 450, 451
Rowe, Michael, 418
Ruble, Raymond J., 205

S

Sabatino, Casper, 459, 463
Safran, Ronald A., 234
St. Denis, Joseph, 30
Sakai, Margaret, 353–355
Sanders, Teresa Rubio, 367
Saunder, Brent, 324
Sawyer, Diane, 94
Scavo, Frank, 297
Schilit, Howard, 298, 303, 389
Schipper, K., 287
Schlicksup, Daniel, 206
Schultz, Tyler, 162, 163, 393, 394, 397
Scrushy, Richard, 53–55, 60, 111, 129, 240, 367, 368
Shandwick, Weber, 14
Shaw, Brian, 187
Shawver, T. J., 77
Shelton, E. Kirk, 459
Sherman, Marc, 129
Sherman, Mark, 437, 438
Shore, Andrew, 390
Shultz, George, 162–164, 394
Silverstein, Michael A., 439, 440
Sims, Marcus, 43–44
Sims, Randi L., 70, 367
Sisodia, Raj, 124
Skilling, Jeffrey K., 46, 241, 359, 363–364
Skinner, P. J., 287
Sloan, Grace, 215
Smiley, Tavis, 95
Smith, Adam, 118
Smith, Joe, 73, 79
Smith, Lesley, 141
Smith, Weston L., 129

Snoeyenbos, Milton, 71
Snow, Brad, 216
Socrates, 4, 15
Soltani, Bahram, 468
Somers, Paul, 143
Speaks, Steven, 459
Spielberg, Steven, 94
Sprankle, Brandon, 225–226
Stanga, Keith G., 288, 397
Stanley, Morgan, 152
Stanton, John, 165
Stein, Jeffrey M., 205, 392
Stone, Haley, 274
Strine, Leo, 116
Strom, Helen, 216–217
Strong, Jeremy, 376
Strong, John A., 343
Stuebs, Martin, 24
Stumpf, John, 166, 167
Sturgess, Anan, 211
Sugofsky, Ira, 96–97
Sullivan, Scott, 3, 52, 58, 100–101
Sutherland, Edwin, 235
Swartz, Marc, 241
Swartz, Mark, 104, 241
Szeliga, Robin R., 245–246

T

Tanis, Elizabeth, 451
Tate, John, 386
Taylor, David, 398
Tenbrunsel, Ann E., 127, 362, 363
Thibault, Robert H., 243
Thoman, G. Richard, 301
Thompson, Rachel, 355
Thorne, L., 5, 61, 62, 73
Thornton, Grant, 360, 413
Tietz, Wendy, 453n1
Toffler, Barbara Ley, 199
Tracy, Marc, 9
Trevino, Linda Klebe, 362
Turner, Lynn E., 350, 352
Tusa, Stephen, 270
Tversky, Amos, 53
Twaronite, Karyn, 195, 222
Twohey, Megan, 94

U

Uzzi, Donald R., 387

V

Valukas, Anton, 122
Vanstraten, Pete, 337, 338
Vavic, Jovan, 37
Velasquez, Manuel, 72
Vinson, Betty, 3, 12, 21, 52, 54, 61, 63, 101, 109, 110, 235
Viswesvaran, Chockalingam, 367
Voreacos, David, 205, 206

W

Wahlen, J. M., 287
Wald, Beverly, 97
Walker, David, 30
Walker, Jonathan, 92, 104
Walker, Michael, 280
Walravens, Pat, 296
Walter, William J. (Chip) Jr., 49
Wang, Sophia I-Ling, 347
Ward, Karen, 220–223
Watkins, Sherron, 46–47, 52, 53, 55, 76, 77, 365
Webb, Wilse B., 362
Webber, Paine, 390
Webster, Maron, 367
Weinstein, Bruce, 30
Weinstein, Harvey, 11, 55, 94–95
Weirich, Thomas R., 350, 352
Welch, Jack, 383
White, Mary Jo, 307
Wilchfort, Kenneth, 461
Wilkinson, Brett, 24
Williams, Sue, 73–74, 79
Willingham, Mary, 9
Winterkorn, Martin, 51
Wittmer, Dennis P., 55
Wolf, Jennifer F., 453–456
Woodruff, Robert S., 245–246
Woods, Dan, 297
Wynn, Karen, 49

Y

Young, Sarah, 320–322
Yukl, Gary, 357

Z

Zanin, Ryan, 270

Subject Index

Note: Page numbers followed by n indicate notes.

A

absolutes, moral, 22

acceptable payments, 428

accountants, perception of earnings management, 287-288

accounting
  application of ethical reasoning, 27-29
  auditing issues, 461
  culture and ethical leadership, 367-368
  ethical decision making, 71-72
  ethical skills, 364
  moral relativism in (*see* moral relativism)
  for nuts, 272-274
  profession, 24
  public interest in, 24
  Revue product/components, 454-456

Accounting Exemplar Award, 3

accounting fraud. *See* financial fraud; fraud

accounting restatements, 348-350

Ace Manufacturing, 73-75

act-utilitarians, 18

Acts Discreditable, 195

actually foreseen third parties, 405

adverse interest threat, 180, 192

advertising, 198

advocacy threat, 180, 192

affirmative defense, 428

AICPA (American Institute of Certified Public Accountants)
  advertising and solicitation by, 198
  Code of Professional Conduct, 234
  commissions and referral fees, 198
  confidential information, 198-199
  conflicts of interest, 191
  contingent fees, 197
  ethical conflicts, 189-191
  financial statement fraud, 231
  form of organization and name, 199-200
  impair independence, relationships, 183-186
  members in business, conceptual framework for, 191-194

  members in public practice, 179
    conceptual framework of, 179-181
    impair independence, 183-186
    revised Code, 179
    safeguards to counteract threats, 181-182
    SOX: nonaudit services, 182-183
  and professional judgment, 178
  providing nonattest services, 182
  Statements on Standards for Tax Services (SSTS), 201-203
  and tax services, 200-201

AICPA Code of Conduct, principles, 26-27

AICPA Code of Professional Conduct, 18, 25-27
  due care principle, 402

Alexion case, 443-444

Allergan case, 322-326

American Institute of Certified Public Accountants (AICPA). *See* AICPA (American Institute of Certified Public Accountants)

anchoring tendency, professional judgment, 177

Anjoorian, 439-441

anti-fraud controls, 105-106

antisocial behavior, 363-364

application of ethical reasoning, 27-28

Aristotle, 4, 15

Arnold Kilberg & Co., 439-441

Arthur Andersen & Co., Credit Alliance v., 405

AT&T, 303

attest clients, employment/association with, 184-185

audit committees, 131
  communications with, 250
  earnings guidance, 290
  United Thermostatic Controls, 157-161

audit evidence, 239, 243, 245, 250, 251, 253, 257-258

audit opinions, 252-255

audit planning gone awry, 271

audit procedures, 249-250, 257

audit report

  background information, 246
  example paragraphs in, 253-254
  independent, 247
  limitations of, 255-257
  opinion paragraph, 252-253

audit risk, 231, 258. *See also* risk assessment; risk factors

auditing standards, 246-255
  Consideration of Fraud in a Financial Statement Audit (AU-C Section 240), 231

auditor-client relationship, 402-403

auditor independence, SEC approach, 186

auditor defenses to negligence, 412-414

auditors. *See also* certified public accountants (CPAs)
  communication with those charged with governance, 244-245
  communications with audit committees, 250
  defense against third-party lawsuits, 412-413
  defenses of, 412-413
  ethical reasoning in, 71
  external, 367
  FCPA and, 427-429
  internal, 366-367
  legal liability of, 401-405
  professional judgment by, 62
  PSLRA and, 422-424

audits
  definition, 231
  ethical decision making in, 71-72
  ethical leadership, 365-368
  fraud considerations, 239-240
  fraud triangle (*see* fraud triangle)
  KBC Solutions, 215
  Lone Star School District, 40

authentic leaders
  followership and leadership, 362-363
  moral intensity, 365
  overview, 361
  social learning theory, 363-364

transformational leadership, 362

availability tendency, professional judgment, 177

B

banks, income smoothing by, 285–286

Beauda Medical Center, 216

Beazer Homes, 339–343

behavioral ethics, 48–55

    bystander effect, 54–55

    cognitive biases, 49–53

    cognitive dissonance, 54

    situational factors, 54

    system 1 *versus* system 2 thinking, 49

bill-and-hold scheme, 169–170

Bily v. Arthur Young (1992), 406–407

Biotechnologies (cases), 446–447

Black and White, LLP, 359

blind spots, ethical, 10

blow the whistle or don't blow the whistle, 165

Blue Bell, Inc. v. Peat, Marwick, Mitchell & Co. (1986), 406

BMW case, 333–335

board of directors, 111. *See also* audit committees

    and CEO, 12, 28

    WorldCom's, 3

bogus revenue transactions, 299

Bond Linked Issue Premium Structure (BLIPS), 391–392

breach of contract, 402

Buddhism, 4

business judgment rule, 116–117

business relationships, 184

bystander effect, 54–55

C

California, 406

Canadian Institute of Chartered Accountants (CICA), 62

cannabis business, 91

capitalization *versus* expensing, 41

cardinal virtues, 21

caring, 11, 13

Caterpillar tax fraud case, 205–207

cautionary tale for Silicon Valley, 162–165

Cayman Fund, 413

Cendant Corporation, 458–465

CEOs

    ethical behavior, 365

    reports, 426–427

certified public accountants (CPAs), 397. *See also* auditors

    advertising and solicitation by, 198

    commissions and referral fees, 198

    conflicts of interest, 191

    contingent fees, 197

    ethical conflicts, 189–192

    ethical obligations of, 12

    financial relationships, 183–184

    form of organization and name, 199

    providing nonattest services, 185

    reputation of, 14

    spirit of the rules, 200

    Statements on Standards for TaxServices (SSTS), 201–203

    subordination of judgment, 192

    and tax services, 200–207

    threats to independence, 180–181

    the UK experience, 185–186

CFOs

    corporate responsibility for financial reports, 426–427

    earnings quality, 292

    ethical leadership, 368

    followership and leadership, 362–363

    HealthSouth Corporation, 368

    materiality criteria, 255–256

channel stuffing, 285, 388

character, pillars of. *See* Six Pillars of Character

cheating, student, 8–10

cheating on internal training exams at KPMG, 172–173

chefs delight: that slope looks slippery, 97–98

Christianity, 4

Citizens State Bank v. Timm, Schmidt, & Company, 408

citizenship, 11, 13–14

civility, 13

Clean Sweep: A Story of Compromise, Corruption, Collapse, and Comeback (Minkow), 266

Cleveland Custom Cabinets, 43–44

client-auditor relationships, 402–403

cloud computing revenue recognition, 297

cloud credits, 297

code of ethics, 50. *See also* AICPA Code of Professional Conduct

cognitive biases, 49–53

cognitive dissonance, 54

college, cheating in, 8–10

Colonial Bank, 450–452

commissions fees, 198

Committee of Sponsoring Organizations (COSO) framework, 132–133

common-law liability, 402, 407–409

Comp-U-Card (CUC), 458

competence

    ethical leadership, 360–361

    professional services, 194

compliance function, 113

compliance with standards, 194–195

confidential information, 198–199

confirmation tendency, professional judgment, 177

conflicts of interest, 111, 191

Confucianism, 4

conscious capitalism, 124

consequentialism, 16

Consideration of Fraud in a Financial Statement Audit (AU-C Section 240), 231, 235, 244

constructive fraud, 402, 407, 409

contingent fees, 197

contractual adjustment, 285

controllers, 12, 38, 41, 256

cookie-jar reserves, 285, 340

coronavirus, 1. *See also* COVID-19 pandemic

Coronavirus Aid, Relief and Economic Security (CARES) Act, 374

corporate governance, 356–357. *See also* organizational culture/ethics

    agency theory, 118

    case studies, 152, 173

    compliance function, 113

    components of, 117

    conscious capitalism, 124

    corporate social responsibilities, 123

    defining, 115–116

    ethical and legal responsibilities of officers and directors, 116–117

    ethical decision making, 63

    ethics in workplace, 112

    ethics reflection, 102–103

    executive compensation, 118–120

    foundations of, 115–122

    fraud in organizations, 103–109

    internal auditors, 131

    internal controls, 132–134

    millennials, 123–124

    oversight and regulation, 120–122

    signs of ethical collapse in, 109–112

    structures and relationships, 128–130

sustainability, 123

triple bottom line, 123

whistleblowing, 135

corporate responsibility for financial reports, 426–427

corporate social responsibilities (CSR)

economic model, 125

Ford Pinto cases, 126–127

stakeholder model, 125–126

COSO (Committee of Sponsoring Organizations), 242

COVID-19 pandemic, 9, 14, 37, 289, 374, 447

CPAs. *See* certified public accountants (CPAs)

Credit Alliance, 405

Credit Alliance v. Arthur Andersen & Co., 405

Cubic Corporation, 351

cultural relativism, 23

culture, Kohlberg's stages of moral development and, 57–58

cyberbullying, 10

D

Data Systems Solutions (DSS), 320

decision making, ethics, 29

Dell Computer, 320

Deloitte Japan's system

bank accounts with audit client, 187–188

insider trading on client information, 188

Deloitte & Touche LLP

North Face and, 335–339

Vertical Pharmaceuticals Inc. et al. v. Deloitte & Touche LLP, 441–442

Deloitte surveys, 65

deontologists, 19

deontology, 15

AICPA Code, 20

rights of individuals, 19

rights principles, 19–20

rule-utilitarianism, 19

Department of Justice (DOJ), 427

Diamond Foods Inc., 272

Difference Principle, 20

Digital Realty Trust, Inc. v. Somers and, 145

disclaimer of opinion, in audit report, 252, 253

discretionary accruals, 286

distributive justice, 20

diverse, equitable or inclusive, 93–94

diversity *versus* inclusion, 64

dot.com businesses, 420

due care standard, 27, 257, 402

due diligence defense, 417

duties, in deontology, 19

duty of care, 116

duty of good faith, 116

duty of loyalty, 116

E

earnings guidance

audit committee responsibilities, 290

earnings expectations, 289

forward-looking statements, 289

as motivation for earnings management, 284–285

non-GAAP financial metrics, 304–310

pull-in sales, 290–291

social media, 291

earnings management, 356–357, 376

acceptability, 287

earnings guidance, 289–291

earnings quality, 292

Enron case, 304

ethical choices, 286

ethics of, 288–289

ethics reflection, 282–283

financial analysis, 293

financial shenanigans, 298–304

financial statement restatements, 347–348

income smoothing, 285–286

Lucent Technologies case, 302–304

manager/accountant perception of, 287–288

motivation for, 284–285

new revenue recognition standard, 295–296

overview, 283

red flags of, 291–295

revenue recognition, 295–298

SEC enforcement actions, 209

Xerox case, 301–302

earnings manipulation, earnings management, 284–285

earnings quality, 292

eating time (case), 42

Echo Park Sportswear (EP Sports) audit, 280

education, ethics, 26

egoism

enlightened, 16–17

ethical, 16

rational, 17–18

8-K form, 255, 416

emphasis-of-matter paragraph, audit opinions, 252, 253

employment/association with attest clients, 184–185

engagement letter, 225–226

engagement withdrawal, 254–255

enlightened egoism, 16–17

Enron, 304, 365

earnings manipulation, 284

financial statement fraud, 233

moral manager, 361

professional judgment and, 62

social learning theory, 363–364

special-purpose-entities, 62, 299, 311

story of, 47

enterprise risk management, 243

equality *versus* equity, 65

Equifax data breach, 134–135

equity, diversity, and inclusion (EDI), 64

components of, 65–68

Erhart v. BofI Holdings, 144

Ernst & Whinney, 266

Ernst & Young (EY), 243

HealthSouth Corporation, 368

relationships with client personnel, 187

ethical blindness, 10

ethical climate, 64

ethical conflicts, 189–191

ethical culture, 63

ethical decision making

behavioral ethics, 48–49

case studies, 89–101

cognitive biases, 49–53

cognitive development approach, 55–59

Enron and, 46–47

equity, diversity, and inclusion, 64–68

ethical decision making in accounting and auditing, 71–72

Giving Voice to Values, 76

integrated process, 73

models, 72

moral intensity, 63

moral reasoning and behavior, 59–60

organizational influences, 63

professional judgment and, 62

Rest's four-component model of, 59–63

ethical dissonance model, 68–70

ethical egoism, 16

ethical leadership, 357–361
    audit firms, 365–368
    authentic leaders, 361
    competence, 360–361
    ethics reflection, 345–346
    HealthSouth case, 368
    internal audit function, 366–367
    moral person and manager, 361
    overview, 357
    role of CFOs, 368
    traits, 358–359
    whistleblowing implications, 397
Ethical Leadership Scale, 360
ethical (moral) motivation, 61
ethical organization
    business ethics intentions, behavior,
      and evaluations, 70
    ethical climate, 64
    ethical culture, 63
    individual factors, 68
    opportunity, 70
    organizational factors, 68
ethical relativism, 23
ethics
    behavioral, 48–55
    of earnings management, 288–289
    education, 26
    language of (*see* language of ethics)
    and laws, 7
    laws and ethical obligations, 7–8
    philosophical foundations, 4
    and professionalism, 25–26
    and tax services, 200–207
    Tyco fraud and, 241
    virtue, 21–22
    in workplace, employee perceptions of,
      114
Ethics Compliance and Officer Association
    (ECOA), 113
Ethics Compliance Initiative (ECI), 113
Ethics Resource Center (ERC), 113
ethics standards. *See* PCAOB (Public
    Company Accounting Oversight Board);
    PCAOB standards
ethos, 5
executive compensation, 374
expense or capitalize research and
    development costs, 171–172
expensing, capitalization *versus*, 41
external auditors, 131–132
external audits/auditors, 231, 240, 243, 246,
    265, 270, 275, 277

*Extraordinary Circumstances: The Journey of
    a Corporate Whistleblower* (Cooper), 3
EY partner Michael Kamienski, 187
EY partner Pamela Hartford, 187

F
Facebook, 291
Fair Funds, 467
fair presentation of financial statements,
    231, 245, 247, 255–256
fairness, 13
Fairway Capital Corporation (FCC), 439
familiarity threat, 181, 192
Family Games, Inc., 216–217
FASB (Financial Accounting Standards
    Board), 352
    cloud computing arrangements, 297
    Emerging Issues Task Force ("EITF")
      Issue No. 01-9, 377–378
    Revenue from Contracts with Customers,
      295, 457
Faulty Budget case study, 92–93
FDA liability concerns, 89–91
Federal Deposit Insurance Corporation
    (FDIC), 450
fees
    commissions, 198
    referral, 198
financial analysis, 293
financial fraud, 3, 46, 52, 130, 178, 245, 291,
    302, 312, 345, 380, 421, 459
financial reporting
    corporate responsibility for, 426–427
    determination, 233
    fraud, 231–234, 236
    internal control, 237, 240–242
    internal control over, PCAOB rule on,
      425–426
    PCAOB standards, 250
    process and control, 237, 244
    restatements due to errors in, 350–352
financial reporting framework, 248, 257
Financial Reporting Releases (FRRs), 419
financial results, social media reporting, 291
financial self-interest threat, 180
financial shenanigans, 285, 310–311
    accounting for revenue in cloud,
      296–298
    Enron, 299, 304
    examples of, 301–302
    financial statement effects, 298–300
    red flags of earnings management,
      291–295

financial statement fraud, 107–109. *See also*
    material misstatements
    errors, 232
    fraud, 232–233
    illegal acts, 233
    misstatements, nature and causes of,
      232
financial statement restatements, 347–348
financial statements
    failing to record expenses, 300
    one-time gains, 299
    recording bogus revenue, 299
    recording revenue, 298
    shifting current revenue, 299
    shifting expenses, 300
first-in, first-out (FIFO) method, 258
followership, and leadership, 362–363
Foreign Corrupt Practices Act (FCPA),
    233, 427–429
Foreign Leveraged Investment Program
    (FLIP), 391
foreseen third-party concept, 404, 406
form of organization and name, 199
forward-looking statements, 289
Fostermann Corporation, 265
Franklin Industries' Whistleblowing,
    161–162
fraud, 102–103, 235–239. *See also* financial
    fraud; financial statement fraud
    auditor liability for, 407–409
    common-law liability, 407–409
    dark triad personality risk, 240–241
    financial statement audit, 414–416
    incentives/pressures to commit, 236
    occupational, 104–107
    opportunity to commit, 237
    in organizations, 103–109
    rationalization for, 237–238
    risk assessment, 239–240
    statutory law liability, 409–410
    triangle (*see* fraud triangle)
fraud in financial statements, 107–109
    AICPA standards, 231
    confidentiality obligation, 234
    errors, 232
    fraud, 233
    generally accepted auditing standards
      (GAAS), 231
    illegal acts, 233
    nature and causes of misstatements,
      232
    Private Securities Litigation Reform
      Act (PSLRA), 233–234

fraud triangle
　auditing, 235
　conditions, 235
　dark triad personality risk, 240–241
　incentives/pressures to commit fraud, 236
　opportunity to commit fraud, 237
　rationalization, 237–238
　trust, 238–239
　Tyco fraud, 241
fraudulent financial reporting, 232, 233, 235, 244
fraudulent misrepresentations, 410
Fred Stern & Company, 400
full disclosure principle, 18

G

GAAP (generally accepted accounting principles). *See also* non-GAAP financial metrics
　earnings quality, 292
　financial statement restatements, 347
　Krispy Kreme Doughnuts, Inc., 385–387
GAAS (generally accepted auditing standards), 231
General Electric (GE), 331–333, 383–385
General Standards Rule, 194
getting called-out on social media case, 44–45
Giant Stores, 406
Giles and Regas (case), 38–39
Giving Voice to Values (GVV), 193–194
　ace manufacturing, 77–80
　levers, 77
　reasons and rationalizations, 76–77
　values-based leadership, 360
going concern issue, in audit report, 254
Global Human Capital Trends survey, 65
Golden Rule, the, 4–6, 11, 13, 19, 20
Grant Thornton LLP v. Prospect High Income Fund, et al., 413
grease payments, 427–428
Greeks, ancient, 2, 4, 15
Green Mountain Coffee Roasters, 294–295
gross negligence, 403, 407
GVV. *See* Giving Voice to Values (GVV)

H

Halliburton, 167–171
Han, Kang & Lee, LLC, 218–219
Harrison Industries case, 328–329

Harvey Weinstein Case, 94–95
HealthSouth Corporation, 53, 55
Heinz and the Drug dilemma, 56–59
Hertz Global Holdings, Inc., (Hertz), 348
HFS Incorporated (HFS), 458
Higginbotham v. Baxter Int'l., 426
high organizational ethics, high individual ethics (High-High), 69
high organizational ethics, low individual ethics (High-Low), 69–70
Hinduism, 4
honesty, 4, 6, 10, 12, 21
Houbigant, Inc. v. Deloitte & Touche LLP, 409

I

IFRS (International Financial Reporting Standards), 246, 257
illegal acts, 233. *See also* fraud in financial statements
IMA. *See* Institute of Management Accountants (IMA)
In re Lattice Semiconductor Corp., 426
In re WatchGuard Secs. Litig., 426
In the Matter of John J. Aesoph, CPA, and Darren M. Bennett, CPA, 329
In the Matter of Marcum LLP. And Alfonse Gregory Giugliano, CPA, 224
Inclusion Pulse Survey, 66
income smoothing, 285–286
income tax fraud versus tax negligence, 411–412
independence
　in AICPA Code of Professional Conduct, 26
　audit, 18
　auditor, 244, 257
　employment/association with attest clients, 184–185
　ethics education, 26
　financial relationships impairing, 183–184
　PCAOB report, 249
　providing nonattest services, 185
　safeguards, 181
　standards, 230
　threats to, 180–181
　values and ethics, 6
India, 272
individualism, 18
insider trading case, 188
Institute of Internal Auditors (IIA), 26
Institute of Management Accountants

(IMA)
　code, 25
　and IIA, 26
　standards, 26
　statement of ethical and professional practice, 26
instrumental virtues, 62
integrity
　accounting, 2–3
　trustworthiness, 11
integrity and objectivity
　conflicts of interest, 191
　members in business, 191–194
intellectual virtues, 62
internal audits/auditors, 3, 26, 131
internal control assessment, 241–242
Internal Control-Integrated Framework, 245
internal control over financial reporting (ICFR), 242–243, 245, 260, 276, 278, 279, 444–445
internal controls
　FCPA and, 428
　over financial reporting, 425–426
International Federation of Accountants (IFAC), 26
Islam, 4

J

Johnson Pharmaceuticals, 227
Joker & Wild LLC, 436
Judaism, 4
judgment
　moral, 60
　subordination of, 189
justice as fairness, 20–21
Justice Department. *See* Department of Justice (DOJ)

K

Kay & Lee LLP, 442
Kidder's ethical checkpoints, 72
Kiley Nolan's ethical dilemma case, 456–457
Kohlberg's stages of moral development, 55–59
KPMG, 230
　cheating on internal training exams, 172–173
　Maxwell v. KPMG LLP, 420
　SEC sanctions on, 184
　tax shelter, 204–205
　withdrawing audit opinions, 187

Xerox case, 301–302

KPMG LLP, Maxwell v., 420

KPMG professional judgment framework

and AICPA Code of Professional
Conduct (*see* AICPA Code of
Professional Conduct)

and cognitive processes, 177–178

components, 177

professional skepticism, 177

KPMG tax shelter case, 204–205

KPMG tax shelter scandal, 391–393

Kraft Heinz Co., case, 380–383

Krispy Kreme Doughnuts, Inc., 385–387

L

language of ethics

cheating, student, 8–10

definition, ethics, 6

differences, ethics and morals, 5–6

ethical obligations and law, 7–8

and laws, 7

morals, 5

relativism (*see* moral relativism)

social media, 8

values, 6

Laramie Systems, 322

last-in, first-out (LIFO) method, 258

Lattice Semiconductor, 426

lawsuits, 402, 412

leader ethicality, 362

leaders, 361–363

leader's legitimacy, 363

leadership

failures, 364–365

followership and, 362–363

transformational, 362

lease accounting, 301–302

legal and regulatory obligations. *See also*
Sarbanes-Oxley Act (SOX); statutory
liability

of auditors, 401–412

FCPA and, 427–429

PSLRA and, 422–424

third party liability, 405

legal liability

of auditors, 401–405

to third parties, 407

ZZZZ Best, 267

liability

of auditors, 401–405

common-law, 402, 407–409

defending audit-malpractice cases,
403–404

negligent misrepresentation, 404–405

privity relationship with clients,
402–403

professional negligence, 403

proportionate, 422–423

recklessness, 404

Sarbanes Oxley (SOX) legal, 424–427

statutory, 409–410, 416

third-party, 405–406, 439–441

liberty principle, 20

Lockheed Corporation, 427

Logitech International, 452–456

Lone Star school district, 40

Lottery Bonanza case, 41

low organizational ethics, high individual
ethics (Low-High), 70

low organizational ethics, low individual
ethics (Low-Low), 69

loyalty, 2, 11, 12, 24, 110–111

Luckin Coffee case, 468–471

Lucent Technologies, Inc., 300, 302–304

M

MagnaChip Semiconductor, Ltd., 353–355

management. *See also* CEOs; CFOs

earnings management, managers and
accountants perception, 287–288

participation threat, 181

Marcum LLP case, 223–224

margin normalization, 302

material misstatements

nature and causes of, 232

reasonable assurance and, 241

material weakness, 238, 242, 273, 276, 279,
444–445

materiality, 231, 233, 255–256

defense, 417

Maxwell v. KPMG LLP, 420

Medicis, 242–243

Merger reserves, 461

Miller Energy Resources, Inc., 445–446

Milton Manufacturing Company, 95–97

misstatements, material. *See* material
misstatements

modified opinion, in audit report, 252–253

monitoring, 231

Monroe v. Hughes (1991), 425

Monsanto Company Roundup, 377–380

moral behavior, 59–60

moral character, 21, 61

moral courage, 14

moral development

Kohlberg's stages of, 55–59

professional judgment and, 62

moral focus, 61

moral intensity, 63, 365

moral judgment, 60–61

moral manager, 361

moral motivation, 61

moral person, 361

moral philosophies. *See also* ethics

framework for guiding behavior, 15

justice, 20

moral relativism, 22–24

teleology (*see* teleology)

virtue ethics, 21

moral reasoning, 59–60

moral relativism

cultural, 23

ethical, 23

fixed standards of behavior, 23

situation ethics, 23–24

moral sensitivity, 60

morals and ethics, 5–6

more likely than not standard, 392

multi-element arrangements, 296

multibillion-dollar charge, 269–270

multiple deliverables, 296

Murphy v. BDO Seidman, LLP (2003), 407

N

near-privity relationship, 405, 407

Needles' continuum of ethical financial
reporting, 286

new revenue recognition standard, 295–296

New York Stock Exchange (NYSE), 246,
350

non-GAAP financial metrics

compliance and disclosure
interpretations, 309

defining, 307

ethics, 310

external auditor responsibilities, 309

liability for wrongful use, 309–310

requirements under item 10(e) of
regulation S-K, 308

non-GAAP metrics, 326–327, 331–333

nonattest services, 185

nondiscretionary accruals, 286

North Face, Inc., 256, 335–338

NYSE. *See* New York Stock Exchange
(NYSE)

O

objectivity
ACFE, 26
AICPA Code, 26
occupational fraud, 104–107
Offshore Portfolio Investment Strategy (OPIS), 391
Omnibus Trade and Competitiveness Act of 1988, 427
one-time gains, boosting income with, 299
Operation Varsity Blues case, 37
opinions, audit. *See* audit opinions
Oracle's cloud services, 296–297
organizational culture/ethics. *See also* corporate governance
business ethics evaluations and intentions, 70
compliance function, 113
employee perceptions of, 114
individual factors, 68
opportunity, 70
organizational factors, 68
signs of ethical collapse in, 109–112
overconfidence tendency, professional judgment, 177

P

Pacific Business Credit v., 405
Pacific Mutual Life Insurance v. Ernst & Young, 407–409
"Parable of the Sadhu" (McCoy), 152–156
Parmalat, 449
Pascarella & Trench (P&T), 439–440
Paul V. Anjoorian v. Arnold Kilberg & Co., 439
payments acceptable, 428
defining, 427
grease, 428
permissible facilitating, 427
PCAOB (Public Company Accounting Oversight Board), 71
ethics and independence standards, 207
inspections, 210–211
quality control standards, 209–210
Rule 3520-auditor independence, 207
Rule 3521-contingent fees, 207
Rule 3522-tax transactions, 207
Rule 3523-tax services for persons in financial reporting oversight roles, 208
Rule 3524-audit committee preapproval of certain tax services, 208

Rule 3525-audit committee preapproval of nonauditing services related to internal control over financial reporting, 208
Rule 3526-communication with audit committees concerning independence, 209
PCAOB standards
audit deficiencies, 242
audit report, 251
GAAS and, 257–258
Peat, Marwick, Mitchell & Co., 405, 406
permissible facilitating payments, 427
personality traits, Machiavellianism, 240
person-organization fit, 69–70
Phar-Mor v. Coopers & Lybrand, 409
Plato, 4, 15
prescriptive reasoning, 60
present fairly, 247, 252, 254–256
PricewaterhouseCoopers (PwC)
age discrimination, 195
prohibited nonaudit services, 187
prima facie case, 417
Paycheck Protection Program (PPP), 374–375
Private Securities Litigation Reform Act (PSLRA), 422–423
privity relationship, 402–40
procedural justice, 21
professional judgment in accounting, 62
professional practice, rules of
Acts Discreditable, 195–197
advertising and other forms of solicitation, 198
commissions and referral fees, 198
confidential information, 198–199
contingent fees, 197
form of organization and name, 199
General Standards Rule, 194
spirit of the rules, 200
professional skepticism, 6, 27, 176, 233, 239, 243, 257, 260, 352, 430, 446
proportionate liability, 422–423
prudent person test, 417
PSLRA. *See* Private Securities Litigation Reform Act (PSLRA)
public interest in accounting
AICPA Code, 24
CPA license, 24
ethics and professionalism, 25–26
regulation, accounting profession, 24
public trust
auditors, 178

financial reporting, 24
PCAOB inspections, 210–211
Treadway Commission Report, 130
pull-in sales, 290–291, 353
PwC mischaracterizes nonaudit services, 225–226

Q

QSGI, Inc., 437–438
qualified opinion, in audit report, 252, 253
quality of financial reporting, 285

R

rational egoism, 17–18
reasonable assurance
financial statements, 231
internal controls, 241–242
limitations, 255
reasonable basis, 392
reasonable person/observer, 255
reasonableness standard, 417
reasonably foreseeable third parties, 406–408
"reason to expect" vs. "should have known" standard, 410–411
red-flag warnings of fraud, 106–107
referral fees, 198
regulation, accounting profession, 24
Regulation Fair Disclosure, 291
Reisman v. KPMG Peat Marwick LLP, 409
reissuance restatements, 345, 346
related-party transactions, 280, 387
reliability, 12
reporting. *See* financial reporting
representational faithfulness, 282
reprisals, fear of, 110
reputation, 14
reserves, cookie-jar, 285, 340
responsibility, accounting professionals, 13
Restatement (Second) Law of Torts, 406–407
Restatement test, 440
restatements, financial statement
characteristics, 343–344
errors in accounting and reporting, 350–352
Hertz accounting restatements, 348–349
operational issues, 352
Rest's four-component model of ethical decision making, 59–61
revenue recognition, 295–298, 300, 350
rights theory, 15, 22, 24, 28, 29

risk assessment
    audit committee responsibilities for
        fraud, 243–244
    COSO Framework, 132–133
    internal control assessment, 241–242
risk-benefit analysis, Ford Pinto case, 127
risk factors, 240, 241
risk management, 243
    COSO's enterprise, 243
Rite Aid Inventory Surplus Fraud, 156–157
Rosenblum, Inc. v. Adler (1983), 406
Rule 3520-auditor independence, 207
Rule 3521-contingent fees, 207
Rule 3522-tax transactions, 207
Rule 3523-tax services for persons in
    financial reporting oversight roles, 208
Rule 3524-audit committee preapproval of
    certain tax services, 208
Rule 3525-audit committee preapproval of
    nonauditing services related to internal
    control over financial reporting, 208
Rule 3526-communication with audit
    committees concerning independence,
    209
rule deontologists, 19
rule-utilitarians, 18
Rusch Factors, 405
Rusch Factors, Inc. v. Levin (1968), 405, 406

S

SAB 101, 295
safeguards
    to counteract threats, 181
    threats and, 192–193
Sarbanes-Oxley Act (SOX), 71
    false certifications of financial
        statements, 129–130
    internal controls, 132
    legal liabilities, 424–427
    nonaudit services, 182–183
    Section 301, 128
    Section 302, 128, 426–427
    Section 404, 128, 425
    Section 406, 128
    Section 806, 128
scienter, 409, 421
scope and nature of services, in AICPA
    Code of Professional Conduct, 26
Scott London, KPMG, 187
SEC Charges against, 386–387
SEC enforcement, 168, 290
    accounting violations, 355–356

improper revenue recognition, 296
independence rules, 188–189
MagnaChip Semiconductor, Ltd.,
    353–355
MD&A, 289
materiality determinations, 189
new revenue recognition standard,
    295–296
revenue recognition, 295–298
SEC v. KPMG LLP, 234
*SEC v. Vivendi Universal, S. A., Jean-Marie
    Messier, and Guillaume Hannezo*, 465n1
Section 404, 425
Section 179 deduction for equipment
    purchases case, 42–43
Securities Act of 1933, 416–417, 431
Securities and Exchange Commission
    (SEC), 71, 100, 169, 269, 326, 329. *See
    also* SEC enforcement
    auditor independence, 186–189
    Dell Computer, charges against, 320
    explanation, 419–422
    external auditors, 368
    financial statement restatements, 348,
        350
    HealthSouth Corporation, charges
        against, 285
    KPMG sanctions, 302
    Krispy Kreme Doughnuts, Inc.,
        385–387
    nonaudit services, 182–183
    North Face, charges against, 338
    PricewaterhouseCoopers, 386–387
    statutory liability, 416
*Securities and Exchange Commission v. Erik
    K. Bardman and Jennifer F. Wolf*, 454n3
*Securities and Exchange Commission v.
    Walter A. Forbes et al.,* 464n6
Securities Exchange Act of 1934
    intent to deceive or defraud, 420–422
    reliance by plaintiff, 420
    statutory liability, 416
*Securities Exchange Commission v. Luckin
    Coffee, Inc.*, 471n1
*Security Pacific Business Credit, Inc. v. Peat
    Marwick Main & Co.* (1992), 405
Seidman & Seidman, 407
self-interest threat, 192
self-review threat, 180, 192
servant leadership, 362
sexual harassment, 66, 195, 220–222
Six Pillars of Character caring, 11–14
    caring, 13

citizenship, 13–14
fairness, 13
moral courage, 14
reputation, 14
respect, 13
responsibility, accounting professionals,
    13
trustworthiness (*see* trustworthiness)
virtues/character traits, 11
60 Minutes interview, 241
Small Business Administration (SBA), 439
social learning theory, 363–364
social media, 291
social networking, 10–11
Socrates, 4, 15
solicitation, 198
Solutions Network, Inc., 320–322
SOX (Sarbanes-Oxley Act). *See,*
    Sarbanes-Oxley Act (SOX)Staff
    Accounting Bulletins (SABs), 419
Standards (SFAS)
    No. 5, 302
    No. 141, 461
State Street Trust Co. v. Ernst, 409
Statement of Financial Accounting
    Concepts (SFAC), 255
Statements on Standards for Accounting
    and Review Services (SSARS), 194
Statements on Standards for Tax Services
    (SSTS), 201–203
statutory liability, 416–422
    court cases, 419
    explained, 401
    Securities Act of 1933, 416–417
    Securities Exchange Act of 1934,
        419–422
    summary of, 402
subordination of judgment, 192–193
substantial authority, 392
Sunbeam Corporation, 387–391
Sustainability, 123
System 1 thinking, 49
System 2 thinking, 49

T

Taoism, 4
tax avoidance, 203
tax law, auditor responsibility and violation,
    233
tax positions, 392–393
tax practice, 366
tax return position, 201

tax returns, 197

tax rules, 2

tax services
    ethics and, 200–201
    SSTS, 201–204

tax shelters, 204–207, 219–220
    KPMG, 391–393

teaching values, 4

teleology
    deontology, 19–20
    egoism, 16–18
    utilitarianism, 18–19

Tellabs, Inc. v Makor Issues & Rights, 421–423

10-K (annual) reports, 419, 426

10-Q (quarterly) reports, 419, 421

Terms of Engagement (AU-C Section 210), 234

Tesla's case, 119

Texas Supreme Court, 413

Theranos case, 393–398

third parties
    auditor liability, 407–410
    auditor's defense against, 412–413
    foreseen, 405–408

third party liability, 405, 439–441

Thomas Flannigan, Deloitte & Touche (insider trading case), 188

Thorne's integrated model of ethical decision making, 62–63

threats to audit independence, 217

threats to independence, 180–182

3D printing case, 28–29

302 certifications, 426–427

TierOne Bank, 329–331

tort actions, 402

tort liability, 403

Toxic Sales Culture, 165–167

transformational leadership, 362

transparency, 54

Treadway Commission Report, 130

Treasury Circular 230, 203–204, 392

Trigen Laboratories (TLI), 441

Triple bottom line (TBL), 123

trust-based organizations, 361

trustworthiness
    honesty, 12
    integrity, 12
    loyalty, 12
    reliability, 12

Tyco, 283, 359
    fraud, 241

U

uber sexual harassment case, 66–68

Ultramares principle, 405

Ultramares v. Touch (1933), 406
    universality perspective, 403

undue influence threat, 180, 192

unintended consequences case, 39

United Thermostatic Controls (a GVV case), 157–161

University of North Carolina, student cheating, 9–10

unmodified opinion
    in audit report, 254
    nonpublic companies, 247
    public companies, 246

utilitarianism, 16, 18–19

V

values and ethics, 6

values-driven leadership, 359–361

Vertical Pharmaceuticals Inc. et al. v. Deloitte & Touche LLP, 441–442

virtue(s)
    character traits, 11
    ethical decision making, 62
    instrumental, 62

    intellectual, 62

virtue ethics, 21–22

Vivendi Universal, 465–468

Volkswagen "Dieselgate" scandal, 50–51

W

whistleblowing, 12, 29
    bystander effect and, 140
    culture in accounting, 367–368
    defining, 135
    Dodd-Frank provisions, 139–141
    experiences, 141–142
    external, 135, 139
    HealthSouth Corporation, 368
    internal, 135, 136
    morality of, 135–136
    obligation to report fraud, 131
    payouts, 141–142
    rights and duties, 136–139

Whittman-Hart, 420

Winners & Losers, Inc., case, 318–320

Wirecard audit, 271–272

withdrawal from engagement, in audit report, 254–255

workplace behavior, ethics in, 112–114

WorldCom, 3, 100–101
    earnings manipulation, 284
    professional judgment and, 62
    shifting expenses, 299

X

Xerox, 234, 301–302

Z

Zoroastrianism, 4

ZZZZ Best Company, 266–268